ORLANDO
& WALT DISNEY World

© Disney

25th Anniversary Edition
2020
Simon & Susan Veness

foulsham
LONDON • NEW YORK • TORONTO • SYDNEY

W. Foulsham & Co. Ltd

for Foulsham Publishing Ltd

The Old Barrel Store, Drayman's Lane, Marlow, Bucks SL7 2FF

Foulsham books can be found in all good bookshops or direct from www.foulsham.com

While every effort has been made to ensure the accuracy of all the information contained within this book, neither the author nor the publisher can be liable for any errors. In particular, since prices, times and any holiday or hotel details change on a regular basis, it is vital that each individual checks relevant information for themselves.

ISBN: 978-0-572-04796-2

A CIP record for this book is available from the British Library

Dedication: To our special home-grown research team – Ben, Anthony and Mark – who help make our work fun!

Our sincere thanks go to Wendy Hobson, Jane Hotson and all the hard-working people at Foulsham who help to bring our work to life every year.

CONTENTS

Foreword

Simon says... The first edition of the *Brit Guide to Orlando* appeared 25 years ago, and it is amazing to look back on a quarter-century of growth and reflect on the transformation of not just this humble little guidebook but the destination itself. We began with just 184 pages and now boast 352, almost twice the original number (and still struggle to shoe-horn everything in!). That's representative of how much this vast area we call 'Orlando' has grown since 1995. The theme parks have increased in size – and number – and the associated attractions have likewise proliferated. There are more shopping centres, restaurants and sporting activities, too, and we have greatly expanded the scope of the book to include other parts of the Sunshine State. With all that growth, it stands to reason this amazing destination is more complex and demanding than ever – and that's why you have the *Brit Guide*. This is your essential inside track to all that's on offer; we've done all the hard work of laying things out clearly and concisely so you can just head out and have fun. There's a LOT to do, so get cracking, now...!

Susan says... Phew! The opening of *Star Wars: Galaxy's Edge* at Disney's Hollywood Studios left us all breathless, but the pace of change in Orlando doesn't stop just because its attractions stretch to the furthest reaches of the universe (and beyond!) and not one, but two wizarding worlds are drawing visitors in by the millions. Development marches on, and while 2020 promises to be slightly less dramatic in the heart-pounding department, the adrenalin will still be cranked up to 11 with the debut of three major new roller coasters at each of Universal Orlando, SeaWorld and Busch Gardens, plus a gentler but long-awaited dark-ride coming to Disney's France pavillion in EPCOT and a brand new Mickey and Minnie themed dark-ride at Disney's Hollywood Studios. You can bet there will be a slew of new restaurants and minor attractions opening, too, so bring your appetite and a sense of adventure, and, if you see us swigging back a Fuzzy Tauntaun at Oga's Cantina or munching on a Ronto Wrap at Ronto Roasters in Black Spire Outpost, be sure to say hello!

And if you want to make sure you get the most out of your holiday without wasting time or money, let us help with our unique Touring Plans (p39).

So if you're ready, let's get on with the planning...!

Simon and *Susan Veness*
(For feedback, email **britsguide@yahoo.com** and be sure to Follow **Veness Travel Media** on Twitter, Facebook and YouTube)

1 Introduction

Or Welcome to the Holiday of a Lifetime

Fun. Excitement. Thrills. Fantasy. Food (lots of food!). They are all waiting for you in this vast area of Central Florida we call Orlando. It is an amazing array of choice, temptation and all-out holiday appeal that has no equal anywhere else on earth. It is a fully fledged assault on the senses and it draws families, couples and singles, young and old alike. It runs the gamut from astounding theme parks to world-class shopping, superb nature and fabulous nightlife.

Most of all, though, this is a BIG venture in every sense and it's vital you do some 'homework' first. Walt Disney World is the leading attraction and is the size of a small city, plus there's a strong supporting cast with Universal Orlando, SeaWorld and LEGOLAND Florida. There's something for all tastes and ages, but it exacts a high toll. You'll walk a lot, queue a lot and probably eat a lot. You WILL have a fabulous time, but you'll probably end up exhausted, too. But stick with us, and you'll have the best possible preparation for what's in store.

Eight theme parks

In simple terms, there are eight major theme parks, and several need two days to enjoy fully. Add a day at a water park, a trip to one of the nature attractions and the lure of the Kennedy Space Center, and you already have two full weeks of pure adventure mania. Mix in the night-time fun of Disney Springs, Universal's CityWalk and a host of dinner shows, plus superb shopping, and you start to understand the awesome scope of the place. Even with two weeks, something has to give – just make sure it isn't your patience, wallet – or sanity.

The key to all this is Planning. On pages 345–46 is a handy outline guide for a typical two-week stay. Be aware of the time demands of the parks and make sure you build in a quiet day or two by the pool or at one of the smaller attractions. Focus on the attractions that appeal to you most, try not to be too ambitious, and don't underestimate the vast scale involved – this is a *huge* area and it takes time even to get from park to park. But do stop to admire the imagination and detail of what's on offer as it is all world class.

Cinderella Castle at the Magic Kingdom

© Disney

Florida

0   50 miles

N

← Panama City Beach

○ Amelia Island

■ JACKSONVILLE

Atlantic Ocean

○ St Augustine

○ Ormond Beach
○ Daytona Beach
DeLand ○
○ New Smyrna Beach

○ Ocala

Mount Dora ○

Homosassa Springs ○

Winter Garden ○

ORLANDO
○ Sanford
Titusville ○
Cape Canaveral
■ Kennedy Space Center

Walt Disney World

○ Kissimmee
○ Cocoa Beach

New Port Richey ○

Winter Haven ○
Legoland Florida

○ Melbourne

Clearwater Beach ○

Lakeland ○

TAMPA

Lake Wales ○
Bok Tower Gardens

St Pete Beach ○

FLORIDA

FLORIDA TURNPIKE

○ Vero Beach

Gulf of Mexico

Bradenton ○

Sarasota ○

Venice ○

○ Stuart

Lake Okeechobee

Charlotte Harbor ○
Fort Myers ○
Captiva ○
○ Sanibel

○ Palm Beach

○ Delray Beach
○ Boca Raton

Florida

Naples ○

○ Fort Lauderdale

Marco Island ○

Everglades

■ **MIAMI**

○ Key Largo

Florida Keys

Key West ○

© Steve Munns 2019

How far from Orlando to . . .

	mls	-	km
Bradenton	130	-	210
Clearwater Beach	110	-	176
Cocoa Beach	40	-	64
Daytona Beach	60	-	97
Fort Lauderdale	205	-	330
Fort Myers	190	-	306
Jacksonville	155	-	250
Key Largo	294	-	470
Key West	375	-	604
Miami	220	-	354
Naples	230	-	370
Sarasota	140	-	225
St Augustine	120	-	193
St Pete Beach	105	-	169
Tampa	75	-	120
Venice	160	-	257
Winter Haven	40	-	64

Orlando

In tourist terms, 'Orlando' has grown to encompass much of Central Florida, an area almost twice the size of Yorkshire. The city itself is north of the main tourist areas and many people won't even see it as they charge from park to park, which is a shame as it is a happening place. When Walt Disney's dream of a vast resort opened in 1971 with the Magic Kingdom (sadly, he never saw it realised as he died in 1966), it led to a huge and ongoing tourist expansion.

There are seven counties in Central Florida. **Orange County**, home to the city of Orlando, with Walt Disney World in the south-west corner, part of which is also in **Osceola County**, with Kissimmee its main town; **Seminole County**, home of Orlando Sanford International Airport, north-east of Orange; **Lake County** to the north-west, with Mount Dora its principal town; **Polk** to the south-west, home to many vacation villas and LEGOLAND Florida; and east to **Brevard** and **Volusia Counties**, home to the Kennedy Space Center and Daytona Beach.

Orlando hosts 70+ million visitors a year, and the area boasts over 120,000 hotel rooms, 26,000 vacation homes, 4,500 places to eat and 30 malls. Here are the highlights.

Walt Disney World

This is where the magic really starts. This vast resort consists of four separate theme parks, 21 themed hotel resorts, a camping ground, two water parks, a sports complex, five golf courses, mini-golf and a huge shopping and entertainment district (Disney Springs). It covers $47ml^2/122km^2$ and Alton Towers and Thorpe Park would comfortably fit into its car parks! At peak periods, it holds over 200,000 visitors. It maintains a high level of customer service, where everyone who works for them is a Cast Member, not just staff, and they take that ethos to heart.

Magic Kingdom: The essential Disney, with the magic of its wonderful films, the adventures of the Wild West and Africa, the excitement of thrill rides like Space Mountain (an indoor roller-coaster), the eye-catching Fantasyland and splendid parades and fireworks.

EPCOT: Disney's two-part park, with the technology-inspired Future World and a potted journey around the globe in World Showcase. More educational than adventurous, it still has some memorable rides, including the superb Soarin', plus great dining.

Disney's All-Star Music Resort

© Disney

Disney's Hollywood Studios: Ride the movies in style, including the all-new Star Wars: Galaxy's Edge area that is drawing HUGE crowds, along with Toy Story Land, Indiana Jones, the Muppets, and much, much more.

Disney's Animal Kingdom: Realistic animal habitats, including a 100acre/40.5ha safari savannah, captivating shows and terrific rides, like the grand Expedition Everest. Newest 'land' Pandora is a brilliant recreation from the film *Avatar*.

Disney's Typhoon Lagoon Water Park: Splash down waterslides and learn to surf in the world's biggest man-made lagoon.

Disney's Blizzard Beach Water Park: The big brother of all the water parks, with a massive spread of rides in a 'snowy' environment.

Disney Springs: Almost a mile of themed restaurants, bars, shops, a cinema multiplex, bowling centre, House of Blues music venue and new NBA Experience.

Wedding Pavilion: A fairytale venue overlooking Seven Seas Lagoon.

ESPN Wide World of Sports: A huge sporting venue to both play and watch top events.

Taniwha Tubes at Volcano Bay

© Universal Orlando Resort

The other parks
If you think Orlando is only about Disney, prepare to be amazed.

Universal Orlando: The other main resort has two theme parks, an entertainment district, brand new water park, **Volcano Bay**, and seven themed hotels. At **Universal Studios** you encounter The Simpsons, the Rip Ride Rockit roller-coaster, The Fast and the Furious, TRANSFORMERS: The Ride – 3D and the Wizarding World of Harry Potter – Diagon Alley.

Islands of Adventure: IoA features another Wizarding World area, plus a superb blend of thrill rides, family attractions, shows, great design and high-tech features such as the Amazing Adventures of Spider-Man.

SeaWorld: THE place for creatures of the deep, with killer whales, dolphins and penguins, a refreshing atmosphere, great shows, fabulous Antarctica attraction, thrill rides like Manta, Kraken, Mako and the new Infinity Falls, a Sesame Street area of rides and activities just for kids, and vital animal rescue facilities.

Discovery Cove: Its exclusive neighbour offers the chance to swim with dolphins, among other things.

Aquatica: A fab water park providing even more fun and animal encounters in a colourful South Seas setting.

BRITTIP

Be realistic when buying tickets. You simply won't get full use out of, say, a 14-day Disney ticket, a Universal 3-Park Explorer ticket AND a 3-Park SeaWorld ticket in a two-week holiday.

Busch Gardens: In nearby Tampa, SeaWorld's sister park offers creatures of the land, plus great rides and shows. Highlights are coasters Cheetah Hunt, SheiKra, Cobra's Curse and new Tigris, plus the Edge of Africa 'safari' experience and extensive Sesame Street play area. A family treat and a must for coaster fans.

Other key attractions

These include the **Kennedy Space Center**, with its superb Space Shuttle Atlantis exhibit; the surprisingly fun and humorous **Gatorland**; LEGOLAND Florida for the 2–12 age group; **ICON Park**, featuring the 400ft/120m The Wheel; **Forever Florida**, a mix of local nature and zipline adventures; and **Wild Florida,** for a close-up with Kissimmee nature. Plus there's mini-golf almost everywhere and other attractions along International Drive.

Disney tickets

This is where things get complicated and it's important to work out what tickets you need. Most people buy one of three multi-day passes specifically for the UK market that allow visits to more than one park a day. They are great value for a two or three-week visit and provide full flexibility. But they aren't cheap and, if you want only two or three of the Disney parks, you have to buy a Magic Your Way ticket in Orlando. Be aware you can't walk between the parks (they can be miles apart) and trying to do more than one a day is hard work, especially in summer.

—**BRITTIP**

Buy your theme park tickets in advance, NOT at the park gates. You will save time AND money, as most outlets offer an advance purchase discount.

Disney's ticket system is called Magic Your Way and is horribly complicated (although there is a simplified choice for UK visitors; see below). Multi-day tickets offer savings against one-day tickets but unused days expire after 14 days of first use.

Magic Your Way: If you just turn up at the ticket booths (or buy in advance from a US broker), you must choose:

• The number of days you want (up to 10).

• If you want the **Park Hopper** option (giving you the ability to move between parks on the same day) for an extra $60–80/ticket.

• If you want **Park Hopper Plus**, which adds 2–10 visits to the water parks, ESPN Wide World of Sports™, Winter-Summerland or Fantasia Gardens mini-golf, or the nine-hole Oak Trail golf course (book in advance on 407 939 4653; club hire NOT included) for a bargain $20/ticket.

Per-day ticket savings increase with the more days you buy: 1 day = $102–122 plus tax; 10 days = $445 plus tax, or $44.40/day. However, there's also seasonal pricing for one-day tickets, making it more expensive at peak periods.

UK tickets: In the UK, there are three tickets on offer: the 7, 14 and 21-day Ultimate Ticket (see chart p11).

Other tickets

The choice is equally complicated for Universal Orlando, SeaWorld, Busch Gardens and Aquatica. Do check periodic special offers (see Orlando Ticket Deals, p11).

• **1, 2, 3, 4 or 5-day Tickets:** For Universal, for one, two or three parks each day.

• **2 and 3-Park Explorer Ticket:** 14 consecutive days at Universal Studios and IoA, or those two plus Volcano Bay (sold in UK only).

• **1, 2, 3 or 4-Park Tickets:** To any combination of SeaWorld, Busch Gardens, Aquatica and Adventure Island water park, valid for 1, 2 or 3 visits, or, with the 4-Park ticket, for 14 consecutive days and free parking. UK ticket brokers have **2 and 3-Park** tickets valid for 14 consecutive days with parking.

• **Discovery Cove:** Bought in the UK, a day ticket includes a 14-Day Pass for SeaWorld and Aquatica. The Ultimate Package adds Busch Gardens for an extra £20 (plus free parking).

- **Party Pass:** For Universal's CityWalk ($12 plus tax) or a Party Pass with Movie ($15 plus tax) at the 20-screen cinema.

- **14-Day Combo Ticket:** Offered by many UK brokers, for Disney & Universal, plus a **Freedom** ticket (or similar) that includes the SeaWorld parks. This is NOT one ticket but a bundle of two or three.

- **Orlando Flexiticket:** a UK-only ticket that bundles the Universal parks with SeaWorld's, for 14 consecutive days, with free parking at the SeaWorld parks.

- **Go Orlando Card:** Two, three or five days of visits within 14 days to 32 attractions and activities, including Kennedy Space Center, LEGOLAND Florida, Coca-Cola Orlando Eye, WonderWorks, Fun Spot, airboat rides, mini-golf and more ($149–299 adults, $129–266 3–12s). There is also an **Explorer Pass** for three or five visits, and a **Build-Your-Own** choice with 20% savings. All come with a handy attractions guidebook. See **goorlandocard.com**.

- **Eat and Play Card:** A discount card for groups of up to four, valid for 30 days from first use. Save 10–20% off 50-plus restaurants, from McDonald's, Denny's, Pizza Hut and TGI Friday's to upmarket choices like Big Fin Seafood, Café Tu-Tu Tango and Bongos Cuban Café, all in the main tourist areas and some including alcohol; 10–30% on attractions like golf, mini-golf, Gatorland, Ripley's Believe It Or Not and more; and 10–20% off in shops like Macy's and Reebok Outlet Stores, plus the Outta Control Magic Dinner Show and Golfsmith shops. It costs a bargain $25 and covers the entire bill for up to four people each time, so you can make significant savings. Available from **eatandplaycard.com** (or call 001 613 680 7109) or select ticket brokers and tour operators.

With annual price hikes, try to buy your tickets as soon as you can, but be aware that some discounted tickets must be used for the first time in the year of purchase (e.g. 'first use by 31 Dec 2019'). Shop around, as many outlets have sales and special offers, but use a reputable agent and use your credit card for added security. The following companies all come well recommended.

Attraction Tickets Direct: Britain's top direct-sell Florida ticket broker, with a sharp bookings team, no credit card fees, free delivery in seven days and a promise to match any UK brochure price, plus a huge range of dinner shows, excursions, sports, theme park backstage tours and special offers (0800 691 1027, **attraction-tickets-direct.co.uk**).

BRITTIP

Say 'Hello!' to us on the info-packed Forums of **Attraction Tickets Direct** and don't miss their regular News blog, which we also contribute to weekly.

FloridaTix: Independent ticket specialist featuring all the theme parks, plus the likes of Kennedy Space Center, Blue Man Group, dinner shows, many tours and excursions, no credit card fees and a £10 deposit ticket offer (0330 100 3130, **floridatix.co.uk**).

Ocean Florida: Independent Florida specialist also offers a well-priced ticket service, featuring all the theme parks, plus Kennedy Space Center and Clearwater Beach (020 8131 9162, **ocean-florida.co.uk**).

Orlando Attractions: A UK-owned ticket service based in Orlando, it will post tickets to the UK and offers all the parks and the likes of airboat rides, fishing and other activities, plus some good combo tickets. Fully ABTA-bonded. Free shipping, price includes tax and no credit card fees (0800 294 9458, **orlandoattractions.com/tickets**).

BRITTIP

Be sure to download the new **Orlando Attractions** App, from the Apple Store or Google Play, for up-to-the-minute info on ride wait times, maps, special deals, local news and more.

Choosing a ticket

Ticket type	Park	Allowance
1-Day Ticket	Any Disney park, Universal Orlando parks, SeaWorld or Busch Gardens	Access to one park ONLY for one day; not available in advance
7, 14 and 21-Day Ultimate Ticket	All Disney parks	Unlimited access to all Disney attractions, including water parks, *ESPN Wide World of Sports*™ and nine-hole Oak Trail golf course (clubs not included) for 14 days after first use; available only in advance in the UK
Disney Platinum Pass	*Magic Kingdom Park, EPCOT, Disney's Hollywood Studios, Disney's Animal Kingdom;* plus discounts for shops, dining and tours	Unlimited admission and *free parking* for 365 days after purchase date. If ordered online, you get a voucher that must be activated at a park; the 365 days start on the day you activate the pass. Plus free PhotoPass downloads.
Disney Platinum Plus Pass	All Disney parks; plus numerous discounts for shops, dining and tours	Unlimited admission and *free parking* for 365 days after purchase date; plus discounts on sports and recreation, and free PhotoPass downloads.
2, 3, 4 or 5-Day 1-Park Ticket	Universal Studios, Islands of Adventure	Access to one of the Universal parks each day for 2–5 days, plus CityWalk; valid for 14 days
2, 3, 4 or 5-Day 2 or 3-Park Ticket	Universal Studios and Islands of Adventure, or those two plus Volcano Bay	Access to the parks each day for 2–5 days, plus CityWalk; valid for 14 days
2 and 3-Park Explorer Ticket	Universal Studios and Islands of Adventure, or those 2 and Volcano Bay, with CityWalk	14 consecutive days' access to 2 or 3 of the Universal parks, plus CityWalk clubs; sold in UK only
Orlando 6-Park Flexiticket	Universal Studios, Islands of Adventure, Volcano Bay, SeaWorld, Busch Gardens and Aquatica	Access to all parks, with multiple parks on same day, for 14 days from first use, plus CityWalk clubs. Free parking for SeaWorld parks; sold in UK only
2 or 3-Park Ticket; Unlimited ticket	SeaWorld, Busch Gardens, Aquatica and Adventure Island water park	2 or 3 visits to any of the 4 SeaWorld parks; Unlimited Ticket offers admission to all 4, and free parking, for 14 consecutive days
2-Park Ticket and 3-for-2 Ticket	Either SeaWorld and Aquatica or SeaWorld and Busch Gardens; or all 3	14 consecutive days' access to each of the 2 parks; or access to all 3 for 14 days with free parking (available in UK only)

Orlando Ticket Deals: A keenly priced and helpful broker that also issues real tickets (not vouchers), has a next-day delivery service and offers a significant Price Promise for all its attractions, including all the parks, dinner shows and many excursions (0800 984 6707, **orlando-ticket-deals.co.uk**).

There are others, including the main tour operators (p20), while you can also visit the Official Visitor Center on International Drive (**visitorlando.com**), but beware offers for 'free' tickets as these are purely timeshare lures. And NEVER buy resale tickets from a booth in Orlando – they are often unusable. Stick with the main brokers, who offer good products, service and local knowledge. And don't forget to plan with our sample Busy Day Guide (p345–46). You'll be exhausted if you try to do all the parks in one go!

BRITTIP

For theme park tickets, be sure to see *Brit Guide* partner **Orlando Ticket Deals** first, as it features an exclusive offer for our readers (see inside back cover and **bit.ly/brit-offer**).

The climate

Sub-tropical Florida can be hot – *really* hot May–Oct – so be ready for temperatures above 32°C/89°F, with high humidity which makes it feel at least 38°C/100°F. Add fierce – but rarely long – thunderstorms, with lots of lightning (Florida is the lightning capital of the world), and the weather can be a challenge, especially in high summer. Mar/Apr and Nov/Dec can be close to idyllic, while it is also possible for Dec–Feb to see occasional night-time temps drop to 0°C/32°F. Winter sees the biggest temperature range, from 30°C/86°F down to barely 7°C/45°F during the day. Rain rarely lasts for more than a day in winter but can be extremely heavy (be careful when driving on the motorways). If you are governed by school holidays, the latter half of Aug is your best bet.

The mood

Orlando is big, brash and fun, but above all it's American and that means everything is well organised, but with some cultural differences such as tipping (see Brit Tip). It's clean, well maintained and eager to please. Floridians generally are an affable bunch, but they take affability to new heights in the theme parks, where staff are almost painfully keen to make sure you 'have a nice day'.

Mako at SeaWorld

Tipping

With the exception of fast-food restaurant servers, just about everyone who serves in hotels, bars, restaurants, buses, taxis, airports and public amenities will expect a tip, not least because all service industry workers are taxed on the basis of receiving 15% in tips, whether they're given or not.

- Bars, restaurants and taxis: 15%.
- Porters: $1/bag.
- Housekeeping: $1/day per adult.

BRITTIP

Tipping guide	
Bill	Suggested tip
$15	$2.25
$20	$3.00
$25	$3.75
$30	$4.50
$40	$6.00
$50	$7.50

ESTA and immigration

AnyAnyone flying to the USA on the Visa Waiver Programme MUST register online via the Electronic System for Travel Authorization (ESTA) no later than three days before departure.

ESTA: ESTA is a pre-authorisation process prior to arriving at US immigration. The fee is $14 per person and is valid for any visits in a two-year span (so you do NOT pay the $14 fee again in that time).

Apply at **bit.ly/brit-esta** and fill in your basic immigration info – passport, address in the USA, flight and employment details (where necessary), email address and a few security questions. Have your holiday address details available both for the ESTA and your Advance Passenger Information for your flight online.

Ask your tour operator if you don't have a specific address (e.g. for a villa allocated on arrival) as it will have a formula for this. Your application should generate an immediate response of 'Authorization Approved' or 'Pending'. If the response 'Travel Not Authorized' is generated, the applicant is unable to travel under the Visa Waiver Programme and must apply for a visa in advance. Remember to record or print your Application Number during the process so you can amend it for future visits within two years.

BRITTIP

If you need to fill in the white I-94 immigration form for visa holders, do so carefully in block capitals. Mistakes are often sent to the back of the queue. Please be courteous to immigration officials – they do a difficult job in demanding circumstances, and jokes about terrorism are NOT appreciated.

The ESTA speeds up the immigration process and cuts out most form filling. An ESTA must be completed for each member of your group or family travelling under the Visa Waiver Programme. Those who have a US visa because they are not eligible to travel under the Visa Waiver Programme (i.e. because of a criminal record – see p15) still need to fill in a white I-94 form en route (fill in the front only) but they do NOT pay the $14 ESTA fee. However, anyone with a US work visa and who is travelling to America for a holiday, WILL need to fill in an ESTA and pay the fee.

BRITTIP

Beware unofficial websites that offer to fill in the ESTA form for you – for a fee. Stick with the official US government website and just pay the $14/person fee (or 'Travel Promotion Act fee').

Customs: You still need to complete a white customs form en route (it'll be given to you on the plane or at check-in and it's best to complete it in advance). Fill in one customs form per family, with some of the same basic info but also the value of any goods that will stay in the USA (put $0 unless you are arriving with gifts for friends). Hand the documents with your passports to the immigration official who checks

you through and takes a fingerprint scan and photo. The customs form will be handed back to you to present to another official when you exit the baggage hall.

Visa requirements

Holiday visitors to America do not need a visa providing they hold a valid machine-readable British passport (MRP). Each family member must have their own passport, valid for the FULL duration of the holiday. However, British subjects, those without an MRP or those who fail to meet the photo/biometric data criteria DO need a visa ($160), and should apply at least two months in advance to the US Embassy.

US immigration requires ALL visitors aged 14–79 to give fingerprint and photo ID on arrival. It is a simple process – first the four fingers and thumb of one hand, and then the other, then stand still for the camera.

Some travellers may NOT be eligible under the Visa Waiver Programme and will have to apply for a special restricted visa or they may be refused entry. This applies to those who have been arrested (even if it did not result in a conviction), have a criminal record (the Rehabilitation of Offenders Act does not apply to US visa law), have a serious communicable illness (but no

Baby giraffe at Animal Kingdom

© Disney

Main Attractions & Routes

✈ **Sanford International Airport**

Sanford Airport via Interstate 4 has no tolls, but can be far busier, especially during rush-hour

Sanford Airport via 417 has a few tolls, but is much quieter

Daytona

ALTAMONTE SPRINGS

Mount Dora

94

92

4

90

88

87

436

— Toll road (from 50c to $5)

429

441

WINTER PARK

Lake Apopka

OCOEE

50

417

■ Ivanhoe Row
■ Mills 50 District

WINTER GARDEN

WEST COLONIAL DRIVE

50

84

DOWNTOWN ORLANDO

■ Milk District

EAST - WEST EXPRESSWAY

83

408

82

79

80

■ Thornton Park
Orange County History Center

FLORIDA TURNPIKE

KIRKMAN ROAD

WINDERMERE

429

78

441

77

Universal Studios
CityWalk

75

SEMORAN BOULEVARD

Islands of Adventure
Volcano Bay

74B

Cocoa Beach

Kennedy Space Center →

74A SAND LAKE RD

■ Ripley's Believe It or Not
■ ICON Park
— INTERNATIONAL DRIVE

528

BEACHLINE

north exit —

✈ **Orlando International Airport**

Magic Kingdom

TURKEY LAKE RD

535

435

72

71

■ Aquatica

4

SeaWorld
Discovery Cove

423

south exit →

PALM PARKWAY

ORANGE BLOSSOM TRAIL

JOHN YOUNG PARKWAY

BOGGY CREEK ROAD

CENTRAL FLORIDA GREENEWAY

WESTERN BELTWAY

Lake Buena Vista

EPCOT DRIVE

Disney Springs

68

BUENA VISTA DRIVE

Epcot

67

Disney's Hollywood Studios

■ Typhoon Lagoon

Animal Kingdom

■ Blizzard Beach

65

MainGate West

WORLD DRIVE

OLD LAKE WILSON RD

64

63

417

■ Gatorland

OSCEOLA PARKWAY

— Toll road

KISSIMMEE

■ Old Town

Celebration

62

FLORIDA TURNPIKE

BOGGY CREEK ROAD

BOGGY CREEK ROAD

East Lake Tohopekaliga

Champions Gate

60

192

IRLO BRONSON MEMORIAL HIGHWAY

17

58

Kissimmee Airport ✈

◤ Busch Gardens, Bok Tower Gardens, Legoland Florida

55

Tampa, Clearwater, Gulf Coast

ST CLOUD

Lake Tohopekaliga

© Steve Munns 2019

0   5 miles

Miami

N

longer including AIDS/HIV), or have previously been refused admission into, been deported from, or have overstayed in the US on the Visa Waiver Programme. Minor traffic offences do not count. Visa appointments can be arranged online at **bit.ly/brit-visa** or call 020 3608 6998.

Contacts

- **England, Scotland and Wales:** Visa Office, US Embassy, 33 Nine Elms Lane, London SW11 7US (020 7499 9000).

- **Northern Ireland:** US Consulate General, Danesfort House, 223 Stranmillis Road, Belfast BT9 5GR (028 9038 6100).

- **Detailed advice: uk.usembassy.gov/**

Travel information

Luggage is liable to random searches in the US so do NOT lock your suitcases at check-in for the flight home as TSA officials have the authority to break into them. Using zip-lock seals that can be snipped open is okay and some airlines provide them free, or you can also buy TSA-approved reusable locks at some travel shops. Leave any gifts you are taking home unwrapped, and put scissors and other sharp items in checked bags, never in your hand luggage.

BRITTIP

Cabin baggage restrictions often change, so check with your airline in advance for up-to-date info.

© Disney

What's new?

Walt Disney World: Disney's Hollywood Studios continues to be the hottest ticket in town following the August 2019 opening of **Star Wars: Galaxy's Edge**, which created a huge surge in crowds, and that will continue in spring 2020 with the debut of **Mickey's Runaway Railway**. EPCOT won't be far behind, though, with **Remy's Ratatouille Adventure** ride due to open in early 2020, while a brand new night-time spectacular is scheduled for the summer.

Universal Orlando: The success of **Hagrid's Magical Creatures Motorbike Adventure** roller-coaster in the Islands of Adventure park in summer 2019 should be followed up by the fabulous new **Jurassic World** coaster in late 2020.

SeaWorld: Talking of coasters, it is a few years since SeaWorld opened one, but 2020 will see the debut of their next high-speed offering, with a novel fast-launch ride, with several switchbacks, next to the Bayside Stadium. Sister park **Busch Gardens** will also be in on the act, with an all-new steel-wood hybrid coaster – the fastest and highest of its kind – replacing the former Gwazi ride in summer 2020.

Other new highlights to look out for are the fab villa homes of **Balmoral Resort** (p83), the superb natural attractions of **Wekiva Island** (p261), the drive-through safari experience at **Wild Florida** (p253), and **Hopdoddy's**, our fave new burger bar, at Pointe Orlando (p323).

BRITBONUS 💲

Don't forget to keep an eye out for the Brit Bonus, which features special offers and discounts with various hotels, attractions and restaurants. In addition, *Brit Guide* partners Gray Line Orlando now offer an exclusive 15% discount to our readers on a live booking option on our website, **britguideorlando.net.**

Festival of Fantasy parade

BRIT GUIDE 25

When we started the *Brit Guide*, in 1995, there were only:

- SIX theme parks, not eight
- THREE water parks, not five
- And only TWO night-time entertainment districts, not four.

The likes of **CityWalk, ICON Park, Pointe Orlando, Orlando Premium Outlets, LEGOLAND Florida, Discovery Cove, Volcano Bay, Aquatica, Mall at Millenia, Fun Spot, WonderWorks, Restaurant Row, Forever Florida, Wild Florida** and several dinner shows didn't even exist, while **Disney Springs** (the old Disney Village Marketplace, and then Downtown Disney) was less than half its current size.

It cost just **$5** to park at the main theme parks, not **$25**; a burger, chips and coke meal was only **$5.80** (not **$16.50**); and a Disney souvenir T-shirt would have set you back **$16.95**, instead of **$25**.

More importantly, there were no such things as **FastPass+, Universal Express** or **QuickQueue** to complicate your planning, preparation – and enjoyment! – of the parks. Orlando has become a MUCH more complex and challenging place from the

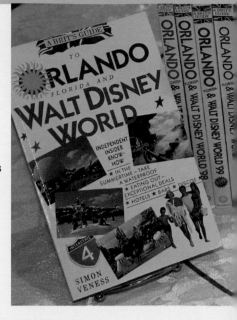

sheer variety and volume on offer, let alone the technology to make it all work. We didn't carry around mobile phones and iPads; many cameras still used regular film; and there was no such thing as **Uber** or **Lyft**.

Orlando International Airport typically handled around 22 million passengers. Today it is more likely to be 47 million – and a return airfare could be as low as £210!

Happily, many things HAVE stayed the same. You will still get an especially warm welcome; everything is just as efficient (OK, the roads may be just a BIT more crowded); and the weather remains wonderful. Even better, we now have many more places to explore than just 'Orlando'. The **city centre**, or 'downtown' has developed into a series of fascinating districts (p296), the beaches have become more open and diverse, **the wildlife** is now a major feature of the state, with a great variety of eco-tours, and many of the smaller towns are now waiting to be discovered for their authenticity and charm. Florida's history dates back more than 500 years in real terms, and it is all so much easier to investigate thanks to the likes of GPS and WiFi.

We moved here in 2004 because we wanted to experience more ourselves, and we urge you to expand your horizons and see more, too. This is a truly fascinating place with WAY more to it than just theme parks. P5: Look out for **BRITGUIDE 25** snippets throughout the book for more highlights from 25 years ago!

Liberty Square in the Magic Kingdom

© Disney

Plan your visit

The next few chapters will tell you all you need to know to plan the ideal holiday. Make a rough itinerary and then fine tune it with this book. You can also take advantage of our unique Touring Plans Service (p39).

2 Planning and Practicalities

Or How to *Almost* Do It All and Live to Tell the Tale

There is one simple key to a memorable Orlando holiday: planning. There are no short-cuts here, you simply have to do some 'homework' in advance, or risk being frustrated and/or exhausted!

This huge, demanding place can pull you in a dozen directions, with a dazzling array of options. Nowhere else in the world can be so complex to navigate, so it's vital to plan your visit in advance.

Start with WHEN you want to go; WHERE you'd like to stay; WHAT sort of holiday you want; WHO to book with; and finally HOW MUCH to try to do. Just remember there's no way you will be able to do it all in 2 or 3 weeks.

When to go

To avoid the worst of the crowds, the best times to go are Oct–Dec (but not Thanksgiving week or Christmas); mid-Jan–mid-Mar; and the week after Easter to the end of May.

Busiest times: Orlando is seldom quiet but is absolutely packed at:

- Christmas/New Year period (about 17 Dec–12 Jan).
- Mid-Mar through Easter.
- From Memorial Day weekend (the last Mon in May, the start of the summer season) to mid-Aug, especially around 4 July.
- Labor Day weekend in early Sept, the last holiday of summer.
- Thanksgiving week (Wed–Sun).

The parks can even close to new arrivals by mid-morning during the Christmas period.

Hagrid's Magical Creatures Motorbike Adventure at Universal Studios

Hurricane alert?

June–Nov is hurricane season, but it is not anything to worry about. Three major storms hit Central Florida in 2004, and Hurricane Irma dropped by in 2017, but there was no major damage and the main inconvenience was losing electricity for a few days. In the unlikely event of a hurricane, switch your TV to the Weather Channel or local news stations WESH, WFTV or WKMG and follow their advice.

BRITTIP

Thanksgiving is the 4th Thurs in Nov; George Washington's birthday, or President's Day, is the 3rd Mon in Feb, and both make for above-average long-weekend crowds.

Best times: The best combination of good weather and smaller crowds are in Apr (after Easter) and Oct. Rain isn't a big factor (although outdoor rides and water parks will close if lightning threatens), but the crowds will noticeably thin out when it does rain and you can take advantage by bringing waterproofs or buying a plastic poncho (cheaper from local supermarkets than at the parks). In the colder months, take warm layers for early morning queues. When it heats up, leave them in the park lockers. When it gets really hot, seek out the air-conditioned attractions. The humidity alone will knock you sideways in summer and it's vital to drink plenty of water.

Simon & Susan's 10 Commandments

1   Drink water frequently
2   Use sunscreen regularly
3   Bring a lightweight rain jacket
4   Pre-book Disney dining
5   Use FastPass+
6   Slow down
7   Remember: you can't do it all
8   Wear comfortable walking shoes
9   Be sure to see some of Florida
10 Don't forget to tip

Where to stay

This is equally important and, again, there's a huge choice. As a rough guide, four main areas make up the great Orlando tourist conglomeration.

Walt Disney World: Some of the most sophisticated, convenient and fun places to stay are Disney's own hotels, built with the same imagination that created the theme parks. They all feature free transport, MagicBand (p95), and the BIG bonus of Extra Magic Hours, which allows Disney resort guests entry to one theme park a day, either one hour before official opening or for two hours after closing, when there are fewer crowds (though evenings can still be busy). However, with the exception of Disney's All-Star, Pop Century and Art of Animation Resorts, its hotels are among the most expensive, especially to eat in, and are

Kumba at Busch Gardens

Virgin's V-Room

Virgin Holidays guests have the option of the V-Room lounge at Gatwick and Manchester, a private haven with a kids' play room, teen zone with video games, photo booth, adults area, free WiFi, breakfast, snacks, fruit, soft drinks, tea and coffee, and fast-track security channel. £20 adults and £12 2–11s in advance (£22/ £14 on day of travel), free with Platinum bookings. Standard Plus adds select beer, wine and spirits for an extra £4/adult (pre-book only on 0344 557 9813).

not close to the other attractions, but they make a good one-week base.

BRITTIP

Beware holiday homes (and some hotels) that insist they are 'just minutes from Disney World' – which may actually mean 30mins or more from the parks. Check the exact address.

Lake Buena Vista: On the eastern edge of Walt Disney World and along I-4, this features a good mix of hotels. It is handy for Disney (and slightly cheaper), with most hotels offering free transport to the parks, plus there is good dining and shopping.

International Drive: The big tourist corridor of I-Drive lies mid-way between Disney and downtown Orlando, running parallel to I-4, and is an excellent central location about 20mins drive from Disney and close to Universal and SeaWorld. It is a well-developed area, with great shops, restaurants and attractions like ICON Park, Ripley's Believe It Or Not, WonderWorks and iFLY Orlando, plus its own transport service, the I-Ride Trolley. The downside is it gets congested in peak times, but it is good value and one of the few areas with extensive pavement, making it easy to explore on foot. A sub-district off I-Drive is the Universal area of Kirkman Road and Major Boulevard.

BRITTIP

I-Drive south of Sand Lake Road offers some of the best hotels and restaurants. To the north, it is more budget hotels, fast food and gift shops.

Kissimmee: Budget holiday-makers flock to the tourist sprawl of Highway 192 (the Irlo Bronson Memorial Highway), an almost unbroken 20ml/32km strip of hotels, motels, restaurants and shops. It offers some of the best economy accommodation and is handy for Disney, though further from Universal and SeaWorld. A car is advisable, although there's extensive pavement, landscaping, bus shelters and benches. **Highway 27** is often referred to as 'Kissimmee' but is actually either in Lake County (north) or Polk County (south). This is prime holiday-home and villa territory.

Split holidays

Florida has so much to offer, many opt to spend a week in Orlando and a week somewhere else. The Atlantic and west coasts have great beaches and the Everglades are 3-4 hours to the south. There's great shopping almost everywhere stunning golf courses and opportunities to play or watch tennis, soccer and basketball, go fishing, boating or kayaking. The tour operators offer a huge variety of packages, plus cruise and-stay options. Budget permitting, the ideal is two weeks in Orlando then a week relaxing on a beach. A two-week, 50/50 split is popular, but a 60/40 split is less hectic in Orlando. Fly-drives are flexible, but there is a lot to tempt you and you may find it better to book a two-centre stay that includes a car and accommodation so you can still travel but avoid too much packing and unpacking (see also Chapter 9).

Ninjago World at LEGOLAND Florida

Dining Plan options

Most tour operators offer the Disney Dining Plan as an optional extra with Disney hotel packages and it can be good value if you spend ALL your time in Walt Disney World, where there are few cheap dining outlets. But, because ALL members of the family must be included for the FULL length of your stay, even the Quick Service plan adds £1,512 for a family of four (with children 3–9) staying for two weeks; the main Dining Plan would be £2,072; and the Deluxe Plan a huge £3,164 (2019 prices). It is a LOT of food, especially when it's hot, and you often need to book the full-service restaurants well in advance. You can eat cheaper elsewhere, so don't book unless you are sure. However, tour operators occasionally offer the Dining Plan as a FREE perk at quieter times of the year – a BIG bonus. See more on p58.

Booking your holiday

The big question is whether to book a package or book the flight, accommodation, car hire, etc, separately. The DIY approach can pay dividends but, at peak periods, a package may still be cheaper. Shop around, and use the Internet. Increasingly, it pays to book early, especially for the summer and Christmas holidays, but you can still pick up some late bargains at quieter times. Always book with ABTA and ATOL-bonded agents. Start by looking at prices with the Big Boys (Virgin, Thomson, etc) then compare with some of the online specialists like Expedia and Opodo and also look up the 'aggregator' websites like Skyscanner and Kayak that check flights/hotels/car hire from a number of sources.

The big boys: You'll find a good range of holidays, featuring Orlando, the Gulf Coast, Miami and the Florida Keys from British Airways Holidays (0344 493 0124, **bit.ly/brit-ba**); TUI (0203 636 1931, **tui.co.uk**); and Virgin Holidays, who remain Britain's top tour operator for Florida, with the widest array of options, including early entry to the Wizarding Worlds of Harry Potter at Universal Orlando, plus return flight check-in at Disney Springs, wedding services and exclusive options in Miami, Marco Island and Key West (0344 739 9390, **virginholidays.co.uk**). TUI (from Birmingham, Bristol, East Midlands, Edinburgh, Glasgow, Gatwick, Stansted, Manchester and Newcastle to Orlando Sanford) also offer flights-only seasonally. Sadly, the collapse of Thomas Cook in 2019 has left the UK with fewer flight options, which will increase prices for 2020.

Tolédo – Tapas, Steak and Seafood at Coronado Springs Resort

© Disney

The specialists: There's also a variety of smaller operators specialising in Florida and the US. Take a look at:

- **America First Coast Travel** (0800 669 6409, **americafirstcoasttravel.com)**

- **James Villa Holidays** (0808 256 8864, **jamesvillas.co.uk)**

- **Jetset** (0161 613 4028, **jetsetholidays. com)**

- **Kuoni** (0800 140 4769, **kuoni.co.uk)**

- **My America Holiday** (020 290 9751, **myamericaholiday.co.uk)**

- **Trailfinders** (020 7084 6500, **trailfinders.com)**

- **Travelbag** (020 3944 3594, **travelbag. co.uk)**

- **USAirtours** (0800 0350 149, **usairtours.co.uk)**

Perhaps the best of the bunch here, though, is **Ocean Florida** (020 8131 6989, **ocean-florida.co.uk)**, who have built up a solid Florida reputation in recent years.

BRITGUIDE 25

Back in 1995, when we still booked holidays by Teletext (!), there were flight choices with Leisure Air, Airtours, Unijet, First Choice and Cosmos, among others. Now, the choice is simpler and more direct.

Online agents: You can also price-check with a variety of online agencies who provide packages, flights, hotels and car hire.

- **Cheap Flights (cheapflights.co.uk)**
- **Dial A Flight (dialaflight.com)**
- **eBookers (ebookers.com)**
- **Expedia (expedia.co.uk)**
- **Flight Centre (flightcentre.co.uk)**
- **Kelkoo (travel.kelkoo.co.uk/)**
- **Kayak (kayak.co.uk)**
- **NetFlights (netflights.com)**
- **Opodo (opodo.co.uk)**
- **Sky Scanner (skyscanner.net)**
- **Travel Supermarket (travelsupermarket.com)**

Scheduled flights

For DIY, book your flights first. These airlines offer scheduled, year-round services to Orlando.

Aer Lingus: Direct flights from Dublin (0333 006 6920, **aerlingus.com**).

British Airways: Flies direct daily from Gatwick to Orlando and Tampa, as well as providing a twice-daily service from Heathrow to Miami (0844 493 0787, **britishairways.com**).

Icelandair: Fly via Reykjavik, Iceland, from Belfast, Birmingham, Heathrow, Glasgow or Manchester (020 7874 1000, **icelandair.co.uk**).

Norwegian: The smart, low-cost carrier flies direct to both Miami and Orlando from Gatwick in the Boeing Dreamliner, with some tempting prices (0330 828 0854, **norwegian.com/uk/**).

Virgin Atlantic: Multiple direct flights each week from Gatwick, Manchester and Glasgow, plus summer peak from Belfast, as well as daily from Heathrow to Miami (0344 874 7747, **virgin-atlantic.co.uk**).

Indirect flights: You can often save money on indirect flights, the obvious drawback being the extra journey time, and the connecting flight may land you in Orlando late in the evening. However, it does break the journey and places like Detroit and Dallas often process international passengers quicker than Orlando, meaning less hassle when you arrive.

EPCOT's International Flower and Garden Festival

© Disney

American Airlines: From Heathrow, Manchester, Glasgow or Dublin via Chicago, Charlotte, Dallas, New York, Philadelphia and Miami (0844 369 9899, **americanairlines.co.uk**).

Delta/KLM: Gatwick, Glasgow, Heathrow, Manchester or Edinburgh via Boston, Atlanta, Minneapolis, Detroit or New York (020 7660 0293, **klm.com**).

United: Heathrow, Belfast, Dublin, Manchester, Birmingham, Glasgow or Edinburgh via Washington, Houston, New York or Chicago (0845 607 6760, **united.com**).

What to see when

The best way to end up exhausted is to head for one theme park after another. Take advantage of quieter park days and include rest days.

Using the Planner on p345 as an example (or with the *Brit Guide* Touring Plans service, p39), list the attractions you want to see, planning around the eight 'must-see' parks. If you have only a week, drop Busch Gardens and focus on Disney, Universal and SeaWorld. Kennedy Space Center is also hard to miss.

- **Magic Kingdom:** 2 days – the biggest hit with young children.
- **EPCOT:** 2 days – one day is not really enough, but there are fewer rides to amuse children.
- **Animal Kingdom:** 1 day – a little short on appeal for the youngest but now with evening entertainment.

Gaston's Tavern at the Magic Kingdom

Our must-do experiences

- Soarin' and World Showcase (EPCOT)
- Wizarding Worlds of Harry Potter at Universal Orlando
- Wild Florida (Kissimmee)
- Pandora: The World of Avatar (Animal Kingdom)
- Happily Ever After fireworks, Pirates of the Caribbean and Haunted Mansion rides (Magic Kingdom)
- Star Wars: Galaxy's Edge (Disney's Hollywood Studios)
- Shopping!
- Infinity Falls and Mako rides (SeaWorld)
- Cheetah Hunt and SheiKra coasters (Busch Gardens)
- Space Shuttle Atlantis (Kennedy Space Center)
- A Disney character meal
- A trip to Winter Park
- A day at a water park

- **Disney's Hollywood Studios:** 1 day – plus two great evening shows.
- **SeaWorld:** 1–2 days.
- **Islands of Adventure:** 1–2 days.
- **Universal Studios:** 1–2 days.
- **Busch Gardens:** 1 day – popular with Brits, 75mins away in Tampa.
- **LEGOLAND Florida**: 45mins away in Winter Haven, is also a full day's outing, while the attractions of **ICON Park** can be fitted around the main parks. Look at the detail in Chapters 5–8 before you plan.

BRITTIP
When making many travel purchases, you can sometimes get cashback on anything from flights to hotels from websites like **topcashback. co.uk** and **quidco.com**. And consult Martin Lewis' **MoneySavingExpert.com**, too.

Smaller attractions

Of the other, smaller-scale attractions, **Forever Florida** is a full day out as it also involves an hour's drive to get there, but everything else can be fitted around your Big Eight itinerary. The **water parks** or the quieter **Bok Tower Gardens** make for a relaxing half-day, while **Gatorland** (at least half a day) is a unique look at some of Florida's oldest inhabitants and is a good combination with **Boggy Creek Airboats** or **Wild Florida**. Then there are the likes of **Ripley's Believe It Or Not** museum, the **WhirlyDome** and the **WonderWorks** house of fun, all offering several hours' entertainment, the thrills of **iFLY Orlando** (an indoor 'sky-diving' wind tunnel) and the lure of old-fashioned go-karts and other fairground-type rides at **Fun Spot, Andretti Indoor Karting** and **Magical Midway**. Many stay open after the parks close.

Each main area is also well served with creatively designed **mini-golf** courses (p268).

Evenings

The evening entertainment features a similarly wide choice. By far the best, and worth at least one evening each, are **Disney Springs** and Universal's **CityWalk** – the latter will keep you busy until the early hours! Dinner shows provide a lot of fun: two-hour cabarets based on themes such as medieval knights, pirates, Al Capone and murder mysteries that all include a hearty meal. Downtown Orlando (the actual city centre) is also well worth a visit (see Chapter 10).

Shopping

Shopping in Orlando is world class (see Chapter 12) and your plan should include at least a day to visit the spectacular malls and discount centres, like the two excellent **Orlando Premium Outlets** centres, **Lake Buena Vista Factory Stores**, **Mall at Millenia** and the **Florida Mall**. Busy at weekends, but handy if it rains.

What to do when

There are several guidelines for avoiding the worst of the tourist hordes, even in high season.

Avoid busy days: Most Americans arrive at weekends and head for the main theme parks first, so Sun and Mon are often bad times to visit the Magic Kingdom, while Tues is usually also busy at EPCOT. New rides like Millennium Falcon and Rise of the Resistance (at Hollywood Studios) and Hagrid's Magical Creatures Motorbike Adventure (IoA) also create longer queues, notably at weekends. Animal Kingdom is the hardest to navigate when crowded, while EPCOT handles the crowds best. Blizzard Beach and Typhoon Lagoon water parks hit high tide at weekends, and Thurs and Fri in summer; avoid Volcano Bay and Aquatica at weekends, too. If Disney is busy early in the week, visit SeaWorld, Busch Gardens or Kennedy Space Center.

Disney's Extra Magic Hours: Allowing Disney guests early and late access (see p59) creates bigger crowds, too. So, if you are NOT staying at a Disney hotel, avoid EMH mornings. For much of the year, they run as: Magic Kingdom, Mon (morning EMH) and Weds (evening EMH); EPCOT, Thurs (morning), Tues (evening); Disney's Hollywood Studios, Sun (morning only); Animal Kingdom, Mon and Sat (morning only). EMH days can change at short notice, and several parks can have multiple successive days at peak periods. Disney's Hollywood Studios had Extra Magic Mornings from 6–9am every day in September and October 2019 following the opening of Star Wars: Galaxy's Edge, while the Magic Kingdom and Animal Kingdom ALSO had EMH mornings each day to try to ease the record crowds at the Studios. See park hours at **bit.ly/brit-discal**

Universal Orlando: The picture is different here as only the two Harry Potter rides have daily early opening privileges (for guests at Universal hotels). This often means heavier crowds early in the week, while the parks also get busiest at weekends.

Rainy-day options

Long, wet days are rare, but here's where to go if they do set in for more than an hour or so.

International Drive: WonderWorks, SeaLife Orlando, Madame Tussauds, Ripleys Believe It Or Not, I-Drive NASCAR, Whirlydome, Andretti Indoor Karting & Games, iFly Orlando, Kings Dining & Entertainment, Main Event Entertainment, The Escape Game, Escapology, Chocolate Kingdom.

Florida Mall: Crayola Experience (great for 3-10s), Build-A-Bear Workshop, M&M's World.

Downtown: Orlando Science Center, Orange County History Center.

BRITTIP

If your hotel is not far away, take a mid-afternoon break from the park and return for a siesta or a swim. Your car park ticket is valid all day, and the evening is often the best time to be in the parks.

Arrive early: Getting the most out of your days at the parks is another art form, and there are several options.

The opening times can be as early as 8am in peak season, and arriving at least 30mins before opening time (or an hour at peak periods) is advisable. You will also be better placed to park in the huge car parks and catch the tram to the main gates

Prioritise: Once you are in pole position, don't waste time on the shops, scenery and other frippery that will lure the unprepared first-timer. Head straight for some of the main rides and get a few big-time thrills under your belt before the hordes arrive. You will quickly work out where the most popular attractions are as the majority of early birds will flock to them. Use Chapters 5 and 6 to plan your park strategies.

Universal's Portofino Bay Hotel

© Universal Resort Orlando

Pace yourself: Disney's parks, notably the Magic Kingdom, stay open late for the main holidays, until midnight at times, and that's a l-o-n-g day for kids. It's vital to pace yourself, especially if you arrive early. There are plenty of options to take time off for a drink or a rest somewhere air-conditioned, which is vital in summer.

FastPass+: Make *sure* you use this Disney system to your advantage in advance (p96).

Meal breaks: Benefit from the American habit of dining at lunchtime (midday–1.30pm) and dinner (5.30–7pm) by planning your meals outside those times. It pays to take an early lunch (before noon), snack in mid-afternoon and then enjoy a relative drop-off in crowds in late afternoon. Try not to have all your meals in the parks; eating here can be expensive ($15–18/person for a basic meal). A good breakfast before you arrive and a light lunch will save you $$$s!

BRITTIP

The water IS safe to drink in the US, but it might not taste great as it's heavily fluoridated. If you buy bottled water, do so at supermarkets, not at the parks, where it is exorbitantly expensive.

Comfort and clothing

Avoiding alcohol and coffee on the plane You may feel jetlagged for the first day and drinking plenty of water can or so after your arrival, but reduce this.

Footy frenzy

You don't need a specialist sports bar for most British football on TV. The Premier League is extensively covered by NBC, while the Champions League is on TNT. Check if your villa/hotel has NBC Sports for some games, as it is a cable channel that not everyone gets. The FA Cup is only offered online on ESPN+. And don't forget to check out our own team – Orlando City – at orlandocitysc.com (p270).

Shoes: These are the most important part of your holiday wardrobe – you'll be on your feet a LOT, even at off-peak periods. The smallest park is 'only' 100acres/40ha, but that is irrelevant to the time spent queuing. This is not the time to break in new sandals or trainers. Comfortable, well-worn shoes or trainers are essential (many rate Croc-type shoes as ideal park footwear).

BRITTIP
Look after your feet and avoid the onset of blisters by buying some moleskin footpads from a supermarket or 'drug-store' like Walgreens and CVS.

Casual clothes: Casual dress is fine in parks and nearly all restaurants, but swimwear is not acceptable away from pool areas. If you want a change of clothes or a sweater for the evening, use the park lockers (unlimited use all day for a small fee).

BRITTIP
Don't be tempted to pack a lot of smart or formal clothing – you really won't need it in hot, informal Florida.

Baby services: All the parks are well equipped with pushchairs, or 'strollers', for hire (although it pays to have your own), and baby services are located at regular intervals. You can even hire pushchairs for your full holiday period from Orlando Stroller Rentals from $100 for two weeks (1800 281 0884, **orlandostrollerrentals.com**).

Measurements

US clothes sizes are smaller than ours, hence a US size 12 dress is a UK 14, or an American jacket sized 42 is a 44. Shoes are the opposite: a US 10 should fit a British size 9 foot. The measuring system is imperial, not metric.

Measurements

Sunscreen: It is VITAL to use high-factor sun creams (30-plus) at all times, even during the winter when the sun may not feel strong but can still burn. Orlando has a subtropical climate and you need higher-factor creams than in the Mediterranean, and waterproof if you are swimming. Use sun block on sensitive areas like nose and ears, and splash on the after-sun liberally at the end of the day. Skincare products are widely available and usually inexpensive (at Wal-Mart, Publix or Target). Wear a hat during the day, and avoid alcohol, coffee and fizzy drinks until the evening as they are dehydrating and make you liable to heatstroke. You must increase your fluid intake SIGNIFICANTLY in the summer, but stick to sports drinks and lots of water.

BRITTIP
One of the best ways to keep cool in the sun is to buy a simple mist spray fan (about $7.99) from a supermarket.

Medical help

Should you need medical treatment consult your tour operator's info about local hospitals and surgeries. In the event of an emergency, dial **911** as you would 999 in Britain. It cannot be

Hotel Radisson Lake Buena Vista

Attractions with warnings for expectant mothers

Animal Kingdom: Dinosaur!, Expedition Everest, Flight of Passage, Kali River Rapids, Kilimanjaro Safari, Primeval Whirl.

Busch Gardens: Cheetah Hunt, Cobra's Curse, Congo River Rapids, Falcon's Fury, Kumba, Montu, Phoenix, Sand Serpent, Scorpion, SheiKra, Stanley Falls Log Flume, Tigris, Ubanga-Banga Bumper Cars.

EPCOT: Mission: SPACE, Soarin', Test Track.

Hollywood Studios: Rock 'n Roller Coaster, Slinky Dog Dash, Star Tours, Twilight Zone Tower of Terror, Millennium Falcon: Smugglers Run.

Islands of Adventure: Amazing Adventures of Spider-Man, Cat in the Hat, Dr Doom's Fearfall, Dudley Do-Right's Ripsaw Falls, Flight of the Hippogriff, Hagrid's Magical Creatures Motorbike Adventure, Harry Potter and the Forbidden Journey, Incredible Hulk Coaster, Jurassic World Coaster, Jurassic Park River Adventure, Popeye & Bluto's Bilge Rat Barges, Reign of Kong, Storm Force Accelatron.

Magic Kingdom: Barnstormer, Big Thunder Mountain Railroad, Seven Dwarfs Mine Train, Space Mountain, Splash Mountain.

SeaWorld: Antarctica: Empire of the Penguin (Wild version of ride), Infinity Falls, Journey to Atlantis, Kraken, Manta, Mako, Rock Wall, Wild Arctic (ride portion).

Universal Studios: ET Adventure, Fast & Furious: Supercharged, Harry Potter and the Escape from Gringotts, Men in Black Alien Attack, Revenge of the Mummy, Shrek 4-D, Despicable Me: Minion Mayhem (stationary seats available), TRANSFORMERS: The Ride – 3D, Woody Woodpecker's Nuthouse Coaster.

Gator safety

Alligators are found in many bodies of water in Florida but they rarely approach humans and are rarely a threat. However, they should NEVER be approached or fed (which is illegal). They usually avoid people but swimming in lakes in the evening is not advised and small children should never be allowed in or near open water on their own.

overstressed, however, you should take out comprehensive travel insurance (p28) for any trip to America, as there is NO National Health Service and any form of medical treatment is expensive. Keep all the receipts and put in a claim on your return home.

———BRITTIP

Look for local insect-repellent brands Cutter, Repel and Off! and use them away from the parks.

Emergency outpatients: These can be found with Centra Care at Florida Hospital Medical Center in more than 20 Central Florida locations (407 200 2273: **centracare.org/florida**), as well as full family and paediatric care.

Open 8am–8pm (5pm at weekends), there are four locations open to midnight Mon–Fri, including at 12500 S Apopka-Vineland Road near the Crossroads shopping centre and Disney Springs at Lake Buena Vista (8pm Sat and Sun; 407 934 2273). Other notable tourist area locations are: 8201 West Irlo Bronson Memorial Highway (192), by Orange Lake Resort (407 465 0846); on Sand Lake Road, between John Young Parkway and Orange Blossom Trail (9am–5pm Sat and Sun; 407 851 6478); and 4320 West Vine Street, near Medieval Times (407 390 1888).

Medical Concierge®: This has doctors throughout the tourist areas, making house calls to hotels and villas 24/7. They also have a clinic at 6000 Turkey Lake Road (near Universal) 8am–8pm Mon-Fri, but you must call for an appointment. Doctors have mobile pharmacies

At-a-glance kids' height requirements

Height	Park	Rides
2FT 8IN/82CM	Disney's Blizzard Beach	Chairlift
MUST BE WITH A CHILD 3FT–4FT 8IN/91–142CM	Islands of Adventure	Pteranodon Flyers
3FT/91CM	Disney's Magic Kingdom	The Barnstormer
	Universal Studios	Woody Woodpecker's Nuthouse Coaster
	Islands of Adventure	The Cat in the Hat, Skull Island: Reign of Kong (3–4 ft with adult)
3FT 2IN/96.5CM	Disney's Hollywood Studios	Millenium Falcon: Smugglers Run
3FT 4IN/101CM	Disney's Animal Kingdom	DINOSAUR!
	Disney's Hollywood Studios	Star Tours, The Twilight Zone Tower of Terror, Star Wars: Rise of the Resistance
	Disney's Magic Kingdom	Splash Mountain, Big Thunder Mountain Railroad, Seven Dwarfs Mine Train Ride
	EPCOT	Test Track, Soarin'
	Islands of Adventure	The Amazing Adventures of Spider-Man
	Universal Studios	The Simpsons Ride, TRANSFORMERS: The Ride – 3D, Harry Potter and the Escape from Gringotts, Fast & Furious: Supercharged
3FT 6IN/106CM	Aquatica	Walhalla Wave, Taumata Racer, Ray Rush
	Busch Gardens	The Wild Surge (3ft 2in/96cm with adult), Congo River Rapids, Ubanga-Banga Bumper Cars, Scorpion, Sand Serpent (age 6 minimum), Cobra's Curse
	Disney's Animal Kingdom	Kali River Rapids
	Islands of Adventure	Jurassic Park River Adventure
	SeaWorld	Journey to Atlantis, Wild Arctic, Infinity Falls
	Universal Studios	Men in Black: Alien Attack
3FT 8 IN/111CM	Disney's Animal Kingdom	Expedition: Everest, Flight of Passage
	Disney's Magic Kingdom	Space Mountain
	EPCOT	Mission: SPACE
	Islands of Adventure	Dudley Do-Right's Ripsaw Falls
3FT 10IN/116CM	Busch Gardens	Stanley Falls
UNDER 4FT/122CM ONLY	Aquatica	Kata's Kookaburra Cove
	Disney's Blizzard Beach	Tike's Peak
	Disney's Typhoon Lagoon	Ketchakiddee Creek
4FT/122CM	Aquatica	Dolphin Plunge, Ihu's Breakaway Falls, Omaka Rocka, KareKare Curl
	Busch Gardens	Jungle Flyers
	Disney's Animal Kingdom	Primeval Whirl
	Disney's Blizzard Beach	Summit Plummet, Slush Gusher, Downhill Double Dipper
	Disney's Hollywood Studios	Rock 'n' Roller Coaster Starring Aerosmith
	Disney's Typhoon Lagoon	Crush 'n' Gusher, Humunga Kowabunga
	Islands of Adventure	Popeye And Bluto's Bilge-Rat Barges, Flight of the Hippogriff, Hagrid's Magical Creatures Motorbike Adventure, Harry Potter and the Forbidden Journey
	Universal Studios	Revenge of the Mummy, ET Adventure
4FT 3IN/130CM	Universal Studios	Hollywood Rip Ride Rockit!
4FT 4IN/132CM	Disney's Magic Kingdom	Tomorrowland Speedway (for child to drive alone)
	Islands of Adventure	Dr Doom's Fearfall
4FT 6IN/137CM	Busch Gardens	SheiKra, Kumba, Montu, Cheetah Hunt, Falcon's Fury, Tigris
	Islands of Adventure	The Incredible Hulk Coaster
	SeaWorld	Kraken, Manta, Mako

and even X-ray units and they specialise in healthcare for overseas visitors. They can often arrange same-day dental and other specialist care and take many UK travel insurance policies, dealing directly with the insurance company. Their switchboard is manned around the clock (1855 932 5252, **themedicalconcierge.com**).

If you need an emergency dentist, **Mobile Dental ER** has a mobile facility that can visit anywhere in the Orlando area, 7 days a week (9am–5pm). Pay with all major credit cards (but save receipts for your insurance). (407 955 0743; **mobiledentaler.com**).

BRITTIP
If you take regular prescription drugs, find out the different UK and US names from your doctor or pharmacist and carry the info with you (e.g. adrenaline is known as epinephrine, paracetamol is acetaminophen).

The Dr P Phillips Hospital, 9400 Turkey Lake Road, also has an emergency outpatients (the Emergency Room, or ER in America) open 24hrs (407 351 8500).

Chemists: The largest chemists ('drug stores') are Walgreens (**walgreens.com**) and CVS (**cvs.com**), and the Walgreens at 12100 S Apopka-Vineland Road (near Disney Springs), 5935 W Irlo Bronson Memorial Highway (Highway 192 in Kissimmee), 6201, 8959 and 12650 I-Drive (among others, plus the one at the corner of I-Drive and Sand Lake Rd), are open 24 hours.

BRITTIP
The Kids Eat Free card (look up **kidseatfreecard.com/**) and the Eat & Play card (p10) are great ways to save money in many tourist-area restaurants. They feature dozens of options, from fast-food places to upmarket choices.

Travel insurance

Don't travel without insurance, but there's no need to pay over the top or to buy your travel agent's policy. Your policy should cover all these options

- Medical cover of at least £2m.
- Personal liability up to £2m (but you still need Supplementary Liability with your car hire firm).
- Cancellation or curtailment cover up to £5,000.
- Personal property cover up to £1,500 (but check as most policies limit single articles to £250).
- Cash and document cover, including your passport and tickets. 24hr emergency helpline.
- If you want to go horse-riding, check your policy includes dangerous sports cover.

Shop around at reputable dealers like:

- **Allianz Assistance** (020 8603 9653, **allianz-assistance.co.uk**)
- **American Express** (0800 028 7573, **insurance.americanexpress.co.uk**)
- **Aviva** (0345 303 8715, **aviva.co.uk**)
- **AXA** (0330 024 1307, **www.axa.co.uk/travel-insurance**)
- **Columbus Direct** (0800 068 0060, **columbusdirect.com**)
- **Direct Travel** (0330 880 3600, **direct-travel.co.uk**)
- **Money Supermarket** compares travel insurers online at **moneysupermarket.com/travel-insurance.**

BRITTIP
To avoid costly overseas roaming charges on your mobile in the US, switch off data roaming and use free WiFi or buy a pre-paid data Sim before you go. To call the US from the UK, dial 001, then the number; from the US to the UK, dial 011 44 and omit the first 0 of the area code.

Florida with children

There is no 'right' age to take children to Orlando. Some toddlers take to it instantly, while some 6–7-year-olds are overwhelmed. Often, the best attractions are the hotel swimming pool or the tram ride to a park gates! Some love the Disney characters instantly, while others find them frightening. At 4½, Simon's oldest boy loved just about every second of his first experience (apart from the fireworks!) and still talks about it. A 3-year-old may not remember much, but will have fun and provide you with great memories, photos and videos. Here are our top tips.

The flight: Pack a bag with lots of little treats and activities (comics, sweets, colouring books, small surprise toys, etc.) and keep vital extras like Calpol (in sachets, if possible), a change of clothes, a small first-aid kit, plasters, antiseptic cream, baby wipes, sunglasses, a hat and sunscreen in your hand luggage.

Once you're there: Take things slowly and let your children dictate the pace to a large extent. In hot, humid summer, only the most placid children (and few under-5s, in our experience) will happily queue for an hour or more, so use Disney's FastPass+ system (p96) judiciously. The heat, in particular, can quickly result in grizzly kids, so take breaks for drinks and splash zones or head for attractions with air-conditioning. Keep your 'extras' kit from the flight with you. Go back to the hotel for an afternoon snooze to dodge the worst of the heat and crowds.

In the sun: Always carry sun cream and sun block and use it often, in queues, on buses, etc. Use a children's after-sun lotion and make sure they drink a lot of water or non-fizzy drinks; tiredness and irritability are often the signs of mild dehydration.

Dining out: Look for Kids-eat-free deals as they can apply to children up to 12, and take advantage of the many buffet options (see Chapter 11) to fill up the family or for picky eaters. Many restaurants do Meals To Go if you want a quiet meal in your own accommodation. And try to let your children get used to the characters (especially their size) before you go to one of the many wonderful character meals.

Having fun: Let your children do some of the decision-making and be prepared to go with the flow if they find something unexpected – such as the many squirt fountains and splash zones in the parks (bring swimsuits and/or a change of clothes!). The Orlando rule of 'You Can't Do It All' applies especially with kids. Be aware some youngsters find the evening fireworks too loud, but the hotels around the Magic Kingdom offer a view from a distance.

Baby centres: All the parks have facilities for nursing mothers (locations are on the park map) and can provide baby food, nappies and even spare children's underpants for those little accidents. All Disney hotel gift shops stock baby food and nappies. Expectant mothers are strongly advised not to ride some of the more dynamic attractions, and there are clear warnings on park maps and at the rides (p26).

Pushchairs: 'Strollers' are essential, even if your children are a year or so out of them. The walking wears kids out quickly. You can take your own, hire them at the parks or buy one for as little as $25 at a local supermarket. Babysitting is available through many Disney resorts and some of the bigger hotels elsewhere.

SheiKra at Busch Gardens

Travellers with disabilities

The parks pay close attention to the needs of visitors with disabilities and Florida is extremely disabled-friendly. (Note: Americans use the word 'handicapped' as we use 'disabled'.)

Access: Wheelchair availability and access is usually good (though there are a few rides that cannot cater for them) and all hotels have disabled-accessible rooms. For hearing-impaired guests, there are assistive listening devices and reflective captioning where a commentary is part of a show. Braille guidebooks are available, plus rest areas for guide dogs, and there are Audio Descriptions for blind guests. Disney, Universal and SeaWorld offer Accessibility Guides for disabled guests in all their main parks (and online). Life-jackets are always on hand at water parks. For Disney disability assistance, call 407 560 2547; for Universal, call 407 224 4233.

Guest Assistance: If you need help with queuing or have children with special needs, visit any Disney theme park Guest Relations office, with the person in question, and request a Disability Access Service card (DAS). It provides a return time based on the current queue at each attraction.

As soon as the Guest finishes one attraction, they can receive a return time for another. This can be used in addition to Disney's FastPass+ service. Universal, SeaWorld and Busch Gardens provide similar assistance through their Guest Services.

Parking permits: To use any of the plentiful designated disabled parking areas in all public areas (including the parks), UK drivers must obtain a **Temporary Disabled Parking Permit**, which costs $15 and is valid for 90 days (although you may renew a permit within 12 months for no fee). Apply in advance via the Orange County Tax Collectors office at **bit.ly/brit-park** as follows:

1. Visit the Contact Us page, enter your name, email, choose 'Parking Placards', provide a brief note of where you are travelling from, and Submit.

2. A customer service specialist will reply with a list of documents.

3. Reply, attaching your completed HSMV 83039 form, copy of driver's licence/state ID or passport and both sides of your UK Blue Badge.

4. After verification, you will be contacted for payment processing.

5. The temporary placard will be mailed to your home address.

There is a $2 processing fee and you should allow two weeks for it to arrive. Alternatively, you can visit any Tax Collectors office in central Florida (most open 8.30am–5pm Mon–Fri only, but you can request an appointment in advance). For tax offices in Orange County (for the Orlando area), call 407 845 6200 or visit **octaxcol.com** and click Locations; in Osceola County (for Kissimmee), call 407 742 4000 (**osceolataxcollector.com**). The main tax office in Kissimmee is located at 2501 E. Irlo Bronson Highway.

- **Walker Mobility:** Electric scooters and wheelchair rentals, with free delivery and pick-up, even from holiday villas (407 518 6000, **walkermobility.com**).
- **Mobility Works:** Specially equipped vans for hire for wheelchair users (1877 275 4915, **mobilityworks.com**).
- **Orlando Medical Rentals:** Wide range of medical equipment for hire, including powered scooters and wheelchairs (1877 356 9943, **orlandomedicalrentals.com**).

The AllEars website has lots of advice on a range of concerns, from children with ADD to vegetarian and vegan food (**bit.ly/brit-allears**).

Repeat visitors

A large part of the Orlando market is repeat visitors. Chapters 8 and 9 are largely designed with this in mind. Here are 10 things worth doing once you have Been There and Done That:

1 Behind-the-scenes tours at the Disney parks

2 Dolphin watch cruise from Dolphin Landings at St Pete Beach

3 Wildlife eco-tour with Island Boat Lines at Cocoa Beach

4 The scenic boat ride and Morse Museum in Winter Park

5 Bok Tower Gardens

6 St John's River Eco Tour Cruise in Debary

7 St John's Rivership lunch or dinner cruises

8 Eco-park at Forever Florida or Orlando Tree Trek

9 Merritt Island National Wildlife Refuge at Titusville

10 Kayaking at Kissimmee Paddling Center

Orlando for grown-ups

You don't need to have kids to enjoy Orlando. There is so much clever detail and imagination, adults usually get the most out of the experience.

In fact, as many couples and singles visit the parks as do families with children and you can see the attraction. There's great entertainment, a brilliant range of bars and fine restaurants, a friendly, sociable atmosphere that's ideal for singles and late opening at the parks and clubs. The downtown area of Orlando is coming back as a happening night-time venue, and the Craft Beer scene is booming, with plenty of ways to sample it (p305).

BRITTIP

Freeze drink cartons in your hotel fridge overnight and they will be cool for much of the next day. Also freeze some water bottles in a cheap coolbag and leave it in the car for the end of the day.

Orlando for seniors

Mature travellers can also benefit from a healthy dose of the Sunshine State, as they are likely to have just as much fun, just within slightly different parameters. Seniors can also take advantage of numerous discounts and special deals at many attractions, restaurants and hotels. The official Visitor Center on I-Drive (p40) publishes a brochure of all the deals.

Hotels: For the older person, staying in a Disney hotel is highly recommended as it removes the stress of driving. The extra cost is offset by the convenience and relaxation factor.

Toy Story Land at Disney's Hollywood Studios

© Disney

Parks: Even if the thrill rides are not a draw, just watching can be entertainment enough! Both EPCOT and Disney's Animal Kingdom have much to engage the older visitor, while the shows of Disney's Hollywood Studios make that a popular choice, too, and the Magic Kingdom, while a bit hectic, is still an essential experience.

Evenings: Disney Springs can feel a bit frenetic for the senior crowd, but the Boardwalk Resort is popular and the whole EPCOT resort area offers much in the way of fine dining and relaxation. It is often a prime area for seniors, notably the quieter Disney's Yacht and Beach Club Resorts, and Swan-Dolphin complex.

Weather: Mar and late Oct/Nov are ideal times to visit, but the summer months are hard going for older folks. Good coats (and gloves) may still be necessary at times in winter.

Attractions: We also highlight the following for the senior age group.

- **Animal Kingdom:** Kilimanjaro Safaris, the Maharajah Jungle Trek, Gorilla Falls Forest Trail, Finding Nemo show, Rivers of Light, Festival of the Lion King and Na'vi River Journey.

- **Disney's Hollywood Studios:** Muppet Vision 3-D, Indiana Jones Stunt Show, Beauty and the Beast, Stars Wars: Galaxy's Edge area and Fantasmic!.

- **EPCOT:** Spaceship Earth, Soarin', all of World Showcase and the live entertainment (plus the superb gardens and architecture).

Rivers of Light at Disney's Animal Kingdom

© Disney

- **Magic Kingdom:** The Haunted Mansion, Jungle Cruise, Pirates of the Caribbean, Mickey's PhilharMagic, Under the Sea – Journey of the Little Mermaid and Festival of Fantasy Parade.

- **Universal Studios and Islands of Adventure:** The amazing Wizarding Worlds of Harry Potter.

- **Others:** Watching the children at the many parades and character greetings; dinner at the California Grill in Disney's Contemporary Resort (and other fine dining locations); shopping at Orlando Premium Outlets.

- **More options:** SeaWorld remains popular for seniors and even Busch Gardens, despite its many roller-coasters, has plenty to offer. The local Segway Tours (in Kissimmee, Mount Dora, St Petersburg, Port Canaveral and Clearwater Beach) are well recommended, while Mount Dora, Winter Garden and Winter Park (see also Chapter 8) are also perfect senior fare.

You've got mail

You won't find many post boxes and some post offices don't seem to know the fees for postage to the UK. All the parks have post boxes and you can get stamp books from most stamp machines and City Hall at the Magic Kingdom. A standard postcard or greetings card in an envelope to the UK both need a $1.15 stamp; standard postage within the US is 55c.

The main post offices are:

- **Disney area:** 10450 Turkey Lake Road (just north of the junction of Palm Parkway and Central Florida Parkway; 8am–7pm Mon–Fri, 9am– 5pm Sat).

- **Kissimmee:** 1415 W Oak Street (8.30am–5pm Mon–Fri, 9am–2pm Sat).

- There is also a small post office inside the **Mall at Millenia**, off the lower level of the Grand Court.

American speak

Many words and phrases have a different meaning across the Atlantic. For instance, when Americans say the first floor, they mean the ground floor, the second floor is really the first, and so on. (NB: NEVER ask for a packet of fags; 'fag' is a crude, slang term for a homosexual.) Here are a few everyday words to help you:

American	English	American	English
ATM	Cash machine	Faucet	Tap
Appetizer	Starter	Fender	Car bumper
Band aid	Plaster	Freeway	Motorway
Bathroom	Private toilet	Fries	Chips
Biscuit	Savoury scone	Gas	Petrol
Broiled	Grilled	Graham cracker	Digestive biscuit
Cellphone	Mobile phone	Hood	Car bonnet
Check	Bill	Intersection	Junction
Chips	Crisps	Nickel	5 cents
Collect call phone call	Reverse charge	No standing	No parking OR stopping
Cookie	Biscuit	'Pound sign'	The # on a phone keypad
Cot/rollaway	Fold-up bed	Purse	Handbag
Crib	Cot	Quarter	25 cents
Diaper	Nappy	Ramp	Slip road
Dime	10 cents	Restroom	Public toilet
Divided highway	Dual carriageway	Seltzer	Soda water
Eggplant	Aubergine	Shrimp	King prawn
Eggs 'over easy'	Eggs fried on both sides but soft	Soda	Fizzy drink
		Stroller	Pushchair
Eggs 'sunny side up'	Eggs fried on just 1 side (soft)	Trunk	Car boot
		Turn-out	Lay-by
Entree	Main course	Yield	Give way
Facecloth/washcloth	Flannel	Zucchini	Courgette

Wedding bells

Florida is a popular choice for couples wanting to tie the knot. Its almost guaranteed sunshine and lush, natural landscape make it a huge hit as a wedding backdrop. Orlando also has terrific services, co-ordinators and venues like Wild Florida, Cypress Grove Estate House, Winter Park wedding chapel, Casa Feliz, Leu Gardens, Ceviche in downtown Orlando and hotels like Rosen Shingle Creek, Walt Disney World Swan and Dolphin and the Omni Orlando Champions Gate. Even scenic golf courses such as Celebration Golf Club and Grand Cypress can stage grand occasions extremely well. More unusual ones include the Hard Rock Café, a hot-air balloon or helicopter, Danville B&B (**danvillebnb.com**), on the beach, a luxury yacht, or even the Wheel at ICON Park. All tour operators feature wedding options, or you can pick a local specialist like Get Married In Florida (p34). Prices vary from £300/couple (for a basic civil ceremony) to more than £5,000.

BRITTIP

Looking for essential travel accessories and useful knick-knacks, like TSA-approved locks, plug adapters and waterproof accessories? Type in 'essentials for travel' on Amazon. Asda supermarkets also sell a good travel range.

Walt Disney World's Wedding Pavilion: True fairytale romance, with the backdrop of Cinderella Castle, you can opt for traditional elegance in this Victorian setting with up to 260 guests or the full Disney experience, arriving in Cinderella's coach with Mickey and Minnie as guests. Disney's wedding planners can tailor-make the occasion for you (407 828 3400) but at a price – rates START at $7,000 for the basic ceremony and can top $60,000!

Licence: To obtain a marriage licence, visit a local courthouse: Osceola County Courthouse, Courthouse Square, Suite 2000, Kissimmee (just off Bryan Street in downtown Kissimmee) 8am–4pm Mon–Fri (407 343 3500); Orange County Courthouse, 425 N Orange Avenue (downtown Orlando) 7.30am–4pm Mon–Fri (407 836 2067); or Clermont Courthouse at Minneola City Hall, 800 North Highway 27, Minneola, 8.30am–4.30pm (closed noon–1pm; 352 394 2018). All are closed on US bank holidays. Both parties must be present to apply for a licence, which costs $93.50 (in cash, travellers' cheques or by credit card) and is valid for 60 days, while a ceremony (equivalent to a British register office) can be performed at the same time by the clerk for an extra $30. You'll need passports, birth certificates and, if you have been married before, your decree absolute. After acquiring a licence, a couple can marry anywhere in Florida. It is also possible to obtain a licence BEFORE arriving in Florida (see **floridamarriagelicencebypost.com**). For flowers and floral design, be sure to look up Flourish on 407 644 7474 or **flourishproductions.com**)

Space Mountain during Mickey's Not-so-Scary Halloween Party

© Disney

Top 10 romantic restaurants

1. Victoria & Albert's, Disney's Grand Floridian Resort
2. Urbain 40, Sand Lake Road
3. California Grill, Disney's Contemporary Resort
4. Todd English's Bluezoo, Walt Disney World Dolphin Resort
5. Jiko, Disney's Animal Kingdom Lodge
6. Capa, Four Seasons Orlando
7. Old Hickory Steakhouse, Gaylord Palms Resort
8. Bice, Universal's Portofino Bay Hotel
9. Cala Bella, Shingle Creek Resort
10. Narcoossee's, Disney's Grand Floridian Resort

We could actually list several dozen more, including Hillstone, Luma on Park and Fleming's (Winter Park), Bull & Bear (Waldorf-Astoria), Primo (JW Marriott Grand Lakes), The Venetian Chop House (Caribe Royale Resort), Seasons 52, Eddie V's and Roy's (Sand Lake Road), and Kres Chophouse (downtown Orlando).

Get Married in Florida: This local business has been dedicated to organising weddings for UK couples since 2002. Ideally placed to deliver great personal service, it offers the complete package for the perfect wedding (321 945 1563, **getmarriedinflorida.com**).

BRITTIP

Looking for a good pay-as-you-go mobile option for the USA? Check out Three and their £25 add-on option (**three.co.uk/feel-at-home/**).

Disney special occasions

Birthday badges: Get free badges from City Hall in the Magic Kingdom and Guest Services at EPCOT, Disney's Hollywood Studios and Disney's Animal Kingdom. Cast Members make a fuss over children (and adults!) wearing a birthday badge.

Top things to do for FREE!

Disney's Boardwalk Resort: Free nightly entertainment includes jugglers, comedians and live music. Time your visit to coincide with the 9pm EPCOT Forever show at nearby EPCOT.

Downtown Orlando Historic Tour: From the Visitor Center on Orange Avenue, local historian Richard Forbes leads a free tour of downtown at 9.30am on the first Fri of every month from Oct–May. Must call in advance to check availability on 407 246 3789 (**bit.ly/brit-downtowntour**).

Lake Eola Park: Take a walk on the mild side in downtown Orlando. The kids can play or feed the swans and summer sees live music and films at the Walt Disney Amphitheater (**bit.ly/brit-eola**).

Lake Tibet-Butler Preserve: Just 5mins from Disney but a world away from the theme park bustle (on local highway 535, Winter Garden-Vineland Road) is this local nature preserve, with quiet trails, lake overlook and interpretive centre. Open 9am–dusk (not public holidays), it is on the Great Florida Birding Trail and is a minor gem of native wildlife (**sfwmd.gov**).

Lakeridge Winery and Vineyards: Join one of its fun, free wine-tasting tours and you'll know why Lakeridge (in nearby Clermont) has won more than 700 awards. Designate a driver as sample sizes are generous! 10am–4pm Mon–Sat, 11am–4pm Sun (**lakeridgewinery.com**).

Morse Museum of American Art: This superb little museum in tranquil Winter Park, dedicated to American paintings, ceramics and representative arts from the 19th and 20th centuries, is free 4–8pm every Fri, Nov–Apr (**morsemuseum.org**).

Old Town, Kissimmee: The biggest vintage car parade in the US every Sat, with cars on display from 1pm and the Classic Car Cruise at 8.30pm, plus Thursday Night Bike Night from 5pm and a Muscle Car Cruise 8.30pm each Fri, and live music 7–10pm (**myoldtownusa.com**).

Osceola County History Museum: Part of the new Welcome Center on Highway 192 in Kissimmee (by Marker 15), this offers a great insight into the region's back story and heritage (**osceolahistory.org**; see also p257; daily 9am–5pm, closed on public hols).

PLUS: Watching the participants at iFLY Orlando on I-Drive (p234); the Cornell Fine Arts Museum at Rollins College in Winter Park (p247); and the hiking trails of Ocala National Forest, north of Orlando (**stateparks.com/Ocala.html**).

Birthday cakes: Contact room service at your resort or Guest Services at one of the parks. All Disney restaurants can offer ready-made 15cm/6in cakes ($35 at each restaurant) or something larger ($50–180) if ordered 48 hours in advance on 407 827 2253. If someone in your group has a birthday, tell the Cast Member at check-in (or when you make your reservation), as well as hostesses and/or servers in restaurants. While not guaranteed, Disney staff often go out of their way to make the day special. If characters know it's a birthday when they sign a child's autograph book, they may add a special birthday wish.

Birthday cruise: Celebrate a special occasion with a 90-minute pontoon boat trip from one of five Disney resorts, complete with snacks, drinks, streamers and balloons for a 90min tour for up to 10 from $349, plus tax (407 939 7529).

Disney's Pirate Adventure: This two-hour activity for kids 4–12 sails (on pontoon boats) from two of the resorts (the Yacht/Beach Club and Caribbean Beach at 9.30am) to find pirate 'booty' at different ports of call, with a final stop for snacks; $39–49 per child (407 939 7529, up to 180 days in advance).

Money matters

You'll need to carry ID for both cheques and some credit card purchases (take your UK driving licence card).

Cash: It is worth separating larger notes from smaller ones in your wallet to avoid flashing all your money in view. Losing £300 of travellers' cheques shouldn't ruin your holiday – but losing $600 in cash might. All the theme parks have ATMs (cash machines).

Credit cards: Having a credit card is almost essential (especially for car hire) as they are accepted everywhere and provide extra buying security. Visa, Mastercard and American Express are all widely accepted.

FairFX card: Perhaps the best option is this convenient card, which you preload to a chosen amount (**fairfx.com**). The exchange rate is fixed at loading and you can save 5–10% on High Street currency rates.

Safety and security

While crime is not a serious issue in Florida, this is still big-city America. Tourism is such a vital part of the economy, the authorities have a highly safety-conscious attitude. Just don't ignore the usual safety guidelines for travelling abroad.

━━━━━━━━BRITTIP

Use a business rather than your home address on your luggage. It is less conspicuous and safer should any item be lost or stolen.

Common-sense tips: A bumbag (or 'fanny pack') is better than a handbag

The Space Shop at Kennedy Space Center

Simon and Susan

Apart from the *Brit Guide to Orlando*, we contribute to a wide range of media on many travel subjects. Find out more about our work on **venesstravelmedia.net**, our Facebook page, YouTube (Veness Travel Media), or Twitter (@VenessTravelMe1), including our book *Defying Expectations* about Orlando City Soccer Club and new *Walt Disney World Hacks*.

or shoulder bag in the parks. Make sure bags are always firmly zipped up when not in use. Don't leave camera equipment on view in the car (the heat could damage it anyway).

Dealing with assault: The VERY strong police advice in the unlikely event of being confronted by an assailant is: DO NOT resist or 'have a go', because this can often make a bad situation worse. But it is comforting to know Orlando does not have any no-go areas in the main tourist parts. The nearest is the portion of the Orange Blossom Trail south of downtown Orlando (a selection of strip clubs and 'adult bars').

Hotel security: Always use door peepholes and security chains when someone knocks at the door. DON'T open the door to strangers without asking for ID, and check with the hotel desk if you are not sure. Keep doors and windows locked and always use deadlocks and security chains. Take all valuables when you go out (or put them in the room safe), and don't leave the door open, even if you pop down the corridor to the ice machine.

Most hotels now have electronic card-locks and can offer deposit boxes as well as in-room mini-safes. Ask reception staff for safety advice for surrounding areas or if you are travelling somewhere you are not sure about. Safety is a major issue for the Central Florida Hotel & Lodging Association (**cfhla.org**) and hotel staff are well briefed to be helpful.

Christmas cheer

We're often asked our favourite time of year here and it has to be the festive season, from late Nov–early Jan. Every park adds a fab Christmas overlay and there is more to enjoy everywhere, even at the smaller attractions and places like Disney Springs and the town of Celebration. It can get seriously crowded 17 Dec–10 Jan, but visit in early Dec and you get all the festivities with fewer crowds.

Walt Disney World: Every park has its own extensive decorations and magnificent Christmas tree, with a daily lighting ceremony at the **Magic Kingdom**, plus Mickey's Once Upon A Christmastime Parade, the Castle Dream Lights (a stunning effect on Cinderella Castle) and the chance to meet Santa, as well as the extra-ticket event of Mickey's Very Merry Christmas Party (p114). At **EPCOT**, the standout feature is the Candlelight Processional, a choral retelling of the Nativity story with a guest narrator, as well as Holidays Around The World, with traditional storytellers at each World Showcase pavilion. Mr and Mrs Claus visit at the American Adventure pavilion, where vocal group Voices of Liberty become carollers for the season. **Disney Springs** features the Spirit of the Season, with Santa's chalet, school choirs and more lavish decorations, including the character-filled Christmas Tree Trail. Each resort also boasts plenty of Christmas cheer, with the best being Disney's Grand Floridian, offering a life-size Gingerbread House.

Universal Orlando: Miles more garland, lights and tinsel are on offer here, plus three daily features. At **Universal Studios**, Universal's Holiday Parade is a fabulous cavalcade of floats, giant balloons, Father Christmas and a tree-lighting ceremony at dusk each day, as well as carollers, hot cocoa kiosks and a Christmas Village of traditional fare and gifts. The Wizarding World of Harry Potter: Diagon Alley adds its own festive overlay, buskers in Kings Cross Station and a special Celestina Warbeck show. **Islands of Adventure** offers Christmas both Harry Potter and Dr Seuss style. Grinchmas can be found in Seuss Landing, including the family-friendly stage show *The Grinch Who Stole Christmas*. The Wizarding World of Harry Potter: Hogsmeade features the stunning projection show *The Magic of Christmas at Hogwarts Castle* multiple times each evening.

SeaWorld: Arguably the biggest Christmas celebration is here, with magnificent shows, special effects and extravagant theming. It starts with the Sea of Trees, a fabulous musical sequence of well-lit 'trees' spread over the main lagoon, and continues with the Christmas Marketplace at one end of the park. Two unmissable seasonal shows are Winter Wonderland On Ice and O Wondrous Night, a nativity tale with a difference, while nightly 'snowfalls', dancers, musicians and the Christmas Celebration fireworks round out a glittering seasonal occasion.

Busch Gardens: The centrepiece is Christmas Town, another after-dark spectacular throughout the park, with themed areas, shows and decorations (each Fri, Sat and Sun from late Nov/early Dec, and nightly from mid-Dec). Highlights include the Carol of the Bells, an Ice Show, the Three Kings Journey and a lavish array of seasonal dining and shopping, plus Santa's 'North Pole' home and some more superb lighting effects.

Gaylord Palms Resort: Equally astounding is their annual ICE! exhibition, a mind-boggling presentation of 2 MILLION pounds of ice in marvellous tableaux, hand-carved by 40 Chinese artisans in the special 'Florida Freezer,' including four huge ice slides. There are festive presentations, shows, musicians, trees, kids' activities, character meet-and-greets and the chance to meet Santa, making for an amazing Christmas offering. Book in advance, though, at **bit.ly/brit-gaylord**.

Celebration: This pretty Disney-inspired town offers nightly 'snow-falls' 6–9pm on Market Street in Dec and also features ice-skating for kids, horse-drawn carriage rides, carollers and other festive touches.

And more: Downtown Orlando is well worth a visit for its many festive touches, notably around **Lake Eola**, which has Christmas trees, ice-skating and the nightly Holiday Lights show. The child-sized fun of **LEGOLAND Florida** boasts a superb array of decorations and the daily Tree Lighting, while all the dinner shows add in suitably festive theming and extra Christmas elements. One final amazing event is staged at the huge First Baptist Church on John Young Parkway just off I-4, where The Singing Christmas Trees is a stunning choral show presentation of music, stage and lighting each Fri, Sat and Sun for the first two weeks in Dec. Find out more at **bit.ly/brit-trees**.

British Consulate-General, Miami

Top Five Travel Aware Tips when travelling to Florida, Puerto Rico & US Virgin Islands:

1   Secure **appropriate travel insurance** for the duration of your holiday. Hospital visits in the US can cost thousands of pounds out of pocket. Ensure you travel with enough medication to see you through your holiday.

2   Check your **passport's validity,** fill out the emergency details page. Keep your passport safe at all times. Take a photo of it on your smart phone and send it to a relative or friend who may need to access it on your behalf. Don't leave your passport, luggage or valuables unaccompanied in your rental vehicle.

3   The British Consulate-General, Miami, provides **Consular Services** to British nationals in Florida, Puerto Rico and US Virgin Islands when things go wrong abroad. Consular Services can assist in matters such as Hospitalization, Emergency Travel Documents, Death(s) and Arrest/Detention. Remember to respect local laws and customs.

4   The British Consulate-General, Miami can provide British nationals with an **Emergency Travel Document** to return home should your passport be lost, stolen or damaged. These documents are also available in Orlando via our Consular Agency at Orlando International Airport by appointment. Apply for one of these documents on 305 400 6400 or gov.uk/emergency-travel-document.

5   Hurricane Season runs from 1 Jun–30 Nov each year. For the latest **Travel Advice updates**, visit travelaware.campaign.gov.uk and follow us on Twitter **@UKinFlorida**. Phone 305 400 6400 should you require Consular Services during your holiday.

BRITTIP

If your room has been cleaned before you go out for the day, put the 'Do Not Disturb' sign on the door. Always keep valuables out of sight whether in the hotel or car.

Car safety: Make the basic safety checks of your hire car straight away and familiarise yourself with the car's controls BEFORE driving away. Try to memorise your route in advance, even if you just remember the road numbers. Most hire firms now give good directions to all the hotels, so check them before you set off (or, better still, hire a GPS system). Make sure the fuel tank is well filled and never let it get near empty so you risk running out of 'gas' in an unfamiliar area. If you do stray off your pre-determined route, stick to well-lit areas and ask for directions only from official businesses like hotels and petrol stations, or the police. Try to park close to your destination where there are plenty of lights and DO NOT get out if there are suspicious characters around. Always lock the car when you leave it – note that not all rental cars have central locking.

More info: For more info on safety, contact the Orange County Police (407 254 7000 or **ocso.com**) or the I-Drive police team office (407 351 9368). If you are the victim of theft in Orange County, call 407 836 4357.

Emergencies

Emergency services: For police, fire department or ambulance, dial 911 (9-**911** from your hotel room). Make sure your children know this number.

General: For smaller-scale crises (e.g. mislaid tickets, lost passports or rescheduled flights), your holiday company should have an emergency number in the hotel reception.

Let us take the stress out of your holiday …

…with our unique Touring Plans

The *Brit Guide* Touring Plans will ensure you get the most out of your time in central Florida. This is a service no one else can offer, as we provide you with daily touring plans for the parks, attractions and shopping in central Florida.

Your full Touring Plan (which usually runs to 40 pages for a 2-week holiday) will: walk you through your day so you make the most of your time and your tickets; highlight any rides that may be closed for refurbishment; include shopping guides if you plan to take advantage of all the savings to be had at the malls and outlets; provide key advice right from the source of the fun, as well as a host of Brit Tip Extras and Brit Picks (our special favourites) we can't fit into the book, plus a special Busy Day Guide for your visit. Just go to **britguideorlando.net** and click Touring Plans.

Fill out the online form with your travel dates, choose the type of Plan you need (be sure to see our FAQ to help you decide which Plan is right for you), and indicate which parks/shopping/etc you want to fit into your visit. Submit the form, with your payment, and you'll receive, by email, your unique Touring Plan, which will consist of:

1   An official *Brit Guide* welcome from Susan and Simon Veness.

2   A daily plan for each of the parks, water parks and shopping centres you will visit.

3   Touring strategies in each day's plan to help you avoid the longest queues and take advantage of the latest developments.

4   Alternative suggestions in case of bad weather.

5   A note of any rides/shows that are closed during your visit (please see our FAQ for further info).

6   A special selection of Brit Tip Extras and local advice.

7   Our Brit Picks – a guide to a range of personal favourites, from restaurants to shops.

8   The ultimate insider knowledge, as Susan and Simon are based in the heart of the Orlando magic and are fully up to date on all developments.

9   Our special bonus: an EXCLUSIVE Platinum VIP Passport for Orlando Premium Outlets (not available to the public), with extra savings at select stores at this great shopping venue.

10 Best of all, you will receive a Busy Day Guide especially for your holiday dates so that you can assemble the best possible day-by-day plan.

All in all, it adds up to the most comprehensive package of specialised holiday info anywhere, and it represents the secret to the most fun, in the most hassle-free way, in the most exciting place on earth. What more could you ask for? Just check out our website and we'll do the rest.

Please note: There is a minimum order period, so check online and apply in good time before your holiday (*at least* 10 days). Book owners receive a discount on the price of the Touring Plans, so have it with you when you register as you'll need a password from the book.

The password is random and expires on 31 Dec of the edition's year, NO EXCEPTIONS. We are not a travel agency or ticket service and you MUST know your park and shopping requirements in advance.

We urge you to read our FAQ before ordering, as it will assist you in choosing the right plan for your holiday, answer the most common questions we receive, and ensure you order with confidence.

You'll find masses of info on all things Orlando on the discussion forums at **attraction-tickets-direct. co.uk** and, as we are both Moderators on the site, you can come and 'talk' to us and pass on your own ideas and experiences. It's a fun, friendly community and we're always happy to see new faces.

Know before you go

Here are the best sources for additional info before you go.

- **Kissimmee:** More useful online info and an e-guide to download on this link, **experiencekissimmee.com/ request-guide.**

- **Fan websites:** Check out **thedibb. co.uk** ('Disney with a British accent', including busy forums, villa pages and more); the comprehensive **allears.net** (notably for its Disney dining section); the huge **wdwinfo. com**; and specialist UK Universal podcast **uuopodcast.blogspot.com.**

- **Orlando Attractions mag:** (which we also write for) offers a superb feature-full site at **attractionsmagazine. com**, plus a weekly magazine-style programme called *The Show.*

- **Orlando Sentinel:** The online local paper (**orlandosentinel.com**) is packed with info, especially for shopping, dining and nightlife, while the Orlando Weekly is also handy (**orlandoweekly.com**).

- **Orlando Visitor Center:** It's worth checking Orlando's ONLY official Visitor Center, 8am–9pm daily at

Fabulous Florida beaches

8102 International Drive (next to Mango's Tropical Café; 407 363 5872 or email **info@visitorlando.com**) for discounted attraction tickets, and free brochures, accommodation advice, info pamphlets and maps (**visitorlando.com**).

Seeing the real Florida

Central Florida is an amazing place (it's one of the reasons we live here) but it's not all about the theme parks. Venture beyond the main tourist areas and you'll discover the *real* Florida, which is bursting with great scenery and wildlife. It's not hard to see alligators, deer, raccoons, armadillos and even bobcats in the wild. There are also panthers, bears, wild pigs and foxes. The exotic birdlife includes eagles, ospreys, herons, cranes and egrets, and the waterways boast manatees, dolphins, rays and dozens of types of fish. Chapters 8 and 9 highlight how to discover these great opportunities and we urge readers to try at least one to experience what truly makes Florida special. There are many state parks and wildlife reserves and, increasingly, nature tours and trails to enjoy them. There is also more history – dating back to the 16th century – than you'd imagine, plus fabulous museums and other cultural aspects. Florida had cowboys (or 'crackers') before the Wild West and is still a huge cattle-producing state. Cute towns and suburbs like Gulfport, Mount Dora, Winter Park, Stuart, DeLand, Dunedin, Winter Garden and Tarpon Springs abound, while the beaches are simply superb – everywhere. The varied tropical terrain boasts lakes, marshes, cypress forests, sandhills, flatwoods and prairies, and is about as different to most European landscapes as it's possible to get. It all adds up to way more than you thought when you decided Orlando was the place for you – just make sure you see some of it!

Now, on to the next step of the holiday, your transport….

3 Getting Around

Or The Secret of Driving on the Wrong Side of the Road!

A rriving and driving in Orlando are among the biggest concerns for visitors, especially first-timers, but there's no need to worry. Although most people begin their holiday by leaving the airport in a newly acquired, automatic, left-hand-drive hire car on roads that can appear bewildering, driving here is a lot easier and more enjoyable than in the UK. Anyone familiar with the M25 should find Florida FAR less stressful.

Before you get to your hire car, though, you need to be aware of the arrival process at the two airports.

> **BRITTIP**
> Don't forget you must have filled your ESTA form and immigration details online before you travel (p12). For country of residence put UNITED KINGDOM; for Passport Issuing Country, put UK – BRITISH CITIZEN. You must give a valid US address for your accommodation.

Orlando International

This is one of the most modern and enjoyable airports in the world, but anywhere new can be confusing. All flights arrive at one of four satellite terminals and you then take a shuttle tram to the main terminal. Allow at least an hour from landing to ground transportation.

International arrivals: If you arrive with British Airways, Virgin Atlantic, Aer Lingus, Lufthansa, Norwegian or Thomas Cook, you disembark at the satellite for Airside 3 (gates 70–99). Most US domestic airlines use Airside 1 (gates 1–29), Airside 2 (30–59) or Airside 4 (100–129). Join one of the two main queues that feed into the immigration kiosks. Once through Immigration, collect your baggage from the carousel and go through the Customs check. The airport now has a series of self-service kiosks where you input your flight info and passport details, fingerprints and photo before reaching the Immigration officer, which can save considerable time. Just follow the instructions and take your receipt, with your passports and customs form, to the officer. Be aware of a full biometric scan system for arrival and departure at Orlando International, with facial recognition booths that speed up the immigration process still further.

> **BRITTIP**
> Visit **orlandoairports.net** for info including a photo preview of the arrival process at Orlando International Airport (click *Getting Around MCO*, then *Airport Guide*, followed by *Arrival & Departure Guides*, and *International Arrival Guide*).

Option 1: Deposit your checked luggage on a second conveyor belt to take it to the main terminal while you go upstairs to the shuttle with your hand luggage. Once in the main terminal you are on Level 3 and you follow signs down to Baggage Claim B on Level 2 (BA, Lufthansa and Thomas Cook), Baggage Claim A on Level 2 (Aer Lingus and Norwegian) or Baggage Claim A Level 1 (Virgin).

Option 2: If you can manage your luggage without a trolley, take it on the escalator up to the shuttle and go straight to pick up your transport on Level 1 (or, if a specific driver is meeting you, Level 2).

Domestic arrivals: For anyone arriving on a US domestic flight (from another US gateway), you disembark at the satellite terminal and proceed straight to the main terminal on the shuttle to collect your baggage on Level 2 (either A or B side, depending on arrival gate). Once at the main baggage claim, porters can help you to Level 1 (tip $1/bag) for car hire, shuttles and buses. Trolleys need $3 in change (or a credit card).

BRITTIP
Don't follow signs yet for the South Terminal, which is now under construction and due to open in 2021. The tram link is fully operational, but only for parking garage C.

Transfers: Kerbside pick-up – including for taxis, Uber and Lyft – is outside the doors on Level 2, at the bottom of the escalators or by your baggage reclaim. Some tour operators have help desks here, while Virgin has a reception desk on Level 1, side A.

The public bus system, Lynx (p44), operates ONLY from the A side of Level 1 (6am–10.30pm; 9.30pm

Mars Rover Concept Vehicle at Kennedy Space Center

on Suns and public holidays), in spaces 38–41. Links 11 and 51 depart every 30mins (less often on Sun or bank holidays) for Orlando city centre (45mins), while Link 42 serves I-Drive (1hr) and Link 111 goes to SeaWorld via the Florida Mall.

Car hire: All the main hire companies are on site (with 20 off-airport). The main 11 to choose from include *Brit Guide* partner **Alamo** (with new automated self-service kiosks), **Dollar, National, Thrifty, Hertz** and **Avis**, and all offer a full service. Complete your paperwork, then walk out of Level 1 across the road to the multi-storey car park.

BRITTIP
Hiring a car from an on-airport company? Save time by sending the driver to complete the paperwork BEFORE collecting your luggage on Level 2.

If you arrive late, consider staying overnight at the Hyatt Regency hotel at the airport rather than driving tired. You will be fresher and ready to drive next day (and the car hire queues will be shorter). Several tour operators also offer an arrival-day transfer, with car hire pick-up the next day.

Leaving the airport: When you drive out of the airport, DON'T follow signs to 'Orlando'. The main tourist areas are south and west of the city, so follow the signs for your accommodation.

The Martin Andersen Beachline Expressway (528) and Greeneway (417) are both toll roads, so make sure you have some US currency before leaving the airport. Toll booths hate to change notes above $20, while some auto-tolls take ONLY coins.

- **For International Drive:** (I-Drive), take the north exit and the Beachline Expressway (Route 528) west until it crosses I-Drive just north of SeaWorld at exit 1 (it costs $2.50 in toll fees). Most hotels on I-Drive are to the north, so keep right at the exit. NB: there is now

© Kennedy Space Center

Florida Rail

Considering Florida was originally opened up by railways in the late 1800s by railroad baron Henry Flagler, travelling by rail hasn't been a modern option, until recently. Central Florida's commuter rail system **Sunrail** arrived in 2014 and, while it is mainly for locals, it offers a few possibilities as it runs over a 49ml/78km, 16-station stretch from Poinciana, south of Kissimmee, to the city of DeBary north of Orlando. The best stretch for visitors to know about is from Sand Lake Rd station, at the junction with S. Orange Ave, to Church Street in downtown Orlando (2 stops) and Winter Park (5 stops). However, it ONLY operates Mon–Fri (and not public holidays), every 30mins in peak periods and every 2hrs otherwise, 5.30am–10pm. Fares are modest ($3.75/adult for a round-trip from Sand Lake Rd to Winter Park while an unlimited seven-day weekly SunCard is $34) and tickets can be bought in machines at each station using cash or credit card. Just tap your ticket on the validator machine on the platform before you board and at your destination. There are also Lynx bus connections at every Sunrail station, including Link 111 from SeaWorld and Link 42 from I-Drive to the Sand Lake Rd station (**sunrail.com**).

Florida's first high-speed rail system, rebranded as **Virgin Trains USA**, opened in 2018, from West Palm Beach to Miami, with an extension to Orlando in 2022. Orlando International Airport to downtown Miami will take just under 3hrs and feature the latest trains, two classes of travel and on-board comforts (including dining and free WiFi). Once complete, it will make the journey to Miami far more enticing, with day-trips from 16 departures each way every day. Check out **gobrightline.com** for the latest info.

only one toll kiosk on this route but the fee is still $2.50.

- **For Kissimmee, Disney and villas in Clermont/Davenport:** Take the south exit for 3ml/5km and pick up the Central Florida Greeneway (Highway 417) west.

- **For most Disney resorts:** Take exit 6 and follow the signs ($3 in tolls).

- **For Animal Kingdom resorts:** Use exit 3 and take Osceola Parkway west ($3.75).

- **For eastern Kissimmee:** Come off Highway 417 at exit 11, the Orange Blossom Trail (Highway 17/92), and go south ($2.25 in tolls).

- **For west Kissimmee and Clermont/ Davenport (Highway 27):** Take exit 2, turn right on Celebration Avenue and left (west) on Highway 192 all the way to Highway 27 (you will need $3.75 in toll fees).

BRITTIP

For traffic news and reports, tune to 96.5FM (WDBO) or **news965. com**. Call 511 on a mobile phone for motorway traffic info or **fl511.com**.

Orlando Sanford International Airport

Arriving at Sanford (in Seminole County) couldn't be easier. The list of airlines visiting this easy-to-use airport includes TUI (to the UK and Brussels seasonally, and Amsterdam year-round). It generally takes only 30–40mins from arrival to leaving the baggage hall, but there may be delays in peak season. It's a short walk from the plane to the immigration hall (where two queues feed through to the kiosks); you then collect your baggage, pass through Customs and walk straight out to car hire, shuttle or taxi pick-up.

Car hire: As you exit the Customs Hall, the TUI welcome desks are across the road in front of you, next to the Car Rental centre. The one exception is for *Brit Guide* partner Alamo, which has its own centre via a covered walkway and boardwalk behind this building, and its British-dedicated operation is very smooth. Look up more on **orlandosanfordairport.com**.

BRITTIP

If you don't want to drive in Orlando, staying on International Drive is your best bet for being close to most of the attractions. Most hotels have regular shuttles to the parks while Uber is popular and relatively cheap.

Leaving the airport: It may be 35ml/56km to the north and involve more driving (and taxis and shuttles are much more expensive – a town car service would be around $120–135 one-way to Walt Disney World and a taxi $90–115, while one-way shuttle services are around $65/person), but you usually save time by your quicker exit. There is one main road out, on to Lake Mary Boulevard, and you then take Seminole Expressway (Highway 417, which becomes Central Florida Greeneway in Orange County) south. The slip road to this toll motorway is just under the flyover on your LEFT, and you need $8 to reach Disney or Kissimmee or $6.50 for I-Drive (via the Beachline Expressway). You can avoid the tolls by staying on Lake Mary Blvd for 6ml/10km until you get to I-4, but you're going to hit major traffic through the city. The Expressway/Greeneway is an easy-driving introduction to Orlando, even if it does cost a few dollars.

BRITTIP

If you suspect you may need more boot space, upgrade when you book at home as it is usually more expensive to upgrade when you arrive.

Disney's Magical Express

© Disney

WITHOUT A CAR

Although being mobile is advisable, you can survive without a car. However, few attractions are within walking distance of hotels, and taxis can be expensive. You also need to plan in extra travelling time (and with children, taking buses can be tiring). For non-drivers, your best base is either Walt Disney World itself (free transport throughout, but harder to get to the rest of Orlando) or I-Drive for its location, 'walkability' and the great I-Ride Trolley. Many hotels have free shuttles to some of the parks or a cheap, regular mini-bus service. The main options are: public transport; shuttle services; town cars and limousines; and taxis.

BRITTIP

Although Disney has free and extensive transport services, it can be slow, with bus rides from many hotels to the parks taking up to 30mins. The big bonus, though, is the free **Disney's Magical Express** coach service from Orlando airport direct to all Disney resorts. See p59.

Public transport

Lynx bus system: Reliable and cheap but slightly plodding, it covers much of metro Orlando. Its online system map shows all its routes (or 'links') and main attractions (407 841 5969, **golynx.com**).

- **Link 18:** Kissimmee to downtown Orlando (from Osceola Square Mall, east on Highway 192 north on Boggy Creek Road, Buenaventura and Orange Ave).

- **Link 38:** I-Drive to downtown Orlando (from the Convention Center via Kirkman Road and I-4).

- **Link 42:** Orlando International Airport to I-Drive.

- **Link 50:** Disney's Transportation & Ticket Center (TTC) to downtown Orlando (via SeaWorld and I-4).

- **Link 55:** Kissimmee to Four Corners (from Osceola Square Mall west via Highway 192 and Summer Bay Resort).

Park maps

Each of the park maps contains a QR code that you can scan with your smartphone or tablet to take you to a high-res online map. Download a QR reader from iTunes or Play Store

- **Link 56:** Kissimmee to Disney's Magic Kingdom (from Osceola Square Mall, along Highway 192 via Old Town and Celebration to TTC.
- **Link 300:** Disney Springs to downtown Orlando (via I-4).
- **Link 304:** Top of I-Drive to Disney Springs (from Oak Ridge Road via Sand Lake Drive).

BRITTIP

Lynx buses use the Disney Springs West Side Transfer Center as their Disney hub, with Links 301, 302, 303, 305 and 306 going to the parks and resorts.

Lynx fares are $2/ride (free transfers) or $16 for a weekly pass (children six and under free with a full-fare passenger). The service is every 30mins in the main areas, every 15mins 6–9am and 3.30–6.30pm, but you must have the right change. All buses are wheelchair accessible and stop at the pink paw-print Lynx stops.

There can be *long* bus queues at park closing. Taking a taxi can save a lot of hassle to return to I-Drive – about $30–40 from EPCOT and the Studios park; about $40–50 from Magic Kingdom and Animal Kingdom. Uber or Lyft can often be half that.

I-Ride Trolley: Great-value, two-route service along a 14ml/23km stretch of this tourist corridor.

- **The Main/Red Line:** 38 stops from Orlando International Premium Outlets at the top of I-Drive to SeaWorld and Aquatica via Westwood Boulevard and Sea Harbor Drive, then Orlando Vineland Premium Outlets.
- **The Green Line:** 29 stops from the Universal resort (Windhover Drive and Major Boulevard) south to Vineland Premium Outlets via Universal Boulevard, the Convention Center and SeaWorld.

Every day, 8am–10.30pm roughly every 20mins (30mins on the Green Line), it costs $2/trip ($1/kids 3–9, 25c/seniors) – have the right change – or you can buy Unlimited Ride Passes for 1, 3, 5, 7 or 14 days at $5, $7, $9, $12, $18. If you need to transfer between routes, ask for a transfer coupon when you board (not needed with Unlimited Ride Passes). All trolleys have hydraulic wheelchair lifts. Buy a pass at 100+ locations in the I-Drive area, including the Official Visitor Center and most hotel desks, plus online, but NOT on the trolleys themselves (407 248 9590 or US freephone 1866 243 7483, **iridetrolley.com**).

Busch Shuttle Express: Seven departure points in this regular daily service, 8.15–9.40am, from SeaWorld to Busch Gardens. This is FREE with any advance ticket for Busch (notably the 3-Park Ticket with SeaWorld and Aquatica). For more info, call 1800 221 1339 in Orlando toll-free.

BRITTIP

The cheapest way to get from I-Drive to Disney is the $2 Lynx bus Link 50 from SeaWorld – 6600 Sea Harbor Drive – to the TTC next to the Magic Kingdom. All Disney transport then operates from there. Use the I-Ride Trolley to get to SeaWorld.

The Wildlife Express at Walt Disney World

© Disney

Shuttle services

Alternatives to public transport are more than a dozen firms offering set-fee shuttles – from Hummers to buses – from hotels to attractions.

Lake Buena Vista Factory Stores: Shuttle collects guests free each day from 60 hotels in the Orlando and Kissimmee areas (407 363 1093, or **lbvfs.com/free-hotel-shuttles**).

Maingate Transportation: with scheduled services from the airport to all the main tourist areas, and most hotels to the attractions (407 390 0000, **maingatetaxi.com**).

Mears: The most comprehensive service, with a 1,000-vehicle fleet from limousines to town cars and coaches. Typical round-trip shuttle fares: Airport to WDW, $38 adults, $29 under-12s, under-4s free ($24 and $19 one way); Airport to I-Drive, $34 and $26 ($22 and $17 one way); Airport to Highway 192 in Kissimmee, $40 and $32 ($29 and $23 one way); Walt Disney W to Universal Orlando, $22 round trip; I-Drive to Walt Disney World, $22.

You can book a shuttle on arrival at the Mears' desks in the luggage halls, but it can be a longish trip if it has a full van stopping at several hotels before yours (407 423 5566, **mearstransportation.com**).

BRITGUIDE 25

Car hire prices could be as low as $30/week (plus insurance and taxes) 25 years ago, but most car hire companies were based off-airport. Now everything is much more convenient.

Theme Park Express: This innovative service from City Sightseeing Orlando (p265) offers daily services on an open-top double-decker bus *direct* to Disney or Universal from International Drive. The Disney version goes from nine I-Drive locations to EPCOT from 8am–12.05pm daily, returning at 6.30 and 8.30pm from EPCOT and 11pm from Magic Kingdom for $14/person. The Universal service goes from seven locations from 7.15–11.15am for $8/person (407 352 4646, **bit.ly/brit-express**).

Excursions: There are also excursion services offered by *Brit Guide* partners Gray Line Orlando (407 522 5911, **graylineorlando.com**) and Florida Dolphin Tours.

BRITTIP

Drivers should obtain an online code from the DVLA website (**gov.uk/view-driving-licence**) to show the rental company, in case it is requested, although Alamo have said it is unlikely that they will ask for it.

Town cars and limos

There's a huge choice (more than 150 at the last count), but the following all earn a *Brit Guide* recommendation:

Destination MCO: A choice of luxury cars, limos and vans, with a reliable, dedicated service to all the main tourist points, including airport pick-up and transfer to Disney from $88 one-way (407 722 8286, **destinationmco.com**).

BRITTIP

Be firm with the car hire check-in clerk if they push you for extras, like car upgrades you won't need.

FL Tours: A popular, well-established company specialising in airport–Disney routes and Port Canaveral transfers. One-way trips from $75 and round trips from $140 ($140 and $250 from Orlando Sanford), plus tip; also a free 30min grocery stop and kids' booster and car seats; 24-hour online reservation; no extra charge for late pick-ups (407 857 9606, **fltours.com**).

Orlando Airport Towncar: Popular service specialising in efficient airport pick-ups from Orlando International and Sanford, using Lincoln towncars and luxury SUVs. Prices from $60 for four one way from Orlando International to Disney to $290 round-trip for six from Orlando to Port Canaveral (407 754 8166, **orlandoairporttowncar.com**).

Taxis

For groups of four or five, taxis can be more cost-effective than shuttles. Orlando International to I-Drive would be around $45 (plus tip); $45–75 for the Kissimmee area; $55–68 to Disney resorts; $15–20 I-Drive to Universal Orlando; and $30–40 I-Drive to Disney Springs. You'll find plenty of taxis in ranks at parks, hotels and shopping centres, but they don't cruise for fares. Elsewhere, you should pre-book. Reliable companies will show a driver's ID, insurance and rates. It's illegal for drivers to look for fares in the airport baggage hall. All taxis will be on Level 1. Most are metered but you can ask what the fare is likely to be. Some hotels have Town Cars at their ranks which don't have meters.

Reliable firms: Mears operate Checker Cabs Yellow Cabs and City Cabs (407 422 2222); **Ace Metro Cab** (407 855 1111); **Star Taxis** (407 857 9999); **Diamond Cab** (407 523 3333).

App-based ride-sharing services **Uber** and **Lyft** are both popular, with the usual caveat about prices varying with demand and drivers who are not licensed in the same way as taxi drivers. **bit.ly/brit-uber.**

Minnie Vans: Disney's own smart taxi/shuttle service offers rides for up to six throughout WDW for a flat-rate $15 fee, plus mileage (anywhere from 4–10 miles, adding around $14–30). It is available via the Lyft app or 407 828 3500. A flat-rate Disney-Orlando Airport service cost $150 one way.

WITH A CAR

Having a car is the key to being in charge of your holiday. There are dozens of hire companies and rates can be as low as $150/week for the smallest car.

BRITTIP
Your first call for car hire should be to Brit Guide partner Alamo. See inside the front cover for our special offer or visit **alamo.co.uk/brits**.

The cars will be mainly American – Chevrolet, Dodge, Buick, plus international makes like Kia, Hyundai, Honda and Nissan.

- **Economy or Subcompact:** Usually a Vauxhall Corsa-sized hatchback.
- **Compact:** Small family saloon like a Nissan Versa.
- **Midsize or Intermediate:** 4-door, 5-seater like a Toyota Corolla.
- **Fullsize:** Larger-style executive car like a Ford Mondeo.
- **Premium, Luxury, Convertible, SUV and Minivan:** Upmarket options, while the Minivan is a Ford Galaxy or Renault Espace type.

Most holiday companies offer 'free car hire', but it is only the rental cost that is free. You must still pay the insurance and taxes (which makes all-inclusive packages more attractive).

Also beware low starting rates. Essential insurances and surcharges can take the weekly rate above $300/week. However, most companies now offer all-inclusive rates that work out cheaper if booked in advance.

BRITTIP
Be sure to pick the right car for your group size – and luggage. You simply won't get seven people AND all their cases in a seven-seater van!

Car rental companies: Alamo is our Brit Guide partner and offers excellent rates and service (see inside front cover). You also benefit from choosing your own car in each range, where most other companies assign a specific car. Or try Dollar (**dollar.co.uk**), Avis (**avis.co.uk**; 0808 284 0014), Budget (**budget.co.uk**, 0808 284 4444), or **Thrifty** (**thrifty.co.uk**, 0333 332 1222), or try comparison website **carrentals.co.uk**.

Insurance: You must have a credit card. There are two main kinds of insurance: Loss or Collision Damage Waiver (LDW or CDW) costs $26–31/day and covers any damage to the car. You can do without it, but you'll pay a hefty deposit on your credit card, and you are liable for ANY damage. Liability Insurance Supplement (LIS) or Extended Protection costs $12–15/

day. It is not essential but covers most damage you might cause.

BRITTIP

The Central Florida Expressway Authority was testing a money-saving option for automated toll payments for Orlando International Airport car rentals in 2019. Called Visitor Toll Pass, it is available online in advance at **visitortollpass.com**.

Another option is Underinsured Motorists Protection (in case someone with minimal cover runs into you) at around $8 a day.

Specialist insurance: You can cut costs by taking specialist insurance like Insurance4CarHire (0844 892 1770, **insurance4carhire.com**), offering an annual policy, including CDW/LDW and LIS, for £120. **iCarHire Insurance** also features independent insurance, including CDW/LDW from £8/day (**icarhireinsurance.com**).

Other costs: Drivers must be at least 21, and those under 25 pay an extra $25 a day. Other costs include local and state taxes, plus Airport Access and 'Facility' fees, which can add more than $40 a week. Many companies also offer a Roadside Plus (around $5/day), which covers flat tyres, running out of fuel or locking your keys in the car, but this is optional.

Fuel: 'Gas' is still cheaper than in the UK. You can either pre-pay for a full tank (so you bring it back empty; the charge is usually slightly under the local rate/gallon for this); fill it up yourself so you have a full tank on return; or pay a fuel surcharge at the end for the company to refill the tank (the most expensive option).

Pre-pay tolls: You can also opt for the SunPass auto-pay system, so you just drive through; all your tolls are auto-recorded for payment when you return the car. It is called PlatePass or TollPass and there is a flat-rate fee ($5–11/day, depending on the company, up to a maximum of $20–53/month). This is easy but

Enter Mapman

By far the best area map is a British production, created by Disney fan and cartographer Steve 'Mapman' Munns, who is also our *Brit Guide* mapman. It is superbly detailed for the I-4 corridor, Highway 192 and Walt Disney World, with special sections on I-Drive and the Highway 27 villa locations. All the main attractions, hotels and restaurants are marked, with text and photos, and there is plenty of other info packed in. Great value at £8.65 (plus p & p), the latest version now comes as a full A5 booklet. There is also a PDF version for smartphones and tablets (£6): **orlandomaps.co.uk.**

can be expensive unless you are using the toll roads a *lot*.

BRITTIP

You must stop at the toll booths marked 'Change Given' (in green) or 'Exact Change Only' (in blue) unless you have accepted the SunPass pre-pay auto-toll option from the car rental firm, in which case, use 'Sunpass' or 'E-Pass'.

Getting used to your car

Most people find driving in America is a pleasure, mainly because almost all hire cars are automatics and nearly new. And as speed limits are lower (and rigidly enforced), you are rarely rushed into taking a wrong turn.

- All cars have air-conditioning, which is essential for most of the year. Turn on the fan as well as the A/C button or it won't work! A small pool of liquid will form under the car from condensation.

- Power steering is universal.

- Larger cars have cruise control, so you can set the desired speed and take your foot off the accelerator. There will be two buttons on the steering wheel, one to switch on cruise control, the other to set the speed. To cancel, either press the first button or touch the brake.

- Keep your foot on the brake when you are stationary as automatics

The satnav solution

The best way to navigate is by a GPS. All car hire companies offer this as an extra (at $75–95/week) or you can bring your own. If your system has only the base-level (i.e. UK) maps loaded, download the maps for the USA for around £35. If you are thinking of buying a GPS system, the likes of Wal-Mart offer new systems, fully loaded for the US, for as little as $50.

tend to creep forward. Always put the gear lever in 'P' (Park) when switching off.

- To start, put the gear in 'P' and depress the brake, then put in 'D' to drive. D1 and D2 are extra gears for hills (none in Florida)!

- Not all cars have central locking, so make sure you lock ALL the doors before leaving it. With an automatic, you won't be able to take the keys out of the ignition unless you put the gear lever in 'Park'.

Fuel: All local gas stations are self-service and you usually pay before filling up. However, the pumps should allow you to pay by credit card without having to visit the cashier (some stations ask for a local zip code with a credit card swipe, which means you DO need to go inside). To activate the petrol pump, you may need first to lift the lever underneath the pump nozzle.

BRITTIP

RaceTrac and the three Speedway stations in Walt Disney World are among the cheapest, while the Wal-Mart on Vineland Road is also a cheaper option. Petrol stations just *outside* Disney and the airport are the most expensive.

Finding your way

Your car hire company should provide you with a basic map of Orlando, plus directions to your hotel.

BRITTIP

Be organised – get your directions in advance off the internet at sites like **mapquest.com** or use Google Earth to source maps, directions and even check out the lie of the land in advance. Download it free from its website at **google.com/earth**.

Signposting: Getting out can be more difficult than getting to the main attractions as the exit road may be different. Familiarise yourself with the main roads in advance and learn to navigate by road numbers (given on the signposts), exit numbers off the main roads, and directions around the attractions (i.e. if you want I-4 east or west or 192 as you exit Walt Disney World).

Lanes and exits: Exits off motorways can be on EITHER side of the carriageway, not just on the right, and you don't get much notice. You can overtake in ANY lane on multi-lane highways, so sit in the middle lane until you see your exit.

Road names: Around town, road names are displayed at every junction suspended ABOVE the road underneath the traffic lights. This road name is NOT the road you are on, but the one you are CROSSING.

Again there is little advance notice of each junction and the road names can be hard to read as you approach, especially at night, so keep your

You will soon get used to driving in the US

© Visit Florida

speed down if you think you are close to your turn-off to allow time to get into the correct lane. If you do miss a turning, most roads are on a grid system, so it's easy to work back.

Occasionally you will meet a crossroads where no right of way is obvious. This is a Four-Way Stop, and the priority goes in order of arrival. So, when it's your turn, just indicate and pull out slowly (America doesn't have many roundabouts, so this may be the closest you get to one).

Local maps: Those supplied by the rental companies and the free tourist maps are pretty basic. AA members have their own map options (p51), but we recommend getting the Orlando Map by Steve Munns (p48).

BRITTIP
On nearly all toll roads, for the manned toll booths you have to pull in to a slip road on the right to pay. It is SunPass/E-Pass only on the main carriageway. This can catch you out when you have just left the airport.

The Gauntlet at Gatorland

© Gatorland

Rules and regulations

As well as driving on the opposite side of the road, there are several differences in procedure.

Tolls: For toll roads, have some change handy in amounts from 25c to $3. Most give change (in the GREEN lanes), but you will get through quicker if you have the correct money (in the BLUE lanes). On minor exits of Osceola Parkway and the Greeneway, there are auto-toll machines *only*, so keep some loose change to hand. Several exits of the Florida Turnpike will now take SunPass **only**, not cash, hence PlatePass is valuable if you plan to travel widely (p48). Look up the main Toll Calculator site for central Florida on **cfxway.com/for-travelers/#**.

Traffic lights: The most frequent British errors occur at traffic lights (which are hung above the road). At a red light, you can still turn RIGHT providing there is no traffic coming from the left. Stop, check there are no pedestrians crossing and make your turn – unless there is a sign indicating 'No turn on red'. Turning left at the lights, you have the right of way with a green ARROW but must give way to traffic from the other direction on a SOLID green. A YELLOW flashing arrow means it is OK to turn left providing the way is clear.

Left turns: The majority of accidents involving overseas visitors take place on left turns, so take extra care. There is also no amber light from red to green, but there IS from green to red. A flashing amber light at a junction means proceed but watch for traffic joining the carriageway, while a flashing red light indicates it is okay to turn if the carriageway is clear.

BRITTIP
The Osceola Parkway toll road (522) that runs parallel to Highway 192 is a better route to Walt Disney World from east Kissimmee and costs only $2. Use Sherberth Road for Disney access from west 192 or the new Western Beltway (Highway 429).

Speed limits: Speed limits are well marked with black numbering on white signs and the police are hot on speeding, with steep fines. There are varying limits of 55–70mph/88–113kph on the Interstates, where there is also a 40mph/64kph minimum speed limit. It can be just 15–25mph/24–40kph in built-up areas.

BRITTIP

Parents, to make sure of a professionally trained driver for your taxi or transfer, download the KidMoto App to ensure the right car seats, etc, at **https://kidmoto.taxi**.

Seat belts: These are compulsory for all passengers, while child seats must be used for under-4s and can be hired from the car companies at $10–15 a day (so bring your own or buy one locally for $70–80). Also 4 and 5-year-olds *must* use either a car or booster seat, depending on the child's size.

Parking: It is illegal to park within 10ft/3m of a fire hydrant or a lowered kerb, and never park in front of a yellow-painted kerb – they are stopping points for emergency vehicles and you will be towed away – and never park ON a kerb. Park bonnet first – reverse parking is frowned upon because number plates are only on the rear of cars and police then can't see them. If you park parallel to the kerb, you must point in the direction of traffic.

Other traffic laws: Flashing orange lights over the road indicate a school zone, and school buses must NOT be overtaken in either direction when they are unloading and have their hazard lights on. U-turns are forbidden in built-up areas and where there is a solid line down the middle of the road. You must pull to the side of the road to allow emergency vehicles to pass, in either direction, when the lights and/or sirens are on. Also, on multi-lane highways in Florida, the Move Over law means you must pull into an adjacent lane if you see a police car on the hard shoulder, or slow right down if you can't move over. And you must put on your lights in the rain.

Finally, DON'T drink and drive. Florida has strict laws, with penalties of up to 6 months in prison for first-time offenders. The blood-alcohol limit is lower than in Britain, so it is safer not to drink at all if you are driving. It is also illegal to carry open containers of alcohol in the car.

Bonus for AA members: Produce your AA card where you see the AAA 'Show & Save' signs to enjoy some handy discounts. Visit **autoclubsouth.aaa.com** and click Discounts & Rewards for the full range, which includes shopping and dining, like 10% off at Hard Rock Café and Dennys restaurants (use the zip code 32819). You can also get maps and books from their office in Lake Mary in Seminole County (near Sanford).

Accidents

In the unlikely event of an accident, no matter how minor, you must contact the police before moving the cars (except on the busy I-4). Car hire firms will insist on a full police report for the insurance. If you break down, there should be an emergency number for the hire company in its literature or, if you are on a main highway, raise the bonnet and wait for one of the frequent police patrol cars to stop (or dial *FHP on your mobile). *Always* carry your driving licence and car hire forms when driving, in case you are stopped.

The entrance to the Magic Kingdom

© Disney

Key routes

All main motorways are prefixed I, the even numbers going east–west and odd numbers north–south. Federal Highways are the next grade down, with black numerals on white shields, while state roads are prefixed SR (black numbers on white circular or rectangular signs).

All American motorways have their junctions numbered in mileage terms, which makes it easy to calculate journey distances. I-4 starts at exit 1 in Tampa and goes to exit 132 at Daytona, 132ml/211km away. In Orlando, the main junctions run from exit 55, at Highway 27, to exit 87 (Winter Park) and exit 101 for the Seminole Expressway (417) and Orlando Sanford International Airport. Downtown Orlando can be found off exits 82B to 85.

BRITTIP

Be ready for MAJOR roadworks on I-4 north of Universal (at Kirkman Rd) all the way to north of downtown. It is a road widening project that will add toll lanes for the first time. Completion date 2021! See **i4ultimate.com**.

Interstate 4: I-4 is the main route through Orlando, a four, six or eight-lane motorway linking the coasts. Interstates are always indicated on blue shield-shaped signs. For most of its length, I-4 travels east–west but, around Orlando, it swings north–south, though directions are still given east (for north) or west (for south). All the attractions of Walt Disney World, plus SeaWorld and Universal Orlando are well signposted from I-4. LEGOLAND Florida in Winter Haven, Lake Wales and Bok Tower Gardens are a 45min drive from Orlando west on I-4 and then south on Highway 27, while Busch Gardens is 75–90mins down I-4 to Tampa. Be aware I-4 can be packed in the morning and evening rush hours. You can check for major roadworks on **cflroads.com**.

International Drive: I-Drive is the second key local roadway, linking a 14½ml/24km ribbon of hotels, shops, restaurants and attractions like ICON Park, Pointe Orlando and Orlando Premium Outlets (I-Drive South, from Highway 192 in Kissimmee north to Route 535 is NOT the main stretch and the two sections are linked via Route 535 and World Center Drive). From I-4, take

The Leaky Cauldron at Universal's Wizarding World of Harry Potter

exits 71, 72, 74A or 75A going east, or 75A, 74A or 72 going west. To the north, I-Drive runs into Oak Ridge Road and the South Orange Blossom Trail, which leads to downtown Orlando (junctions 82B, 83A and 85 off I-4). I-Drive is also bisected by Sand Lake Road and runs into World Center Drive (536) to the south, also convenient for Disney.

I-Drive is a major tourist centre and makes an excellent base, especially around the Sand Lake Road junction, as it is fully pedestrian-friendly. It's a 20min drive to Disney and 10mins from Universal. However, at peak times, heavy traffic means it's best to avoid the stretch from the Convention Center north. Use Universal Boulevard instead.

Also, try to avoid I-4 from exits 60–68 in the morning and evening rush-hours as traffic can be severe here. Equally, I-4 westbound from 78–74B will be really congested through 2019 as the Kirkman Rd junction completes a major reconstruction.

Kissimmee: The other main tourist area, south of Orlando and south-east of Disney, its features are grouped along a 20ml/32km stretch of the Irlo Bronson Memorial Highway (192), which intersects I-4 at junction 64B, and is close to Walt Disney World (though a good 25mins from SeaWorld and Universal). Downtown Kissimmee is off Main Street, Broadway and Emmett Street, and is ideal for walking.

Highway 192: A handy visual along here is the Marker Series from Formosa Gardens (number 4) to just past Medieval Times (number 15). These highly visible signs are good locators for hotels, restaurants and attractions, and much of this stretch is also walkable (though few places are close together). Try to avoid the area of the 192 east of Marker 15, though; it is rather run-down and unappealing. For downtown Kissimmee (which we DO recommend) use the Osceola Parkway and S Orange Blossom Trail (441).

The unique Disney-inspired town of Celebration is also here (just south of Walt Disney World).

Highway 27: At the west end of Highway 192, running north to Clermont and south to Davenport (and Haines City) is a major area of holiday villas, convenient for Disney – although some owners claim to be 'only 5mins from Disney' when they are 20–30mins away! The area has a spread of shops and restaurants, notably in the Cagan Crossings junction just north of where 192 meets 27, which includes a large Wal-Mart.

Western Beltway: Highway 429 provides a western Orlando bypass, avoiding the often-crowded I-4 to link with the Florida Turnpike and Apopka to the north. It offers Disney entry at exit 8 (Western Way), which is handy for the Davenport/Clermont areas. This junction is also being developed as Flamingo Crossings at the junction of 429 and Western Way, with two budget hotels now open and more to follow, plus shops and restaurants.

ChampionsGate: Right on I-4 at exit 58 is this mushrooming area of hotels, shops, apartments and restaurants, which makes for a handy self-contained destination as an alternative to Highway 192. Dining includes Red Robin, Chili's, Miller's Ale House, First Watch Café, 4 Corners Tavern and the British-owned Fish & Chip Shop, among a growing array of choice (**championsgate.com/restaurants**).

BRITTIP

Sadly, the morning traffic on I-4 east can be almost solid from Exit 55 to 68. You're often better off staying on 27 to go north, then east on 192; getting on the (toll) 429 to get to Disney via the Western Way; or getting off at ChampionsGate to take Osceola Polk Line Rd east to Old Lake Wilson Rd and north to Highway 192.

Now, let's go on to the next vital step – your holiday accommodation….

4 Accommodation

Or Making Sense of American Hotels, Motels and Villas

Choosing your accommodation is the first major decision in store and, as with everything Orlando, there is a massive array of options. There are some 500 hotels, 26,000 villas and even more possibilities with Airbnb. Finding the right place for you will be the key to a memorable holiday.

The main choice is between a traditional hotel and one of the many self-catering villas/vacation homes or condos. Do you want the extra space, style and amenity of a villa, or do you prefer having your room made up every day? Prefer to save money by doing your own cooking and laundry or do you want resort facilities on tap?

Those are the main differences between villa and hotel, along with the all-important question of location. Most vacation homes are some distance from the parks and, with traffic to deal with as well, you could be a 30 or 45-minute drive from Disney or Universal each day. But hotels close to Disney all come at a premium, so you can save money if you don't mind a longer journey.

BRITGUIDE **25**

Back in 1995, Disney's All Star resorts were the newest thing. Now Universal is adding its own variation on the theme with the Endless Summer Resort. *Plus ça change!*

Stormalong Bay at Disney's Beach Club Resort

The right location

Being on-site at Disney or Universal is obviously the ideal way to enjoy the parks, but their hotels are among the most expensive. The closest areas to Disney are Lake Buena Vista and West Highway 192 in Kissimmee, which allow you to avoid busy motorway I-4 for the most part. There is a good range of budget-priced hotels on the 192 in particular. International Drive is ideal for Universal and SeaWorld, and not too far from Disney, and has the highest concentration of hotels as well as good public transport (p44–47). There is an increasingly sophisticated choice, too, with upmarket brands like Four Seasons, Ritz-Carlton and Waldorf Astoria on offer. We therefore break down the hotel choice by area, starting with Disney and Universal, then I-Drive, Lake Buena Vista and Kissimmee, plus a few off-the-beaten-track options.

Go south of Highway 192 and you find all the main villa developments (in purpose-built sub-divisions), especially on Highway 27, which runs north-south on the western edge of the Kissimmee area. There are some beautiful properties to choose from, nearly all with their own private pools, and some positively mansion-esque, but there are far fewer restaurant choices nearby and you will need a hire car, and longer drives to the attractions. Some villa developments are now as far south as Haines City on Highway 27, which is 27ml/43km from the Magic Kingdom and 31ml/49km from Universal.

Suite things

Suites hotels provide a combination of hotel and apartment, with extra value for large families or groups. Typically, a suites room gives you a living room and kitchenette, including microwave, coffee-maker, fridge, cutlery and crockery, while many offer a complimentary continental breakfast (or better). All have pools and grocery stores or snack bars and several have restaurants. They vary only in the number of bedrooms and can usually sleep 6–10.

Prices

Hotel and villa rates are cheaper out of the main holiday periods, with special deals at times. Always ask for rates if you book directly and check if special rates apply during your visit (don't be afraid to ask for their 'best rate' at off-peak times, which can be lower than published or 'rack' rates). There may be an extra charge for more than two adults sharing a room ($5–15 per person), plus there is state tax and, sometimes, a sneaky Resort Fee that can add $15–35/day. Once you move away from Walt Disney World, the hotel choice becomes more diverse. Budget types are common, and *where* you stay affects the price. East on Highway 192, hotels and motels are cheaper (and more basic)l. On I-Drive, hotels south of Sand Lake Road are more expensive than the northern stretch. Shop around, and feel free to ask to see a room before you book.

Deals and bookings: If you've just arrived and need a hotel, visit the official Visitor Center at 8102 I-Drive, just south of Sand Lake Road (next to Mango's Tropical Cafe; 8am–9pm daily; 407 363 5872), where they have brochures on all current deals. Or look at online specialists like Priceline (**priceline. com**), Expedia (**expedia.co.uk**), Hotels. com (**hotels.com**), Orbitz (**orbitz.com**), Trivago (**trivago.com**), Agoda (**agoda. com**), Hotel Tonight (**hoteltonight. com**), Trip Advisor (**tripadvisor.com**), Booking.com (**booking.com**) and Hotwire (**hotwire.com**). It also pays to check out a hotel's rates on their own website, as many have special deals and price guarantees.

Disney's Boardwalk Inn

© Disney

HOTELS

Orlando is very heavily chain-hotel territory. All the big brand names are here, plus a handful of independents and local groups, like the Rosen hotels. The general standard is consistently good, with rooms often much larger than in Europe. Many feature two queen-sized beds but couples without children can request a king room for extra space. All US hotels charge per room, and not per person, and a family of four (with younger children) can usually fit in one room. Meals are rarely included, but many budget choices provide a simple buffet breakfast. Most budget hotels don't have a restaurant or bar, but there'll be plenty nearby.

Most hotels are big, clean, efficient and great value. You'll find plenty of soft-drink and ice machines (though it's cheaper to buy drinks from a supermarket), with ice buckets in all rooms. Rooms are all air-conditioned, hence you'll need to get used to the drone of the A/C unit. If you need a more spacious room, look for one of the many suite hotels, which provide sitting rooms and mini-kitchens, as well as 1–3 bedrooms.

Budget hotels

The main chain hotals are at the cheaper end of the market. All have pools, but not many have restaurants, bars or lounges (though some provide a free continental breakfast and many offer fridges, microwaves and free wi-fi).

- **America's Best Value Inn** (1888 315 2378, **bit.ly/brit-value**).
- **Days Inn** (1800 225 3297, **bit.ly/brit-daysinn**).
- **Econo Lodge** (1877 424 6423, **bit.ly/brit-econolodge**).
- **Howard Johnson** (1800 221 5801, **wyndhamhotels.com/hojo**).
- **Knights Inn** (1800 477 0629, **redlion.com/knights-inn**).
- **Motel 6** (1800 899 9841, **motel6.com**).
- **Red Roof Inn** (1800 733 7663, **redroof.com**).
- **Rodeway Inn** (1877 424 6423, **choicehotels.com/rodeway-inn**).

- **Super 8 Motel** (1800 454 3213, **wyndhamhotels.com/super-8**).
- **Travelodge** (1800 525 4055, **wyndhamhotels.com/travelodge**).

BRITTIP

Hotels designated Maingate East or Maingate West should be close to Disney's main entrance on Highway 192, though it is wise to check.

Value choices

As you go up the scale of the bigger chains, you find more modern facilities and a better array of amenities. Many still don't have their own restaurant, but do provide a breakfast option. Choose from:

- **Baymont Inn & Suites** (1800 337 0550, **wyndhamhotels.com/baymont**).
- **Best Western** (1800 780 7234 in US, **bestwestern.com**).
- **Choice Hotels Group** comprising **Comfort Inn, Comfort Suites, Clarion Inn** and **Quality Inn** (1877 424 6423, **choicehotels.com**).
- **Country Inn & Suites** (1800 830 5222, **countryinns.com**).
- **Doubletree by Hilton** (1800 560 7753, **bit.ly/brit-doubletree**).
- **Extended Stay America** (1800 804 3724, **extendedstayamerica.com**).
- **Fairfield Inn** (1888 236 2427, **fairfield.marriott.com**).
- **Hampton Inn and Suites** (1800 560 7809, **bit.ly/brit-hampton**).
- **Hawthorn Suites by Wyndham** (1800 337 0202, **bit.ly/brit-hawthorn**).
- **Holiday Inn and Holiday Inn Express** (1888 465 4329, **bit.ly/brit-holidayinn**).
- **Homewood Suites** (1800 445 8667, **bit.ly/brit-homewood**).
- **La Quinta Inn and Suites** (1800 753 3757, **wyndhamhotels.com/laquinta**).
- **Radisson** (1800 967 9033, **radisson.com**).
- **Ramada** (1800 854 9517, **wyndhamhotels.com/ramada**).

Kidsuites = happy families

Orlando has pioneered a great family accommodation style, worth seeking out if you have kids who enjoy bunk beds. Basically, a kidsuite is a separate area within the hotel room that gives the kids their own 'bedroom' (with bunks), usually also with their own TV and games consoles.

- **Residence Inns** (1888 236 2427, **residenceinn.marriott.com**).
- **Springhill Suites** (1888 236 2427, **springhillsuites.marriott.com**).
- **Staybridge Suites** (1877 238 8889, **bit.ly/brit-staybridge**).
- **Wingate Inn** (1800 337 0077, **wyndhamhotels.com/wingate**).

Moderate hotels

If you're looking for more amenities, including the guarantee of a restaurant and bar, this range of big-brand hotels is worth considering. All provide a good pool (often with extras like a waterslide, kids' pool and/or playground), a gym and at least one restaurant, bar and café, plus extra in-room comforts.

- **Courtyard by Marriott** (1888 236 2427, **courtyard.marriott.com**).
- **Crowne Plaza Hotels rooms** (1877 227 6963, **ihg.com/crowneplaza**).
- **Embassy Suites** (1800 445 8667, **embassysuites3.hilton.com/en/ index.html**).
- **Hilton Garden Inn** (1800 445 8667, **bit.ly/brit-hilton**).
- **Hyatt Place** (1800 233 1234, **bit.ly/ brit-hyatt**).
- **Sheraton Hotels** (1800 325 35353, **sheraton.marriott.com**).
- **Westin** (1800 937 8461, **westin. marriott.com**).
- **Wyndham Hotels** (1877 999 3223; **wyndhamhotels.com/wyndham**).

Deluxe hotels

Then there are the Deluxe brands like Autograph Collection, Four Seasons, Hyatt Regency, Loews, Marriott, Omni and Ritz-Carlton. We highlight some of the best choices and personal favourites area by area, but always be sure to check the latest reviews on TripAdvisor and other review websites.

BRITTIP
Buy soft drinks at the supermarket, and (if your hotel room doesn't have a fridge) buy a polystyrene cooler for about $5 that you can fill from your hotel ice machine to keep drinks cold.

DISNEY HOTELS & RESORTS

Our review of Orlando's hotels starts with Walt Disney World. Situated conveniently for all its attractions – and linked by an excellent free transport system of monorail, buses, boats and new Skyliner (p61) – Disney's hotels, villas and campsites are all magnificently appointed and maintained. Their categories are:

BRITTIP
It is usual to tip hotel housekeeping staff by leaving $1/adult each day before your room is made up.

- **Value:** Pop Century, All Star and Art of Animation Resorts.
- **Moderate:** Port Orleans, Caribbean Beach and Coronado Springs Resorts.

La Quinta Inn by Wyndham, I-Drive

© Wyndham Hotels

- **Deluxe:** Contemporary, Polynesian Village, Boardwalk Inn, Wilderness Lodge, Grand Floridian, Yacht and Beach Club, Swan and Dolphin, and Animal Kingdom Lodge resorts.

- **Deluxe Villas:** (Disney's timeshare properties, or Disney Vacation Club) – Old Key West, Saratoga Springs, Bay Lake Tower, Animal Kingdom Villas, Beach Club Villas, Boardwalk Villas, Polynesian Village Villas, Grand Floridian Villas, Wilderness Lodge Villas and new Riviera Resort.

- **Campground:** Fort Wilderness (cabins, campsites and RV sites).

They range from $112/night (All Star Sports resort) to over $3,000 (Grand Floridian), while dining at Disney resorts is not cheap as there are few fast-food options. However, staying with the world-famous Mouse is one of the great thrills, for the style, service and extras.

The 25 resorts, with 30,000 rooms, offer superb facilities that children especially love. The benefits are:

- **MagicBand:** Every guest receives this wristband, which is the room key, theme park entry, FastPass+reservations and PhotoPass collector, as well as a 'charge card' for almost all on-site purchases. Disney hotel guests can also book FastPass+ 60 days in advance instead of 30.

- **Package delivery:** Park purchases can be sent back to your hotel (for a small fee).

Disney Dining Plan

This is another perk of staying onsite with Disney. Hotel guests can pre-pay most meals at a set fee per day. However, it is an EXPENSIVE option if you are staying for a week or more. There are 3 plans to choose from (prices as of summer 2019):

Quick Service Dining Plan: Provides two counter-service meals and two snacks a day, plus one refillable resort mug/person. Counter-service meals are an entrée or combo meal, plus a dessert and a drink (alcoholic for guests 21 and older) for lunch or dinner; and an entrée or combo meal and a drink for breakfast.

Snacks can be any item such as an ice-cream, popcorn, pastry, a piece of fruit, a bag of crisps, a bottled drink, a medium soda or tea/coffee. Cost: $52.50/day for adults, $23.78 for 3–9s (children must order off the Children's Menu).

Disney Dining Plan: Provides one table-service meal, one counter-service and two snacks per person per day, as well as a refillable drink mug. Table-service meals are an entrée, a dessert and a drink (alcoholic for guests 21 and up). Cost: $75.49 and $27.98/day (slightly more in peak season).

Deluxe Dining Plan: Provides three meals (table or counter-service) and two snacks per person per day, plus one refillable resort mug per person. Cost: $116.25 and $43.49/day (more in peak season).

All meals do NOT have to be used per day and can be spread over the duration of your stay, so you can miss a table-service meal one day, then use two credits another day for a signature restaurant or dinner show. Gratuities are NOT included. When you check in at a Disney hotel, your MagicBand is loaded with all your Dining Plan meals and that monitors your daily usage. The Dining Plans CAN be used for Character Meals, when one table-service meal is required per person (two at ultra-popular Cinderella's Royal Table in Magic Kingdom), and for the 14 signature restaurants in Walt Disney World (like Jiko at Animal Kingdom Lodge, California Grill at the Contemporary Resort and Citricos at the Grand Floridian Resort), which all require two table-service meals. They can even be used at Disney's Dinner Shows (p297), subject to availability, at two table-service credits per person.

However, ALL members of the group must book the Plan for the full duration of the stay and inclusive of park tickets. It is also advisable to pre-book (on 407 939 1947 or 0800 16 60 748 in the UK) full-service meals well in advance as the sit-down restaurants usually book up early. Not all restaurants are on the Plan but you still have more than 100 options. More info at **bit.ly/brit-disney** where you can book all table service restaurants online.

- **Free parking:** At all the parks.

- **Refillable mugs:** All Disney resorts sell drinking mugs, which are well worth buying (at $21.99 for your stay) as you then get free refills at their self-service cafés.

- **Dining priority:** Many Disney restaurants hold tables for guests, and you can book 180 days in advance, *plus* the length of your stay if you're staying in a Disney resort. Call 407 939 1947 or 0800 16 90 748 in the UK.

- **Children's services:** All resorts have in-room or group babysitting (subject to availability) and there is the Captain Hook's Pirate Crew activity evening for 4–12s at the Beach Club Resort (4.30–8.30pm, $55/child).

━━━━━━━BRITTIP

All Disney's deluxe resorts offer valet parking. If you use it, the average tip is $3–5, handed to the valet when he or she returns with your car.

- **Mickey on call:** An alarm call from the Mouse (or other Disney characters) himself.

- **Extra Magic Hours:** The BIG bonus is getting into one of the parks each day either 1hr early or for 2hrs after regular park closing to enjoy rides with reduced crowds.

- **Disney's Magical Express:** The free airport transfer service for guests at Disney hotels. Book at least 10 days before arrival through **bit.ly/brit-disney** or a travel agent.

Value resorts

Disney's All-Star Resorts: Here you can stay in one of five Sports-themed blocks centred on a massive food court, two swimming pools, a games arcade and shops; the Music-themed version; or the Movies complex – possibly the most imaginative, with its Fantasia pool and kids' play areas. Standard rooms are bright and compact (read 'tight' for families with older children), but well designed for those who want the Disney convenience but not the price. The All-Star Music Resort (Jazz and Calypso buildings) also has 192 impressive two-room Family Suites (combining two standard rooms) that sleep six, each with two bathrooms, kitchenette, lounge and master bedroom. All three centres, with 5,794 rooms, have pool, bars, shops, laundries, video games rooms and pizza delivery. Resort transport is by an efficient bus service.

━━━━━━━BRITTIP

To make a reservation at any Walt Disney World hotel call 407 939 1936, 0800 028 0778 in the UK, or see **bit.ly/brit-disney**.

Treehouse Villas at Saratoga Springs

© Disney

Disney's Pop Century Resort: In a similar vein, themed to the decades from 1950s–90s are five blocks with giant icons – yo-yos, Rubik's cubes and juke-boxes – and a riot of period sayings and visual gags. It features a pool like a 10-pin bowling lane (others shaped like a computer and a flower), a huge table football set-up and open-air Twister mats. Blocks are grouped around a main building housing the check-in area (with a large-screen TV showing Disney films), an imaginative food court, a lounge (with quick-breakfast bar), a Disney store and a games arcade. The 177acre/72ha complex also features a central lake and lots of bright landscaping, plus a reliable bus service to the parks, and the Skyliner system to EPCOT and Hollywood Studios (see p61). The drawbacks: long queues to check in and a rather hectic feel. Rooms are on the small side.

Disney's Art of Animation Resort: This suites-style hotel builds on the popularity of the Family Suites at the All-Star Music Resort and is a four-part, 1,984-room complex based around *The Lion King*, *The Little Mermaid*, *Finding Nemo* and *Cars*. It has a themed main pool and play areas, two 'quiet' pools, the excellent Landscape of Flavors food court, huge games arcade and Ink and Paint gift shop. The four courtyards are heavily themed, with larger-than-life icons, interactive sculptures, fountains, photo ops and play features, and theming in all the rooms (look for fun 'character reveals'), with the suites offering a master bedroom, two bathrooms and three separate sleeping areas in the living space, plus a kitchenette with mini fridge, microwave and coffee-maker. All park transport is by bus or Skyliner.

Moderate resorts

Disney's Caribbean Beach Resort: This 1,550-room complex is spread over five Caribbean 'islands' (with a connecting bus service). Basic rooms are quite plain, but comfortably sleep four, while the Pirate Rooms (request at booking) take the theme to a new level, with ship-shaped beds and other decor. The heart of the resort is Old Port Royale, with the main lobby, food court style of Centertown Market (with grab-and-go option), Calypso Trading Post (gift shop), and the treat of the full-service Latin and Caribbean menu of Sebastian's Bistro. The main pool, Fuentes del Morro, features water slides and cannons, and there's a separate kiddie pool for those under 4ft/122cm. There are bike and boat rentals, and each 'island' has its own pool. Transport to all parks is by bus and the Skyliner system to EPCOT and Hollywood Studios.

BRITTIP

Disney resort restaurants can (and, we think, should) be visited even if you aren't staying there. Advance book at any of the parks (407 939 1947 or 0800 16 60 748 in the UK **bit.ly/brit-disney**).

The new lobby at Disney's Caribbean Beach Resort

This imaginative new transport system opened in late 2019. A glorified cable-car service, it starts at Pop Century and Art of Animation, runs to a hub at Caribbean Beach, then splits to either Hollywood Studios (helping to ease traffic congestion from the new Star Wars area) or EPCOT, via the Riviera Resort. Be aware, its operation may be affected by stormy weather.

Disney's Coronado Springs Resort: Possibly the best value of this trio, it has slightly more facilities for its 2,466 rooms spread over 125acres/50ha: four pools (including the massive Lost City of Cibola activity pool with waterslide), two games arcades, three restaurants, food court, convenience store/café, lounge bar, gift shop, beauty salon, health club, business centre and two launderettes. There's also the Rix Sports Bar & Grill, serving classic bar food and craft beers to go with all the sports action on multiple TVs.

Constructed on a scenic Mexican/Spanish theme in four areas (the 'villages' of Casitas, Ranchos and Cabañas, plus the new 15-storey Gran Destino tower), Coronado Springs is an often-overlooked treasure. The addition of Gran Destino has given the resort an imposing new hub, along with a fabulous rooftop restaurant, Toledo – Tapas, Steak and Seafood, with an indoor/outdoor lounge, as well as the eye-catching new Three Bridges Bar & Grill set on an island on Lago Dorado, the 14acre/5.6ha lake. Check out the Maya Grill and its New Latino cuisine; sample food court-style Pepper Market; or a snack or drink from Café Rix to enjoy with the splendid lake views from the terrace. Coronado Springs is 5mins from Animal Kingdom and well served by the bus network.

Disney's Port Orleans Resort: This is a two-part complex. The 2,048-room Riverside has a steamboat reception area, a great Riverside Mill food court, Boatwright's full-service restaurant, the River Roost lounge (live entertainment on certain nights) and an old-fashioned General Store (gift shop). It also features Royal Guest Rooms, themed for princes and princesses right down to headboards that perform fibre-optic fireworks! Also here is the 1,008-room French Quarter, with the Sassagoula Floatworks and Food Factory court, two bars, games room and shopping arcade.

The Riverside includes the great Ol' Man Island, a 3½acre/1.5ha playground with swimming pool, kids' area and a fishing hole, while the French Quarter has Doubloon Lagoon, with Mardi Gras dragon slide, alligator fountains and a play area. The design varies from rustic Bayou backwoods to turn-of-the-century New Orleans. Transport for both is by bus to the parks and bus or boat to Disney Springs.

Deluxe resorts

Disney specialises in high-quality deluxe hotels with grand design features, amenities and restaurants. All nine offer a concierge level, which adds an exclusive private lounge with drinks and snacks.

Disney's Animal Kingdom Lodge: This stunning 'private game lodge' is set on a 33acre/13ha animal-filled savannah, which many rooms overlook. The pervasive African theme and the effect of opening your curtains to a vista of giraffes and zebras is immense. The lavishness and detail are superb, right down to the guides who can tell guests about the animals and their habitats, the African folklore around the outdoor fire pit and the chance for children to become junior safari researchers while Mum and Dad do some wine-tasting (from a huge collection of South African wines).

All this creativity comes before you consider the amenities: two restaurants, café, bar, elaborately themed 'watering-hole' main pool (with waterslide) and kids' pool, Spa and fitness centre, large gift shop, children's play area and an awesome four-storey atrium. The main restaurant, Jiko, is spectacular, but there is also the superb buffet-style Boma, a 'marketplace' restaurant featuring African-tinged dishes from a wood-burning grill and rotisserie for breakfast and dinner.

BRITTIP

Wine aficionados take note: Jiko at Disney's Animal Kingdom Lodge offers a fabulous array of South African wines in a wonderfully romantic setting.

Rooms range from standard doubles to one and two-bedroom suites, some of which have bunk beds. The newer Kidani Village wing adds still more (p68). All transport is by bus (with the Animal Kingdom barely 5mins away).

Disney's Boardwalk Inn and Villas:
One of the Crescent Lake resorts next to EPCOT is this 45acre/18ha extravagant inn and entertainment 'district'. It features a 512-room hotel, 383 villas, four themed restaurants, a TV sports club and two nightclubs, plus shops, sports facilities and a huge, freeform pool with a waterslide, all on a semi-circular boardwalk around the lake. For dining, the Big River Grille is a great bar/restaurant with its own micro-brewery while the Flying Fish is an upmarket seafood option with a creative (if a bit pricey)

menu and magic-themed lounge-bar AbracadaBar. Trattoria al Forno offers creative Italian 'comfort food', wood-oven pizza and risottos. There's also the Boardwalk Bakery for a snack and Ample Hills Creamery for ice cream treats. Transport is by boat to EPCOT and Hollywood Studios and bus to the other parks.

Disney's Contemporary Resort:
On the monorail next to the Magic Kingdom, this 15-storey resort boasts 655 rooms, a cavernous foyer, five shops, four restaurants, four lounges, a sandy beach, a marina, two pools (one with waterslide), two tennis courts, a video games centre and health club – and fab views, especially from the superb, hotel-top California Grill (one of the most romantic settings in Orlando; aim to go to coincide with the park's fireworks). Don't miss Chef Mickey's for a breakfast or dinner buffet with your favourite characters, while the monorail runs *through* the hotel – great for kids. Rooms are some of Disney's largest, with elegant décor, dark-wood furniture and comfy duvets. Chic restaurant/lounge The Wave features a modern bar and dining area with a varied menu and is well worth trying for dinner or just a cocktail, while the Contempo Café adds a light meal option 6am–midnight. Within walking distance of the Magic Kingdom, transport to other parks is by bus.

Gran Destino tower at Coronado Springs

Disney's Grand Floridian Resort & Spa: This true five-star hotel is like an elaborate Victorian mansion, with 867 rooms, an impressive domed foyer, and staff in period costume. One stop on the monorail from the Magic Kingdom, it is truly deluxe hence the high price-tags, though it's worth a look if you're not staying. Its six restaurants include the top-of-the-range Victoria and Albert's (where a set seven-course dinner with wine costs $250, or the Chef's Table $400/p with wine), the chic seafood-based Narcoossee's, with its excellent view over Seven Seas Lagoon, and forthcoming Victoria and Albert's Bistro, an all-new restaurant-and-lounge set-up. There are also four bars and impressive sports and relaxation facilities, notably the fabulous Senses Spa. There's a main pool and a great second pool area with zero-depth entry and waterslide. The 1900 Park Fare restaurant is very popular for character breakfasts and dinners, plus children's activities, while the new Beauty and the Beast lounge evokes the magic and romance of the classic animated film with three themed rooms and a garden terrace. Also new is an outlet of the Bibbidi Bobbidi Boutique for girls (3–12) to enjoy a full Princess makeover ($65-$230).

The Garden View Lounge serves a variety of traditional afternoon teas 2–5pm daily, $35–150/person ($24 for 3–9s). Transport to the Magic Kingdom is by boat and monorail; by bus to the other parks.

BRITTIP

Watch out for the free nightly Electrical Water Pageant on Bay Lake and Seven Seas Lagoon, on view from all the Magic Kingdom resorts.

Disney's Polynesian Village Resort: This is a South Seas tropical fantasy, with modern sophistication and comfort. Beautiful beaches, lush vegetation and architecture are home to 853 rooms built in wooden long-house style, all with balconies and superb views. Also on the monorail

opposite the Magic Kingdom, it boasts a lovely three-storey atrium, with landscaped seating areas and an iconic Tiki god. The dining is excellent: 'Ohana is a stylish dinner venue with lively character breakfasts. Kona Café is less formal but still with an extensive menu. Captain Cook's Snack Company has more basic counter-service fare. Interactive tropical lounge Trader Sam's Grog Grotto (4pm–midnight) offers appetisers and exotic cocktails. Then there is a beautiful 'Volcano' pool area with waterslide, a games room, shops and children's playground. Catch the monorail or boat to the Magic Kingdom and buses to the other parks.

The 360 Disney Vacation Club deluxe studios feature a private balcony or porch and room for five. Then there are 20 gorgeous lakefront two-bed, two-bath bungalows (on stilts over Seven Seas Lagoon) that sleep eight, boasting full kitchens, living and dining rooms, outdoor deck with individual plunge pool, and a grandstand view of the fireworks. But beware the price – from $2,845/night!

Disney's Wilderness Lodge: A picturesque and romantic resort, this is a re-creation of a National Park lodge, from the stream running through the massive wooden balcony-lined atrium into the gardens, past the swimming pool (with hot and cold spas) to a geyser that erupts every hour. Offering backwoods charm with luxury, the

Bora Bora Bungalows at Disney's Polynesian Village
© Disney

Walt Disney World and Lake Buena Vista Accommodation

© Steve Munns 2019

Toll road

Lake Buena Vista Resort & Spa

Home 2 Suites Orlando

Hilton Grand Vacation Suites

Floridays

Quality Suites Lake Buena Vista

Courtyard by Marriott, Fairfield Inn, SpringHill Suites

Holiday Inn LBV Resort

Bryan's Spanish Cove

Blue Heron Beach Resort

Grand Beach Resort

Caribe Royale

Buena Vista Suites

Worldquest Resort

Marriott Village

Marriott Vacation Club

Orlando World Center Marriott Resort

Holiday Inn Resort Orlando Suites

Hilton Grand Vacations

Hilton Garden Inn

Embassy Suites

Hampton Inn

Clarion Inn

Crowne Plaza

Hyatt Place LBV

Crossroads Center

Radisson Lake Buena Vista

Holiday Inn

Vistana Resort

Parc Soleil by Hilton Grand Vacations

Residence Inn

Holiday Inn Express

TownePlace Suites

Extended Stay America

Hawthorn Suites

Courtyard

Cypress Pointe Resort

Staybridge Suites

Fairfield Inn & Suites

Sheraton LBV Resort

Delta Orlando Resort

Doubletree Guest Suites

Best Western LBV

Wyndham LBV Resort

Hilton Orlando Resort

Hyatt Regency Grand Cypress

Hilton Buena Vista Palace Resort & Spa

Saratoga Springs Resort & Spa, & Treehouse Villas

DISNEY SPRINGS

LBV

Four Seasons Hotel and Disney's Golden Oak Villas

Port Orleans Riverside Resort

Port Orleans French Quarter Resort

Old Key West Resort

Typhoon Lagoon

Waldorf-Astoria, Hilton Orlando, Wyndham Grand and JW Marriott at Bonnet Creek

Riviera Resort

Caribbean Beach Resort

Pop Century Resort

Disney's Art of Animation Resort

Beach Club

Boardwalk

Yacht Club

Dolphin

Swan

Epcot

Car Park

Disney's Hollywood Studios

Fort Wilderness Resort & Campground

Walt Disney World

Contemporary Resort, & Bay Lake Tower

Wilderness Lodge

Transportation & Ticket Center

Car Park

monorail

WORLD DRIVE

Blizzard Beach

Coronado Springs Resort

Magic Kingdom

Seven Seas Lagoon

Grand Floridian Resort & Spa

Polynesian Village Resort

Bay Lake

BAY LAKE

Animal Kingdom

Animal Kingdom Lodge Resort & Kidani Village

All-Star Resorts

Sand Lake

PALM PARKWAY

APOPKA - VINELAND ROAD

BUENA VISTA DRIVE

EPCOT CENTER DRIVE

WORLD CENTER DRIVE

INTERNATIONAL DRIVE SOUTH

OSCEOLA PARKWAY

VICTORY WAY

WESTERN WAY

BUENA VISTA DRIVE

N

→ Flamingo Crossings

resort is connected to the Magic Kingdom by boat and bus (and buses to the other parks). Rooms are spacious and well furnished, while the Courtyard View rooms are the best of the regular rooms (though at a slight premium). Superb Deluxe rooms sleep up to six, but at up to £1,298/night. It has two restaurants: the brilliant Artist's Point (lunch and dinner) and the Whispering Canyon Café (lively breakfast and huge all-you-can-eat family meals), plus a snack bar, pool bar and Geyser Point Bar & Grill, with views over Bay Lake. **Copper Creek Villas** and **Cabins** at Wilderness Lodge are a Vacation Club development of 136 studios and one and two-bed villas. Facilities include living areas, kitchens, private balconies and whirlpool baths. There is a quiet pool, hot-tub and Health Club, with fitness centre, sauna, and massage and facial treatments.

Disney's Yacht and Beach Club Resorts: There is more refined quality with this duo, featuring 630 and 580 nautical-themed rooms respectively. Set around Crescent Lake next to the EPCOT park, they help to form a massive resort area that is a delight to walk around at any time but especially at night. For dinner, the Yachtsman Steakhouse offers friendly, elegant dining at the Yacht Club, while the sister hotel features Cape May Café for lovely character breakfasts and a nightly New England-style clambake buffet. Beaches & Cream can also be found here, a classic 1950s-style diner for burgers, shakes and sundaes. Both resorts are set along a white-sand beach like a tropical island paradise and share water fun at Stormalong Bay, a superb 2½acre/1ha recreation area with waterslides and a sandy lagoon. You can go boating or catch a water-shuttle to EPCOT or Disney's Hollywood Studios; other park transport is by bus.

BRITTIP

The Crew's Cup Lounge in the Yacht Club Resort is a true hidden gem, ideal for a cocktail before dinner, or to unwind after a day in the parks.

Walt Disney World Swan & Dolphin Resort: These unmistakable twin hotels are not owned by Disney but conform to the same high standards, with some of the best facilities, location, restaurants and a night-time view second to none, while usually slightly cheaper than most Deluxe resorts. They're within walking distance of EPCOT and Hollywood Studios, Disney's Boardwalk Resort and the Fantasia Gardens Miniature Golf Courses, but also have a boat service to both parks (and bus to the others). The unique architecture is extensive, with the Swan (758 large rooms including 55 suites) topped by a 45ft/14m statue, while the Dolphin (1,509 rooms, 112 suites) is crowned by two even bigger statues. Both have been extensively refurbished to include the Westin Heavenly Bed® and high-speed wi-fi, while adding a sumptuous Grand Deluxe room category with enhanced bathrooms, personalised in-room fridge, new furniture and contemporary décor. The Dolphin also boasts the Balinese-inspired Mandara Spa, with a tea garden and Meru Temple. The resort has 16 restaurants and lounges, five pools (one an amazing grotto pool with hidden alcoves and waterslide), a kids' pool and white-sand beach, two health clubs, a range of shops, a video arcade and the Camp Dolphin centre for 4–12s (5.30pm–12am, $12/hour/child).

Dolphin's Shula's Steak House and Todd English's Bluezoo are especially worth seeking out. Fresh, a Mediterranean-style market, serves

Disney's Wilderness Lodge

breakfast and lunch, featuring all made-to-order menu items and both à la carte and tableside dining. Picabu is open 24 hours with all-American favourites, while The Fountain is great for ice creams, sundaes, milkshakes and other speciality desserts, as well as classic diner fare. In the Swan, you'll find Il Mulino Trattoria, New York's top Italian restaurant, and the lovely Garden Grove Café, with Disney characters each evening and breakfasts at the weekend. The intimate Kimonos offers sushi and a karaoke bar (407 934 1609, **swandolphin.com**). A new 14-storey tower expansion is under way, and **The Cove** should be completed by March 2021, adding 349 rooms and suites, an elevated pool deck, restaurant, lounge, health club and lobby cocktail bar.

Four Seasons Resort: (see Golden Oak, p68).

BRITTIP

Most Disney hotel rooms will sleep four, except Port Orleans Riverside (which can take an extra child on a truckle bed). For larger groups, consider Old Key West, Saratoga Springs, the Boardwalk Villas, the villas at Animal Kingdom Lodge, Wilderness Lodge Villas, Fort Wilderness cabins or two-room suites at the All-Star Music and Art of Animation Resorts.

Campground & cabins

Disney's Fort Wilderness Resort & Campground: Possibly the best value of all the Disney properties, on Bay Lake opposite the Magic Kingdom, it offers impressive camping facilities and chalet-style cabins housing up to six in a 750acre/304ha spread of countryside. Two 'trading posts' supply fresh groceries and there is a lounge/bar and full-service restaurant. The on-site activities include two swimming pools, the thrice-nightly Hoop-Dee-Doo Musical Revue, (a traditional hoedown-style song-and-dance dinner show, p298), campfire programme, open-air films, sports, games and a prime position to view the nightly Electrical Water Pageant. You can rent bikes or boats or take horse rides around the country trails from the Tri-Circle D ranch. There is even a Segway Tour (the great two-wheeled personal transports), the Wilderness Back Trail Adventure, providing a two-hour trundle around the many trails ($96/person, over-15s only; 8.30 and 11.30am Tues, Fri, Sat; call 407 939 8687 to book).

The Trail's End restaurant offers a great buffet breakfast and dinner, while Crockett's Tavern serves pizza and appetisers (dinner only).

Cabin at Fort Wilderness Campground

Buses and boats link the resort with other areas (and the short boat ride to the Magic Kingdom is a great start to the day). If you need a break from the Magic Kingdom, hop on the boat and try Trail's End for dinner (4.30–9.30pm; $35/adult, $19/3–9s).

BRITTIP

For a different dining experience try the fab Weekend Brunch (7.30am–2pm) every Sat and Sun at the Trail's End restaurant at Fort Wilderness. It is buffet-style at $28 adults, $16 3–9s.

Disney Vacation Club resorts

Disney's Old Key West Resort

Disney's first Vacation Club resort, this is primarily a five-star holiday ownership scheme (one of 10 resorts), but the one, two or three-bed studios in a Key West setting can be rented nightly when not in use by members. Facilities include four pools, tennis courts, a games room, shops and a fitness centre, plus the lovely Olivia's restaurant. Transport to all parks is by bus, plus boat to Disney Springs.

BRITTIP

Looking for a diversion from Disney Springs? Take the boat from The Landing to Old Key West and try a meal at Olivia's for a laid-back vibe.

Disney's Saratoga Springs Resort & Spa: The most extensive DVC resort, this 65acre/26ha apartment complex is opposite Disney Springs, next to scenic Lake Buena Vista Golf Course with wonderful views over the lake. It boasts 828 units, from standard two-bed hotel-style studio rooms to massive two-storey, three-bed apartments sleeping 12. The theme is the 1880s' New York resort of the same name, with a gracious look and great facilities, from the freeform, zero-depth entry main pool (with waterslide and squirt-fountains), a

smaller quiet pool, varied dining (the Artist's Palette for counter-service breakfast, lunch and dinner, the Paddock Grill for more quick-service fare and the upscale Turf Club Bar & Grill, with a cocktail lounge, pool table and food shop), a large video arcade, tennis courts and a wonderful full-service spa and gym. Also here are 60 three-bed Treehouse Villas, beautiful chalets raised 10ft/3m off the ground among a heavily wooded area next to Sassagoula River. Sleeping up to nine, they feature sumptuous furnishings, including granite counter-tops and flatscreen TVs, two full bathrooms and outdoor barbecue grills. They also have their own leisure pool and whirlpool spa. Transport to all parks is by bus.

Bay Lake Tower at Disney's Contemporary Resort: Linked to the Contemporary Resort by a 5th-floor bridge, this features its own pool, waterslide and whirlpool spa, kids' water-play area, shuffleboard and bocce courts. The 14-storey, 295-room Tower, studio rooms and spacious one, two and three-bed villas have modern decor. The studios (sleeping up to four) have small fridges, microwaves and coffee-makers, while the villas (up to 12) have full kitchens and laundry facilities. The Tower affords wonderful views over the Magic Kingdom and nightly fireworks from its exclusive rooftop lounge and viewing deck (DVC members only).

There's a pool bar and grill, and easy access to the Contemporary Resort

Bay Lake Tower

© Disney

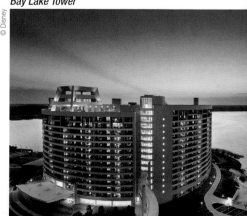

restaurants. Transport by monorail or bus (or on foot to Magic Kingdom).

Disney's Animal Kingdom Lodge – Kidani Village: An addition to Animal Kingdom Lodge, this features hotel-room studios (sleeping four) and one, two and three-bed villas (sleeping five, nine or 12), offering full kitchens and laundry facilities. There is a separate wildlife preserve in four animal savannah areas, a fab pool and kids' play area, and another restaurant, Sanaa, which continues the Lodge's reputation for fine dining. Dazzling Samawati Springs – a huge zero-depth entry pool – is open to all Lodge guests, while children will make a beeline for Uwanja Camp, a three-part interactive water playground (for ages 4 and under, 5–7s, and 8+). Other amenities include a video arcade, basketball court, fitness centre, gift shop and animal programmes, from flamingo-feeding to campfire story-telling. Transport to all parks is by bus.

Grand Floridian Villas: These sumptuous additions to the DVC inventory provide 147 stylish one and two-bed villas sleeping 5–9, plus 'grand villas' that sleep 12 and include a media room with home theatre system. The elegant building, with subtle Mary Poppins theming, has a reception, laundry room and lovely private gardens.

Riviera Resort: Just opened next to the Caribbean Beach Resort – and on the Skyliner route to EPCOT and Hollywood Studios – is this 300-room, nine-storey homage to classic French

Samawati Springs at Kidani Village

Riviera hotels. It offers stylish one, two and three-bed villa-style rooms with a grand Cote d'Azur feel, including elaborate gardens and fountains, plus the highlight of rooftop restaurant, Topolino's Terrace, offering classic Italian and French cuisine as well as views of the fireworks at the two nearby parks. It is open to non-DVC guests but is highly sought-after, with restaurant reservations highly advisable. Breakfast features a Character Dining experience.

The other four DVC resort centres are at the Yacht and Beach Clubs, The Boardwalk, Polynesian Village and Wilderness Lodge.

Disney's Golden Oak

Golden Oak: In an ultra-exclusive corner of Walt Disney World is this small-scale community of holiday homes for private sale. Like most villa developments, it has its own luxurious Clubhouse, but homes are NOT rented out and feature VIP perks such as concièrge service, private transport to the parks and special events. The prices are equally exclusive – they START at $2m!

Four Seasons Resort: Within Golden Oak but a separate entity (and also open to non-guests for its spectacular dining), is this fabulous five-star brand, featuring 444 capacious rooms and even larger suites, with marbled bathrooms, and in an oasis of tranquillity within the Disney confines. Built in luxurious Spanish Revival style, it has an amazing array of amenities, including five restaurants, three pools, a lazy river and water-play area, tennis courts, extensive spa, state-of-the-art gym and its own golf course. The kids club (for 4–12s; 10am–6pm) is free to guests, with a superb spread of activities, and there's a good choice of connecting family rooms, plus adults-only rooms with luxurious king beds and great views. Rooms with views of the Magic Kingdom fireworks come at a premium, while rooftop steakhouse restaurant Capa is one of Orlando's most spectacular. Italian restaurant Ravello, with its show kitchen, is a show-stopper and golf clubhouse

Universal's Aventura Hotel

diner Plancha features Cuban–American cuisine in a lakeside setting. The whole ambience is superb, but room rates *start* at $645/night. Park transport is by bus (1800 267 3046, **fourseasons.com/orlando**).

BRITTIP

Time your dinner booking at Capa at the Four Seasons to get a superb high-level view of the Magic Kingdom fireworks.

Disney Hotel Plaza

If Disney's hotel prices are out of your range, consider the seven on-site 'guest' hotels that come with a less hefty price-tag, on Hotel Plaza Boulevard on the doorstep of Disney Springs. There's a free bus service to the parks, guaranteed admission (even on the busiest days), and you can make reservations for shows and restaurants before the general public, plus they now have Extra Magic Hours privileges, too. For more info on these, go to **disneyspringshotels.com**.

- **Best Western Lake Buena Vista:** Solid budget-priced choice that makes for great value.
- **B Resort & Spa:** Chic, high-tech contemporary hotel with a lot of built-in style and fab dining.

- **DoubleTree Suites by Hilton:** Well-priced and versatile option, with extra-large rooms.
- **Hilton Orlando Buena Vista Palace:** Extensive, recently refurbished resort with a lot packed in.
- **Hilton Orlando Lake Buena Vista:** Ultra-smart executive resort with many mod cons.
- **Holiday Inn:** One of our faves, a surprisingly fresh and modern style, with excellent dining.
- **Wyndham Garden:** Wonderfully stylish resort opposite Disney Springs with a huge array of amenities.

BRITTIP

Look out for a 'Free Breakfast' and special Advance Purchase offers at the Holiday Inn Walt Disney World. Book 5–10 nights and qualify for free breakfast for two adults. Look them up on **hiorlando.com/specials.htm**.

UNIVERSAL ORLANDO

Disney hasn't cornered the market when it comes to smart, creative hotel designs, and Universal has seven that are equally attractive and highly themed. And, like Disney, they offer their own special park benefits.

- Free transportation to the Universal parks, SeaWorld and Aquatica.
- Early entry to the Wizarding Worlds of Harry Potter 1hr before park opening, and select attractions at Volcano Bay water park.

Hard Rock Hotel Future Rock Star Suites

- Resort-wide charging privileges with room key.
- In-park merchandise delivered to hotel room.
- Character appearances.
- Special golf privileges at a number of nearby courses.
- FREE Universal Express ride access (for Portofino Bay, Royal Pacific and Hard Rock hotels).
- Unlimited club-to-club access to select CityWalk entertainment venues.

Aventura Hotel: New in 2018 was this 16-storey all-glass tower, featuring a dramatic roof-top bar and great views over the whole Universal resort – including the neighbouring Volcano Bay water park – as well as 600 rooms (notably with kids suites) boasting floor-to-ceiling windows. An elaborate pool area includes a kids' splash pad and hot-tubs, while there is a high-tech fitness centre, free wi-fi, an innovative market-style food court called Urban Pantry and a Starbucks. It has its own walking route to the parks as well as a shuttle, but is at the more modest end of Universal's hotel pricing (**loewshotels. com/universals-aventura-hotel**).

Cabana Bay Beach Resort: This Value-priced hotel is split into two parts either side of a central reception with classic 1950s styling. There are 2,200 standard rooms and family suites with kitchenettes, sleeping up to six, set

The Fire Pit at Sapphire Falls Resort

© Universal Orlando Resort

around an efficient 600-seat Food Court. Other options include a retro Starbucks coffee shop, lobby bar and two elaborate pool bars offering signature frozen drinks and smoothies. The Lazy River Courtyard also offers the Hideaway Bar & Grille for lunch and dinner. Guests can even have pizza delivered to rooms that feature all mod cons, with flatscreen TVs, mini fridge, wi-fi and a clever bathroom that features two wash-basins and separate bathtub/shower. Amenities include a 10-lane bowling alley with its own bar/restaurant, and two feature-packed resort pool areas, with zero-depth entry, sandy beaches, waterslide and Universal's first lazy river, all with extensive period theming. It has its own shuttle bus to CityWalk, or a 15min walk (407 503 4000, **loewshotels.com/cabana-bay-hotel**).

Hard Rock Hotel: Possibly the coolest hotel in Orlando, this icon of rock chic is themed as a former rock star's home, with 650 rooms and suites in California mission style: high ceilings, wooden beams, marble floors and eclectic artwork. The rock-star theme is in most public areas, with music memorabilia, black-suited staff and fairly constant music. The hotel features three bars (including the ultra-cool Velvet Bar), two restaurants (the full-service The Kitchen and five-star, dinner-only Palm Restaurant), plus a takeaway café, fitness centre, gift shop and games room. The lido area features a huge, freeform pool with underwater sound system and 240ft/73m waterslide, two Jacuzzis, beach volleyball, shuffleboard and life-size chess and draughts. The 650 big rooms (with 12 kidsuites and 10 king suites) are beautifully furnished and comfortable (407 503 2000, **loewshotels.com/hard-rock-hotel**).

Portofino Bay Hotel: The jewel in Universal's crown is a splendid re-creation of the famous Italian port. Elaborate porticos, *trompe l'oeil* painting and elaborate harbourside piazza make it a five-star setting. With 750 rooms, even standard rooms are sumptuous, with huge beds, spacious bathrooms, mini-bar and coffee facilities, ironing board and hairdryer. The 94 Club Rooms offer concierge service with private lounge, extra room amenities and free entry to the Mandara Spa fitness centre. There are 18 *Despicable Me* themed kidsuites with separate bedrooms (complete with missile beds!). Resort facilities are equally smart – a Roman aqueduct-style pool with waterslide, an enclosed kids' play area and wading pool, a separate quiet pool, Jacuzzis, the Mandara Spa, business centre, an array of gift shops and a video games room. The hotel has eight restaurants and lounges, including the superb Bice Ristorante (p313), boisterous Trattoria del Porto, family dining at Mama Della's (watch out for Mama herself!), an aromatic deli, pizzeria, gelateria and swanky Bar American. It is only a short distance from the parks, but light-years away in terms of its tranquil ambience (407 503 1000, **loewshotels.com/ portofino-bay-hotel**).

BRITTIP

For a romantic dinner, book a table at the Portofino Bay's Bice for early evening, when the restaurant is serenaded at sunset by opera singers Musica della Notte from the piazza below.

Royal Pacific Resort: This 1,000-room resort has an exotic 1930s South Seas style, and you feel as if you have stepped into another world as you cross the bamboo bridge into the elegant lobby. Extensive use of rich, dark woods, stone floors and masses of greenery give it an opulent, colonial feel. Standard rooms feature hand-carved Balinese furniture among many refined touches, and there is also a Club level, with separate lounge and extended facilities, and 51 superlative suites – including eight Jurassic Park-themed kidsuites (dinosaurs not included!). The Islands Dining Room offers breakfast, lunch and dinner in an oriental setting (children have their own buffet area with TV

screen, plus a Saturday *Despicable Me* character breakfast), while the Bula Bar & Grille is the ideal poolside dining venue. The luau garden area features the Wantilan Luau Saturday nights, featuring a Polynesian feast and dinner show ($75–96 adults, $38–54 under-13s; 407 503 3463 to book). The huge freeform pool is ideal for kids, with zero-depth entry and a boat-shaped interactive play area of squirting fountains. Add a health club (with Jacuzzi, sauna and gym), kids' club (with computer games, TVs and activities), video arcade and two shops and you have excellent value, even at this end of the scale (407 503 3000, **loewshotels.com/royal-pacific-resort**).

Sapphire Falls Resort: This Caribbean-themed tropical oasis features 1,000 rooms (including 77 ultra-spacious suites and kidsuites) and a glittering array of amenities. A resort-style pool features a waterslide, children's play area, sand beach, Jacuzzi, private cabañas and fire pit, forming a central courtyard surrounded by guest rooms. A full-service Caribbean restaurant, Amatista, offers scenic views and outdoor dining, while there's also a quick-service marketplace, a lobby lounge and fancy poolside bar, Drhum Club Kantine, plus state-of-the-art fitness centre with saunas. Like the three deluxe resorts, there is water taxi and shuttle access to CityWalk and it is one of Universal's most picturesque hotels. The new Caribbean Carnaval dinner-show is held every Fri (6–8.30pm; $71–81 adults, $36–41 3–9s), with authentic entertainment, food and music from the islands (1888 430 4999, **loewshotels.com/sapphire-falls-resort**).

BRITTIP

Don't miss the superb Strong Water Tavern at Sapphire Falls. It features a unique array of vintage rums, plus a fabulous Caribbean small-plate menu.

Endless Summer Resort: This new twin-centre resort opened part 1, the Surfside Inn & Suites, in summer 2019 while the second stage, Dockside Inn & Suites opens in March 2020. On the site of the former Wet 'n Wild water park on I-Drive, they are more Value-conscious hotels offering a mix of standard rooms and two-bed suites sleeping up to six. The former has 750 rooms while the latter will have 2,050, but both feature a strong beach theme, free transport to Universal and early entry to the Wizarding World areas and Volcano Bay. **Surfside** boasts a resort-style pool and splash pad, a fitness centre, games room and food court (407 503 7000, **loewshotels. com/surfside-inn-and-suites**), while the **Dockside** version will be similar but with two pools, a lobby bar and a larger food court (407, 503 8000, **loewshotels.com/dockside-inn-and-suites**).

INTERNATIONAL DRIVE

Moving away from the theme park hotel style, this more traditional area of hotels, attractions, shops and restaurants remains a go-to choice for many, with a strong mix of options. We'll use Disney's three hotel categories – Value, Moderate and Deluxe – and add a Budget range.

Budget hotels

Avanti Resort: An ideal location is boosted by a fab resort pool (including kids' section), fitness centre, coffee shop and pool bar and grill, with free shuttles to Universal, SeaWorld, EPCOT and Aquatica (407 313 0100, **avantiresort.com**).

Drury Inn & Suites: A smart choice with a LOT included for your money (free wi-fi, parking, hot breakfast, evening meal, local phone calls, and popcorn and soft drinks in the lobby 3–10pm; 407 354 1101, **druryhotels.com/ locations/orlando-fl**).

Midpointe Hotel: This quality-conscious choice near the Convention Center was acquired by Rosen Hotels in 2017 and given the group's signature budget-with-style makeover, ensuring a clean, well-maintained basic property with 2 pools, free wifi and parking (407 351 5100, **midpointehotelorlando.com**).

Ramada Plaza Resort & Suites: Great value choice in a good I-Drive location with free wi-fi, breakfast and Disney transport, plus over-sized rooms (407 345 5340, **michotel.com**).

Rosen Inn at Pointe Orlando: One of I-Drive's 'old faithfuls', this continues to be a reliable and sound choice, with plenty of amenities and a good bar and restaurant (407 996 8585, **roseninn9000.com**).

Rosen Inn International: Another long-serving hotel still providing great value in budget territory but with more facilities and comfort than you might expect (407 996 1600; **roseninn7600.com**).

Midpointe Hotel

Rosen Inn I-Drive: Completing the trio of clean-and-cheerful value-conscious hotels in this group, this is another well-designed but well-priced option with some nice family-friendly touches (407 996 4444; **roseninn6327.com**).

Staybridge Suites SeaWorld: A surprisingly chic big-brand choice, featuring an excellent free hot breakfast, spacious one and two-bed suites with kitchen facilities, a relaxing pool area, fitness centre and laundry (407 917 9200, **ihg.com/staybridge/hotels/us/en/reservation**).

StaySky Suites I-Drive Orlando: This Brit-friendly resort just off the main drag of I-Drive is nicely located and features over-large one and two-bed suites and a good free breakfast buffet (407 956 6101, **stayskysuites idriveorlando.com**). It is also part of the smart StaySky Hotels & Resorts group that features well-priced hotels throughout the area (**staysky.com**).

Value hotels

CoCo Key Water Resort: This feature-packed hotel offers excellent amenities with its extensive water park, chic lobby and 391 rooms, all with flatscreen TVs, smart bedding and furniture, coffee-maker and free wi-fi. The water park is hugely child-friendly (407 351 2626, **cocokeyorlando.com**).

Four Points Orlando International Drive: A 21-storey icon near Universal Orlando, this features a heated tropical pool and paddling pool, games room, mini-golf and fitness room, while the Tropical Palms restaurant is great value for breakfast, lunch or dinner (407 351 2100, **fourpointsorlandointernationaldrive.com**).

Home2 Suites International Drive South: A new, creative brand, featuring excellent rooms with self-catering facilities and plenty of space (ideal for long stays). A free breakfast, wi-fi, gym and laundry provide lots of value, while its location next to Orlando Premium Outlets (and several restaurants) is another bonus (407 944 1705, **home2suites3.hilton.com**).

Sonesta ES Suites: This refreshing, spacious and Brit-friendly choice features one and two-bed suites sleeping 4–8 in three versatile layouts, including full kitchens. It includes a full breakfast buffet, and the pool area and hot tub provide a great end-of-day retreat (407 352 2400, **bit.ly/brit-sonesta**).

The Point Hotel & Suites: Nicely tucked away just off I-Drive but close to all the action is this chic, modern condo-hotel that has wonderfully comfy rooms and a laid-back vibe, notably around its freeform pool deck and hot tub. The Cabana Bar & Grill is a great place to sit with a drink or two in the evening (407 956 2000, **thepointorlando.com**).

Wyndham Orlando Resort: This well-equipped resort puts guests in the heart of I-Drive's entertainment district. It features lush gardens, winding lagoons, two pools, fitness centre, sauna and steam rooms, plus a fab poolside bar and restaurant. A recent multi-million dollar renovation added upscale amenities – including pillow-top mattresses, massaging showers and 40in/100cm flatscreen TVs – to the guest rooms, which also offer family-friendly suites with bunk beds, but without the hefty price tag of similar resorts (407 351 2420; **wyndhamorlandoresort.com**).

BRITBONUS

Save 15% off rates at the **Wyndham Orlando Resort** when you book and pay in advance. Use the online rate code 'SSP' when booking.

Castle Hotel

© Castle Hotel

The SeaWorld bonus

For anyone planning on a lot of SeaWorld and Aquatica visits, consider a **SeaWorld Official Hotel** for a range of benefits and money-saving offers. All 11 feature free Quick Queue at SeaWorld, a free behind-the-scenes Rescue Tour, free shuttle service to SeaWorld, Aquatica and Universal, priority entry on select days, 10% off dining and 10% off merchandise purchases of $50 or more. Alternatively, there are another five Partner hotels that offer priority entry and 10% discounts. See **bit.ly/brit-seaworld**.

Moderate hotels

Castle Hotel: A one-off boutique hotel in the heart of I-Drive, with a luxury touch that gives it a Bavarian feel. Plush rooms, heated pool, fitness centre and creative dining combine for an unusually individual style in mass market territory (407 345 1511 **castlehotelorlando.com**).

BRITTIP

Coffee-makers are standard in most hotel rooms, but tea-making facilities are rare. Bring your own teabags or look for PG Tips and Yorkshire Tea in the International aisles at Publix and Wal-Mart.

Crowne Plaza Orlando – Universal: With a spectacular atrium, two restaurants, cocktail lounge, fitness centre and huge heated pool, this provides plenty of value in an ideal location on Universal Boulevard (407 355 0550, **cporlando.com**).

Doubletree by Hilton Orlando at SeaWorld: A recently remodelled hotel just off I-Drive set in 28acres/11ha. It offers two pools (including kids' pool), two restaurants, fitness centre and extra-large suites for a luxury feel (407 352 1100, **doubletree3.hilton.com**).

Embassy Suites International Drive Convention Center: A consistent 'old faithful' in the heart of I-Drive, with spacious rooms, great outdoor pool deck, kids' splash pool and indoor pool, plus gym and good dining options, with a free breakfast (407 352 1400, **embassysuitesorlando.com**).

Rosen Centre: This spectacular 24-storey property, one of the area's largest, caters heavily to the Convention Center next door but also offers excellent facilities. It has a huge swimming grotto, tennis courts, an exercise centre and high-quality restaurants, including the must-try steak-and-seafood Everglades and 98Forty Tapas & Tequila bar. The style is luxurious, yet prices aren't (1800 204 7234, **rosencentre.com**).

Hilton Orlando

International Drive Accommodation

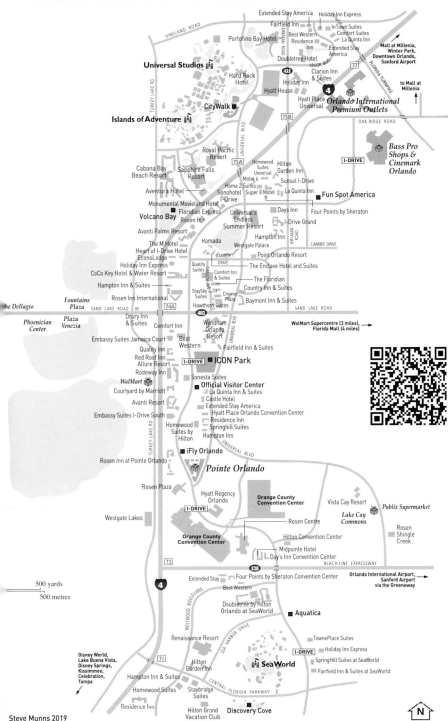

Steve Munns 2019

Rosen Plaza: Another trademark I-Drive hotel that continues to be well looked after and gracious. It offers an excellent pool deck, state-of-the-art gym, business centre and a great array of dining and evening entertainment, including the swish Jack's Place, for great steaks and seafood, and its own nightclub, 3NINE. It is especially good for Kosher guests (407 996 9700, **rosenplaza.com**).

Deluxe hotels

Hilton Orlando: This impressive 1,400-room hotel next to the big Convention Center boasts superb leisure facilities and fabulous dining. There is a full-service spa, state-of-the-art fitness centre, two pools, lazy river (in a 'tropical island' setting), tennis, volleyball and basketball. (407 313 4300, **thehiltonorlando.com**).

Hyatt Regency Orlando: This huge resort appeals largely to convention business but is well stocked for holiday fun. Between its two towers, it boasts an Olympic-size rooftop pool and a lushly landscaped 3acre/1.2ha recreation area with three pools, tropical pool bar and cabañas; tennis courts; a huge fitness centre and spa; and no fewer than seven restaurants, bars and lounges. Rooms are gorgeous and wonderfully spacious, but conference business can make it a bit hectic at times (407 284 1234, **bit.ly/brit-hyattregency**).

Radisson Lake Buena Vista

© Radisson Hotels

Renaissance Orlando Resort: This superb hotel – and *Brit Guide* favourite – opposite SeaWorld features a fab children's water-park and gorgeous resort amenities. It has a massive 10-storey atrium lobby and huge rooms and suites, a lavish spa and fitness centre and video arcade. Impressive dining consists of Mist Sushi & Spirits, Boardwalk Sports Bar, the upscale but casual Tradewinds for breakfast, lunch and dinner, Palms Pool Bar & Grill, a Starbucks café and ice-cream parlour (407 351 5555, **bit.ly/brit-renaissance**).

Rosen Shingle Creek Hotel: This 230acre/93ha resort ranks among the grandest for its location, quality and style, and is another *Brit Guide* fave. Set amid Shingle Creek Golf Club on lower Universal Boulevard, it boasts 1,500 rooms and suites, all with sumptuous decor and comfort, as well as a full-service spa and fitness centre. Amenities include no less than five restaurants, four bars, a lounge, coffee house, deli and ice-creamery, plus three outdoor pools, tennis, basketball and volleyball courts and nature trails, plus a chic shopping gallery (407 996 6338, **rosenshinglecreek.com**).

> **BRITTIP**
>
> Not all hotels provide hairdryers, but they can usually be ordered from the front desk. For your own, you will need a US plug adaptor (with two flat pins). The voltage is 110–120AC (ours is 220) so UK appliances will be sluggish.

LAKE BUENA VISTA

This area either side of I-4 features a number of fairly smart alternatives that are a bit cheaper than Disney but live up to the standard of the area, and are all close to some good restaurants.

Value hotels

Buena Vista Suites: This extensive resort offers terrific value for money just a bit further away from the parks, with spacious rooms and quality amenities, right next to sister (upmarket) resort Caribe Royale (407 239 8588, **buenavistasuites.com**).

Extended Stay America Lake Buena Vista: A good choice in a quieter area but still convenient for Disney that usually delivers top value for money (407 239 4300, **bit.ly/brit-extended**).

Holiday Inn Express & Suites: New on Palm Parkway, just around the corner from the busy Crossroads area and entrance to Disney Springs, is this smart and well-appointed hotel featuring a great free breakfast (407 230 1508, **bit.ly/brit-holidayinnexpress**).

Radisson Lake Buena Vista: Convenient for Disney, with sleek decor and furnishings, it boasts a stylish bar and grill, small gym and free wi-fi, plus spacious rooms (407 597 3400, **bit.ly/brit-radisson**).

Hyatt Place Lake Buena Vista: In an ideal location, close to the Disney hustle-bustle but just out of the way, it is a great example of this contemporary brand, as everything looks and feels like new (407 778 5500, **bit.ly/brit-hyattlbv**).

Sheraton Lake Buena Vista Resort: A popular choice with Brits, with spacious, well-furnished rooms, spectacular pool complex and fitness centre, and impressive restaurant and lounge (407 239 0444, **sheratonlakebuenavistaresort.com**).

Moderate hotels

Caribe Royale Resort: A huge, quality-conscious suites hotel boasting dazzling amenities (including a tropical pool with waterslide, tennis courts, basketball and fitness centre), plus great dining, notably at the award-winning Venetian Chop House, which offers genuine gourmet fare (1800 823 8300, **cariberoyale.com**).

Delta Orlando: Ideally located close to Disney Springs, this trail-blazer for the Delta brand offers chic dining, excellent family pool and super-comfy rooms. Organic breakfast choices, low-energy features and outdoor patio with fire-fountain feature highlight this as well above average (407 387 9999, **bit.ly/brit-deltaorlando**).

Embassy Suites Lake Buena Vista South: This well-kept example of the brand is an oasis of calm and modernity, close to Disney and with smart features (407 597 4000, **embassysuites3.hilton.com**).

Holiday Inn Resort Orlando Suites: The former Nickelodeon Suites, the amenity choice here is huge, with its own water-park, video arcade, mini-golf, laser tag and a quieter adults pool. The Marketplace boasts a fine array of shops and dining, with a bar, pizzeria, Deli and Lakeside Café. Rooms come in excellent one-bed

La Luce restaurant at the Hilton at Bonnet Creek

© The Hilton Orlando

kitchen suites and two and three-bed kidsuites. Close to Disney and with free transport, it's a mini theme park in its own right (407 387 5437, **bit.ly/ brit-holidayinnresort**).

─────**BRITTIP**

La Luce at the Hilton at Bonnet Creek is a wonderfully chic and individual dinner venue, featuring modern Mediterranean cuisine with a Napa Valley flair.

Deluxe hotels

Hilton at Bonnet Creek Resort: Extensive and unique development inside Walt Disney World but privately owned (the one piece of land Walt was unable to buy in 1966), it's part of a 482acre/194ha resort with the Waldorf-Astoria and shares some facilities. It features 1,000 rooms, four restaurants, a lagoon pool complex with lazy river and waterslide, golf course, tennis courts and the adjoining full-service Spa and fitness centre. Just minutes from Disney's parks, it benefits from the full Hilton package of stylish accommodation and excellent kids' activities (407 597 3600, **hiltonbonnetcreek.com**).

Hyatt Regency Grand Cypress: The area's first genuine deluxe hotel in 1984, this is still one of the best. A mature 1,500acre/608ha resort with a unique mix of facilities, including a golf academy, boating lake and superb pool complex with a kids' water park, rock-climbing wall and snack bar. The elegant lobby boasts Zen-inspired décor, while all 779 recently-renovated rooms have a bright, contemporary, amenity-laden finish. The dining choice is among

Orlando World Center Marriott

the best of any Orlando resort, and the location remains ideal, almost on the doorstep of Disney yet blissfully reclusive. The restaurants include intimate Hemingway's, a Key West-styled venue with a Cuban twist, and stylish LakeHouse, the all-day option with its two-storey atrium and beautiful lake views (407 239 1234, **bit. ly/brit-hrgrandcypress**).

Orlando World Center Marriott: We love this iconic resort on Disney's outskirts, set in 200 landscaped acres and surrounded by a beautiful golf course. With eight restaurants and a food court, and a series of pools, including a huge freeform tropical pool and three water slides, it is a monumental prospect but it offers a Jack Nicklaus Golf Academy, tennis courts, volleyball, basketball, spa and state-of-the-art gym. Highlights are the Mikado Japanese Steakhouse, Hawk's Landing Steakhouse, Siro Urban Italian Kitchen, Latitude & Longitude restaurant and High Velocity Sports Bar. The picturesque pool complex offers true relaxation and the spacious rooms are equally impressive (407 239 4200, **bit.ly/brit-wcmarriott**).

JW Marriott Bonnet Creek Resort & Spa: Due to open in early 2020 is this eye-catching development near the Hilton and Waldorf-Astoria complex, featuring an extensive resort pool, salon and spa, elegant rooms and swish rooftop bar with views of the Disney fireworks, plus lobby bar, Market Café and two full-service restaurants. Families will enjoy the kids' activity centre, while couples will be well catered for at the Spa by JW (1888 236 2427, **bit.ly/brit-marriottbc**).

Waldorf-Astoria: A sister Bonnet Creek resort to the Hilton, this was the first US Waldorf outside New York in 2009. Stately and serene, the famous-name hotel features gorgeous standard rooms with Italian marble bathrooms and HD flatscreen TVs, plus grand suites with butler service. The zero-entry pool has cabañas and waiter service, while the dining choice is superb, from the poolside grill and classic Bull & Bear Steakhouse to the small-plate cuisine of Peacock Alley, gourmet style of Oscar's brasserie and private club atmosphere of Sir Harry's Lounge. The renowned WA Kids Club provides active, creative fun for 5–12s from 10.30am–2.30pm weekly and 6–10pm Fri and Sat (407 597 5500, **waldorfastoriaorlando.com**).

Wyndham Grand: Another high-quality resort inside the Bonnet Creek area, with more sumptuous style in a Mediterranean character. Beautifully fitted rooms are matched by excellent dining, notably Deep Blu Seafood Grille, Tesoro Cove (for an extensive buffet breakfast) and Back Bay Bar and Grill overlooking the 10acre/4ha lake. An excellent fitness centre, lagoon-style pool and blissful spa complete a superbly appointed resort (407 390 2300, **wyndhamgrandorlando.com**).

KISSIMMEE/HIGHWAY 192

When it comes to this extensive stretch of busy highway right through the Kissimmee area, there is an enormous choice.

Budget–Value hotels

These are mostly of the chain variety, but a few individuals also stand out.

Champions World Resort: Converted Howard Johnson on west Highway 192, a sound choice with three pools, free theme park transport and wi-fi (407 396 4500, **championsworldresort.com**).

Destiny Palms Hotel Maingate East: Well situated for Disney, this pleasant motel also offers free wi-fi and a continental breakfast (407 396 1600, **destinypalmsmaingate.com/web**).

Park Inn by Radisson: Ideally located for Disney, this extremely well-equipped value-for-money resort boasts spacious rooms and a good dining choice (407 396 1400, **parkinn. com/orlando**).

Royale Parc Suites: Spacious one and two-bed suites, free Disney shuttle, hot buffet breakfast and fun poolside bar add up to excellent value in this hotel, conveniently located next to Old Town on Highway 192 (407 396 8040, **royaleparcsuitesorlando.com**).

Moderate hotels

Galleria Palms Hotel: At Maingate West, just off Highway 192, this has a smart, contemporary look, ultra-comfy rooms, a great location close to Disney, free shuttle to the parks, free breakfast and wi-fi (407 396 6300, **gphkissimmee.com**).

Holiday Inn Orlando SW: Between Markers 8 and 9, with well-maintained rooms (including kidsuites) in two high-rise towers, and a great range of amenities, plus a Kids-eat-free programme and varied dining (407 396 4222, **hicelebration.com**).

Delta by Marriott Orlando Celebration: The former Grand Orlando Resort is due to complete an extensive renovation in early 2020 that will convert it into the smart Delta brand, offering sleek, modern rooms, expanded lobby and smart pool deck (407 396 7000, **deltaorlandocelebration.com**).

Deluxe hotels

Bohemian Hotel: In the Disney-inspired town of Celebration just off Highway 192, this boutique hotel offers refreshing small-town America style that is a long way from the usual tourist hurly-burly. With just 115 rooms in its 1920s' wood-frame design, it has a classy ambience and a wealth of high-quality touches, notably in the ultra-comfy rooms and highly-regarded Lakeside Bar & Grill. It is just a short stroll to the town's shops, restaurants and lakeside walks and makes a great romantic choice (407 566 6000, **celebrationhotel.com**).

Bohemian Hotel Celebration

© Marriott Hotels

BRITTIP

The Gaylord Palms features the stunning Christmas celebration ICE!, a wonderland of ice sculptures, snow scenery and ice slides, plus other festive touches. Early Nov–3 Jan, tickets $30 adults, $29 over-55s and $17 4–12s, extra for snow tubing.

Gaylord Palms Resort: One of the most dramatic hotels, with 1,406 rooms, it features 4½acres/2ha of indoor themed gardens, fountains and landscaped waters under a glass dome in three Florida-themed sections. The restaurants and bars include spectacular Wreckers sports bar, fine steakhouse dining at Old Hickory, MOOR (featuring fine seafood), Mediterranean buffet-style Villa de Flora and Cuban-inspired Socio bar, with fab cocktails.

The Cypress Springs Family Fun Water Park is a huge zero-entry pool featuring seven water slides, surf simulator, massive water-play structure, lagoon and toddler splash area. Grown-ups appreciate the relaxed ambience of the South Beach Pool (with private cabañas). Standard rooms are some of the smartest and most spacious, while suites are enormous. One area is themed like the Everglades (with alligator feeding!); another copies St Augustine's old-world charm, with a replica Spanish fort; and the third is eclectic Key West, with a marina and sailboat. Then there is

Melia Orlando

the signature Relâche Spa, one of the area's largest, with 25 treatment rooms, fitness centre and beauty salon. Find unique shopping along the indoor 'retail street', plus the Cocoa Bean coffee shop, grab-and-go Marketplace and Honeybells Frozen Yoghurt. The hotel stages regular special events and is a great wedding venue (407 586 0000, **bit.ly/brit-gaylordpalms**).

Meliã Orlando Hotel: One of the finest condo-hotels, on Highway 192 at the entrance to Celebration, this is a luxury 5-storey, 240-unit property set around a spectacular 'vanishing edge' swimming pool and boasting upmarket dining at 360 American Bistro & Bar. The beautifully furnished one and two-bed suites feature full kitchens and ultra-comfy bedrooms, with designer toiletries. Balconies overlook the infinity pool or lush landscaping. There is also privileged use of the Celebration Spa and Golf Club (407 964 7000; **bit.ly/brit-melia**).

BRITTIP

If you're like many travellers who have trouble falling asleep with a whirring air conditioner in your room, pick up a pack of soft foam earplugs from Wal-Mart, Walgreens or CVS – effective enough to filter out the drone without making you deaf to 'important' noises.

FURTHER AFIELD

There are also a handful of deluxe hotels worth pointing out that are not in the main areas already covered but still have great appeal.

Alfond Inn: In an ideal quiet part of Winter Park, but handy for the shops, restaurants and museums, this gorgeous boutique hotel is owned by nearby Rollins College and run with great style. The rooms are opulent, the service is gracious and the dining is some of the best in the area. There is also a fabulous roof-top pool, gym and outdoor patio, plus a popular cocktail bar and library lounge (407 998 8090, **thealfondinn.com**).

Kissimmee Accommodation

Blue Heron Beach Resort
Grand Beach Resort
Caribe Royale
Buena Vista Suites
Lake Buena Vista Resort & Spa
Lake Buena Vista Factory Stores
Hampton Inn & Suites Orlando South
Calypso Cay
Embassy Suites
Publix
Palm Lakefront Hostel
Saratoga Resort Villas
Super Target
Sam's Club
Club Cortile
Villas at Seven Dwarfs Resort
Econo Lodge
Knights Inn Kissimmee
Sevilla Inn
HoJo Tropical Palms (further east)
Medieval Times
WalMart

Lake Bryan
Lake Cecile

Vistana Resort
Orlando World Center Marriott Resort
Marriott VC
Holiday Inn Resort Orlando Suites
Worldquest Resort
Holiday Inn Express LBV East
Lake Buena Vista East
Traveledge East Gate
WalMart
Toll Booth
Magic Castle Inn, Fantasy World
EconoLodge Kissimmee
Days Inn Kissimmee
Magic Moment Resort
Comfort Inn
Quality Inn & Suites Eastgate
Golden Link Motel
Magnuson Hotel Kissimmee Maingate

LBV
DISNEY SPRINGS

Gaylord Palms
Super 8, Motel 6
Holiday Inn Orlando SW
Seralago Hotel
Comfort Suites Maingate East
OLD TOWN KISSIMMEE
Regal Oaks

Epcot

Pop Century Resort

The Palms Hotel & Villas, Vacation Village at Parkway
Parkway International
Rodeway Inn Maingate
Fairfield Inn & Suites
Delta by Marriott Resort (2020)
Publix
Celebration Suites, Royale Parc Suites
Metia Orlando Suite Hotel

Boardwalk

Disney's Art of Animation Resort

Bohemian Hotel

CELEBRATION

Disney's Hollywood Studios

Walt Disney World

All-Star Sports Resort
All-Star Music Resort
All-Star Movies Resort
Baymont by Wyndham Celebration
Days Hotel by Wyndham
Hawthorn Suites
Knights Inn Maingate
Ramada Gateway
WalMart
Magic Tree Resort
Oakwater

Animal Kingdom

Coronado Springs Resort

Animal Kingdom Lodge Resort
Kidani Village
Quality Inn & Suites by the Lake
Silver Lake
Magic Village Yards
Galleria Palms
Maingate Lakeside Resort
Grand Lakes Resort
Westgate Towers
Quality Inn & Suites By The Parks
Island H2O
Live Margaritaville Resort
Clarion Suites Maingate
Formosa Gardens Village

Windsor Hills
Mystic Dunes

Formosa Gardens
Rolling Hills
Tempus Palms
Windsor Palms
Oak Island
Indian Creek

Indian Ridge

Highway 27
Town Center at Orange Lakes, Publix

© Steve Munns 2019

N

WESTERN BELTWAY (TOLL)

BRITTIP
Even if you don't stay at the Alfond Inn, it is worth a visit if you are in Winter Park, especially for Hamilton's Kitchen, an award-winning restaurant that serves modern Southern cuisine with panache for lunch and dinner (p328).

Grande Lakes Orlando: You'll find extensive luxury at this 500acre/200ha combination of a 584-room, Ritz-Carlton hotel, a 1,000-room JW Marriott, grand spa, 18-hole Greg Norman golf course, tennis centre and upscale shops and restaurants. On the edge of a forestry preserve, it feels secluded and remote – quite a feat in this area. It is slightly off the beaten track, at the junction of John Young and Central Florida Parkway, yet is only 10ml/16km from Disney and Orlando Airport. It also features its own eco-tours, including kayaking, fishing, bird-watching and nature walks. The **JW Marriott** has Spanish-Moorish design and fabulous dining, including the fresh organic produce of Whisper Creek Farm: The Kitchen (with its own craft brewery), classic Italian at Primo and a pool bar and grill.

Omni Orlando at Champions Gate

It has a great lazy river mini-water park, plus a kids' pool and splash fountain. Rooms are plush and ultra-comfortable, with 64 grand suites and 70% with balconies. The **Ritz-Carlton** offers lush gardens, abundant lakes and streams, Venetian-inspired architecture and a wealth of antiques. It has a large, sloped-entry pool, kids' pool, three floodlit tennis courts, a shop and five dining choices, plus a separate children's check-in and the excellent Ritz Kids Club (5–12s; also for JW Marriott guests). It also includes the fab Southern-inspired Highball & Harvest (one of our faves; p328), Fairways Pub and Bleu pool bar and grill. Rooms are beautifully furnished, with marbled bathrooms, plasma-screen TVs, mini-bar, slippers and robes. There are 66 spacious suites and 92 Club rooms on the top two floors, with concierge and butler service. The beautiful citrus-tinged spa boasts a huge fitness centre and aerobics studio, lap pool (all free to guests at both hotels), lovely restaurant and a huge range of treatments. Prices are suitably upmarket, but it is a rare treat (407 206 2300/2400, **grandelakes.com**).

Omni Orlando Resort at Champions Gate: This imposing hotel offers 720 rooms overlooking a superb golf set-up, with two Greg Norman-designed courses. The impressive facilities include the HQ of the renowned David Leadbetter golf academy, a main swimming pool and activity pool (including a lazy river, fountains and waterslide), four restaurants (notably the superb Asian cuisine of Zen and chic David's Club bar-grill), coffee bar, deli, three lounge bars, state-of-the-art health club and full-service spa. Just 15mins south of Disney off I-4, this is well situated yet off the beaten track for those (especially golfers) looking for something different. It also has 59 superb two- and three-bed villas, affording a more private stay, with full kitchens and opulent furnishings (407 390 6664, **bit.ly/brit-omni**).

SELF-CATERING

This is now a big choice for British visitors, many of whom prefer the extra space and convenience of the villa communities, town homes, studios and condo resorts, all of which are essentially self-catering (although some still offer restaurants and other hotel-type amenities). They tend to be further away from the parks but represent a flexible option, especially for larger groups. They usually have fewer amenities than a hotel but can be more comfortable for a two-week (or longer) stay, and you can save money on not having to dine out all the time and doing your own laundry.

Bahama Bay Resort: A wonderful lakeside location in Davenport (south of Highway 192), this is spread over 70acres/28ha, with 498 condos in 38 two and three-storey buildings. It is woven with tropical landscaping that includes water features, a recreation centre and clubhouse, excellent dining, Cenote Day Spa, fitness centre, tennis, basketball and volleyball, four heated pools and kiddie pools. You can fish in the lake, plus there are nature trails and billiard tables. You can arrange shuttle transport to the parks for a small charge. The four types of condo offer two-bed, two-bath (sleeping six, with a sofa-bed in the lounge) and three-bed, two-bath (sleeping eight, again with sofa-bed), with fitted kitchen, laundry room, living room and dining area. The huge Grand Bahama three-bed condo is as large as some villas (1877 299 4481 or **bit.ly/brit-bahama**).

━━━━━ **BRITTIP**

If you prefer a tranquil Lake View room at the Blue Heron Beach Resort, you can still get a view of Disney's fireworks at night from the outdoor corridor/terrace on each floor.

Balmoral Resort: New in Haines City, on Highway 27 south of I-4, is this ultra-smart 115acre/47ha lakeside development of 160 villas, made up of three-bed town-homes sleeping six, and three, four, five and six-bed pool-homes sleeping 6–14. The resort is maintained by builders Feltrim, hence it keeps a consistent level throughout, with every home decorated and furnished in the same way (unlike many developments), which makes for a hotel level of quality. The high standard of fixtures and fittings is impressive, along with the superbly outfitted Clubhouse, featuring a games arcade, Balmoral Bar & Grill, fitness centre and extensive pool-deck, with firepits, loungers, cabañas and movie nights, plus a child-friendly water park and mini-golf. There is also a wedding pavilion, lake fishing (for catch-and-release) and home delivery to every villa from the restaurant. Balmoral is just 13mls/21km from LEGOLAND Florida and 25/40 from the Magic Kingdom, and it makes for a blissfully relaxed retreat after the frenzy of the theme parks. There is more to come, too, with a Sports Center and Ronaldo Soccer School due to open in late 2019 (1866 584 5527, **feltrimresorts.com/balmoral-resort**).

━━━━━ **BRITBONUS**

Stay seven nights in a row at Balmoral Resort and the final night is free, or stay 14 nights and get two free. Applicable on all pool home bookings (3–6 bedrooms) made by end of 2020, subject to availability. Some block-out dates apply, including Christmas period. Quote code 'Brit Guide 2020' when booking on 001 866 584 5527, email **bookings@feltrimresorts.com**, or online chat at balmoralresortflorida.com.

Balmoral Resort

© Balmoral Resort

Blue Heron Beach Resort: A superb complex of two high-rise towers on Apopka-Vineland Rd (Highway 535) in Lake Buena Vista, this features 283 beautifully furnished one and two-bed condos, with two bathrooms, a balcony and fully equipped kitchen, including washer-dryer. There are bunk beds in the spacious one and two-bed units, which comfortably sleep 6–8. All master bedrooms include a whirlpool tub. All have balconies overlooking Lake Bryan while the two-bed Deluxe suites have a second balcony with a Disney fireworks view. There is a superb lido deck, with a large pool, kids' pool and hot tub, plus a boardwalk fronting the lake and watersports (jet-skis and water-skiing, for an extra charge), with the Hawaiian Rumble mini-golf course next door, as well as two fitness centres, but no restaurant (although there are plenty nearby). Housekeeping is available for a charge, but there's a free daily shuttle to Disney and the local outlet shops and, for $14/person, to Universal (407 387 2200, **blueheronbeachresort.com**).

Encantada Resort: A lovely development of two and three-bed town-homes, this offers a lot of facilities at the central clubhouse and a great location south of west Highway 192 but still close to Disney. Each home has two bathrooms and a separate WC, kitchen, dining area and living room with big-screen LCD TV and home cinema, a private terrace, sunbeds and Jacuzzi. The clubhouse has a heated zero-entry pool with a Jacuzzi, children's play area and private lake surrounded by a walking/jogging trail. It also has a restaurant and pool bar, cyber café, games arcade and well-equipped gym, as well as a fishing pier (407 997 9478, **clcworldflorida.com/encantada**).

Encore Club: Adjacent to the huge Reunion Resort (p87), this is the latest community of high-quality villas surrounding a well-appointed clubhouse. The homes vary from four bedrooms (all with en suite) to massive 12-bed mansions, all with private pools, designer kitchens and many including Jacuzzis, games rooms and home theatres. Some even come with themed bedrooms. The wonderful clubhouse includes an Aquapark with slides, flumes and water features, as well as a resort pool, large fitness centre, kids' club, Grab & Go market,

The Grove Resort and Spa

© The Grove

Self-catering definitions

To avoid confusion, here's the correct terminology for self-catering accommodation (but check with the operator for the exact type if it's not clear):

Villa: Detached vacation home, usually with its own screened-in pool, in self-contained residential communities.

Town-home: Two-storey terraced-style house, rarely with its own pool; found in many Resorts.

Condo: One, two or three-bed apartment-style unit, usually in a low-rise block but sometimes 10 or more storeys.

Studio: One-room accommodation unit with kitchen facilities.

Resort: Collection of condos (or town-homes) built around central features like pools, recreation facilities and, sometimes, a restaurant/bar or two.

full-service restaurant (the excellent Finns) and bar/lounge. There is a fully staffed reception desk and a concierge that can arrange tickets and transportation to the parks, plus services like baby-sitting, personal chefs for special occasions and grocery deliveries (407 396 9000, **encoreresorthomes.com**).

BRITTIP

If the designer homes of the Encore Club sound good, check out the rental options with British-owned Jeeves Management (p92) for a great selection.

Floridays Resort: One of the smartest of the area's condo-hotels, this is situated in a quieter part of I-Drive, but close to Orlando Premium Outlets and with a free shuttle to the parks. The 18 tropical acres feature six towers (each with 72 rooms), two pools (including the elaborate main zero-depth entry pool and water-play area), a pool bar and grill, fitness centre, stylish Welcome Center, kids' activity centre and games room, a small grocery store, plus concierge services, business centre and meeting facilities.

The spacious two and three-bed suites are beautifully furnished, sleep 6–10, and have either a balcony or patio. Living rooms include flatscreen TV and high-speed wi-fi, while there are two bathrooms, one with a Jacuzzi tub. There's also a delivery service (8am–10pm) from the Café & Marketplace, which serves Starbucks coffee. All rooms are wheelchair-accessible and some have roll-in showers (1866 994 6321, **floridaysresortorlando.com**).

The Grove Resort & Spa: This complex is a wonderful mix of full-scale hotel and self-catering suites. Just off Highway 192 in Kissimmee (on Avalon Road), it is set in a landscaped 106acres/43ha, with seven-storey accommodation blocks grouped around the pools, bars, luxury Spa and dining options, plus its own water park and feature-packed Family Activity Center, with arcade games and glow-in-the-dark mini-golf. The hugely spacious one, two and three-bed units are fully equipped with kitchen and laundry facilities, all with balconies. There are two indoor bars, the smart Alfresco Market for snacks, coffees and grab-and-go items, Springs pool bar and the swish full-service Valencia restaurant. The pool complex is geared for children and couples (with separate sections, and private cabañas), and there is a private lake with boating and fishing (407 545 7500, **groveresortorlando.com**).

Hapimag Orlando Resort: A rare mix of vacation home and resort, this is Hapimag's only US property, set inside the hide-away Lake Berkley villa community (almost behind Medieval Times). It consists of a self-contained circle on one half of the community with one, two or three-bedroom town-homes. Within the reception is an office area, small library and ticket office for local attractions. The Hapimag club house features a pool, children's splash-pad and fitness room. There is a scenic walkway around the lake, with two white-sand beaches, barbecue picnic area, beach volleyball and a dock for fishing (407 390 9083, **orlando-hapimag.com**).

BRITBONUS

Use promo code 'britbonus' when booking on the direct booking website **orlando-hapimag.com** for an additional 5% discount off their special rates. Email **orlando@hapimag.com** for further information.

Lake Buena Vista Resort Village & Spa: This stylish condo-hotel features five tower blocks of two, three and four-bed condos, next to Lake Buena Vista Factory Stores on Highway 535. The impressive facilities include a superb freeform swimming pool, with pirate play-ship, a quiet pool, a state-of-the-art fitness centre, video games room and kids' club. There is a convenience store and gift shop, a Pizza Hut Express, Frankie Farrell's Irish Pub & Grille and pool-side bar and grill, as well as a shuttle to the theme parks. The rooms (all with kitchens and Jacuzzi bathtubs) are comfortable and stylish, with the four-bed condos super-spacious. Housekeeping is available either daily or weekly for a charge, while the $14/day resort fee covers parking, wi-fi, theme park shuttle, pool towels and fitness room use. The Reflections Spa & Salon offers some wonderful relaxation (407 597 0214, **lbvorlandoresort.com**).

BRITTIP

Visiting Lake Buena Vista Factory Stores? Relieve aching limbs by popping next door to the Reflections Spa in the Resort Village for a soothing pedicure, massage or other treatment (407 597 1695).

Magic Village Yards triplex living room

Magic Village Yards: Beautiful community of three and four-bed town-homes, close to Disney but in a quiet location, and with a Brazilian/Mediterranean design quality. The central clubhouse features a gorgeous main pool, kids' play-room, gym and an excellent restaurant, Villaggio, which features gourmet pizza in a creative menu. The bar offers beer, wine and sake, which can all be served poolside, with a view of the Disney fireworks at night. There is a free shuttle to Disney's Magic Kingdom, 24hr reception and a concierge desk that can arrange in-home private parties, private chefs and grocery delivery, plus free parking and wi-fi. The homes are equally stylish, with ultra-modern kitchens, bathrooms with each bedroom and a first-floor balcony with sun-loungers. Some have outdoor barbecue grills or Jacuzzis, and all have washer/dryers and flatscreen TVs (407 507 5900, **magicvillagevacationhomes.com**).

Margaritaville Resort Orlando: New in 2019, this immense resort on Highway 192 in Kissimmee is based on the 'Floribbean' style of musician Jimmy Buffett, and features a 184-room hotel, vacation homes, timeshare units *and* condos, making it the most multi-use resort in town. The array of features – including a huge freshwater swimming lagoon, water-park, wedding pavilion, signature St Somewhere Spa, kids' clubs and multiple pools – is dazzling, along with waterfalls and other water features that invoke a Key West feel. The hotel features three standout restaurants – notably the fine dining and open-air kitchen of Euphoria – while the Sunset Walk district of shops and restaurants includes Rock & Brews (a brew-pub by rock band KISS), classic 1920s burger bar Ford's Garage, mega candy store It'Sugar, and New York-style coffee bar Café D'Avignon. Estefan Kitchen – a new Cuban-cuisine concept restaurant from Gloria and Emilio Estefan – was due to open in late 2019. There is live music throughout the resort, while the Studio Movie Grill offers films-

© Magic Village

while you-dine, and Avalon features a nails and spa service. Hotel rooms are gorgeously fresh and inviting, and the cottage-style vacation homes range from one to a massive eight bedrooms. There is even a grocery delivery service, to make this one of the most eye-catching, and all-round action-packed, resorts in Florida (407 479 0950, **margaritavilleresortorlando.com**).

Mystic Dunes Resort & Golf Club: This holiday ownership property is tucked away in a quiet corner of Kissimmee and offers hotel-type rentals, often at terrific rates. It features just about every facility, including four pools, waterslide and water-play area, plus one, two and three-bed condos that sleep up to 12, a championship-quality golf course, mini-golf and great dining (1877 747 4747, **mystic-dunes-resort.com**).

Holiday Inn Club Vacations at Orange Lake Resort: This 1,450acre/623ha resort on west Highway 192 offers a mixture of well-furnished one, two and three-bed condo-style villas and studios that sleep 4–12, plus wonderful family-friendly amenities, from world-class golf to no less than seven pools. Villas all have full kitchens, TVs in each room, DVD players, hot-tubs, living and dining areas and a patio or balcony. At the heart of Orange Lake is the amazing River Island water park, with a 1,200ft/365m lazy river style pool, two zero-depth entry pools and pool-bars, mini-golf, hot-tubs and a clubhouse with arcade and fitness centre, as well as three restaurants and a coffee/ice cream café. There are another six pools, four dining choices, two arcades and four championship-quality golf courses spread over the three Villages that make up this immense complex, which has free wi-fi and parking (1866 892 5890, **bit.ly/brit-orangelake**).

BRITTIP

Staying at Orange Lake Resort? Don't miss the Key West-inspired menu at Breezes Restaurant & Bar – or the decadent milkshakes at River Island Grilling Company!

Holiday Inn Club Vacations Orlando Breeze Resort: This timeshare resort on Highway 27 in Davenport features ultra-spacious three-bed condo-style suites with all mod cons, including TVs in every room, free wi-fi and parking. There are two outdoor pools, a kiddie pool, fitness centre and activity centre with kids' activities. Families also enjoy the arcade and pool table, movie theatre and 18-hole mini golf course, plus tennis, basketball and volleyball courts. A casual grill/snack bar provides a handy extra amenity at the activity center (1855 441 2617; **bit.ly/brit-breeze**).

Regal Oaks at Old Town: This mix of stylish three and four-bed town-homes (with two or three baths), follows the successful blueprint of accommodations set around an elaborate clubhouse, with fabulous water features (zero-entry pool, waterslide, whirlpool and twin slides), new restaurant, bar, tennis courts, fitness centre and kids club for 4–12s. All the homes feature an enclosed patio with a hot tub. Next to all the fun and shopping of Old Town in Kissimmee, it offers terrific value (407 997 1000, **regaloaksorlando.com**).

Regal Palms Resort & Spa: Next door to the serene Highlands Reserve villa community on Highway 27 is this mix of three and four-bed town-homes and four and five-bed villas set around a beautiful clubhouse that includes a mini water park (with

Sheraton Vistana Villages

© Sheraton Vistana

lazy river and waterslides), pools, Jacuzzis, extensive sun terraces and free wi-fi. The sister resort to Regal Oaks, it also boasts a tiki bar, business centre, gym and health centre, plus a shop/grocery store (407 965 3887, **regalpalms.com**).

Reunion Resort & Club: One of the most extensive resorts, this will interest golfers who appreciate the chance to stay where they play and lovers of the high life. On Highway 532 in Kissimmee (just off I-4 south of Disney), it boasts a vast line-up of condos, town-homes and luxury villas set around three superb golf courses designed by Arnold Palmer, Tom Watson and Jack Nicklaus, backed up by a full Golf Academy. The deluxe choice features one, two and three-bed condos (many with stunning golf-course views); modest three-bed villas to 15-bed mansions; a stylish golf clubhouse with excellent bar and restaurant; a full-service spa; 11 pools, including the scenic Seven Eagles pool, complete with The Cove bar and grill; fitness room; kids' play centre; floodlit tennis courts; an amazing water park consisting of lazy river, slides, pools, waterfalls and interactive kids' area; and miles of biking and hikng trails. High-rise condo Reunion Grande offers 82 luxurious one and two-bed suites, brilliant Italian bistro Forte, a modern gym and chic rooftop pool-bar and steakhouse, Eleven, offering premium steaks, cocktails and panoramic views. It all comes with concierge service that marks this out as one of Florida's most upmarket resorts. Only those staying here or members can play on the courses,

Reunion Resort

but the scale is superb (407 662 1000, **reunionresort.com**).

BRITTIP

At both Sheraton Vistana properties, for a nominal fee, you can arrange to have your condo pre-stocked with food and laundry products.

Sheraton Vistana Resort: This huge family-friendly complex in Lake Buena Vista, close to WDW, is a mature development of modern, roomy one and two-bed/two-bath condos, sleeping four to eight, with full kitchens, plus magnificent resort facilities. Multiple TVs, DVD player and a screened-in private patio or balcony, plus large washer-dryers, serve to underline the great self-catering value of this type of accommodation. There is a wide variety of dining, from Castaways Bar & Grill to a food court, full-service restaurant and pool bars. Massages are available by appointment and there are mini-golf, volleyball, tennis, bike rentals and a sauna, as well as lots of family-orientated activities, poolside parties, crafts and more. There is scheduled transport to select Disney parks ($10/person, round-trip, per day; bookings required), plus free wi-fi, parking and no resort fee (407 239 3100, **bit.ly/brit-sheraton**).

Sheraton Vistana Villages: The sister property, on I-Drive south of SeaWorld, this upmarket family resort offers spacious one and two-bed/two-bath condos with fully equipped kitchen or kitchenette, dining area, washer-dryer and more, in five and six-storey blocks set around scenic landscaping or pool areas. The beautiful lobby opens on to a stunning pool with waterfalls, Jacuzzis and children's play areas, while there's the smart Breeze Restaurant & Bar for breakfast, lunch and dinner and a mini-market/deli. Less than 6ml/10km from Disney, guests enjoy extensive amenities like scheduled transport to select Disney parks ($10/person, per day, bookings required), daily activities, three pool areas (some with slides

Rental Accommodation

© Steve Munns 2019

and water-play areas), a state-of-the-art fitness centre, games rooms, basketball and tennis courts and a grocery store, plus there is a Publix supermarket and Premium Outlets shops nearby (407 238 5000, **sheratonvistavillages.com**).

Tuscana: This Mediterranean-inspired condo-resort bordering the Champions Gate golf courses offers 288 large, elegant two and three-bed condos, each with two baths, balcony, fully equipped kitchen, washer and dryer. The excellent clubhouse boasts the Tavern Bar & Grill, poolside sports bar, kiddie pool, fitness centre, 30-seat cinema and picnic area (407 787 4800, **bit.ly/brit-tuscana**).

Villas at Grand Cypress: Arguably Orlando's top golf resort, this is also an upmarket option in a beautiful setting behind Walt Disney World, making it among the most convenient villa choices. It offers 146 single-room club suites and one, two, three and four-bed condo-style villas furnished in luxury style, with fully equipped kitchens and patios or balconies. There is a pool with sauna, hot-tub and bar, fitness centre, bike rentals, fishing, the Golf Academy for private lessons, and great dining at the Clubhouse Restaurant and Sports Bar and the Oasis Pool & Bar. Villa guests also get full use of all the amenities of the nearby Hyatt Regency Grand Cypress (p78), a

5min ride on the free on-demand shuttle service. Literally just minutes from Disney, the villas' relaxed ambiance and lush surroundings make you feel light years away (407 239 4700, **grandcypress.com**).

Vista Cay: This timeshare resort offers some of the most extensive facilities in the I-Drive/Universal Boulevard area (behind the Convention Center North). Convenient for the attractions but away from the main bustle, it has beautiful two and three-bed executive suites and three-bed town-homes, plus a large clubhouse and pool set in tropical grounds; whirlpool spa and kids' pool; games room, cinema, business centre and fitness centre. The spacious suites offer full kitchens, large HD TVs with DVD players, dining rooms, master bedrooms with separate Roman tubs and showers, private balconies and free wi-fi (407 996 4647, **vistacayholidays.com**).

Windsor Palms Resort: Just off west Highway 192 in Kissimmee, this popular gated community has a mix of two-bed condos, two and three-bed town-homes, and three to six-bed private pool villas. Amenities include a large clubhouse and fitness centre, tennis courts, an Olympic-sized pool, a kiddie pool and spa, basketball, billiard room, volleyball court, video arcade, playground and a 58-seat cinema. Sister resort **Windsor Hills** on Old Lake Wilson Road offers the same amenities, like its lagoon-style pool with waterslide and state-of-the-art fitness centre and is even closer to the parks. **Windsor at Westside** in Davenport features four and five-bed town-homes and gorgeous six to nine-bed private pool villas. The clubhouse facilities are equally impressive, with huge resort pool, lazy river, waterslide, tiki bar, fitness centre, video arcade and sports courts (407 396 0642, **globalresorthomes.com**).

Vista Cay

HOLIDAY HOMES

This is in many ways the biggest area of accommodation for UK visitors as it has become hugely popular, as well as being a cost-effective way for large families and groups to stay together. The homes – individual or in communities – are sometimes gated, and most have a private pool, while some have access to communal facilities like pools and recreation areas. They are always equipped with full kitchen, laundry facilities and multiple TVs. Some are classed as 'executive', which means more facilities (games rooms, barbecues, Jacuzzis, etc.) rather than an increase in size. A hire car is usually essential, but the savings can be significant. Prices can be as low as $450/week off-peak, but expect to pay at least $1,600/week for a five or six-bed villa in high season. A word of warning: once you've experienced pool-at-home life, you may never go back to a hotel!

If you book independently, there are several key questions. Do you need to go to an office to pick up the keys or is there a combination lockbox at the house? Is there a local contact if anything goes wrong, and is the property maintained by a local company? Does it offer a secure bonding for your booking, and is it a member of a reputable organisation, such as the Better Business Bureau of Central Florida? In winter, is the pool heated, and what is the charge for heating? Is it as close to Disney as it says (some can be half an hour away, but still insist they are 'just minutes from Disney')?

There are more than 26,000 villas across Osceola, Polk and Lake Counties to the west and south-west of Disney, most in well-established developments. Be aware homes within a particular community can still vary in quality depending on the care and attention of owners and/or managers, hence just being in, say, Cumbrian Lakes, is not a guarantee of executive quality. You can rent direct from the owners or a property management company

that will look after multiple villas. For direct rentals, check sites like **vrbo. com, lastminutevillas.net and thedibb. co.uk/forums/villa-search.php. Owner Direct** also have a well-vetted Orlando selection of more than 800 properties and are often good for late deals at **bit. ly/brit-late**.

There are increasing numbers of terrace-style town-homes, so, for a 'detached' house, ask for a 'single family home'. You must do your homework and shop around for recent reviews. The following all pass the *Brit Guide* credibility test.

Advantage Vacation Homes: In the villa business for more than 20 years and one of the largest companies, it keeps its 2–6 bed homes (the majority on west Highway 192 and Highway 27 in Clermont and Davenport) fresh while also managing a range of condos (notably in the Bahama Bay Resort) and town-homes. It offers 24hr management, with courteous and efficient staff at its office just off Highway 192 (9am–10pm daily). Its holiday homes are rated Silver, Gold or Platinum, with the difference measured in extras rather than size (flatscreen TVs, tiled floors rather than carpeting, a Jacuzzi or games room, etc.), though some of the more exclusive villas might

Top Villas

be in a golf community or have tennis courts (407 396 2262; **advantagevacationhomes.com**).

Alexander Holiday Homes: Family-owned Alexander manages more than 200 properties in Kissimmee, from standard two, three and four-bed condos to luxury seven-bed executive homes sleeping 14, all with pools and immaculately furnished, within 15–20mins of Disney, including some of the closest to the parks. It was the first of its kind in Orlando (in 1981) and only the third management company to earn the distinguished AAA (American Automobile Association) Three Diamond rating, as well as being fully accredited with the official Walt Disney World Vacation Rental Home Connection (where homes are inspected quarterly) and definitely gets our approval. It shows prices in UK and US currency and offers a free concierge service to ensure you get to your home, as well as arrival grocery packages, barbecue rentals, scooter and wheelchair hire (0871 711 5371 in the UK, 1800 621 7888 in the US, **floridasunshine.com**).

Elite Vacation Homes: This is another company with a long and solid track record of villa management in the Kissimmee area, with the majority of their 3–7-bed villas just a 10–15min drive from Disney. With a lot to choose from, including the latest executive-style homes with hot-tubs, large-screen TVs and games rooms, there is something for all budgets here (407 397 0850, **elitevacationhomes.com**).

——BRITBONUS $

Get $15 off regular nightly rates per night with Elite Vacation Homes by using the code UKFRIENDS when you call or book online (proof of UK residency required at check-in).

Florida Leisure Vacation Homes: Another reliable company that has been around for 20 years, it pays great attention to detail, with an upscale approach that sets it apart from many operators. With 100 homes (3–7 beds) in the Kissimmee area, most just a few years old, it prides itself on a personal touch (even down to providing personal chef, massage and concierge services) and offers some of the biggest and newest properties, as well as an online booking system. Many are in the Executive range, with the fullest array of amenities as well as private, screened pools, and often in gated communities. All villas have lockboxes, so you don't need to visit the office to check in. You can see all its homes online (with extensive photo galleries) plus lots of local info, while its testimonial sections provide first-hand feedback (407 870 1600; **floridaleisurevacationhomes.com**).

Jeeves Holiday Homes: For the deluxe villa touch and immaculate style, British-owned and award-winning Jeeves is one of the best in the business. They specialise in high-end properties – including some of the largest and most sumptuous mansions in Reunion Resort, with up to 15 bedrooms – and have a boutique approach, offering bespoke services and concierge luxury. Need an in-villa private chef, spa treatment or butler? Ask Jeeves! They have also selected some of the most eye-catching properties in Central Florida, notably several with fully themed bedrooms that wouldn't be out of place in the theme parks. They offer welcome packs, special-occasion services and a 'Car on the Drive' option for those who don't want to pick up their hire car straight away. Their knowledge of the area is first class and they feature villas in the gorgeous Encore Club resort (407 706 3870, **jeevesfloridarentals.com**).

——BRITBONUS $

Receive 5% off regular rates PLUS a welcome grocery pack with stays of 10 nights or more with **Jeeves Management**. Use the code BRITS5% when booking online or by phone.

Loyalty Homes: For a luxury touch, this British-owned company (since 1999) offers three to eight-bedroom homes, all within a genuine short drive of Disney and with true 'executive' style, including digital door locks (no key collection required), cable TV, free wi-fi and games rooms. The website offers video tours, too (call 0121 468 0016 in the UK or 863 420 1010 in the US, **loyaltyusa.com**).

Premier Home Management: A good range of properties with 3–7 bedrooms, sleeping up to 12, in secure residential communities within a 15–20min drive of Disney. All are privately owned and have been furnished as holiday homes, with screened pools, two TVs, fully equipped kitchens, at least one king or queen bed and free local phone calls. In addition to the villas, there are town-home and condo options (863 421 6115, **premiervacationhomesorlando.com**).

BRITTIP

You'll find Marmite, Ribena, McVities and a handful of other British groceries at Publix and Winn-Dixie supermarkets, and most Wal-Marts (International aisle).

Think Vacation Homes: Another company offering a wide variety, from two-bed condos to massive 14-bed homes, all located within 10mls/16km of Disney, plus properties in the Miami and Delray beach areas. All homes feature luxurious amenities, including pools with spas, multiple master suites, games rooms and home theatres (321 281 4966, **thinkvacationhomes.com**).

Top Villas: For a one-stop shop, UK-owned booking agent, **Top Villas** takes some beating. A specialist in villa rentals worldwide – but especially in Orlando – they work with local management companies to offer hundreds of properties, from one-bed condos to 15-bed villas, including luxurious resorts

like Reunion and Encore. They also feature extras such as car hire, private catering and housekeeping for a bespoke experience (1866 341 8086 in the US, 0800 433 4567 in the UK; **thetopvillas.com**).

Villa Direct: Another major Orlando specialist, and one of the biggest, with an extensive range of properties in the area, from two-bed condos to luxury 10-bed villas, and a good user-friendly website, plus an excellent range of guest services, including arrival groceries, a personalised concierge service, car hire and mobility equipment rental. Also on the Walt Disney World Vacation Rental Home Connection, their office is uniquely located in the town of Celebration (407 397 1210, **villadirect.com**).

Air BnB

While all the main villa developments are in Osceola, Lake and Polk counties, the advent of Airbnb has opened up a lot more possibilities for Orlando/Orange County, which traditionally has not allowed short-term rentals. You will still find plenty of typical vacation villas on offer but also a mix of downtown apartments and even homes and condos closer to the parks. If you are comfortable with the unique Airbnb style (where you are renting a room in someone's home), it can work out cheaper than hotels or villas (**airbnb.com/s/Orlando--FL**).

OK, that's enough accommodation advice. Now it's on to the parks….

Weikiva Island

5 The Theme Parks: Disney's Fab Four

Or Mickey, Magic, Movies - and Star Wars!

Now let's prepare you for the main business of any visit to Orlando: Walt Disney World. This is the heart of all the excitement and fun in store (along with the other big theme parks of Universal Orlando, SeaWorld and Busch Gardens).

A fortnight is barely enough to see all of Disney on its own – especially now Star Wars: Galaxy's Edge is open in Disney's Hollywood Studios! – let alone the other parks and smaller attractions, so you start to realise the awesome scope of an Orlando holiday. Disney's designers – called Imagineers – have set an incredibly high bar for creativity and imagination, and these are true 'themed' parks for a very good reason.

Buzz and Woody in Toy Story Land

© Disney

BRITTIP
Before you leave home, photocopy the back of your park passes and your passport info page, then you'll have the info you need should you lose them.

Buying your tickets in advance saves time and is often better value, but work out your requirements first – you won't get full value for the 14-day Disney, Universal AND SeaWorld tickets in just a fortnight. Try to use your credit card for all purchases for the built-in extra security (for our list of recommended ticket outlets; p10).

Discount options: You will find a welter of discount coupons for many of the smaller attractions in tourist publications distributed in Orlando (or from your hotel Guest Services desk – it's often worth asking). What you won't find is discounted Disney tickets (unless it is a timeshare lure). Disney never discount, apart from occasional '5th Day Free' offers through the official outlets.

BRITTIP
I-Drive has the only genuine Official Visitor Center. Offers of 'free' Disney tickets usually mean timeshare firms, which also claim to have 'official' visitor centres.

Official Visitor Center: Check this out for discounts (and a handy currency exchange) at 8102 International Drive next to Mango's Tropical

Cafe (407 363 5872). It IS possible to bag free tickets by attending timeshare presentations but they can easily take half a day of hard-sell out of your precious holiday.

Timeshare: If you DO want to look at timeshare options, look first at Disney Vacation Club for the guarantee of memorable holidays. A tour (for which you will be picked up) will take about 3hrs and you'll receive a small parting gift (dining coupon, etc). Call 0800 783 2893 or visit **disneyvacationclub.disney.go.com.**

BRITTIP

Smoking is not permitted in the restaurants or in the parks, apart from in a designated area outside each park's gates.

Ratings

Our unique rating system splits attractions into thrill rides and scenic rides, earning **T** or **A** ratings out of 5.

- **TTTTT** is as exciting as they get and, along with **AAAAA** is unmissable. These will have the longest queues, so you should plan your visit around them.
- **TTTT** or **AAAA** should be high on your 'must do' list.
- **TTT** or **AAA** should be seen if you have time.
- **TT** is worth seeing only if there is no queue, **AA** is likely to be twee and missable.

Some rides have height restrictions and are not advisable for people with back, neck or heart problems or for expectant mothers. Where this is the case we say, for example, '**R**: 3ft 6in/106cm'. Height restrictions (strictly enforced) are based on the average five-year-old being 3ft 6in/106cm tall, those aged six being 3ft 9in/114cm and nines being 4ft 4in/132cm. You can also refer to our Height Restriction Guide, p27.

My Magic+

This high-tech system of guest interaction is designed to personalise

and enhance many aspects of park visits. Free for Disney resort guests, but available for offsite guests to buy, the MagicBand wristband acts as an all-purpose ticket, optional payment card, FastPass+ and PhotoPass card, and allows various special features, like pre-booking FastPass+ and cataloguing your dining reservations. It works in conjunction with My Disney Experience (see below), where you fill in your trip details (as much or as little as you prefer) and use the mobile app for all the latest info, such as queuing wait times and dining reservations. MagicBands come in different colours and styles and are designed to be collectible. Intended to be 'transformational' in how we enjoy the parks, My Magic+ can be tough to navigate, and the need to pre-book 60 days in advance for onsite guests (30 for offsite guests) can take some of the fun and spontaneity out of the experience. You don't have to sign up for My Magic+, but you won't be able to access all the perks available if you choose not to.

Disney has an App for that

Get essential Park info on your Mobile device, from park hours and wait times to menus, ride info and FastPass+ reminders, plus the new **Play Disney Parks app,** (especially for Star Wars: Galaxy's Edge) all free for iPhone and Android, from **bit.ly/disney-app.** The App also allows you to order food and drinks. Go to Mobile Food Orders, choose the restaurant you'd like to order from and press

Magic bands

© Disney

Character dining

Having a meal with Mickey and Co is one of the great Disney experiences – even without children – and is often the best way to meet your favourite characters without a wait. Make reservations up to 180 days in advance (180 plus your length of stay if you are booked at a Disney hotel) by phoning 407 WDW DINE (939 3463), calling at any Guest Services desk in a hotel, or on **disneyworld.com**.

Some meals are difficult to get. Breakfast at Cinderella's Royal Table or Be Our Guest at the Magic Kingdom usually sell out within minutes of the 180-day window being open. Chef Mickey's and the Princess meals also go quickly. If you cannot book in advance, try calling the day you'd like to dine or, as a last resort, show up to see if there have been any cancellations. You must check in at the podium 10mins before your time and you will be given the next available table. Some characters don't enter the restaurant so, if they are in the lobby, meet them before you are seated. Dining is all-you-can-eat, served buffet, pre-plated or family-style. Inside the restaurant, characters circulate among the tables, giving attention to each group (particularly when children are holding the camera!).

Character interaction is top-notch, especially if you dine off-hours when the restaurant is quieter. Bring your autograph book, a fat pen or marker (easier for the characters to hold) and a large capacity digital card. Some characters are huge, and children may be put off by them. If you aren't sure how they'll react, see how they are with the characters in the park before booking. Price range: breakfast $28-72 adults, $18–44 children; lunch $50–90 and $26–54; dinner $50–90 and $25–54 (NB: beware peak season price rises – Disney raises its rates in high season and even weekends, and some of those children's prices are outrageous, in our opinion).

Order Food. Make your selections, and pay via credit card or debit card (Disney Dining Plan users must order at the restaurant). When you arrive at the restaurant, tap 'I'm Here, Prepare My Order', and your food will be made while you wait. Pick it up at a special Mobile Order Pickup Window.

────BRITTIP
Free wi-fi is available throughout Walt Disney World to ensure you can access the online facilities, including all the benefits of MyMagic+.

My Disney Experience

This is the online platform that allows guests to make dining reservations, schedule FastPass+ times, add Photopass, and link their Disney resort reservations and theme park admission. You must have a My Disney Experience account and valid theme park admission to schedule FastPass+ selections in advance. Using the online system, guests are also able to connect Friends and Family in-park experiences. To create an account, visit **disneyworld.disney.go.com/plan.**

Disney's FastPass+

Most of the attractions have this essential aid to queuing (free with admission), which allows you to roam while you wait for your scheduled ride time. Onsite guests can schedule three FP+ times in one park per day, up to 60 days in advance (30 days for offsite guests; starting at 7am US Eastern Standard Time, or noon UK time) using the online My Disney Experience system or Disney's free mobile app. Guests may also schedule FP+ times at in-park kiosks or by using the mobile app. Buy your park passes, create a My Disney Experience account, and follow instructions for scheduling FP+, booking dining reservations, and adding 'reminders'. You can then link your experiences to others in your party, make changes as needed, and customise your account with additional options. However, each guest can choose their own FP+ selections if they would like to experience attractions separately. **Club Level** guests at Disney's Deluxe hotels can purchase 3 additional

Character Dining: the meals

MAGIC KINGDOM: Crystal Palace for breakfast, lunch or dinner with Winnie the Pooh and Co – especially good for smaller children; and **Cinderella's Royal Table** for the (expensive) Once Upon A Breakfast, with Cinderella and her Princess Friends; Lunch (Cinderella and Friends); and Dinner (Fairy Godmother only). Breakfast (off-peak) is $73 adults, $44 children; lunch and dinner $90 and $54. Credit card payment in full is required to book and you WILL be charged the full price if you cancel less than 24hrs in advance (photo package and gratuity included, additional photos for a fee).

EPCOT: Garden Grill for lunch or dinner with Farmer Mickey, Pluto, Chip and Dale; Princess Storybook Dining at **Restaurant Akershus** (Norway) for breakfast, lunch and dinner; an alternative to Cinderella's, with some of Belle, Jasmine, Snow White, Mulan, Aurora (Sleeping Beauty) and Mary Poppins. Breakfast $52 adults, $31children; lunch and dinner $62 and $37. Credit card needed to book; full charge applied for cancelling less than 24hrs in advance.

DISNEY'S HOLLYWOOD STUDIOS: Hollywood & Vine for breakfast or lunch with the Play 'n Dine pals, including Doc McStuffins, Sophia the First, Vampirina and Goofy ($38/$23). At peak times, Minnie's Seasonal Dining (with Goofy, Donald and Daisy) features lunch and dinner ($52/$31).

DISNEY'S ANIMAL KINGDOM: Donald's Dining Safari Breakfast and Lunch at **Tusker House** with Donald, Goofy, Pluto and sometimes Daisy and Mickey.

DISNEY RESORTS

Beach Club Resort: At **Cape May Café**, breakfast with Goofy, Minnie and Donald.

Contemporary Resort: At **Chef Mickey's**, breakfast or dinner with Mickey, Minnie, Goofy, Pluto, Donald Duck – peak times book up quickly.

Four Seasons Hotel: At **Ravello**, Thurs and Sat (plus Tues during peak seasons) breakfast with Goofy and pals, $46 adults and $24 3–9s.

Grand Floridian: At **1900 Park Fare**, breakfast with Alice, Mary Poppins, Tigger, Pooh Bear and Mad Hatter; dinner with Cinderella, Anastasia, Drizella, Lady Tremaine and, sometimes, Prince Charming – book early. Wonderland Tea Party 2–3pm Mon–Fri, 4–12s only, $49, meal, activities and storytelling with Alice and friends. Perfectly Princess Tea Party with Princess Aurora, 10.30am–12pm on select mornings, 3–11 with an adult, $333.64 for 1 adult with 1 child age 3–11. Meal (tea, cake, finger sandwiches), singalong, story time, Princess Aurora doll, bracelet, necklace, rose, tiara, and stickers and 'best friend' certificate.

Polynesian Resort: At **'Ohana**, breakfast with Lilo, Stitch, Pluto and Mickey.

Walt Disney World Swan: At **Garden Grove Café**, Mon–Fri, dinner and Sat and Sun breakfast, both with Goofy and Pluto

FastPasses for $50/person and book them up to 90 days in advance.

BRITTIP

Disney's FastPass+ system makes it essential to schedule your ride times well in advance using MyMagic+. It is likely FP+ times for the major attractions will be gone if you leave it until the day, especially in peak season.

EPCOT, Disney's Hollywood Studios and Disney's Animal Kingdom use a tiered system for FastPass+. Tier 1 indicates attractions from which you must choose only one; Tier 2 allows you to schedule two attractions. Watch for FP+ (choose two) and FP+1 (choose one) in our attraction descriptions. Guests who opt out of My Disney Experience can still use their regular ticket for park admission.

Onsite guests will each receive a MagicBand (waterproof wrist band with RFID chip) in place of an admission ticket, which can also be used to open their room door, charge purchases (if desired), allow FP+ access, and more. MagicBands will not be shipped overseas, but will be presented on check-in. However, you can still book FP+ in advance with a confirmation code. Offsite guests can buy MagicBands to replace their admission tickets, if they like.

BRITTIP

You can schedule additional FP+ using the My Disney Experience app on your phone rather than queuing up at the FastPass kiosks, once you have used your initial three FP+.

All Disney parks offer pushchair ('stroller') hire, and you can save money by buying a multi-day rental at your first park. Children of ALL ages seem to get a big thrill from collecting autographs from the various Disney characters, and most shops sell autograph books ($9.99). Parents wanting healthier dining options for kids in Disney parks and resorts should look on the menu for Mickey Check, a standard for more nutritious meals. You should find at least one choice at every counter-service and full-service restaurant (**disneymickeycheck.com**). The Power Pack lunch at some counter-service options serves healthier snacks in boxes, containing things like juice, yoghurt, string cheese, crackers, carrots and apple sauce.

PhotoPass

This worthwhile scheme is available in all Disney's parks and in Disney Springs. Disney photographers take photos of guests that are linked to an online account via a card you receive with your first photo or via Memory Maker (see below). There is no charge for a card or for viewing them online, but there is if you want to download and print them. Photos can be enhanced with Disney characters and special effects, while there are 'magical' photos where photographers ask guests to pose in a fun way and Tinker Bell (or Stitch, or Simba or Mickey) will appear in the frame.

Guests have 30 days after the photos are taken to decide if they want to buy at **mydisneyphotopass.com.**

Memory Maker: This package links to a My Disney Experience account (p96), collecting each PhotoPass, on-ride and character dining photo for $199 ($169 in advance) for the full duration of your visit or $69 for one day of photos. Images can be put on mugs, mouse pads and more. Just swipe your card or Magic Band with every photo (ride photos add automatically with a Band). Annual Passes and the UK Ultimate Tickets include Memory Maker.

Cast Members

Disney employees are called Cast Members or CMs (never 'staff' as they all play a role in the entertainment) and they're renowned for their helpful, cheerful style, always willing to assist, advise or chat. If you've had exceptional service or a CM has gone out of their way to help, let Disney know (at Guest Relations or City Hall) as it values feedback and CMs get credit for it.

Rider Switch

If you have children under a height restriction, or one person in your group who does not wish to ride but cannot be left alone, you needn't queue twice. At the entrance, tell the operator you want to do a Rider Switch. Then riders can enjoy the ride while non-riders wait in a quiet area, and then they swap. You will be given a Rider Switch ticket while you wait.

Park security

Visitors with bags must go through a security check at the Transportation and Ticket Center for Magic Kingdom or at park entry for EPCOT, Hollywood Studios and Animal Kingdom. There is a separate lane for those without bags, but all visitors can be asked to go through additional metal detector screening. When you put your ticket or MagicBand across the electronic terminal, you must give a finger scan (which stops others from using your ticket). Be aware there is no smoking inside any theme park (smoking sections are located outside each park's entrance), pushchair size is limited to 31 x 52in/79 x 132cm, and selfie sticks, stroller wagons, loose ice and dry ice are banned.

MAGIC KINGDOM PARK

The starting point for any visit, the Magic Kingdom – the original development that sparked the Orlando tourist boom in 1971 – best embodies the genuine enchantment Disney bestows on its visitors. A few rides are the same as those in Disneyland Paris or Disneyland in LA, but there are key differences, notably on Pirates of the Caribbean,

Big Thunder Mountain Railroad, Haunted Mansion and especially Space Mountain. And, even if a couple of attractions are closed for refurbishment, you won't be short of things to do! Here's our guide to a typical day, including the rides, shows and places to eat; how to park, how to avoid the worst of the crowds – and how much you should expect to pay.

Magic Kingdom Park at a glance

Location	Off World Drive, Walt Disney World
Size	107 acres/43ha in 6 'lands'
Hours	9am–7pm off peak; 9am–10pm President's Day (see Brit Tip, p18), spring school holidays; 8am–11pm or midnight high season (Easter, summer holidays, Thanksgiving and Christmas)
Admission	Under-3s free; 3–9 $104–154 (1-day base ticket, priced seasonally), $392-550 (5-day Magic Your Way), £385 (14-day Ultimate, includes Memory Maker); adult (10+) $109–159, $410–568, £399. US prices do not include tax.
Parking	$25; $50 premium
Lockers	To the right of the main entrance $10 and $12
Pushchairs	$15 and $31 (underneath Main Street Train Station; $13 and $27 per day for multiple days)
Wheelchairs	$12 or $70 ($20 deposit refunded) underneath Main Street Train Station
Top attractions	Splash Mountain, Space Mountain, Seven Dwarfs' Mine Train, Big Thunder Mountain Railroad, Pirates of the Caribbean, Haunted Mansion, most rides in Fantasyland
Don't miss	Festival of Fantasy Parade and Happily Ever After fireworks (most nights)
Hidden costs	**Meals** Burger, chips and coke $17.98 / 3-course dinner (Tony's Town Square) $38–68 / Kids' counter service meal $6.49–7.49 **T-shirts** $24.99–44.99 Kids $14.99–29.99 **Souvenirs** $1.99–31,500 **Sundries** Chalk colour portraits $18.95–$37.90, or Silhouettes $10, with oval frame $19.95

The Magic Kingdom takes up just 107acres/43ha of Disney's near 31,000acres/12,555ha but attracts almost as many as the rest put together. It has six 'lands', like slices of a cake, centred on Florida's most famous landmark, Cinderella Castle. More than 40 attractions are packed into the park, plus shops and restaurants. It's easy to get overwhelmed, especially as it gets so

busy (even the fast-food restaurants have long queues in high season), so plan around what most takes your fancy, but do look out for the interactive queues at some rides, including Big Thunder Mountain Railroad, Haunted Mansion, Peter Pan's Flight, Space Mountain, Little Mermaid, Winnie the Pooh and Seven Dwarfs Mine Train.

Location

The Magic Kingdom is situated at the innermost end of Walt Disney World, with its entrance Toll Plaza three-quarters of the way along World Drive, the main entrance off Highway 192. World Drive runs north–south, while the Interstate 4 (I-4) entrance, EPCOT Drive, runs east–west. Unless you are staying at a Disney resort or are an Annual Pass holder, you must pay the $25–45 parking fee at the Toll Plaza to bring you into the massive car park (we really don't believe the Premium Parking is worth it, by the way).

BRITTIP

For the smoothest entry by road from Highway 192, take Seralago Boulevard (opposite the Seralago Hotel & Suites next to Old Town), turn left on to a non-toll stretch of Osceola Parkway and follow the signs to your chosen park. On West 192, turn off on Sherberth Road, go north to the first traffic lights and turn right, then pick up the Disney signs.

The car parks are busiest from 9.30–11.30am, so it's vital to get here EARLY. If you can't arrive by 9am at peak times, wait until after 1pm, or later when the park is open late. Remember to note where you park: there are Heroes (Woody, Simba, Rapunzel, Aladdin, Peter Pan and Mulan) and Villains (Ursula, Jafar, Zurg, Hook, Scar and Cruella) sections of the 'parking lot'. Note the side, section and number you're in (e.g. Ursula row 94) as many hire cars look the same!

BRITTIP

Take a photo of the Section and Row number on your camera or phone so you know where you've parked.

A tram takes you to the Transportation and Ticket Center, where you go through a security check. Unless you already have tickets (which saves valuable time), you visit the ticket booths here. Then, to get to the Magic Kingdom itself, the monorail is quicker if there isn't a queue, otherwise take a ferryboat. For Disney hotel guests, the resort buses drop you almost at the front door. Minnie Vans drop off and pick up at the same location, while Uber and Lyft drop off at the Transportation and Ticket Center.

Princess Fairytale Hall

ADVENTURELAND

1 Swiss Family Treehouse
2 Jungle Cruise
3 Magic Carpets of Aladdin
4 The Enchanted Tiki Room
5 Pirates of the Caribbean

FRONTIERLAND

6 Splash Mountain
7 Big Thunder Mountain Railroad
8 Country Bear Jamboree
9 Raft to Tom Sawyer Island

LIBERTY SQUARE

10 Liberty Tree Tavern
11 Liberty Square Riverboat
12 The Haunted Mansion
13 The Hall of Presidents

FANTASYLAND

14 'It's a Small World'
15 Prince Charming Regal Carousel
16 Mad Tea Party
17 The Many Adventures of Winnie The Pooh
18 Princess Fairytale Hall
19 Dumbo The Flying Elephant
20 Mickey's PhilharMagic
21 The Barnstormer starring The Great Goofini

22 Casey Jr Splash 'n' Soak Station
23 Peter Pan's Flight
24 Castle Forecourt Stage
25 Cinderella's Royal Table
26 Brave – Meet Merida
27 Enchanted Tales with Belle
28 Be Our Guest Restaurant
29 Under The Sea – Journey of the Little Mermaid
30 Ariel's Grotto
31 Seven Dwarfs Mine Train

TOMORROWLAND

32 Space Mountain
33 Tron Coaster (2021)
34 Tomorrowland Indy Speedway
35 Walt Disney's Carousel of Progress
36 Astro Orbiter
37 Tomorrowland Transit Authority
38 Buzz Lightyear's Space Ranger Spin
39 Monsters Inc. Laugh Floor

TRANSPORT

40 Walt Disney World Railroad Stations
41 Boat Dock
42 Monorail Station
43 Bus Station

MAGIC KINGDOM

Main Street USA

Hopefully, you've arrived early and are among the first to swarm through the entrance. The opening time may say 9am but the gates can open up to 45mins earlier, bringing you into the first of the 'lands'. On your right is **Town Square Theater**, the place to meet Mickey Mouse and Tinker Bell. On the left is **City Hall** for any queries, problems and restaurant bookings (highly advisable). Main Street also has the park's best shopping (notably the massive **Emporium**) and **Walt Disney World Railroad** (AAA), a Western-themed steam train that circles the park and is a good choice when queues are long elsewhere (though Town Square station is often the busiest).

Sorcerers of the Magic Kingdom: This interactive game takes place around the park, but has its HQ at The Firehouse in Town Square, where guests sign up for a role in saving the Magic Kingdom from various Disney villains, with the help of role-playing cards. There are 20 'magic portals' (cleverly disguised video screens) to unmask the villains and help ensure Merlin defeats them. AAA

Dining: The Italian-style **Tony's Town Square Restaurant** serves lunch and dinner; **The Plaza Restaurant** offers salads and sandwiches, with beer and wine (lunch and dinner); and **The Crystal Palace** (breakfast $38 adult, $24 ages 3–9; lunch and dinner $52 & $31) is buffet-style food with Winnie

Mickey and Minnie celebrate at Town Square Theater

© Disney

the Pooh and Co. Quick bites can be bought from **Casey's Corner** (hot dogs, chips and soft drinks); **Main Street Bakery** (a Starbucks coffee shop, also serving wonderful pastries); **Main Street Confectionery** (chocolate and sweets); and the **Plaza Ice Cream Parlor**. Disney characters also appear periodically throughout the Square.

Info: Check the **Guest Information Board** at the top of Main Street (on the left) as it gives waiting times for all the attractions. The **Baby Center** (for nursing mothers) is also at the top of Main Street, to the left next to Crystal Palace, along with the **First Aid** station.

BRITTIP

Can't find your favourite characters? **City Hall** can tell you exactly who will be out, where and when. Character meet-and-greets are also shown on park maps with a 'Mickey glove' icon.

Beating the queues: Unless you are late, skip Main Street and head for the end of the street to the real entrance to the park, where you await official opening hour. Adopt one of three tactics, each aimed at doing some of the most popular rides before the queues build up (wait times of 2hrs for Splash Mountain are not unknown). 1: If you fancy the five-star, log-flume Splash Mountain, keep left in front of the Crystal Palace with the majority, who will head the same way. 2: If you have young children who can't wait to try the Fantasyland rides (especially the Seven Dwarfs Mine Train, which is *very* hard to get on FP+), stay in the middle and pass around the Castle. 3: If the thrills of indoor roller-coaster Space Mountain appeal, move right by The Plaza Restaurant for Tomorrowland. Now you're in pole position for the initial rush (and it will be a rush; take care with children).

BRITTIP

The Move It! Shake It! MousekeDance It! Street Party begins in Town Square, but the real action takes place around the Castle Hub. Stake out a spot in advance if you want an up-front view.

Other entertainment: The day starts with **Let The Magic Begin**, a five-minute welcome show on the Castle Forecourt stage, with a royal herald and a few well-known Disney faces appearing to mark the official opening of the park. The **Move It! Shake It! MousekeDance It! Street Party** performs up to three times daily, from Town Square, along Main Street, ending up in the Hub area as Disney characters, stilt walkers and dancers lead a high-energy party. The **Main Street Trolley Show** happens 3–4 times a day, with a horse-drawn trolley arriving for a 6min song-and-dance interlude. Fun barbershop quartet the **Dapper Dans** and brass band **Main Street Philharmonic** (who also play in Storybook Circus) add lively musical interludes, as does **Casey's Corner Pianist**, and don't miss the **Glass Blowing Demonstrations** at Crystal Arts Shop. There is a daily **Flag Retreat** at 5pm, with a military veteran helping the Security Colour Guard to bring down the national flag.

Adventureland

Head left (going round clockwise) to enter Adventureland. If you're going to Splash Mountain first pass the Swiss Family Treehouse on your left and bear right through an archway (with toilets) into Frontierland, where you turn left and Splash Mountain is ahead. Stopping in Adventureland, these are the attractions.

Swiss Family Treehouse: This imitation banyan tree is a clever replica of the treehouse from Disney's 1960 film *Swiss Family Robinson*. It's a walk-through attraction where the queues (rarely long) move steadily if not quickly, providing a neat glimpse of the ultimate tree house. **AA**

BRITTIP
Disney sells an autograph book and pen set, but it's cheaper to buy them separately. Buy a fat pen, which is easier for characters to hold.

Jungle Cruise: It's not so much the scenic, geographically suspect boat ride (where the Nile suddenly becomes the Amazon) that is so amusing as the non-stop yarn about your adventure from the boat's captain. Long queues, so visit early morning (opens 10am) or late afternoon (evening queues are shortest, but you'll miss some of the detail in the dark). **AAAA FP+**

Pirates of the Caribbean: One of Disney's most impressive attractions that involves Walt's pioneering work in audio-animatronics, life-size figures that move, talk and, in this instance, lay siege to a Caribbean island! Your 8min underground boat ride visits a typical pirate adventure and the world of Captain Jack Sparrow and nemesis Captain Barbossa as they search for buried treasure. It's terrific family

Main Street USA

fun (though perhaps a bit spooky for young children, with one small drop in the dark). Queues are longest from late morning to mid-afternoon. AAAAA (**TTTT** under-10s) FP+

The Enchanted Tiki Room: A classic bird-laden, South Seas audio-animatronic show starring various parrots, macaws and other tropical feathered friends – plus the angry Tiki Gods! Queues are rare and it is air-conditioned. AA

Magic Carpets of Aladdin: In an Agrabah-themed area, this ride spins you up, down and around as you try to dodge the spitting camel! Your 'flying carpet' tilts as well as levitates, simple stuff geared for younger children (like the Magic Carpets of Agrabah ride in Disneyland Paris). T (**TTTT** under-5s), FP+.

A Pirate's Adventure: Treasure of the Seven Seas: A variation on the Sorcerers of the Magic Kingdom interactive card game (p102), with the chance to help Captain Jack Sparrow fight off his foes and locate different treasures around Adventureland, using a pirate map and magic talisman. Visit the special kiosk

through the archway past the Pirates ride to get started. AAA

Disney characters from the movie Aladdin also turn up next to the Magic Carpets ride.

Shopping: The best shopping is in **Pirates Bazaar**, where **Pirates League** (9am–2.45pm) offers a chance for young swashbucklers to transform into fully fledged pirates, empresses or mermaids with various packages ($19.95–109.95) that include accessories like earrings, eye patches, swords, coin necklaces and temporary tattoos, or mermaid make-up and nail polish, sash, jewellery, hairstyle and dress (photos sold separately).

Dining: Skipper Canteen is casual full service 'adventure dining' themed like the Jungle Cruise and in three different dining rooms. It features 'World Famous Jungle Cuisine', served by Jungle Cruise skippers, and is an excellent choice for lunch or dinner, offering surprisingly upscale food for a theme park. **Aloha Isle** adds signature Dole Whips and **Sunshine Tree Terrace** has ice cream and drinks, and **Tortuga Tavern** (open seasonally) features ribs, turkey legs and hot dogs.

Big Thunder Mountain Railroad

Magic Carpets of Aladdin

Frontierland

This Western-themed area is one of the busiest and is best avoided from late morning to late afternoon.

Splash Mountain: Based on classic Disney cartoon *Song of the South*, this is a watery journey with Brer Rabbit, Brer Fox and Brer Bear. It features jolly cartoon scenery and fun with the main characters and several minor swoops in your log boat, followed by a five-storey plummet into a mist-shrouded pool! A huge adrenalin rush, but busy almost all day (try it first thing or during one of the parades to avoid the longest queues). Be ready to get VERY wet! **R:** 3ft 4in/101cm. **TTTT** FP+

Big Thunder Mountain Railroad: When Disney does a roller-coaster it will be one of the classiest, and here it is – a runaway mine train that swoops, tilts and plunges through a mock mine filled with clever scenery. You have to ride it at least twice to appreciate all the detail, but again queues are heavy, so go early (after Splash Mountain) or late in the day. **R:** 3ft 4in/101cm. **TTTT** FP+

Country Bear Jamboree: Here's a novelty: a 16min musical revue by audio-animatronic bears! It's great family fun with plenty of novel touches (watch for the talking moose head). Crowds are rare, so it's a good one when it's busy elsewhere. AAA

Frontierland Shootin' Arcade: The park's single attraction that costs extra ($1 for 35 shots), as you take aim at a series of animated targets. **T**

Tom Sawyer Island: Take a raft over to an overgrown playground of mysterious caves, grottos and mazes, rope bridges and Fort Sam Clemens, where you can fire air guns at passing boats (opens 11am). A good choice in early afternoon when the queues are long elsewhere. Aunt Polly's Dockside Inn allows time off your feet, but the only drinks are from a vending machine. **TT**

Other entertainment: The **Hoedown Happening** with the Country Bears provides musical interludes.

Shopping: Frontierland shops sell cowboy hats and badges, as well as Native American and Mexican crafts. Look out for the themed **Briar Patch** and **Prairie Outpost** for interesting gifts.

Dining: Try **Pecos Bill Tall Tale Inn & Café** (burgers, Tex-Mex, Fajitas), **Golden Oak Outpost** (chicken nuggets, waffle fries, cookies and drinks) or **Westward Ho!** (breakfast sandwich, corn dog, chicken skewer, snacks, drinks).

Splash Mountain

The Muppets present Great Moments in American History

Liberty Square

The clockwise tour brings you to a homage to post-independence America. A lot of the historical content will go over the heads of British visitors, but it still has some great attractions.

Interactive Fun at the Haunted Mansion

Liberty Square Riverboat: Cruise America's 'rivers' on an authentic paddle steamer, be menaced by river pirates and thrill to the stories of How the West Was Won (9.30am–7 or 8pm). This is also good at busier times of the day, especially early afternoon. **AAA**

The Haunted Mansion: A clever delve into the world of Master Gracey's ghostly bride that is neither too scary for most kids nor too twee for adults. Not so much a thrill ride as a scenic adventure. Watch out at the end when the 'hitch-hiking ghosts' might drop in! Longish queues for much of the day, however, so try to visit late on. **AAAA** (**TTTT** under-6s), **FP+**

The Hall of Presidents: The attraction likely to mean least to us, a two-part show that is a film about the US Constitution and an audio-animatronic parade of all 45 US presidents (opens 9am). Technically impressive, it may bore young 'uns (though it is air-conditioned). **AAA**

The Muppets Present…Great Moments in American History: Kermit, Miss Piggy, Fozzie Bear, Gonzo and Sam Eagle join town crier James Jefferson in humorous sketches retelling great moments in history – but, as they point out, just the American parts. Sketches include The Declaration of Independence and Paul Revere's Midnight Ride, and the outdoor 'show' runs several times daily.

Shopping: Look for **Ye Olde Christmas Shoppe** and the fabulous Haunted Mansion-themed **Memento Mori**.

Dining: Eating options are the full-service **Liberty Tree Tavern** (hearty soups, salads, and traditional dishes like roast turkey, roast pork and pot roast), **Columbia Harbor House** (counter-service platters, good soups, salads and sandwiches, notably for vegetarians), **Diamond Horseshoe** (lunch sandwiches and platters, dinner buffet of pork, chicken, sausage, beef, sides, and desserts), **Liberty Square Market** (hot dogs, turkey legs, snacks and drinks) and **Sleepy Hollow** (a picnic area serving corn dogs, sweet and savoury waffles, snacks and drinks).

Fantasyland

Leaving Liberty Square, you come to the park's spiritual heart, the area that most enchants young children. The attractions, in three areas, are designed with kids in mind, but the shops are sophisticated and the Tangled 'village' (basically a courtyard with restrooms) is wonderfully scenic.

'It's a Small World': This could almost be Disney's theme ride, a family boat trip around the world, each continent represented by hundreds of dancing, singing audio-animatronic dolls in delightful set-piece pageants. If it sounds twee, it actually creates a surprisingly striking effect, accompanied by an annoyingly catchy theme song that young children adore. Crowds peak in early afternoon. AAAA FP+

BRITTIP

Watch for enhanced allergy-friendly menus in the parks. If you're still not sure, a chef is always happy to speak to you directly. Just ask!

Peter Pan's Flight: This may seem a rather tame ride but is another Walt classic and a big hit with kids. Its novel effect of flying with Peter Pan is good fun and there's a lot of clever detail as your ship sails to Neverland. An interactive queue helps pass the time in air-conditioned comfort. AAA (AAAAA under-6s) FP+

Mickey's PhilharMagic: This special-effect laden 3-D film show features Donald's hapless attempts to conduct the Enchanted Orchestra, immersing guests in the world of *Beauty and the Beast, The Little Mermaid, The Lion King, Peter Pan* and *Aladdin* before Mickey saves the day. The lavish theatre, animation and special effects (you can 'smell' the food!) make for a hugely enjoyable family attraction. AAAA FP+

Prince Charming Regal Carrousel: The Fantasyland centrepiece shouldn't need any more explanation other than it is a vintage carousel that kids love. Long queues for much of the day, though. T (TTT under-5s)

The Many Adventures of Winnie the Pooh: Building on the timeless popularity of Pooh, Piglet and Co, this family ride offers a musical jaunt through Hundred Acre Wood with some clever effects (get ready to

The queue for The Many Adventures of Winnie the Pooh

© Disney

'bounce' with Tigger!) and an original soundtrack. Wait times are made easier by hands-on elements throughout the queue. AAA (AAAAA under-5s) FP+

Mad Tea Party: The kids will insist you take them in these spinning, oversized tea cups that have their own 'steering wheel' to add to the whirling effect. Actually, they're just a heavily disguised fairground ride. Again, go early or expect crowds. Characters from *Alice in Wonderland* also visit periodically. **TT** (TTTT under-5s) FP+

Princess Fairytale Hall: This elaborate 'royal' residence features a dramatic castle gallery area where visitors gather before being summoned for an audience with some of the Disney princesses (choose from Cinderella or Princess Elena, who then have another princess friend with them; characters alternate) AAA (AAAAA under 13 girls!) FP+

Enchanted Tales with Belle: A wonderfully clever Beauty and the Beast character show, here you visit Maurice's Workshop, nestled in the shadow of the Beast's Castle, and guests are transported via a magic mirror to the Castle Library for a memorable interactive story-time with Belle and Lumière. AAAA FP+

Under the Sea – Journey of the Little Mermaid: Be a part of her world as you journey under the sea with Ariel in this gentle ride aboard stylised clamshells, past colourful scenes from the movie. Ariel, Prince Eric, Flounder, Scuttle, Sebastian, King Triton and evil sea witch Ursula all make appearances, while favourite songs add to this charming adventure (with some surprising special effects!) that is sure to have a happy ending. AAAA. FP+

The Seven Dwarfs Mine Train

© Disney

Ariel's Grotto: Next door is the elaborate setting for a meeting with the Little Mermaid. FP+

The Seven Dwarfs Mine Train: It's 'off to work we go' in this charming ride through a gem-laden mine. Your trip begins as a family-friendly coaster, enters the mine for a gentle journey past the Dwarfs as they dig, dig, dig, then plunges back outside again for the grand finale. The mine cars have the swaying motion of a real mine train, all the charm of the fairytale and the sense of being 'in the film'. TTT (TTTTT under 10s) FP+

Storybook Circus
Themed for the classic film *Dumbo*, this colourful circus-inspired land features more family-friendly fun.

Dumbo the Flying Elephant: Young children cannot pass this one by and, with a clever interactive, air-conditioned queue, parents can survive a long-ish wait. It's a 2min ride on the back of a circling flying elephant, and its charm is undeniable. **TT** (TTTT under-5s) FP+

The Barnstormer: Get ready for a junior-sized coaster in the company of classic stunt pilot The Great Goofini as this surprisingly whizzy (but very short) ride takes some sharp twists and turns in best circus style. **R:** 2ft 11in/89cm. **TTT** (TTTTT 4–8s) FP+

Casey Jr Splash 'n' Soak Station: The Circus Train has pulled into a siding – and sprung a leak! In fact, it is a cleverly disguised water-play area, with all manner of squirting fountains, pop-jets and dumping buckets guaranteed to get the kids good and wet – so don't forget swimsuits OR a change of clothes. AAAA (under 10s).

Pete's Silly Sideshow: More themed fun under the Big Top as Minnie, Goofy, Donald and Daisy (in fancy circus outfits) line up for a clever meet-and-greet. AAA

Other entertainment: The Castle Stage hosts **Mickey's Royal Friendship Faire,** featuring Mickey, Goofy, Donald and Daisy with guests Princess Tiana and Prince Naveen, Rapunzel and Flynn Rider, and

Olaf, Anna and Elsa in a festival of music, dance and the celebration of friendship. **AAA**

In Storybook Circus, look out for **The Royal Majesty Makers** group of strolling performers in the Castle Courtyard, with a variety of regal routines (including the revived Sword in the Stone ceremony). Other **character experiences** include Meet Merida from the 2012 film *Brave* in the Fairytale Garden, Pooh and friends next to the Winnie the Pooh ride, Gaston outside Gaston's Tavern and *Alice in Wonderland* characters next to the Mad Tea Party.

Shopping: Shop at **Castle Couture**, the excellent **Sir Mickey's**, **Fantasy Faire**, **Hundred Acre Goods**, **Big Top Souvenirs** and **Bonjour! Village Gifts**. There is also an outlet of the **Bibbidi Bobbidi Boutique** here (the others are at Disney Springs and the Grand Floridian Resort), where 'little princesses' three and older can choose from three makeover styles ($70–510), the Crown, Courtyard and Castle packages, with three different hairstyles, Disney Diva, Color Star and Fairytale Princess, plus The Knight Package for young dragon-slayers ($25–81) from 7.50am–6.50pm (reservations highly recommended on 407 939 7895).

Dining: Eating opportunities are at **Pinocchio Village Haus** (flatbreads, salad, pastas, and sandwiches), **Storybook Treats** (ice-cream), the **Cheshire Cafe** (Cheshire Cat Tail pastry and drinks) and **Friar's Nook** (mac and cheese, hot dogs, brats, tots and drinks). **Cinderella's Royal Table** is a fine setting for the popular character breakfast, lunch and dinner with various Disney princesses (Cinderella greets guests in the foyer only). The majestic hall, waitresses in costume and well-presented food – salads, beef, fish, pork tenderloin and chicken – provide a memorable experience. Be aware you pay in FULL by credit card when you book, and, if you cancel less than 24hrs in advance, there is NO refund. More fun (and better value) is the spectacular **Be Our Guest** restaurant

inside the Beast's Castle, a unique set-price breakfast and quick service lunch option and full-service dinner restaurant, with beer and wine (reservations required). Set in three themed sections – the Ballroom (complete with snow on the terrace!), Rose Gallery and dark and moody West Wing – it's one of the most ornate dining options. Breakfast includes pastries, sandwiches and quiche ($28 adults, $15 kids; 8–10am); lunch ($13–17/$9; 10.30am–2.30pm) offers salads, quiche, sandwiches and braised pork; and prix fixe dinner ($60/$36; 4pm–10pm or park closing) offers French-influenced dishes like Poulet Rouge Chicken and Seafood Bouillabaisse. Dinner books up FAST, so try to get a reservation at the 180-day mark (407 939 3463 or online at **disneyworld.com**; credit card deposit required, $10/person charge if you don't turn up).

Gaston's Tavern is a counter-service cafe featuring an eclectic menu of sandwiches, snacks and drinks, again with some great *Beauty and the Beast* theming.

BRITTIP
The unique LeFou's Brew (frozen apple juice with marshmallow) is a must-try drink! Try LeFou's Winter Brew (hot cocoa) when temperatures drop.

Be Our Guest restaurant

© Disney

Tomorrowland

This area's cartoon-like space-age styling, novel shops and varied rides provide guaranteed all-round appeal.

Space Mountain: One of the three most popular attractions, its reputation is deserved. Launching from Starport 75, this is a high-thrills, tight-turning roller-coaster, completely in the dark save for occasional flashes as you whiz through the galaxy. Don't do this on a full stomach! The only way to beat the crowds is to go either first thing, late in the day or during one of the parades (or get a FastPass+). Ride photos are available for $20.96–26.95 (included with Memory Maker, p101). **R:** 3ft 8in/111cm. **TTTTT** FP+

Tomorrowland Speedway: Despite the long queues, this is a rather tame ride on supposed race tracks that just putt-putts along on rails with little real steering required (children must be 4ft 4in/132cm to drive alone). **T** (**TTTT** under-6s) FP+

Astro Orbiter: A jazzed-up version of Dumbo in Fantasyland, this ride is a bit faster and higher and features rockets. Long, slow-moving queues are a reason to give this a miss unless you have young children. **TT** (**TTTT** under-10s).

Walt Disney's Carousel of Progress: This overlooked gem will surprise, entertain and amuse. It is a journey through 20th-century technology with audio-animatronics in a revolving theatre that reveals different periods in history. Its 22min duration is rarely threatened by crowds. **AAA**

Tomorrowland Transit Authority: A neat 'future transport system', this

Tomorrowland

© Disney

offers an elevated view of the area, including a glimpse inside Space Mountain, in electro-magnetic cars. Short queues. **AAA** (**TTT** under-8s)

Buzz Lightyear's Space Ranger Spin: Ride into action against evil Emperor Zurg and the robot army – and shoot them with laser cannons! A sure-fire family winner, especially as you keep score. **TTT** (**TTTTT** under-8s) **FP+**

Monsters Inc Laugh Floor: With 'live' animation, special effects and voice links, guests can match wits with Mike, Sulley and Roz from *Monsters Inc* and be entertained by their patter. Billy Boil introduces comedians like two-headed jokester Sam-n-Ella in order to capture the audience's laughter. Watch the screen – you may be featured! **AAA FP+**

Other entertainment: Disney characters are often on hand by the Carousel of Progress, notably Buzz Lightyear. The **Rockettower Plaza Stage** features live entertainment and greetings with the likes of The Incredibles and other recent release film characters.

Shopping: Highlights are provided by **Mickey's Star Traders** and **Merchant of Venus**.

Dining: For food, try **Cosmic Ray's Starlight Café** (good burgers, chicken, sandwiches, soups, salads and flavoured iced coffees); **Auntie Gravity's Galactic Goodies** (ice-cream, smoothies and juices); the **Lunching Pad** (hot dog, beef sandwich and frozen drinks) or **Tomorrowland Terrace** (burgers, chicken strips, wraps and salads; open seasonally).

Look out for a new ride being built at the back of Tomorrowland (next to Space Mountain). The Tron Lightcycle Power Run coaster will be open for the 50th anniversary celebrations in 2021.

Having come full circle you're now back at Main Street USA and it's best to return here in the afternoon to avoid the crowds and enjoy the impressive shops.

Incredibles 2 backdrops in Tomorrowland

© Disney

Disney parades

Disney really knows how to do a parade. Coupled with its range of special seasonal events, there is always much more to look forward to than just the rides.

BRITTIP

To watch a parade, sit on the left side of Main Street USA (facing the Castle) to stay in the shade if it's hot, or grab a spot in the Hub or Frontierland. People start staking out the best places an HOUR in advance.

Festival of Fantasy Parade: A dazzling and unmissable pageant of creative floats, costumes, dancers and music. The seven featured floats include The Little Mermaid, Disney Princes and Princesses (including *Frozen*'s Anna and Elsa), Maleficent (with a magnificent fire-breathing steam-punk style dragon!), Tangled and Peter Pan and friends, plus a special balloon-like vehicle for Mickey and Minnie. The energetic dancers, stilt-walkers and rather menacing outfits of the 'Raven' men combine for dramatic effect. AAAAA FP+ for special viewing area.

Festival of Fantasy Parade

© Disney

Main Street USA closes 30mins after the rest of the park, so you can avoid the inevitable mad rush for the car parks by lingering here to shop or enjoy an ice-cream.

Once Upon A Time: This stunning nightly state-of-the-art projection show uses the Cinderella Castle as its backdrop, incorporating animated special effects and video that make the castle seem to come alive, transforming again and again with a sequence of Disney characters and films in dynamic colour. Watch as a magical montage brings to life favourite scenes from classic Disney films, with the imagery weaving visual trick after trick to leave your eyeballs breathless! AAAA

Happily Ever After: Most nights finish with this spectacular fireworks show over Cinderella Castle. A panorama of laser and lighting effects mix with castle projection mapping to set the tone for 18mins of heart-tugging magic. Memorable moments from Disney classic like *The Lion King, Frozen, Moana* and *The Little Mermaid* play out across the castle, backed by special pyrotechnics. It is a triumph of visual storytelling, and the perfect farewell to a memorable day. AAAAA FP+

BRITTIP

After the fireworks crowd exits, you are allowed to take the Resort Only monorail back to the Transportation & Ticket Center, rather than queue for the main Express monorail.

Happily Ever After Cruises: If you prefer not to fight the crowds for a fab view of Happily Ever After, book one of three speciality cruises to view the fireworks from Seven Seas Lagoon. The Basic Cruise holds up to eight guests onboard a 21ft/6m pontoon boat and costs $299; the Premium Cruise holds up to 10 on a 25ft/7.6m pontoon boat (for $349). Both include water, soft drinks, snacks and an audio feed to the fireworks music; or splash out for the Celebration Cruise, which adds special occasion decorations to the Basic and Premium Cruises for an added fee,

MAGIC KINGDOM PARK with children

Here is a rough guide to the attractions that appeal to different age groups (height restrictions have been taken into account):

Under-5s
Country Bear Jamboree, Mickey's Royal Friendship Faire, Dumbo the Flying Elephant, Enchanted Tales With Belle, The Enchanted Tiki Room, Festival of Fantasy Parade, 'It's a Small World', Journey of the Little Mermaid, Jungle Cruise, Liberty Square Riverboat, Many Adventures of Winnie the Pooh, Mickey's PhilharMagic, Monsters Inc Laugh Floor, Move It! Shake It! MousekeDance It! Street Party, Peter Pan's Flight, Prince Charming Regal Carousel, Tomorrowland Speedway (with a parent),Tomorrowland Transit Authority, Walt Disney World Railroad.

5–8s
Astro Orbiter, The Barnstormer, Big Thunder Mountain Railroad, Buzz Lightyear's Space Ranger Spin, Country Bear Jamboree, Enchanted Tales With Belle, The Enchanted Tiki Room, Festival of Fantasy Parade, Haunted Mansion, Journey of the Little Mermaid, Jungle Cruise, Liberty Square Riverboat, Mad Tea Party, Magic Carpets of Aladdin, Many Adventures of Winnie the Pooh, Mickey's PhilharMagic, Mickey's Royal Friendship Faire, Monsters Inc Laugh Floor, Move It! Shake It! MousekeDance It! Street Party, Pirates of the Caribbean, Seven Dwarfs Mine Train Ride, Space Mountain (with parental discretion), Splash Mountain, Swiss Family Treehouse, Tom Sawyer Island, Tomorrowland Speedway (with a parent),Tomorrowland Transit Authority, Walt Disney's Carousel of Progress, Walt Disney World Railroad, Happily Ever After fireworks.

9–12s
Astro Orbiter, Big Thunder Mountain Railroad, Buzz Lightyear's Space Ranger Spin, Country Bear Jamboree, Festival of Fantasy Parade, The Haunted Mansion, Journey of the Little Mermaid, Mad Tea Party, Mickey's PhilharMagic, Monsters Inc. Laugh Floor, Move It! Shake It! MousekeDance It! Street Party, Pirates of the Caribbean, Seven Dwarfs Mine Train Ride, Space Mountain, Splash Mountain, Tomorrowland Speedway (without a parent), Happily Ever After fireworks.

Over-12s
Astro Orbiter, Big Thunder Mountain Railroad, Buzz Lightyear's Space Ranger Spin, Festival of Fantasy parade, Haunted Mansion, Mad Tea Party, Mickey's PhilharMagic, Move It! Shake It! MousekeDance It! Street Party, Pirates of the Caribbean, Seven Dwarfs Mine Train, Space Mountain, Splash Mountain, Happily Ever After fireworks.

Over-12s
Astro Orbiter, Big Thunder Mountain Railroad, Buzz Lightyear's Space Ranger Spin, Festival of Fantasy parade, Haunted Mansion, Mad Tea Party, Mickey's PhilharMagic, Pirates of the Caribbean, Seven Dwarfs Mine Train, Space Mountain, Splash Mountain, Happily Ever After fireworks.

depending on decorations. All can be booked 90 days in advance.

Pirates & Pals Fireworks Voyage: This kid-friendly cruise includes a dessert party and meet-and-greet with Mr Smee and Captain Hook before cruising the Lagoon to view the Electrical Water Pageant and fireworks show. Snacks and drinks are provided while you enjoy sing-alongs trivia during your cruise, then meet with Pan himself at the end of your voyage ($75 adults, $45 3–9; can be booked 180 days in advance).

BRITTIP

For a final bit of typical Disney entertainment head outside the Magic Kingdom at 10.25pm and catch the Electrical Water Pageant passing by on Seven Seas Lagoon in front of the park.

Leaving the park

When it comes to leaving, the monorail is quicker than the ferry but it can still take up to an hour to get back to your car. Also, if the crowds get too heavy during the day, you can escape by leaving in the early afternoon (your car park ticket is valid all day) and returning to your hotel for a few hours' rest or a dip in the pool. Alternatively, catch a boat to one of the Disney resorts. Fort Wilderness is especially fun for kids and boasts the good value Trails End restaurant for lunch or dinner.

Halloween and Christmas

Two additional annual events in the Magic Kingdom provide a separate, party-style ticketed event 7pm–midnight, with most of the rides open and extra themed fun and games.

Mickey's Not So Scary Halloween Party: Aug–Oct sees many visitors dress up for the American trick-or-treat fun, with plenty of treats for all. With special features, shows, Mickey's Boo To You Halloween Parade and a brand new projection, laser and fireworks night-time spectacular that tells a Trick-or-Treating story, tickets ($79–135 adults, $74–130 for children 3–9), go on sale about five months in advance and sell quickly.

Once Upon a Merry Christmas Parade

© Disney

Mickey's Very Merry Christmas Party: The Christmas party (Nov–Dec; variously from $99–139 adults, $94–134 children 3–9) sees 'snow' on Main Street and magnificent festive decorations and theming. There is free hot chocolate and cookies, a parade and more fireworks. The atmosphere is enchanting, though the evening can be prone to unfriendly weather.

━━━━━━BRITTIP

Although the special evening parties don't start officially until 7pm, you can use the ticket to gain entry to the park from 4pm, which gives you 8 full hours to enjoy all the attractions.

Park tours

Keys to the Kingdom: One of the park's little-known secrets is this 4–5hr guided tour of many backstage areas, including the service tunnel under the park, and entertainment production buildings. It's an extra $99 (including lunch; not available for under-16s) but is a superb journey into the park's creation.

Disney's Family Magic: This is a 2hr guided adventure that takes you on a search for clues throughout the park at $39/person. Mon, Tues, Fri and Sat.

Magic Behind Our Steam Trains Tour: A 3hr tour ($54/person; no under-10s) that joins the crew that prepares the park's trains each day. Sun–Thurs.

Walt Disney: Marceline to Magic Kingdom: A 3hr tour on how the inspiration of Walt's early years in Marceline, Missouri, culminated in the creation of the Magic Kingdom ($49/person; no under-12s). Wed–Sun.

Ultimate Disney Classics VIP Tour: A 4hr tour ($249/person) with a Disney VIP guide, including special access to 8 attractions. 10am, Sun, Wed and Thurs.

EPCOT

EPCOT originally stood for 'Experimental Prototype Community of Tomorrow', but it might be more accurate to say Every Person Comes Out Tired. For this is a BIG park, with a lot to see and do, and much legwork required to cover its 300acre/122ha extent. Actually, it is not so much a vision of the future as a look at the world and technology of today, with a strong educational message. The park is undergoing a massive transformation, with a new-look entry, two major new attractions, a space-themed table service restaurant, giant indoor play area, updated shows in China and Canada, and a Beauty and the Beast sing-along in France, all slated to open from 2020–21. Visit the new Experience Center between Future World and World Showcase for interactive exhibits that will track the transformation's progress.

At almost three times the size of the Magic Kingdom Park, it is more likely to require a two-day visit (though under-5s might find it less entertaining) and your feet will notice the difference! Remember FP+1 means you can pick only ONE of these FastPass attractions, while FP+ indicates you can select two.

Location

EPCOT opened in October 1982 and its giant car park can hold 9,000 vehicles, so a tram takes you to the main entrance (though if you are staying at a Disney hotel you can catch the monorail, boat or bus service to the gates; International Gateway is a separate entrance for guests at the EPCOT resort hotels). Don't forget to note where you have parked

EPCOT at a glance

Location		Off EPCOT Drive, Walt Disney World
Size		300 acres/122ha in Future World and World Showcase
Hours		9am–9pm Future World (except Imagination 9am–7pm), 11am–9pm (World Showcase)
Admission		Under-3s free; 3–9 $104–154 (1-day base ticket, priced seasonally), $392-550 (5-day Magic Your Way), £385 (14-day Ultimate, includes Memory Maker); adult (10+) $109–159, $410-568, £399. Prices do not include tax.
Parking		$25; $50 premium
Lockers		Through the main entrance to the right hand side and at International Gateway $10 small, $12 large
Pushchairs		$15 and $31 to the left after the main entrance and at International Gateway; $13 and $27 per day for multiple days
Wheelchairs		$12 or $70 ($20 deposit refunded) with pushchairs
Top attractions		Mission: SPACE, Test Track, Spaceship Earth, Soarin' Around The World, American Adventure
Don't miss		Disney Character Spot, Turtle Talk With Crush, live entertainment (including JAMMitors and Voices of Liberty in America), the night-time show and dinner at any of the World Showcase pavilions
Hidden costs	Meals	Burger, chips and coke $16.97 3-course dinner $45–58 (La Hacienda, Mexico) Kids' meal $6.19–7.49
	T-shirts	$24.99–34.99 Kids' T-shirts $19.99–29.99
	Souvenirs	$1.99–8000
	Sundries	EPCOT 'Passport' $12.99

(e.g. Create, row 49). If you have your ticket or MagicBand, you pass through the gate area and wait in the immediate entrance plaza for Rope Drop, which is signalled by Mickey and Co arriving to greet guests.

Beating the queues: EPCOT is divided into two distinct parts arranged in a figure of eight and there are two tactics to avoid the worst of the crowds. The first or upper half of the park is Future World, with five pavilions arranged around Spaceship Earth, which dominates the skyline.

The second part is World Showcase, a global journey around 11 international pavilions that highlight each one's culture, entertainment and cuisine. Once through the entrance plaza, aim first for the three big-time rides – Test Track, Mission: Space and Soarin' Around the World™ – then move into World Showcase, which opens at 11am. Continue in World Showcase until 4–5pm, then return to Future World for the other attractions, as the majority will have moved on (apart from the three main rides).

As a general tactic, head first for the fab Soarin' Around the World, then head to the other side of Future World for Test Track (you can get a FP for only one of them with the two-tiered system). While you wait for your FP ride time, you can queue for the Mission: SPACE ride. Alternatively, if the rides don't appeal as much as a visit to such diverse cultures as Japan and Morocco, have a lie-in, then head into World Showcase at 11am and you'll be ahead of the crowds for the first hour.

Look out for big changes coming to EPCOT in future, though, as the park undergoes a transformation by 2021, including splitting Future World into three new areas: World Nature in the centre, World Discovery to the left and World Nature on the right.

Planning your visit

If you plan a two-day visit, try to get an early FastPass+ for either Test Track or Soarin' Around the World, then, after riding it, head straight to World Showcase for its 11am opening as the majority will stay in Future World for a while. Book an evening meal for around 5.30pm, then linger around the lagoon for the evening entertainment.

For your second visit, look to get a FP+ for whichever of Test Track or Soarin' you didn't do first time. If you can add Mission: Space, even better (or just head there first). If you linger in Future World, you should find queues for Spaceship Earth, Mission: Space and Journey into Imagination much shorter in mid-afternoon. You CAN do EPCOT in a day – if you arrive early, put in some speedy legwork and give most of the detail a miss. But, of all the parks, it is a shame to hurry this one. Browse in the 60-plus shops when the rides are busiest.

Kidcot Fun Stops: At 11 activity centres around EPCOT (each country in World Showcase), children can decorate a cardboard character and get a stamp from each country on the handle attached to the character.

US Blue Angels fly over EPCOT

© Disney

Future World

1 Mission: SPACE
2 Test Track
3 Odyssey Center
4 Journey into Imagination with Figment
5 The Land (including Soarin' Around the World)
6 The Seas with Nemo and Friends
7 Spaceship Earth
8 Guardians of the Galaxy (2021)
9 Play Pavilion (2021)

World Showcase

10 Mexico
11 Norway
12 China
13 The Outpost
14 Germany
15 Italy
16 The American Adventure
17 Japan
18 Morocco
19 France
20 International Gateway (to EPCOT resort hotels)
21 United Kingdom
22 Canada
23 Friendship Boats
24 America Gardens Theater
25 Showcase Plaza
26 Monorail Station

EPCOT

Buses to *Disney* Resort hotels

Trams to Guest parking

Monorail to Transportation and Ticket Center

ENTRANCE

The Seas with Nemo & Friends®

FUTURE WORLD WEST

The Land

FUTURE WORLD EAST

Imagination!

Complimentary Wi-Fi
Wi-Fi is available in most areas. Some attractions and shows may have limited availability.

22 **CANADA**

23

25 **SHOWCASE PLAZA**

23

10 **MEXICO**

11 **NORWAY**

21 **UNITED KINGDOM**

12 **CHINA**

International Gateway

20

IllumiNations: Reflections of Earth FP+
Presented by Siemens

Breathtaking fireworks, colors and lights set to a musical score. *See Times Guide.*

Boat & walkway to *Epcot®* Resorts & Disney's Hollywood Studios®

WORLD SHOWCASE

13 Outpost

19 **FRANCE**

America Gardens Theatre

24

14 **GERMANY**

18 **MOROCCO**

15 **ITALY**

17 **JAPAN**

16 **THE AMERICAN ADVENTURE**

Future World

Here's what you'll find in the first part of your EPCOT adventure.

Guardians of the Galaxy: This brand new attraction isn't due to open until 2021, but it will be a hybrid dark ride and one of the longest indoor roller coasters in the world.

Interactive City: Housed in the former Wonders of Life pavilion, this hands-on play area – due to open in 2021 – will be filled with interactive exhibits themed to a working city, and will feature character meet-and-greets plus other engaging entertainment.

Mission: SPACE: This is a high-tech journey into the future at the International Space Training Center, where a major adventure awaits. As you enter, there are superb models and graphics to look at while you queue for Team Dispatch, where groups become Pilot, Navigator, Engineer or Commander, each with different functions. You have the choice of the full, dynamic blast off to Mars (Orange version) or a less intense adventure around Planet Earth that avoids the 'spinning' effect (Green version). Once briefed, enter the Preparation Room to learn your mission, then board the ride vehicle, capsules that close down tightly with shoulder restraints and screens that move forward to just in front of your face (this is not ideal for those with claustrophobia, prone to motion sickness, or expectant mothers). The sense of realism, with the consoles, individual speakers and countdown is magnificent, though.

For those on the full version, the blast-off simulates some of the genuine rocket launch forces (thanks to its huge centrifuge, which is part-ride and part-simulator). Each team member has to perform duties on cue and you experience a simulated sling-shot around the moon and on to Mars. It's an original, aggressive ride, but you should heed the advice to keep your head still and look straight into the screen or you WILL feel sick (unless you are on the tamer version, where the capsules just tilt and turn). We think the full experience is too intense for youngsters, and there is no backing out once you board (parents could try it first). **R:** 3ft 8in/112cm. **TTTTT** FP+

Elaborate post-show and activities include **Space Base** – an excellent play area for children who can't ride (and those who just like to climb, slide and crawl); **Space Race** – a great game for two teams of 60 players to propel a rocket back to Earth via a series of on-screen challenges;

Guardians of the Galaxy concept

Expedition Mars – a computer game to rescue stranded astronauts; and **Postcards from Space** – where you can email a 'space video' to friends and family. There is then the inevitable (and well-stocked) gift shop. All in all, it's a terrific experience.

Test Track: This equally big-scale production – a 5½min whirl along Disney's longest, fastest track – travels into the world of Chevrolet car design. It starts with an interactive queue that invites riders to design their own car, which they carry on to a prototype vehicle. Once aboard, it is off through a digital computer world of performance tests, including hair-pin bends, rough surfaces, temperature extremes and a high-speed section outside the building at up to 67mph/108kph. Each car design is computer tested alongside the vehicle and scored according to how it fares. The post-ride area shows more about the testing process and its design elements. The vivid lighting, which feels like you're inside a computer (like the film *Tron*), sharp twists, turns and other special effects add up to a unique whirl through this high-tech world, but it does draw BIG queues and the FP+ option often runs out well in advance. If you're riding solo or don't mind your group being split up, the Single Rider option is handy here. **R:** 3ft 4in/101cm. **TTTT (TTT teens) FP+1**

Dining: Take an elevator to 'outer space' and view Earth from 'an international space station' at the **Space 220** table service restaurant. This was due for a late 2019 opening as EPCOT's most immersive dining experience, featuring international cuisine and special wine and craft beer selections.

The Odyssey Center: Baby-care, first-aid, telephones and restrooms.

Imagination!: This three-part attraction starts with **Journey into Imagination with Figment**, an uneven but quirky ride into experiments with imagination with Eric Idle (as Dr Nigel Channing of the Imagination Institute) and the cartoon dragon Figment. The sight laboratory sees Figment having fun with a vision chart, the sound lab is a symphony of imaginative melodies and Figment's house is a truly topsy-turvy world (watch out for the skunk in the smell lab!). It's gentle fun and rarely draws a crowd. AAA FP+ You exit into **Image Works – The 'What If' Labs**, an interactive playground of sight and sound, which usually amuses kids more than adults (though you might be tempted to buy cartoon images and select-your-own CDs). Also here is the **Disney & Pixar Short Film Festival** featuring three 3-D short films in the Magic Eye Theater. FP+

The Land: This three-part pavilion features positive environmental messages and two huge rides. **Living with the Land** is an informative 14min boat journey through food production, which may sound dull but is revealing and enjoyable, with plenty to make children sit up and take notice of its three different communities, especially the greenhouse finale. AAAA FP+ Film-show **Awesome Planet** will be a unique special-effect laden presentation on the beauty and ecological challenges of our planet when it opens in 2020. AAA (expected). **Soarin' Around the World™**: One of Disney's most imaginative attractions, this 'flight simulator' offers an exhilarating global journey for all ages, visiting the Great Wall of China, Sydney Harbour Bridge, the Matterhorn and

Soarin' Around the World

© Disney

other world icons. An interactive game for mobile devices leads to a 'departure lounge', with passengers embarking on rows of seats that are hoisted over a giant screen. A bit like a hang-glider ride, the sounds and scents become all-encompassing as you soar up, over and around great sights such as the Pyramids and Eiffel Tower, with the projection system, special effects, magnificent music and superb technology ensuring a five-star experience. Queues build up fast, so use FastPass+ or visit early or in the last two hours of the day. **R:** 3ft 4in/101cm. **AAAAA FP+1**

Dining: The **Sunshine Seasons Food Court** offers the chance to eat some of Disney's home-grown produce, while the **Garden Grill** restaurant is a slowly revolving platform that offers Harvest Feasts (eggs, breakfast meats, hash browns and waffles at breakfast; beef, turkey, sausages and salad at lunch and dinner), all in the company of Mickey, Goofy, Pluto and Chip 'n' Dale.

BRITTIP

Queues for Soarin' and Test Track are notably shorter in the last hour of the day, and you're guaranteed to get on provided you are in the queue before 9pm.

The Coral Reef Restaurant

© Disney

The Seas with Nemo & Friends: This pavilion does for the oceans what The Land does for terra firma, starring the characters from *Finding Nemo*. You start with the ride, which takes you underwater to meet Nemo and Co (brilliantly interwoven into the huge aquarium). Nemo has gone missing (again), hence it becomes a quest to reunite him with the rest of the class in a rousing musical finale. **AAAA FP+** You exit into **Sea Base**, a two-level development featuring stories of undersea exploration and marine life, including a research centre for the endangered manatee. Crowds are steady, but queues rarely get too long – except for **Turtle Talk with Crush,** a brilliantly interactive meet-and-greet with the surfer dude turtle, plus Dory and other characters from *Finding Nemo* and *Finding Dory*. Crush is the star, though, as he engages children with some fun live banter. **AAAA FP+** Next door, **Bruce's Sub House** is a kids' play area including photo opportunities (**TTT** under-6s). **Nemo and Friends** is more hands-on fun for kids, while **Mr Ray's Lagoon** showcases real stingrays.

Dining: The pavilion includes the highly recommended **Coral Reef Restaurant** that serves great seafood with a grandstand view of the massive aquarium. Dinner will be $41–64.50 (starter, main and dessert), depending on your choices, which isn't cheap, but the food is first class (kids' menu $11–13).

Spaceship Earth: Spiralling up 18 storeys, this attraction is a convincing time-travel story into various technologies narrated by Dame Judi Dench. From cave paintings to the internet (with a superb depiction of Michelangelo's Sistine Chapel), the gentle ride unfolds in imaginative historical stages, culminating in an interactive finale that invites riders to 'predict' the future. There is then a clever post-ride area with futuristic interactive games and challenges. Queues are heavy all morning, but almost non-existent late in the day.

BRITTIP

See all the changes in store for the park at the Odyssey Center, where the **EPCOT Experience** will provide an elaborate hands-on preview centre for future attractions.

Other entertainment: Live fun is also provided periodically around Future World by the unique JAMMitors percussion group, while the **EPCOT Character Spot** (9am–9pm at peak times, 10am–6pm off-peak, FP+) offers a fabulous themed meet-and-greet with many Disney characters (though the characters may move to a new location in ImageWorks as EPCOT undergoes its big transition throughout 2020). A rotating selection of characters can also be found just inside the main entrance. The majestic **Plaza Fountain** choreographs to musical performances every 15min. It will be removed during the 2020 transition.

Shopping: Mouse Gear, on the left side of the central plaza, features a massive variety of EPCOT and Disney merchandise (this shop is due for a whole new look in 2020), while the **Art of Disney** features superb signature art and animator drawings.

Dining: Food outlets include the counter-service **Electric Umbrella Restaurant** for lunch and dinner (sandwiches, burgers and flatbread) and the **Fountainview Café** for Starbucks coffees, cold drinks, pastries and sandwiches. Look out also for **Club Cool** presented by Coca-Cola®, where you can enjoy international Coke products and souvenirs, along with various free tastes from around the world (beware the Beverly!). Fountainview Café and Club Cool will close by 2020 as part of the big EPCOT makeover.

BRITGUIDE 25

The only Future World attraction that remains largely unchanged from 1995 is Living With The Land (albeit, with Soarin' added and minus 2 other attractions). The others were The Living Seas, Journey Into Imagination. Horizons, World of Motion, Wonders of Life, Universe of Energy and Innoventions.

The Seas with Nemo and Friends

© Disney

World Showcase

If you found Future World amazing, prepare to be astounded by the imaginative pavilions around the World Showcase Lagoon, each featuring a glimpse of a different country in dramatic settings. Several have rides or films to showcase their main features, while the restaurants offer some outstanding fare and many character greeting spots can be found here (check the daily Times Guide for locations and timings).

Agent P's World Showcase Adventure: Download this interactive family-friendly challenge game, based on the *Phineas & Ferb* TV series, using the app at **agentpwsa.com**. Using their own mobile phone, guest 'agents' follow clues around World Showcase to help pet platypus Perry (Agent P) foil his nemesis Dr Doofenschmirtz. Complete all the tasks and you also free Perry from his predicament.

---BRITTIP---

Don't waste your precious FastPasses on attractions such as Journey Into Imagination, Living with the Land or the night-time show's viewing location. Queues for the two rides are generally non-existent in late afternoon, and it usually isn't difficult to find a good spot for the evening show.

Mexico: Starting at the bottom left of the circular tour of the lagoon and moving clockwise, your first encounter is inside the spectacular pyramid. Here you have the amusing boat ride **Gran Fiesta Tour Starring The Three Caballeros**, a 9min journey through the people and history of the country guided by Donald, Panchito and José Carioca. Queues build up in mid-afternoon but are usually light otherwise. AAA

Other entertainment: As in all of the World Showcase pavilions, there is live entertainment, with periodic 25min music shows from **Mariachi Cobre**, while Donald Duck puts in character appearances.

Shopping: Much of the pavilion comprises market-style gift shops.

Dining: The San Angel Inn is a romantic Mexican restaurant (lunch from 11.30am–4pm, dinner 4.30–9pm), and **La Cava del Tequila** has tempting cocktails, light bites and tequilas. Outside, choose from the counter service **Cantina de San Angel** (open-air, serving tacos, nachos and tortillas) and full-service **La Hacienda de San Angel** (dinner from 4pm) serving authentic Mexican fare with a superb lagoon view and grandstand seat for the nightly fireworks show. This gets our thumbs-up as a stand-out choice.

Norway: A reproduction of Oslo's splendid Akershus Fortress is the exterior façade, while the interior is given over to headline attraction, **Frozen Ever After**. This delightful boat ride through the realm of Arendelle features a 'Winter in Summer' celebration that visits Queen Elsa in her Ice Palace, as well as Troll Valley and the Bay of Arendelle to share in some of *Frozen*'s iconic moments. Clever animatronics, projection screens and animated scenes bring the journey to life in classic Disney style, while *Frozen* fans can then visit Elsa and Princess Anna in their **Sommerhus**, a themed location for character meet-and-greets. FP+ (for ride AAA) and FP+1 (for meet-n-greet AAAAA).

Other entertainment: Look out for periodic comedic appearances by those colourful **Norway Vikings** in front of the pavilion, and the historical exhibit, **Gods of the Vikings**, in the Stave Church Gallery.

Shopping: Gift shop **Wandering Reindeer** features all things *Frozen*, while **The Fjording** stocks Norwegian clothes, toys, perfume, camera needs, food and spirits.

Dining: The Akershus Royal Banquet Hall offers the Princess Storybook dining for breakfast, lunch and dinner, complete with a host of Disney Princesses, while the counter-service café serves sandwiches, flatbreads, soft pretzels and drinks.

China: The spectacular landscapes of China are well served by the main attraction here, the stunning **Reflections of China**, a 360° film in the circular Temple of Heaven, offering the sights and sounds of this enigmatic country. Queues are rare and it is fully air-conditioned. AAAA There will be an updated film here in 2020, Wondrous China, using new, seamless 360° technology.

Other entertainment: Don't miss the periodic shows from the spectacular **Jeweled Dragon Acrobats** on the plaza in front of the temple, while Disney characters from *Mulan* also appear throughout the day.

Shopping: Yong Feng Shangdian Dept Store is a warehouse of Chinese gifts and artefacts.

Dining: Two restaurants, the **Nine Dragons** and the counter-service **Lotus Blossom Café** offer tastes of the Orient.

The Outpost: Between China and Germany features hut-style shops and snacks, with crafts from Africa and the Caribbean.

Germany: There is more in the way of shopping and eating than entertainment, though you still find a magnificent re-creation of a **Bavarian Biergarten**, with lively Oktoberfest shows featuring the resident Musikanten brass band at regular intervals. It also offers hearty portions of German sausage, sauerkraut and rotisserie chicken. The Sommerfest is fast food German-style (bratwurst and strudel), while there are eight shops, more than anywhere else in EPCOT,

including chocolates, wines, crystal, porcelain, toys and cuckoo clocks.

Other entertainment: An elaborate outdoor **model railway** is popular with children, while the fun **Groovin' Alps** percussion band add the sound of Bavaria. Look out for **character appearances** from Snow White.

Italy: Similarly, Italy has pretty, authentic architecture, including a superb reproduction of Venice's St Mark's Square, three gift shops with wine, chocolates, Armani gifts, fine crystal, porcelain and Venetian masks, and two full-service restaurants. **Tutto Italia** is the fine-dining option, designed like the Medici Palace, complete with a gluten-free menu and a splendid cellar-style wine bar, **Tutto Gusto**, that offers small plates and light bites (reservations not needed), while the superb **Via Napoli** is a delightful pizzeria, featuring wood-burning ovens and genuine Neapolitan style, as well as an outdoor terrace.

Other entertainment: Watch out for the fun entertainment of **Sergio**, a madcap juggler who loves to involve his audience.

Tutto Italia

© Disney

The American Adventure: At the top of the lagoon and dominating World Showcase is this huge edifice, not so much a pavilion as a celebration of the country's history and Constitution. It boasts a wonderful singing group that adds authentic sounds to the 18th-century setting, overlooked by a reproduction of Philadelphia's Liberty Hall. Inside, you have the **American Adventure** show, a magnificent half-hour film and audio-animatronic production that details the country's founding, its struggles and triumphs, presidents, statesmen and heroes. It's a glossy, patriotic display, featuring some outstanding technology and, while some of it will be unfamiliar to foreign visitors, it's difficult not to be impressed. A good choice at most times of the day – and it's all in the cool! AAAA Also here is the new *Creating Tradition* exhibit featuring Native American art and artefacts.

Other entertainment: Superb à *capella* group **Voices of Liberty** appear in the pavilion's rotunda several times a day, while the **America Gardens Theater**, next to the lagoon, presents concerts with major bands during the International Art, Flower & Garden and Food & Wine Festivals.

Shopping: Antiques and handcarts provide touches of nostalgia, along with the **Heritage Manor Gifts** store.

Dining: Liberty Inn offers fast-food lunch and dinner and the **Block & Hans** kiosk has craft beers, wine and pretzels.

Japan: Next up on the clockwise tour, you are introduced to typical Japanese style and architecture, including a five-storey 8th-century Pagoda, some magnificent art exhibits, notably in the **Bijutsu-kan Gallery**, featuring art and insights into Japanese history and culture, a tranquil **Bonsai garden** (complete with carp pond) and landmark Torii gate.

Other entertainment: Don't miss the periodic presentations from the amazing **Matsuriza** taiko drummers.

Shopping: The huge **Mitsukoshi** store adds fascinating shopping, from traditional calligraphy, tea kettles and wind chimes to Hello Kitty souvenirs.

Dining: Great food is a real highlight, and the restaurant line-up consists of the wonderful fine dining of **Teppan Edo** (with its traditional chefs at each table) and **Tokyo Dining**, featuring Japanese cuisine and ingredients, showcasing sushi and innovative presentation. **Katsura Grill** is its fast-food equivalent, with great soups, teriyaki and sushi dishes while the **Kabuki Café** serves sake, beer, plum wine, tea and soft drinks. New in 2019 was **Takumi-Tei**, the Japan pavilion's signature dining restaurant operated by Mitsukoshi and drawing inspiration from nature and art.

Morocco: As you would expect, this is another shopping experience, with bazaars, alleyways and stalls selling a well-priced array of carpets, leather goods, clothing, brass ornaments, pottery and antiques.

All the building materials were imported for the pavilion, which was hand-built to give Morocco a greater degree of authenticity, even by World Showcase's high standards. The **Gallery of Arts and History** offers more historical and cultural insights, while the **Fez House** depicts a typical Moroccan home.

Other entertainment: Characters from Disney's *Aladdin* appear from time to time.

Dining: Restaurant Marrakesh provides a full dining experience, complete with traditional musicians and their own belly dancer. It's rather pricey but the lively atmosphere is entertaining. Better value can be had at **Tangierine Café**, with its roast lamb, hummus, tabbouleh, couscous, lentil salad and Moroccan breads ($10.95–16.95;

kids' meals $9.95). **Spice Road Table**, a clever indoor/outdoor café and bar, offers superb small-plate, Mediterranean-style meals and snacks plus signature cocktails and other drinks, all with a great Lagoon view (select tables can see the nightly EPCOT Forever show).

BRITTIP

The **Tangierine Café** in Morocco is a peaceful haven in which to enjoy a quiet, healthy lunch, especially if you are vegetarian, plus there is a tempting coffee and pastry counter. **Spice Road Table** can often accommodate late-comers for a good table-service lunch or dinner.

France: Predictably overlooked by a replica Eiffel Tower, this is a clean and cheerful pre-World War I Paris, with comedy street theatre adding to the rather dreamy atmosphere and pleasant gardens, plus stylish shopping and dining. Don't miss **Impressions de France**, a big-film production that serves up all the grandest sights of the country to the music of Offenbach, Debussy, Saint-Saëns and Satie. Crowds are rarely heavy, and it's air-conditioned.

AAAA New for 2020 will be a **Beauty and the Beast Sing-Along** show that will alternate with Impressions de France

Rémy's Ratatouille Adventure: Like its counterpart in Disneyland Paris, this 4D dark ride will be an absolute delight of storytelling for visitors in May 2020. The big-screen technology, trackless vehicles and other special effects ensure a grand adventure in best animated style. Enter Gusteau's restaurant, where you 'shrink' to the size of a rat and follow Chef Rémy in a mad chase through the kitchen, dining room, duct work and finally, safely into Bistrot Chez Rémy. Cue the popping champagne corks! **FP+1 AAAAA** (expected)

Other entertainment: Look out for the visual comedy and amazing balancing act of **Serveur Amusant** (not when it's too windy), while **Princess Aurora** (Sleeping Beauty) makes regular appearances, along with **Belle** from *Beauty and the Beast*.

Shopping: Suitably chic, there's an authentic **Wine Shop** and elegant **La Signature** perfumery (ask about the

EPCOT's Festival of the Arts

Les Halles Boulangerie Patisserie

© Disney

free perfume tour during the Flower and Garden Festival)

Dining: This is THE pavilion for a gastronomic experience provided by three restaurants, of which **Les Chefs de France** and **Monsieur Paul** are major discoveries. The former is a classic, full-service establishment featuring top-quality French cuisine for lunch and dinner, while the latter, upstairs, is named (and themed) for late, great chef Paul Bocuse, with his staff still overseeing both

l'Artisan de Glace

© Disney

restaurants. Monsieur Paul is a touch more formal and upscale, with a 4-course prix fixe menu ($89/person), and, while an expensive meal (dinner only; appetisers from $15–29 and main courses $37–46), it is a fabulous choice. Also here is the **Les Halles Boulangerie Patisserie**, a genuine French patisserie featuring freshly made baguettes, croissants, salads, quiches and fab pastries, and **L'Artisan des Glaces**, an artisan ice-cream and sorbet shop, with everything made fresh in-house every day (and with liqueur treats for grown-ups!). New in 2020 will be **La Crêperie**, next to the Ratatouille ride, featuring table-service dining with the culinary accent of Brittany and a counter-service option with both savoury and sweet crepes.

United Kingdom: The least inspiring of all the pavilions, and certainly with little to entertain those who have ever visited a pub or shopped for Royal Doulton or Burberry goods, it is partly offset by some good live entertainment and pleasant gardens, but that is about it.

Other entertainment: Live music is provided by **British Revolution**, offering the sounds of the 60s, 70s and 80s up to five times a day, while the **Pub Musician** performs several times daily. Mary Poppins and Alice can also be found here.

Shopping: The best shops are the **Tea Caddy**, the **Queen's Table**, **Crown and Crest** (perfumes and heraldry), **Sportsman Shoppe** (sweaters, kilts, football shirts) and **Toy Soldier** (traditional games and toys), but prices are WAY above what you'd pay at home.

Dining: The Rose and Crown Pub is antiseptically authentic but you can get better elsewhere at these prices (shepherd's pie $22, bangers and mash $21 or fish and chips $22, and a pint of Bass for a whopping $9.75). **Yorkshire County** offers takeaway fish and chips.

Canada: Completing World Showcase, the main features here

EPCOT with children

Here is our rough guide to the attractions that appeal to different age groups:

Under-5s
Frozen Ever After, Gran Fiesta Tour Starring The Three Caballeros, Journey into Imagination with Figment, Kidcot stops, Living with the Land, The Seas with Nemo and Friends, Soarin Around the World'™ (if tall enough), Spaceship Earth, Turtle Talk with Crush.

5–8s
All the above, plus The American Adventure, Image Works, JAMMitors, Test Track, Agent P's World Showcase Adventure, Rémy's Ratatouille Adventure, Awesome Planet.

9–12s
All the above, plus Guardians of the Galaxy, Impressions de France, Matsuriza Drummers, Mission: SPACE, O Canada!, Reflections of China, Sergio, Serveur Amusant.

Over-12s
The American Adventure, Bijutsu-kan Gallery, JAMMitors, Impressions de France, Living with the Land, Matsuriza Drummers, Mission: SPACE, The Seas with Nemo and Friends, O Canada!, Reflections of China, Soarin' Over the World™, Spaceship Earth, Test Track, Guardians of the Galaxy, Rémy's Ratatouille Adventure, Awesome Planet.

are **Victoria Gardens**, based on world-famous Butchart Gardens on Vancouver Island, Rocky Mountain scenery, and 360° film, *O Canada!* As with China and France, this highlights the epic sights and traditions in a terrific national showcase, led by comedian Martin Short. *Canada Far And Wide* replaces it in 2020, with a new story and scenes. AAA

Other entertainment: Live music is provided by the traditional styles of various groups. In 2019 it was the **Suroît** and others.

Shopping: The Trading Post and **Northwest Mercantile** provide a range of Canadian clothing and souvenirs, notably wonderful glass ornaments and Deauville perfume.

— BRITTIP
Best way to tour World Showcase? Start in Canada and continue anticlockwise or jump on Friendship Boats and go straight to Italy or Morocco.

Dining and shopping: Le Cellier Steakhouse is an excellent dining room, offering great steaks, prime rib, seafood, chicken, fish and poutine for lunch and dinner.

EPCOT Forever
Following the end of the classic IllumiNations evening spectacular in September 2019, this new show takes over for 10 months, offering a story of EPCOT through laser effects, choreographed kites and pyrotechnics. It gives way to all-new **HarmoniUS** in summer 2020, celebrating the global inspiration of Disney music, interpreted by artists from around the world in an extravaganza of floating set-pieces, custom-built LED panels, lasers, moving fountains and fireworks. AAAAA+ (expected)

Behind-the-scenes tours
EPCOT also has a big range of tours. Book all tours on 407 939 8687.

Dolphins in Depth: This is a 3hr dip into the research areas of The Seas pavilion, including a chance to meet the dolphins ($199, with refreshments, photo and T-shirt; 13–17s must be accompanied by an adult; swimming costume required).

Undiscovered Future World: A 4½hr journey into the creation of EPCOT, Walt's vision and backstage areas like Test Track ($69).

Behind the Seeds: This 1hr tour, every 45mins from 9.45am–4.30pm at The Land pavilion, looks at Disney's innovative gardening practices ($25 adults, $20 3–9s).

Dive Quest: A 3hr experience, with a 40min dive into The Seas aquarium, plus a backstage look at the facility at 4.30 and 5.30pm daily, Must have scuba certification; park admission not required ($179/person, 10 and over, includes T-shirt and certificate).

Seas Aqua Tour: A similar tour without the scuba diving, daily at 12.30pm ($145/person, 8 and over; under-18s accompanied by an adult).

Backstage Magic: The most comprehensive tour goes behind the scenes of EPCOT, Magic Kingdom and Hollywood Studios on a 7hr foray into little-seen aspects, like the backstage areas of the Studios and tunnels below Magic Kingdom ($275, 16+).

DestiNations Discovered: This 4.5hr walking tour highlights the history, culture and cuisine behind World Showcase, including a cultural demonstration, peek behind the scenes, exclusive Festival experience and a snack. Tours run on select days during EPCOT festivals ($79/person, 16 and over, no photography backstage).

Day Cruise Around The World: Poodle around the waterway between Disney's Yacht Club resort marina and Crescent Lake into World Showcase Lagoon on this 1hr pontoon boat tour with bagged snacks and soft drinks ($149 per 10-passenger boat).

Annual festivals

There are also three annual EPCOT events to watch out for.

International Festival of the Arts: Showcasing a wide variety of arts Jan to Feb, from painting and printing to performance art and concerts (including a Disney on Broadway series at the America Gardens Theater), there are also seminars and workshops, delicious food offerings and a hands-on wall mural to try out.

International Flower and Garden Festival: This puts the whole park in full bloom with an amazing series of set-pieces, topiaries, seminars and mini-exhibitions from Mar to May. All exhibits and some lectures are free, and they add a beautiful aspect to an already scenic park, along with new food kiosks around World Showcase that offer regional tastes and drinks.

Food and Wine Festival: From late Aug to late Nov, this showcases national and regional cuisines, wines and beers, with the chance to attend grand Winemakers' Dinners and Tasting Events, or just sample more than 30 food booths dotted around World Showcase.

Each offers free concerts three times a day at the America Gardens Theater.

Epcot Forever

DISNEY'S HOLLYWOOD STUDIOS

Stand by for the biggest thing to hit Walt Disney World in more than 20 years. Fans have been clamouring for a Star Wars 'land' almost since the first film came out, and, in August 2019, their wish came true with the opening of **Star Wars: Galaxy's Edge** – and Disney's Hollywood Studios will never be the same again! This park has always been a journey into the movie world, but it has been transformed into a different, more immersive experience as Toy Story Land (in 2018) raised the bar, and now Galaxy's Edge takes it several stages further, redefining theme park design and enhancing the level of all-encompassing storytelling Disney is known for. There is more in store, too, with an adjoining Star Wars hotel under construction and Mickey and Minnie's Runaway Railway due to debut in 2020. A new entrance plaza, via Osceola Parkway, has opened, along with novel transport system the Disney Skyliner, and it all makes for a fascinating prospect for a park that is bigger than the Magic Kingdom at 124acres/50ha but smaller than EPCOT, but aims to be as big as both.

Location

The new entrance is officially on S. Studio Drive, between Victory Way and Osceola Parkway, and once again you catch a tram to the main gates, where you wait for the official opening time. If queues build up quickly (quite likely with Galaxy's Edge now open), the gates will open

Disney's Hollywood Studios at a glance

Location	Off Osceola Parkway, Walt Disney World		
Size	154 acres/62ha		
Hours	9am–7pm off peak; 8am–10pm high season.		
Admission	Under-3s free; 3–9 $104–154 (1-day base ticket, priced seasonally), $392-550 (5-day Magic Your Way), £385 (14-day Ultimate, includes Memory Maker); adult (10+) $109–159, $410-568, £399. Prices do not include tax.		
Parking	$25; $50 premium		
Lockers	From the Crossroads kiosk through the main entrance; $10 small, $12 large		
Pushchairs	$15 and $31 Oscar's Super Service Station; $13 and $27 per day for multiple days		
Wheelchairs	$12 or $70 ($20 deposit refunded), from Oscar's		
Top attractions	Millennium Falcon: Smuggler's Run, Star Wars: Rise of the Resistance, Toy Story Mania, Twilight Zone™ Tower of Terror, Rock 'n' Roller Coaster, Slinky Dog Dash, Star Tours, Voyage of the Little Mermaid, Muppet*Vision 3-D		
Don't miss	Indiana Jones™ Epic Stunt Spectacular, Beauty and the Beast – Live on Stage, Fantasmic!, Stars Wars: A Galactic Spectacular		
Hidden costs	**Meals**	Burger, chips and coke $16.97, 3-course dinner $35–58, child's $12–15 (Mama Melrose) Beer $8–12.50 Kids' meal $6.19–7.39, Kid's power pack $6.19	
	T-shirts	$19.99–34.99 Kids' T-shirts $19.99–29.99	
	Souvenirs	$1.99–3,500	
	Sundries	Rock Your Face Painting $16–$20	

early, so be ready for a running start. Once through, you are in Hollywood Boulevard, a street of shops, then you must decide which attraction to head for first, as these are where the queues will be heavy most of the day. Try to ignore the shops as it is better to browse in the afternoon when the attractions are at their busiest.

BRITTIP

It is crucial to schedule your Hollywood Studios FastPass+ times 60 days in advance if you are staying onsite, or 30 days in advance if you are staying offsite. The major rides book up well in advance.

The main attractions

The park is laid out in a more confusing fashion than its counterparts, with their neatly packaged 'lands', so have your map handy to keep your bearings.

Beating the queues: The opening crowds will surge in one of three directions. By far the biggest will be towards **Star Wars: Galaxy's Edge**, with LONG waits for its two main attractions, so head here first if you arrive for park opening. If Toy Story Land is more important, and you don't have a FastPass+ for **Slinky Dog Dash** or **Toy Story Mania**, make this your first land of the day. The other major crowd-pullers are **Twilight Zone™ Tower of Terror**, a magnificent haunted hotel ride that ends in a 13-storey drop in a lift, where queues hit 2hrs at peak periods, and **Rock 'n' Roller Coaster**. Head straight up Hollywood Boulevard, turn right into Sunset Boulevard and you'll see them at the end of the street. They

Millennium Falcon: Smugglers Run

are both FP+ rides (p96). Although the FastPass+ service wasn't initially available for **Millennium Falcon: Smuggler's Run** or **Star Wars: Rise of the Resistance**, we believe they will be Tier 1 FP+ attractions by 2020, very much like the Pandora area of Animal Kingdom.

Star Tours, this Star Wars™ simulator ride (not a part of the new development) is another of the park's serious queue-builders (and also a FP+ attraction). If you are not up for the really big thrills (or the really big waits!) schedule a FP+ for Toy Story Mania if there are any available, then head for Star Tours (across the main square past the Indiana Jones™ show). After Star Tours and Toy Story Mania, another gentler experience (and also worth doing early on) is the hilarious Muppet*Vision 3-D show, which also has the benefit of being air-conditioned for when you need a rest.

Hollywood Boulevard

Move around the park in a (roughly) clockwise direction, starting along this street of shops and services that are best visited in early afternoon when it's busier elsewhere.

Immediately to the left through the turnstiles are the Guest Relations and First Aid offices, plus the Baby Care centre. An up-to-the-minute check on queue times at the attractions is kept on a Guest Information Board on Hollywood Boulevard, just past its junction with Sunset Boulevard, where you can also book restaurants. To the right is Oscar's Station for pushchair and wheelchair hire, while locker hire is obtained at the Crossroads kiosk in front of you. At the top of the Boulevard (behind the Center Stage) is where **Mickey and Minnie's Runaway Railway** is located, opening in spring 2020.

Other entertainment: A series of **Citizens of Hollywood** acts enliven Hollywood Boulevard throughout the day, staging impromptu movie shoots, casting calls or even detective investigations. Have fun with them–

you just might end up the star of the show! Also, look out for **Disney characters** during the morning. **Star Wars: A Galaxy Far, Far Away** stage show features film clips and live appearances by Darth Vader, Darth Maul, Chewbacca, R2-D2, C-3PO, Boba Fett, Stormtroopers, BB-8 and more in an epic showdown between good and evil on the Center Stage.

Shopping: Hollywood Boulevard has the best of the park's shopping (nine of the 21 stores), including **Keystone Clothiers** (some of the best clothing), **Mickey's of Hollywood** (souvenirs and gift items) and **Celebrity 5&10** (kitchen and home decor).

Dining: The Brown Derby is the park's signature restaurant, offering fine dining in best vintage Hollywood style (reservations usually necessary) while the **Brown Derby Lounge** offers outdoor dining with a full bar (beer $7.50–12.50, wine $11–18, cocktails $12.25–16) and terrific people-watching (noon–8pm). **Trolley Car Café** quick-service offers breakfast all day, plus cakes and Starbucks coffee.

Echo Lake

Turn left out of Hollywood Boulevard to find another area that pays homage to the movies of the 1930s and 40s.

For The First Time in Forever: Join Anna and Elsa and the Royal Arendelle Historians for a *Frozen* Sing-Along Celebration, with music and clips from the movie. AAA (AAAAA+ under 8s). FP+

Indiana Jones™ Epic Stunt Spectacular: Consult your park Times Guide for show times as a special movie set creates three different backdrops for Indiana Jones'™ stunt people to put on a dazzling demonstration of scenes and special effects from the films. Audience participation is an element and there are some amusing sub-plots. Queues for the 30min show begin up to 30mins beforehand, but the auditorium holds more than 2,000 so everyone usually gets in. TTTT FP+

Star Tours – the Adventure Continues: Climb into your StarSpeeder 1000 for a stunning high-speed journey through the worlds created by George Lucas, including Coruscant, Naboo, Kashyyyk (the Wookiee planet) Jakku from *The Force Awakens*, and Crait from *The Last Jedi*. Droids R2-D2 and C-3PO (with help from Master Yoda) must save your Speeder from disaster as you bid to evade the Imperial Forces, which include Boba Fett and Darth Vader. The ride has 96 different options from four key points, so you never quite know how it will turn out! The realism of the Star Wars™ world, from the queue to the post-ride gift shop, is immersive and lots of fun. R: 3ft 4in/101cm, no under 3s. TTTT AAAAA FP+

Other entertainment: Kids should make a beeline for **Jedi Training: Trials of the Temple**, on stage outside Star Tours up to eight times a day. Here, young Jedi hopefuls try their light-sabre technique under the eyes of a Jedi master, before taking on Darth Vader, Kylo Ren or the Seventh Sister Inquisitor. Great fun just to watch. **Celebrity Spotlight** offers a chance to meet cuddlesome snowman Olaf from *Frozen* (TTTT for under-12s).

BRITTIP

Youngsters (ages 4–12) keen to try Jedi Training should sign up at the Indiana Jones Adventure Outpost first thing in the morning, as it is popular and availability is limited.

Shopping: Shop for Star Wars™ goods at **Tatooine Traders** (at the exit to Star Tours) and Indiana Jones souvenirs at the **Indy Truck and Adventure Outpost**.

Dining: There are also two good dining choices: the **'50s Prime Time Café** is fun as you sit in mock stage sets from 1950s American TV sitcoms and eat meals 'just like Mom used to make' (the waiters all claim to be your aunt, uncle or cousin and warn you to take your elbows off the table – good fun) while a varied

Hollywood Boulevard

1 Hollywood Brown Derby

2 Brown Derby Lounge

Echo Lake

3 For the First Time in Forever

4 Indiana Jones™ Epic Stunt Spectacular

5 Star Tours

6 '50s Prime Time Café

7 Hollywood & Vine

8 Center Stage

9 Mickey and Minnie's Runaway Railway (spring 2020)

Grand Avenue

10 Jim Henson's Muppet®Vision 3-D

11 Mama Melrose's

12 PizzeRizzo

Star Wars: Galaxy's Edge

13 Millennium Falcon: Smugglers' Run

14 Star Wars: Rise of the Resistance

15 Oga's Cantina

16 Docking Bay 7

Commissary Lane

17 Mickey and Minnie in Red Carpet Dreams

18 Sci-Fi Dine-In Theater Restaurant

Toy Story Land

19 Toy Story Mania

20 Slinky Dog Dash

21 Alien Swirling Saucers

Animation Courtyard

22 Voyage of the Little Mermaid

23 Disney Junior Dance Party

24 Walt Disney Presents

25 Star Wars Launch Bay

Sunset Boulevard

26 Rock 'n' Roller Coaster

27 The Twilight Zone™ Tower of Terror

28 Beauty and the Beast – Live on Stage

29 Fantasmic!

30 Lightning McQueen's Racing Academy

DISNEY'S HOLLYWOOD STUDIOS

Toy Story Land

Star War: Galaxy's Edge

Star Tours – the Adventure Continues

buffet dinner is served at **Hollywood & Vine** as well as the Play 'n Dine character breakfast with the Disney Junior Pals (8–10.30am; breakfast $38 adults, $23 3–9s, lunch $52/$31), while Minnie Mouse and friends take over on select dates in Spring and Summer, plus at Halloween and Christmas, with Minnie's Seasonal Dine ($52/$31).

Grand Avenue

The former Streets of America area of the park has been renamed as a new section that is home to the Muppets (and great dining).

Muppet*Vision 3-D: The 3-D is crossed out here and 4-D substituted, so be warned strange things are about to happen! A wonderful 10min holding-pen pre-show takes you into the Muppet Theater for a 20min experience with all the Muppets, 3-D special effects and more – when Fozzie Bear points his squirty flower at you, prepare to get wet! It's a gem, and the kids love it. Queues build up from late morning, but Disney's queuing expertise makes them seem shorter. AAAAA FP+

Dining: Try **Mama Melrose's Ristorante Italiano,** for a fab table-service Italian option (one of our faves) or Muppet-themed **PizzeRizzo** for pizza, meatball subs, salads and drinks. Another great choice is **Baseline Tap House**, a Los Angeles 'neighbourhood pub' in keeping with the Grand Avenue style, serving craft beers, cocktails and a limited small-plate menu.

Star Wars: Galaxy's Edge

Welcome to the planet of Batuu, a remote outpost in the Outer Rim Territories (hence the Galaxy's Edge). This may very well be the most immersive, imaginative and downright exciting 'land' in any Disney park, as, from the second you walk through the entry tunnel to the heart-pounding moment you see the iconic Millennium Falcon, it all comes to vivid life around you. Black Spire Outpost is a relative backwater in the Star Wars universe, but is home to smugglers, rogues and renegades, as well as a Resistance base. That sets the scene for mysterious shops, cantinas and dining outlets, each hidden from view until you round *this* corner or take *that* turn in the pathway. At 14acres.5.6ha, it isn't huge, but the creative forced-perspective used to design this canyon outpost makes it feel enormous. With two main attractions (for which you can only choose one FP+ at a time), a Cantina lounge/bar, an epic counter-service diner, three food stalls, a 'marketplace' gift shop, and a whole array of character meet-and-greets, there is a LOT to see, and visitors who take the time to explore are richly rewarded. Batuu is not a well-known planet in the Star Wars realm, but you should notice many sights (and sounds) that are familiar from the general style. Just be aware this is THE big draw in Walt Disney World these days and a lot of patience is required to experience it.

Star Wars: Galaxy's Edge

© Disney

Star Wars: Galaxy's Edge Rise of the Resistance

Star Wars: Rise of the Resistance:
Due to open in late 2019, this
immense experience puts riders –
travelling on unique First Order
Fleet Transports – at the heart of a
skirmish between Supreme Leader
Snoke's men and The Resistance,
with stormtroopers galore, droids,
blaster-fire and many of the
trademark vehicles from the films,
including two full-size AT-ATs. Guests
are recruited by Resistance hero Rey
to help in a daring off-planet mission
that involves being drawn into a
Star Destroyer, escaping from a jail
cell and then being in the middle of
a pitched battle between the First
Order and Resistance fighters. Be
ready for the grandest, most involving
and multi-sensory ride in Disney
history – plus a total Star Wars geek-
out! AAAAA+/TTTT (expected) FP+1.

Millennium Falcon: Smuggler's Run:
Here's the one every fan has been
eagerly anticipating, the chance to
walk into the most famous spaceship
in movie history, become part of
its six-person crew – and pilot it
into action! The level of detail and
immersion is stunning, and each of
the six 'crew members' has specific
tasks to fulfil during the mission to

aid the Resistance, as Pilots, Gunners
or Engineers, including manning the
quad guns and prepping the navi-
computer for hyperspace. Be sure
to complete your tasks well, as your
skills will come under scrutiny in
the Spaceport after you have helped
Chewbacca and Hondo Ohnaka on
their quest. AAAAA/TTTTT FP+1.

BRITTIP
Arguably the best photo opportunity
in Walt Disney World is on the
Millennium Falcon ride as you get to
hang out in the ship's crew room – and
sit at the iconic 3-D chess table where
Chewbacca played C-3PO in *Star Wars: A
New Hope.*

Other entertainment: The level of
interaction with the 'inhabitants'
of Batuu is outstanding, and
the reputation you build as you
experience the land will determine
how they react to you, so choose
wisely! There are also roaming meet-
and-greets for Chewbacca, R2-D2,
BB-8, Kylo Ren, Hondo and others,
which adds a delicious element of
realism. Be sure to ask the locals
about their planet – they all have a
story to tell.

Shopping: Shopping (and dining)
here is as much a heavily themed
experience as the land's two
attractions. Visit **Black Spire
Outfitters** for intergalactic clothing,
Creature Stall for cuddly toys and
Dok-Ondar's Den of Antiquities
for unique 'artefacts' and rare
lightsabres. You can create a personal
lightsabre at **Savi's Workshop** and
build your own droid or pick up one
ready-made at the interactive **Droid**

Star Wars: Galaxy's Edge custom droids

© Disney

Oga's Cantina

Depot. **First Order Cargo** outfits those whose allegiance lies with the Dark Side, and **Toydarian Wares** is the shop for toys and collectibles. You may even see store owner Zabaka's silhouette through a window at the back of her shop. Of course, all this Star Wars merchandise magnificence comes at a price – creating your own R2 or BB unit costs $99, while a custom-made lightsabre is $200.

Dining: Oga's Cantina is a wildly run den by Black Spire Outpost's local crime boss (based on the Cantina in Mos Eisley from *Star Wars: A New Hope*), with a terrific array of themed drinks. It features 'DJ' Rex and a range of specially prepared cocktails, mocktails and ales (including a Beer Flight in a souvenir board with Rancor teeth for $75) in another wonderfully inventive setting. Look out for owner Oga Garra lurking in the shadows! Counter-service **Docking Bay 7** is part of the spaceport's working area, themed as a food freighter and serving familiar dishes such as meatloaf and ribs, made 'other-worldly' through unusual presentations. **Kat-Saka's Kettle** carries drinks and flavoured popcorns, **Milk Stand** offers the iconic Star Wars drink of Blue or Green Milk (a non-dairy, frozen treat) while **Ronto Roasters** features grilled meat wraps, snacks and themed drinks.

It all adds up to an evocative experience inside an all-encompassing location of genuine star quality that has all the feel of the films, and even more of that close-up detail Disney does so well. The scenic splendour is a triumph of the Imagineers' art and well worth a AAAAA+ rating – before you even go on a ride!

BRITTIP

Be SURE to use the **Play Disney Parks App** (p95) in Galaxy's Edge to maximise the Star Wars experience. It's the secret to a wealth of special interactions as it transforms into a Star Wars Datapad, a unique interface that communicates with droids, reveals stories in the areas around you, translates galactic languages and hacks into the land's control panels. Create your own persona as hero or villain, earn digital rewards and interact with the characters around you!

Commissary Lane

This is another street of dining and character meetings. The **Sci-Fi Dine-In Theater Restaurant** is huge fun, a mock drive-in cinema, with cars as tables, and a big film screen showing old science-fiction movie clips. It offers burgers, steak, pasta and sandwiches, as well as signature milkshakes and sodas ($32–46 for three-course lunch, $10–15 kids' meal). The counter-service **ABC Commissary** serves standard fare including ribs, burgers, sandwiches and salads.

Mickey and Minnie Starring in Red Carpet Dreams: Meet the main Mouse and his best girl at this themed meet-and-greet, with Mickey dressed for his role in The Sorcerer's Apprentice and Minnie in a dazzling show-stopper gown.

Slinky Dog Dash

Toy Story Land

Get ready to shrink down to toy-size in this *Toy Story* themed land set in Andy's backyard and bedroom, including giant Tinker Toy sets, crayons, the Green Army Men and Woody's pals Rex, Wheezy and Jessie among the clever scene-setting.

Toy Story Mania: This family fun 3-D ride dives into a fantasy fairground of games with the *Toy Story* characters aboard carnival vehicles (with individual spring-action shooters) through Andy's Bedroom. There are five challenges, plus a practice round and, thanks to 3D glasses, riders can 'see' everything their shooter fires at the targets, while there are air-bursts and water effects – if you hit a water balloon, watch out! Throw virtual eggs at barnyard targets, launch darts at prehistoric balloon targets, break plates with baseballs, land rings on Buzz Lightyear's alien friends and finish up in Woody's Rootin' Tootin' Shootin' Gallery, before totting up your scores. It is a touch raucous and chaotic, but kids love the shooting element and the whole family can enjoy the amusing ride through the toys' world. (**AAA TTTT** FP+1). It's busy from mid-morning, so get a FP or get here *early*.

Slinky Dog Dash: This child-friendly coaster is the main element of the backyard area, a fast-turning whiz through the garden surrounded by many of Andy's other toys. It doesn't feature any big drops or high speed, though it does give riders delightful air time through its section of camelbacks. It's a "transitional" coaster that will seem quite big for youngsters (larger than The Barnstormer but not quite the size of Big Thunder Mountain Railroad at the Magic Kingdom). It is a fast-launch coaster (i.e. without a lift hill) and covers much of the expansion area in scenic style. **TTTT** (**TTTTT** under-12s) FP+1 Again, you'll need a FP or to be here early.

Alien Swirling Saucers: The other eye-catching garden ride is primarily for kids, a hectic whirl in classic fairground fashion with the green aliens from the *Toy Story* films as they bid to escape the clutches of The Claw. It is designed as a toy set Andy got at Pizza Planet, but is basically a variation on the spinning tea cups ride at Magic Kingdom, but with special lighting, music and sound effects. **TT** (**TTTT** under-5s) FP+1 Another one that's popular for much of the day with the younger set.

Alien Swirling Saucers

© Disney

Woody's Lunch Box

© Disney

Other entertainment: Look out for **Sarge and the Green Army Patrol** and the **Green Army Drum Corps** here, with the chance to take part in an army 'Boot Camp'. **Woody**, **Buzz** and **Jessie** also appear for regular meet-and-greets.

Shopping: A Toy Camper and Toy Dump Truck offer a good range of Toy Story souvenirs and gifts.

Dining: Woody's Lunch Box serves classic American fare, including sandwiches, BBQ brisket and old-fashioned soda floats for breakfast, lunch and dinner. **Roundup Rodeo BBQ** table service restaurant will open in 2020, with Andy's rodeo play set as its theme. Menu items had not been announced when we went to press, but expect American barbecue foods such as grilled meats and traditional picnic dishes.

━━━━BRITTIP

Look out for the signature drink of Toy Story Land, the Mystic Portal Punch (or Powerade Mountain Berry Blast), which is offered in a souvenir Alien Sipper Cup.

Animation Courtyard

Get ready for a series of wonderful family-friendly shows in this area of the park, plus the stop-gap until Galaxy's Edge opens.

Voyage of the Little Mermaid: A 17min live performance that is primarily for children who have seen the Disney animated film. It brings together a mix of actors, animation and puppetry to re-create the film's highlights. Parents will still enjoy the special effects, but queues tend to be long, so go early or late. You may also get a little wet. AAA (AAAAA under-9s; FP+)

━━━━BRITTIP

Try to sit at least halfway back in the Mermaid Theatre, especially if you are with young children, as the stage front is a bit high.

Mickey and Minnie's Runaway Railway: Located inside the Chinese Theatre and replacing The Great Movie Ride in spring 2020, this 'train ride' with Goofy as your engineer takes guests directly into the world of cartoon shorts with Mickey, Minnie and their pals. Follow Mickey and Minnie as they set out for a picnic, but be prepared for anything, because this is a wacky romp through cartoon-land, where 'the rules of physics don't apply.' AAAA FP+ (expected)

Disney Junior Dance Party!: The latest incarnation of Disney Junior Live on Stage, with a lively musical presentation featuring popular Disney Junior TV shows like Mickey, Doc McStuffins, Timon and Vampirina. Hosted by Finn Fiesta and DJ Deejay, the interactive

Mickey and Minnie's Runaway Railway

© Disney

fun also has classic character appearances (AAAAA under-5s) FP+

Walt Disney Presents: Step into Walt's world for a multi-media look at the creativity behind his films and theme parks, including original concept art for Walt Disney World, forthcoming new attractions, and a short film highlighting his amazing catalogue of work. AAA.

Star Wars Launch Bay: More Star Wars toys and collectibles are on offer here, along with dozens of prop replicas and exhibits, plus meet-and-greets for Chewbacca, BB-8 and Kylo Ren. A 10min film in **Launch Bay Theater** gives a behind-the-scenes look at the making of the movies.

Other entertainment: Youngsters can meet all their favourite Disney Junior characters in **Animation Courtyard**, several times daily. Meet popular movie characters, such as Star Lord and Baby Groot from Guardians of the Galaxy inside **Walt Disney Presents**.

Sunset Boulevard

The final area contains the two high-thrill rides, and the night-time finale, but it's also the busiest from midday on, so go here first or use FastPass+.

Rock 'n' Roller Coaster: Disney's first inverted coaster is a big draw for thrill-ride addicts, with a great indoor setting and fast-launch ride. It features a clever holographic-style film show starring rock group Aerosmith, leading to their 'super-stretch' limos for a memorable whiz through 'Los Angeles' (watch out for a close encounter with the Hollywood sign. Go first thing or expect long queues. Ride photos cost $20.95–26.95, $16.95 digitally, or $199

for Memory Maker ($69 single day). R: 4ft/124cm. TTTTT FP+1 NB: Strong rumours insist the Aerosmith theming will be dropped in the near future.

BRITTIP

If only one or two in your group want to ride Rock 'n' Roller Coaster, or you want to save time, opt for the Single Rider queue. You'll be split up, but the wait will be much shorter.

The Twilight Zone™ Tower of Terror: This 199ft/60m landmark invites you to experience another dimension in the Hollywood Tower Hotel that time forgot. The exterior is intriguing and the interior suitably spooky, and, just when you think you've reached the ride, there's another queue, so enjoy the superb detail. Eventually, you board elevator cars for a journey into the 'Twilight Zone' and things take a quick turn for the quirky and bizarre, in a 13-storey lift shaft that seemingly has a mind of its own! R: 3ft 4in/101cm. TTTTT FP+1

Lightning McQueen's Racing Academy: Lightning McQueen, from the hit movie *Cars*, has opened his own racing academy, and is teaching rookie drivers the rules of the road—until his nemesis, Chick Hicks, challenges him to a definitive race. Lightning's friends pitch in to save the day in this cute stage and screen show, featuring one of Disney's most convincing audio-animatronics to date. AAA

Beauty and the Beast – Live on Stage: An enchanting live musical song and dance performance of the highlights of this Disney classic will entertain the whole family for 30min up to five times a day in the Theater of the Stars. Check

Rock'n Roller Coaster

© Disney

DISNEY'S HOLLYWOOD STUDIOS with children

Here is our guide to the attractions that appeal to the different age groups in this park:

Under-5s
Beauty and the Beast – Live on Stage, Disney Junior Dance Party, Fantasmic!, For The First Time In Forever, Voyage of the Little Mermaid, Lightning McQueen's Racing Academy.

5–8s
All the above, plus Alien Swirling Saucers, Indiana Jones™ Epic Stunt Spectacular, Jedi Training: Trials of the Temple, Muppet*Vision 3-D, Slinky Dog Dash, Toy Story Mania, Star Wars: A Galactic Spectacular, Mickey and Minnie's Runaway Railway.

9–12s
All the above, plus Millennium Falcon: Smuggler's Run, Star Wars: Rise of the Resistance, Rock 'n' Roller Coaster, Star Tours, Twilight Zone™ Tower of Terror.

Over-12s
Millennium Falcon: Smuggler's Run, Star Wars: Rise of the Resistance, Fantasmic!, Indiana Jones™ Epic Stunt Spectacular, Muppet*Vision 3-D, Rock 'n' Roller Coaster Starring Aerosmith, Slinky Dog Dash, Star Tours, Toy Story Mania, Twilight Zone™ Tower of Terror, Star Wars: A Galactic Spectacular, Mickey and Minnie's Runaway Railway.

the daily schedule for show times, usually starting at 11.45am. AAA FP+

Fantasmic!: A not-to-be-missed special-effects spectacular. Staged nightly (twice nightly in peak periods) in a 6,900-seat amphitheatre, it features the dreams of Mickey, portrayed as the Sorcerer's Apprentice, through films such as *Pocahontas, The Lion King* and *Snow White,* but hijacked by the Disney villains, leading to an epic battle, with Our Hero emerging triumphant. Dancing waters, shooting comets, animated fountains, swirling stars and balls of fire combine in a breathtaking presentation, especially the giant, fire-breathing dragon! The 25min show begins seating up to 2hrs in advance and it's best to head there at least 30min before (watch out for the splash zones!). AAAAA FP+

Book the **Fantasmic Dining Package** at Mama Melrose, Hollywood and Vine or Hollywood Brown Derby for special reserved show seating (starter, main, dessert, non-alcoholic drink from $43–60 adult, $18–36 child).

Star Wars: A Galactic Spectacular: Nightly fireworks (with some stunning pyrotechnic special effects) take on a whole new meaning in this dramatic battle between good and evil, where bursts look like TIE Fighters, battle scenes, the twin suns of Tatooine and more, all set to John Williams' original Star Wars scores. Watch for the 'wow'

moment as columns of flames and giant lightsabres rise into the night sky. AAAAA Book the **Galactic Spectacular Dessert Party** for access to a special viewing area (Star Wars themed desserts savouries buffet, alcoholic and non-alcoholic drinks, souvenir stein, character meet-and-greets, $79 adult, $45 child).

Other entertainment: Look out for the **Wonderful World of Animation** projection show on the Chinese Theater each night, preceding the Galactic Spectacular firework extravaganza. It lasts for just 10mins but features a cavalcade of clips from just about every Disney animated movie imaginable. Sunset Boulevard is also home to more of the park's **Citizens of Hollywood** characters.

BRITTIP
While the Galactic Spectacular fireworks show is genuinely breathtaking, the full effects can only be viewed from the Center Stage hub area

Shopping: Legends of Hollywood, **Beverly Sunset Boutique** and the **Once Upon A Time** shops (for limited edition watches, clothing and other collectibles) are the best.

Dining: Rosie's All-American Café (chicken, burgers) and **Catalina Eddie's** (pizza, salads) are the best of Sunset Boulevard's five market-style eateries.

DISNEY'S ANIMAL KINGDOM THEME PARK

This version of the Disney theme park represents a very different experience, emphasising conservation and nature instead of non-stop thrills. Its more relaxing pace still has Disney's seamless entertainment style – and two excellent rides – but the attractions are relatively few. However, there are two elaborate wildlife trails, six shows (including two that are almost worth the entry fee alone), a huge adventure playground, conservation station and petting zoo. Pandora: The World of Avatar opened in 2017, adding even more to the park's appeal, plus huge crowds!

It is wonderfully scenic, notably with the huge Tree of Life, Kilimanjaro Safaris, Asian village of Serka Zong (home to the Expedition: Everest™ ride) and stunning Valley of Mo'ara, but it won't overwhelm you with Disney's usual grand fantasy. Rather, it is a chance to explore, experience and soak up the gentler, more natural ambience. It is not a zoo in the conventional sense, but it is home to 200-plus species of birds and animals. The educational tone is fairly strong, but children in particular may pick up easily on the conservation undertones of things like Kilimanjaro Safaris and Maharajah Jungle Trek. However, the park does get crowded, especially in Pandora, and there are fewer places to cool down. It is definitely advisable to be here on time and use FastPass+ (p99) to minimise queuing.

Disney's Animal Kingdom Theme Park at a glance

Location	Directly off Osceola Parkway, also via World Drive and Buena Vista Drive		
Size	500 acres/203ha divided into 6 'lands'		
Hours	8 or 9am–6, 8, 9 or 11pm seasonally		
Admission	Under-3s free; 3–9 $104–154 (1-day base ticket, priced seasonally), $392-550 (5-day Magic Your Way), £385 (14-day Ultimate, includes Memory Maker); adult (10+) $109–159, $410–568, £399. Prices do not include tax.		
Parking	$25; $50 premium		
Lockers	Either side of Entrance Plaza; $10 small, $12 large		
Pushchairs	$15 and $31 at Garden Gate Gifts, through entrance on right; $13 and $27 per day for multiple days		
Wheelchairs	$12 or $70 ($20 deposit refunded) with pushchairs		
Top attractions	Avatar Flight of Passage, Na'Vi River Journey, DINOSAUR!, Kilimanjaro Safaris, It's Tough to Be a Bug!, Kali River Rapids, Festival of the Lion King, Finding Nemo – The Musical, Expedition: Everest™		
Don't miss	Gorilla Falls Exploration Trail, Maharajah Jungle Trek, Rafiki's Planet Watch, dining at Rainforest Café, Rivers of Light and Tree of Life Awakens night-time shows.		
Hidden costs	Meals	Burger, chips and coke $16.78 3-course meal at Yak & Yeti $40.97–53.97 (kid's entrée and dessert $13.49) Beer $8–10.25 Kids' meal $8.69–$9.99	
	T-shirts	$24.99–39.99 Kids' T-shirts $19.99–29.99	
	Souvenirs	$1.99–2,700	
	Sundries	Pressed Penny Holder $12.99	

Location

If you are staying in the Kissimmee area, Disney's Animal Kingdom is the easiest of the parks to find. Just get on the (toll) Osceola Parkway and follow it all the way west to the entry plaza. Alternatively, coming down I-4, take exit 65 on to Osceola Parkway. From West Highway 192, come in on Sherberth Road and turn right at the first traffic lights. If you arrive early, you can walk to the Entrance Plaza, otherwise the tram system takes you in. Again, note where you park (e.g. Unicorn, row 67). The entrance plaza is overlooked by the Rainforest Café, which is open for breakfast, lunch and dinner (but is busy 12.30–3.30pm and an hour before closing). With Orlando so hot in summer, the animals are more evident early in the day, especially on Kilimanjaro Safaris. If you don't arrive early, plan this attraction for its latest daytime excursion.

Beating the queues: If you arrive *before* opening time, head straight to **Avatar Flight of Passage** and **Na'vi River Journey** (if you don't have a FastPass+). Otherwise save them for late afternoon. They have peak waits from as early as 8.30am, all the way to 5pm. After your early Pandora excursion, take in **Kilimanjaro Safaris** and **Gorilla Falls Exploration Trail** in succession and you will have experienced the busiest ride and two of the park's best animal encounters before it gets too hot. Alternatively, thrill-seekers should head for Asia, where the **Expedition: Everest™** ride is the big draw. Then head to Kilimanjaro Safaris or the nearby **Kali River Rapids** raft ride, followed by the scenic **Maharajah Jungle Trek**. The best tactic is to get a FastPass+ for Avatar Flight of Passage or Na'vi River Journey in advance (but be aware the Pandora rides book up *quickly*), or, failing that, for Expedition Everest. Do Kilimanjaro Safaris first then, once you have done that (and depending on your FP+ time), either do your FastPass ride or go to Kali River Rapids. Those are your main tactics – here is the full rundown.

The Oasis

Tropical Garden: A gentle, walk-through introduction to the park, this is a rocky, tree-covered area featuring animal habitats, streams, waterfalls and lush plant life. Here you meet miniature deer, exotic boars, waterfowl, a giant anteater and wallabies in an understated environment that leads you across a stone bridge to the main park area. AAA

Shopping: Stop at **Garden Gate Gifts** (on the right) for pushchair, wheelchair and locker hire, while Guest Relations is on the left.

Dining: The fun **Rainforest Café** also has an entrance inside the park here. If you haven't seen the one at Disney Springs, call in to view the amazing jungle interior with its audio-animatronic animals, waterfalls, thunderstorms and aquariums. A 3-course meal costs $31–59, but the setting alone is worth it and the food is above average. Try breakfast or an early dinner to avoid the crowds.

Discovery Island

This colourful village is the park hub, themed as a tropical artists' colony, with animal-inspired artwork, nature trails, four main shops and four eateries. You will also find the Baby Center and First Aid station here.

The Tree of Life: This arboreal edifice is the park centrepiece, an awesome creation that seems different from wherever you view it. It is covered in 325 carvings representing the Circle of Life, from the dolphin to the lion. Trails around the Tree are interspersed with fish and animal habitats. It has 103,000 leaves (all attached by hand) on more than 8,000 branches! AAAA

Discovery Island Trails: These pretty trails around the Tree of Life feature habitats for flamingoes, lemurs, kangaroos and more. AA

It's Tough To Be A Bug!: Winding down among the Tree's roots brings you 'underground' to a 430-seat theatre and another example of Disney's artistry in 3-D films and

The Oasis

1 1 The Oasis Tropical Garden

Pandora – The World of Avatar

2 Na'vi River Journey
3 Avatar: Flight of Passage
4 Windtraders
5 Satu'li Canteen
6 Pongu Pongu

Discovery Island

7 The Tree of Life
8 It's Tough To Be A Bug
9 Discovery Island Trails
10 Flame Tree Barbecue
11 Pizzafari
12 Adventurers' Outpost
13 Tiffins

Dinoland USA

14 DINOSAUR!
15 The Boneyard
16 Finding Nemo – The Musical

17 Chester And Hester's Dino-Rama!
18 TriceraTOP Spin
19 Primeval Whirl
20 Restaurantosaurus

Africa

21 Harambe
22 Kilimanjaro Safaris
23 Rafiki's Planet Watch
24 Gorilla Falls Trail
25 Tusker House Restaurant
26 Festival Of The Lion King
27 Harambe Market

Asia

28 UP! A Great Bird Adventure
29 Kali River Rapids
30 Maharajah Jungle Trek
31 Expedition: Everest™
32 Rivers of Light

Rafiki's Planet Watch

Complimentary Wi-Fi
Wi-Fi is available in most areas. Some attractions and shows may have limited availability.

Train to Rafiki's Planet Watch

AFRICA

Curiosity Animal Tours kiosk

ASIA

Discovery River

DISCOVERY ISLAND

DINOLAND U.S.A.

OASIS

ENTRANCE

Buses to Disney Resort hotels

Trams to Guest parking

PANDORA – THE WORLD OF AVATAR

DISNEY'S ANIMAL KINGDOM

special effects. This hilarious 10min show, in the company of Flick from the Pixar film *A Bug's Life*, is a homage to 80 per cent of the animal world, featuring grasshoppers, beetles, spiders, stink bugs and termites (beware the 'acid' spray!) as well as several tricks we couldn't possibly reveal. Sit towards the back in the middle (allow a good number of people in first as the rows are filled up from the far side) to get the best of the 3-D effects. AAAAA FP+

BRITTIP

The special effects and mock creepy-crawlies in It's Tough To Be A Bug can be VERY scary for young 'uns.

Other entertainment: The Island is home to the lively **Viva Gaia Street Band** and various **Disney characters**, notably Pocahontas along Discovery Island Trails, Russell and Dug from *UP!* opposite Discovery Trading Company, Kevin from *UP!* (wandering character) and Timon and Rafiki at the **Hakuna Matata Time Dance Party** on the Discovery Island Stage. **Adventurers Outpost** is the setting to meet Mickey and Minnie. FP+ Children can also sign up for the novel **Wilderness Explorers** programme here (also based on *UP!*), with the chance to visit kiosks around the park for interactive lessons and animal experiences, earning stickers on the way that act as a gentle educational story. **Winged Encounters – The**

Kingdom Takes Flight free-flight macaw show takes place over Discovery Island several times daily.

Shopping: You will find a huge range of merchandise, souvenirs and gifts here, notably in **Discovery Trading Company** (clothes, accessories, gifts) and **Island Mercantile**.

Dining: Counter-service restaurants **Pizzafari** (pizza, salads, flatbreads; or a buffet of salad, pasta, pizza and dessert at dinner) and **Flame Tree Barbecue** (barbecued ribs, chicken and pork, mac & cheese and salads) are good choices. If it's not too hot, the Flame Tree is a picturesque option among the gardens and fountains alongside Discovery River, but air-conditioned Pizzafari is better in summer. Full-service **Tiffins** features an imaginative lunch and dinner menu in a creative, art-gallery style setting, with extensive artefacts from Disney Imagineers' travels. It features a 'global culinary expedition' menu, with the likes of Butter Chicken, Whole-Fried Sustainable Fish, Pork Belly, Lamb Shank, vegetarian Crispy Sadza corn cake and Guava Mousse, plus other creative dishes (three-course meals from $49–94). It includes the laid-back **Nomad Lounge** (our favourite haunt!) with a River view, great cocktails and small-plate dining. **Creature Comforts** carries Starbucks coffee and pastries, while **Isle of Java** has pastries, pretzels, coffees and soft drinks.

Hakuna Matata Time Dance Party

© Disney

© Disney

Avatar Flight of Passage

Pandora: The World of Avatar

One of Disney's most immersive and dazzling lands, especially at night, this delve into James Cameron's *Avatar* film is a full-on recreation of the Valley of Mo'ara on the planet Pandora, with masses of scenery, special effects and a totally convincing setting. Guests enter a pristine valley, where mystical 'Floating Mountains', bioluminescent plants, native totems and remnants of the planet's occupation by the predatory forces of the Research Development Administration (RDA) are among the host of stunning set-pieces and captivating place-making. It would be easy to spend a day just taking in the scenery, but there are two major attractions as well.

Na'vi River Journey: This pleasant river boat ride is a gentle journey into the mysteries and wonders of Pandora's bioluminescent forest and caves, where the only sounds you hear come from the world of nature that surrounds you. It is a large-scale diorama that gives visitors a close-up view of the native wildlife, the peaceful Na'vi and the astounding Shaman of Songs, who connects all living things through her mystical chants. AAAAA FP+1.

Avatar Flight of Passage: Swoop and soar over Pandora on the back of a Mountain Banshee in this 3-D simulator ride that is so realistic you'll believe you *have* taken part in an adventure like no other. Enter a cavern deep inside a mountain, pass through the former RDA facility hidden inside, and continue on to the Pandora Conservation Initiative's research centre, where your DNA is 'scanned' for a match with an Avatar. Riders are then paired with a Banshee via 'linking chairs' (bike-style ride vehicles) and the journey of a lifetime begins. Fly with the Na'vi over forests and mountains, dive and twist through tangled treetops and along thundering waterfalls, catch your breath in a magnificent bioluminescent cave and experience up-close encounters with Pandora's wildlife – some of it friendly, some of it not (cue the fearsome Great Leonopteryx!). It is a traditional Na'vi 'right of passage' so exhilarating it leaves you breathless, and we challenge you not to queue up immediately for a second go! (R: 44in/111cm; children under 7 must be accompanied by a 14 or up. No expectant mothers). TTTTT+ FP+1 Be aware wait times here can top three hours.

BRITTIP
Return to Pandora after dark, when the entire land is even more dramatic than in daylight with the special lighting effects.

Other entertainment: Find Na'vi inspired face painting at **Colors of Mo'ara**. There is a **Wilderness Explorer** challenge in this area as well. The 15min **Na'Vi Drum Ceremony** is performed multiple times a day, and you should look out for the PCI's **Utility Suit**, with its pilot interacting with guests periodically each morning.

Shopping: Windtraders is an unusual shop, not only for its elaborate theming, but also because it sells Pandora-related merchandise *only*, from clothes and unique gifts to the must-have souvenir, a robotic mini Banshee that sits on your shoulder.

Dining: Counter service **Satu'li Canteen** offers an imaginative lunch and dinner (chicken, beef, fish and tofu bowls, and cheeseburger bao buns) plus desserts, soft drinks and an intriguing selection of cocktails, beer and wine. Kid-friendly choices include hot dogs and cheese quesadillas.

Pongu Pongu quick-serve counter has creative alcoholic and non-alcoholic cocktails, pineapple lumpia, pretzels and beer, plus an egg and sausage savoury scone and French toast at breakfast.

Africa

The park's largest land recreates the forests, grasslands and rocky homelands of East Africa in a rich landscape that is part vintage port town and part savannah. Central Harambe Village is a superb Imagineer's eye-view of a Kenyan port town, with white coral walls and thatched roofs, and the starting point for adventure. The Arab-influenced Swahili culture is also depicted in the tribal costumes and architecture.

BRITTIP
It is difficult to take photographs during the Sunset Kilimanjaro Safari, so ride during the day when the animals are most visible.

Festival of the Lion King: This not-to-be-missed, high-powered 25min production (seven to 10 times a day) brings the film to life in spectacular fashion, with giant moving stages, huge animated figures, singers, dancers, acrobats and stilt-walkers, plus some fun audience participation. All the well-known songs are given an airing in a fiesta of colour and sound, with the usual Disney quality. Queuing often begins an hour in advance for the 1,000-seat (air-conditioned) theatre, so use FastPass+ or take in one of the early shows. AAAAA FP+ Sign language shows are performed at 4pm each Tues and Sat; arrive at least 25mins early and ask a Cast Member if you can sit in the Warthog section.

Festival of the Lion King

© Disney

Kilimanjaro Safaris: The queue alone earns high marks for authenticity, preparing you for the 110acre/45ha savannah beyond. You board a safari truck, with your driver describing the flora and fauna on view and a bush ranger-pilot overhead relaying facts and figures on the wildlife, including the dangers of poaching. Scores of animals are spread out in various habitats – with fences all cleverly concealed – as you splash through fords and cross rickety bridges for close-ups with lions, rhinos, elephants, giraffes, antelope, hippos and ostriches. The animals roam over a wide area, though, and can disappear from view. Not recommended for expectant mothers or those with back/neck problems. AAAAA FP+

Kilimanjaro Safaris – Nocturnal Encounters: The route may be the same, but the night-time safari feels very different. Most of the Reserve is lit only by moonlight once the sun goes down, allowing guests to see the animals in a 'whole new light' – and a new level of activity. Other areas are softly illuminated as if by the rising moon, while a 'sunset' section creates stunning silhouettes as animals roam past. AAAAA FP+

Gorilla Falls Exploration Trail: As you leave the Safari, this nature trail showcases gorillas, hippos, okapi, zebras, meerkats and rare tropical birds. You wander at your own pace and visit 'research' stations to learn more about the animals, including the underwater view of the hippos and the savannah overlook, where giraffes and antelope graze and the meerkats frolic. There is a walk-through aviary, but the real centre-piece is the extensive silverback gorilla habitat. Again, the natural aspect is fabulous and it provides many photo opportunities. AAAAA

Rafiki's Planet Watch: This subsection of Africa involves a (rather dull) rustic train ride, with a peek into some of the backstage areas, as a preamble to the park's educational exhibits (especially for children). The three-part journey starts with **Habitat Habit!**, where you can see cotton-top tamarins and learn how conservation begins at home. **Conservation Station** offers exhibits and information about the environment and threats to its ecology. Animal Encounters Stage features live animal shows, while the Veterinary Treatment Room and the Science Center provide a glimpse into the park's working facilities. Finally, the **Affection Section** petting zoo consists of a collection of goats, sheep and a miniature donkey. AAA

Other entertainment: There's plenty more to enjoy here, with the splendid African sounds of **The Burudika Band** and the pageantry and rhythms of **Tam Tam Drummers of Harambe**. The melodic harp sounds of **Kora**

Kilimanjaro Safaris

© Disney

Kali River Rapids

Tinga Tinga provide more live engagement, along with the **Harambe Village Acrobats**. With luck you'll also spot the wonderful **DiVine**, a 'moving' part of the foliage (also in The Oasis at times). Doc McStuffins and Rafiki meet guests outside the clinic at **Rafiki's Planet Watch**.

Shopping: Harambe is home to **Mombasa Marketplace**, where you can suit up safari-style and buy African-inspired art, carvings and drums. **Mariya's Souvenirs** offers apparel, Vinylmation collectibles, housewares, camera accessories and toys.

Dining: Tusker House Restaurant (featuring Donald's Dining Safari for breakfast at $38 adults, $23 children, and lunch and dinner at $52 and $31;

pricing is seasonal) is one of the best diners in the park, with a mouth-watering array of salads, rotisserie chicken, salmon, beef, pork, curry and vegetarian dishes. There are also four snack and drink bars, most notably the **Kusafiri Coffee Shop** (pastries, curry, sandwiches and drinks), while **Tamu Tamu Refreshments** offers some ice cream and soft drinks, and the **Dawa Bar** is a great place to sit with a beer or cocktail and soak up the scenery. The Harambe Market has Kitamu Grill (chicken bowl), Famous Sausages (sausages), Wanjohi Refreshments (beer, wine, speciality drinks) and Chef Mwanga's (ribs).

Asia

The next 'land' is elaborately themed as the gateway to the imaginary south-east Asian region of Anandapur, with temples, ruined forts, landscape and wildlife. The elaborate ruined temple exhibits for the gibbons and siamangs are worth looking out for – and you may well hear them wherever you are in the park!

UP! A Great Bird Adventure: This gentle show features Russell and Dug from the Pixar film *UP!* in a 25-minute presentation that showcases the world of exotic birds. It includes vultures, eagles, toucans and a singing parrot, and highlights many of the conservation issues facing their cousins in the wild. **AAA**

Rafiki's Planet Watch Conservation Station

DISNEY'S ANIMAL KINGDOM THEME PARK with children

Here is our guide to the attractions that appeal to the different age groups in this park:

Under-5s
Affection Section, The Boneyard, Discovery Island Trails, Festival of the Lion King, Finding Nemo – The Musical, Gorilla Falls Exploration Trail, Kilimanjaro Safaris, Maharajah Jungle Trek, Na'vi River Journey, Rivers of Light, TriceraTOP Spin.

5–8s
All the above, plus Avatar Flight of Passage (if tall enough), Conservation Station, DINOSAUR! (with parental discretion), UP! A Great Bird Adventure, Habitat Habit!, It's Tough To Be A Bug (with parental discretion), Kali River Rapids, Primeval Whirl.

9–12s
All the above, plus Expedition: Everest

Over-12s
Avatar Flight of Passage, DINOSAUR!, Expedition: Everest™, Festival of the Lion King, UP! A Great Bird Adventure, Gorilla Falls Exploration Trail, It's Tough To Be A Bug!, Kali River Rapids, Kilimanjaro Safaris, Maharajah Jungle Trek, Na'vi River Journey, Primeval Whirl, Rivers of Light.

Kali River Rapids: Part thrill-ride, part scenic journey, this bouncy raft ride will get you pretty wet (not great for early morning in winter). It starts out in tropical forest territory before launching into a scene of logging devastation, warning of the dangers of clear-cut burning. Your raft then plunges down a waterfall (and one unlucky soul – usually the one with their back to the drop – gets seriously damp) before you finish more sedately. Queues can be long through the main part of the day, so use FastPass+ here. **R:** 3ft 6in/106cm (a few rafts have adult-and-child seats allowing smaller children to ride). **TTT AAAA FP+**

Maharajah Jungle Trek: Asia's version of the wildlife trail is another picturesque walk past decaying temple ruins and animal encounters. The first few exhibits – the water buffalo, Komodo dragon and a bat enclosure (including the flying fox bat, the world's largest) – lead to the main viewing area, the 5acre/2ha Tiger Range, whose pool and fountains are a popular playground early in the day for these magnificent big cats. An antelope enclosure and walk-through aviary complete this breathtaking trek. **AAAAA**

Expedition: Everest™: This clever roller-coaster takes you deep into the Himalayas for an encounter with the mythical Yeti. The queuing area alone will convince you of its authenticity (try to do the main queue at last once to appreciate all the detail) as you reach an abandoned tea plantation railway station to undertake a ride to the foothills of Mount Everest, trying not to disturb the hidden menace of the Yeti. Will the beast be in evidence? You bet! And the ride becomes a typically fast-paced whiz, forwards AND backwards, as you attempt to escape the creature's domain. It is a

Expedition Everest

© Disney

memorable ride but draws big crowds, so try to head here first or take advantage of the Single Rider queue if you don't mind being split up. You can get ride photos here, too ($20.95–26.95; $16.95 digital download $169 for full Memory Maker or $69 single day). **R:** 3ft 8in/115cm. **TTTTT** FP+

BRITTIP

Although Expedition: Everest™ is a FastPass+ ride, its popularity means FP+s often run out, so schedule in advance, if possible. Don't leave it too late.

Other Entertainment: Don't miss Bollywood Beats, an energetic (and interactive!) dance performance backed by traditional Indian rhythms and tunes from Bollywood musicals.

Shopping and dining: The retail options are limited to two minor kiosks and **Serka Zong Bazaar** for Expedition Everest gifts, but it boasts the fab **Yak and Yeti** combination diner. Outside is counter-service **Local Foods Café** (honey sesame chicken, Teriyaki beef bowl, vegetable tikka massala and chicken salad), while inside is the full restaurant. Yak and Yeti offers imaginative cuisine, from a Dim Sum basket to Chicken Tikka Masala and Bhakapur Duck, as well as Asian-fusion dishes like Soy-Herb Glazed Ribeye, Seared Miso Salmon and Pork Pot Stickers.

A good range of drinks and cocktails complement this tempting eatery. Extra incentive to visit: a full range of drinks to go, while you can just sit at the bar for a drink or full meal. The **Anandapur Ice Cream Truck** is also popular and **Mr Kamal's** features falafels, seasoned fries and hummus. **Thirsty River Bar and Trek Snacks** offers popcorn, soft pretzels, fruit, hummus, ice cream and drinks.

DinoLand USA

The final area of the park is somewhat at odds with the natural theme of the rest, a full-scale palaeontology exercise, with the accent on a 'university fossil dig'. Energetically tongue-in-cheek (the students who work the area have the motto 'Been there, dug that', while you enter under a mock brachiosaurus skeleton, the 'Oldengate Bridge' – groan!), it also features the character-filled Donald's Dino-Bash.

DINOSAUR!: This is a herky-jerky ride experience, rather dark and intense (and often too scary for young children). It is also a wonderfully realistic journey back to the end of the Cretaceous period, when a giant meteor put paid to dinosaur life. You enter the high-tech Dino Institute for a history show that leads to a briefing room for your 'mission' 65 million years in the past. However, one of the Institute's scientists hijacks your trip to capture a dinosaur, and you

Dinosaur!

career back to a prehistoric jungle in a 12-passenger Time Rover. The threat of a carnotaurus (quite frightening for children; try to sit them on the inside of the car) and the impending doom of the meteor add up to a whirl through a menacing environment. You will need to ride at least twice to appreciate all the detail, but queues build up quickly, so go either first thing or late in the day. **R:** 3ft 4in/101cm. **TTTT** AAAA FP+

The Boneyard: An imaginative adventure playground, offering kids the chance to slip, slide and climb through the 'fossilised' remains of triceratops and brontosaurs, explore caves, dig for bones and splash through a mini waterfall. **TTTT**

Finding Nemo – The Musical: This show is a first for Disney, taking an animated film and turning it into a musical. It combines colourful puppets, dancers, acrobats and animation with innovative lighting, sound and special effects. The basic idea remains faithful to the story of Nemo, his dad Marlin and friends Dory and Crush via larger-than-life puppetry, all designed by Michael Curry, who created the award-winning West End version of Disney's *The Lion King* show. It's a spectacular performance, and the 30min show is staged up to six times a day. AAAA FP+

BRITTIP

Finding Nemo – The Musical is popular, but although it draws long queues, the theatre seats 1,500, so most people usually get in.

Chester & Hester's Dino-Rama!: This mini-land of rides, fairground games and stalls is rather garish but is designed to have a quirky, tongue-in-cheek style from 1950s' American roadside attractions. There are two rides. **TriceraTOP Spin:** Another version of the Dumbo/Aladdin rides in the Magic Kingdom, where a flying, twirling, spinning top bounces you up and down with a surprise at the top. AA (**TTTT** under-5s). **Primeval Whirl:** Coaster fans will get a laugh out of this wacky offering that sends riders over curves, hills and (quite sharp) drops that make it seem faster than it is. It's basically a lampoon of the DINOSAUR! ride, a journey 'way back in time', with plenty of cartoon fun, as the cars also spin, giving each ride an unpredictable element. The queuing area is a riot of visual gags, but the ride isn't recommended for those with back/neck problems. **R:** 4ft/122cm. **TTTT** FP+

Finding Nemo – the Musical

Donald's Dino-Bash: This character carnival crates a showcase for Donald, Daisy and friends around Dino-Rama, with each of Launchpad McQuack, Goofy, Pluto and Chip 'n' Dale having their own meet-and-greet areas, with colourful costuming and backdrops, culminating in the Dino-Riffic Dance Party at 5pm daily. AAA

Other entertainment: Dino-Rama also features the **Fossil Fun Games**, six fairground-type stalls (costing $5 for a single ticket, $10/3 tickets, $15/5, $20/7, $30/10) designed to tempt you to try to win a cuddly dinosaur.

Shopping: Chester and Hester's Dinosaur Treasures offers a wide range of dino-related souvenirs.

Dining: Restaurantosaurus serves burgers, hot dogs, sandwiches, chicken nuggets and salads while **Dino Bite Snacks** offers ice-cream and pastries.

Other entertainment

Rivers of Light: We Are One: This nightly spectacular is a special effects extravaganza in front of the lake amphitheatre between Discovery Island and Expedition Everest. It tells the story of our connection to the animal world through live artistry, puppetry, glowing lanterns, 'water lily' fountains, sensational animal-themed floats and immense water-screen effects featuring special footage from Disneynature films. Combined with a superb soundtrack, lighting and staging, it is a beautiful finale to the day. AAAA FP+

The Tree of Life: Night-time Awakenings: Projected onto the Tree of Life each night, this series of short shows tells stories as the carvings on the tree's trunk 'magically' awaken, and its branches glow with the light of thousands of fireflies. Through colour and imagery, the animals 'come to life' in 3min vignettes, transitioning into a procession of clips from classic Disney nature-inspired films. Viewing is from the entry to Discovery Island and is standing-room only. AAA

Tours: Join an animal specialist and a cultural representative for a fascinating insight into the park's African elephants with the 1hr **Caring for Giants** tour (several times daily; $30, no under 4s). **Savor the Savanna: Evening Safari Experience** takes guests on an evening safari, stopping to enjoy tapas, beer and wine, plus stories about the wildlife, in a secluded viewing area (5 and 6.15pm daily, $169, no under 8s; 21 and up only for alcoholic beverages). For something really different, try the **Wild Africa Trek**, a 3hr ride-and-trek into the savannah. From a precarious rope bridge crossing to a VIP safari in open-air vehicles and a visit to Harambe's private camp, this exclusive experience in groups of up to 12 is open to ages 8+ (minimum 4ft/122cm tall; under 18s with adult), six times daily. Closed-toe shoes required, dresses/skirts not advised; weight limit 310lb/141kg (407 939 8687, $189–249/person).

That's the full Disney theme park story, but there is still PLENTY more in store...!

Donald's Dino-Bash

© Disney

Five More of the Best

or Wizards, Wildlife and Wonders

It's time to leave the wonderful world of Disney and explore the rest of Central Florida's attractions. And there's still a terrific amount in store, including some of the most thrilling rides and dazzling creativity. Yes, Universal Orlando and the SeaWorld parks are that good.

Diagon Alley

© Universal Orlando Resort

Universal is an increasingly dynamic proposition, and more centralised than Disney. For UK visitors, the 2 and 3-Park Tickets are extremely well priced. It does not offer a free FastPass+ system like Disney but you can buy the **Universal Express** pass that covers a one-time front-of-queue access to all the main rides. It is not cheap – from $80–120 at one park, and from $90–130 for two, for one-time use at each attraction – but it can save a LOT of queueing at busy times. A limited number go on sale at park opening and are snapped up, but they can also be bought online for a specific day at **universalorlando.com**. The Park-to-Park Unlimited Express provides Express access to both parks for $110–170.

Universal hotel guests at Portofino Bay, Royal Pacific Resort and Hard Rock Hotel benefit from Express ride priority all day by showing their room key and all eight hotels enjoy the major perk of early access to The Wizarding Worlds of Harry Potter each day. In addition, some rides have Single Rider queues, which save time if you want to

Universal Dining Plan

Visitors can choose to add a daily meal allowance to their hotel bookings, or a daily Quick Service meal plan if they are just visiting the parks. The full Dining Plan can only be booked via Universal's own reservation system as part of a vacation package – **universalorlandovacations.com** – and offers one table-service meal (entrée, dessert and soft drink), one quick service meal (entrée and soft drink), one snack (popcorn, ice-cream, etc) from food carts or counter service restaurants, and one additional soft drink per day for about $64/day per adult and $25/day per child. It can be used at most dining venues in the parks and eight in CityWalk (but, strangely, none in the hotels). The Quick Service option costs $24/adult and $16/child per day and offers one counter service meal (entrée and soft drink), one snack and one soft drink per day. The Quick Service option can be purchased on the day or in advance online. There is also the Coca-Cola Freestyle cup at $15/person (plus $8 for additional days) with unlimited free refills all day at the special Coca-Cola Freestyle outlets (eight in each park), offering more than 100 different drinks.

go by yourself or don't mind splitting up your group. Once again, height/health restrictions (R) are noted in ride descriptions. Universal is also home to some of the best (and most grisly!) Halloween celebrations on earth, with their Halloween Horror Nights programme (p164).

BRITGUIDE 25

Of all the changes since we first started, Universal has transformed most of all, from a one-park set-up with no hotels, to three parks with seven! Plus, the whole of CityWalk is new since 1995.

Hollywood Drive-in Golf

© Universal Orlando Resort

UNIVERSAL STUDIOS FLORIDA

Universal opened its first Florida park in 1990 and quickly became a serious rival to Disney. For the visitor, it means a consistently high standard and good value (though the choice can be bewildering), but there are few similarities to their Los Angeles park. Universal is also a different proposition to Disney, with a more edgy style that appeals especially to teens. Younger children are still well catered for, though. Universal parks can also need more than a full day in high season. Strategies are the same: arrive EARLY (up to 30mins before opening), do the big rides first, avoid main meal times and take an afternoon break (try shopping, dining or visiting the cinemas at CityWalk) if it gets too crowded.

Location

Universal Studios Florida® is divided into seven main areas, set around a lagoon, but there are no great distinguishing features. The main resort entrance is just off Interstate 4 (I-4 eastbound take exit 75A; westbound take exit 74B) or via Universal Boulevard from I-Drive. Parking is in its massive multi-storey car park and there is quite a walk (with moving walkways) to the front gates.

My Universal Photos

Universal's photo sharing system allows guests to collect all their ride photos in one source and is cheaper than buying them individually. Go online before your visit at **universalorlando.com/web/en/us/ my-universal-photo/index.html#** and buy the 1-day package for $70 (a $10 saving on buying it at the park). Take your confirmation email to a My Universal Photo location in the park to activate. You will receive a themed lanyard for your Photo card, unlimited

Universal Studios Florida® at a glance

Location	Off exits 75A and 74B from I-4; Universal Boulevard and Kirkman Road		
Size	110 acres/45ha in 7 themed areas		
Hours	9am–6 or 7pm off peak; 9am–10pm high season (Washington's birthday, Easter, summer holidays, Thanksgiving, Christmas)		
Admission	Under-3s free; 3–9 $110–119 (1-day ticket), $275 (2-day Park-to-Park ticket), £278 (UK 3-Park Explorer ticket); adult (10+) $115–124, $285, £278. Prices do not include tax.		
Parking	$25 (preferred parking $35; valet parking $65)		
Lockers	Immediately to left in Front Lot $10 and $15		
Pushchairs	$15 and $25, Kiddie cars $18–28		
Wheelchairs	$12, ECV $50, $70 with sun shade (with photo ID as deposit), with pushchairs		
Top attractions	Fast & Furious – Supercharged, Harry Potter and The Escape From Gringotts, Hogwarts Express, Revenge of the Mummy, Men in Black, Despicable Me: Minion Mayhem, TRANSFORMERS: The Ride – 3-D, The Simpsons, Hollywood Rip, Ride Rockit!		
Don't miss	Universal's Cinematic Celebration, Universal's Superstar Parade, Curious George Playground (for kids), The Blues Brothers, Tales of Beedle the Bard		
Hidden costs	**Meals**	Burger, chips and coke $15.18 2-course lunch $16.19–23.48 (Leaky Cauldron)	
	T-shirts	$25–40, kids $20–29	
	Souvenirs	95c–$2,000	
	Sundries	Temporary tattoos $7–20	

digital downloads of your photos, photo gift product discounts and two colour photos.

BRITTIP

A good way to enjoy the Universal Express perk is to book a night's stay at one of their three deluxe hotels. Check in early (they will store bags for you) and you get your hotel room key, with Express feature, for use that day AND the next day.

Beating the queues: With the opening of The Wizarding World of Harry Potter – Diagon Alley, this has become THE place to visit first, with heavy queues building up quickly and lasting all day. It is at the back of the park, so try to avoid all the other attractions if this is your top target. Turn right on Rodeo Drive, continue through Sunset Boulevard and the Springfield area of The Simpsons, and go left across the bridge straight to the Wizarding World. If you are not a Potter fan (although you should

still give Diagon Alley a look at some stage) and want some of the big-time thrills, stop first at Hollywood Rip Ride Rockit (on your left in Production Central) and then take in TRANSFORMERS: The Ride – 3-D, Fast & Furious – Supercharged, and the nearby Revenge of the Mummy in New York. For interactive fun, take in Despicable Me first, then head back to the Springfield area and do The Simpsons and Men In Black. Many of the other attractions are now easier to do with the crowds flocking to Diagon Alley.

Here's a full guide to the Studios (for CityWalk, see Chapter 10).

BRITTIP

Watch out for the helpful mobile electronic Wait Times boards around both parks. Better still, get the free **Universal Orlando App** on iTunes or Google Play and have all the essential info at your fingertips, with free Wi-Fi throughout the parks.

Diagon Alley at night

Hollywood Rip Ride Rockit!

Production Central

Coming straight through the gates brings you into the administrative centre, with a couple of large gift stores plus Studio Sweets. Call at **Guest Services** for guides for disabled visitors, TDD and assisted listening devices, and to make restaurant bookings, which can also be made at a kiosk to the right after the turnstiles, next to the Today Café. **First aid** is available here (and on Canal Street between New York and San Francisco), while there are facilities for nursing mothers at **Family Services** by the bank through the gates on the right. Coming to the top of the Plaza of the Stars brings you to the business end of the park.

Shrek 4-D: This adds a fun dimension to 3-D films as the original cast (Mike Myers, Eddie Murphy, Cameron Diaz and John Lithgow) reprise their Oscar-winning roles. The amusing 7min pre-show leads into the 500-seat main theatre, where you don your Ogre Vision 3-D glasses and enter a new world. The film is funny enough as Shrek and Donkey save the Princess, but the special effects (watch out for the spiders!) and moving seats add a startling extra

element. Queues stay long for much of the day. AAAAA+

Despicable Me – Minion Mayhem: This outrageously funny 3-D simulator ride is based on the animated films starring Steve Carell. You enter the home of super-villain Gru and visit his lab where you are 'shrunk' to undergo Minion training. In the company of Gru's daughters, Margo, Edith and Agnes, the zany scheme goes awry and his 'recruits' suffer some hair-raising adventures that need Gru's intervention to save the day. It ends happily, of course, with a fun Minion dance party (and gift shop). With dynamic, motion-based seats, things can get bumpy, so those with heart, neck, or back problems should ask for the stationary seats. TTT+ AAAA (TTTTT under-10s)

Hollywood Rip Ride Rockit!: This iconic ride is a high-tech colossus, with an onboard system that allows you to select your own ride music – then take home the DVD. It starts with a video intro while you queue that reveals five music choices (Rap/Hip Hop, Country, Classic Rock/Metal, Pop/ Disco and Club Electronica), each with six tracks. You're then strapped into an open-sided car that goes straight up a 17-storey vertical lift-hill, then into a steep dive followed by the signature Double Take, the world's first non-inverted loop (you don't actually go upside-down but it feels like it!). You will soar over the heads of people in the queue, dive below ground level and fly around a 150° banked turn, all in the course of the 1min 40sec ride. The innovative open cars make the experience feel even faster and more dynamic, while the mix of pounding music (from your headset and speakers along the track) and concert-style lighting (flashy

Despicable Me, Minion Mayhem

during the day, stunning at night) ensure this ride really rocks (ride photos $20–35). Ride early or leave it for the evening when queues tend to drop off. R: 4ft 3in/130cm. **TTTTT+**

BRITTIP

Universal Orlando has metal detectors at the bag check area that all guests must walk through. To help move crowds through faster, be sure to have your bags open and coins, mobile phones and keys removed from pockets.

TRANSFORMERS: The Ride – 3-D: The latest generation of Universal's dramatic 3-D technology allied with a dynamic ride vehicle, this puts guests at the heart of an explosive battle between the Autobots, led by Optimus Prime and the evil Decepticons of Megatron. It feels like walking into a movie as the long, elaborate queuing area prepares riders for joining the planet-defending forces of NEST, and then a larger-than-life whirl through a Decepticon attack in a bid to defend the AllSpark – and the earth's existence! The combination of ultra-HD film, real scenery and dramatic special effects is breathtaking (if loud).

Even those who have never seen one of the films will not feel left out as the whole scenario is explained while you queue. Crowds build up quickly, hence you need to ride early on or late in the day. R: 3ft 4in/101cm. **TTTT**

Character appearances: Optimus Prime, Bumblebee and Megatron have a brilliant set-piece **Transformers photo spot** next to the ride, or meet Shrek, Fiona and Donkey at **Meet Shrek & Donkey**, well worth catching for the amusing patter. You'll find **Minion photo ops** in the Super Silly Stuff shop.

Shopping: Great shops here, including **Supply Vault** for all things Transformers, **On Location** (film, clothes, sundries and 2-way radio rentals), **Super Silly Stuff** (Despicable Me merchandise), the massive **Universal Studios Store** (with everything) and **It's A Wrap** (discounted items).

Dining: The main eating outlet is the wonderful **Monsters Café** (peak season only) offering ribs, chicken, burgers, turkey legs and pizza. The counter-service area is themed like Frankenstein's lab, with the dining areas showing black-and-white horror film clips.

TRANSFORMERS: The Ride

© Universal Orlando Resort

Revenge of the Mummy

New York

Now head to New York with its impressive architecture, street scenes and park.

Race Through New York Starring Jimmy Fallon: Comedian and *Tonight Show* host Jimmy Fallon stars in this 3-D simulator ride experience through the streets of New York. Enter through 'Studio 6B' in the city's famous NBC Studios at 30 Rockefeller Plaza, where Jimmy challenges his audience (you) to a 'race through New York.' Fly on your special vehicle through subway tunnels, around the Empire State Building, into the Hudson River, and even to the moon! Popular *Tonight Show* characters The Ragtime Gals and Hashtag the Panda also appear in this special-effects filled, high-adrenalin laugh-fest that is part show, part character meet-and-greet, part ride, and all family-friendly fun. The best part? There is no queuing. Instead, visitors get a time to return to enjoy the pre-show areas with their TV exhibits, games and live entertainment. **AAAA/TTT**

BRITTIP

Don't miss the hilarious song routines of The Ragtime Gals before the Jimmy Fallon attraction. This is an amusing 'barbershop quartet'.

Revenge of the Mummy: This superb offering is a high-thrill, high-fun journey into the Ancient Egypt of *The Mummy* film series, fusing coaster technology with special effects. It starts out as a slow, dark ride through curse-ridden Hamunaptra, but soon takes an ingenious launch into something more dynamic, using the idea of the film studio becoming a full archaeological discovery, with a host of special effects and audio animatronics as you brave the Mummy's realm. The high-speed whiz in the dark (backwards to start with) doesn't involve inversions but is still a thrill with its tight turns and dips, while there are several clever twists (the front row may get damp!). It is a hugely immersive experience but may be too scary for under-8s. Preview your ride photos ($20–35) as you enter the gift shop. **R:** 4ft/122cm. **TTTT½**

Race through New York with Jimmy Fallon

© Universal Orlando Resort

BRITTIP

For the best ride experience on Revenge of the Mummy, try to get a back row seat. You are not allowed to carry anything on the ride – loose items must be left in the (free) lockers provided.

The Blues Brothers: Fans of the film will not want to miss this live show as Jake and Elwood Blues cruise up in their Bluesmobile and put on a stormin' performance of a series of the film's hits on New York's Delancey Street several times a day before heading off into the sunset, stopping only for autographs. AAAA

Other entertainment: The energetic can try the 42nd Street Wall Climb (rock wall) on 5th Avenue ($10). New York also boasts an **amusement arcade**. Or just grab a drink at **Finnegan's bar** and listen to the live music from their fun singer-guitarist.

Shopping: Check out **Sahara Traders** for Mummy souvenirs, as well as

The Blues Brothers

© Universal Orlando Resort

jewellery and toys, and **Rosie's Irish Shop** for all things Irish.

Dining: Finnegan's Bar and Grill offers shepherd's pie, fish and chips, corned beef and cabbage, along with steak, burgers, fries and a good range of beers, plus Irish-tinged entertainment, while **Louie's Italian Restaurant** has counter-service pizza and pasta, ice-cream and tiramisu. There's also a **Ben and Jerry's** store for ice-cream and smoothies, and a **Starbucks** for coffee and pastries.

San Francisco
Cross Canal Street to get to this area that has undergone a major rebuild.

Fast & Furious – Supercharged: This fab ride-and-show experience is based on the underground street racing world from the films starring Vin Diesel, Paul Walker and Dwayne Johnson. It takes visitors on an all-new adventure with the high-speed stars, using the latest ride technology and giving it an immersive twist thanks to digital film and sound effects, with a mix of clever simulation and real physical motion. Most of all, it is just pure fun, with plenty of humour mixed in, while guests have the chance to get up close with some of the super-charged cars from the films in an elaborate queue area. AAAA/TTTT

Other entertainment: Although the **Jaws** ride is gone, you can still get a photo with the 'Great White' next to the **Chez Alcatraz** dockside bar, or try the **Amazing Pictures** kiosk and have your face added to a famous view, poster or magazine ($19.95–150).

Shopping: The **Fast & Furious** gift shop offers some great souvenirs.

Dining: Lombard's Seafood Grille offers excellent seafood, steak, pasta and sandwiches (high season only; reservations accepted), while **San Francisco Pastry Co** serves up desserts and coffee, **Richter's Burger Co** has some tempting burgers and **Chez Alcatraz** is a neat dockside bar with appetisers.

The Wizarding World of Harry Potter – Diagon Alley

This is where Universal really raises the bar for theme park entertainment. The second part of the hugely impressive Potter-verse not only repeats the immersive, film-like setting of Hogsmeade in Islands of Adventure (with a unique link between the two), it goes even deeper into JK Rowling's creation and leaves you in awe of the design and innovation. And that's before you get to the two rides, the live entertainment and the food!

Diagon Alley: Hidden behind a realistic setting of The Embankment lies the secret wizarding street and a full array of complex theming, with the entrance next to a façade of Leicester Square tube station. The external design is modern London, right down to the ¼-scale King's Cross Station and Piccadilly's Eros Statue, where you will also find the iconic Knight Bus. Other elements include Grimmauld Place and the Wyndham Theatre but then visitors walk through the jumbled red-brick barrier next to the tube station and emerge in the jaw-dropping recreation of Diagon Alley, where the towering shop-fronts and mysterious businesses envelop visitors with the full visual effect of the films. Also here is brooding Knockturn Alley, where every nook and cranny is sinister as it is always night. Another area, Carkitt Market was created by JK Rowling purely for Universal. AAAAA+

Harry Potter and The Escape From Gringotts: Prepare to be mesmerised as you enter the vaults – and dangers – of the wizarding world's bank. A fire-breathing dragon sits high atop the building and, if that doesn't take your breath away, the stunning entry hall will, with its amazing animatronic goblin staff. The queue twists and turns through the filing office and backrooms before reaching Bill Weasley's office, where you learn you have arrived during the famous episode when Harry, Ron and Hermione break into the vaults. Then you take the elevator deep underground and climb a flight of steel stairs into a vast cavern that only *feels* like it's miles below the bank. Here you board the ride to share in the perils of Harry and Co as they search for a crucial Horcrux. Half coaster and half 3-D simulator ride, it changes pace as riders brave the various guardians of the vaults, including the dangerous Bellatrix Lestrange, a fire-breathing dragon, an enchanted waterfall, goblin guards and, finally, a close encounter with Lord Voldemort.– Just be aware this draws the longest queues in the park from first thing, so head here straight away or expect a l-o-n-g wait. **R: 3ft6in/106cm. TTTTT+**

Escape from Gringotts

© Universal Orlando Resort

Hogwarts Express: This neat, realistic ride operates between the two parks, as guests journey to Hogsmeade from King's Cross Station. Again, the sense of realism is superb as you arrive at Platform 9¾ to board a replica of the famous Hogwarts train, complete with separate compartments and pulled by a Hull-class locomotive. While it runs on a special track backstage, the enclosed carriage 'windows' show highlights of the journey north to Scotland, including a close encounter with Hagrid on his flying motorcycle, the flying Ford Anglia – and some dangerous Dementors. Oh, and look out for Harry, Hermione and Ron on the train! As this ride goes from park to park, you will need a 2-park ticket to ride. The queue area here is vast but waits rarely top 30mins. AAAAA+

Other entertainment: Look out for two original shows in Carkitt Market, where **Celestina Warbeck & The Banshees** take the stage several times a day to deliver a rollicking four-song performance. The 'Singing Sorceress' is not dissimilar to Shirley Bassey in a 1940s big-band jazz style, and the songs are all originals, including the classics 'You Stole My Cauldron But You Can't Have My Heart' and 'A Cauldron Full of Hot, Strong Love.' AAAA. Also on the Market stage is the elaborate story-telling of **Tales of Beedle the Bard**, a combination of live actor and puppetry show. It's especially engaging for children, and Potter fans. AAA. Other live entertainment is provided by **Ollivander's** shop, where 'the wand chooses the wizard.' AA. Look out also for the **Knight Bus Conductor**, who engages visitors entering the Wizarding World, and don't miss the Talking Shrunken Head. His wisecracks might be aimed at YOU!

Shopping: Another key experience, with eight immersive stores to please the eye and tease the wallet. **Weasley's Wizard Wheezes** is a multi-storey joke shop with all manner of gags, then there is **Wiseacre's Wizarding Equipment** (for all your essential school gear), **Quality Quidditch Supplies, Madam Malkin's Robes** (school uniforms and accessories), **Borgin & Burkes** (the Dark Arts store in Knockturn Alley), **Magical Menagerie** (a soft toy emporium – listen for the animals scurrying about in the upper levels!) and **Scribbulus**, for other Hogwarts mementoes. The shops also feature interactive windows that work with the special wands on sale at **Ollivander's** and **Wands By Gregorovitch** at $44–50 each. Look for the markers in the pavement, say the magic command and wave your wand for a host of surprises. You can even change dollars into wizarding notes at the **Money Exchange**, complete with a Goblin host.

Dining: The essential reality of the Wizarding World is continued into the main dining outlet of **The Leaky Cauldron**, a superb recreation of Diagon Alley's hallmark pub. The food may seem standard pub fare, but the Cottage

Weasley's Wizard Wheezes

Halloween Horror Nights

Universal's massively popular Halloween celebration occurs through mid-Sept to early Nov each year and is a wonderfully bloodthirsty – and thoroughly entertaining! – series of evening events. The Horror Nights have become a real trademark and add a suitably grisly touch to park proceedings. The park is transformed with imaginative set pieces from various horror movies, plus live shows and character interaction. The general mix is 10 indoor Scare Houses, each with its own macabre theme (such as Stranger Things and Walking Dead), plus open-air Scare Zones, with atmospheric dry ice and characters (zombies, chainsaw guys and various beasts!) lurking in dark corners, and two or three live presentations that include the likes of the amazing **Academy of Villains dance** troupe and their wonderfully creative routines, which perfectly fit the mood. All horror genres are well represented, and the Scare Houses feature some superb 'scare actors' and special effects. The rides are all open (and often with fairly short queues), adding more novelty to the park experience, but this over-the-top (and occasionally downright gruesome) extravaganza is definitely not for kids, especially as the atmosphere can get a bit raucous late in the evening as alcohol is widely available. It goes down a treat with adults with the right sense of humour, though, and begins every evening at 6.30pm until 1 or 2am. It is a separate event costing $63–89/person, depending on the day, when purchased in advance, online. It is a flat rate of $115 if purchased at the gates, no matter which night you visit. Best value is the Frequent Fear Pass at just $108 for multiple visits on select evenings (not Fri or Sat, when Scare Houses queues can top 2 hours). A Rush of Fear ticket for the first three weeks is only $97, while a HHN Express pass is $80–160, depending on dates. A Frequent Fear Plus Express Pass (including Fridays) costs $420. No costumes are allowed on any evening, though. Look up more at **halloweenhorrornights.com**.

Pie is excellent, as is the Beef, Lamb and Guinness Stew, while their Ploughman's Platter is positively indulgent with its array of three cheeses, pickle, salad, scotch egg and fresh bread (priced variously from $11–22). There is also Toad in the Hole, Fish 'n Chips, two types of sandwich (sausage and chicken) and a Fisherman's Pie. Kids can choose from a mini-pie, mac and cheese and their own fish 'n chips ($6.99). There are then four tempting desserts, of which the Sticky Toffee Pudding is to die for. All this can be washed down with

drinks such as Fishy Green Ale (a variation on bubble tea, and non-alcoholic), Otter's Fizzy Orange Juice, Tongue-Tying Lemon Squash and Gilly Water, as well as two outstanding beers – the IPA-like Dragon Scale Ale and porter-style Wizards Brew. There is a separate menu for breakfast. Still hungry? Head for **Florean Fortescue's Ice Cream Parlour** where Universal's culinary wizards have come up with a superb array of flavours that are all worth trying, including Earl Grey & Lavender, Apple Crumble, Chocolate Chilli and Clotted Cream. You can also grab a drink – alcoholic and otherwise – at the **Hopping Pot** and **Fountain of Fair Fortune**.

Halloween Horror Nights

© Universal Orlando Resort

World Expo

Continuing around the park brings you to an extensive area that is home to Fear – and Aliens.

Men in Black – Alien Attack: This combination thrill/dark ride takes up where the hit films, starring Will Smith, left off. Visitors are introduced to the MIB Institute in an inventive mock-futuristic setting and enrolled as trainees for a battle around the streets of New York with a horde of escaped aliens. Your six-person car is equipped with laser zappers for an interactive shoot-out that is like a real-life arcade game, as the aliens can also shoot back to send your car spinning. The finale features a close encounter with a giant bug that is all mouth. Only your collective shooting skills can save the day, and there are numerous ride variations according to your accuracy. Fast, frantic and a bit confusing, you'll want to come back until you can top 250,000 (for Defender status). **R:** 3ft 6in/106cm.

---BRITTIP

For a big score in Men In Black, when you meet the Big Bug – push the big red button!

Fear Factor Live: (high season only) This live-action version of the reality TV show asks audience volunteers to take part in some hair-raising (and stomach-churning!) challenges, with a head-to-head competition to find the biggest daredevil. Auditions take place 70mins before each show, and the audience then gets to see the chosen few battle it out, with clips from the TV show interspersed with live action.

Shopping: Visit **MIB Gear** (at the exit to the ride) for Men In Black clothing and souvenirs, plus photo opps with the MIB themselves.

The Simpsons Ride

© Universal Orlando Resort

Springfield: Home of the Simpsons

The Simpsons Ride: The headline attraction here, this brings the TV characters to vibrant life in a colourful and amusing production, even if you're not a fan of The Simpsons. It is themed as Krustyland amusement park, brainchild of irascible Krusty the Clown, a bizarre funfair that is the setting for a hectic, breathtaking ride in the company of the Simpson clan. A wicked sound system and state-of-the-art motion simulator technology ensure a frantic race through outlandish attractions (watch out for the Tooth Chipper!). The feel of the 'ride' is amazing and the huge domed screen ensures an outrageously comical sensory experience. **R:** 3ft 4in/101cm. TTTTT

Kang and Kodos' Twirl 'n' Hurl: A standard fairground whirligig with some clever touches as the alien duo take 'foolish humans' into 'orbit' and provide a challenge as you twirl. **TT** (**TTTTT** under 6s).

Other entertainment: In Springfield, chance your hand at a series of fairground-type games that require $6 to play ($25 for five games), like the groan-inducing Sledge-Homer. Look out for Simpsons **character meet-and-greets** at regular intervals, and **photo ops** with Springfield icons like the Lard Lad Donuts statue, Founders statue and The Seven Little Duffs.

Shopping: To complete the immersive Springfield effect, visit the **Kwik-E-Mart** for Simpsons souvenirs (plus more gags).

Dining: Clever counter-service offerings of the **Fast Food Boulevard** food-court are found here, and you can dine in true Homer fashion (albeit with better quality) at **Krusty Burger, Luigi's Pizza, Frying Dutchmen, Cletus' Chicken Shack** and **Flaming Moe's** (complete with the non-alcoholic Flaming Moe cocktail, $8.99). For a specially made brew, visit the **Duff Brewery & Shop** with a fab view of the Lagoon. **Bumblebee Man's Taco Truck** completes the picture.

KidZone

A great place to let the kids loose on their own, this also features several great family attractions, but is likely to be next on Universal's agenda for redevelopment.

Animal Actors On Location!: An amusing mix of video, animal performance and audience interaction, several children are invited to help present some unlikely feats and stunts featuring a range of wildlife, from parakeets to pigs. Many have been rescued from animal shelters and gone on to feature in films before finding a home at Universal. The theatre also provides an escape from the queues. AAAA

Fievel's Playland: Strictly for kids, this playground, based on the enlarged world of the cartoon mouse, offers the chance to bounce under a 1,000-gallon hat, crawl through a giant boot, climb a giant spider's web and shoot the rapids (a 200ft/61m waterslide) in Fievel's sardine can. TTTT (young 'uns only!)

Woody Woodpecker's Nuthouse Coaster: This junior-sized coaster is a whizzy little racer with plenty of kid-appeal. While its highest speed is just 22mph and its tallest hill is 28ft/8m, it does have a height restriction. **R:** 3ft/91cm TTTT (youngsters only).

A Day in the Park with Barney: Again strictly for the younger set (2–5), the purple dinosaur from kids' TV is brought to super-dee-duper life in a large arena that features a pre-show before the 15min main event, plus an interactive post-show area. AA (AAAAA under-5s)

ET Adventure: This glorious scenic ride comes with a grand queuing area and spectacular leap on flying bicycles to save ET's home planet. Steven Spielberg has added some new characters to the story, and queues rarely build up here. **R:** 3ft/91cm. AAAA

BRITTIP

If you want to let your youngsters loose in the Curious George playground, it is advisable to bring swimsuits or a change of clothing.

Curious George Goes To Town: Kids of all ages love this adventure playground with plenty of ways to get wet. It combines toddler play, water-based play stations and a huge interactive ball pool, and is a real bonus for harassed parents. The town theme includes buildings to climb, pumps and hoses to spray water, a ball factory in which to shoot, dump and blast thousands of foam balls and – the tour de force – two huge buckets of water that flood the street below at regular intervals. TTTTT (under 12s)

Other entertainment: For kids under 36in/91cm tall, **Barney's Backyard** is a neat indoor (and air-conditioned!) play area, while there is also a fun **character meet-and-greet**.

Shopping and dining: Shop at the fun **Spongebob Storepants** for everything to do with Spongebob and friends in an immersive environment, complete with character photo opportunity, plus the **Barney Store** and **ET's Toy Closet** and **Photo Spot**. For a quick bite, **Kidzone Pizza Company** offers pizza and chicken fingers.

Woody Woodpecker's Nuthouse Coaster

© Universal Orlando Resort

Hollywood

Finally, your circular tour of Universal returns you to the main entrance via Hollywood (where else?).

Universal's Horror Make-Up Show: Not recommended for under-12s, this demonstrates some of the ways in which films have terrorised us, from classic black-and-white to modern horror movies. Using film clips and special effects 'experts', the audience is treated to a slapstick approach to horror make-up. It's a 20min show, queues are rarely long and the special effects are amusing. AAA

Hello Kitty: Fans of this popular Sanrio character (and others like Chococat) will love this extensive retail opportunity; also includes Betty Boop and a section on Hollywood Stars.

Other entertainment: The **Hollywood Character Zone** provides character appearances throughout the day along Hollywood Boulevard, from Scooby Doo and Shaggy to Dudley Do-Right and The Flintstones, plus music from the **Studio Brass Band**. **Character Party Zone** features various members of the Superstar Parade periodically next to Mel's Drive-In.

BRITTIP
Ever wanted to take home a truly unique souvenir from the Universal parks? **Williams of Hollywood** is the place to find original props and artifacts for sale.

Shopping: Look for all manner of headgear in **The Brown Derby** and designer clothes and sunglasses in **Studio Styles**.

Universal's Superstar Parade

© Universal Orlando Resort

Dining: Choose from **Mel's Drive-In**, a re-creation from the film *American Graffiti*, serving burgers and hot dogs, and the new **Today Cafe**, with breakfast fare, yummy pastries, some of the park's best sandwiches, plus salads and drinks.

Parade time!

Universal's Superstar Parade: The daily performance takes place at 3, 5 or 7pm in a vibrant and lively style, with dozens of performers and interactive characters. The four main sets of 'superstars' are led by Gru and his Minions from *Despicable Me* and followed by Spongebob Squarepants and his Bikini Bottom pals, including skaters and stilt walkers – and with the world's biggest pineapple! The characters from *The Secret Life of Pets* add to the fun, while Nickelodeon stars Dora and Diego from *Dora The Explorer* and *Go, Diego, Go!* complete the line-up, with aerialists and other high-energy performers. The huge floats – especially for the Minions – are feature-packed, and the parade has two dance stops to allow characters to meet guests. It is just 15mins but there are up to four other meet-and-greet performances during the day when characters come into the park for their own Street Parties. AAAA

BRITTIP
The two best viewing spots for the Parade are halfway along the main New York street (opposite the Palace Arcade) or on Hollywood Boulevard, by Schwab's Pharmacy.

Universal's Cinematic Celebration This night-time special effects extravaganza brings down the curtain each night, viewed from a three-tiered spectator area in Central Park section for a grandstand view of the Lagoon, where a massive underwater platform provides all the razzamatazz. This special 'stage' is equipped with more than 120 fountains, pop-jets, fog effects, water-screens and more. Combined with fireworks, lasers and projection equipment, it builds into a massive

UNIVERSAL STUDIOS with children

Our guide to the attractions that generally appeal to the different age groups:

Under-5s
Animal Actors On Location!, Curious George Goes To Town, A Day in the Park With Barney, ET Adventure, Fievel's Playland, Kang & Kodos' Twirl 'n' Hurl, Universal's Superstar Parade.

5–8s
All the above (minus Barney), plus Despicable Me, Hogwarts Express, Men In Black, Shrek 4-D, The Simpsons, TRANSFORMERS: The Ride – 3-D (with parental discretion), Woody Woodpecker's Nuthouse Coaster.

9–12s
All the above, plus Hollywood Rip Ride Rockit, Fear Factor Live!, Fast & Furious, Harry Potter and The Escape From Gringotts, Revenge of the Mummy, TRANSFORMERS: The Ride – 3-D, Race Through New York Starring Jimmy Fallon.

Over-12s
The Blues Brothers, Despicable Me, ET Adventure, Fast & Furious, Race Through New York Starring Jimmy Fallon, Fear Factor Live, Hollywood Rip Ride Rockit, Men In Black – Alien Attack, Revenge of the Mummy, Shrek 4-D, The Simpsons, TRANSFORMERS: The Ride – 3-D, Universal's Horror Make-Up Show.

cinematic spectacular that goes through a repertoire of Universal films, including blockbusters like *Jurassic World, The Fast And The Furious, ET, Despicable Me, Transformers, Kung Fu Panda* and *Harry Potter*. With 300 outdoor speakers and digital projectors that use the New York area façade as a clever 3-D backdrop, it is an eye-popping performance. AAAA. Other live entertainment is offered periodically by **Marilyn and the Diamond Bellas** and the **Studio Brass Band**.

Special programmes
Universal Studios features some brilliant extra seasonal entertainment for **Mardi Gras**, with a hectic, bead-throwing parade, plus music, street entertainment and authentic New Orleans food each Sat at 6pm mid-Feb–mid-Apr (and free with park admission). The spectacular Parade alone is worth coming to see, along with authentic Zydeco bands in the French Quarter Courtyard. The day culminates in a live concert with well-known acts (including Macklemore, Steve Miller

Band and Pitbull in 2019), but it does draw HUGE crowds. Universal also throws a party for **Fourth of July**, when the park presents a major firework spectacular. And don't miss the Studios at Christmas (p37).

Hogwart's Castle at Christmas

© Universal Orlando Resort

ISLANDS OF ADVENTURE

With the arrival of Diagon Alley at Universal Studios, you'd think there might be slightly less focus on the original Harry Potter development here, but not a bit of it. In fact, with the Hogwarts Express ride now connecting the two areas, and the new Hagrid's Magical Creatures Motorbike Adventure, it is busier than ever.

The Islands of Adventure opened in 1999 under the supervision of creative consultant Steven Spielberg, and it provided one of the most complete and thrilling theme parks you could imagine, containing an upbeat collection of high-adrenalin rides, shows and entertainment, plus some fine dining. Then JK Rowling's boy wizard arrived and added a whole new 'world' of excitement.

The park has a full range of attractions, from out-and-out thrills to pure family entertainment. OK, so they aren't really islands (the areas form a chain around the central lagoon), but that's the only illusion. And you get a lot for your money here, unless you have extremely timid children or under-5s. Seuss Landing will usually keep pre-schoolers amused for several hours, while Camp Jurassic is a clever adventure playground for 5–12s, but the rest of the park, with its eight 5-star thrill rides and other attractions, is primarily geared to kids of 10 and over, their parents and especially teenagers. There are several elements that look alarming, but don't be put off – they all deliver immense fun as well as terrific spectator value! If any one ride sums up IoA, it is Harry Potter and the Forbidden Journey, which took theme park ride technology to a whole new level.

Private nursing facilities, an open area for feeding and resting (with high chairs) and nappy-changing stations, can be found at the **Family Service Facility** at Guest Services (to the right inside the main gates), while ALL restrooms throughout the park are equipped with nappy-changing facilities. First aid is provided in Sindbad's Village in the Lost Continent, just across from Oasis Coolers, and in Port of Entry.

Harry Potter and the Forbidden Journey

Port of Entry
1 Ocean Trader Market
2 Confisco Grille

Marvel Super-Hero Island
3 Incredible Hulk Coaster
4 Dr Doom's Fearfall
5 Café 4
6 Captain America Diner
7 The Amazing Adventures of Spider-Man
8 Storm Force Accelatron

Toon Lagoon
9 Popeye and Bluto's Bilge-Rat Barges
10 Dudley Do-Right's Ripsaw Falls
11 Me Ship, The Olive
12 Comic Strip Café
13 Toon Lagoon Amphitheater

Jurassic Park
14 Jurassic Park River Adventure
15 Pteranodon Flyers
16 Camp Jurassic
17 Discovery Center
18 Skull Island: Reign of Kong

19 Raptor Encounter
20 Jurassic World Coaster

The Wizarding World of Harry Potter
21 Harry Potter and the Forbidden Journey
22 Filch's Emporium
23 Flight of the Hippogriff
24 Olivander's
25 Dervish and Banges
26 Three Broomsticks
27 Zonko's
28 Hogwart's Express
29 Hagrid's Magical Creatures Motorbike Adventure

The Lost Continent
30 Mythos Restaurant
31 Mystic Fountain
32 Poseidon's Fury

Seuss Landing
33 Circus McGurkus Café Stoo-pendous
34 High in the Sky Seuss Trolley Train Ride
35 Caro Seuss-el
36 If I Ran the Zoo
37 The Cat in the Hat
38 One Fish, Two Fish, Red Fish, Blue Fish

ISLANDS OF ADVENTURE

Port of Entry

You arrive for IoA as you do for Universal Studios, in the big multi-storey car parks off I-4 and Universal Boulevard and pass right through the CityWalk area, where you come to the main entrance plaza (head for the huge Pharos Lighthouse). As with Universal Studios, you can purchase the Universal Express pass (p154) for Islands of Adventure at various locations throughout the park and at Guest Services. Once through the gates, the lockers, pushchair and wheelchair hire are on your left as the Port of Entry opens up before you. This elaborate 'village' consists of shops and eateries, so push straight on to the main lagoon, but do take in the wonderful architecture throughout Port of Entry, which borrows from Middle East, Far East and African themes and uses bric-a-brac from all over the world.

Shopping: Later in the day, return to check out the extensive retail experience at places like **IoA Trading Company** and **Ocean Trader Market** for a full range of Islands of Adventure merchandise.

Dining: You can enjoy a coffee and pastry at the inevitable **Starbucks** or the **Croissant Moon Bakery** (also with croissants and sandwiches), or sample the huge cinnamon rolls and pastries of **Cinnabon**. Alternatively, try lunch or dinner at **Confisco Grille** with tastes from around the world including Italian, Mexican and Asian as well as American, and a range of dishes from sandwiches and burgers to salads, Fajitas, ribs and pasta. Or just grab a beverage and a snack at the **Backwater Bar**.

Beating the queues: At the end of the street, you will need to decide which way to head first as there are eight attractions where the queues build up quickly and remain that way. If you are among the majority lured by Harry Potter, turn right (through Seuss Landing and The Lost Continent). If you're after the big thrill rides, turn left into Marvel Super-Hero Island and head straight to Spider-Man, then do Dr Doom's

Islands of Adventure at a glance

Location	Off exits 75A and 74B from I-4; Universal Boulevard and Kirkman Road
Size	110 acres/45ha in 6 'islands'
Hours	9am–6, 7 or 8pm off peak; 8 or 9am–9 or 10pm high season (Washington's birthday, Easter, summer holidays, Thanksgiving, Christmas)
Admission	Under-3s free; 3–9 $110–119 (1-day ticket), $275 (2-day Park-to-Park ticket), £278 (UK 3-Park Explorer ticket); adult (10+) $115–124, $285, £278. Prices do not include tax.
Parking	$25 (preferred parking $35; valet parking $65)
Lockers	Immediately to left through main gates; $10 and $15
Pushchairs	$15 and $25
Wheelchairs	$12, ECV $50, $70 with sun shade (with photo ID as deposit), with pushchairs
Top attractions	Harry Potter and the Forbidden Journey, Hagrid's Magical Creatures Motorbike Adventure, Hogwarts Express, Amazing Adventures Of Spider-Man, Incredible Hulk Coaster, Jurassic Park River Adventure, Skull Island: Reign of Kong
Don't miss	Jurassic Park Discovery Centre, If I Ran The Zoo playground (for toddlers), Three Broomsticks restaurant and Ollivander's Wand Shop
Hidden costs	**Meals** Burger, chips and soda $15.19 / 3-course lunch $24–44 (Confisco Grill) / Kids' meal $9.99
	T-shirts $25–40, Kids $20–28
	Souvenirs 99c—$6,500
	Sundries Butterbeer $7.50 regular or frozen

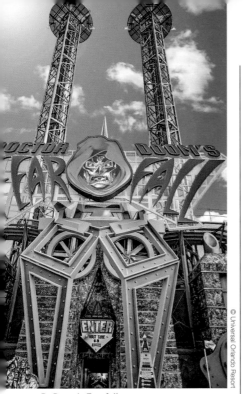

Dr Doom's Fearfall

Fearfall and the Incredible Hulk Coaster. The King Kong attraction (between Toon Lagoon and Jurassic Park) is a big draw, too, so you may want to head here first, and then visit Hogsmeade.

BRITTIP

There are two entrances to the Wizarding World of Harry Potter: from Jurassic Park and The Lost Continent. The latter is much more dramatic and offers the full Hogsmeade Village panorama.

Dinosaur fans should go left around the lagoon to Jurassic Park for the River Adventure before the majority arrive. Once you are wet, go back to Toon Lagoon for Ripsaw Falls and the Bilge-Rat Barges. Or those with younger children, turn right into Seuss Landing and enjoy The Cat in the Hat and High In The Sky Seuss Trolley Train Ride prior to the main crowd build-up.

Turning right, in an anti-clockwise direction, here's what you find.

Seuss Landing

There is not a straight line to be seen in this vivid 3-D working of the Dr Seuss children's books. Even if the characters are unfamiliar, everyone can relate to the fun (though queues build up quickly). Take your time and try not to miss the clever detail, from squirt ponds to beach scenes, while the lagoon-front area provides a quieter corner to escape the crowds.

Caro-Seuss-el: This intricate carousel ride on some of the Seuss characters – cowfish, elephant-birds and dog-a-lopes, for example – has rider-activated features that are a big hit with children. AA (AAAA under-5s).

One Fish, Two Fish, Red Fish, Blue Fish: A fairground ride with a twist as you pilot these Seussian fish up and down according to the rhyme that plays while you ride. Get it wrong and you get squirted! More fun for the younger set. TTT (TTTTT under-5s)

The Cat in the Hat: Prepare for a ride with a difference as you board these crazy six-passenger 'couches' to meet the world's most adventurous cat and friends Thing One and Thing Two. You literally go for a spin through this storybook world, and it may be a bit much for very young children.

Seuss Landing

The slow-moving queues are a bit of a drag, so try to get here early or leave it until later in the day. **AAAA/TTT**

If I Ran the Zoo: Interactive playgrounds don't get much better for the pre-school brigade than with these Seuss character scenarios, some of which can be pretty wet! Hugely imaginative and great fun to watch. **TTTTT** (under-5s)

The High in the Sky Seuss Trolley Train Ride: This fun family adventure high above Seuss Landing has terrific appeal to youngsters as you board a trolley to journey into the world of the Sneetches, visiting the Inking and Stamping Room, the Star Wash Room and a tour inside the Circus McGurkus Café Stoo-pendous. It is slow-paced and scenic, but it does draw slow-moving queues, so head here early with under-9s. **AAAA**

Character appearances: Look out for The Cat in the Hat, Thing One and Thing Two and The Grinch outside the Circus McGurkus, and the character-filled celebration of the Oh! The Stories You'll Hear street show.

Shopping: If the land has captivated you, you can buy the books at **Dr Seuss' All The Books You Can Read Store**, or a full variety of character merchandise at the **Mulberry Street Store**. **Snookers and Snookers Sweet Candy Cookers** is a super sweet shop.

Dining: Snacks and drinks can be had at **Hop On Pop Ice Cream Shop**, **Moose Juice Goose Juice** and **Green Eggs and Ham Café** (sandwiches and burgers). The **Circus McGurkus Café Stoo-pendous** is a mind-boggling eatery for fried chicken, spaghetti, burgers and pizza – with clowns and pipe organs.

One Fish, Two Fish, Red Fish, Blue Fish

© Universal Orlando Resort

© Universal Orlando Resort

Flight of the Hippogriff

The Lost Continent

This land underwent a rather drastic reduction to accommodate Harry Potter, but it still offers some eye-catching locations.

Poseidon's Fury: A walk-through show that puts its audience at the heart of the action as a journey in the company of a hapless young archaeologist takes a turn for the worse in the lost temple of Poseidon. You pass through an amazing water vortex before your expedition awakens an ancient demon. There is an element of suspense, but the special effects showdown between Poseidon and the demon is amazing. Queuing is tedious, but it is inside. **TTT**

Other entertainment: Try a bit of mystic manipulation with **Star Souls** psychic readers. But beware **The Mystic Fountain**; it can strike up a conversation – and then soak you!

Shopping: Find some original souvenirs at **Treasures of Poseidon** (jewellery and clothing).

Dining: Food options include **The Fire-Eater's Grill** (chicken fingers, hotdogs, salads, fries and drinks) and **Doc Sugrue's Kebab House** (kebabs, hummus, salad and churros). The ornate **Mythos Restaurant** provides the best dining in IoA; the food (salads, beef, risotto, fish, pad thai and pasta) is first class, but the setting (inside a dormant volcano with fountains and clever lighting) is a real attraction (3-course meal $31.50–46.50, kids' meals $7–10).

Wizarding World of Harry Potter – Hogsmeade

This 'Island' has significantly boosted the park's attendance since it opened in 2010 and draws BIG crowds. The magnificent edifice of Hogwarts Castle looms large but the whole area is completely immersive as it uses the design genius behind the films. Entering from The Lost Continent area provides the grand view, through Hogsmeade and with Hogwarts seemingly towering above (the use of architectural perspective is masterful), and you are drawn into an all-encompassing realm where chimneys smoke, icicles glitter, owls roost, visitors are warned to 'Observe the spell limits' and Butterbeer is real!

Hogsmeade Village: Walk through the grand archway into the Wizarding World and a powerful sense of realism envelops you. This is a shimmering, snow-covered version of the magical settlement Harry, Ron and Hermione inhabit. It is the shopping and dining heart of the Wizarding World, but is an attraction in itself. Here you will find a wonderful photo opportunity with the **Hogwarts Express**, while nearly all the shop windows feature 'wizardly' animatronic touches. The Owl Clock comes to life every 15mins; the wooden-raftered Owlery is a work of art; and you may just encounter Moaning Myrtle in the loos! Numerous other clever effects and design touches all help to transform this corner of Florida into JK Rowling's authentic creation AAAAA+

BRITTIP

Don't forget your interactive wizard's wand in Hogsmeade. They were originally designed for the Diagon Alley area, but were added to the Islands of Adventure section in 9 different windows.

The Flight of The Hippogriff: This junior-sized coaster is aimed primarily at youngsters and features a journey into Hagrid's realm, where his love of outlandish creatures gives rise to this swooping ride. Hagrid offers instructions and warnings as you wind through the queue, and you may even hear Fang barking from inside his hut. There are no big drops, but it delivers a surprisingly fast-paced whirl. Be sure to bow to the Hippogriff at the start. R: 3ft 4in/92cm. TTT (TTTT for 6–12s)

Harry Potter and the Forbidden Journey: This is the Big One: a trip inside the legendary halls of Hogwarts, and a breathtaking plunge on a state-of-the-art ride, Quidditch and all. The basic premise is that 'muggles' (non-wizarding types, i.e. you!) have been invited to tour the school. The immense queuing area is part discovery, part storytelling and part entertainment, so be ready for a LONG time on your feet as you traverse the corridors, traipse through the greenhouse, tiptoe along the Portrait Hall (where the paintings of the four founders of Hogwarts come to life in magical fashion) and tread the stone floors of the Gryffindor common room. Along the way, you'll

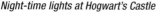

Night-time lights at Hogwart's Castle

be greeted by Professor Dumbledore in his study (complete with more talking portraits), be accosted by the Fat Lady (another painting-come-to-life) and enter the Defence Against the Dark Arts classroom, where Harry, Ron and Hermione urge visitors to abandon their 'boring' tour and come to the Quidditch match (with the aid of a magic spell).

BRITTIP

Once again, this is an unpredictable, dynamic ride, with sudden twists, turns and tilts. You are strongly advised to leave all loose items in the free-to-use lockers just inside the castle.

Finally, you reach the Room of Requirement (past the Sorting Hat), where your mode of transport to the match is revealed – magical flying benches. With some pre-ride warnings, you are then strapped in to your 'bench' and are up, up and away. Only things don't go as planned and, before you can say 'Expecto Patronum' you're on a crazy dash through some of the young wizard's most dangerous adventures. Your unique ride vehicle sweeps you through dramatic settings that combine film technology with full-scale scenery, creating a convincing effect as you move up, down, backwards and even sideways.

Blast-ended Skrewt

© Universal Orlando Resort

© Universal Orlando Resort

Hagrid's Magical Creatures Motorbike Adventure

BRITTIP

Look for the Single Rider queue at Harry Potter and the Forbidden Journey – it can save a LOT of time

There is a close encounter with a fire-breathing dragon, an army of giant spiders, a Death Eater and a narrow escape from the clutches of the Whomping Willow before the big finale in a spooky underground cavern where it's up to Harry, naturally, to try to save the day. It is an astounding theme park experience, but it WILL scare small children (and those with arachnophobia!), and it draws queues in excess of 2hrs, so head here early in the day. **R:** 4ft/122cm. **TTTTT+** You exit through **Filch's Emporium of Confiscated Goods**, where you'll find plush Hedwig owls, Crookshank cats, Scabbers rats and three-headed dogs (watch out, he growls!), plus a range of tempting Azkaban and House-related clothing and gifts. You also pick up your ride photos here ($20–45).

BRITTIP

Look out for the Marauders Map in Filch's Emporium, plus other clever Hogwarts signature gadgets and gizmos among the merchandise.

Hagrid's Magical Creatures Motorbike Adventure: New in summer 2019 was this hugely elaborate and distinctly novel coaster that dives into the world of Hagrid and the magical creatures inhabiting the Forbidden Forest surrounding Hogwarts. Themed as a Care Of Magical Creatures class with Hagrid (beware his creation of the Blast-Ended Skrewts!), this roller-coaster hybrid – with pauses in the action to take in various set-pieces – hurtles riders on a manic journey, both inside and outside, with several surprises (including a sudden backwards section and a vertical drop). It has seven fast-launch moments but also a slow crawl through the Forest, featuring a meeting with Hagrid in his Hut, an encounter with a centaur, unicorns, Cornish pixies, Hagrid's three-headed dog Fluffy, and a scary moment in the clutches of the Devil's Snare, the deadly constricting plant from *Harry Potter and the Philosopher's Stone*. But the real danger here is being incinerated by the fire that shoots out of the Blast-Ended Skrewt's scorpion-like tail! There is excitement around every turn, and fans of the books and films will be thrilled to see Arthur Weasley's famous flying Ford Anglia and other notable Potter icons along the way. The queueing area is immense, and hugely detailed (look out for mysterious eggs – could they be dragons? – and Hagrid's magical creatures laboratory), while your coaster vehicle is also unique, a multiple-car version of Hagrid's motor-cycle and side-car. Riders need to choose which of the two seats to sit in before they ride, then it's off in

suitably madcap fashion for a genuine Hogwarts adventure. **R:** 4ft/122cm. **AAAAA+**/**TTTTT**. Be aware the queues build up quickly here, as they do at Forbidden Journey.

Hogwart's Express: This is the 'northern' end of the famous train ride from King's Cross Station. With its own station (and queue area), it provides the full effect of arriving at or departing from this mythical Scottish village. The station is almost completely enclosed to allow the designers to build up the illusion, and then you pass through a small section of the Forbidden Forest to reach Hogsmeade itself and enjoy your first full view of the village with Hogwarts towering behind it. The ride from Hogsmeade to King's Cross is also different, screen-wise, from the one that brings you here, with more scenes of London and some of Harry's other exploits. Don't forget, you need a 2-park ticket to ride the Express, or you can pay the extra fee at the ticket office. **AAAAA+**

BRITTIP

Try all three sweet, non-alcoholic Butterbeers: 'regular', frozen (slushie style) or hot. It's usually easier to get served in the Hog's Head rather than at the busy street carts.

Other entertainment: The **TriWizard Spirit Rally** celebrates the upcoming tournament, with the Beauxbatons Academy ribbon dancers and staff-fighting wizards from Durmstrang Institute. Hogwarts is represented by

Hogwart's Express

the **Frog Choir** (four students and two huge frogs!), making for an entertaining show. The periodic **Nighttime Lights at Hogwarts Castle** each evening is a delightful 4min film show on the Castle, using state-of-the-art projectors, sound effects and a few pyrotechnics to provide more visual wizardry. It goes into overdrive for **The Magic of Christmas at Hogwarts** during the festive holiday season, with an even more dramatic 7min version that includes snow, ghosts and the Weasley's Wizard Whiz-Bangs. A whiz of a show!

BRITTIP

The best viewing point for the Hogwarts Castle projection shows is in front of the TriWizard Rally stage, but the crowds are also heaviest here. Good alternatives are the outdoor dining area behind the Three Broomsticks and the bridge from Jurassic Park. Or just wait for the last half-hour each evening, when the hordes thin out.

Shopping: The intricate level of detail given to shopping and dining locations makes them attractions in their own right. Be sure to have a wander through each to soak up the atmosphere, especially the famous sweetshop **Honeydukes**, the place to buy Cauldron Cakes, Bertie Bott's Every Flavour Beans, Chocolate Frogs and more. **Dervish and Banges** supplies 'students' with Quidditch gear and school-related clothing, Luna Lovegood's 3-D Quibbler, and even the Nimbus 2001 broomsticks. **Ollivander's** has 13 varieties of wand to choose from. 'The wand also chooses the wizard' with surprising special effects similar to those Harry experienced. This is the same as in Diagon Alley but that one is

much bigger, hence with shorter queues. AAAAA

Dining: There is only one sit-down dining location here, but it's a corker. A 'Cathedral to Butterbeer', the **Three Broomsticks** menu features British favourites such as shepherd's pie, fish and chips and Cornish pasties, along with the Great Feast, a family-style meal of salad, ribs, chicken, roast potatoes and corn on the cob ($60 for 4; $15 per extra person). Entrées $10–17, with desserts $3.49–5.49, including strawberry and peanut-butter ice cream, found only in the Wizarding World. They also serve a different menu for breakfast. Next door is the **Hog's Head Pub**, complete with animatronic boar's head, where you'll find Hog's Head Brew ($8.50–9.50 a pint).

BRITTIP

Of all the buildings, the Three Broomsticks is a must-see experience of dramatic interior design and special effects. Look in the rafters for owls, magical maids and the roaming House Elf!

All in all, it's an immense collection of dramatic and charming elements (witness the animated Prisoner of Azkaban poster in Hogsmeade) that add up to a vivid portrayal of JK Rowling's work. You don't need to be a fan to enjoy it and, like the Diagon Alley area in Universal Studios, the only snag is the huge crowd it draws for much of the day, as most of the shops are quite small and quickly feel congested. Arriving early is highly advisable (the early entry perk with Universal hotels is so valuable here), but also try to see it after dark, when the lighting effects make it even more magical.

Honeyduke's at Hogsmeade

Jurassic Park

Now travel back to the Cretaceous age and the make-believe dinosaur film world where extravagant scenery will have you looking out for stray dinos.

Jurassic Park River Adventure: From scenic splendour, the mood changes to hidden menace as your journey into this waterborne realm brings you up close and personal with some realistic dinosaurs. Inevitably, your passage is diverted to the hazardous, and the danger increases as the 16-person raft travels through the main building – with raptors loose everywhere. You are aware of something large lurking in the shadows – will you fall prey to the T-Rex, or will your boat take the 85ft/26m plunge to safety (plus a good soaking)? Queues usually move briskly but will top an hour in mid-afternoon. **R**: 3ft 6in/106cm. The ride photo comes in various packages ($20–35).**TTTT**

BRITTIP

Keep your valuables dry on the River Adventure by leaving them in the lockers at the start of the queue.

Pteranodon Flyers: The slow-moving queues are a major turn-off, especially for a fairly average ride, which glides gently over much of Jurassic Park (though it reaches a height of almost 30ft/9m). **R**: It is designed mainly for kids, and anyone OVER the height range of 3ft–4ft 8in/91–142cm (usually 11+) must be accompanied by a child of the right height. **TT** (**TTTT** under-9s). The Universal Express pass is not valid here.

Camp Jurassic: More excellent kids' fare with the mountainous jungle giving way to an 'active' volcano for youngsters to explore, climb and slide down. Squirt guns and spitter dinosaurs add to the fun (for kids, but parents can explore!). **TTTT**

Discovery Center: This indoor centre offers various interactive games, like creating a dinosaur via DNA sequencing, mixing your own DNA with a dino on a touch-screen, playing the fun Jurassic trivia game and handling 'dino eggs', plus other hands-on exhibits. It's ideal in summer as it's fully air-conditioned (10am–5pm; 7pm peak season). **AAA**

Jurassic World Coaster: A brand new coaster is due to open in this area in late 2020, with a track so long it reaches from the Discovery Center area all the way to the lagoon side of Mythos restaurant. Theme and details had not been announced as we went to print.

Other entertainment: If you're not easily frightened, seek out the **Raptor Encounter**, where you can learn some interesting dino facts, then have your photo taken with the rather terrifying velociraptor, Blue. Sports minded guests can try the **Rock Climbing Wall** (just outside River Adventure) for an extra $10, while there are also fairground games at an extra $6 a time, or $25 for five games.

Shopping: Visit **Dinostore** and **Jurassic Outfitters** for the best shopping.

Dining: Try **Burger Digs** (huge burger platters), **Pizza Predatoria**, **Thunder Falls Terrace** (counter service rotisserie chicken, ribs, burgers, turkey legs and salads, plus a great view of River Adventure) or the **Watering Hole** (hot dogs, snacks and drinks).

Raptor Encounter at Jurassic Park

© Universal Orlando Resort

Skull Island

There is only one attraction here, but it's a good one! This is your chance to step back in time and meet the great ape himself.

Skull Island: Reign of Kong: In a world created by Peter Jackson's 2005 remake of *King Kong*, this is themed around a 1930s expedition to a mysterious isle, where it all goes seriously wrong, and prehistoric predators are determined to eat your crew. Part ride, part 3-D film spectacular, this large-scale truck journey encounters all manner of scary beasts, culminating in a big finale with a giant animatronic version of Kong that leaves riders convinced they face a terrible fate! The use of high-def projection equipment, wrap-around film screens, superb sound systems and other effects make for a realistic environment, and the immense nature of the queue area (beware the lurking natives!) is worth seeing on its own. **R:** 36in/92cm, 36in–48in/123cm with adult. Parental discretion advised, no expectant mothers. But, although there are no ride age restrictions, this may be too intense for many youngsters. TTTT/AAAAA.

Toon Lagoon

The thrills continue here with a watery theme and more comic-book elements from (US) newspaper cartoon characters. Children will also love the fountains, squirt pools and overflowing fire hydrants!

Popeye and Bluto's Bilge-Rat Barges: Every park seems to have a variation on the white-water raft ride, but this is one of the wettest! Fast, bouncy and unpredictable, it has water coming at you from every direction, a couple of sizeable drops and a whirl through the Octo-plus Grotto that adds to the fun. If you don't want to get wet, don't ride, because there is no escaping the deluge here. This is also one of the top five for long queues (at least when it's hot), but it's worth the wait. **R:** 1ft/122cm. Look for the Water Blasters (for 1 token; $5 for 12 tokens) on the bridge to give riders a wet start. TTTTT

BRITTIP

A change of clothes is often advisable after the Barges, unless it's mega hot. Bring a waterproof bag for your valuables or leave them in a locker.

Dudley Do-Right's Ripsaw Falls: A flume ride that sends its passengers on a wild (and steep!) journey in the company of guileless Mountie

Skull Island: Reign of Kong

Popeye and Bluto's Bilge-Rat Barges

© Universal Orlando Resort

Dudley Do-Right, bidding to save girlfriend Nell from the evil Snidely Whiplash. The action builds to an explosive finale at the top of a 75ft/27m abyss that drops you through the roof of a ramshackle dynamite shack to the lagoon below. Wet? You bet! **R**: 3ft 8in/111cm. **TTTTT** More Water Blasters on the bridge overlooking the final drop get riders even wetter.

Me Ship, The Olive: A kids' playland designed as a three-storey boat full of interactive fun, including water cannons, bells and slides (ideal for squirting riders on the Bilge-Rat Barges below), in best Popeye style. **TTTT** (for youngsters).

Other entertainment: Comic Strip Lane is the place to meet the Classic Comic Book Characters like Beetle Bailey, Hagar the Horrible, Betty Boop, Popeye and Dudley Do-Right. Plus various **fairground stall games** for $6, or $25 for five.

Shopping: There is the usual array of character shops, like **Gasoline Alley**, **Betty Boop Store** and **Toon Extra.**

Dining: Grab a humongous sandwich at **Blondie's** (home of the Dagwood), a trademark burger at **Wimpy's**, sample the food court of **Comic Strip Café** (burgers, fish, chicken, Chinese dishes, pizza and pasta), or pick up something cool at **Cathy's Ice Cream**.

Marvel Super-Hero Island

Finally, you arrive at total immersion in super-hero comic-book pages, with some of the best rides in the park.

The Incredible Hulk Coaster: Roller-coasters don't come much more dramatic than this giant green edifice that soars over the lagoon, blasting 0–40mph/64kph in 2secs, and reaching a top speed of 65mph/105kph. It looks awesome, sounds stunning and rides like a demon as you enter the gamma-ray world of Dr David Banner, aka the Incredible Hulk, and zoom into a weightless inversion 100ft/30m up.

BRITTIP

At the Hulk Coaster, keep left where the queue splits up and you will be in line for the front car for an even more extreme Hulk experience.

Just watching is mind-boggling, and the effects are brain-scrambling! Deposit ANY loose articles in the lockers at the front of the building as the ride is guaranteed to shake anything out of your pockets. Crowds build up rapidly but queues move reasonably quickly. **R**: 4ft 6in/137cm. Ride photos are available from $20–35, and also on My Universal Photos.

The Amazing Adventures of Spider Man

© Universal Orlando Resort

ISLANDS OF ADVENTURE with children

Our guide to the attractions that generally appeal to the different age groups:

Under-5s
Caro-Seuss-el, The Cat in the Hat, High In The Sky Seuss Trolley Train Ride, If I Ran The Zoo, Jurassic Park Discovery Center, Me Ship, The Olive, One Fish, Two Fish, Red Fish, Blue Fish.

5–8s
All the above, plus Amazing Adventures Of Spider-Man, Camp Jurassic, Eighth Voyage of Sindbad, Flight of the Hippogriff, Harry Potter and the Forbidden Journey (if tall enough), Hogwarts Express, Jurassic Park River Adventure (with parental discretion), Pteranodon Flyers, Storm Force Accelatron.

9–12s
Amazing Adventures Of Spider-Man, Camp Jurassic, The Cat in the Hat, Dr Doom's Fearfall, Dudley Do-Right's Ripsaw Falls, Eighth Voyage Of Sindbad, Flight of the Hippogriff, Harry Potter and the Forbidden Journey, Hogwarts Express, Hagrid's Magical Creatures Motorbike Adventure, Incredible Hulk Coaster, Jurassic Park Discovery Center, Jurassic Park River Adventure, Popeye and Bluto's Bilge-Rat Barges, Pteranodon Flyers, Skull Island: Reign of Kong (with parental discretion), Storm Force Accelatron.

Over-12s
Amazing Adventures Of Spider-Man, Dr Doom's Fearfall, Dudley Do-Right's Ripsaw Falls, Eighth Voyage Of Sindbad, Harry Potter and the Forbidden Journey, Hogwarts Express, Hagrid's Magical Creatures Motorbike Adventure, Incredible Hulk Coaster, Jurassic Park Discovery Center, Jurassic Park River Adventure, Popeye and Bluto's Bilge-Rat Barges, Skull Island: Reign of Kong, Storm Force Accelatron.

Dr Doom's Fearfall: Dr Doom's latest creation is a device for sucking fear out of his victims, and YOU are about to test it, strapped into chairs at the bottom of a 200ft/60m tower. The dry ice rolls, and whoosh! Up you go at breakneck speed, only to plummet back seemingly even faster, with a split second when you feel suspended in mid-air. Summon up the courage to do this and we promise an astonishing (if brief!) experience. R: 4ft 4in/132cm. TTTTT+

The Amazing Adventures Of Spider-Man: A visit to the Daily Bugle, home of ace reporter Peter Parker (aka Spider-Man) turns into a mission in a 'Scoop' vehicle – and an audio-visual extravaganza. This roving 3-D motion simulator takes you into a battle with super-villains that includes a convincing 'drop' off a skyscraper. There are special effects aplenty and the whole ride is loaded with the 'wow' factor. Go early on or wait until late in the day – queues often top an hour by mid-morning. R: 3ft 4in/101cm. TTTTT+ PS: If this seems similar to the TRANSFORMERS ride at Universal Studios, it's because they use the same ride platform.

BRITTIP

You can beat some of the queues on the Spider-Man ride at busy times by opting for the Single Rider queue.

Storm Force Accelatron: This ride, primarily for kids, puts you in the middle of a battle between X-Men heroine Storm and arch-nemesis Magneto. It's basically an updated spinning-cup ride but with some neat twists (like a 3-way rotation where the cars look set to collide). **TTT** (**TTTTT** under-12s).

BRITTIP

For some of the park's best shopping bargains, visit Port Provisions right by the exit gates (to the left as you come through) where all the merchandise is 30–50% off.

Other entertainment: The **Marvel Super-Heroes** appear here periodically for photos and autographs, while **Spider-Man** has his own meet-and-greet booth at The Marvel Alterniverse Store. A high energy **video arcade** can be found at the exit to Dr Doom's Fearfall.

Shopping: Each ride has its own character merchandise, while the **Comic Book Shop** and **Marvel Alterniverse Shop** sell other souvenirs.

Dining: For a bite to eat, try the Italian buffeteria **Café 4** (pizza, pasta, sandwiches and salads) or a burger, chicken fingers or salad at the **Captain America Diner**. Want the full Super-hero experience? Try the **Marvel Character Dinner** at Café 4 (5pm Thurs–Sun) with each of Captain America, Spider-Man, Storm, Cyclops, Rogue and Wolverine. The Super Six are surprise guests at this special celebration meal and provide great character interaction, as well as photo opportunities ($50 for adults, $25 for 3–9s).

And that, folks, is the full low-down on a truly immersive and exciting theme park. Miss it at your peril!

The Incredible Hulk Coaster

© Universal Orlando Resort

SEAWORLD

SeaWorld is firmly established as one of the most popular parks for its more peaceful and naturalistic aspect, the change of pace it offers and lack of substantial queues. It is large enough to handle big crowds well (though it still gets busy in peak season) and is a big hit with families in particular, but it has some fabulous rides and imaginative attractions too, including Antarctica: Empire of the Penguin, Turtle Trek, three superb coasters, the Infinity Falls raft ride and Sesame Street area for younger children.

Part of SeaWorld Parks & Entertainment with Discovery Cove, water-park Aquatica and Busch Gardens in Tampa, this makes for excellent multi-day adventures, notably with the UK Discovery Cove Ultimate Package, which includes all four. SeaWorld's recent additions and brilliant Christmas overlay (p37) ensure this remains an exciting and meaningful place to visit. SeaWorld is a good starting point if this is your first Orlando visit as it gives you the hang of negotiating the vast areas, navigating by maps and learning to plan around the show times. There are special offers for booking online at **seaworld.com**, where you can print your tickets to save waiting in the queue, plus a website for UK visitors – **seaworldparks.co.uk**

SeaWorld at a glance

Location	7007 SeaWorld Drive, off Central Florida Parkway (Junctions 71 and 72 off I-4)		
Size	More than 200 acres/81ha, incorporating 26 attractions		
Hours	9am–6pm off peak; 9am–7, 8 or 9pm some weekends; 9am–9pm high season (Easter, summer holidays, Thanksgiving, Christmas)		
Admission	Under-3s free; ages 3 and up $105 (1-day ticket), $150 (2-Park ticket, with 2nd day at SeaWorld, Aquatica or Busch Gardens), 14 days with UK Discovery Cove tickets, from £131, pricing seasonal		
Parking	$25, $35 preferred parking		
Lockers	Inside Entrance Plaza (next to the Emporium shop), $15–25		
Pushchairs	$25, to right of Guest Services		
Wheelchairs	$12 manual, $60 electric, $65 ECV with canopy; with pushchairs		
Top attractions	TurtleTrek, Antarctica: Empire Of The Penguin, Infinity Falls, One Ocean, Shark Encounter, Journey To Atlantis, Kraken, Manta, Wild Arctic, Mako, Dolphin Days		
Don't miss	Manatee Rehabilitation, behind-the-scenes tours, Dolphin Nursery, dining at Sharks Underwater Grill, Sesame Street land (with kids)		
Hidden costs	Meals	Burger, chips and coke $15.98 3-course lunch $40–61 (Sharks Underwater Grill) Kids' meal $7.50–10, $13 at Sharks Underwater Grill	
	T-shirts	$21.95–31.95 Kids, $12–21.95	
	Souvenirs	$0.99–4,900	
	Sundries	Face paint $12.49–18.49	

Port of Entry
1   Entrance plaza
2   Dolphin Nursery

Sea of Shallows
3   Stingray Lagoon
4   Flamingo Cove
5   Dolphin Cove
6   Dolphin Theater
7   Dolphin Underwater Viewing
8   Turtle Trek and Manatee Rehabilitation
9   Manta

Sea of Legends
10 Journey To Atlantis
11 Kraken

Sea of Ice
12 Antarctica: Empire of the Penguin

Sea of Delight
13 Pacific Point Preserve
14 Sea Lion and Otter Stadium
15 The Waterfront

16 Seaport Theater
17 Seafire Grill & Flamecraft Bar
18 Sky Tower
19 Voyager's Smokehouse

Sea of Mystery
20 Shark Encounter
21 Nautilus Theater
22 Mako
23 Sharks Underwater Grill
24 Infinity Falls
25 Mama's Pretzel Kitchen

Sesame Street at SeaWorld
26 Sesame Street Party Parade

Sea of Power
27 Shamu Stadium
28 Wild Arctic
29 Ice Breaker
30 Bayside Stadium

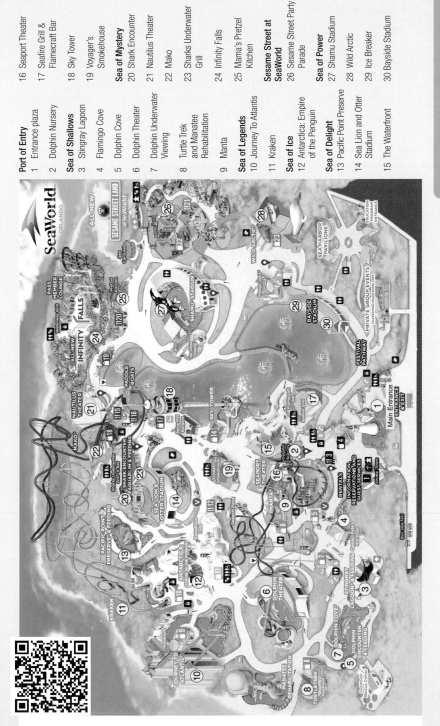

Tours

Private VIP Tour: 4, 6, or 8hr tours for your family or group, with individual guide, front-of-the-queue ride access and reserved seats for one, two or three main shows, preferred parking, animal interactions and lunch or All Day Dining ($200–400/person; perks and price according to duration).

BRITTIP

The variety of behind-the-scenes tours provide great insight into the park's conservation and research programmes, as well as its entertainment resources. Book in advance: online, call 407 545 5550 or visit the Guided Tours counter.

Dolphins Up-Close Tour: Meet the park's resident dolphins during this 30min hands-on tour, and learn the hand signals trainers use to communicate with the dolphins ($45/person).

Sharks Up-Close Tour: A chance to go backstage at the 700,000-gallon aquarium and learn how SeaWorld cares for its sharks. Visitors will also touch a small shark and hear about vital conservation issues ($20/person).

Sea Lions Up-Close Tour: A 1hr walking tour focusing on the care and training of the stars of the Clyde & Seamore show, including a photo with them and a chance to feed the Pacific Point Preserve sea lions ($40/person).

Penguins Up-Close Tour: This 45min family walk goes behind the scenes at Antarctica: Empire of the Penguin to learn the proper care for these cute birds and gives visitors the chance to interact with and touch a penguin ($70/person).

Behind The Scenes Tour: Join a knowledgeable tour guide for a 1hr look backstage at the Shark Encounter and Avian Research Center, as well as touch a shark and interact and have a photo taken with a penguin ($35/person).

Also: the **Killer Whale** ($115/person), **Beluga** ($40/person) and **Walrus Up-Close Tours** ($30/person) add more backstage discoveries of these wonderful animals.

The entrance to SeaWorld

Location

SeaWorld is located off Central Florida Parkway, between I-4 (exit 71 going east or 72 heading west) and International Drive. It is still best to arrive before the opening time so you're in good position to book a backstage tour, dash to one of the attractions that draws a crowd, like Mako, Manta and Antarctica, or buy QuickQueue, the park's limited number of paid-for passes that provide front-of-the-line access to each of the main rides (priced seasonally at $20–35). There is also a Signature Show Seating option at $15–30/person.

The park covers more than 200acres/81ha, with four shows, seven major rides, 12 large-scale continuous viewing attractions and several smaller ones, plus a smart range of shops and restaurants. Try to eat before midday or after 2.30pm for a crowd-free lunch, and before 5.30pm if you want a leisurely dinner (better still, book Sharks Underwater Grill).

SeaWorld is arranged in various 'seas' on the park map but they are hard to follow, hence you will need to keep the map close to hand to navigate, as there is also a fair bit of to-ing and fro-ing to catch all of the shows, with the show schedule listed on the back of the map. Going in a clockwise direction, here's what you find.

Port of Entry

Coming through the main entrance brings you to the park's functional area, including the Information & Reservations counter, Lost & Found, and lockers, pushchair and wheelchair hire. You will also find some good shopping and snack options here. Look for the **Emporium** for the full range of souvenirs; **Sea World Rescue** for gifts and clothing; and **Adventure Photos** for all park pictures taken by SeaWorld photographers. Grab a quick breakfast (pastries and coffee) at **Starbuck's Coffee & Bakery** or something colder from the **Ice Cream Shop**. This is also the place for a photo opportunity with a cuddly Shamu.

All Day Dining Deal: Also worth considering, a wristband gives unlimited visits to nine restaurants (including Spice Mill, Voyager's, Seaport Pizza and Seafire Grill), claiming an entrée, side dish or dessert and standard non-alcoholic drink each time (once per hour; seasonal pricing starts at $40 adults, $20 ages 3¬9). It's good value if you eat at least twice in the park and can be booked at the Information & Reservations desk.

Photokey: If you'd like to collect all your SeaWorld photos digitally, including ride photos and character meet-and-greets (but not backstage tours), sign up for this service, online or when you arrive at the park, for $70 at **bit.ly/brit-seaphotos**.

Dolphin Days

Aquarium at Manta

Other entertainment: The **Dolphin Nursery** provides wonderful close-ups of the park's younger dolphins, with different levels for viewing mothers and their babies, as well as digital displays that offer key conservation info.

Sea of Shallows

A whole collection of exhibits is grouped together here, as well as the eye-catching Dolphin Theater and one of the signature rides.

There is a clever Key West theme, starting with **Stingray Lagoon**, where you can feed ($6 per tray, 3 trays for $13) and touch fully grown rays, and there's a nursery for newborns. The centrepiece is the 2.1acre/0.8ha **Dolphin Cove**, a spectacular, naturalistic development that hosts a frisky community of Atlantic bottlenose dolphins, who make for great viewing, including from a special underwater window. The Key West area is designed

Manta

in the eclectic, tropical flavour of America's most southerly city, but it also underlines the environmental message through interactive graphics and video displays to make it a fun educational experience. AAA

Dolphin Days: This 'edutainment' spectacular features the park's bottlenose dolphins in an informative and fun pageant of fascinating natural behaviours. Learn about their relationships with their trainers, discover how strong bonds are formed, and delve into the importance of protecting these magnificent animals in the wild. Key themes of conservation are delivered in inspirational style – with a splash of colour when a flock of macaws joins the fun! The show features plenty of breaching and splashing (heed the Splash Zone warning, especially with cameras or phones!), and one lucky guest is invited to interact with a cheeky dolphin by using hand signals. AAAA

Manta: This turns a coaster into a unique mixture of ride and animal encounter. The elaborate queuing area winds through rocky caverns, passing waterfalls and floor-to-ceiling windows showcasing some 300 rays and thousands of fish, which lead to the 'undersea world' of the manta ray. Themed like a giant ray, riders are swung face-down before being launched into an exhilarating series of four inversions, reaching nearly 60mph/96kph and 140ft/43m high as well as skimming the surface of the lagoon. The 'flying' nature of the coaster and smooth ride make

this an original with great spectator appeal. There is a separate walk-though aquarium with its own entry while lockers next to the queue entry can be used during your ride ($2/2hrs). **R**: 54in/137cm. **TTTTT**. For the most powerful effects of the G-forces, opt for the back rows.

TurtleTrek: Right behind Dolphin Theater is this thrilling part exhibit and part show that introduces you to the undersea world of the sea turtle and marine conservation. A host introduces the story and doors open to reveal a domed cinema where you don 3-D glasses. Suddenly, you are in the world of the sea turtle, sharing the dangerous journey from beach to open ocean and back again, in an immersive 3-D environment with graphic encounters with a marauding crab and sharks. You exit to two open-air pools (the top of the lagoons you see below) where you learn more about sea turtle life and see them and manatees being fed. There is also a video game for kids, plus an exhibit showcasing Florida alligators. AAAAA NB: The menace of the crab in the early scene may be scary for young children.

Manatee Rehabilitation: Learn all about the fabulous work SeaWorld and their small army of volunteers does in rescuing and rehabbing endangered manatees, with information boards and animal keepers on hand. Well worth making time for. AAA

Shopping: There are three main gift shops here, the best being **Coconut Bay Traders** and **Trek Treasures**

Turtle Trek

(apparel and soft toys), as well as **Manta Photo & Gifts**.

Dining: You can grab a hot dog, chili dog or fries at **Captain Pete's Hot Dogs** or ice cream at **Dippin' Dots**, plus drinks, snacks and refills and several cart-style kiosks.

BRITTIP

For a great soft drink deal, buy any souvenir cup for $14.99 ($12.99 for 2, $10.99 for 3) and get $.99 refills all day.

Sea of Legends

Continue past Dolphin Theater and you come to the park's serious thrill quotient.

Journey to Atlantis: This terrific water-coaster is a combination of special effects and water-ride that becomes a runaway roller-coaster. The discovery of Atlantis in your eight-passenger 'fishing boat' starts gently through the lost city. But evil spirit Allura takes over and riders plunge into a dash through Atlantis, dodging gushing fountains and water cannons before a 60ft/18m drop and entry to the roller-coaster finale back in the candle-filled catacombs. Be ready to get soaked, which is fine in summer but not so clever on a winter morning. **R**: 3ft5in/106cm. **TTTTT**

Kraken: One of Florida's most breathtaking coasters, based on the mythical sea monster, this is an innovative ride that plunges an initial

Journey to Atlantis

Antarctica: Empire of the Penguin

144ft/44m at 65mph/105kph, diving underground, adding seven brain-scrambling inversions and a flat spin before riders escape the beast's lair. It's not for the faint of heart, but it is a mega-thrill of the highest order. **R**: 4ft 5in/137cm. **TTTTT+**

Shopping: Don't miss **Golden Seahorse Gifts** as you exit Journey to Atlantis, a combination gift shop and aquarium full of tropical fish (remember to look up), while there are coaster-orientated souvenirs in **Kraken Gifts**.

Dining: High Seas Market offers convenient grab-and-go snacks and drinks, and there is a **Dippin' Dots** for ice cream.

Sea of Ice

Getting back to the animal side of the park brings you to one of the most eye-catching sections. Both an extensive, themed area in its own right and an amazing ride, it features an epic journey into the snow and ice-covered realm of the South Pole.

Antarctica: Empire of the Penguin: Once you walk between the towering snow-capped 'mountains,' the ride awaits, starting with a dramatic presentation about penguin life and taking visitors on a unique expedition into the heart of the continent, following the story of young Gentoo

penguin, Puck. Guests board special vehicles and choose their level of ride experience, either 'Mild' or 'Wild', and set off through a mix of simulation and film elements that offer a stylistic taste of the polar region, moving seemingly at random and with no obvious track. The dangers – including a typical storm – and beauty of life in this realm are graphically depicted as you track Puck's journey through the world's most extreme landscape before you arrive in a real penguin colony to experience more of their 'empire.' And it is cold; like, *really* cold (the temperature drops to an icy -1C by ride's end) and you may want to visit the gift shop for a scarf or gloves before you set off! The Wild version is quite fast-paced, with various bumps, slides and spins, while 'Mild' is designed for all the family, with no height restriction. **R**: under 3ft 5in/106cm must be accompanied by an adult. **AAAAA+** This can also draw long queues by mid-day.

BRITTIP

Take a look at the main 'mountain' in Antarctica. Does the shape look familiar? Yes, that's right – the whole edifice has been shaped like a towering mother penguin on the left, with her baby to the right.

Other entertainment: After the ride, there is a spectacular **underwater viewing area** where you can see the different species of penguin – Rockhopper, King, Adelie and Gentoo – at play. Back out in Antarctica you can marvel at this realistic environment, which includes a **Penguin Wall** for photo opportunities, and flatscreen TVs for more info about the region.

Shopping: Lone gift shop **Glacial Collections** has a huge selection of all things penguin-orientated and cuddly.

Dining: Expedition Café provides Italian, Asian and American food choices from their show kitchen which you can then enjoy in one of two clever 'Quonset Huts' that provide a South Pole setting.

> ────── BRITTIP 🇬🇧
> Be sure to see Antarctica at night as the brilliant blue lighting makes the setting even more impressive.

Sea of Delight

This extensive area features two more live shows plus some of the park's best dining and shopping.

Sea Lion and Otter Theater: The venue for another live show, this features the resident pinnipeds in *Clyde* and *Seamore's Sea Lion High*, and offers 25mins of slapstick and watery stunts, with guest appearances by Opie Otter and Sir Winston Walrus. The basic premise is that Clyde and Seamore are in danger of flunking their high school exams and need help to get the necessary grades, which is the cue for all manner of school-type jokes and amazing antics from the animals (often at the expense of their human assistants!). The best part, though, may be the pre-show fun with the resident Pirate Mimes, who provide all manner of interactive antics with arriving guests – not to be missed! AAAA

Pacific Point Preserve: A natural rocky habitat for the park's seals and sea lions with a hidden wave machine and lively talks from park attendants. You can also buy smelt ($6 per tray or three trays for $13) to feed the animals. AAA

Pets Ahoy!: Just inside the Waterfront is the air-conditioned haven of the Seaport Theater, which hosts this cute

Glacial Collections

25min giggle featuring an unlikely menagerie of dogs, cats, birds, rats, pot-bellied pigs and others, most from local animal rescue shelters. AAA. The Theater is also home to the seasonal show *Elmo's Christmas Wish*, when the Sesame Street characters help Elmo discover his Christmas wish.

Sky Tower: This 400ft/122m landmark offers slowly rotating rides for a bird's-eye view of the park for $5/person (closed when windy). AAA

Other entertainment: Look out for the zany antics of **The Longshoremen** periodically, as the hapless trio try their hand at various maintenance tasks.

Shopping: The linked series of **Waterfront** shops offer an extensive shopping plaza with a stylish range of souvenirs and other gift items, while the **Guy Harvey** shop features unique branded art and clothing from the eminent artist and conservationist, whose giant mural adorns the wall next to Mako. **Oyster's Secret** features the chance to select and open a real oyster and discover the pearl inside.

Dining: The excellent eateries are: **Seafire Grill** (chicken tenders, salads and wraps); **Voyagers Smokehouse** BBQ (smoked chicken, barbecue ribs, salads and a children's menu with chicken nuggets, hot dog, macaroni and cheese, chicken nuggets or junior portion of ribs); and **Spice Mill** (flame-grilled burgers, salads, sandwiches and a vegetarian 'Impossible' burger), plus **Seaport Pizza** with four varieties of pizza. There are also three snack bars: **Café de Mar** for pastries, coffees,

smoothies and soft drinks; and **Turkey Legs** for huge smoked turkey legs. The **Flamecraft Bar** is a water's edge hideaway, serving beer, wine and snacks – THE place to watch the sun go down each evening (15 craft beers at $9.99 for 20oz or $14.99 for a flight of six 7oz samples).

Sea of Mystery

Continuing the clockwise tour brings you towards the back of the park and this newly re-themed 'underwater' area with the showpiece, must-do Mako ride.

Shark Encounter: Top of the bill, the world's largest collection of dangerous sea creatures can be found here, brought dramatically to life by the walk-through tubes that surround you with more than 50 prowling sharks (including sand tigers, black tips, nurse sharks and sandbars), sawfish, tropical fish and gigantic groupers. It's an eerie experience, but brilliantly presented and highly informative. AAAA TTTT

BRITTIP

Busch Gardens' Twisted Tails Pretzels has proved so popular in that park that SeaWorld has copied the formula here, including the must-sample Bacon Pretzel Twist, at *Mama's Pretzel Kitchen*.

Nautilus Theater: This is home to weekend and special events throughout the year, notably Jack Hanna's Animal Adventure. Watch out for the latest information.

Sea Lion and Otter Theater

Mako: SeaWorld's dramatic steel rollercoaster – the tallest and fastest in Orlando – rises up between the Shark Encounter and Nautilus Theater, giving the park another iconic ride for its growing collection. It reaches 200ft high and 73mph and is named and themed for the world's fastest shark, hence it's sure to give adrenalin junkies a real blast. Although there are no inversions, its big initial drop, tight twists and turns, fast pace and multiple 'air time' moments provide plenty of thrills, including a breathtaking U-shaped 'Hammerhead' turn and several camelbacks. **TTTTT R**: 54in/137cm.

BRITTIP

Throughout the summer, SeaWorld offers a FREE beer (one 14oz pour per person, per day) at the Patio Bar next to Mama's Pretzel Kitchen, plus buy-one-get-one-free Happy Hour weekdays from 4pm to closing time at Flamecraft Bar, Sharks Underwater Grill Bar and Waterway Grill Bar.

Infinity Falls: The river raft ride will never be the same again after you experience this expedition-style adventure through Class IV rapids with a SERIOUS final splashdown! Your journey passes a flock of flamingos before reaching the tightly-winding rapids and a huge waterfall, where an outrageous vertical lift hints at what's to come. But there's no preparing for the final splashdown as your 8-person raft plunges 40ft/13m into a turmoil of white-water. Expect a good soaking! **AAAA/TTTTT** R: 3ft 5in/107cm. There are interactive touch-screen games at the front of Infinity Falls that teach about the rainforest and encourage conservation.

BRITTIP

If the day is cool but you still want to ride Infinity Falls, watch for the family-sized drying stations near the attraction. For a small fee, you can dry off quickly.

Other entertainment: The **flamingo pedal-boats** on the lagoon rent for $6 per 20min (for two). You can also feed the sharks and stingrays outside **Shark Encounter** ($6 per tray, $13 three trays).

Shopping: Check out **Fins Gifts** for toys, apparel and jewellery and **Reef's Treasures** for Mako souvenirs and all things shark-like, while **The Village Store** has all manner of Infinity Fall souvenirs to complete your journey – and future expeditions – in style.

Dining: At the entrance to Shark Encounter is top dining choice, **Sharks Underwater Grill**, with an amazing backdrop for your meal in a subterranean environment (check out the mini-aquarium bar), and a menu blending local and spicy Caribbean fare. The emphasis is on seafood, plus pasta, steaks and chicken, as well as fab desserts, cocktails (including non-alcoholic) and a kids' menu. Open from 11.30am to an hour before park closing, it's busy at lunch but quieter in late afternoon, so we advise booking (at the restaurant) as soon as you arrive. The **Panini Shore Café** (high season only) offers fresh-grilled panini sandwiches, salads and drinks. Grab a drink and an ice cream treat at **Soft Serve & Starbucks Coffee**, while you should try **Mama's Pretzel Kitchen** for freshly baked pretzels with a variety of dipping sauces. At Infinity Falls, **Waterway Grill** is a commissary-style restaurant serving succulent barbecue meals, salads, sandwiches and other family favourites, as well as a tempting selection of domestic and craft beers.

Infinity Falls

Sesame Street at SeaWorld

This section is primarily for kids, with a fabulous children's play area, water splash-pad, junior-sized rides, food trucks and meet-and-greets.

Sesame Street: Themed to the popular children's television programme, this is a nostalgic step back in time for parents and a chance to visit the most famous TV street for youngsters. Children can visit Mr Hooper's store, enjoy story time with Big Bird and meet their favourite characters at **Photos with Elmo and Friends**. It's all cleverly designed as an interactive 'community', with a playground and 11 hands-on stations where kids can ring Bert and Ernie's doorbell, transform their voice into a monster voice, peek into Elmo's window to watch him dance and sing, and more. Six rides purely for the 2–5 age group are also sprinkled through the land.

Abby's Flower Tower: A fairground-style ride that raises riders to the top for a spin around the tower in cute flowerpots. R: 3ft 5in/107cm. **Cookie Drop!:** Bounce up, then down again on this pre-schooler friendly samba tower themed to Cookie Monster. R: 3ft 5in/107cm. **Elmo's Choo-Choo Train**: This classic train ride offers a gentle trundle through a garden setting. Watch for cleverly-placed bugs, including Elmo's friends the Twiddlebugs, hiding in the landscaping. R: 3ft/92cm **Super Grover's Box Car Derby**: Bigger thrills are found on this junior-sized coaster, a good introduction for youngsters with enough zip to be enjoyable for adults. R: 3ft 1in/97cm. **Big Bird's Twirl 'N' Whirl**: Hop into Big Bird's nest for a dizzying spin in this tea-cup style attraction. R: 3ft/92cm. **Slimey's Slider**: Big thrills for young 'uns can be found on this dynamic ride that rocks, spins and slides through Oscar's compost collection. R: 3ft 5in/107cm. **Rubber Ducky Water Works**: Kids can cool off in this delightful water-playground splash area with pop jets, fountains and water wheels. Ideal for spontaneous play on a hot day!

Other entertainment: The superb **Sesame Street Party Parade** takes place here each day, with Elmo and friends leading a series of colourful floats. Children are encouraged to join in during stops in the parade when the characters lead youngsters in singing, dancing and child-friendly games. Watch for **character meet-and-greets** that pop up periodically along Sesame Street.

Shopping: Pick up Sesame Street gifts and apparel at **Hooper's Store**.

Dining: Enjoy a meal or snack at **ABC Eats** (3 varieties of chicken tenders, fries, cookies and drinks) or **Yummy Yummy Nom Noms** (Hawaiian, Italian, Turkey or Veggie grilled cheese sandwich platters, and grilled cheese kids meals, $9.99). **Sesame Sips** drinks stand carries 4 yummy smoothies (pineapple, strawberry, blueberry and raspberry) plus string cheese, salads, fruit and cookies.

Sesame Street at SeaWorld

Sea of Power

The final main area of the park features the iconic Shamu Stadium, plus another engaging ride/animal attraction, and the high-season fireworks finale.

BRITTIP
The first 14 rows at Shamu Stadium get VERY wet (watch out for your cameras). When a killer whale leaps into the air in front of you, it displaces a LOT of water on landing. In fact, the Splash Zones should be renamed Soak Zones!

Shamu Stadium: 'What can one person do?' That is the message One Ocean brings to SeaWorld in a spectacular show filled with brilliant splashes of colour – especially of the black and white variety! In the past, the whales' relationship with their trainers was the main focus, and while that bond remains strong, the heart of One Ocean lies with the relationship between the whales themselves. Behaviours common to whales in the wild combine with learned behaviours in a celebration of joyful play, reminding us we are all connected and, when we pull together, we can do amazing things. And if the biggest thrills in past Shamu shows came from seeing these magnificent animals jump, spin, and cover the Splash Zone in a wall of water, you're in for a real treat! Even better, the charming Side By Side scene features the connection between mother and baby, so have those cameras ready. Shamu Stadium is extremely popular, so try to take in an early show. And, if you think it looks good during the day, return in the evening (in high season) for an even more dramatic, music-orientated presentation under the lights, **Shamu's Celebration: Light Up The Night**. AAAAA+

BRITTIP
Be sure to arrive early for One Ocean, especially if you have a smart-phone. You may get a sneak peek behind the scenes during the pre-show!

All guests can then enjoy the **Shamu Underwater Viewing area**.

Wild Arctic: This interactive ride-and-view is an exciting simulator jet helicopter journey into the white wilderness, where passengers see seals, beluga whales and walruses. This one is not to be missed (but avoid just after One Ocean when the hordes descend). **R:** 3ft 6in/106cm. **TTTT** AAAAA. Those who don't want to do the (dynamic) ride can just walk to the Base Station.

Bayside Stadium: The final element is this large outdoor arena facing the central Lagoon. It's home to various seasonal entertainments, including the Seven Seas Food Festival concerts and an ice-skating show at Christmas.

BRITTIP
Any purchases can be sent to Package Pick-up in The Emporium to collect on your way out, if you give at least an hour's notice.

Up Close Dining: Get a close-up view of SeaWorld's rescued pilot and killer whales as you learn how the animal care specialists establish a special relationship at this fascinating and informative dining experience ($29–37 adult seasonally, $15 children). Buffet includes chicken, pork loin, roast beef, salmon, salads, sides, desserts and drinks (kids' choices are chicken nuggets, hot dogs and penne pasta with marinara). Book online or on 407 545 5500.

New roller coaster Ice Breaker will go into this area in 2020, occupying the footprint that formerly housed Mango Joe's Burgers and the landscaped area along the lagoon. With its high-speed launch, massive drop, inversions and extended ground-level track with a long banked turn, it will be a thrilling addition to SeaWorld's current line-up. Riders will have a magnificent view of the lagoon – if they can keep their eyes open! **R:** 4ft/120cm (expected); **TTTTT** (expected)

Shopping: Wild Arctic Gifts has a wide range of items, plus a year-round Christmas-themed section.

BRITTIP
Learn more about SeaWorld's conservation and environmental efforts at scaworld.org.

SEAWORLD with children

The following gives a general idea of the appeal of the attractions to the different age groups:

Under-5s
Antarctica: Empire of the Penguin, Clyde and Seamore's Sea Lion High, Dolphin Cove, Dolphin Days, One Ocean, Pacific Point Preserve, Pets Ahoy!, Sesame Street, Wild Arctic (without the ride).

5–8s
All the above, plus Infinity Falls, Shark Encounter, Turtle Trek, Wild Arctic (with the ride).

9–12s
All the above (with the exception of Sesame Street), plus Journey to Atlantis, Kraken, Manta and Mako.

Over-12s
Antarctica: Empire of the Penguin, Clyde And Seamore's Sea Lion High, Dolphin Days, Infinity Falls, Journey To Atlantis, Kraken, Mako, Manta, One Ocean, Shark Encounter, Turtle Trek, Wild Arctic.

Summer extras

During the summer (weekends and some week-days late May to Sep 1), SeaWorld has extended hours to 9.30pm and offers live entertainment as part of its **Electric Ocean** programme. The party atmosphere is generated by live DJs and other entertainers and features extra shows, notably **Sea Lions Tonight** (a parody of the day-time shows) and **Shamu's Celebration: Light up The Night**, which adds a more high-energy version of the main show. Dolphin Stadium adds party-style **Touch The Sky** show, while **Club Sea Glow** features a fun dance party, with more performers, sea-characters and dancing fountains. Finally, the big finale, **Ignite**, lights up the lagoon with a dazzling array of lasers, fireworks and other special effects, all set to a memorable soundtrack. It makes for the best summer show in town, so don't miss it! For the park's fab **Christmas Celebration** (late Nov–31 Dec each year) see p37.

And there's more

Other seasonal events (all FREE with park admission) include the superb **Seven Seas Food Festival**, each weekend from mid-Feb through to mid-May, featuring samplings of 60 international street foods, 55 craft brews and 13 wine offerings ($3.75–$6.50/sample; sampling lanyards $30/5 samples, $50/10, $65/20), plus unique cocktails at multiple kiosks around the park, along with free live concerts; and the ultra child-friendly **Halloween Spooktacular**, when there are fun activities for kids of all ages, including trick-or-treating, Penelope's Party Zone, sweet treat decorating and strolling entertainers (weekends from late Sept–Oct).

Killer Whales Up-Close

DISCOVERY COVE

Fancy a day in a tropical paradise, swimming with dolphins, eyeballing sharks, snorkelling in a coral reef and diving through a waterfall into a tropical aviary? Discovery Cove is all that, and more. The only drawback is the price. This park comes at a premium because it admits just 1,300 guests a day, creating an exclusive experience that's reflected in the price. The weather can get distinctly cool in winter, but the water is always heated (apart from the dolphin lagoon, which remains at 72°F/22°C) and full wetsuits are available to keep out the chill. The attention to detail is superb, guest ratings are extremely high and it is hugely popular with British visitors. Discovery Cove is also a Certified Autism Center.

The costs

Ticket pricing varies ($199–380 for Resort & Dolphin Swim; plus $21 for 14 days at SeaWorld & Aquatica; plus $46 for Busch Gardens, too), making UK Ultimate tickets good value (£153–301 for all four parks, plus free parking). Under 3s are free but 3–5s must pay the Day Resort price ($149–250). So, what do you get for your money? Well, it's a supremely personal park. You check in at the beautiful entrance lobby as you would for a hotel rather than a theme park. All your basic requirements – towel, mask, snorkel, wet-jacket, lockers, beach umbrellas, animal-safe suncream, food and drink – are included, and the level of service is excellent. Then there is a full breakfast, snacks, beverages (including beer and cocktails) and an excellent lunch at the Laguna Grill. But gift shop and photo prices reflect the entry fee – expensive. It is also an extra $199–429 (priced seasonally) to hire one of their swanky cabañas for the day (which include tables, chairs, loungers, towels and a fridge stocked with soft drinks, and must be booked in advance).

Therefore, for all its style and dolphin appeal, Discovery Cove will take a BIG bite out of your holiday budget. A family of four, with children old enough to do the Dolphin Swim, could pay $1,520 in peak season. Even with a free SeaWorld and Aquatica pass, it's a big outlay. The charge for ages 3–5 is also pretty steep, in our opinion. Your sundries can add up, too. Photo packages are $99–$299. The Island Package (4 6x8 prints) is $99, Adventure Package (8 6x8 prints, 2 frames) is $169, and Discovery Package (8 6x8 prints, 2 photo frames, 1 All-Image digital Photo Key, 1 digital downloaded photo print) is $229. Poster-size photos (16x24 and 24x36)

Sea Venture

are $20 and $25, while a single 6x8 photo is $10.

However, despite the fees, the feedback we get is almost unfailingly positive and most people are captivated by the experience. One handy free perk, though, is the Horticulture Tour, twice a day, which takes guests through the care and maintenance of the park's tropical plant and tree life (sign up at Guest Relations).

BRITTIP

Try to pick up your Discovery Cove photos before 4pm or you might find everyone else trying to do the same!

Trainer for a Day: This programme is an exciting opportunity to go behind the scenes into the park's training, feeding and welfare. You get to work with the experts as they interact with dolphins, birds, sharks, stingrays and tropical fish, including a behavioural training class, the chance to experience two deep-water swims, a professional photo session, and a behind-the-scenes tour, all with the use of a waterproof camera (SIM card given to you at end of programme). Participants must be at least six and in good health, and it costs $399–510 (seasonally). For all Discovery Cove bookings, call 1 877 577 or visit **discoverycove.com**.

Location

Situated on Central Florida Parkway, almost opposite the SeaWorld entrance (open year-round 9am–5.30pm; parking free), the whole 30acre/12ha park is magnificently landscaped, with thatched buildings, palm trees, lush vegetation, white-sand beaches, gurgling streams – even hammocks to chill out in. The overall effect is of being transported to a relaxing tropical paradise away from the hurly-burly. The 5-star resort feel is enhanced by a high staff-to-guest ratio, there are no queues (though the restaurant may get busy at lunchtime), and the highlight Dolphin Encounter is world class. Visitors with disabilities are well catered for, with special wheelchairs that can move in sand and shallow water, and an area of the Dolphin Lagoon that allows those who can't enter the water to touch a dolphin.

The main attractions

Freshwater Oasis: This combination of animal environment, walking trails and pools offers the chance to get a close-up of the park's otters and marmosets in realistic, natural habitats. Children especially love watching the otters, and the way the animals are incorporated into the lush tropical scenery is a real gem of clever design. AAAA

Wind-away River: This 800yd/732m circuit of gently flowing bath-warm water is a variation on the lazy river feature of many of the water parks, though with a far more naturalistic aspect and none of the inner tubes. It is primarily designed for snorkellers and features rocky lagoons, caves, a beach section, a tropical forest segment and sunken ruins. The lack of fish makes it a bit bland after the Grand Reef, but it is as much about relaxing as having fun. It is up to 8ft/2.4m deep at points, so non-swimmers are advised to use a flotation vest. It finishes in the freeform Serenity Bay pool, which provides more idyllic relaxation. AAA

Explorer's Aviary: This three-part adventure is both an area in its own right and a 120ft/37m section of the Tropical River. You can walk in off the beach or swim in through the waterfall from Wind-away River, fun for snorkellers. Some 250 tropical

Swimming with the Dolphins

birds fill the main enclosure and, if you stand still, they are likely to use you as a perch. There is a small-bird sanctuary – full of finches, honeycreepers and hummingbirds – and a large-bird enclosure, featuring toucans and the red-legged seriema. Guides will introduce you to specific birds (which you can hand-feed) and tell you about their habitats and conservation issues. **AAAA**

Dolphin Swim: The headline attraction is the encounter with the park's Atlantic bottlenose dolphins. A 15min orientation programme in one of the beach cabañas, with a film and instruction from two trainers, sets you up for this thrilling experience. Groups of 6–8 go into the lagoon and, starting off standing in the waist-deep (slightly chilly) water as one of the dolphins comes over, and you gradually become more adventurous until you are swimming with them. Timid swimmers are well catered for and there are flotation vests for those who need them. The lagoon is up to 12ft/3.6m deep so there is a real feeling of being in the dolphins' environment. You learn how trainers use hand signals and positive reinforcement to communicate, and get the chance to stroke, feed and even kiss your

dolphin. The encounter concludes dramatically as you are towed ashore by one of these awesome animals (which weigh up to 600lb/272kg), though activities vary according to their attention span. You spend around 30mins in the water and it is unforgettable. Under-6s are not allowed in the lagoon. **TTTTT+**

The Grand Reef: This area features a massive artificial reef with 125 species, including fish, rays, eels, sharks, urchins and lionfish (the dangerous ones are behind glass!). Beaches, meandering pathways and bridges lead to shallow wading areas, waist-deep paddling pools and deep-water snorkelling, while underwater canyons and inviting grottos combine with coloured artificial coral reefs for a convincing experience. It's like paradise, only better! For extra relaxation, stake out a hammock on the central island or consider hiring one of eight private cabañas. There is a drinks kiosk here but no food outlets. **AAAAA**

> **BRITTIP**
>
> The Sea Venture area is not accessible to snorkellers during tours, but you can swim there when a tour is not running.

Swimming with Rays

Sea Venture: One of the most innovative features of the Grand Reef is this underwater walking tour. Equipped with special dive helmets, guests make a 20min trek along the bottom of the reef, passing sharks and lionfish and interacting with schools of fish and gentle rays. This is a totally immersive experience and a sensation like no other (how often can you explore underwater while standing up straight?). There are handrails throughout the journey, which takes groups of 4–9 at a time. Total tour time is 1hr, including preparation and underwater trek (for an extra $49–69 per person). Ages 10 and up only. **TTTT**

Discovery Cove 'extras'

This isn't a cheap day out, but the extra quality is everywhere. The Laguna Grill lunch is excellent and you can visit as often as you want, while a Calypso band adds to the tropical paradise feel. Conservation Cabaña allows guests to meet a neat selection of the park's small mammals (like an anteater and tree sloth); parking is free and you also receive an 8x6in/15x20cm welcome photo. While official opening time is 9am, they will check you in as early as 8am for the free breakfast.

Other extra elements are a 90min **Animal Trek** programme taking up to 12 guests behind the scenes, including a private aviary tour and the chance to meet one of the park's animal ambassadors for $79/person. Then there is **Ray Feeding**, a chance for an early-morning (7–8.45am) close-up of the park's rays with an Aquarist, including a chance to hand-feed these gentle creatures ($59/person). The **Shark Swim** offers a unique close-up with the other denizens of the Reef, including a shallow-water encounter and then a free swim among them ($109–169/person, seasonally). A **Premium Drink Package** upgrades your choice of beer, wine and spirits for $30pp. Discovery Cove also has a Celebration Package ($129–179) that includes tote bag, beach towel, souvenir buoy delivered by a dolphin and 20% off Ultimate photo package.

You are advised to book all packages at least two months in advance as they do sell out in peak periods and, in winter, the park is closed on some midweek days. There is also a 10% advance discount periodically for online bookings. See **discoverycove.com**.

Reef Shark Tank

BUSCH GARDENS

While the Orlando parks may get more publicity, the 335acre/136ha Busch Gardens in Tampa offers just as much in terms of attractions and – especially – Brit appeal. In fact, the sister park to SeaWorld, which started as a mini-menagerie for the wildlife collection of the brewery-owning Busch family in 1959, is often one of the most popular of all Florida attractions with UK visitors for its nature appeal – and superb roller-coasters. It is a major, multi-faceted family park, the biggest outside Orlando and just an hour from International Drive. It is rated among the top four zoos in America, with more than 2,700 animals representing over 320 species of mammals, birds, reptiles, amphibians and spiders. But that's just the start. It boasts a safari-like section of Africa spread over 65acres/26ha of grassy veldt, with special tours to hand-feed some of the animals. Interspersed among the animals are more than 20 bona fide theme park rides, including the mind-numbing coasters Kumba, SheiKra, Montu, Cheetah Hunt, Cobra's Curse and Tigris, plus the dramatic drop-tower ride, Falcon's Fury, with guaranteed fun for coaster addicts, plus plenty of scaled-down rides for children. New in 2020 will be a hybrid wood-steel roller coaster in the Morocco area of the park, adding yet another high-adrenalin thrill-ride to this undisputed leader in mega-thrill attractions. Then there are animal shows, musicians and big-stage show productions.

The overall theme is Africa, hence the park is divided into areas like Nairobi and Morocco, and dining and shopping are just as good as the other parks. It doesn't quite have the pizzazz of EPCOT or Universal, and the staff are a bit

Busch Gardens at a glance

Location	Busch Blvd, Tampa; 75–90mins' drive from Orlando		
Size	335 acres/136ha in 11 themed areas		
Hours	10am–6 or 7pm off peak; 9am or 10am–9 or 10pm Easter, Thanksgiving, Christmas; 10am–10pm summer		
Admission	Under-3s free; ages 3 and up $110 (1-day ticket), $150 (2-Visit ticket, with 2nd day at SeaWorld, Aquatica or Busch Gardens); UK 3-for-2 ticket (all 3 parks for 14 days) £114 adults, £109 children 3-9		
Parking	$25; $28 preferred parking		
Lockers	$15, $20, $25, in Morocco, Congo, Egypt and Stanleyville		
Pushchairs	$20		
Wheelchairs	$20 and $50, sun cover $12; with pushchairs		
Top attractions	Congo River Rapids, Kumba, Montu, Cheetah Hunt, SheiKra, Falcon's Fury, Cobra's Curse, Tigris		
Don't miss	Jungala, Edge of Africa, Animal Care Center, Myombe Reserve, Animal Care Experts		
Hidden costs	Meals	Burger, chips and coke $15.68 3-course meal $22–32 (Zambia Smokehouse) Kids meals: $7.49	
	T-shirts	$25–38, Kids $20–25	
	Souvenirs	99c–$2,000	
	Sundries	Face Painting $10.50–19.50	

Morocco
1 Moroccan Palace Theater
2 Myombe Reserve
3 Iron Gwazi

Bird Gardens
4 Festival Walkway
5 Lory Landing
6 Walkabout Way

Sesame Street Safari of Fun
7 Air Grover
8 Sunny Day Theater
9 Big Bird's 123-Smile With Me

Stanleyville
10 Sheikra
11 Stanley Falls Flume
12 Stanleyville Train Station
13 Stanleyville Theater
14 Skyride Station
15 Zambia Smokehouse
16 Tigris

Jungala
17 Jungle Flyers, The Wild Surge and Treetop Trails

18 Tiger Habitat
19 Orang Outpost

Congo
20 Kumba
21 Congo River Rapids
22 Ubanga-Banga Bumper Cars

Pantopia
23 Falcon's Fury
24 Sand Serpent
25 Grand Caravan Carousel
26 Pantopia Theater
27 Scorpion
28 Desert Grill

Nairobi
29 Animal Connections
30 Elephant Habitat
31 Animal Care Center

Edge of Africa
32 Cheetah Run
33 Cheetah Hunt and Skyride Station
34 Edge of Africa

Egypt
35 Cobra's Curse
36 Montu

more laid back, but it has guaranteed 5-star family appeal, especially with its rides just for kids. It's a bit like the big brother of Chessington World of Adventures in Surrey, though on a grander scale and in a better climate – albeit Busch Gardens can be more affected by bad weather than most, especially the threat of lightning, as so many of the attractions are outdoors. To avoid the queues at the ticket kiosks, there are self-serve machines to the right of the park entrance if you haven't bought in advance.

BRITTIP

Like SeaWorld, Busch Gardens offers QuickQueue, the limited number front-of-the-line pass for all the park's main rides. Price varies (seasonally), $15–80 for One-Time use.

All Day Dining Deal: For just $35 ($20 3–9s) you can enjoy all-you-care-to-eat-and-drink privileges at seven restaurants throughout the park. With your special wristband, choose one entrée, one side or dessert and a soft drink each time you pass through the dining queue (child's price valid for kids' meal only; baby back ribs excluded).

Photokey: If you'd like to collect all your park photos digitally, including ride photos and character meet-and-greets (but not backstage tours), sign up for this service, either online in advance or when you arrive at the park, for $50 (**photokeyonline.com**).

Animal Care Experts: Look out for sessions where the animal handlers explain various features of husbandry, notably with the gorillas, cheetahs and hippos. You'll find them at the Alligator Habitat, Myombe Reserve, Edge of Africa, Jungala and Animal Connections.

Location

Busch Gardens can be hard to locate on the sketchy local maps but it's pretty simple. From Orlando, head west on I-4 for almost an hour (it is 55ml/88km from I-4's junction with Highway 192) until you hit intersecting motorway I-75. Take I-75 north for 3½ml/5.5km to the exit for Fowler Avenue (Highway 582). Go west on Fowler for another 3½ml/5.5km, then, just past the University of South Florida on your right, turn LEFT into McKinley Drive. A mile/1.6km down McKinley Drive, the car park is on your *left*, where it costs $25 ($28 preferred) to park (those with disabled badges should continue on, then turn *right*).

Those without a car can use the free **Busch Gardens Shuttle Express** bus, which makes several round trips a day from Orlando; riders must have a Busch Gardens park ticket to board. You board at SeaWorld, Orlando Premium Outlets, Universal Studios, Ramada Maingate West, Best Western Lakeside or Old Town in Kissimmee and pick-up times range from 8.30 to 9.40am, returning at 6 or 7pm. Take note, arrival time at the park is occasionally as late as 11.30am, with up to 3 stops en route. Call for time and stops. Book at Guest Services at SeaWorld or call 1800 221 1339.

Beating the queues: Don't think you've left the high-season Orlando crowds behind. It's still advisable to be here at opening time, if only to be first to ride the dazzling roller-coasters, which all draw big queues (especially SheiKra, Cobra's Curse, Tigris and Cheetah Hunt). The Congo River Rapids and Stanley Falls Log Flume ride (if you want to get wet) are

Tigris

also prime draws in peak season. But queues take longer to build here, so for the first few hours you can enjoy a relatively crowd-free experience.

Busch Gardens is divided into 11 main sections, with the major rides all a bit of a hike from the main entrance. Check your park map for times and locations of various small-animal encounters throughout the park – then watch for passing flamingos as they take the first of their twice-daily promenades in the main courtyard!

Coaster fans flock to SheiKra, the world's second highest and fastest dive coaster, and peak-season queues can top an hour by mid-afternoon. So, if you want to ride this first, bear left through Morocco past the Zagora Café, through the Bird Gardens and up into Stanleyville. Tigris is also in this area. Then continue through Stanleyville to Congo for Kumba, and retrace your steps to do Congo River Rapids and the other two water rides. To start with the superb Cheetah Hunt coaster, veer right into Morocco and go past the Moroccan Palace Theater, opposite Serengeti Overlook restaurant. After riding the Cheetah, try Cobra's Curse and Montu in nearby Egypt, then return to take the SkyRide to Stanleyville and the other big rides there. Here is the full layout of the park in a clockwise direction.

Gorillas at Myombe Reserve

Morocco

Come through the main gates to the home of all the guest services and a lot of shops. EPCOT's Moroccan pavilion sets the scene better, but the architecture is still impressive and this version won't tax your wallet as much as Disney's! Turning the corner brings you to the first animal encounter, the alligator pen. Morocco is also home to one of the park's biggest shows.

Moroccan Palace Theater: The setting for the skilful 25min production **Turn It Up!**, a glittering cavalcade of super-slick ice dancing and stunts set to popular music in air-conditioned comfort. AAA

Myombe Reserve: One of the largest and most realistic habitats for the threatened highland gorillas and chimpanzees of Central Africa, this 3acre/1.2ha walk-through has a convincing tropical setting with high temperatures, lush forest landscaping and water mist sprays. Take your time, especially as there are good, seated vantage points, and catch these magnificent creatures on their daily routine. It is highly informative, with attendants on hand to answer questions. AAAAA

Iron Gwazi: A hybrid wooden rail coaster with steel tracks, this will be the tallest, steepest and fastest of its kind, using elements of the tracks from the former Gwazi coaster but without any of the brain-rattling Gwazi was known for. The steel track allows for inversions, loops and turns not possible with a standard wooden coaster. With its tallest hill topping out at a whopping 210ft/64m, watch for serious air time! **R**: 4ft 6in/137cm (expected). TTTTT

Other entertainment: Basketball fans can try the 3-Point Shootout (for $10), Slapshot Hockey challenge ($6) or Gwazi Climb ($3–10).

Shopping: The Emporium and Marrakesh Market are the best of three shops.

Dining: For a quick meal, try **Zagora Café,** or the enticing **Sultan's Sweets,** serving Starbucks coffee, sandwiches and pastries.

Bird Gardens

The most peaceful area and the original starting point of the park in 1959, you can unwind here from the usual theme-park hurly-burly. The exhibits and shows are all family-orientated, too, with an elaborate kids' playground and more animal exhibits.

BRITTIP

The Bird Gardens area is a good place to visit in mid-afternoon when most of the rides are busy.

Lory Landing: Walk through this tropical aviary featuring lorikeets, hornbills, parrots and more, with the chance to become a human perch and feed the friendly lorikeets. A cup of nectar costs $6, but makes for a great photo opportunity. AAA

Walkabout Way: This charming Australia-themed attraction offers the chance to meet free-roaming wallabies and wallaroo's, and visit Kangaloom to feed the kangaroos ($6, or 2 for $10, ages 5 and up only). It is a surprisingly captivating area, perfect for a relaxed stroll. AAA Other encounters include the lush, walk-through Kookaburra's Aviary and Flamingo Island.

Other entertainment: Festival Walkway is home to the seasonal live musical entertainment during summer and other special events, like the **Food & Wine Festival** (Mar/Apr).

Shopping: A real novelty here is the eye-catching **Xcursions** eco-friendly gift shop. Its live frog and gecko displays and conservation info on interactive touch-screens make it worth visiting whether you buy or not (but all proceeds contribute to the Busch Gardens Conservation Fund).

Dining: Garden Gate Café offers excellent sandwiches, pizza, sandwiches, flatbreads and craft beers, with pleasant outdoor seating. This is also where you can get two free beer samples per person (ages 21 and up only).

Sesame Street Safari of Fun

This impressive children's interactive play area is the cheerful 'home away from home' for much-loved Sesame Street characters, dressed in best African Safari finery. You will be hard pressed to get pre-schoolers away when they catch sight of this land's five rides (including a junior-sized coaster, a gentle flume ride and character-themed fairground style rides), entertaining stage show and the wonderfully extensive water play and climb-and-slide areas. The huge treehouse climb, ball pools and adventure play structures alone will keep most kids busy for hours! But there's more:

Air Grover: A whizzy little dip-and-turn coaster packing plenty of junior-sized thrills, piloted by everyone's favourite blue guy, Grover. **R:** 2ft 9in/97cm accompanied; 3ft 5in/104cm unaccompanied.

Sunny Day Theater: Get ready for lots of Sesame Street fun with Elmo, Zoe, Cookie Monster and the gang as they hit the stage for *Let's Play Together*, a kid-friendly story of friendship and diversity. Children (and adults!) can't help but sing along, and it is a great photo opportunity as the characters come out for a meet-and-greet afterwards.

Lory Landing

BRITTIP

Arrive early and find a seat in the first five rows for an unobstructed view at the Sunny Day Theater. Seat children on the ends for the best character interaction.

Big Bird's 1-2-3 Smile with Me:
Big Bird and friends have their own meet-and-greet area, near Air Grover. The big bonus here is 1-on-1 time with the characters in a quiet, air conditioned room (photo packages $15–25).

Bert and Ernie's Watering Hole:
Thoughtfully designed with even the smallest guests in mind, this gentle water-play area is filled with bubblers, water jets, dump buckets, geysers and splash tubs. Swimwear and sun block are available at Cookie Monster's trading Post if you forgot yours. Convenient seating surrounds the area. **TTTTT** (young 'uns only!)

Shopping: Look for **Abby Cadabby's Treasure Hut** for Sesame Street gifts and souvenirs.

Tigris track with SheiKra

Stanleyville

This brings you back into true ride territory, with the park's biggest coaster, and a water ride. You'll also find one of the three Train Stations here (next to SheiKra), for a gentle 35min journey round the park.

SheiKra: The park's outstanding big-thrill attraction is the giant steel structure of this monstrous coaster. At 200ft/62m tall and hitting 70mph/112kph, it puts Alton Towers' fearsome Oblivion in the shade. Higher, longer and faster, it features an initial drop at an angle as near vertical as makes no difference (with a delicious moment of stop-go balance as you teeter on the edge!), a second drop of 138ft/42m into an underground tunnel, an Immelman loop (an exhilarating rolling manoeuvre) and a water splashdown. The whole ride lasts less than 3min and is almost as much fun to watch as to ride. It also draws big queues, so get here early or expect a long wait (or use the paid-for QuickQueue system). You can buy ride photos for $17–25. R: 4ft 6in/137cm. **TTTTT+**

Stanley Falls: Almost identical to Log Flume rides at Chessington, LEGOLAND, Thorpe Park and Alton Towers, this guarantees a good soaking at the final 40ft/12m drop. R: 3ft 10in/116cm. **TTT**

BRITTIP

Nervous about taking young children into such a big park? Stop by Guest Relations for a kid-friendly wristband with info that will help you reconnect quickly if you get separated.

Tigris: You can't miss this hugely imposing coaster, which reaches 150ft/46m at its highest point and features three launches, forward and backward movement, an inverted heartline roll, and a massive corkscrew drop that barrels into a final loop, just for good measure. It launches forward to the first hill's midpoint, barrels backwards, and then launches forward again as it gains full

Skyride

momentum and crests the first hill, straight into the iconic twisted top at more than 60mph/96kmh – and with enormous spectator value. Although the ride is silky-smooth, you may not want to do it just after eating! **R:** 4ft 6ins/137cm. **TTTTT+**

Skyride: The other end of the park's cable-car ride (from Cheetah Hunt), it offers spectacular views over the Serengeti Plain (with a thrilling moment as Cheetah Hunt races above!). However, it closes when it's windy and queues can build up here in late afternoon. **AA**

Other entertainment: Try **Bahati Hoops** and other fairground games (next to SheiKra) for an extra fee.

Shopping: The **Kariba Marketplace** has the best of the shopping, and there is a small gift shop just outside Tigris.

Dining: For a hearty meal (and a great view of SheiKra), try **Zambia Smokehouse**, where its wood-smoked ribs platter is a delight among a heavily barbecue-orientated menu (also with salads, sandwiches and kids' meals).

Jungala

This eclectic land contains some superb animal habitats and a hugely elaborate children's play area. It gets busy in the afternoon, so visit either early on or late in the day.

The Wild Surge: Get ready to 'surge' 4 storeys into the air on this tower ride from inside a giant waterfall, with a (brief!) glimpse over Jungala before bouncing back down again. Be aware queues are long and slow-moving as the ride takes just 14 at a time. **R:** 3ft 6in/106cm to ride solo (3ft 2in/96cm with a parent). **TTT (TTTTT under-12s)**

Treetop Trails: Climbing nets, elaborate bridges, crawl tubes and a multi-level maze are the basis of this fab 3-storey children's playground, with smaller-scale adventures at ground level, including squirt fountains and other watery fun (swimsuits or a change of clothes are advisable). It cleverly mixes in two different animal habitats, for the fun-loving gibbons, flying fox-bats and the rare tomistoma (an Asian crocodile). **TTTT (young 'uns only)**

---BRITTIP

The toddler play area in Treetop Trails is very thoughtfully in the shade.

Tiger Habitat: One of the park's most creative animal environments is this multi-level tiger exhibit (including its rare white tigers). Tiger Lodge is an air-conditioned overlook including conservation info and issues, and Tiger Trail is a walkthrough section with close-up opportunities, including a unique pop-up turret (with a separate queue) in the main enclosure and a rope-pull for guests to 'test their strength' (periodically) against the big cats. Huge windows provide maximum viewing of the animals at play, especially in their plunge pool. AAAA

Orang Outpost: Another brilliant animal habitat, the orang-utans love to look in on guests, viewing them as much as vice versa. A series of close-up windows, including a glass floor over a hammock play area and a kids' tunnel, provide superb observation of the specially designed forest environment. AAAA

Shopping: Shop for gifts at **Tiger Treasures** (organic cotton T-shirts and conservation-related items).

Dining: Stop to eat at **Bengal Bistro** (fish, burgers, veggie wraps, salads and sandwiches).

Congo

Continue into Congo, an area that is geared around three rides and has a stop along the Serengeti Railway.

Kumba: Another of the park's signature coasters, this unmistakable giant turquoise structure looms over the area. It's one of the largest and fastest in south-east USA and, at 60mph/97kph, features three high-thrill elements: a diving loop plunging a full 110ft/33m; a camel-back, with a 360º spiral; and a vertical loop. For good measure, it dives underground! It looks terrifying close up but is absolutely exhilarating, even for non-coaster fans. R: 4ft 6in/137cm. TTTTT

Congo River Rapids: These look pretty tame after Kumba, but don't be fooled. The giant rubber rafts will bounce you down some of the most convincing rapids outside of the Rockies, and you will end up with a fair soaking. R: 3ft 6in/106cm. TTTT

Ubanga-Banga Bumper Cars: Fairly typical fairground dodgems, you won't miss anything if you pass them by. R: 3ft 6in/106cm. TT

Shopping and dining: There is just the **Congo River Outfitters** gift shop here, plus three refreshment kiosks.

Congo River Rapids

Pantopia

This dramatic land boasts the park's most eye-catching ride. There is also a full back-story, as Pantopia was created by a mystical Key-Master who arrived by hot air balloon to create a place where travellers could meet. The doors of Pantopia tell a tale of the original owners and travellers who passed this way and the land includes clever kinetic sculptures and re-purposed vehicles, like an Asian tuk-tuk and various bikes and wagons.

Falcon's Fury: The land's signature ride, this awe-inspiring tower lifts 32 riders at a time (slowly) up to its 300ft/91m height, tilts them forward so they are face down – then drops in best free-fall style. It's the world's highest drop-tower ride and is for adrenalin addicts only as it really has that sky-dive feeling for several seconds before the brakes kick in and bring you more gently back to earth. It is aptly named for the 160mph vertical dive of a falcon) and provides an amazing view from the top – if you can keep your eyes open. We think it's as much a spectator opportunity as something you'll actually want to ride but it does provide an iconic look to the park. It's a relatively brief experience and queues move slowly, so you may want to try this early on – or chicken out completely! R: 3ft 6in/106cm. TTTTT

Sand Serpent: This family-orientated 'Crazy Mouse' coaster is surprisingly energetic, rising 46ft/14m and adding tight turns and swift drops. Top speed is 22mph/35kph, but it seems faster and thrills younger kids. **TTT** (**TTTTT** under-10s)

Scorpion: A vintage 1980 roller-coaster, this features a dramatic drop and 360° loop. It lasts just 120secs, but *seems* longer! Queues rarely top 30mins. **R:** 3ft 6in/106cm. **TTTT**.

Grand Caravan Carousel: Join this 'Bedouin caravan' in its layers of tapestries and tenting for a genuine carousel ride. **TT** (**TTTT** under 5s).

The Phoenix swinging boat ride looks relatively tame, until it starts swinging! At its height, it performs a 360° loop guaranteed to disorient even the heartiest riders. Queues can be long at mid-day. Don't ride straight after eating! **R:** 4ft/122cm. **TTTT**.

Pantopia Theater: This indoor arena features hilarious animal show, *Critters Inn Charge*. Staff at Critters Inn are getting ready for a VIP guest in advance of their big Conservation Celebration, but the actual critters at the inn (rescued dogs, cats, birds and more) make sure things don't run smoothly! It's a delightful break in air-conditioned comfort, and you can meet the trainers and animals afterwards. **AAAA**

Other entertainment: The **Games Area** offers fairground-style games that require a few extra dollars, while the **Dragon Fire Grill & Pub** – a Moroccan-influenced nightclub that is Pantopia's gathering place for artists from around the world – offers a show while you dine (or just sit and watch). In 2019 it was Rock-A-Doo-Wop, a 20-minute live song-and-dance extravaganza featuring the 'greatest hits' in music history's past eras.

Shopping: Painted Camel Bazaar offers a wide range of creative merchandise, some of it made from recycled materials from around the world, as well as Falcon's Fury and other souvenir items.

Dining: Headline restaurant the Dragon Fire Grill is an innovative food court-style offering including Italian, American, Asian and Southwestern cuisine, as well as a grab-and-go Starbucks coffee station and an extended selection of craft beers. Look out for rotisserie chicken, flatbread pizza, salads and sandwiches. **Twisted Tails Pretzels** is a delightful offering of fresh-rolled pretzels (don't miss the signature Bacon Pretzel Fury, along with the beer mustard sauce!), artisan sandwiches, pizza and pretzel dogs, as well as craft beers. **Lynx Frozen Treats** adds snowcones, smoothies and other icy delights and **Kettle Corn** is a haven for popcorn-lovers as well as serving turkey legs, potato twisters, chicken strips and drinks.

Falcon's Fury

Nairobi

It's back to the animals as we enter this area, with five different habitats.

Serengeti Plain: A 49acre/20ha spread of African savannah, this is home to buffalo, antelope, zebras, giraffes, wildebeest, ostriches, hippos, rhinos and many exotic birds, and can be viewed for much of the journey on the Serengeti Express, a full-size, open-car steam train that chugs slowly from its main station in Nairobi to the Congo, Stanleyville and back. AAA

BRITTIP

Take the Serengeti Railway from Nairobi (or Congo or Stanleyville) in mid-afternoon to give your feet a rest when it's busy elsewhere.

Lions on the Serengeti Plain

Animal Connections: The park's nursery is an interesting animal encounter, with some friendly flamingos, small critters (lemurs, sloths, possums and babies needing extra care) on view through the large windows. This is the place to meet the park's Animal Ambassadors for education and conservation issues. AA

Hippos

Animal Care Center: This is a peek into the way Busch Gardens cares for its residents, even down to performing live surgical procedures. The state-of-the-art facility is in three parts, for the Treatment Room, Nutrition Center and Pathology Lab, with live audio links to the vets and technicians working behind the big glass windows and keepers on hand to answer questions, whether it's a snake getting an ultrasound check-up or the daily preparation of mealworms for the possums! AAAA

Other entertainment: Look out for the **Elephant Interaction Wall** and periodic sessions with animal staff (notably the afternoon Elephant Wash), while you can see more park inhabitants at the **Reptile House, Penguin Point** (with its South African penguins) and **Tortoise Habitat**. The meeting area for park tours is also here, next to Kenya Kanteen.

Shopping and dining: Caravan Crossing (safari apparel and hats) has the best shopping here while **Kenya Kanteen** offers drinks and snacks.

Edge of Africa

This animal-rich area features the park's wonderful cheetah habitat – and signature ride.

Cheetah Hunt: This beast of a coaster re-creates the thrill of a cheetah pursuing its prey. With a fast-launch start from the loading station, the hunt is on. A second launch spirals you 10 storeys up the signature figure-of-eight tower before taking an exhilarating 130ft/40m drop into a subterranean gorge. Then you're off again, low and fast across the Serengeti. A final launch zips riders back across the grasslands (leaping over onlookers below and above the SkyRide!) and, just before you're completely out of breath, the hunt comes to an end after a sensational 2mins. The smooth ride, extensive theming and superb eye-appeal mark this out as one of Florida's finest rides, but it draws BIG queues, so try to do it early on. **R**: 4ft/120cm; **TTTTT+**

Skyride: Take to the air with this one-way cable car trip to Stanleyville, getting a fabulous aerial view of the park, including part of the Serengeti Plain. **TT**

Cheetah Run: Here you have the chance to see these magnificent cats up close, either chasing their favourite toy alongside Cheetah Hunt or just lounging around the splendid habitat designed especially for them. Sprints occur up to four times daily (check park map for times). Then, take time to learn more about the park's conservation efforts through touch-screen technology. **AAA**

Edge of Africa: This clever 15acre/6ha 'safari experience' guarantees a close-up almost like the real thing. The walk-through puts you in an authentic setting of native wilds and villages from which you can view giraffes, lions, baboons, meerkats, crocodiles, hyenas and vultures, and even an underwater hippo habitat. Wandering naturalists offer informal talks, and the attention to detail is superb.

Shopping and dining: Grab a souvenir at **Cheetah Gifts** or quick bite or drink from **Cheetah Snacks**. Victorian-style **Serengeti Overlook Restaurant** offers views of Cobra's Curse and Serengeti Plain, with a varied buffet Fri-Sun ($20 adults, $10 kids) featuring chicken, fish, pizza, mac and cheese and side dishes, plus dessert and soft drinks. Beer and wine available. **Serengeti Overlook Pub** offers salads, sandwiches and pizza, with an adjoining bar for a selection of craft beers, including various local breweries ($9.50, or a flight of four for $11).

BRITTIP

Busch Gardens offered FREE beer throughout its 60th anniversary in 2019 and we expect it continue in summer 2020, with two 7oz samples available per person daily at Garden Gate Café and Serengeti Overlook Pub.

Cheetah Hunt

Egypt

The final area of Busch Gardens is somewhat tucked away, so it's best visited either first thing or late in the day. It sits in the park's bottom right corner and much of it is re-created pharaoh country, dominated by suspended coaster Montu, named after an ancient Egyptian warrior god. Thrilling family coaster Cobra's Curse can also be found here.

Montu: You cannot miss the area's main attraction, another breathtaking inverted coaster, covering nearly 4,000ft/1,219m of track at up to 60mph/97kph and peaking with a G-force of 3.85! Like Kumba, it looks terrifying but really is a 5-star thrill as it leaves your legs dangling and twists and dives (underground at two points) for almost 3min of brain-scrambling fun. R: 4ft 6in/137cm. TTTTT

Cobra's Curse: This novel coaster starts with an impressive vertical lift hill that brings riders face to fangs with a 70ft snake (well, an 'ancient cobra statue', at least!). From a height of 70ft/21.3m, it zips out into the African plain with multiple swoops and dips, twisting and turning as it snakes along more than 2,100ft/640m of track. It is a high-speed ride with a difference, as the cars will *reverse* and then spin at various points to provide a first-of-its-kind coaster experience. The clever theming, like an archaeological dig, plus live snake exhibits through the queuing area, ensure this is good family fun. TTTTT, R: 3ft 6/106cm.

BRITTIP

Edge of Africa offers some fantastic photo opportunities but, in the hot months, come here early in the day as many animals seek refuge from the heat later.

Shopping: Montu Gifts sells clothes, handbags and other merchandise, while **Cobra's Crypt Marketplace** offers clothes, plush toys and gifts.

BRITTIP

We find the upstairs restaurant at Serengeti Overlook a blissful lunch stop in the hotter months when its cool interior and elegant ambience offer a welcome change of pace after all the rides.

Montu

New hybrid coaster

Special tours

Busch Gardens features many great behind-the-scenes tours and expeditions that add an extra dimension to the park. For all tours, book at the Serengeti Outpost in Nairobi or, better still, in advance on 1888 800 5447 or **buschgardens.com/tampa/tours**.

Serengeti Safari: A 30min excursion (five times a day, up to 20 at a time) aboard flat-bed trucks, takes you to meet some of the Serengeti Plain's residents and feed the beautiful giraffes while learning about the park's environmental efforts. It fills up quickly and costs $29–49/person seasonally (ages 5+, 5–15s must be accompanied by an adult).

Guided Adventure Tour: This takes just 15 at a time on a 5hr VIP trek, with your own guide, front-of-line access for major rides, counter-service lunch and close encounters with many of the animals, including the Serengeti Safari ($99/person).

Elite Adventure Tour: The ultimate personal park tour, a 7hr journey with front-of-line access to all rides, the Serengeti Safari, reserved seating at shows, free bottled water throughout, plus breakfast and lunch ($199/person, ages 5+).

Keeper for a Day: An exclusive 6½hr behind-the-scenes walking tour where you join the keepers as they feed, train and care for giraffes and antelope, then move on to assist the avian team on the Serengeti ($250/person, including park admission and lunch; ages 13+ and 4ft 3ins/132cm, book at least two weeks in advance).

Tiger Insider: A fascinating 45min group visit behind the scenes in Jungala to meet the keepers, see how they care for the magnificent tigers (you might even help to weigh one!) and learn some zoo husbandry secrets ($29/person, ages 5+).

Animal Care Center Tour: A 45min walking tour with the park's vets and zoological staff, with hands-on opportunities, as they showcase medical check-ups and other treatments (limited dates; $29/person, ages 8+).

Heart of Africa Insider Tour: A 30min behind-the-scenes walking tour to get close to hippos and lions with their keepers ($29/person, ages 10+).

Penguin Insider Tour: Spend 30mins meeting and learning about the park's African Penguins (12pm daily; $29/person, ages 5+).

Elephant Insider Tour: Take a 30min tour behind the scenes to find out how the park cares for its biggest inhabitants ($29/person, ages 10+).

Also look for **Cheetah Insider, Gorilla Insider** and **Aldabra** (giant tortoise) **Insider** tours.

Special programmes

Food & Wine Festival: This imaginative event runs each weekend from Mar–Apr and is well worth sampling. Based in the Festival Walkway area, it consists of a series of themed food and beverage 'cabins' offering dozens of fresh dishes, with menus created especially by the park's culinary team. The festival runs from noon–9pm and starter-size samples range from $5–9, with wine and beers from $7–12, plus bourbon and tequila tasting. It concludes each evening with a concert from the likes of Boyz II Men, Daughtry and Foreigner, all as part of regular park admission. There are food and wine sampler packages from $30–55 for 5, 8 or 12 samples while giant topiaries and food sculptors add extra colour.

Summer Nights: Busch Gardens is open until 10pm for this programme featuring live entertainment with themed food and drink that runs from late May to early Aug. With three distinct Party Zones – in Cheetah Hunt Plaza, Pantopia and Stanleyville – offering DJs, dancing and special food kiosks, it adds to the thrill of riding the big coasters at night as well as showcasing the high-energy summer ice show, Turn It Up!, at the Moroccan Palace, with its skating feats and memorable pop tunes.

Howl-O-Scream: Don't miss the park's special Halloween presentation each Sept–Oct. A separately ticketed event ($55–90/person; see online for early-booking discounts) offering grisly goings-on and themed houses, it also offers the chance to ride all the big coasters at night (7.30pm–midnight or 1am). It features some imaginative shows with all the shock-horror effects, plus a dance party, but it is definitely not advised for young children. It is similar to Universal's Halloween Horror Nights programme (p164), with eight elaborately themed haunted houses – like Death Water Bayou and Meat Market – plus a series of scare zones that change annually. The Busch Gardens version is more spread out and less frenetic than Universal's, but you may want to try both (**buschgardens.com/tampa/events/howl-o-scream**).

Christmas: See p37.

Adventure Island: For a really full family day out, you can combine Busch Gardens with sister water park Adventure Island (on McKinley Drive), which is blissful when it's hot. The 25acres/10ha of watery fun, in a Key West theme, offer a full range of slides and rides, such as the **Colossal Curl,** a massive family raft ride, **Wahoo Run** raft ride, the exciting four-lane mat slide **Riptide,** leisurely **Rambling Bayou** lazy river, spiralling tube ride **Calypso Coaster** and new freefall drop-slide **Vanish Point**. Open mid-Mar to late Oct (weekends only Sept and Oct) 10am–5pm (9pm in summer). Tickets are $60 (ages 3 and up), while a Busch Gardens–Adventure Island combo is $150.

Well, that's the low-down on the main theme parks, but there's still a LOT to discover…

Riding Tigris during the Summer Nights programme

7 The Other Attractions

One Giant Leap for Tourist Kind

If you think you can 'do' Orlando just by sticking to the main theme parks, think again! There is still a LOT more to discover, starting with Kennedy Space Center, which we rate as an essential place to spend a day.

Then there's LEGOLAND Florida – ideal for the 3–12 brigade – and Gatorland, another great-value experience. There are unique venues like WonderWorks, ICON Park and Ripley's Believe It Or Not and, for more individual tastes, the amazing 'skydive' experience of iFLY Orlando and WhirlyDome fun centre, plus some great water parks. The choice is yours, but it's an immense selection. Let's start with One Giant Leap for Mankind.

> ──────**BRITGUIDE**
> When we first started, the likes of
> Cypress Gardens, Splendid China,
> Disney's Discovery Island and River Country,
> Mystery Fun House, Fantasy of Flight, Wet
> 'n Wild and Water Mania were all included
> in this chapter. Sadly, not any more!

KENNEDY SPACE CENTER
Welcome to the past, present and future of NASA's space programme, and one of the most fascinating places in Florida. In addition to Space Shuttle *Atlantis*, there are a series of exhibits and shows (including two splendid IMAX films), a children's play area,

Cosmic Quest Adventure interactive game, the daily Astronaut Encounter, poignant Astronaut Memorial, and the essential Space Center bus tours, which all add up to great value.

Getting there: Take the Beachline Expressway out of Orlando (Route 528, and a toll road, see map p214) for about 45mins, bear left on SR 407 (don't follow signs to Cape Canaveral or Cocoa Beach at this point) and turn right at the T-junction onto SR405. The Visitor Center is located 9ml/14km along on the right. Tours and IMAX presentations start at 10am (**KennedySpaceCenter.com** – check the website for periodic online ticket discounts).

> ──────**BRITTIP**
> Kennedy Space Center's handheld
> **SmartGuide** ($9) allows you to
> customise your touring through audio,
> photos and interesting facts, plus
> information on each exhibit and attraction
> you visit.

Once inside the Visitor Complex, the attractions are as follows. Start with Space Shuttle *Atlantis*, as this has proved THE big draw since it opened in June 2013. Late arrivals should do the Bus Tour first, though, then visit the Shuttle complex.

Atlantis: This dramatic $100m exhibit is the core experience of the new-look KSC, offering the 30-year history of the Shuttle programme

Orlando's Other Attractions And Main Shopping Outlets

✈ **Sanford International Airport**

Sanford Airport via Interstate 4 has no tolls, but can be far busier, especially during rush-hour

Mount Dora →

Daytona ▲

ALTAMONTE SPRINGS

Altamonte Mall

Sanford Airport via 417 has a few tolls, but is much quieter

Sanford-Central Florida Zoo ↑

94
92
4

Toll road (from 50c to $5)

90

Lake Apopka

441

88

436

Winter Park ■

87

Leu Gardens ■

429

OCOEE

441

417

WINTER GARDEN

Amway Center ■
Orlando City Soccer Stadium ■

50

84
85
83
82

50

WEST COLONIAL DRIVE

Downtown Orlando ■
Lake Eola

408

EAST - WEST EXPRESSWAY

Camping World Stadium ■

Winter Garden Village

429

WINDERMERE

79 80

Mall at Millenia ■

441

528

FLORIDA TURNPIKE

78

KIRKMAN RD

Universal Studios
Universal Citywalk
Islands of Adventure
Volcano Bay

77
75
74B

Orlando International Premium Outlets

Cocoa Beach

Port Canaveral →

SAND LAKE RD
74A

Pirates Dinner Adventure ■
Sleuth's Mystery Dinner Shows ■

Florida Mall

BEACHLINE

SEORAN BOULEVARD

TURKEY LAKE RD

INTERNATIONAL DRIVE

Magic Kingdom
■

535 435

72

71

SeaWorld

Orlando Watersports Complex ■

✈ **Orlando International Airport**

Hoop-Dee-Doo Musical Revue

4

423

Lake Buena Vista

ORANGE BLOSSOM TRAIL

JOHN YOUNG PARKWAY

BOGGY CREEK ROAD

CENTRAL FLORIDA GREENEWAY

WESTERN BELTWAY

Epcot Drive
Epcot
Disney Springs

68

Orlando Vineland Premium Outlets ■
Buena Vista Watersports ■

Disney's Hollywood Studios
■ Fantasia Gdns Mini-golf

67

Animal Kingdom
■

■ Winter-Summerland Mini-golf

65

Lake Buena Vista Factory Stores

417

The Loop & Loop West

Island H2O Live ■

WORLD DRIVE

MainGate West

64

63

OSCEOLA PARKWAY

Toll road

OLD LAKE WILSON RD

62

Old Town
Celebration

Capone's Dinner Show ■

KISSIMMEE

Osceola County Pioneer Museum ■
Osceola County Historical Museum ■

East Lake Fish Camp ■

Silver Spurs Arena ■

East Lake Tohopekaliga

60

■ Orlando Tree Trek

Medieval Times ■
Kissimmee Paddling Center ■
Warbird Adventures & Museum ■

192

IRLON BRONSON MEMORIAL HIGHWAY

Downtown Kissimmee ■

FLORIDA TURNPIKE

BOGGY CREEK ROAD

Champions Gate

58

17

Kissimmee Airport ✈

Kissimmee Lakefront Park ■

Forever Florida, Reptile World Serpentarium

Dinosaur World →

Wild Florida

ST CLOUD

55

Tampa, Clearwater, Gulf Coast

Boggy Creek Airboat Rides

Lake Tohopekaliga

Miami

0   5 miles

N

© Steve Munns 2019

through a mix of interactive media. Both hands-on and immersive, it features one of the three surviving orbiters (*Discovery* is on show at The Smithsonian in Washington and *Endeavour* at the California Science Center in Los Angeles). The six-storey building is dominated outside by full-size replicas of the external fuel tank and solid rocket boosters, illustrating the power needed to put the Space Transport System (STS) in orbit. It starts with a film pre-show into how the Shuttle programme was devised, then offers a vivid sense-surround presentation into the life and missions of *Atlantis* (stand about two-thirds of the way back for the full effect of the wrap-around screens). The specially written musical score reaches an emotional crescendo that is accompanied by a real 'wow' moment as…no, we won't reveal it! It is a breathtaking show that leads into the main exhibit hall, with the orbiter displayed with its payload bay doors open and robotic arm extended alongside an elevated viewing platform. The hall is subdivided into areas for the International Space Station, Hubble Space Telescope and Astronaut Training Simulation Gallery (complete with the chance to land a Shuttle and dock with the Space Station). In all, there are more than 60 interactive touch-screen experiences and simulators, Cosmic Quest Adventure game (p217) and climb-through Space Station, with its clear plastic tube suspended two storeys up. You can easily spend a couple of hours in here and we strongly advise heading here first as queues build up quickly. AAAAA+ The gift shop offers a great variety of souvenirs.

BRITTIP

Not sure what to do first at KSC? Visit the Information Center just to the left before the main turnstiles and they can provide a schedule for the day, working on your arrival time and what you'd like to see.

Shuttle Launch Experience: After seeing *Atlantis*, walk up the long gantry for this well-made presentation into a real-life launch – with you on board! A clever pre-show – with fog, moody lighting and sound and

Kennedy Space Center at a glance

Location	Off State Road 405 in Titusville
Size	Visitor Complex 70 acres/28.3ha
Hours	9am–6, 7pm or 8pm seasonally
Admission	Under-3s free; 3–11 $47; adult (12+) $57; Atlantis annual pass $78–96; Explorer annual pass $116–146. Prices do not include tax.
Parking	$10
Lockers	$6 and $8, just inside turnstiles to left.
Pushchairs	$6 and $8 at Information (through entrance on left)
Wheelchairs	$10 and $25 (electric scooter) at Information
Top attractions	Space Shuttle Atlantis; Shuttle Launch Experience; IMAX films; Astronaut Encounter; KSC Bus Tours
Don't miss	Apollo-Saturn V Center on Bus Tours; Astronaut Memorial; Rocket Garden

Hidden costs	Meals	Burger, chips and coke $16 Kids' meal $6–8
	T-shirts	$18–35, Kids $8–28
	Souvenirs	$1.99–12,000
	Sundries	Bus tour photos $20–35

vibration effects – paves the way to the 'ready room' to prepare for your own blast-off. The capsules look like crew cabins in the cargo hold of the Shuttle, and you go through the launch procedure as the vehicle moves into a near vertical position for take-off. On the command 'Go for engine start', you are at the heart of a 5min simulation providing the features of a realistic launch, with vibration generators, sound effects, cabin movements and screen visuals. You get a taste of the G-forces involved, the Rocket Booster and External Tank separations, and a moment of 'weightlessness' as you enter Earth's orbit. Finally, the cargo doors open to reveal an awe-inspiring view. There is then a 'space walk' back to Earth via a spiral walkway surrounded by the stars and more satellite views of the planet. **R:** 3ft 8in/112cm. **TTT** AAAAA

Forever Remembered: Space Shuttle Memorial: Also inside the Atlantis exhibit is this moving two-part tribute to the astronauts who lost their lives in the *Challenger* and *Columbia* disasters. A short hallway features display cases dedicated to each astronaut, with artefacts, personal belongings and insights. A second hallway shows news footage of the physical recovery of shuttle parts, and the emotional recovery of the families. AAAA.

Heroes and Legends: This exhibit is part interactive 3-D adventure and part memorial, taking guests along on the earliest space missions and telling the astronauts' stories, for a real you-are-there experience using liberal touches of virtual reality. View the **EVA 23** documentary, which tells the gripping story of Italian astronaut Luca Parmitano's near-fatal spacewalk at the International Space Station. Then, you can interact (virtually) with the inductees into the fabulous Astronaut Hall of Fame. AAAA.

BRITTIP

All of the Shuttle Launch Experience is fully wheelchair accessible, and there is a seat outside for potential riders to test their comfort level. For anyone wary of the full ride (although there is no need to be, unless you are pregnant or have neck or back problems), there is a bypass room where you can experience the attraction without the motion.

Bus tours: The KSC's signature coaches depart every 15mins from 10am and are newly narrated to provide a full overview of the Space Center. Each tour makes a main stop in addition to driving around much of the working area, including past the massive Vehicle Assembly

Apollo Saturn V Center

© Kennedy Space Center

Building and the former shuttle launch pads. The main stop is the Apollo/Saturn V Center, one of the KSC's great exhibits, where you can easily spend 90mins. It highlights the Apollo missions and first Moon landing with two impressive theatrical presentations on the risks and triumphs, a full-size 363ft/111m Saturn V rocket (with a special projection-mapping display on its flank) and a hands-on gallery of space exploration. A moving tribute exhibit to the crew of Apollo 1 – who were tragically killed during testing in 1967 – was added in 2017 and is well worth taking in. Allow a couple of hours to do the tour justice but be aware the last bus leaves the Visitor Complex at 3pm. AAAAA

IMAX films: Back at the Visitor Complex are the IMAX cinemas, twin 55ft/17m screens that give the impression of sitting on top of the action.

Journey To Space is a 42min look at the story of the space shuttle programme and what comes next – a mission to Mars. The detailed and exciting film traces some amazing new developments in NASA's future. New in 2019 was **Touch The Stars: The Journey Has Begun 3D**, a spectacular 38-minute, high-definition exploration of the solar system with NASA's robotic spacecraft, touching on the sun, the moons and the planets with a view that truly sets your heart pounding and makes you feel as if you are really there. Both films dazzle with the spirit of human achievement. AAAA Also in the IMAX building, you'll find **Science on a Sphere**, making use of projections on a 6ft/2m globe, teaching complex lessons about the Earth and the planets in an easy-to-understand way. Experts are on hand to narrate and answer questions. **NASA Now** features the original capsules from Orion's EFT-1 mission, SpaceX Dragon from COTS-2 mission, Boeing CST-100 Starliner crew capsule, plus scale models of the NASA Space Launch System and Sierra Nevada Dream Chaser Cargo Vehicle, and Vector Space Systems' Vector-R rocket.

Astronaut Encounter: This engaging feature is a daily talk and Q&A session, with personal observations and stories from various veterans of the space programmes, including Shuttle astronauts. It is held up to three times a day at the Universe Theater. AAAA

Journey To Mars: Explorers Wanted: What will it take to explore deep space? This interactive exhibit inspires thinking through live presentations, interactive games, simulators and a mock-up of NASA's Orion crew capsule. AAAA

Other exhibits: A covered **Children's Play Dome** has a range of climbing/crawling/sliding elements. Also primarily for young 'uns is the splash fountain in the **Rocket Garden**, which showcases the full variety of spacecraft that have journeyed beyond the Earth's atmosphere since the 1950s. The Garden also features the chance to sit inside replicas of the tiny capsules of the Mercury and Gemini astronauts. Free tours are given up to four times a day (times vary) and are well presented for all ages. Don't forget to stop at the moving **Astronaut Memorial**. AAAA

Cosmic Quest Adventure: This interactive computer game challenges trainees (i.e. you) to test their space knowledge with various missions, culminating in a final Adventure Challenge to decide if they're ready for promotion, or need a bit more training. Four Adventures are located around the Space Center, from building a Martian colony (Journey to Mars building), capturing a rogue asteroid (IMAX), launching a rocket (Apollo/Saturn V Center) or performing experiments on the International Space Station (Atlantis). Doing them all can take several hours, so this is best for a second or third

The Rocket Garden

© Kennedy Space Center

visit ($19.95 for game-activating badge, lanyard, and Training Manual; admission required; best for 8–16s).

Shopping: The Visitor Complex has an excellent **Space Shop** (the world's largest store for space memorabilia and gifts, with some fun interactive elements, including selfies as an astronaut!), **Shuttle Express** in the Atlantis building and **The Right Stuff Shop** at the Apollo/Saturn V Center.

Dining: Stop for lunch at **Orbit Cafe**, a modern counter-service diner where you order your food – a tempting array of salads, sandwiches, focaccia, burgers and kids meals – at touchscreen kiosks (and can see some of the lettuce and herbs being grown in hydroponic towers), or the excellent **Rocket Garden Cafe**, for tasty sandwiches, salads, flatbreads and burgers, plus hot and cold breakfast 9–11am. Also find hot dogs, pastries and drinks at **Red Rock Grill** window-service, scooped ice cream at **Milky Way**, plus various **Space Dots** (Dippin' Dots) kiosks. **Rocket Fuel Food Truck** is in the entry plaza and **Moon Rock Cafe** is at the Apollo/Saturn V Center on the bus tour.

BRITTIP

Photographers are stationed at various locations around the Visitor Complex, and it's worth considering the $55 **Digipass** for unlimited digital-download photos.

The Center then has additional optional extra tours and features.

KSC Explore Tour: Travel almost within the perimeter security fence of Launch Pad 39-A and get a close-up of the complex, including the flame trench and emergency escape system – with a photo-op stop near the pad. Other sites include drive-by views of Launch Pad 39-B, the Vehicle Assembly Building, mobile launch platforms and a stop at the Apollo/Saturn V Center ($25 adults, $19 for 3–11s).

Cape Canaveral: Early Space: If you want to learn more about NASA history, try this 3hr+ guided tour (Thurs–Sun only) into the early days of space exploration around the older part of the facility. Highlights include the Air Force Space & Missile Museum, Mercury launch sites and Memorial, original astronaut training facility and several active launch pads, all of which are otherwise off-limits. For this tour, international guests (including children) must have a valid passport at check in with the visitor complex security officers 9–11am ($25 and $19). Reserve online or call 1866 737 5235.

Astronaut Training Experience (ATX): This 5hr simulator, virtual reality and high-tech, hands-on experience features astronaut 'training' based on a mission to Mars. Participants will 'land' on Mars, walk and drive on the surface of the planet, feel what it's like to "live" on Mars, and experience microgravity, through a series of 35–40min stages (ages 10 and up only, $175). Companion programme **Mars Base 1** includes working in the Plant Lab, operating robotics and taking on the engineering challenges real astronauts will one day face on the Red Planet. This day-long adventure is made all the more realistic through the use of floor-to-ceiling 4K screens that create an entirely convincing atmosphere (45 min, ages 10 and up only, $150). Try the VR Mars **Exploration Simulator Training** (land, walk and drive on Mars) for $40 or **Spacewalk Training** simulator for $30. Both are for ages 10 and up, and require KSC admission.

BRITTIP

The Space Center still has an extremely active rocket launch programme and you can see full details at **nasa.gov/launchschedule**.

Astronaut Training Experience

© Kennedy Space Center

Fly with an Astronaut: Explore Space Shuttle Atlantis, Shuttle Launch Experience and the motor coach tour with an astronaut as your guide on this 4.25hr tour, which includes admission to the Space Center complex, a Shuttle Launch Experience ride, catered lunch and a photo with your astronaut ($199/$174).

Launch Director Tour: Former launch director Mike Leinbach conducts this 3hr tour around Space Shuttle Atlantis, Launch Complex 39 and Shuttle Launch Experience, plus a tour of the Forever Remembered memorial ($65, includes signed lithograph; subject to availability).

Lunch with an Astronaut: For another fully engrossing feature at the Kennedy Space Center, a small group gets to dine with the star of the daily Astronaut Encounter. The featured person gives their own special briefing, adding extra insight into their space missions, plus answers individual questions, gives autographs and poses for photos. $30 adults, $16 children, at noon daily. Buy tickets online or call 1866 737 5235. We recommend this – the buffet-style lunch in the new dining centre is pretty good, too!

LEGOLAND Florida

Children aged 2–12 – plus their parents and even grand parents – will all enjoy this bright and expansive park, which opened in 2011. In a beautiful lakeside setting on the site of the former Cypress Gardens – and including the old tropical gardens – it offers 150acres/60ha of guaranteed fun with its extensive main park and water park. In fact, while the typical LEGOLAND age range is 2–12, the Floridian version probably appeals to kids as old as 14 with its bigger rides and water flumes. There is plenty to do, with no fewer than 26 rides, two main shows, an extensive adventure play area, the amazing Miniland, LEGO Friends area and new LEGO Movie World. It has two LEGO-themed hotels and the **LEGOLAND Beach Retreat**. There is also great shopping, and their two-day ticket is terrific value. Even the dining options are fresh, healthy and appealing, and there are plenty of quiet corners and gardens in which to chill out.

Getting there: Take I-4 west to Exit 55, then Highway 27 south for 18 miles to State Road 540. Turn right and the park is 4mls/6.4km along, on the left.

It does require a lot of legwork to see it all, though, as it sprawls round

Saturn V Rocket

the southern shore of Lake Eloise and, when it's hot, there aren't many places in the air-conditioned cool. But there is definitely something for all but older teens and we enjoy the clever landscaping and fun use of LEGO characters and features.

Location and tactics

LEGOLAND Florida is in Winter Haven, about 45mins south-east of the Disney/Kissimmee area. Shuttle service is available from the ICON Orlando complex on International Drive at 9am next to the multi-storey car park, for $5/person round trip, reservations required on 1877 350 5346 or the Legoland website.

You arrive into the large car park where the parking fee is $23 and walk to the entrance. The Preferred Parking area (closer to the entrance; $33) features solar panel technology that provides power to local homes. The park's 150acres/60ha spreads

people out well but still draws queues at peak periods, hence your best bet is to head for LEGO Movie World, LEGO Kingdoms, Land of Adventure, and DUPLO Valley (girls may also want to check out Heartlake City), returning to Fun Town and Miniland later in the day. If your kids love the Ninjago characters, Ninjago World will be the area to go first. For a second day, start with your favourite rides, then cool down in the water park (which closes an hour before the main park). Once through the gates, here's what you'll find, moving in an anti-clockwise direction (advisable). NB: All ratings are indicated for younger children rather than adults!

BRITTIP

LEGOLAND employees are called Model Citizens, and each wears at least one Mini-Figure on their name badge. Bring along (or purchase) your own mini-figure and they'll trade with you!

LEGOLAND Florida at a glance

Location	Off State Road 540 in Winter Haven	
Size	150acres	
Hours	10am–6 or 7pm in high season (Easter, summer, Thanksgiving and Christmas), 10am–5pm off peak; closed Tues and Wed off peak; Water Park 10.30am–5 or 6pm in summer; 11am–4pm off peak (closed some weekdays); weekends 10.30am–5pm Sept– Oct.	
Admission	Under-3s free; $100 (1-day ticket); $125 (1-day plus water park); $120 (2-day ticket); $145 (2-day plus water park), Discounts if purchased online	
Parking	$25; Preferred parking $33	
Lockers	$9 small $12 large, $15 jumbo	
Pushchairs	$16 and $22	
Wheelchairs	$14 and $56	
Top attractions	The Dragon, Coastersaurus, Driving School, Boating School, The Great LEGO Race, Wave Racers, Royal Joust, Ninjago The Ride, Masters of Flight	
Don't miss	LEGO Movie World, Miniland, Heartlake City, Fun Town 4-D Theater, Pirates Cove Water Ski Show, Cypress Gardens	
Hidden costs	Meals	Burger, chips and coke $13.30 Kids' meal $6.99
	T-shirts	$16.99–22.99 kids, $24.99–27.99 adults
	Souvenirs	$2.99–350
	Sundries	Face Painting $12.99–18.99; Photo Digipass $44.99, $10 second day

The Beginning: This offers the ticket centre, Guest Relations and functional elements like the lockers, pushchair and wheelchair hire.

Shopping and dining: Immediately to the left of the entrance is **The Big Shop** (one of the largest LEGO merchandise stores in the world). Find a quick-bite counter and coffee bar across from The Big Shop, and pizza, salads and drinks at next door's **Pepper & Roni's Pizza Stop** ($7–8).

Fun Town: Here is where the squeals of delight really begin! In true LEGOLAND style, you have entered a charming village complete with a working factory, 4-D cinema and carousel. Take a **Factory Tour** and watch working machinery as it goes through the process of making LEGO bricks, from moulding to packaging, then let the kids ride **The Grand Carousel** (**TT**; under 4ft/122cm must be accompanied by adult). Just beyond is **4-D Theater**, featuring three 12min 4-D movies.

The LEGO Movie 4D: A New Adventure: This features the further madcap exploits of Emmet, Wyldstyle, Unikitty, Benny and Metalbeard as they encounter evil villain Risky Business; **LEGO NINJAGO: Master of the 4th Dimension** offers kids the chance to be part of the action as they join the ninjas in saving the universe; and **LEGO City 4D: Officer in Pursuit**, a special effects-filled romp around the LEGO metropolis hot on the trail of a thief! Each are good family fun, and kids can meet their favourite characters at meet-and-greets outside the theatre after the show. **TTT**

> **BRITTIP**
> Plan your visit to 4-D Theater during the hottest part of the day and enjoy a break in blissful air-conditioned comfort.

Shopping: LEGO Studio Store is full of themed merchandise (including Star Wars, SpongeBob, Indiana Jones, and Batman), and at the **Minifigure Market**.

Dining: Granny's Apple Fries serves up the park's signature dessert (apples, cinnamon and a creamy sauce; $7.25, $8.00 a la mode), and **Fun Town Slushies** offers great cold treats. **Pizza & Pasta Buffet** is a value-conscious choice ($16.99 adults/$10 under 13s).

DUPLO® Valley: Turn right out of Fun Town to the perfect place for toddlers to let their imaginations run wild as they explore a village sized just for them. This area features a junior-sized train that winds through the 'countryside', passing farms, campgrounds and fishing holes. Toddlers will love helping the 'farmer' find missing animals and plough the fields, and then cool down in the water play area. **TTTT** under-6s.

LEGO Movie World: This immersive 'land' is themed as Bricksburg, Emmet's home town from *The LEGO Movie*, and features characters and experiences from the original film and its sequel. Let kids loose in **Benny's Play Ship** play structure, or brave three new rides. The feature attraction is **The LEGO MOVIE: Masters of Flight**, a dynamic 3D 'flying theatre' with wind, mist and scent effects that takes riders on a madcap chase through Bricksburg on Emmet's Triple Decker Flying Couch. The sense of movement comes from on-screen visuals more than the actual movement, but it's a powerful sensation none the less. **R**: under 3ft/101cm and under age 3; 3ft-4.3ft/101-132cm; and age 3-8 with companion age 14 or up; 4.3ft/132cm and age 9 and up can ride alone. **TTTT**. **Unikitty's Disco Drop** is a cute

Lego Ninjago: Master of the 4th Dimension

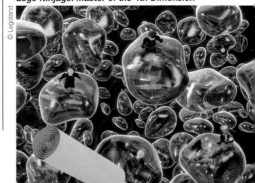

© Legoland

35ft drop tower that gives youngsters a thrill as it rises to 'Cloud Cuckoo Land', then bounces and spins on its way down. **R:** under 3ft/101cm and under age 3; 3ft-4ft (101cm-122cm) and age 3-6 with companion age 14 or up; 4ft/122cm and age 7 and up can ride alone. **TTT** Water ride **Battle of Bricksburg** offers the chance to get wet while defending Bricksburg from DUPLO alien invaders. Kids love firing the water cannons from their boat – and shore-side onlookers love firing back! **R:** Ages 6 and under or less than 4ft (122cm) must ride with companion age 16 or up. **TTTT**

Shopping: The Awesome Shop carries merchandise themed to Emmet, Wyldstyle and friends.

Dining: Taco Every Day serves chicken or beef tacos and drinks.

Other Entertainment: Kids will find their favourite characters from The LEGO MOVIE at **Emmet's Super Suite** meet-and-greet and photo opportunity.

LEGO Kingdoms: The next large-scale land features three major rides and a cool play area. Climb aboard **The Dragon** for a backstage view of life in an enchanted castle, then take off on a thrilling flight as this scenic dark ride becomes a dynamic outdoor coaster! **R:** 4ft/122cm or 3ft 4in/102cm with adult. Child Swap and ride photo available. **TTTT** Then, saddle up on LEGO-themed horses for **The Royal Joust**, where youngsters gallop through an enchanted forest, jousting with LEGO knights along the way. **R:** 3ft/91cm;

The Great Lego Race

© Legoland

max 12 yrs and 170lb/76kg. **TT** Another climbing structure, **The Forestmen's Hideout**, lets kids climb, slide and swing off extra energy. Also here is **Merlin's Challenge**, a fairly standard but quite whizzy fairground circular ride (4ft/122cm or 3ft 4in/102cm with adult). **TTT AAAA** There are also the **Jester's Games** ($5–10).

Shopping: The Kings Market carries suitably themed gifts.

Dining: Castle Burger serves tasty burgers and chicken sandwiches, while **Kingdom Cones** has soft serve ice cream.

Land of Adventure: Next is another BIG land, with two major rides and three other great kiddie attractions. The excitement continues at **Lost Kingdom Adventure** as you hunt for treasure while fighting off baddies with laser blasters. Youngsters will want to ride several times to better their score. **R:** 4ft 6in/137cm or 2ft 10in/86cm with adult. **TTT** Child Swap, ride photos available.

Another top thrill comes with **Coastersaurus**, a classic wooden coaster that zips through a prehistoric jungle and past animated LEGO dinosaurs. **R:** 3ft/91cm or 4ft/122cm with adult. **TTTTT** Then you can just let young 'uns loose at **Pharaoh's Revenge** multi-level climbing structure, with the added fun of being able to shoot soft foam balls at each other. **Beetle Bounce** shoots riders 15ft/4.5m high on this kid-friendly tower ride **R:** 3ft/91cm; **TTTT Safari Trek** is the classic children's car ride, through a clever LEGO-themed African savannah full of lurking animals. **R:** 2ft 10in/86cm, or 4ft/122cm with adult, max age 12; **TTT Adventure Games** are more fairground side-stalls for an extra few dollars.

Dining: Adventure Snacks is a good choice for hot dogs, nachos and cheese, and drinks and **Dino Slush** offers slushies.

Ninjago World: This extensive area is set up around the characters and exploits of the Ninjago warriors from the TV series, which spun off the LEGO sets. It features four outdoor experiences, designed to test visitors' balance and agility before they venture to the main event. **Ninjago – The Ride** is an indoor interactive 4-D adventure that sets up a battle to test your ninja skills in a series of 13 animated Dojo challenges. Using only hand and arm gestures, you fire lightning bolts, fireballs, shockwaves and ice at various targets, building up to a battle with the Great Devourer and the chance to earn full Spinjitzu Ninja status. R: Riders under 4ft/122cm must be accompanied by a responsible rider 4ft or taller. TTTT Kai and Nya have a meet-and-greet here, too.

Shopping: Check out the 22 Ninjago building sets – and more – at **Wu's Warehouse**.

LEGO City: This popular area features some of the most classic attractions, themed like a real working town, starting with **Rescue Academy**, where families race each other to 'put out the fire'. But these fire trucks only move when you pump the levers! R: 4ft/122cm or 2ft 10in/86cm with adult; guests in wheelchairs must transfer. TTT LEGOLAND's ultra-popular **Ford Driving School** (ages 6–13), **Ford Jr Driving School** (3–5s) and **Boating School** (4ft/122cm or 2ft 10in/86cm with adult) are all here too, giving kids the chance to navigate electric cars and small boats to earn official LEGOLAND driving licences. TT–TTTT For something more dynamic, try **Flying School's** suspended steel coaster, one of the biggest thrills in the park and a major hit with coaster fans. R: 3ft 8in/111cm or 4ft 4in/130cm with adult. TTTTT There is an indoor **Tot Spot** play area here, too.

Shopping: Pick up some souvenirs at the **Driving School Store**.

Dining: Grab a tempting chicken lunch or dinner at the indoor **Kick'n Chicken**, a tasty burger at **Burger Kitchen** or a sweet treat at **Firehouse Ice Cream**.

BRITTIP

See LEGOLAND's website for periodic discounts. They sometimes offer up to $15 off ALL tickets if booked in advance for a specific day.

LEGO Technic: This area is packed with fun and thrills for older children as it offers three super rides. The **Great LEGO Race** is the big attraction, a tall, fast-turning steel coaster that adds a fun Virtual Reality element by turning the ride into an action-packed Road Race. Riders whirl, brake and bank in life-size LEGO cars, with the added thrill of (optional) VR headsets that immerse them in a crazy race against madcap minifigure teams. R: 4ft/122cm or 3ft 6in/99cm with adult; must be 6 years and 4ft/122cm to ride with VR headset. TTTTT Ride the waves and dodge soaking blasts of water on the airboat-style **Aquazone Wave Racers**, a ride so cool you'll want to queue up straight away for another go! R: 4ft 4in/132cm or 3ft 4in/102cm with adult; TTTT). Kids can also try the more sedate **Technicyle** (TT) and have a go at the **Extreme Games** (for a few extra dollars), while toddlers will gravitate to **Technic Tot Spot** soft play area.

Dining: The **Funnel Cake Factory** kiosk sells sweet, fried pastries.

Imagination Zone: Next up is the creative heart of the park, where kids put their imagination to work at seven hands-on indoor play areas. They include the chance to try out touch-screen technology in the **Water Zone**; invent crazy aerial creations in **Flight Zone**; build and test race cars in the **Wheels Zone**; build on the walls of the **Creation Zone**; and conjure up loose-brick creations at **Building Zone**. Then there are the latest LEGO video games in the **Warner Bros. Games Zone** and computer-controlled robots in the **LEGO Mindstorms** area. Outside, the **Kid Power Towers** then burn off excess energy as kids (and adults!) use ropes and pulleys to ascend colourful towers – and let go for a 'free fall' back down. R: 4ft/122cm or 3ft 4in/100cm with adult; TTT Child swap available, guests in wheelchairs must transfer.

Dining: Try **Panini Grill** for a tasty toasted sandwich, salad and drink.

Cypress Gardens: The beautiful gardens this park was originally known for are now lovingly restored and a haven for strolling, complete with beautiful gazebo, tropical displays and banyan tree. AAAA

Pirates Cove: Come back out of the Gardens and you'll find the place where swashbuckling meets water in an exciting battle on the 'high seas' in The Battle for Brickbeard's Bounty. LEGO characters and a life-sized pirate ship add to the fun of this water stunt show, with water-skiers, ski-jumping and other stunts that young children will not want to miss. AAA

Dining: Grab a take-away at one of the nearby quick-serves and have an al fresco lunch at the lakeside Imagination Pavilion picnic area.

Heartlake City: This area is dedicated to the LEGO Friends, with

Mia's Riding Adventure offering junior-sized horse-themed fun on a back-and-forth disk coaster. **The Heartlake Stepping Tones Fountain** is another interactive feature with LEGO instruments that play music.

Shopping: Pick up all the latest LEGO Friends collections and accessories at the **Heartlake Mall**.

Miniland USA: Completing the big LEGOLAND tour brings you to the park's other crown jewel, an iconic area featuring eight themed US locations in miniature – and the big bonus of a Star Wars-themed area.

Florida shows off some of the state's gems, with separate areas devoted to a magnificent replica of the Kennedy Space Center (complete with Shuttle countdown!) and the huge Daytona International Speedway.

Las Vegas boasts the glittering resorts and other icons of Nevada's most famous city while **Washington DC** re-creates the White House, US Capitol, Smithsonian museum and the Washington and Jefferson monuments. No mini-land would be complete without **New York City**, and this representation includes Rockefeller Plaza (complete with squirt fountains!), Times Square, Lady Liberty, the Empire State building, Bronx Zoo and Grand Central Station. **California** features icons including the Golden Gate Bridge and the Hollywood Bowl. Finally, there is a section devoted to the ever-popular subject of **Pirates**, plus an extensive **Star Wars** zone, complete with scenes from seven films and one from animated series the Clone Wars, plus spectacular photo ops with LEGO versions of Darth Vader, BB-8, R2-D2, Darth Maul, Chewbacca and Rey.

Miniland's detail is amazing, with a riot of visual gags and fun touches (try to spot the surprised gent in the loos at Grand Central Station!), and you can easily spend an hour or more browsing here.

A LEGO Movie World room at the LEGOLAND Hotel

Haven dining

If you stay in Winter Haven for dinner, there are two great locals' choices. **Harry's Old Place**, on Cypress Gardens Rd, fronting Lake Ned (left out of Legoland, then second right) features classic Floridian style and cuisine, including some excellent seafood and great daily specials, with large portions, a friendly welcome and hand-crafted cocktails (5–9pm, Tue–Sun only; harrysoldplace.com). Popular local chain **Manny's Chophouse** is on Highway 17 (3rd Street SW; left out of Legoland, go 3mls/5km then turn right on to 3rd St SW), with its signature steaks, chops and ribs, plus lively style and eclectic decor. With a good kids' menu and full bar service, it is easily the equal of its Brit-friendly Highway 27 counterpart and, while they don't take reservations, waits rarely top 20–30 mins (p325; mannyschophouse.com).

Water Park: This fabulous extra (for $25/person) is an opportunity to have fun in best LEGO style. Not as large as the likes of Blizzard Beach and Aquatica, but designed completely with young children in mind and easier to navigate, it offers the full array of lockers, changing rooms, towel rental and gift shop (with swimming costumes for sale if you make a late decision to try it), plus **Beach-n-Brick Grill**, complete with shaded Tiki Bar for tired parents! There is also an ice cream kiosk and **Beach Street Tacos**. Cabaña hire is $79-$99. There are six main areas and it will require at least half a day of your time. As ever, have plenty of high-factor, waterproof suncream.

DUPLO Splash Safari: This is Toddler Central, featuring small-scale slides and interactive DUPLO creatures, all in just 6in/15cm of water (and within view of the Tiki bar!). **AAAA**

Joker Soaker: Older children will love this huge water-feature adventure playground and its slides, fountains, climbs, squirt guns and more, including a 300-gallon bucket that fills and tips periodically! **R**: 3ft/91cm on 3 lower slides, 3ft 6in/ 99cm on upper 4; under 3ft 6in/99cm must be accompanied by an adult. **AAAAA**

Build a Raft River: An imaginative variation on the lazy-river idea, with riders able to build their own floating raft with special LEGO bricks and then complete the 1,000ft/330m-long 3ft/91cm deep circuit. **AAA**

LEGO Wave Pool: Enjoy some gentle surf fun in this wide, walk-in pool that allows young children to splash happily while their older siblings can brave the 3ft 4in/100cm-plus depths. **AAA**

BRITTIP

There is no shade in the Miniland area, so be SURE to apply lots of high factor suncream before spending time here.

Twin Chasers: Older children will love the chance to ride these double flumes – one open, one enclosed – on individual rafts that sloosh down the 375ft/114m tubes, with a grand splash-down at the end. **R**: 4ft/122cm; **TTTT**

Splash Out: The ultimate thrill-ride for kids, a selection of 3 intertwined body-slides with a drop of 60ft/18m that afford a great view of the surrounding area – before you 'drop in'! **R**: 4ft/122cm; **TTTTT**

Creative Cove: Here you'll find the hands-on Build-a-Boat attraction, where kids can create and race LEGO watercraft through fast-flowing rivers in a setting inspired by the popular LEGO City Coast Guard sets.

Seasonal fun: LEGOLAND adds more entertainment at different times of the year, notably **Star Wars Days** (weekends in early May), **Knight Lights** (mid-Jun to late Jul), with

Imagination Zone

© Legoland

extended hours, more character appearances, Master Builder sessions and a big fireworks finale over Lake Eloise; meet a firefighter on **Firefighter Fridays** (Oct), **Brick-or-Treat** for the Halloween season (Oct) with trick or treating, scavenger hunts and a fireworks show; the **Christmas Bricktacular**, with festive decorations, a LEGO Santa and sleigh, Master Builder sessions, character appearances and more nightly fireworks; and even a **Kids New Year's Eve**, with the chance to party and celebrate at a more kid-friendly time.

If that's the park, here are some add-ons that may be worth including in your visit.

VIP Experiences: Tour the park with a VIP host who shares fascinating facts about the park and the models. **Red Brick Carpet** VIP tour offers priority access to rides, shows and attractions; a tour of the model shop; VIP lanyard; minifigure; 10% retail discount, as well as park admission (starting at $300pp). **Silver Brick Carpet** adds valet parking; family photo and digital package; and refreshments (starting at $500pp). **Gold Brick Carpet** further adds Q&A with a Master Model Builder; building session and take-home build; lunch and all-day snacks; VIP gift bag and lanyard (starting at $700pp). **Red Brick Carpet & Water Park** adds water park admission, mystery minifigure; brick storage container; beach towels; knapsack; misting fan; and refreshments (starting at $100pp). Book VIP experiences on 1855 753 7777 or **legoland.com/florida/buy-tickets/vip-experiences/vip-experiences**.

LEGOLAND Beach Retreat

© Legoland

Be Aware: LEGOLAND closes on Tues and Wed at quiet times of the year and the water park is only open in the hotter months (and closes weekdays in the spring and autumn). Check in advance on 1877 350 5346 or **florida.legoland.com**.

LEGOLAND Hotel: This is a great way to stay in the heart of the fun and take full advantage of those 2-day tickets. With 152 brightly coloured and themed rooms, there is bags of LEGO style throughout, from the giant dragon at the entrance to dozens of individual pieces in the rooms, where there is a special Treasure Hunt for kids to solve (and find a prize). Chose from Kingdom, Adventure, Pirates, LEGO Friends and THE LEGO MOVIE for the individual room themes, which all feature bunk beds and an entertainment unit for kids, while the two-room suites add a living room, pullout sofa and play area. The VIP Suites sleep up to six. There are king-sized beds for adults, two flatscreen TVs, a mini-fridge and coffee maker in every room. Premium rooms add more LEGO décor and models for kids to play with. The hotel includes a fabulous heated outdoor pool and its own buffet-style diner, Bricks Family Restaurant and themed Skyline Lounge. A full breakfast is included in the daily rate, with exclusive Master Model Builder sessions (a major hit with children), early park admission, nightly LEGO building competitions and live entertainment, and there is also a lovely boardwalk on the edge of Lake Eloise. There are interactive play areas for kids throughout the hotel, and it doesn't get much better than walking straight out of the hotel – and straight INTO the park!

BRITTIP

Don't miss the 'Disco Elevators' at the LEGOLAND Hotel – you might not want to get out when it's your floor!

LEGOLAND Pirate Island Hotel: Open in Spring 2020, this 150 room, 5-storey hotel, connected to the LEGOLAND Hotel, takes the LEGO experience up another notch, adding a massive pirate ship photo opportunity at the entry, an enormous pool area, themed rooms with a prize-filled treasure chest, Master Builder sessions and nightly entertainment. Rooms sleep up to 5 and include a semi-private kids' area with boat-shaped bunks and a trundle bed, a TV in the entertainment centre and in-room puzzles and treasure hunts each day of your stay. A stylish adults area features a king bed, coffee/tea facilities, mini-fridge, TV and plenty of USB ports. Kid-friendly bathrooms have a tub and shower combo. A pirate-themed restaurant, which serves breakfast and dinner, is designed with little buccaneers in mind, and grown-ups appreciate the lobby bar for an evening drink. Family-style breakfast, character meet-and-greets, building activities and nightly entertainment are included in the room rate.

LEGOLAND Beach Retreat: This lakefront resort features 83 village-style bungalows for a total of 166 rooms. Along with a cool Lego beach/surfer theme, each of 13 horseshoe-shaped 'coves' of 5-8 duplex-style bungalows is named for a mini-figure. Rooms have a king bed, bunk beds and a trundle bed to accommodate up to five, with a curtain between the kids room and the adults. They are heavily themed and feature a coffee/tea maker, USB ports, LEGO building bricks, safe, mini-fridge and tub/shower combo. Check-in takes place in your car as you enter the property. The resort's central building, The Lighthouse, features a themed pool, sandy 'beach', climbing structure, games and competitions, a gift shop and buffet-style Sandy's Castle Restaurant serving breakfast and dinner. Bricks Beach Bar serves beer, wine, and speciality cocktails (with limited food at lunch) but it closes by 9pm. Extensive LEGO theming throughout the resort makes it a super-fun choice for families.

GATORLAND

For a taste of Florida wildlife, this is as authentic as it gets and is popular with children of all ages. The 'Alligator Capital of the World' was founded in 1949 and is still family owned, so it has a natural, homespun charm few of its big-name rivals can match. And, when the wildlife consists of several thousand menacing alligators and crocodiles in various natural habitats and three fascinating shows – plus a fabulous Zip Line attraction that is disabled accessible – you know you're in for a different experience (although there is a LOT more to Gatorland than just gators – including their Bobcat Bayou). Overall, Gatorland is something you're unlikely to get anywhere else, and the sense of being in the 'real' Florida is terrific.

Getting there: Gatorland is on the South Orange Blossom Trail, 2ml/3km south of the Central Florida Greeneway and 3ml/5km north of Highway 192 (see map p14). Admission: $29.99 adults, $19.99 3–12s, 10am–5pm, parking free. Annual passes are only $44.99 and $29.99 if you plan more than one visit (407 855 5496, **gatorland.com**). Check website for current coupons.

BRITTIP

If you have an evening flight home from Orlando International, visit Gatorland for half a day on your final day as it is just 20mins' drive from the airport.

Stompin' Gator Off Road Adventure

© Gatorland

Gatorland Express tours: Start by taking the 15min train ride around the park to get an idea of its 110acre/45ha expanse. This has an added fee but is good for multiple rides, is amusingly narrated and is especially fun for kids. You also get a good look at the native animal habitat, which features whitetail deer, wild turkey and quail.

BRITTIP

If you are at Gatorland first thing in the morning, take the Swamp Walk straight away. There will be far more wildlife activity then and the peaceful ambience is quite invigorating.

Attractions: Breeding pens, baby alligator nurseries and rearing ponds are also situated throughout the park to provide an idea of the growth cycle of the gator and enhance the overall feeling that it is the visitor behind bars here, not the animals. A nursery exhibit gives close-up views of eggs hatching and baby gators in a special habitat.

Many of the small-scale attractions have been designed with kids in mind and there is plenty to keep everyone amused. **Allie's Barnyard** is a petting zoo, while you can feed some friendly lorikeets at the **Very Merry Aviary**, and view the pink inhabitants of **Flamingo Island**. The **Breeding Marsh Walkway** provides the best overview of the main gator habitat, with a three-storey observation tower for full panoramic effect.

Gatorland babies

© Gatorland

White Gator Swamp: Don't miss this remarkable showcase for four rare and completely white alligators, which are totally leucistic (without pigment), with startling blue eyes, not pink like albinos. Other animals include owls, turtles, flamingos, tortoises, snakes, spiders, emus and deer; also hundreds of wading birds, providing a fascinating close-up of the nests during Mar–Aug.

Bobcat Bayou: This is the place to find Gatorland's two bobcats, while the park also showcases two rare Florida panthers in the **Panther Springs** exhibit.

BRITTIP

Lucy and Neiko, brother and sister panthers who live at Gatorland, are at their most lively first thing in the morning when they have been let out of their night quarters – just like any domestic cat!

Shows: The 800-seat **Wrestling Stadium** sets the scene for some real cracker-style feats (a 'cracker' is a Florida cowboy) as Gatorland's resident 'wranglers' catch a medium-sized gator and proceed to point out the animal's features, with the aid of some daredevil stunts that will have you questioning their sanity. The **Gator Jumparoo** is another eye-opening spectacle as some of the park's biggest creatures use their tails to 'jump' out of the water and be hand-fed tasty morsels, like whole chickens! **Up-Close Encounters** is another amusing showcase of creatures, from the expected snakes to less obvious cockroaches and scorpions. Great photo opportunities for brave children!

Gator Gully: This superb little water park features numerous ways for kids to cool down, get wet and generally have fun. The ½acre/0.2ha park features five elements, including a giant jalopy with water jets for spokes and a fountain radiator, an old shack that 'explodes' with water, and giant gators with squirt guns. The neighbouring dry play area and chairs and tables allow parents to sit and watch the kids expend some energy, perhaps with a drink from one of the kiosks.

But wait… that's not all!

Screamin' Gator Zip Line: Gatorland has fixed its eyes firmly on the brave of heart, introducing a first-of-its-kind zipline experience, with four zips soaring high above the park's most notorious residents. At 1,200ft/366m long and up to 56ft/17m high, the lines afford spectacular views of jumping Cuban Crocodiles and the scenic Alligator Breeding Marsh. Start at Tower One, where the 'bunny hill' builds up your courage (and your excitement). Tower Two soars over croc pools (look down – the view is outrageous!); Tower Three is the tallest launch point at 75ft/23m, and its 600ft/182m run zips straight over the breeding marsh at up to 35mph/56kph. Take the walking bridge over to Tower Four where you're met by a thrilling double zipline for a final race to the finish.

BRITTIP

Book the Screamin' Gator in advance to avoid disappointment. Capacity is limited to groups of 12 up to 7 times a day and demand is high. Reserve by phone or online.

The experience includes orientation, full equipment check, the zipline and a trek across a swinging bridge. There is a separate fee, but at $69.99/person, it includes all-day admission to the park. A photographer will also chart your journey for purchase back on terra firma! **R**: Min weight 75lb/34kg, max 250lb/113kg. Must be able to climb stairs. Wear closed-toe shoes and trousers or long shorts. Screamin' Gator also includes a brilliant wheelchair-accessible, one-segment zip line for guests with lower-body disabilities (must transfer to specially designed harness), providing a thrilling 350ft/106m glide over the gator marsh.

The hilarious **Stompin' Gator Off Road Adventure** is a 12ft/3.5m high monster buggy ride that takes guests into the wilds of Gatorland for a thrilling excursion through real Florida ecosystems – including a gator pond! It costs extra ($10/adults and kids), but it is a thrilling journey into the swampy backwoods that make up much of the local countryside. Ticketing for all Gatorland's added experiences is at the new onsite **Gator Joe's Adventure Outpost**.

Shopping: In addition to three gift stores and the **Gator & Snake** photo opportunity, you should visit the **Gift Shop** complex at the entrance, which incorporates the trademark Gator Mouth entryway.

Dining: Grab a bite or drink at three snack bars: try **Gator Jake's Fudge Kitchen** or dine on fried gator nuggets (as well as burgers and hotdogs) at **Pearl's Good Eats**, with excellent kids' meals at $6.99.

Special events: Some unique options if you really want to get to know your gators are: **Trainer for a Day**, with the chance to work behind the scenes at the park 8–10am, finding out what it takes to handle such dangerous animals, behavioural training and novice gator wrangling ($130 12s and over, max five people; includes park admission); **Gator Night Shine**, which takes guests into the Breeding Marsh after dark for a one-hour tour with a senior gator expert, with torches and gator food to lure the 'locals'. You can then marvel at how gator eyes shine like red beacons in the torchlight and learn more about the habits of these amazing animals – a real family treat, which kids seem to love (dusk, around 8.15pm summer, 6.30pm autumn and winter; $25 all ages; bug spray provided; reservations required); and **Adventure Hour**, a chance to go truly 'behind-the-scenes' in the Breeding Marsh to feed and pose for photos with the gators here (1pm, $10/person). **Meet-A-Gator** is every kid's chance to show his or her bravery and have the picture to prove it ($10 to kneel over a gator's back; extra for the photo).

International Drive

The 14½ml/23km tourist corridor of I-Drive (see maps p14 and 214) continues to be an ever-changing source of hotels, restaurants, shopping and fun. There are more than 42,000 hotel rooms, 150+ restaurants and almost 500 shops, as well as 22 attractions, and four mini-golf courses. The I-Ride Trolley links it all in transport terms and the website **internationaldriveorlando.com** highlights all the options. Its Official Visitors Guide has an I-Ride map and valuable money-off coupons, which you can download to get you started, plus a hotel booking facility. The I-Ride Trolley section provides 'NextTrolley' info as well as maps and listings of what is near each trolley stop.

Here's a look at the area's attractions (see also Chapter 10, Orlando By Night, and Chapter 12, Shopping, to get the full picture).

ICON Park

This entertainment venue is the biggest attraction on I-Drive. It boasts four family-friendly attractions, including the 400ft/121m The Wheel at ICON Park, 11 restaurants, eight shops and a bar/ nightclub, plus free multi-storey car parking. The landscaped centre also has an elaborate fountain and lighting and is worth visiting both by day and night.

The Wheel at ICON Orlando: Formerly Orlando Eye and Icon Orlando 360, this observation wheel offers a 20min journey that lifts visitors up in air-conditioned 15-passenger capsules for a panoramic view of this

The Wheel at ICON Park

part of Central Florida (as far as the Kennedy Space Center on a clear day). The experience starts with a green-screen photo and a fab 4-D film of Florida's highlights, then passengers are loaded on the slow-moving Wheel, which is especially impressive in early evening. There is narration of the major sights, plus info pads, and the vista is fabulous from the top, including the vast spread of Walt Disney World. It costs $30 adults and $25 4–12s (10am–10pm; midnight Fri and Sat). There is also a Champagne Experience with a glass of champagne for $35 (4.45–8.45pm), or a private capsule for 3–12guests at $80.

Madame Tussauds: An extensive range of celebrity waxworks allows you to rub shoulders (and take selfies) with famous people, past and present. The experience starts with a meeting with Spanish explorer Juan Ponce de Leon in 1513 as he discovers Florida. There is a quick history tour featuring President Lincoln, Uncle Sam and Martin Luther King, and then the journey continues with famous inventors and innovators (notably the man who brought Mickey to Orlando in the first place!). The Madame Tussaud story is well illustrated at the half-way point, and then the centre really turns on the style with a dazzling range of celebrities such as David Beckham, Elvis, Madonna, Jim Parsons, Jennifer Lawrence and Taylor Lautner. The A-list Party adds mega-stars like Samuel L Jackson, Brad Pitt and Angelina Jolie. But the major appeal here is the **Justice League: A Call For Heroes** interactive area that takes you through Metropolis and Gotham City, helping Wonder Woman, Superman and Batman avert disaster. You'll need at least 90mins to see everything, and taking photos with the 'stars' is actively encouraged ($40 and $35; 10am–10pm, 11pm Fri, Sat).

BRITTIP

If you are worried by heights on the ICON ride, there is a seat in the middle of the capsule with a central pole that provides a secure vantage point to enjoy the view with an extra feeling of reassurance.

SeaLife Orlando: The third part of the attraction is a huge indoor aquarium that features some fabulous exhibits and hands-on displays, ideal for children of all ages. The highlight is the 360-degree immersive tunnel through the main aquarium, with fish – including giant rays and sharks – floating all around you, but there are then a variety of smaller tanks and other underwater scenes, including a Rockpool experience, Stingray Cove and Everglades tableau. In all there are more than 5,000 animals to see and investigate, along with some clever 'Talking Aquarium' interactive talks and animal feedings throughout the day, as well as the chance to see the centre's divers feeding and cleaning at regular intervals. There is a Scavenger Hunt for children to follow along the way, and the different vantage points are geared towards smaller visitors, with a strong eco-friendly message throughout ($30 and $25, under 3s free; 10am–9pm). There is a 1hr Behind The Scenes tours for an extra $15/person. Combo tickets for two or three of these adventures are well priced at $40 and $35; $50 and $45 (advance discounts available online). There is also a Gift Shop for each attraction and a Food Court, making it a well-rounded and enjoyable half-day option, while the additional dining (p320) around the complex is excellent (10am–9pm, last entry at 8pm; **iconorlando.com**).

BRITTIP

Didn't bring a camera to Madame Tussauds? Not to worry – there are photographers at regular intervals to make sure you have great memories of the visit.

Separate to the three headline attractions is **Skeletons: Museum of Osteology**, a fascinating museum-with-a-difference boasting a look at some 400 animals of all types (including a great Africa section and a rare Sumatran rhino) in amazing anatomical detail, with full-size skeletons displayed in active poses and cool but educational dioramas that provide great photo opportunities. ($20 adults, $13 3–11s;

10am–10pm; **skeletonmuseum.com**; also available with ICON Orlando for $40 and $35). There's also **Arcade City**, high-energy games arcade with all the latest video challenges and activities, including some high-tech variations on familiar games (with prizes to match; 10am–10pm, midnight Fri–Sat, 9pm Sun).

Kings Bowl: This part of the complex is a bowling centre with restaurant and bar, including 22 high-tech bowling lanes in a grown-up atmosphere that is also family-friendly. Its elegant multi-bar and dining room set-up features big-screen TVs, billiard tables, table tennis, shuffleboard, Foosball and bocce ball. The food – from standard diner fare like burgers, pizza and tacos, to succulent steak tips, baby back ribs and great cocktails – is worth coming in for on its own, while the beer list is impressive and the desserts decadent. Bowling is 2pm–midnight Mon–Thurs, noon–2am Fri–Sat, noon–midnight Sun at $6.75/person Tues–Thurs, $7.50 Fri– Mon before 6pm and $7.50 Sun–Thurs and $9.50 Fri–Sat after 6pm. Shoe hire $4.75 (407 363 0200; **kingsbowlamerica. com/orlando**).

StarFlyer: Towering above I-Drive is this 425ft/129m chair swing ride, the tallest of its kind in the world. Not for the faint-hearted, its 24 double seats

Museum of Osteology

revolve at up to 45mph at its full height and it offers a unique view of the surrounding area. Alternatively, you can just sit and watch with a drink at ground level at the Star Bar! (10am-2am daily; $12.21/person).

BRITTIP

Call ahead for a Priority Lane Reservation when you dine at Kings Bowl and your group will be bumped up to the next available lane once you have finished eating.

Orlando Slingshot: This will also be the highest ride of its kind at 300ft tall, with a "slingshot" effect that catapults riders a whopping 450ft in the air, when it opens in 2020.

Orlando Gyro Drop Tower: At 400ft high, this is the tallest drop tower in the world, in keeping with ICON Park's penchant for all things vertically impressive. Riders wind their way up and around the tower until they reach the top, then make a heart-pounding 350ft, 75mph free-fall back down again. Also slated to open in 2020.

Ripley's Believe It Or Not

You can't miss this extraordinary tilted attraction as it's designed to seem as if it's falling into a Florida 'sinkhole'. But once inside you soon get back on the level and, for an hour or so, you can wander through this quirky museum dedicated to the weird and wonderful. Robert L Ripley was an eccentric explorer and collector (a real-life Indiana Jones) who for 40 years travelled the world to assemble a collection of the greatest known oddities. The Orlando branch of this chain features 8,900ft^2/830m^2 of displays in 16 galleries, including authentic artefacts, interactive exhibits, illusions, video presentations and music. The elaborate re-creation of an Egyptian tomb showcases a mummy and three rare mummified animals, while the Primitive Gallery contains artefacts (some quite gruesome) from tribal societies around the world. There are then Human and Animal Oddities, Big and Little galleries, Illusions and Dinosaurs, plus extra interactive elements. The collection of miniatures includes the world's smallest violin and a single

Ripley's Believe It or Not

grain of rice hand-painted with a tropical sunset. Larger-scale exhibits include a balloon-powered chair that flew over the Rocky Mountains and a 2/3-scale 1907 Rolls-Royce built in matchsticks. You can also attempt various puzzles and brain teasers, and try the unusual shooting gallery.

Admission: $21 adult, $14 3–11s; 9am–12am (last entry 11pm; 407 345 0501, **ripleys.com/orlando**). AAA Ripleys is also included with Go Orlando Card.

Titanic – The artefact exhibit

Go back in time at this fascinating attraction just north of Sand Lake Road. Guided tours start on the hour and weave through full-scale re-creations of the Titanic's famous rooms, including her grand staircase, first-class parlour suite, Verandah Café, Marconi Room, third class cabin and bridge. Costumed actors portray characters such as Captain Smith and Molly Brown, sharing stories of passengers and crew during the one-hour journey of the famous ship. The 17-gallery attraction features an interactive Underwater Room, including a 15ft/4.5m 'iceberg' and a detailed replica of the vessel as she appears on the bottom of the Atlantic today. More than 400 artefacts and treasures, including memorabilia from James Cameron's blockbuster movie Titanic are also on display here, notably some ultra-rare pieces, including the 2nd-largest piece recovered from the wreck site.

Admission: $21.95 adults, $15.95 5–11s, $19.75 Seniors ($2 off online; under-3 free); tours Sun–Thurs 10am–8pm, Fri–Sat 10am-6pm (last tours 7pm and 5pm) **premierexhibitions.com**). AAAA Titanic is also included with Go Orlando Card.

Titanic Gala Dinner: Try this 3hr theatre/dining occasion with the cast of the Exhibit. Starring Molly Brown, Captain Smith, Thomas Andrews and other high-society luminaries, it offers each table a front row seat for the whole Titanic story, setting the scene and delivering a dinner party with a difference, all in period style. Enjoy a sumptuous three-course meal, featuring fillet of beef and chicken, with tea, coffee and soft drinks (extra for unlimited beer and wine) in a splendid atmosphere, recreating Titanic's first-night sailing each Fri and Sat from 6.30pm ($69 for adults, $42 for ages 3-10; not recommended for under-6s; book in advance on 407 248 1166).

Fun Spot America

Just off I-Drive on Fun Spot Way (look for the 250ft/76m SkyCoaster past the junction with Kirkman Road) is this extensive amusement park that offers a whole raft of family fun with coasters, go-karting, kiddie rides and arcade action. The go-kart thrills come from four challenging tracks, including the enlarged Quad Helix, the triple level corkscrew track of Conquest, the fiendish Thrasher and multi-level Commander. Then there are bumper cars and boats, five daring fairground-type rides (including the huge Happy Swing ride and whizzy Scramblur), one of the largest and most up-to-date video arcades in Florida, a Big Wheel, 10 Kiddie Rides – including a classic two-storey carousel – and a Cadet track for the little ones. Fun Spot also boasts the world's second-largest SkyCoaster (a massive, free-fall swing) and three coasters – the impressive long steel-wooden hybrid of White Lightning, which races along at up to 48mph/76kph with a max drop of 75ft/23m; the tight-turning suspended ride of Freedom Flyer (select seats feature Virtual Reality); and the child-friendly Sea Serpent. Another fun option is the high-spinning Enterprise, while the large Food Court serves hotdogs, burgers, salads, pizza, nachos, popcorn and ice-cream. Also check out **Gator Spot**, a separate area featuring almost 120 residents of Gatorland, including an albino gator, gift shop and some great photo opportunities (photos for a fee). Parking and admission are free, with a series of ride Passes geared around children's height (above and below 4ft 4in/1.32m), with younger children getting free run of all the rides (and as a passenger on the two-seater go-karts with an adult).

Admission: Free; Single Day ticket (all day on all 4 tracks, plus all rides and unlimited Free Play arcade; Skycoaster not included) $49.95; SkyCoaster $40 single rider, $35ea double, $30ea triple, $20ea with Single Day pass. Open daily 10am–midnight (2pm–midnight off-peak; 407 363 3867, **fun-spot.com/orlando**). TTTT Also with Go Orlando card.

Magical Midway

Magical Midway back on I-Drive (just north of Sand Lake Road) offers more go-karts, games and thrill rides, including the Sling Shot (400ft/120m straight up!) and the whirling StarFlyer, a 230ft/70m tower with chair swings that lift and rotate for a dizzying view at 54mph/87kph. The two elevated kart tracks, the double uphill corkscrew of The Avalanche and sharply banked Alpine are its signature rides (you must be at least 12 and 4ft 8in/147cm tall to drive, at least 16 to drive a passenger, and at least five and 3ft1in/91cm to be a passenger). Junior Track, a flat concrete track with a 25° bank turn (riders must be 4ft/122cm to drive; single cars only) completes the line-up. There are also bumper cars, boats, trampolines, a large arcade and an ice-cream counter.

Admission: Free, then 3hr Armband (unlimited go-karts and midway rides for 3hrs, not Sling Shot) $25; All-Day

Fun Spot America

Unlimited Armband (not Sling Shot) $32. Or $25 Sling Shot, $7 Starflyer), $8/$6 go-karts, $3 all other rides. Must be 4ft/121cm for Bumper Cars, 3ft 6in/106cm for Bumper Boats and Kiddie Track; noon–midnight daily, (407 370 5353, **magicalmidway.com**). TTTT See website for discounts and promotions.

BRITTIP

ICON Park, WonderWorks, Fun Spot, Magical Midway, Andretti Indoor Karting and WhirlyDome are all open until at least midnight in high season, long after most theme parks are shut, so you can have a day at the park, then let the kids loose to tire them out completely!

WonderWorks

This interactive fun centre is an I-Drive landmark, a three-storey chamber of family fun with a host of novel elements – all built upside-down (the result of a 'tornado experiment that went wrong'!). You have to give full marks for imagination and there's a lot here, especially for 6–12s. You enter through an 'inversion tunnel' that orientates you the same way round as the building, then progress to various chambers of entertaining and mildly educational hands-on experiences that demand several hours to explore fully. The six WonderZones include natural disasters (earthquakes, hurricanes, famous disasters) and Google Earth virtual globe and map; physical challenges (Bubble Lab, Bed of Nails and the chance to make an impression of your body in 40,000 plastic nails at Wonderwall!); Light & Sound (challenges to beat the clock, shape the music and strike a pose); Imagination Lab (with physical and mental challenges to create and have fun); and Space Discovery, where you have the Astronaut Training gyroscope, Shuttle Landers (your chance to pilot the Space Shuttle), a Mercury capsule mock-up and Wonder Coaster (a pair of enclosed 'pods' that let you design and ride your own coaster). There is also a three-storey glow-in-the-dark ropes course with 20 obstacles, Laser Tag game and the 4D XD Motion Theater with two simulator rides, plus Gift Shop and Café.

Also here is the fun of The Outta Control Magic Comedy Dinner Show (p300), with a good-value combo ticket.

Admission: Tickets are $34 adults, $25 4–12s; $32/$22 for The Outta Control Dinner Show; $60/$42 for both; 9am–midnight (407 351 8800, **wonderworksonline.com/orlando**). **TTT** Also included with Go Orlando Card.

iFly Orlando

Next door to WonderWorks is this unmistakable blue and red construction housing one of the most fun 'rides' in town, a 'free-fall skydiving adventure' that is clever, addictive, difficult but exhilarating, with the bonus of being a great spectator sport! It's basically a huge upright wind chamber that provides the feeling of a freefall. The standard 1hr programme provides a full briefing with an instructor, then you're given helmet, pads, goggles, earplugs and flight suit, and your group of 8–12 returns to the flight deck, where you get two 1min supervised 'flights' (which seem a lot longer!). Just watching makes it seem all too easy but, as soon as you hit the chamber, you discover how fiendishly tough it is to just 'hang' in this 125mph/200kph column of air. However, it's a fun, absorbing experience and is almost guaranteed to make you want to try again. There is no fee to watch from the observation area, and you can turn up to see for yourself at any time.

Admission: Standard flight, which includes a certificate, is $69.95; add a photo download for $3.95 or video clip download for $7.95. Discount coupons (for return visitors) and gift certificates can be found on its website. Try the 3 Flights package for $89.95, 4 at $111.95 or 5 for $131.95. Try the 2-flight package with Virtual Reality headset for $109.95.

For real addicts, a 10 Flight package offers 10 1min flights within 30min

for $299.95, including video clips. Open noon–8pm Mon–Thurs, 10pm Fri, 9am–9pm Sat, 9am–7pm Sun, reservations recommended (407 337 4359, **orlando.iflyworld.com**). **TTTT**.

Whirlydome

This indoor fun centre boasts a unique game, full-service restaurant, arcade and other novel elements.

Their stock in trade is the hilarious **WhirlyBall** game, a cross between bumper cars, basketball and lacrosse (!) as two teams of five battle for possession of a whiffle ball and try to hit a target at either end. There are two courts of 4,000ft^2/370m^2 and the centre provides a ref. It is open to all-comers or groups and games are timed in periods of 10min. Guests must be at least 4ft 6in/137cm to play but it is easy to pick up and the Whirlybugs, like fancy bumper-cars, are easy to drive. It is free just to turn up and watch (and is great spectator fun). Playing time is $8/player for 10min, or you can hire the court at $250/hr. In addition, the Dome also offers **Arcade Machines** ($5 play card), a huge **Laser Tag** venue ($8/10min) and a novel **Laser Frenzy** room, where players try to navigate a maze of laser beams, haze and mirrors ($3). More arcade games, and billiards and pool in **The Bar** upstairs fill out the entertainment, while the **Bloodhound Brew Pub & Eatery** is a surprisingly smart restaurant, with great local microbrews and a tempting menu (Happy Hour 5–7pm, 10pm–midnight Fri–Sat). The Dome is open 4–10pm Tues– Thurs, 4pm–midnight Fri, 11am– midnight Sat, 11am–10pm Sun.

I Fly Orlando

See more, including Monthly Specials, at **whirlydome.com** (407 212 3030).

> ──**BRITTIP** ◄▮▶
> Check out Whirlydome's website for special offers, including Unlimited Whirlyball or laser tag discounts.

Andretti Indoor Karting

This amazing indoor centre features some of the best go-karting in Florida – and a LOT more besides. Billed as the longest indoor track in the world, the state-of-the-art racing is terrific and features three different levels, Adult (at least 15 and 4ft 6in tall), Intermediate (12–15 and 4ft 6in) and Junior (at least 4ft tall). But then there is an excellent Ropes Course, 10-pin bowling, Laser Tag, high-tech race-car simulators, a massive array of the latest arcade games, Gear Coaster virtual reality roller coaster, plus an XD Dark Ride 3-D interactive film experience, which adds a thrilling extra element to the usual shoot-'em-up games against zombies and monsters! (Kart races from $21.95; Ropes Course $11.95 for 10min session; $11.95 XD Dark Ride; Bowling $25–35/hour, plus $3.50 shoe rental; Laser Tag $12.95; Gear Coaster $5.95; 10am–midnight Sun–Thurs, 1am Fri–Sat; 407 374 0085, **andrettikarting.com/Orlando**).

> ──**BRITTIP** ◄▮▶
> If you're likely to go for multiple rides or visits at Andretti Indoor Karting, consider their $25 Family Membership deal, with discounts on all the activities, plus food at the Andretti Grill.

Helicopter rides

These are another local staple, and you can try any one of nine tours with **Air Florida Helicopters** at 8990 International Drive. Each flight requires at least two passengers, and the choice includes a basic 8ml/13km flight around SeaWorld and I-Drive, tours of Disney, Universal and Downtown Orlando, plus a grand 30ml/48km journey that covers the homes of the rich and famous in Windermere. Just $25 for the short flight to $364 for the longest ($25–335 under 12s; see website for discounts). No need to book; just turn up and go. They fly 9.30am–sunset daily (407 354 1400, **airfloridahelicopter.com**).

Escape games

These have become all the rage in Orlando recently, with eight opportunities on I-Drive to test your wits in a Crystal Maze-type challenge. Here are two of the best.

The Escape Game: Choose from six intensely themed games (Prison Break, Gold Rush, The Heist, Mission: Mars, Special Ops: Mysterious Market and Playground), then test your ability to solve puzzles and unscramble clues in rooms filled with props and special effects, with a strict one-hour time limit that determines whether you succeed or meet a dire fate, at least symbolically. A Game Master helps out with hints if you get stuck, but there is a real sense of pressure, and ages 13 and up get the most out of the experience. Single players can make up the number with other groups but this is good family fun and also a great place to come in case of bad weather. Booking is highly advisable, but not required. They also list a handy 'degree of difficulty' with each game, so you can judge the level you're happy to tackle ($34.99/person in groups from 2–4, up to 4–12 players, depending on game; 9am–11.45pm daily; 407 501 7222, **bit.ly/brit-escape**).

Escapology: This venue on southern I-Drive (in a shopping/office plaza just north of Sheraton Vistana Villages resort) offers a sophisticated style with a 'living room' to encourage visitors to relax before their briefing for one of seven games (which change periodically), and enjoy a complimentary photo and debrief afterwards. Designed for families and friends in private groups of 2–6, the game rooms can even be used for side-by-side games to test each group. Visitors should book online and then turn up at the allotted time, get locked into their chosen game for 60mins and have to find the clues to escape from situations like Under Pressure, Mansion Murder, Narco, Cuban Crisis, Budapest Express, 7 Deadly Sins, and Antidote. Again it's a real test of initiative, teamwork and lateral thinking, and each room has a Game Master to monitor progress and provide a few clues if needed (11am–11pm daily; from $30/person; 407 278 1515, **escapology.com/orlando**).

BRITTIP

Players are advised to arrive 15mins early for escape games to allow time for paperwork and briefing. No entry once the clock has started. It's important to select a leader and work as a team. Oh, and visit the loo first!

Also on I-Drive (on Hawaiian Court next to the Rosen Center hotel) is an outlet of the **Chocolate Kingdom** (see p237).

Mini-golf

For those in need of more holiday fun, don't miss the mini-golf outlets along International Drive (see p268).

Kissimmee

Old Town: This shopping and entertainment attraction in the heart of tourist Highway 192 in Kissimmee has recently undergone a major overhaul. As well as the shopping (p334), it's worth trying the live events, rides and attractions. Look for the high-energy games arcade **Happy Days Family Fun Center** and **Rootin and Tootan's Shooting Alley**, which is great fun for kids (and dads with a competitive streak). More family entertainment is provided by **The Great Magic Hall**, with live magic shows at 3, 7 and 9pm daily ($15/person) and terrifying **Mortem Manor** haunted house with live actors ($15/person, 6–10pm Wed–Thurs, midnight Fri–Sat, 11pm Sun). Old Town is open 10am–11pm, restaurants 11am–11pm (407 396 4888, **myoldtownusa.com**). Old Town

also features the **Saturday Classic Car Cruise**, the **Friday Muscle Car Cruise** and **Bike Night** each Thurs.

Fun Spot America: Next to Old Town is another version of this amusement park, with a good selection of rides, including the high-adrenalin **Hot Seat** swinging ride, go-kart tracks and Mine Blower coaster. The big daddy of them all is the **SkyCoaster** (or optional **SkySled** harness for those who want to sit upright), a 300ft/90m tower that sends up to three riders at a time on a free-fall plunge that turns into a giant swing – at 85mph/136kph! The more down-to-earth rides consist of two multi-level tracks, the labyrinthine **Chaos** and **Vortex**, with its challenging banked bowl section. The other 14 rides are almost as much fun, like the fairground **Flying Bobs**, **Fun Slide** and **Paratroopers**, and the giant swing of **Headrush 360**. More swinging fun is provided by the **Screaming Eagles** and **YoYo**, while standard **Tilt-A-Whirl** and **Bumper Kars** add to the line-up. There's a well-stocked indoor **Snack Bar** when you need to cool down, as well as an **Ice Cream Kiosk**, while kids will gravitate to the **Midway** and **Arcade** (perfect for a wet or super-hot day), plus the thrilling **Rock Star** wild mouse coaster. The big ride is **Mine Blower**, a unique, tight-turning wooden coaster that includes a rare barrel roll and steep 115-degree overbanked turn that adds real thrills for adrenalin junkies.

Admission: Free, then ride prices are Single Day Pass ($49.95 per person not including SkyCoaster, and Arcade); SkyCoaster is $40 for one rider ($35ea double rider, $30ea triple,

Orange County History Center

$20ea with Single Day pass). Open 10am–midnight, 2pm–midnight off season (407 363 3867, **fun-spot.com/kissimmee**).

Chocolate Kingdom: Sandwiched between Old Town and Fun Spot is this cute and ultra child-friendly opportunity to see how chocolate is made – and get some tasty samples! Sign up for their 1hr tour (on the hour) and you join a quest to help a handsome prince woo a chocolate-loving princess – and get a history lesson in the process. Select the pre-tour Chocolate Bar option and you can have a custom-made bar created before your eyes at the end of the tour (10.30am–6pm daily, $16.95 adults, $12.95 4–12s; 407 705 3475, **chocolatekingdom.com**).

BRITTIP

To visit the downtown Orlando Information Center, take exit 82B off I-4 and there are four multi-storey car parks, including the Library (take 4th right on Central Boulevard). Or take 2nd right, Church St, go across Orange Ave and left into the Plaza multi-storey, more expensive but more central.

DOWNTOWN ORLANDO

The last few years have seen a major revitalisation of Orlando's city centre ('downtown'), with new offices, apartments, shops and restaurants. This makes it a tourist attraction in its own right and it is well served by the Information Center on Orange Avenue (10am–5pm, Mon–Fri; 407 246 2555, **downtownorlando.com** – click 'Visit Downtown'). Start here to get a full overview, with a 3-D city model and ultra-helpful staff (plus free wi-fi). They can provide free maps of the area, several tour guides (including food, cocktail, and art tours) and

Lake Eola

info on riding the free LYMMO bus service around downtown. There is also a free guided tour at 9.30am on the first Fri of each month with local historian Richard Forbes (Oct–May). Much of the former Church Street Station area is also vibrant again, **churchstreetdistrict.com**.

Orange County History Center

This smart part of the downtown scene offers an imaginative journey into central Florida history, from the wildlife and Native Americans to today's tourists and the space programme. The accent is on hands-on exhibits and audiovisual presentations, and it is very much a journey through time, starting with the Natural Environment and First Peoples and moving on to the 1800s, with an authentic pioneer 'cracker' home, tales of Florida's ranching days, a Seminole settlement, and tourism pre-Disney. Aviation explores World War II bombers to the outer reaches of space and the Theme-Park Era explores the opening of Walt Disney World and beyond. An exhibit on African American history and a series of travelling exhibits round things off.

Getting there: On E Central Boulevard (exit 82B off I-4, go across South St and take 3rd right; see also map p214), park at the Public Library multi-storey car park on Central (10am–5pm Mon–Sat, noon–5pm Sun; $8 adults, $7 seniors (60+), $6 5–12s; 407 836 8500, **thehistorycenter.org**).

Getting around: Everywhere is walkable downtown, but the free Lymmo bus service connects the central area along Magnolia Avenue, from South Street and City Hall up to the Centroplex area. Or try the **Hop Around Orlando** service, a bike-sharing scheme allowing rentals from specific hubs around the city, for $1 per ride, then 15 cents per minute/$15 all day, unlimited rides; **gohopr.com/orlando** to download the HOPR app).

Theatre and more

Orlando loves its theatre, and those wishing to take in a performance should look for the **Dr Phillips Center for the Performing Arts**, which features touring Broadway shows, ballet, concerts and more (1844 513 2014; **drphillipscenter.org**); the amazing Amway Center, home to the Orlando Magic basketball team, Orlando Predators Arena League outfit and Orlando Solar Bears minor-league ice-hockey team, plus major concerts (407 440 7900; **amwaycenter.com**); the improv of **SAK Comedy Lab** at Eola Capital Loft on S Orange Avenue (407 648 0001, **sakcomedylab.com**); and **CityArts Factory** featuring local and national artists (407 648 7060, **orlandoslice.com**). Downtown also has a thriving public arts scheme, **See Art Orlando** (**seeartorlando.com**).

Dining: The restaurant/bar choice is also pretty good here, too. Take your pick from **Wall Street Plaza** (a lively collection of bars and lounges that are the heart of downtown nightlife), the upscale **Kres Chophouse**, and Church Street Station, the remains of the old entertainment district, which still includes a cluster of fine restaurants and bars, notably the stylish Spanish cuisine of **Ceviche**, the fun **Harry Buffalo** and outrageous **Hamburger Mary's Bar & Grille**, plus the first US outlet of the famous **Ace Café**. See more in Orlando By Night (p296).

Lake Eola: Once you have sampled the hustle-bustle of downtown, head out to this gem, with more restaurants and shops, plus a beautiful lakeside walk, children's play area, swan paddle-boats, new artwork and a peaceful ambience. There are regular open-air concerts at the **Disney Amphitheater** and the **Sunday Farmers Market** (around Lake Eola, 10am–4pm) is another focal point, with vendors including local artists as well as wonderful fresh produce.

Dining: Stop for a great meal, with a view, at **310 Lakeside** (407 373 0310, **310parksouth.net**. Continue on to Thornton Park Central (at the junction of Summerlin Avenue and

Central Boulevard, just south-east of Lake Eola), offering a mix of unique boutiques and trendy restaurants. **Soco** is a fabulous choice for Southern contemporary cuisine (traditional southern comfort food given an all-new twist) and is a real locals' favourite (407 849 1800, **socothorntonpark.com**). **Anthony's Pizzeria** is a great upmarket pizza restaurant (407 648 0009, **anthonyspizza.com**) and **Dexter's** is a smart café/wine bar with a fab Sunday brunch (407 648 2777, **dextersorlando.com**).

BRITTIP

Don't miss the annual Spring and Fall Fiestas around Lake Eola, with hundreds of vendors, live entertainment and special fun for kids, the first weekend in April and Nov (**fiestainthepark.com**).

Loch Haven park

Continue north and you travel the 'Cultural Corridor' to Loch Haven Park and the area's fine collection of theatres, museums and the Orlando Science Center.

Getting there: On Princeton Street in downtown Orlando, just off exit 85 of I-4 (go east on Princeton; the Science Center is on the left but the multi-storey car park is on the RIGHT, see map p214).

Orlando Science Center: The Orlando Science Center is more than a mere museum and far more fun than the average science centre. Here you are given a series of hands-on experiences and habitats that

Orlando Shakespeare Theatre

entertain as well as inform, and school-age children in particular will benefit greatly from it. It has seven main permanent exhibits, plus periodic travelling ones (in 2019 it was Teenage Mutant Ninja Turtles), a night sky observatory, an inviting café, Science Store and a giant screen cinema.

NatureWorks gets you up close and personal with some of Florida's most fascinating reptiles (including gators and turtles) while you step back into the prehistoric age at **DinoDigs**.

Visitors discover the dynamic forces and systems that shape Earth, and other planets, in **Our Planet** (be sure to experience the Category One hurricane), and take on the challenges of **Kinetic Zone**. And there is more to explore with electricity, magnetism, lasers, soundwaves and nature's forces in **Dr Dare's Lab. Flight Lab** virtual reality cockpit simulatoris for ages 8 and up, while pre-schoolers will appreciate **KidsTown**, an interactive playground dedicated to smaller explorers. Each Jan also sees the fun **Otronicon**, a four-day event celebrating the best in video game technology. If you like gaming and simulators, you'll LOVE Otronicon! In addition, the centre has several programmes in **Dr Phillips CineDome**, a 310-seat cinema that surrounds its audience with large-

Volcano Bay

© Universal Orlando Resort

format films and digital planetarium shows. The **Digital Adventure Theater** adds educational films and Science Live! real-life experiments and interactive programmes in partnership with National Geographic.

Admission: $21 adults, $19 seniors (55+) and students with ID, $15 3–11s; parking $5, includes a mainscreen film (Fri, Sat and Sun). 10am–5pm daily (closed Easter Sunday, Thanksgiving Day, Christmas Eve and Christmas Day; osc.org) AAA

The extensive **Orlando Museum of Art** (407 896 4231, omart.org) is here, and, the diverse **Mennello Museum of American Art**, with a permanent collection by painter Earl Cunningham (407 246 4278, mennellomuseum.com) and the **Orlando Philharmonic Orchestra** (407 896 6700, orlandophil.org). For something different, **Orlando Shakespeare Theater** produces classic, contemporary and children's plays in partnership with the University of Central Florida. Their ambitious, high-calibre productions include 2019's *Hamlet* and 2018's *Shakespeare in Love*, and provide a thoroughly innovative theatrical experience while showcasing William Shakespeare's legacy (407 447 1700, orlandoshakes.org).

BRITBONUS

Save $10 on tickets to signature series shows with **Orlando Shakespeare Theater**. Use code BRITGUIDE at checkout for all A and B level seats on orlandoshakes.org (not valid for Previews, Senior Matinees or *Henry IV, Part 2*).

Parents should also note the superb **Orlando Rep**, a company specialising in family theatre, with youth academies, summer camps for kids and special sensory-friendly shows. Their 2019 season included *Sussical the Musical; L'il Abner, Shrek The Musical Jr* and *Beat Bugs: A Musical Adventure* (407 896 7365, orlandorep.com). Highly recommended.

THE WATER PARKS

Florida specialises in elaborate water parks, and Orlando boasts the very best. Predictably, Disney's two water parks are the biggest, but Universal's Volcano Bay is a brilliant addition, and SeaWorld's Aquatica may be the most laid-back. They adopt a variety of styles that owe much to the flair of the theme park creators, and are imaginative for both the rides and imagery around them. All require at least half a day of splashing, sliding and riding to get full value from their rather high prices. Lockers are provided for valuables and you can hire towels.

Disney's Typhoon Lagoon Water park

When Typhoon Lagoon opened in 1989, it was the biggest and finest in Florida. And, although it has since been superseded, in high season it is still the busiest, so be prepared for queues. Arrive half an hour early if possible as entry often begins before the official opening hour. The park's 56acres/23ha are spread out around the 2½acre/1ha lagoon fringed with palm trees and white-sand beaches. It is extravagantly landscaped and the walk up Mount Mayday provides a terrific overview. However, you need to arrive early to bag a decent spot. Or, for $42–75 extra, you can reserve two beach loungers, two towels, an umbrella and a small table by stopping in at High 'n Dry Rentals (or calling in advance). Really want to splash out? Opt for a Beachcomber Shack (cabaña), which includes a locker, drinks mug, cooler with ice, bottled water, towels, loungers and table, and waiter service. Full day rental for up to six guests will cost $239–362. Reserve in advance on 407 939 7529 (we're fans of arriving early and getting your loungers for free!).

BRITTIP

Take water shoes or socks to all the water parks. They are cheap in local supermarkets.

Getting there: On Buena Vista Drive, ½ml/800m from Disney Springs (see map, p214). Admission: $69 adults, $63 3–9s (under-3s free); included with Ultimate tickets; parking free; 9am (10am off season) to dusk daily. **TTTT** AAAAA

BRITTIP

Water parks provide both a great way of cooling down and an easy way of getting sunburn. So don't forget the high-factor *waterproof* suncream, and reapply often.

Beating the crowds: To avoid the worst of the summer crowds (when

Blizzard Beach
© Disney

the park often reaches its 7,200 capacity), Monday morning is best (steer clear of weekends at all costs) and, on other days, arrive either before opening or in mid-afternoon, when many decide to dodge the daily rainstorm. Early evening is also pleasant when the park lights up.

BRITTIP

Want to learn to surf? Typhoon Lagoon offers Surfing School 2hrs before park opening every day. Call 407 939 7529 in advance to book at $190/person.

Slides and rides: The park is overlooked by **Mount Mayday**, on top of which is perched the luckless Miss Tilly, a shrimp boat that legend has it landed here during the typhoon that gave the park its name. Watch out for the water fountains that shoot from Miss Tilly's funnel at regular intervals, accompanied by a blast from the ship's siren, signalling another round of BIG waves in the **Surf Pool** (and they are big; take care with toddlers). Circling the lagoon is **Castaway Creek**, a 3ft/1m deep, lazy flowing river offering the chance to float along on rubber rings.

The slides and rides are all clustered around Mt Mayday and vary from the

Miss Adventure Falls

© Disney

breathtaking body slides of **Humunga Kowabunga** that drop you 214ft/65m at up to 40mph/48kph down some steep inclines (make sure swimming costumes are securely fastened!) to **Ketchakiddee Creek**, which offers a selection of slides and pools for youngsters under 4ft/122cm. In between, you have the **Storm Slides**, body slides that twist and turn through caves, tunnels and waterfalls, **Mayday Falls**, a wild 460ft/140m single-rider inner-tube flume down a series of banked drops, **Keelhaul Falls**, a more sedate tube ride, and **Gangplank Falls**, a family ride inside rafts that take up to four people down 300ft/90m of mock rapids. **Crush 'n' Gusher** is a fabulous trio of 'water-coaster' tube rides, plus a large heated pool with zero-depth entry (great for toddlers). It also has an extensive sandy beach, ideal for sunbathing.

Miss Adventure Falls is another family raft ride to rival Crush and Gusher. It features a long lift hill and then a wild white-water adventure over the 'Falls' in a bid to spot some of the treasures acquired by the ocean-going Captain Mary Oceaneer. At fully two minutes long, it is longer than any other Disney water park ride.

BRITTIP

'Buy a disposable waterproof camera to tie around your wrist when you visit the water parks. We bought one cheap at Wal-Mart and have some lovely photos from Typhoon Lagoon,' says reader Judith Bingham.

Keeping out of the sun can also be a problem as there's not much shade. A quick plunge into Castaway Creek usually prevents overheating but do remember your sunscreen. There are height restrictions (4ft/122cm) on Humunga Kowabunga and Crush 'n' Gusher and they're not suitable for anyone with a bad back or neck, or expectant mothers.

Shopping: You can buy anything you have forgotten – even a swimsuit – at **Singapore Sal's**. You CAN'T bring your own snorkels, inner tubes or rafts, but inner tubes are provided on Castaway Creek.

Dining: **Lowtide Lou's** and **Let's Go Slurpin'** both offer snacks and drinks, while **Typhoon Tilly's** and **Leaning Palms** serve a decent mix of sandwiches, burgers, salads and ice-cream. Avoid main mealtimes if you want to eat in relative comfort. You can bring your own picnic (unlike the main parks), although no alcohol or glass.

Disney's Blizzard Beach Water Park

Ever imagined a skiing resort in the middle of Florida? Well, here it is. This park opened in 1995 and is still the largest, with all 66acres/27ha arranged as if it were in the Rocky Mountains rather than the subtropics! That means snow-effect scenery, Christmas trees and waterslides cunningly converted to look like skiing pistes and toboggan runs. The same 'premium' offer at Typhoon Lagoon applies here for two beach loungers, two towels, an umbrella and a small table for $42–74.55. Or, if the price doesn't scare you off completely, you can hire a Polar Patio (cabaña), which includes a locker, drinks mug, cooler with ice, bottled water, towels, loungers and table, and waiter service. Full day rental, accommodating up to six, is $239–362 (admission not included). Reserve in advance on 407 939 7529.

Getting there: Just north of Disney's All-Star Resorts off Buena Vista Drive (see map p14). **Admission:** $69 adults, $63 3–9s (under-3s free); included with Ultimate tickets; parking free; 9am (10am off-season) to dusk daily. TTTTT AAAAA

BRITTIP

Adjacent to Blizzard Beach are the amazing Winter Summerland Miniature Golf Courses (where Santa's elves hang out!), with two elaborate courses that are a great diversion for children (p269).

Slides and rides: Main features are **Mount Gushmore**, a 90ft/27m mountain down which all the main slides run. A ski chair-lift operates to the top, providing a magnificent view. Don't miss the outstanding rides, including the world's tallest

free-fall speed slide, the terrifying 120ft/37m **Summit Plummet**, which rockets you down a 'ski jump' at up to 60mph/97kph. For those not quite up to the big drop, the brilliantly named **Slush Gusher** is a slightly less terrifying body slide. Then there is **Teamboat Springs**, a wild family inner-tube adventure and arguably the best of all the water rides; **Runoff Rapids**, a choice of three tube plunges; **Snow Stormers**, a daring head-first 'toboggan' run; and **Toboggan Racers**, the chance to speed down the 'slopes' against seven other head-first riders. All four provide good-sized thrills without overdoing the scare factor. The side-by-side **Downhill Double Dipper** tubes send you down 230ft/70m tubes in a timed race, with a real jolt half-way down! **Tike's Peak** is a kiddie-sized version of the park's slides and a mock snow-beach, and **Ski-Patrol Training Camp** is a series of challenges and slides for pre-teens.

Melt-Away Bay is a 1acre/0.4ha pool fed by 'melting snow' (actually blissfully warm), and **Cross Country Creek** is a lazy-flowing 1½ml/800m river round the whole park that also floats guests through a chilly 'ice cave' (look out for the ice-water waterfalls!).

Shopping and dining: There is a 'village' area with a **Beach Haus** shop and **Lottawatta Lodge**

Blizzard Beach

© Disney

fast-food restaurant (pizzas, burgers, salads and sandwiches), offering a grandstand view of Mount Gushmore. Snacks are also available at **Avalunch** (ouch!), the **Warming Hut**, **Polar Pub** and **Frostbite Freddie's Frozen Refreshments**.

Volcano Bay

Universal's brand new park with a South Seas theme is 'the next generation of water theme parks', with a novel range of attractions and experiences, plus the free queue-beating system of TapuTapu Wristbands, which allow guests to reserve a return time for most rides.

Getting there: Just off I-4 at the Universal Blvd exit (see map p14). Parking is in Universal's main car park, with a dedicated shuttle to Volcano Bay. **Admission**: $80–85 adults, $75–80 3–9s seasonally (under-3s free; included with the UK 3-Park Explorer Ticket); 9 or 10am to 6, 7, 8, 9 or 10pm daily. TTTTT/AAAAA

Crowned by the iconic Krakatau, the 28acre/11.3ha park features four main areas, with a huge central lagoon and an outstanding mix of attractions. The centrepiece is a 200ft/60m volcano, which erupts with 100ft/30m jets of water throughout the day. More than anything, though, this is a scenic triumph, and it offers many places just to sit back and enjoy the view (with a choice beverage or two!).

Slides and rides: The **Volcano** area features the headline ride of **Krakatau Aqua Coaster**, four person 'canoes' that zoom into and around the volcano; the 70-degree trap-door drop of **Ko'okiri Body Plunge**; the **Kola and Ta Nui Serpentine Body Slides,** which drop two riders at a time down a pair of intertwined tubes; and **Punga Racers**, a four-lane mat plunge through mystical underwater sea caves.

BRITTIP

There are a lot of stairs to climb to reach the entry to most slides, and much of the queuing is not covered, so apply high factor waterproof sun cream often.

No water park would be complete without a lazy river, and Volcano Bay boasts two. **Kopiko Wai** provides a lush, tropical float past pretty scenery and partially hidden lounge areas, while **TeAwa The Fearless River** is a fun, faster-moving river, with rapids and sudden waves to navigate.

Rainforest Village is the biggest area of the park, with four main attractions, including **TeAwa**, and **Taniwha Tubes**, a series of four flumes (two Tonga and two Raki) with crazily twisted tracks and mischievous statues that spray water at riders. The main attraction is the six-person **Maku Puihi Round Raft Ride**, while the **Ohyah** and **Ohno Drop Slides** each end with a significant drop into the pool below, hence their names!

River Village offers water-play areas, **Tot Tiki Reef** and **Runamukka Reef**, with child-sized slides and pop-jets to keep the young 'uns happy. Finally, **Wave Village** features **Waturi Beach** wave pool and **The Reef** serene pool, to round out the offerings. Oh, and don't miss the chance to use your TapuTapu to activate a variety of interactive moments, from firing water cannons at riders on the lazy river to taking selfies at a tiki photo booth.

Tiki-hut style cabanas with towels, locker, loungers, fruit and snacks, and mini-fridge with water are available for hire starting at $199 single cabana (up to 6 people) or from $599 for a family suite (up to 16), per day. Or you can hire two loungers with a shade canopy and lockbox for $49.99. To save time, sign up in advance for the Universal Orlando Resort App so you can add paying privileges to your TapuTapu wristband (**bit.ly/brit-uni**).

Shopping and dining: Each Village has its own high-quality dining outlet, and there are two themed boat bars with an array of cocktails and craft beers (including Volcano Blossom tropical fruit pilsner). Signature restaurant **Kohola Reef**, and tropical **Whakawaiwai Eats**, **Bambu**, and **The Feasting Frog** serve healthy (and tasty!) island-inspired dishes, notably a coconut chicken curry with tacos. There are even four smart shops to complete a pretty picture.

Aquatica by SeaWorld

This eye-catching water park has a wonderful range of children's attractions and facilities, innovative rides and an all-you-can-eat-meal option, spread over 59acres/24ha of South Seas-inspired landscaping.

Getting there: Just across the road from SeaWorld on International Drive, exit 71 or 72 off I-4.

Admission: $67 ages 3 and up; 2-Visit Ticket (with SeaWorld) $150; (discounts with online booking; included with UK 2-and 3-Park tickets); parking $25, preferred parking from $30, locker rental $15 and $20, towels $7; 9am–6, 7 or 8pm (late May–Aug) or 10am–5pm (winter, spring and autumn; aquaticabyseaworld.com) TTTT AAAAA

Slides and rides: Aquatica's signature attraction is the **Dolphin Plunge** (4ft/122cm), a twin body slide that sends riders down 300ft/91.5m of tubes and through a lagoon of playful, black-and-white Commerson's dolphins (it's a touch gimmicky as you catch only the briefest glimpse of them on the way down, but it is an exhilarating slide). You can then view the Dolphins at the end of the ride through the huge lagoon window. Another standout attraction is **Ihu's Breakaway Falls**, with three enclosed tubes featuring break-away floors (complete with heartbeat effect while you're waiting for the drop!) and one outrageous non-breakaway tube that is every bit as scary. Each offers a completely different slide. **Whanau Way** is a quadruple raft ride with two distinct variations that twist and turn before landing with a resounding splash, while **Tassie's Twisters** are double bowl rides that send riders down single or double tubes into giant bowls before splashing back into the **Loggerhead Lane** lazy river (which also has a coral reef viewing section). **Taumata Racer** (3ft 6in/107cm) is a

fast-paced mat slide set up like an eight-lane racing toboggan run, partly enclosed and then with a double drop into daylight (queues can look long here but they usually move quickly). Family raft ride **Walhalla Wave** features a winding, enclosed section before a big splash finale while **Ray Rush** is a thrilling family raft ride in three distinct sections, featuring a fast-launch start followed by a massive water sphere and then a hilarious plunge into an open-air half-pipe before the final splashdown (3.5ft/107cm).

Omaka Rocka features two high-speed single-rider tube flumes, each with three sets of funnels that send you coursing up one side and down the other with a sensational 'feel it in your tummy' weightlessness before final splash-down. New in 2019 was **Karekare Curl** double raft ride that plummets down an enclosed tube, then climbs a massive vertical "wave" wall on its way to the splash-down zone (4ft/122cm). **Big Surf Shores** wave pool offers big dynamic waves, while sister wave-pool **Cutback Cove** features gentler rolling surf. A huge sandy beach offers a large array of sun loungers and umbrellas, and private cabanas (from $59–169 in low season, depending on location, to the Ultimate Cabaña, including upgraded furniture, dining table and a second cabana with couch, coffee table and additional seating for up to eight, at $299–699 seasonally). Call 407 545 5550 to book or go online.

BRITTIP

Head for the Beach area when you first arrive to stake out a place to base yourselves and try to grab one of the bigger fixed umbrellas that offer the most shade.

Dolphin Plunge at Aquatica

© Universal Orlando Resort

Rainy Day Options

For that occasional day when the rain sets in and you need to be inside, here are the attractions that offer excellent indoor activities:

I-Drive: WonderWorks, Ripley's Believe It Or Not, Whirlydome, SeaLife Orlando, Madame Tussauds, Andretti Indoor Karting, Kings Bowl, Titanic, Chocolate Kingdom, Putting Edge mini-golf, Main Event Entertainment (Pointe Orlando), iFly Orlando, The Escape Game, Escapology. **Disney Springs**: NBA Experience, The Void, Splitsville. **Downtown Orlando**: Orange County History Center, Orlando Science Center. **Winter Park**: Morse Museum, Cornell Fine Arts Museum. **Florida Mall**: Crayola Experience. **Kissimmee**: Chocolate Kingdom.

As well as the gentle **Loggerhead Lane** (under 4ft/122cm must wear life vest), you should try the dynamic **Roa's Rapids** (under 51in/129cm must wear a life vest), which provides a helter-skelter whirl along this river feature, with a series of fountains, jets and other watery boosts to keep you bobbing along with no effort.

Ihu's Breakaway Falls

Free life vests are on offer here and it is worth trying one for the feeling of floating along in high style!

Kids' features: The big success of the park, though, is its extensive features for children, from the youngest to young teens. **Kata's Kookaburra Cove** is an exclusive area for those under 4ft/1.2m tall, with a whole range of scaled-down slides, rides, pools and fountains to provide a gentler experience for the young 'uns. By contrast, **Walkabout Waters** is a vast and frenzied 60ft/18m-high water play structure with every kind of climb, slide and water eruptions and outpourings, including two giant buckets that fill and dump in spectacular fashion over those below. Small animal encounters are also designed to appeal to children, so watch out for these around the park (featuring macaws, leggy spoonbills, anteaters, tortoises and a kookaburra).

Shopping and dining: The imaginative **Kiwi Traders** is the biggest of the four shops, but both **Adaptations** and **Beachies** are worth a look. For dining, try **Waterstone Grill** (chicken tenders, burgers, salads, sandwiches, wraps), **Mango Market** (chicken tenders, sandwiches, salads, hot dogs and desserts) or **Banana Beach Cookout** buffet (pizza, chicken, pork, ribs, salads, desserts, non-alcoholic drinks; all-day pass $40 adults, $20 ages 3–9; add refillable souvenir bottle for $7).

BRITTIP

Youngsters can learn to swim at Aquatica, with a week-long course of 45min lessons starting at $89/student. Book on 407 545 5550.

Aquatica features unique elements in Roa's Rapids, Ray Rush and Kookaburra Cove. And, if you buy the two-park ticket with SeaWorld, it's great value in summer, with the day in Aquatica and then the sister park for the evening.

That's the large-scale attractions, but let's explore some alternatives to the mass-market experience…

8 Off the Beaten Track

or When You're All Theme-Parked Out

Orlando's main attractions are undoubtedly a lot of fun, but they can also be tiring and you may need a break from all the hectic theme-park activity. Or you may be visiting again and looking for a different experience. Either way, this chapter is for you.

This chapter could easily be subtitled 'A Taste of the Real Florida', as it introduces the towns of Winter Park, Winter Garden, Celebration and Mount Dora, plus natural delights like the state parks, day-trips, eco-tours and sports.

ORLANDO/Orange County

Winter Park: Foremost among the 'secret' hideaways is this elegant northern city suburb, little more than 30mins from the hurly-burly of I-Drive yet a world away from the frenzy. This is the 'real' Orlando in many ways, with museums, art galleries, boutique shopping, restaurants, walking tours, a delightful 50min boat ride around the lakes and, above all, a chance to slow down. Take exit 87 from I-4, Fairbanks Avenue; turn right on Fairbanks, go east for 2ml/3km and then left onto Park Avenue. The dining and shopping are all one-offs, there are superb annual festivals and a great sidewalk café vibe (**cityofwinterpark.org/visitors**).

Morse Museum of American Art: A must for admirers of American art pottery, American and European glass, furniture and other decorative arts of the late 19th and early 20th centuries, as it includes one of the world's foremost collections of works by Louis Comfort Tiffany. The dazzling chapel restoration from the 1893 Chicago World Expo is on display in its original form for the first time since the late 19th century. It also has special Christmas

Morse Museum

exhibitions and periodic family programmes (9.30am–4pm Tues–Sat, 1–4pm Sun, also 4pm–8pm Fri only Nov–April; adults $6, Seniors $5, students $1, under-12s free; free 4–8pm each Fri Nov–April; **morsemuseum.org**). More local heritage is on offer at **Winter Park History Museum** (10am–4pm Tues–Fri, 9am–2pm Sat; free) and the magnificently preserved **Casa Feliz** historic home (free open house 10am–noon Tues and Thurs, noon–3pm Sun).

Park Avenue: The heart of Winter Park is a classy street of restaurants, shops and a shaded park. At one end is Rollins College (founded in 1885), housing the beautiful **Cornell Fine Arts Museum**, with a vibrant collection of Floridian paintings, sculpture and decorative arts (10am–7pm Tues, 10am–4pm Wed–Fri, noon–5pm Sat–Sun, closed Mon and holidays; admission free; **rollins.edu/cfam**). For shops both unique and fun, look for **Lilly Pulitzer** (women's clothing), **Ten Thousand Villages** (international arts and crafts), **Bebe's & Liz's** (children's clothes), **Tuni** (women's clothing) and the **Writer's Block** bookshop, plus **Peterbrooke Chocolatier**. Street parking allows 3hrs free, but the SunTrust car park on Comstock Ave is a good all-day option.

Hannibal Square is an up-and-coming district within Winter Park, featuring more unique shops, restaurants and cafes, including the chic **Rifle Paper Co** (stationery and creative paper goods), **DeVanes** (gifts). **CFS Coffee, Dexter's**

Cornell Fine Arts Museum

A dining delight

Winter Park boasts some of Orlando's finest dining. **310 Park South** is the epitome of elegant, European café culture while pavement bistro **Briarpatch** (breakfast and lunch), Italian style **Pannullo's**, and fab gastropub **Luma on Park**, (daily specials from simple burgers to gourmet offerings are worth sampling **lumaonpark.com**). The gorgeous **Ravenous Pig** has a wide-ranging choice, from its fine microbrewery to steaks and seafood (**theravenouspig.com**). Or try neighbourhood bar-kitchen-market **Boca** (**bocawp.com**) and the fun Southern-style fast-food joint of **The COOP** (**asouthernaffair.com**). For more variety, seek out any of **Garp & Fuss** (especially their Sunday brunch; **garpandfuss.com**), charming French café **Mon Petit Cheri** (notably for their signature Orlando honey-nougat dessert) or **Prato**, a wildly popular Italian 'gastropub' with superb home-made pastas and pizza, plus craft beer and cocktails (**prato-wp.com**). **Hamilton's Kitchen** at the ritzy Alfond Inn combines fresh food and creative cuisine for a great lunch or dinner (p326). **Hillstone** is also an elegant choice (p329); and local BBQ institution **4 Rivers Smokehouse** is practically essential (p326).

(American comfort food), **Armando's** (Italian patio restaurant) and the fine cocktail lounge of **Hannibal's On The Square**.

Look out for the **Taste of Winter Park** (Apr) and **Autumn Art Festival** (Oct) among a series of high quality annual festivals, while it's also wonderful to visit at Christmas (**experienceparkavenue.com**).

You can also get to Winter Park Mon–Fri on the Sunrail train service (p43).

BRITGUIDE 25

This chapter didn't even exist in our first edition, but has grown significantly with reader demand for more things to do beyond the main attractions. It's now one of our favourites to update each year.

© Cornell Fine Arts Museum

For something different, try **Winter Park Distilling Company** on N. Orange Avenue for great small-batch whiskey, rum, bourbon and vodka, with daily tours, including tastings ($11/person, subject to availability; call 407 801 2714, **wpdistilling.com**). The distillery adjoins the **Bear & Peacock Brewery**, with excellent craft beers and taproom (4–11pm Mon–Thurs, midnight Fri, 11am–midnight Sat, 11am–11pm Sun). Coffee-lovers should head for the next-door **Foxtail Coffee Co**, a Winter Park institution for unique fresh-roasted coffees, cold brews, pastries and merchandise, as well as a real local ambience (6am–10pm daily; **foxtailcoffee.com**).

Park Avenue Walking Tour: Free maps are provided at the Welcome Center for this tour of the area highlights (W. Lyman Ave; 8.30am–5pm Mon–Fri, 9am–2pm Sat; 407 644 8281). **Scenic Boat Tour:** On East Morse Boulevard, this offers a charming one-hour narrated tour for a fascinating look at the local lakes, canals and fabulous houses (several of which top $10m!). Tours run every hour 10am–4pm daily (not Christmas) at $14 adults, $7 2–11s, cash only (407 644 4056; **scenicboattours.com**).

Winter Park Village: For more retail and dining, this large-scale centre features a cinema, big-name shops like Pier 1 Imports, Loft, GameStop, White House/Black Market and Ulta Beauty, and fab dining from Cheesecake Factory, Brio Tuscan Grille, Ruth's Chris Steakhouse and more (**shopwinterparkvillage.net**).

Winter Garden: A taste of small-town America 18mls/28km north of Disney, its historic district along Plant Street consists of boutique shops and cafés, plus the chic Garden Theatre (**gardentheatre.org**). There are two small museums, an art centre, water fountains for children to play in, walking and cycling paths on the West Orange Trail and Farmers' Market every Sat (9am–2pm). For dining, Urban Flats, Moon Cricket Grille, vegetarian-friendly Market To Table, Thai Blossom and the Chef's Table at The Edgewater are all highly recommended, while **Plant Street Market** boasts the fab **Crooked Can Brewing Co** among a variety of fresh food and crafts kiosks (**plantstmarket. com**). Parking is free and there is a lot for the casual wanderer to enjoy here (**cwgdn.com**). Nearby is the 11ml/18km **Lake Apopka Wildlife Drive**, which offers a great look at the local wetlands with its many gators and abundant birdlife. It takes a good 1hr to complete the drive and there are plenty of stopping points and photo spots. It is open Fri–Sun dawn to dusk and is free (**bit.ly/brit-apopka**).

Lake Tibet-Butler Preserve: This small nature reserve is in south-west Orange County (just north of Disney) on SR535 (Winter Garden–Vineland Rd) and features 4ml/6.5km of trails and elevated boardwalks where the cypress swamps, freshwater marshes, scrub and pine flatwoods are home to gopher tortoises, turtles, armadillos and especially birds (it is on the Great Florida Birding Trail; 10am–5 or 6pm Wed–Sun).

Scenic Boat Tours

© Scenic Boat Tours

MOUNT DORA/Lake County

To the west and north of Orlando is this large, rural county that is home to unspoiled Florida charms and small-scale attractions.

Mount Dora: This smallish town on beautiful Lake Dora is one of Florida's hidden gems. It is also renowned as a festival city, with 19 annual galas. Check your dates on **mountdora.com** (4 July and Christmas are notable, while the April Sail Boat Regatta is one of Florida's finest). Start with a stroll sssssround the quaint shops, cafés and bars in the compact centre. Antique hunters are spoiled for choice but should visit **Village Antique Mall**, with more than 80 vendors, and **Renninger's Vintage Antique Center** (weekends only), while other stores include **Papilio** (gifts), **Gold In Art** (jewellery) and **La Petite Maison** (aromatherapy gifts, weekends only). The town even boasts the **Rocking Rabbit Brewery**, with live music on Thurs 7–10pm, Fri and Sat 8–11pm (closed Tues and Wed; **mountdorabrewing.com**). Other stops of interest include **Mount Dora Historic Museum** (the old town jail), which displays more (free) local history, and the **Museum of Speed**, a homage to high-powered American sports cars of yesteryear, plus other memorabilia such as vintage jukeboxes (10am–5pm Mon–Fri, $15/person, no under-14s, cash only; **classicdreamcars.com**).

Central Florida Glides: One of the best ways to see Mount Dora is with these fully narrated tours using two-wheel Segways to take small groups downtown, on to the iconic **Mount Dora lighthouse** and around scenic **Palm Island Park**. They pass some of the city's many fine B&Bs (including the award-winning Magnolia Inn on East 3rd Avenue) and the genteel 125-year-old **Lakeside Inn**, on the National Register of Historic Places, where you can stop for a drink in Tremain's Lounge or dine in the Beauclaire Dining Room (great Sunday brunch – **lakeside-inn.com**). The Segway is easy to master (after a brief hands-on lesson) and ideal for the quiet streets. If you enjoy the 1hr tour, there is a second guided tour

Try a leisurely lunch at the excellent **Copacabana Cuban Café** or **One Flight Up**. **Village Coffee Pot** is the place for coffee and the **Windsor Rose** is an English tea-room. For something stronger, there are notable pubs like **Tremain's Tavern** or **Magical Meat Boutique**. All also offer dinner, but our top three – especially at sunset – are **Pisces Rising**, a lovely Key West-themed restaurant, with a grandstand view of sunsets over Lake Dora, plus fresh Florida seafood and steaks (352 385 2669, **piscesrisingdining.com**); the charming **Goblin Market** bistro tucked away in a quiet corner of town (352 735 0059, **goblinmarketrestaurant.com**); and **1921**, a modern gourmet take on classic Floridian fare with a genuine farm-to-table philosophy, all set in a converted 1920s home (11.30am–2pm Wed–Sun, 5–10pm Tues–Sun; 352 385 1921, **1921mountdora.com**).

of nearby Dogwood Mountain. Each one costs $55/person and tours run daily 9.30am, 11.30am, and 1.30pm (reservations advised; 352 460 2039, **centralfloridaglides.com**; save $6 if booking online). Riders must be 14 and 100–260lb/45–118kg.

Premier Boat Tours: See more via the *Captain Doolittle* from the Lakeside Inn for a fascinating eco-tour of the beautiful lakes and Dora Canal. As well as gators, you may see raccoons, turtles, otters, birds of prey and other nesting birds, with narrated 2hr tours daily at 11am and 2pm ($28 adults, $15 children) and 1hr Sunset Tours ($18 and $12, bring your favourite beverages; reservations advised on 352 434 8040, **doracanaltour.com**). Pontoon rentals are also available.

Getting there: On US Highway 441 north-east of Orlando, take the (toll) Florida Turnpike to exit 267A for the (toll) Western Beltway (429), and the Beltway north to its junction with 441, from where Mount Dora is 10ml/16km further north. **More info:** Mount Dora Chamber of Commerce (352 383 2165, **mountdora.com**). The visitor centre is at 341 Alexander Street.

Lake Louisa State Park: Another gem just off Highway 27 (at the west end of Highway 192), this offers beautiful countryside, with six lakes and rolling hills. There are over 20ml/32km of hiking trails, a picnic pavilion, swimming in Lake Louisa (with lifeguards late May–Aug), plus 20 cabins, sleeping up to six (8am–dusk daily, entry $5/car; 352 394 3969, **floridastateparks.org/park/Lake-Louisa**). Further up Highway 27 is the **Citrus Tower**, built in 1956, with panoramic views from its 22-storey glass observation deck (7am–7pm Mon–Sat, $10 adults $6 3–11s; 352 394 4061, **citrustower.com**); and **Lakeridge Winery**, a 127acre/51ha producing some award-winning wines with free tours and tastings (10am–5pm Mon–Sat, 11am–5pm Sun; 1800 768 9463, **lakeridgewinery.com**).

Revolution Off Road: Perfect for families seeking to enjoy the real Florida beyond the theme parks, this is set in 220acres/89ha of glorious countryside with a private lake. They offer self-drive guided ATVs (quad-bikes), Polaris Razors (buggies), and Mucky Ducks (amphibious vehicles), plus Target and Tag Archery (in teams similar to dodgeball), Clay Shooting and fishing. The purpose-built trails feature two driving sessions (18 or older with photo ID to drive, but no licence required). After a safety briefing, it's off over the sandhills and grasslands on dirt trails and tracks.

Whatever the weather, you'll get dirty, so wear old clothes and close-toed shoes or trainers. Nominated as Central Florida's top off-road adventure park, the fishing lake was named as one of the top 10 private lakes. On the self-drive **Mucky Duck** tour, the amphibious vehicles seat up to four passengers and includes training in the Argo UTVs, then a drive around the trails and into the main lake. Drivers must be at least 18 with a full licence, and passengers at least four (with safety vest). They also feature **Target Archery** on an Olympic range with Level 3 coaches, **Clay Shooting**, for over 16s, and **Fishing** for large trophy bass. Reservations required on 352 400 1322 or **revolutionoffroad.com**. Prices start from $95/drivers, $45/

passengers. A 4hr fishing trip, which includes licence, boat and guides, starts at $250 for two, $350 for three. Archery is $45/person; Clay Shooting, $85 for 30 clays and shots. Take Highway 192 west to Highway 27; go north on 27 for 3 traffic lights; turn left on CR 474 to SR 33; then go right for 2ml/3km and it's on the right. Check-in is 1ml/1.6km down the dirt road.

BRITBONUS
Receive $5/person off any activity at Revolution Off Road by showing your Brit Guide or mentioning it when booking.

OSCEOLA COUNTY
You'll find some of Florida's most scenic natural attractions in the Kissimmee area – you just need to know where to look!

BRITTIP
Dresses are not advisable for balloon trips and hardwearing shoes for the set-up and landing areas are essential.

Balloon trips
Florida is popular for ballooning and you will often see them in Osceola County. The smooth way in which you lift off is breathtaking, but the tranquillity and stunning views are awesome. It's not cheap, but it is appealing to all but young children or those with a fear of heights. It can also be a highly personal ride, with basket capacity starting at just four people.

Revolution Off Road

Orlando Balloon Rides: The main operator in central Florida flies every day, weather permitting, meeting at their smart Reception Center on Highway 27 (near the junction with I-4) at 5.30–6.30am depending on season, as the best winds are nearly always early, then transferring in their vans to the take-off site. Here you can help the friendly crew set up their balloons (which take 16–20 passengers in comfort).

━━━━BRITBONUS

Save $40 per adult and $20 per child on regular flights with Orlando Balloon Rides, weekdays or weekends. Use code OBRBG when booking.

After your 1hr flight, enjoy a champagne landing ceremony before returning to the Center for free snacks and drinks. It lasts 3–4hrs and costs $195/adult, $99 ages 6–14 ($225 and $109 at weekends; no under-6s or expectant mothers). Select hotel pick-ups are available at $20/person for the round trip, or, for $30, you can be part of the chase crew and enjoy the champagne landing. Balloonist Certificates can be downloaded from the website. Book well in advance on 407 894 5040 or **britballoon.com**.

Thompson Aire: Top local pilot Jeff Thompson, with 40 years' flying experience, also flies every day (weather permitting), meeting at the Maingate Lakeside Resort on Highway 192, and returning there for a hearty buffet breakfast. Fares are $185 ($105 10–15s; 1 child 5–9 can fly free with a paying adult; discounts for four or more adults travelling together). Chase package available for non-flyers ($20). Call 407 421 9322 or visit **thompsonaire.com**. Hotel pick-ups can be arranged at $15/person.

Airboat rides

The thrill of airboat rides – like flying at ground level – can be experienced on many of Florida's waterways, but especially in Osceola County. You can explore areas otherwise inaccessible to boats, skimming over the marshes to give you an alternative, close-up view. Travelling at up to 50mph/80kph means it can be loud (you will be given ear protectors) and sunglasses are also a good idea to keep stray flies out of your eyes. It is NOT the trip for you, however, if you are spooked by crickets, dragonflies and similar insects that occasionally land in the boat! In summer, a good insect repellent is essential.

━━━━BRITTIP

Want an airboat ride but don't have a car? Taxis are seriously expensive but Gray Line Orlando feature a ride with Wild Florida plus round-trip transportation from $59 (see p264).

Boggy Creek Airboat Rides: Get out into rural Osceola County at **Southport Park**, all the way down

Orlando Balloon Rides

Poinciana Boulevard, off Highway 192 between markers 10 and 11, and across Pleasant Hill Road into Southport Road – about a 35min drive. Southport Park feels a million miles away from the main tourist areas and you can also enjoy the authentic Native American Village and delicious Boggy Bottom BBQ restaurant and Tiki Bar. Boats go every 30 mins, bookings not necessary (9am–5pm daily; half-hour tour, $28.95 adults, $26.61 3–10s; 1hr $48.95 and $41.61; Sunset and Night tours $59.95 and $50.96; book on 407 344 9550 or **bcairboats.com**).

Wild Florida: A superb operation on tranquil Cypress Lake, this airboat ride and wildlife reserve features 30min, one-hour and night-time rides from their purpose-built dock (a great place for wildlife watching) with the chance to see gators, turtles, birdlife and even snakes from the safety of their six and 17-passenger airboats. It also features a self-contained 13acre/5.2ha **Gator and Wildlife Park** that is home to their growing collection of emus, porcupines, lemurs and sloths, plus plenty of Florida wildlife like raccoons, bobcats, crocodiles and a huge gator pond, plus two albino gators. There is also an aviary and a peaceful boardwalk cypress swamp walk. You can feed some of the animals (for a small fee) and there is an excellent gift shop (remember, you can't bring alligator products back to the UK) and the yummy **Chomp House Grill**, for a snack or lunch (we dare you to try the Swamp Sampler, with gator and catfish!) under their lovely covered pavilion. Their alligator handling and photo opportunities (single photos $15–20; percentage of all photos goes to Florida Panther Conservation Society) are good, too, and you won't see any sign of human habitation out on the Lake. Due to open in late 2019 was the 75acre/30ha, drive-through **Safari Park**, featuring more than 100 exotic animals plus Florida wildlife. Zebras, giraffes and watusi cattle will rub shoulders with white-tail deer, wild boar and cracker cattle, alongside a separate gator pond (home to various nuisance gators

relocated by the Florida Fish & Wildlife Conservation Commission), and you can either drive your own car or take the guided Swamp Buggy tour. A full zipline course is also in the works once the Safari Park is open (see website).

BRITTIP

Want a real Florida dining experience after visiting Wild Florida or the Lazy H Ranch (see p254)? Head back on to Highway 192 in St Cloud for The Catfish Place, a real locals' hotspot serving up specialities like catfish, gator and turtle (as well as steaks, chicken and shellfish). It's as authentic as it gets – see **http://thecatfishplacestcloud.com**.

Booking is advisable but they do go out regularly from 9am–6pm Mon– Sat (closed Sun). The ½hr tour is $29 for adults and $26 for 3–11s; 1hr is $49.50 and $41; 1hr private tour or night-time tour $68/person (must pre-book), or the private night-time tour $78/person (pre-book). All tours include Gator and Wildlife Park, or $10 and $8 on its own. There are also animal encounter add-ons, for up-close experiences with lemurs, a sloth, or a porcupine ($41/person, ages 8 and up), plus 'Dine with Crusher' (lunch in a gator pen! $41/person, ages 12 and up), a Behind the Scenes guided tour ($50/person, 8 and up), the incredible Keeper for a Day, including an airboat tour and lunch

Riding with the Lazy H Ranch

($207, 12 and up), and more. We're big fans of Wild Florida's dedication to providing a home for rescued animals, and their commitment to showcasing Floridian wildlife with a message of conservation (407 957 3135, **wildfloridairboats.com**). To get there, take Highway 192 east to St Cloud (about 20mls/32km), turn right on Vermont Ave (12mls/19km), which becomes Canoe Creek Rd, then right on to Lake Cypress Rd for the final 2mls/3.2km. From Orlando, you can take the (toll) Florida Turnpike to 192 at Exit 244, then continue east to Vermont and follow the other directions from there.

BRITBONUS **$**
Receive $7 off all one hour airboat tours with Wild Florida when you use promo code WILDBRITS when booking online.

Paddling, climbing and horse-riding

Kissimmee Paddling Center: Here's a great chance to get up close with the heart of Osceola County nature, with kayaks, canoes and paddleboards on offer at this site ideally located on Highway 192. Shingle Creek forms the headwaters of the Everglades and is a haven of peace and quiet, perfect for a paddling adventure whether for 1hr or a half day. You can just turn up and go but bookings are advisable. Open daily, 8am–5pm (last rental 3pm), kayaks are $30 for 2hrs, tandem kayaks $43, paddle-boards $20 for 1hr, $30 for 2hrs, while 2hr guided tours are $55 adults, $40 4–11s and 3hr Adventure Challenge is $69 (located in Shingle Creek Regional Park just past Medieval Times; 407 344 0881, **paddlingcenter.com**).

Orlando Tree Trek: Adventure-seekers will want to test out this challenging aerial ropes course in a forested area of Kissimmee south of Disney. There are two kids' courses (ages 7–11; must be able to reach 4ft 7in/140cm), three junior courses (ages 9–11; must be able to reach 5ft 9in/175cm) and four for ages 12

and up (must be able to reach 5ft 11in/180cm), from beginner to advanced in skill level, plus a dual giant zipline to finish. There is a full instruction session, then it is off into the treetops for a series of obstacles ranging from short ziplines to cargo nets, ladders, cable bridges, Tarzan swings and more. It is huge fun but the full four-course challenge will take at least 2hrs, and bottled water, stout shoes and older clothing are essential. Priced from $54.95 ($39.95 Junior courses, $32.95 Kids course), first departure daily at 8.30am (closing time seasonal). Take Old Lake Wilson Rd south from Highway 192 to Sinclair Rd, turn right and it is on the right. Bookings advisable (407 390 9999, **orlandotreetrek.com**).

BRITBONUS **$**
Get 20% off at Orlando Tree Trek when you book in advance. Use the code 'BritGuide' at checkout.

Lazy H Ranch: For a horse-back view of the Osceola County country-side, head to this wonderful family-owned ranch in rural Kissimmee. It can accommodate groups up to six, by reservation only, for trail rides of 1–1½hrs into the neighbouring Twin Oaks Conservation Area, bordering beautiful Lake Tohopekaliga. A former 370acre/1530ha cattle ranch, the scenery now includes grassland, live oak hammocks, wet prairies and marshes, and the birdlife is usually plentiful. You may even spot a gator or two lurking in the lake! It is a wonderfully refreshing escape from the theme park hubbub only 19mls/30km from Disney and, while the trail-ride is designed for beginners, owner Abby Horner also offers full riding lessons and even a **Total Horse Experience**, with the chance for horse fans to spend 2hrs grooming, tacking and riding, as well as untacking and horse-bathing at the main horse barn ($125/person). The trail rides operate year-round (mornings-only in summer) and cost $50 and $70/person but must be booked in advance on 407 414 3113 or **lazyhranch.net** (see website for age and weight restrictions).

A cause for Celebration

Dining in Celebration is a real highlight. Try **Market Street Diner**, a 50s-style diner serving down-home favourites such as turkey dinners and meatloaf, plus milkshakes and desserts. Spanish-Cuban **Columbia** uses unique combinations of authentic ingredients (407 566 1505, **columbiarestaurant.com**); **Celebration Town Tavern**, a casual ambiance, specialising in New England seafood; **Ari Sushi**, is the place for sushi and hibachi dishes; and the **Imperium Food & Wine** is an excellent option for fine wines and cocktails, plus a tempting light bite menu, including sandwiches, salads and flatbreads (407 566 9054, **facebook. com/imperiumfoodandwine**). You should also consider the **Lakeside Bar & Grill** at the Bohemian Hotel, a contemporary American steakhouse with old-world Florida charm, while **Kilwins** is great for chocolate and ice-cream treats and **Wonderland Cookie Dough Co** offers scoops of delicious edible cookie dough!

Celebration

In 1994, the Walt Disney Company set out to build a 'new urban' neighbourhood, a model community with a friendly, welcoming spirit and strong traditional values. The result was Celebration, where picture-perfect Victorian homes mingle with smart town-houses with an array of shopping, dining and entertainment options. Today, it is a self-sufficient, bustling town with a hospital, schools and two hotels. On Disney's southern border off Highway 192, enter at the landmark water tower via Celebration Ave, then follow signs to the Bohemian Hotel in the town centre.

BRITTIP

For Celebration, don't stop at the first set of shops and services you come to off Highway 192. Keep going until you find Market Street and the centrepiece lake that is the proper downtown area.

Market Street shops: Look out for delightful boutiques like **Dazzling** (jewellery), **Little Thimble** (arts and crafts), **Soft as a Grape** (casual wear for the family), **Le Macaron** (French pastries) and **Woof Gang Bakery** (pet needs). There are miles of bike and walking paths, with the pretty lakefront setting, children's play area and periodic festivals. A huge event is held on American Independence Day 4 July, with picnics, entertainment and face-painting (parking is at the town entrance, with a park-and-ride bus), while the Christmas period also sees festive events and nightly snowfall on Market Street (**celebrationtowncenter.com**). You can also take a 20min carriage ride (Fri–Sun, 6–10pm, weather permitting).

Segway Tours

ZE Tours: An outstanding feature in Kissimmee/Celebration is this super opportunity to try out the fab two-wheeled Segway transporter and get a guided audio tour of the area. Ideal for young and old alike (14 and older), they're easy to master and fun to ride as you trundle along Highway 192 and around the most scenic parts of Celebration in eco-friendly style. Choose from three separate tours with a personable guide (10am, 1pm & 3pm daily), from their store in the Rock Church plaza on Highway 192 (by Marker 10) and rolling along for 70, 100 or 130mins to discover Celebration, its lakes, paths and byways, plus

Celebration

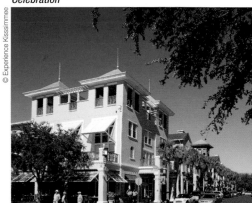

© Experience Kissimmee

its wildlife – from playful squirrels (which you can feed) to gators (which you can't!). There is a quick ride-around to get your 'Segway legs', then it is off in single-file, with the tranquil tour enabled by small helmet walkie-talkies. There are plenty of stops to ask questions, and your guide is a great source of knowledge about the area. Tours cost $60, $75 and $90/person (70, 100 and 130mins; 14–17-year-olds must be accompanied by a parent; minimum weight 100lb/45kg, max 250lb/113kg), or you can just try a ride on a Segway at $10 for 10min, $20 for 20mins, and $30 for 30 mins (closed Sun). Reservations highly recommended (863 512 0256, **zetours.com**).

───**BRITTIP**───

Long trousers and closed-toed shoes are essential for Forever Florida's Horse Safaris. Early morning rides are especially enjoyable.

Forever Florida

This is one of the most outstanding non-theme-park attractions in Florida. Both a 4,700acre/1,900ha wilderness preserve and working ranch, it offers a close-up of the flora, fauna and conservation issues. They specialise in authentic cowboy experiences, plus ziplines, camping, nature trails, cabin rental and the only zipline 'roller-coaster' in the USA!

Charolais Café and Visitor Center: Start here with its essential 30min orientation programme into the

Forever Florida

© Cornell Fine Arts Museum

preserve's creation. Beginning as a dream of gifted biologist and ecologist Allen Broussard, it was completed after his death (from complications of Hodgkin's disease) by his parents, Dr William and Margaret Broussard as a non-profit-making memorial to their son. The education element alone is awesome, and tours feature a strong conservation message. The three **Trail Buggy Adventures** offer a tranquil trundle in a large-wheeled, open buggy around the woods, swamp and prairie of the Crescent J Ranch and Conservancy. You're likely to see alligators, turtles, deer, armadillos and a host of bird life – including bald eagles and wild turkeys – as well as native cattle and horses, and you'll leave with a good insight into the REAL Florida. Try the 45min tour ($21.50 adults, $10.75 6–12s); the 2½hr Big Cat Trail Buggy Adventure, including a visit to the neighbouring **Central Florida Animal Reserve**, with its lions, tigers and cougars ($70 and $43); or the 1½hr Sunset Trail Adventure ($40/person).

Horseback Adventure: For ages 10 and over, here's the chance to enjoy Western trail rides for 45mins with a 'cracker' (Florida cowboy) guide ($50/person, book in advance on 407 957 9794 or online).

Cattle Drive Adventure: Learn cracker skills like rounding up cattle on this 2hr horse-ride, taking the herd out to pasture and back ($105/person, ages 10 and up).

Cowboy For A Day: Experience life on the ranch, riding alongside the foreman for a day on the Crescent J, driving cattle from pasture to pasture, checking fences and caring for livestock, all on horse-back, and complete with hat and lunch ($149/person). The **Overnight Horseback Camping Adventure** takes things a step further with a 3hr trail ride, campfire steak dinner, a night in a tent, breakfast, and then the return 3hr trail ride ($270/person).

EcoPark: Central Florida's must-not-miss attraction for thrill-seekers, featuring a seven-tower zipline course, zipline roller-coaster, hair-raising straightaway zipline, free-fall attraction and climbing wall. The 2hr **Zipline Safari** starts with a short scenic hike to the launch point, which provides a superb view of the preserve at up to 78ft/23.7m high. It includes seven ziplines, 10 observation platforms and three sky-bridges over three eco-systems. The longest run is 750ft/229m at top speeds of 25mph/40kph. The final zip brings you to the wildlife interaction area, including a Florida panther, alligators and other animals ($80/person, ages 10 and up). There is also a **Nightime Zipline** every Fri and Sat night ($90).

Adventure Pack – The Rattlesnake, Peregrine Plunge & Panther Pounce: The Rattlesnake is 'next generation ziplining' at its best, a 1,000ft/205m long, 20mph/32kph diving and soaring 'roller-coaster' ride from the 65ft/20m high tower. Peregrine Plunge launches from a 71ft/22m tower with 1,300ft/396m of line – the longest single zipline in Florida, at up to 30mph/48kph – and not for the faint of heart. But do it once and you'll want to go again. Want to get to the ground quicker? Tethered to an overhead crane and fitted into a secure harness at Panther Pounce, step off the 78ft/23.7m tower and go straight into free-fall! The effect is mindboggling, with serious bragging rights when it's over ($80/person ages 10 and up; weight limits, 55–265lb/25–120kg). Forever Florida is a 60-80min drive from Orlando, 40ml/64km east on Highway 192, through St Cloud as far as Holopaw, then 7½ml/12km south on Highway 441, but is well worth the journey to experience the charm and tranquillity (407 957 9794, reservations necessary for all experiences, **foreverflorida.com**).

Osceola County History Center & Pioneer Village

Highway 192 (just by Marker 15) features the **Osceola County Welcome Center** and **History Museum**, a collaboration between the County and Historical Society, providing a small-scale but engaging look at the area's history and nature. There is a 'steamboat' entryway inside, then a tour of local history from 1867 to the present, through the four main 'habitats' (swamplands, pinc flatwoods, oak hammocks and lakefront) with a series of tableaux and nature exhibits that depict the nature of central Florida, plus the original Indian tribes. Outside, you can wander alongside Shingle Creek, the headwaters of The Everglades (free admission daily 9am–5pm; 407 396 8644, **osceolahistory.org**). After seeing the museum, cross over Highway 192 to Shingle Creek Regional Park for a chance to wander the hiking trails and experience Osceola nature.

Next, head for the **Pioneer Village**, just off Highway 192 on Babb Road. This delightful discovery pays real-life homage to 19th-century Florida life, with a preserved 'cracker' homestead, blacksmith shop, Seminole Village and other buildings portraying how settlers lived in the 1880s. The charming outdoor museum traces more Osceola County history and includes an array of homes owned by historically-known Floridians. The tours are self-guided, or volunteers can take you round, providing a

Cracker House at the Pioneer Village

© Osceola History

fascinating view of life here more than 130 years ago (2491 Babb Road, just off Highway 192. Take Old Vineland Rd to Babb Rd and turn left; 10am–4pm daily; $7 adults, $3 4–12s, under-4s free).

Warbird Adventures and Kissimmee Air Museum

This is the most exhilarating ride in town, bar none – guaranteed. It's the only place we know of where, 20mins after walking in with no previous experience, you can actually be flying a 1945 T-6 Texan fighter-trainer plane… and doing all manner of aerobatics. It's enhanced by in-flight video and wingtip camera to record every moment. Roller-coasters? They're for wimps! Mind you, this is not cheap – a 15min flight costs $290, 30mins is $490, 45mins is $690 and an hour $790 (aerobatics included, if desired, on 30–60 minute flights). Nevertheless, the memory will last a lifetime and just the thought of it is thrilling. New in 2019 was a truly unique opportunity to fly in a dual-seat P-40 Warhawk World War II fighter, with flight options from $990–2,850. Max weight is 18st/115kg and minimum height is 4ft/122cm. Also on the same site at Kissimmee Gateway Airport is **Kissimmee Air Museum**, combination warplane showcase and restoration centre where you can get up close with 22 exhibits, which include a 1947 Hiller Raven helicopter, a 1928 Arrow Sport, a Boeing Stearman biplane, three T-6 Harvards and the amazing one-off Aerocar, plus small-scale offerings like

a WWII rifle collection and Luftwaffe memorabilia. Other aircraft include a racing P-51 Mustang, a French Fouga Magister and a MiG 17. It can all be found just off Hoagland Boulevard, ½ml/800m south of Highway 192, on the left (Air Museum open 9am–5pm Mon–Sat; $12/person, ages 6–12 $6, under-6s free; 407 870 7366, **warbirdadventures.com**).

Stallion 51: If the T-6 Texan isn't thrilling enough, how about a P-51 Mustang? Yes, seriously. This two-plane operation also flies out of Kissimmee and offers orientation flights in their special dual cockpit WWII fighters, from basic manoeuvres to full aerobatics. It is a real connoisseur's experience, hence very pricey but just watching the planes in flight is a thrill, while being in the cockpit is truly mind-blowing (407 846 4400, **stallion51.com**; call or email for latest pricing).

POLK COUNTY

Head south from Kissimmee/Osceola County and you head into Polk territory, another of Florida's oldest-established and most authentic areas. It is home to the large-scale attractions of LEGOLAND Florida (p219) but also has its share of off-the-beaten-track experiences.

Bok Tower Gardens

This national monument and garden centre at Lake Wales, 50ml/80km to the south-west of Orlando (go west on I-4, then south on Highway 27) boasts one of the most unusual attractions in the state – a majestic 205ft/62.5m pink-and-grey marble Carillon Tower. Set in 50acres/101ha of parkland, the Singing Tower, a 1920s-built carillon, is the centrepiece and concerts are given every day at 1 and 3pm.

Gardens: Around the Tower is a wide moat, a pond and semi-formal gardens. At one of the highest points on Florida's peninsula (all of 298ft/90m above sea level), the view is inspiring and uncluttered. The gardens also provide a wildlife observatory, nature trails, an endangered plant exhibit, butterfly and woodland gardens and

Bok Tower Gardens

Pioneer Days Festival at Lake Wales

Lake Wales

Continue on to the Lake Wales area after Bok Tower Gardens and you encounter some other local gems.

Head into the quaint 1920s town of Lake Wales and you discover **Spook Hill** (where cars mysteriously roll uphill!), **Grove House Visitor Center** (home of Florida's Natural fruit juice products – as fresh as it gets; 10am–5pm Mon–Fri; 10am–2pm Sat, seasonally. Closed Memorial Day– end of Sept) and the quaint **Museum and Cultural Center** (set in a restored 1928 Atlantic Coast Line railroad station; 9am–5pm Tues–Sat).

pine forests. There is a kids' play area, plus brass rubbing and family-friendly guided tours.

Education and Visitor Center: The award-winning centre illustrates the story of Edward Bok (don't miss the film about his impact on US society) and his vision for Bok Tower Gardens. The Blue Palmetto Café adds a pleasant opportunity for a light lunch and snacks, while the Tower & Garden Gift Shop offers souvenir items. Kids can borrow free Discovery Backpacks, which make exploration interesting and educational.

Westgate River Ranch: In rural Polk County is this superb ranch and activity centre that boasts great accommodations (including 'glamping' for those who like to camp in style, plus Luxe Tepees and stand-alone Saddle Club Rail Cars) and the chance to try horse-riding, fishing, airboating, trap shooting and archery, as well as take in the exciting Saturday night Westgate Rodeo in the 1,200-seat arena. You can visit just for the day to try any of the activities or the weekly rodeo (followed by live music, line dancing and a family-friendly Street Party), but the accommodations are excellent and you can sample the River Ranch Saloon without having to drive afterwards – guaranteed family fun and a taste of Florida's cowboy country. See more at **westgatedestinations.com** and click on River Ranch, FL.

BRITBONUS $

Show your *Brit* Guide to receive a $3 discount off regular adult combo admission tickets at Bok Tower Gardens (Gardens and Pinewood Estate).

Pinewood Estate: For an additional fee ($6 adults, $5 5–12s, 10am–4pm in spring, 11am–3pm in summer, 10am–5pm Christmas week), you can tour the Mediterranean-style architecture in this 20-room mansion, built as a winter retreat for a Pennsylvania steel tycoon in the early 1930s and lovingly maintained to show a slice of period opulence.

Getting there: Off US Highway 27 on Burns Avenue; take I-4 west to exit 55, go south on US 27 for 25ml/40km, then left on Mountain Lake Cutoff Road (two traffic lights past Eagle Ridge Mall) and follow the signs. Admission: $15 adults, $5 5–12s (under-5s free), apart from occasional ticketed events (mainly carillon festivals and recitals). Open 8am– 6pm daily (last entry 5pm; Visitor Center 9am–5pm only; 863 676 1408, **boktowergardens.org**).

Westgate River Ranch swamp buggy

SEMINOLE COUNTY

You may have flown into the airport at the historic town of Sanford and there are plenty of diversions to get you well off the beaten track. If you want to finish your holiday with a day or so in the area, there are many good hotel choices (often significantly cheaper than their big-name rivals elsewhere) and, after all the hectic theme-parking, you can catch your breath here in Orlando North, as they like to call it!

Adventures in Florida: Get into the wilds with this specialist company that features kayaking adventures along the picturesque Econlockhatchee and Wekiva rivers, with expert guides and an in-depth understanding of the flora and fauna. They offer 2–3hr trips, all-day tours and even night-time paddles, manatee kayak encounters and bioluminescent tours, as well as expeditions and lodge-based trips further afield. Along the Wekiva River you may encounter gators, manatees, turtles and all manner of birdlife, all in safety and with personable guides. Trips must be booked in advance and cost $45–80/person (407 924 3375; **adventuresinflorida.com**).

Central Florida Zoological Park: This private, non-profit organisation is a natural zoo, set in a wooded 116acres/47ha of unspoilt countryside with boardwalks and trails around over 100 species of animal, with weekend feeding demonstrations, educational programmes, a picnic area, giraffe feeding, children's barnyard zoo and a butterfly garden, plus the Zoofari Outpost gift shop, train ride, carousel and Tropical Splash Ground water play area. It's good value at $19.50 adults, $15.95 seniors (60+) and $13.75 3–12s and is open 9am–5pm daily (not Thanksgiving Day or Christmas Day). Also try **Seminole Aerial Adventures**, a separate series of eco-friendly rope bridges, ziplines, guide wires and other aerial challenges through the Zoo's treetops. The two courses can be taken separately or combined (4ft 6in/137cm to take part), plus there is a children's course (for 3–12s). It costs $35.95 for the Upland course and $14.95 for kids, while the combo Upland and Rainforest costs $47.95. Opens at 9am, last adventure 2.30pm (off exit 104 of I-4; 407 323 4450, **centralfloridazoo.org**).

BRITTIP

Keeper Chats and Demonstrations take place daily throughout Central Florida Zoo, with fun insights into the park's animals, including rhinos, cheetahs, warthogs, gators and more.

Sanford: The heart of Seminole County, this quaint town on Lake Monroe boasts a historic centre full of brick-paved streets, antique shops and an artist colony regeneration project (Jeanine Taylor Folk Art). It boasts an increasingly sophisticated array of dining and several great micro-breweries. It's small-town America, having lost the growth battle with Orlando decades ago, but it makes a peaceful diversion with the lovely Riverwalk along the lakefront. Head first for the **Historic Sanford Welcome Center** (230 East 1st Street, 10am–5pm Mon-Thurs, 10am-8pm Fri–Sat, noon–5pm Sun) and the **Sanford Museum** (520 East 1st Street) for an overview of city history, founded in 1877 by pioneering lawyer and diplomat Henry Sanford as a hub on the St John's River, the 'Nile of America.' The free museum (11am–4pm Tues– Fri, 1–4pm Sat) illustrates the life and

Wekiva Island

times of the city's founder, its growth as the 'celery capital of the world' and recent life as a naval base. Part of that river-going heritage is on display with the **St John's Rivership Co**, an authentic sternwheel paddle-boat that offers 3–4hr lunch cruises (and some Sat evenings). With a huge array of food, live music and dancing, it is a great way to get a close-up of the river and its wildlife aboard the five-deck *Barbara-Lee* that includes an open-air top deck, 60-seat dining room, dance floor and cash bar serving wine, beer and signature cocktails. It runs 11am–2 or 3pm Wed, Thurs and Sat, noon–3pm Sun and 7.30–10.30pm some Sats ($47–$61/person; book on 321 441 3030 or **stjohnsrivershipco. com**). In the evening, stop for a bite on First Street, with its many restored turn-of-the-century buildings. Try **The Corner Café** (fresh sandwiches, soups and salads) or the down home family cookin' of the **Colonial Room**. **Hollerbach's Willow Tree Café** is a German diner featuring traditional food, beers and live music Fri–Sun evenings (11am–9pm Sun–Thurs, 10pm Fri and Sat; 407 321 2204, **willowtreecafe.com**). If you like the food, visit Magnolia Square Market, a lovely deli run by the Hollerbach family just round the corner. **The Imperial** is an antique store by day and a fabulous bar by night, with cocktails and craft beers. For great burgers, fish and sandwiches, we also like **The Breezeway Restaurant & Bar** (11am–9pm Mon, 10pm Tues–Thurs, 11pm Fri–Sat, 8pm Sun; 407 878 1284, **thebreezewayrestaurantandbar. com**) and **The Corner Café**, a classic American lunch option serving tasty soups, salads and sandwiches (11am–4pm Mon–Sat, 407 322 3779, **thecornercafesanford.com**). There are also six brew-pubs or micro-breweries, of which the **Sanford Brewing Company** is a great example on S. Sanford Ave I a great example (11.30am–10pm Mon–Thurs, 11.30am–midnight Fri, noon–midnight Sat, noon–9pm Sun; 407 732 6419, **sanfordbrewing.com**). Well worth trying for more tastes and history of the area are **Sanford Food Tours** (guided 3hr walking tours of the

town and its growing foodie profile, with plenty of samples and even food demonstrations along the way; $65/person), and the **Limo Cycle**, a great fun 15-person pedal-powered 'limo' that tours the downtown area, stopping at scenic points and for regular drinks. Especially good for birthdays and other celebrations, it runs Thurs–Sun evenings (21 and up only) from $30/person. (424 299 4441, **limocycle.com**).

The second Thurs in every month in Sanford features the **Alive After Five** street party 5–8pm on First Street, with music, street artists, restaurant samples and more. Admission is free, food and drink extra. Look up **sanfordwelcomecenter.com**.

State Parks: You could head for one of the splendid parks and follow the well-marked trails. **Wekiva Springs State Park** offers bike rentals, hiking, canoeing, swimming, picnic areas and shelters, and **Little Big Econ** state forest has 5,048acres/2,045ha of scenic woodlands and wetlands. **Spring Hammock Preserve** offers 1,500acres/607ha of wilderness and the Lake Proctor area has 6ml/10km of equestrian, hiking and biking adventures.

Wekiva Island: This fabulous outdoor recreation area is almost a rustic resort in its own right, with a gorgeous location right on the Wekiva River, and a bar, food servery, cabanas, picnic area, boardwalk with lounger chairs, lawn games, beach volleyball and full range of kayak, canoe and paddle-board rentals. The paddling along this stretch of the river is truly serene, and you're likely to see plenty of fish and turtles in the crystal-clear waters, as well as the all-natural vista of the lush, tropical vegetation, plus the source of the springs, which keep the river at a constant 22°C/72°F. It is popular right through the summer, especially at weekends, so aim for weekday mornings, especially if you rent a cabana (which includes your own parking space). The **Tooting Otter** bar serves craft beer and wine, and has its own General Store, while the **Without A Paddle Café** features a surprising array of tempting dishes, including Florida staples like gator, pulled pork and shrimp, and there is live music on Fri and Sat evenings. Park entry is $2/person, and rentals cost from $30–45, while cabanas are $100–200/day (8am–7pm Sun–Thurs, 11pm Fri and Sat; 407 862 1500, **wekivaisland.com**).

More info: See **doorlandonorth.com** or go to one of the Visitor Centers at Orlando Sanford International Airport (in the Welcome Center as you exit the main building) or the office at the Heathrow junction of I-4 (exit 98, go west on Lake Mary Blvd, right on International Parkway and left at AAA Drive; 9am–5pm, 407 665 2900).

WEST VOLUSIA COUNTY

Between Seminole County and Daytona Beach is this enticing piece of Florida real estate with a growing range of attractions and eco-tours, plus an eclectic mix of shops, restaurants and breweries. It makes for a great day-trip from Orlando (or an even better over-night stay), less than an hour along I-4.

Start in the quaint town of **DeLand**, with its historic downtown, museums, boutiques and brew-pubs (notably Persimmon Hollow Brewing Co), plus a great series of annual events (**mainstreetdeland.org**). **Blue Springs State Park** is home to more manatee encounters, plus fishing, boating and kayaking, while eco-adventures are also on offer at **DeLeon Springs State Park**, which boasts the Old Spanish Sugar Mill (p277) for a must-try dining experience. For something completely different, the spiritualist camp of **Cassadaga** is a true original (**cassadaga.org**), and

Volusia County birdlife

the fabulous 19th-century treasure of **Stetson Mansion** is open to the public (Feb–Sept; adults $20, ages 22 and under $15, reservations required on **stetsonmansion.com**). Dining is a definite West Volusia pleasure, notably **Genuine Bistro & Lounge** for great seafood and American classics in Debary (**genuinebistro.com**), and elegant **Cress Restaurant** (**cressrestaurant.com**), **Byte Bistro** (**bytebistrodeland.com**) and fun **Half Wall Beer House** among several dozen great DeLand choices.

BRITTIP

While the **Stetson Mansion** is superb at any time of year, it is jaw-droppingly stunning for the Christmas period (mid-Nov to mid–Jan), when the whole house is decorated in the most elaborate and comprehensive fashion. The 75min tours cost $27 for adults and $15 for youths.

St Johns River Eco-Tours: At Highbanks Marina & Camp in Debary (take I-4 east to exit 104, turn right and go north on SR600 for 4ml/6.5km, then left on W Highbanks Rd and due west for 3ml/4.5km to the Marina) is this wonderful chance to experience much of what West Volusia is all about on the beautiful St Johns River, with a 2hr pontoon boat ride. You will gain expert insight into the superb flora and fauna as well as seeing birdlife, gators, turtles and even manatees. There is free bottled water and a restroom on the boat. Tours leave Tues–Sun at 10am and 1.30pm, but booking is advisable ($30 adults, $17 under 13s; 386 626 9004, **stjohnsriverecotours.com**). You can also enjoy dining at the fun **Swamp House Riverfront Grill**, with an elevated view of the river and marina and the chance to sample catfish and gator nuggets (**swamphousegrill.com**).

Where to stay: West Volusia has some handsome B&B offerings, including the country cottage style of **Cabin on the Lake** (**cabinonthelake.com**).

More info: Get the online Visitor Guide at **visitwestvolusia.com**.

CITRUS COUNTY

If you want to travel a little further, the two state park delights of Citrus County, on the Gulf Coast north-west of Orlando, are worth seeking out.

Crystal River Preserve State Park: Just north of Homosassa Springs, the Crystal River is home to the endangered manatee and it is possible to go swimming with these wonderful creatures, either on a self-guided or an organised tour. Mid-November to the end of March is manatee 'season', but the park offers year-round adventure, with hiking and biking trails, kayaking, canoeing and fishing – or just pack a picnic lunch and enjoy a relaxing afternoon amid the natural beauty. The park hosts the annual **Florida Manatee Festival** each Jan (18-19 in 2020), with an impressive variety of family-friendly activities and events (**gomanateefest.com**). You can also catch a relaxing and educational ride with **Heritage Eco-Tours** aboard the 24-passenger *Monroe* for a unique 1½hr look at local history and wildlife (seasonally, Sept–May, Mon, Wed, Fri, 10.30am and 1.30pm weather permitting; $15 adults, $10 under 13s, cash only; call to confirm on 352 228 6028).

> ──**BRITTIP**
> Manatees are protected and there are heavy fines, strictly enforced, for disturbing or harassing them.

For something really different in Crystal River, try **Scalloping**. From the last Saturday in June to late September, visitors can snorkel along the extensive grass flats in 4–6ft/1.2–1.8m of water and collect scallops with a net. It is a unique experience, and they also make for great eating! **River Safaris** are a top company for scalloping tours, among a fab range of eco-adventures ($85/person, **riversafaris.com**).

Getting there: Take the (toll) Florida Turnpike north to I-75, then, almost immediately, take SR44 west to Crystal River. Admission: Free (8am–dusk; **floridastateparks.org/crystalriverpreserve**).

Homosassa Springs Wildlife State Park: This park also showcases the manatee (via its underwater observatory), plus whooping cranes, deer, bobcats, black bear and even a hippopotamus among an active display of rehabilitating animals. There are daily programmes on its wildlife (every hour from 10.30am–3.30pm), notably snakes and birds of prey, plus a hands-on children's education centre. The park's 210acres/85ha take in some of the state's loveliest landscape as well as the headwaters of the Homosassa River and this is extremely popular in the spring.

Getting there: As for Crystal River, but turn left on to CR490 just after Lecanto on SR44. Admission: $13 adults, $5 6–12s (9am–5.30pm, last entry 4pm; 352 628 5343, **floridastateparks.org/parks-and-trails/ellie-schiller-homosassa-springs-wildlife-state-park**).

Where to stay: In the heart of Citrus County is the **Plantation on Crystal River**, a mansion-esque resort in Kings Bay on the river itself. It features gorgeous rooms, great dining, 18-hole golf and its own manatee eco-tours, as well as lashings of Southern hospitality. You should definitely try lunch or dinner (or the fab Sunday Brunch) at the West 82° Bar & Grill, and, if you go scalloping, the restaurant will cook them for you! (352 795 4211, **plantationoncrystalriver.com**).

More info: Look up **discovercrystalriverfl.com** or call 352 794 5506.

Swimming with manatees in Citrus County

BREVARD COUNTY

Out on the Atlantic coast is Cocoa Beach's Thousand Islands. Tranquil canals wind past mangrove stands, wildlife flourishes in the still waters and the Indian River Lagoon Estuary is one of the most biodiverse eco-systems in the world.

Island Boat Lines: This family-owned enterprise offers eco-tours, fishing and the wonderful *Indian River Queen* dinner boat, recalling Mark Twain's tales of paddleboats and peaceful gentility. A relaxing 2hr **In Search of Wildlife** eco-tour onboard Coast Guard-certified pontoon boats departs from the Sunset Waterfront Bar & Grill on Highway 520 (W Cocoa Beach Causeway), passing some of the area's most impressive homes before heading into the Thousand Islands. Here you may spot bottlenose dolphins, manatees and coastal birds. Knowledgeable guides offer a wealth of info. Tours run at 10am and 1pm Mon–Sat, 1pm Sun, and there is a daily **Sunset Cruise** from 7–8.30pm ($34 adults, $30 seniors and military personnel, $25 2–12s; $25/person for Sunset Cruise. Call to book on 321 454 7414; **islandboatlines.com**).

Getting there: Take the Beachline Expressway (Highway 528) to Highway 1 south, then Merritt Island Causeway (Highway 520) east, approx. 2ml/3.2km with the Bar & Grill on the right.

BRITTIP

Get $8 off the regular adult price with Island Boat Lines by using code Brit20 when booking online.

Indian River Queen: Also used for private events, this beautifully appointed triple-deck paddlewheel riverboat is open to the public at weekends, with an elegant **Dinner Cruise** one Fri each month featuring live music, dinner buffet and full bar. Captain Todd and owners Penny and John provide authentic Southern hospitality. Boarding begins at 6.30pm, sailing from 7–9.30pm ($60 adults, $40 ages 3–12). The **Sunday Scenic River Cruise** offers 2hr tours with live music for $30/$25, select dates only (booking required on 321 454 7414 or **indianriverqueen.com**).

Getting there: To reach Cocoa Village Marina, take the Beachline (Highway 528) east to Highway 1, go south to Highway 520, make a slight left at Bee Line, continue to N Cocoa Blvd, turn left at King, then left at Delannoy.

Cocoa Beach Sportfishing: Board the fully equipped *Centerfold*, a 33ft/10m Tournament-rigged boat, and get ready for big game

Indian River Queen

© Indian River Queen

fishing! Troll for mahi-mahi, sailfish, wahoo, kingfish, grouper and more with a crew who boast plenty of experience in finding 'the big one'. *Centerfold* offers 5 and 8hr offshore or nearshore trips at $700 and $900 (fishing licence, tackle, bait included; reservations on 321 848 2662, **cbsportfishing.com**). For more Cocoa Beach info, p277.

Port Canaveral: This area immediately adjacent to the busy cruise port (right off Highway 528) is well worth a visit as it boasts some great small-scale attractions as well as tempting places to eat, all with a great view of the port. Start at the **Exploration Tower**, a seven-storey museum and exhibition centre featuring the region's history and livelihood through a range of multimedia presentations and hands-on exhibits (like the Port Navigation simulator). There is also a wonderful top-floor open-air observation deck, plus a café and gift shop (daily 10am–5pm; adults $6.50, seniors $4, children $3.75; closed public holidays; 321 394 3408, **explorationtower.com**). **Space Coast Segway Tours** are a great way to have fun and see the whole area on these two-wheel vehicles, with a tour guide who takes you round and points out the key elements of the Port and its many facilities. Tours for six run five times a day, including an evening tour, (not Tues and Thurs Sept–Feb) and can take anyone from 45–118kg/ 7–18st, following a short training session ($65/person, $75 evening tour, cash only; reservations required; ages 14 and up; 321 652 4169, **spacecoastsegwaytours.com**).

There is great restaurant choice along Glen Cheek Drive. Try any of Rusty's Seafood & Oyster Bar, Fishlips Waterfront Bar & Grill, Seafood Atlantic and, our fave, **Grills Seafood Deck & Tiki Bar**, an indoor/outdoor beach-themed café with nightly entertainment and fresh food, from sushi to burgers (7am–10pm Sun–Thurs, 11pm Fri–Sat; 321 868 2226, **grillsseafood.com/ port-canaveral**).

EXCURSION OPERATORS

For those without a car (or wanting to put their feet up for a bit), there are tours and day trips visiting as far afield as the Everglades, Miami, Florida Keys and even the Bahamas. You can see a lot if you don't mind a long day (up to 16 hours). However, if the main attraction of a trip to the Everglades is the airboat ride, you are better off going to Wild Florida (p253).

BRITTIP

Be sure to look up our *Brit Guide* partners for the full range of Gray Line excursions – with your exclusive 15% discount.

Gray Line Tours: Orlando's biggest excursion company and a *Brit Guide* partner, offering 15% off all tours, from transport-only trips to Kennedy Space Centre to all-day tours to the Everglades, plus limo pick-ups for Disney character dining, all with air-conditioned coaches, and knowledgeable guides. See full-tour options at **graylineorlando.com**.

Kennedy Space Center: Gray Line has an exclusive bonus with their KSC tour as guests are greeted and given a welcome briefing by a bona fide astronaut before they explore the Visitor Complex at their leisure for the day. The KSC can also be combined with an airboat ride, the Dine With An Astronaut experience, or the Small Group VIP Experience for maximum access to the Space Center ($59–189).

Lake Eola in Downtown Orlando

© Brady P for grayline tours

1-Day Miami: Get the best of Miami with this long day-trip to Florida's biggest city, taking in the Bayside Marketplace shopping centre, marvellous South Beach and the Star Island boat cruise. Another option is to include an Everglades airboat ride, or just the Miami hop-on, hop-off bus tour around the city. It does require a whopping 16hr day, but you will see a *lot* ($99-145).

Wild Florida: This is another tour that can be combined in multiple ways, from the straightforward transport and airboat ride, to combos with Keeper For A Day and Ultimate Package additions ($40-222).

Western Ranch Adventure: Another Gray Line exclusive, this takes visitors to Westgate River Ranch in Polk County (see p259) for the Saturday Night Rodeo. As well as comfortable round-trip transport, it includes a barbecue dinner, hayride, live entertainment and line dancing, as well as the weekly rodeo ($89).

St Augustine: Florida's oldest city is well worth visiting, and makes for a great day-trip to tour the famous Castillo de San Marcos, the oldest schoolhouse in America and ride the hop-on, hop-off Trolley that travels around the main area ($75–95).

Clearwater Beach: This is one of the best beaches and, again, is a day-trip that can be combined with several different elements, such as the Clearwater Marine Aquarium (home of Winter the dolphin; p283); a dolphin cruise, Captain Memo's Pirate Cruise and the huge Sea Screamer powerboat ($69–115).

Orlando City Tours

© Grayline Tours

Swim with the Manatees: Head out to the Crystal River with your tour guide for the chance to experience this rare opportunity to swim and snorkel among the gentle manatees that frequently make the river their home ($114).

BRITBONUS $

To claim your Gray Line 15% discount, use the promo code BRITS15 at checkout.

Other Gray Line highlights are the 12-hour fishing tours (from $125–135); Winter the dolphin experience in Clearwater Beach ($85); and a City Tour of Orlando, including Lake Eola and Winter Park ($75). Book tours in advance on 407 522 5911 or **graylineorlando.com**.

City Sightseeing Orlando: This British-owned company (formerly Florida Dolphin Tours) offers several dozen tours, notably swimming with manatees, Gatorland and airboats, beaches, and sports events. No. 1 is the

BRITBONUS $

For something different and uplifting, book Gray Line's Gospel Brunch at Disney Springs' House of Blues, including round-trip transport, admission, buffet, show and a city tour. Sun, from $119.

Florida Adventure Tour: breakfast, a 2hr boat trip (with snorkel to check out the manatees), picnic lunch, then an airboat ride and trip to Homosassa State Wildlife Park to see the manatees being fed ($139 adults, $109 3–11s). Call 407 352 4646 or visit **floridadolphintours.com**.

Of course, you can also have a great day-trip by heading for the beaches in your hire car (see Chapter 9).

SPORT

In addition to virtually every form of entertainment known to man, central Florida is one of the world's biggest sporting playgrounds, with a huge range of opportunities to either watch or play your favourite sport.

Golf

Florida's No.1 sport, with hundreds of courses, offers numerous packages for golfers of all abilities and, with an 18-hole round, including cart hire, from as little as $35 (average around $65), it's an attractive proposition. If you go in for 36-hole days, it's possible to save up to $55 by replaying the same course, while it is cheaper to play Mon–Thurs, and there are lower rates for afternoon tee-times in summer. Sculpted greens, manicured fairways, abundant water features and white-sand bunkers add up to memorable golf. Winter is high season, hence more courses are expensive, but many courses are busy year-round. Some courses pair golfers with little thought for age, handicap, etc, so if two of you turn up, you may be paired with strangers.

BRITTIP

Golf balls are cheap so there's no need to bring them. Good-quality clubs are usually available for hire.

Virtually every course will offer a driving range, plus lockers, changing rooms and showers, while the use of golf carts is universal (including the GPS system, which gives the yardage for every shot). They feature comforts like iced-water stations and drink carts that circulate the course (remember to tip the trolley drivers). Some have swimming pools, and all offer a decent bar and restaurant. **Edwin Watts Golf** on Turkey Lake Rd carries clubs and accessories (9am–8pm Mon–Fri, 9am–7pm Sat, 10am–6pm Sun; 407 345 8451). **Tee-Times USA** (1800 374 8633, **teetimesusa.com/orlando-tee-times**) offers excellent advice and a reservation service. Visit Florida has its own golf section at **visitflorida.com/golf**. Website **golfnow.com** is also a great source of tee times all over Central Florida, and usually at reduced rates. New on the scene – and great for non-golfers with its smart restaurant, bar and family games – is the massive **TopGolf** floodlit driving range on Universal Boulevard (next to Andretti Indoor Karting). This state-of-the-art facility is ideal for golfers of all abilities to sharpen their game, or take a lesson, in air-conditioned comfort (9am–midnight Mon–Thurs, 9–2am Fri, 8–2am Sat, 8am–midnight Sun; 407 218 7714, **https://topgolf.com/us/orlando**). Then you can take your pick from the following representative selection:

Walt Disney World: Disney has three high-quality courses, including the 7,000yd/6,400m Palm, rated by Golf Digest in its top 25 (the 18th hole is reputedly one of the toughest in America), plus a nine-hole par-36 course, Oak Trail. Fees are $79–125 for Disney resort guests and $85–129 for visitors ($25–39 at Oak Trail) varying seasonally, with a third off Twilight Rate. Call 407 938 4653 for tee-times. Private and group lessons are available under PGA pro guidance, with video analysis and club rentals. Former Disney course Osprey Ridge is now part of the magnificent Four Seasons Resort as Tranquilo Golf Club.

BRITTIP

Some of the best tee-times at Walt Disney World golf courses are reserved for those staying at a Disney resort.

Arnold Palmer's Bay Hill Club & Lodge: Here's a chance to play this legendary course (site of the annual Arnold Palmer Invitational event) without the huge membership fees. From late May to early Jan, Bay Hill offers 'Bucket List' packages, with a night in a Lodge guest room, breakfast and 18 holes on the Championship course for around $200/person (1888 422 9445, **bayhill.com**).

ChampionsGate: Two magnificent Greg Norman-designed courses to

Disney's Magnolia Golf Course

© Disney

the south of Disney (exit 58 off I-4), the practice facilities, clubhouse, service and coaching (from the renowned David Leadbetter Academy) are world class (407 787 4653, **championsgategolf.com**).

Dubsdread: The oldest public course in Orlando and the only municipal one, just east of the city centre, this offers a testing 18 holes featuring narrow fairways and 'postage stamp' greens, plus a beautiful clubhouse, restaurant and pub, where the likes of Sam Snead and Ben Hogan rubbed shoulders in the past (407 246 2551, **historicaldubsdread.com**).

BRITTIP

Visit Dubsdread Golf Course and be sure to spend some time in The Tap Room, their speciality bar and restaurant, with a great setting for a memorable meal or just a beer and a burger.

Falcon's Fire: An outstanding course in Kissimmee, with plenty of water around the course to assure a testing 18 holes, but it is highly picturesque (407 239 5445, **falconsfire.com**).

Grande Lakes Orlando: This wonderful resort complex just off John Young Parkway is a Greg Norman masterpiece, offering 18 holes of Florida nature with a caddie-concierge service (407 393 4900, **grandelakes.com**).

Hawk's Landing: At the Orlando World Center Marriott, this beautiful course boasts extensive practice facilities, a superb shop, resort exclusivity and Bill Madonna's Golf Academy (407 238 8660, **marriottworldcenter.com**).

Hyatt Grand Cypress: A luxury experience close to Disney, with three elegant nine-hole courses and a superb 18-hole links-style offering, all designed by Jack Nicklaus (407 239 1909, **grandcypress.com/golf_club**).

Mystic Dunes: Just off Highway 192 near the Disney entrance, this course winds through native oaks and is a real test (407 787 5678, **mysticdunesgolf.com**).

Orange Lake Country Club: Huge vacation resort 4ml/6km from Disney with 2 18-hole, a 9-hole and rare par-3 floodlit 9 (407 239 1050, **orangelakegolf.com**).

Shingle Creek: World-class facility at the five-star hotel, set among beautiful oaks and pines, including the state-of-the-art Brad Brewer Golf Academy (1866 996 9933, **shinglecreekgolf.com** and **bradbrewer.com**).

Be sure to ask if fees are negotiable. There are often reductions for seniors but check the dress code, as they can vary. Typically, you need a collared shirt, Bermuda shorts and no denim.

Fans: For those just looking to see the stars in action, the big annual event is the Arnold Palmer Invitational at the Bay Hill Club off Apopka-Vineland Road in west Orlando each March. It is a major tournament on the US PGA tour, with Tiger Woods, Rory McIlroy and Justin Rose all regular visitors (**arnoldpalmerinvitational.com**). The Players Championship is also held at TPC Sawgrass in Ponte Vedra Beach each March, just 2hrs from Orlando (**tpc.com/tpc-sawgrass**).

Mini-golf

Not exactly a sport, but Orlando's many extravagant mini-golf centres are a big hit. Several attractions and parks offer mini-golf as an extra, but for the best try the self-contained centres.

Disney's Fantasia Gardens: Next to the Swan Hotel just off Buena Vista Drive is a two-course challenge over 36 holes. The style is taken from classic film *Fantasia*. Fantasia Fairways is a cunning putting course, complete with rough, water hazards and bunkers. 18 holes can take more than an hour ($14 adults, $12 children, 10am–10pm daily).

International Drive: Try the 18-hole **Congo River** in front of the Four Points by Sheraton Orlando International Drive ($13.99 adults, $12.49 under-10; 10am–11pm Sun–Thurs, 10am–midnight Fri and Sat) or **Pirates Cove**, the original and most imaginative I-Drive set-up, with a whole Pirate 'village' at its entrance, while the eye-catching courses include caves, waterfalls and rope bridges to test your skill over twin 18-hole challenges (9am–11.30pm daily; $14.50 adults, $12.95 4–12s, or $23.95 and $21.50 for all 36). There is another Pirates Cove set-up at Lake Buena Vista, at the back of the Crossroads shopping plaza ($11.95 and $10.95, 9am–11pm). **Putting Edge** has indoor glow-in-the-dark mini-golf next to the Cinemark cinema at the top of I-Drive (2pm–10pm Mon–Thurs, 11am–midnight Fri–Sat, 11am–10pm Sun; $12.50 adults, $10.50 under-9s). **Gator Golf & Adventure Park**, next to Murphy's Arms Pub, has a variety of gator shows daily, plus some challenging mini-golf (10am–10pm, admission to park $5; golf $10 adults, $8 3–11s; gator photos, feeding and handling for additional fees).

Kissimmee: Here are the scenic 36-hole **Congo River Golf & Exploration Co** on Highway 192 (by Marker 12; $13.99 adults, $12.49 under-10s; 10am–11pm Sun–Thurs, 10am–midnight, Fri– Sat); **Pirates Cove**, a 36-hole course next to Old Town (10am–9pm Sun–Thurs, 10pm Fri and Sat; $12 adults, $9 4–12s, additional rounds $5); **Mighty Jungle Golf**, with two Africa-themed courses on Highway 192 by Formosa Gardens Blvd (10am–9pm Sun–Thurs, 10pm Fri and Sat; $11.50 adults, $10.50 under 12s; $5 extra for 2nd 18 holes); and **Pirates Island Adventure Golf**, off Highway 192 between markers 14 and 15 (10am–9pm Sun–Thurs, 10pm Fri and Sat; $12 adults, $9 4–12s, additional rounds $3).

Universal's Hollywood Drive-In Golf: This creative twin 18-hole set-up at the entrance to Universal's CityWalk has *The Haunting of Ghostly Greens*, a 1950s mock-horror themed selection that includes putting through a cemetery and a giant spider's lair, and *Invaders From The Planet Putt*, 18 holes of best sci-fi humour that feature an alien spaceship and 30ft/9m robot. And, while it looks good during the day, it sparkles at night with LED lighting. It also stays open long after the theme parks have closed (9am–2am; $16.99 for adults, $14.99 3–9s, or $31 and $27 for both courses; **hollywooddriveingolf.com**).

Winter-Summerland Mini-Golf: At the entrance to Blizzard Beach is a half beach, half snow-themed 36 holes. An adult round is $14 ($12 3–9s), and double round is half price (10am–10pm; Blizzard Beach admission not required).

Footgolf

This family-friendly activity is one of the world's fastest-growing sports and the most fun and challenging we have tried to date. A mixture of soccer and golf, it is played on a full golf course, but with a football and extra-large holes. Plan 2½ hours for a full round.

Disney's Oak Trail: This pretty course often sees wildlife roaming the grounds, including deer, wild turkeys and armadillos. Regular golfers share the course, but the 18 footgolf holes are distinct. Book on 407 939 4653 after 1pm daily ($15-25/person, included with the UK Ultimate Tickets; **golfwdw.com/footgolf**).

Hawks Landing: 18 holes at the Orlando World Center Marriott, with tee times available Tues and Sat only, after 4pm. $35/adult, $17.50 under 18s (1800 567 2623, **golfhawkslanding. com/footgolf**)

Reunion Resort: You must be a resort guest to play this challenging 18-hole course, at $35/adult, $18 under 16. Tee times Sun–Wed starting at 3pm, golf cart included (1866 880 8563; **reunionresort.com/golf/foot-golf**).

Pirate's Cove

Freshwater fishing

Freshwater fishing attracts enthusiasts worldwide. The primary draw is the chance to catch giant Florida bass – which grow to record sizes in the area's grassy waters – and view some of the wildlife.

Florida Freshwater Fishing License: To fish here you need to get this from the Florida Fish and Wildlife Commission (**http://myfwc.com/license/ recreational/freshwater-fishing** with a credit card). You'll be issued with a temporary licence number within minutes, enabling you to fish right away. A permanent licence will be mailed within 48 hours. A three-day licence costs $17, seven-day $30. It's advisable to book at least two weeks in advance, especially at peak times.

AJ's Freelancer Bass Guide Service: This long-running company specialises in trophy bass fishing on Lake Toho in Kissimmee, rated the best big bass lake in the USA. AJ's holds the record for largemouth bass – 16lb 10oz/7.5kg! Saltwater trips are also offered. All guides are experienced, full-time professionals and rates start at $195 for 2.5hr trip for 2 people, up to $350 for 8hr guided trip, max three clients per boat ($50 for 3rd person; 12 and under free; 407 288 9670, **orlandobass.com**).

Go bass fishing (catch-and-release) at Walt Disney World for $170–$455 for 2–4hrs for a boat with 2–5 people, all equipment and refreshments. Book 24hrs in advance on 407 939 2277. Also see, **experiencekissimmee.com**, Things To Do; Outdoor Adventures & Activities; Fishing, Boating & Water Sports.

Buena Vista Watersports

Water sports

Florida is mad keen on water sports so, on any area of water bigger than your average pond, don't be surprised to find the locals indulging in many watery pursuits.

Buena Vista Watersports: This is the place for jet-skiing ($60/30 min, $105/hr; seats two adults and one child), water-skiing, wakeboard and tube rides ($55/15 min, $95/30min, $165/hour), plus rent pontoon boats, canoes, kayaks and stand-up paddle-boards ($25 per hour) on Little Lake Bryan by the Holiday Inn on Highway 535 (407 239 6939, **bvwatersports.com**).

Orlando Watersports Complex: Just off the Beachline Expressway (528) near Orlando International Airport, this elaborate facility features wake-boarding and water-skiing, by boat and suspended cable, for novices and experts, as well as the novel Aquapark of interlocking obstacles, pathways and slides for great family fun from 10am–6pm, at $20 for 50min session, $30 for 2 sessions, $40 all day (407 251 3100, **aktionparks.com**).

Walt Disney World: Disney offers all manner of boats (from kayaks and canoes to sailboats and motorboats holding from 2–10) and activities like fishing and surfing (at Typhoon Lagoon; p241). Boat rentals are on offer at the Contemporary Resort, Yacht and Beach Club, Wilderness Lodge, Fort Wilderness, Polynesian Village and Grand Floridian. Prices vary from $13/hr for a kayak to $45/30mins for a pontoon boat. To book, call 407 939 0754.

Spectator events

American sport is well worth trying for a great entertainment event and there is a lot on offer. From the Orlando Predators of the Arena League (an indoor version of American football) to National Cheerleading championships at Disney's ESPN Wide World of Sports, all sports are represented.

Basketball: This is one of the two main sports in town, with the Orlando Magic of the National Basketball Association (NBA). The season runs

Nov–May (with exhibition games in Oct), and the only drawback is the 18,500-seat Amway Center where the team plays (on W Church Street, exit 82B off I-4) can be sold out. Contact the Magic (407 440 7900, **amwaycenter. com**) to see if there are any tickets, but you'll have to call in person to buy them (from $15 in upper seats to over $1,500 courtside), or try StubHub (**stubhub.com** or 1866 788 2482).

---BRITTIP---
You don't need to understand the game to experience some real Americana, just turn up and enjoy the family-friendly excitement.

American football: For the real thing, the nearest teams in the National Football League (NFL) are Tampa Bay Buccaneers, 75ml/120km to the west, Miami Dolphins, 3–4hrs' drive south down the Florida Turnpike, or Jacksonville Jaguars up on the east coast past Daytona, a 3hr drive on I-4 and I-95. Ticket prices and availability from StubHub ($50–300) (Sept–Dec). The Buccaneers also offer 75min tours of their impressive Raymond James Stadium for much of the year ($10 for adults, $7 5–11s; call for times on 813 350 6500 or email **StadiumTours@ TampaSportsAuthority.com**).

---BRITTIP---
Tampa Bay Buccaneers offer an NFL Experience package with round-trip transport to all home games and a discounted game ticket. The coach picks up at Fun Spot on I-Drive, with the return immediately after the game. Tickets cost from $41–242, plus $25 for transport. Email **rtaback@buccaneers,nfl.com** or call 407 487 4366 for more details.

For the best baseball, head to St Petersburg where the **Tampa Bay Rays** play at Tropicana Field (Apr–Sept). Tickets are nearly always available for the superb indoor stadium (p282).

Orlando City Soccer Club: Soccer is firmly entrenched as Orlando's other big sport thanks to our Major League team, playing Mar Oct at their 26,000-seat stadium in downtown Orlando. They have built up a loyal following and games have a superb atmosphere, with tail-gating (a big car park party) at various surrounding venues, food trucks, and live music prior to kick-off. Ticket prices vary from $20–250 (**orlandocitysc.com/ tickets**). The Church Street area is great for pre-game excitement, the weekly 'March to the Match,' and Watch Parties for away games, notably at soccer-themed bar/restaurant, the **Lion's Pride**. For the full inside scoop, check out our very own authorised biography, *Defying Expectations: Phil Rawlins and the Orlando City Soccer Story*, on Amazon.co.uk.

ESPN Wide World of Sports™

Disney's big sports development is an impressive 220acre/86ha state-of-the-art complex, featuring 30 sports. It boasts a 9,500-seat baseball stadium, softball quadraplex, 10-court tennis complex, 5,000-seat indoor facility, athletics and extensive sports fields.

The centre's extensive fields cater for soccer, lacrosse, baseball and softball, and you can often see some keen sporting action just with college and school teams. Disney's Soccer Showcase (Sept–Jan) is a fine example of this, with some 400 skilful youth teams competing under the eye of various scouts. Standard admission is $19 adults, $14 3–9s, but it is also an option with Ultimate tickets (excluding special events). ESPN Wide World of Sports™ is off Osceola Parkway, on Victory Way (**espnwwos.com**).

Run Disney: Marathons, half-marathons and 10k and 5k fun-runs

Orlando City Soccer

are now big business, with some great spectacles up to six times a year. Up to 55,000 runners take part – including some of the world's leading athletes – drawing huge crowds and taking in all four Disney theme parks. Be aware of serious disruption in the parks. The annual half-marathon takes place the day before the main race, which is on Jan 12 2020 (**rundisney.com**).

Rodeo

An all-American pursuit, the **Silver Spurs Rodeo** is staged twice a year at the 8,300-seat Silver Spurs Arena. The biggest event of its kind in the south-east, it is held in Feb and early June (check website for dates). It sells out fast so book in advance on 321 697 3495 (**silverspursrodeo.com**). The event features classic bronco and bull riding and attracts competitors from as far as Canada. The arena is part of Osceola Heritage Park, which includes Osceola County Stadium (for baseball) and the Kissimmee Valley Livestock Show and Fair Pavilion. The Arena is a state-of-the-art facility and there isn't a bad seat in the house.

Making a welcome return in 2019 was the Friday evening **Suhls Rodeo** in Kissimmee, a full western experience featuring bull riding, barrel racing, bronc riding, rope tricks and more. It is great family fun and a genuine taste of Osceola County culture, with a concession stand, saloon and gift shop to ensure you can also look the part! It costs $30 for adults and $20 for children 4–11 and runs most Fridays from 8pm at the Kissimmee Sports Arena just off

All-American Rodeo

Hoagland Boulevard south of Highway 192 (407 933 0020, **suhlsrodeo.com**). There is also a weekly Saturday Night Rodeo at *Westgate River Ranch* (p259).

Motor sport

Race fans will find some big-league thrills at **Daytona International Speedway** (take I-4 east, then I-95 and Highway 92), the renowned track that hosts more than a dozen events a year, including motor-bike, stock car, sports car and go-karts. Highlights are the **Rolex 24** (a 24hr sports car event, late Jan), the famous **Daytona 500** (Feb), and **Coke Zero 400** (early July). The big events attract crowds of 200,000-plus and offer exhilarating sport. A $400m rebuild of the Speedway in 2016 made this a technological marvel as well as a sporting one, and provides some great daily tours. Choose from the basic 30min Speedway Tour, which provides an up-close look at the fiendishly banked track ($19 adults, $13 6–12s); a 1hr All Access Tour that explores the massive 2.5ml/4km tri-oval in more detail, including behind-the-scenes visits and a photo trip to Victory Lane ($26 and $20); and the 3hr VIP Tour, with visits to the Archive and Research Center and other off-limits areas ($55/person). A huge gift shop and café complete the set-up. The integrated **Motorsports Hall of Fame** (**mshf.com**) offers more fascinating, guaranteed fun, even for non-race fans (1800 748 7467, **daytonainternationalspeedway.com**). The **Richard Petty Driving Experience** is a great opportunity to sample the thrills of NASCAR racing first hand, either as passenger or driver, with a range of different on-track experiences. It costs $150/person for the high-speed, three-lap Ride-Along (age 14 and up, under 18s accompanied by an adult); $80 for Junior Ride Along (6–13s); $600 for 3hr Rookie Experience (tuition plus 8 laps of the Speedway); $1,100 for Kings Experience (tuition plus 16 laps); and $2,100 for the Experience of a Lifetime (an intense 24-lap programme). 18 or over for all but the Ride-Along and Junior Ride-Along (1800 237 3889, **drivepetty.com**).

OK, that's the local area sorted out; now let's take you further afield…

9 The Twin Centre Option

or To Orlando – and Beyond!

While Orlando continues to get bigger and better, it is equally true there is a LOT more to see in the rest of Florida, with some magnificent twin-centre options. From Amelia Island in the north-east to Key West in the extreme south (the 'Floribbean'), it's easy to find wonderful resorts, glorious beaches and superbly authentic experiences.

The beaches of the Gulf (west) coast, the Atlantic coast from Ormond Beach all the way to Miami, and the fabulous Florida Keys all feature some of the best seaside escapes in the world, while cities like Palm Beach, Daytona, Fernandina Beach, Stuart, Fort Lauderdale, Tampa, Miami and Naples provide more Sunshine State fascination. Two-centre (or fly-drive) options are common with most tour operators, but it is also easy to arrange your own. A cruise-and-stay holiday is another great choice, with the ports of Tampa, Port Canaveral, Fort Lauderdale and Miami within easy reach.

You can head out from Orlando in any direction in search of a great twin-centre experience. Go East to Cocoa Beach, New Smyrna Beach, Ormond Beach and Daytona Beach, all with terrific appeal and barely an hour's drive away; the sea is a degree or so cooler on the Atlantic side, and the surf and currents are more noticeable, hence this is good surfing territory, but beware possible rip-currents. To the north-east you have beautiful Amelia Island and historic St Augustine 2–3hrs away. To the north-west is the 'Emerald Coast' of Fort Walton Beach, Destin and Panama City Beach. Go West for Tampa and miles of pristine sands, from Clearwater Beach south to Naples and lovely Marco Island; this is better for families with younger children, while the Clearwater-St Pete Beach area is a perfect combo with Orlando (about 1½–2hrs' drive). Go south-east and you hit Vero Beach, West Palm Beach, Fort Lauderdale and Miami (about a 3½hr drive). Continue south and there are the Keys, a superb 110ml/177km chain of islands linked by roads and bridges, culminating in eclectic Key West. So, heading north-east first, here's what you find.

BRITGUIDE 25

Like *Off The Beaten Track*, this chapter also wasn't in our first edition but has become an integral part of the book because people increasingly want to see more of Florida than just 'Orlando'.

St Augustine

A 2hr drive up I-4 and I-95 brings you to America's oldest city. Founded by Spanish conquistadors in 1565, St Augustine is full of authentic buildings and signs of the original settlement around the imposing Castillo de San Marcos. Much of the original walled city still remains and 18th and 19th-century Mediterranean influences are everywhere. Walk the narrow, uneven streets of the Restoration Area to discover colonial architectural treasures, now home to gift shops, cafés, antique shops, quaint B&Bs and more.

BRITTIP

Spanish adventurer Ponce de Leon was searching for the Fountain of Youth when he arrived at the site of St Augustine in 1513. The modern day Archaeological Park tells the story of his arrival and discovery of the continent of America – and offers the chance to drink the famous waters. Visit **fountainofyouthflorida.com**.

Tours: To see as much as possible, hop on a horse-drawn carriage, the **St Augustine Sightseeing Train** or the **Old Town Trolley Tours** for a narrated tour. For a spookier experience, walk the streets with **Ghost Tours of St Augustine**, with your guide in period costume. Other tours reveal the architectural heritage (also the product of British and colonial American rule). The **Old Jail Tour** – by day or night! – is another fascinating insight into the 19th century period

Other attractions: Florida railway mogul Henry Flagler was a huge influence, building magnificent hotels for his 'passengers to paradise'. The ornate **Lightner Museum**, formerly Flagler's Hotel Alcazar, is home to his turn-of-the-century treasures, including Tiffany and other glass works of art, while the former indoor

Merritt Island wildlife

swimming pool is now a café! There's a modern theatre, art galleries, **Potter's Wax Museum, Ripley's Believe It Or Not Museum** and **Whetstone Chocolates. St Augustine Distillery** offers a chance to visit a working small-batch premium distillery and learn the history of the converted ice factory (free tours daily, 10am–5pm Sun–Fri, 5.30pm Sat; **staugustinedistillery.com**). Golf fans should visit nearby Ponte Vedra for the **World Golf Hall of Fame**.

Restaurants: These range from **The Spanish Bakery & Café** and the famous, family-owned **Columbia Restaurant**, to a modern microbrewery, **A1A Ale Works**.

Where to stay: The premier hotel is historic **Casa Monica** (904 827 1888, **casamonica.com**), while the boutique **St George Inn** (1888 827 5740; **stgeorge-inn.com**) is also a good choice, but there are numerous B&Bs, plus chain hotels like the smart **Wyndham TRYP** (904 209 5580, **trypstaugustine.com**).

More info: St Augustine Visitors & Convention Bureau (904 825 1000 or **floridashistoriccoast.com**).

Amelia Island: Just to the north of Jacksonville is a gorgeous self-contained area of pristine beaches, nature walks and surprising history. **Fernandina Beach** is at the heart of things, with its fascinating colonial heritage and downtown shops and restaurants, while each of **Fort Clinch State Park**, the **Amelia Island Museum of History** and **Amelia Island Lighthouse** are worth visiting. River cruises, horse-riding and kayaking are all on offer, along with world-class golf. Sea turtle nesting is another highlight here, plus bird-watching and eco-tours.

Where to stay: Top resorts are the Ritz-Carlton Amelia Island (904 277 1100, **bit.ly/brit-amelia**), and Omni Amelia Island Plantation Resort (1888 444 6664, **bit.ly/brit-plantation**), while Blue Heron Inn is a gorgeous B&B (**ameliaislandblueheroninn.com**).

More info: Amelia Island Tourism (904 277 0717, **ameliaisland.com**).

Daytona Beach/Volusia County

Travel south from St Augustine and you arrive in this famous beach area.

> **BRITTIP**
>
> Look out for Speeding Through Time, a series of memorials and plaques along Daytona Beach's Boardwalk, highlighting the world speed records set on the beaches, including those of Britons Sir Henry Segrave and Sir Malcolm Campbell.

Daytona Beach: 1hr from Orlando along I-4 east, this family-friendly area includes some chic hotels and restaurants. It is busiest mid-June to mid-Aug but there is something for everyone, especially after Easter when there are often good deals. The beaches are the top draw (some of which you can drive on for a $20 toll; speed limit 10mph/16kph). From there, you can go boating, parasailing, biking, jet-skiing and fishing. Stay in the Oceanfront area at the heart of all things beach-related, with the Pier, Bandshell, Boardwalk and the shops and restaurants of **Ocean Walk Village**, notably **Bubba Gump Shrimp Co** and fun diner **Johnny Rockets**.

Daytona Lagoon: Opposite Ocean Walk Village, this is a water park, go-kart track, mini-golf course, arcade and laser tag centre. The water park has a wave pool and lazy river, seven flumes and an area for toddlers (adults $29.99, children under 3ft 6in/108cm $21.99). The 18-hole mini-golf course ($7.99), single and double go-karts ($8.49–10.49), laser tag (must be above 3ft 6in/108cm, $7.99), Island Hopper kiddie ride ($3.49) and Rock Wall ($6.49) are separate items (**daytonalagoon.com**).

Historic Downtown Daytona Beach: The heart of the city is on Beach Street, with a museum of local history, restaurants, nightclubs, coffee bars and Daytona Beach's only art-house cinema, Cinematique. **Angell & Phelps Chocolate Factory** (free tours, **angellandphelps.com**) is another must-see. Head to the Riverfront in early evening when the street takes on a café society style.

There are plenty of good places to eat, but for something different try the lively **Caribbean Jack's** (on the river at Ballough Road) or chic **Chez Paul** (on N Beach St with a river view). Similar upscale choices are **Martini's Organic** (on S Ridgewood Ave) and the Latin American taste sensation of **Chucherias Hondurenas** (**chucheriashondurenas.com**).

Other highlights: The **Manatee Scenic Boat Tour** out of Ponce Inlet is a leisurely 2hr tour year-round at 10am, 1 and 4pm, or there's a 7pm Sunset Cruise Jun–Sept (on Inlet Harbor Rd; $25 adults, $22 seniors, $16 children; reservations on 386 267 8205, or **manateecruise.com**). Go south on Atlantic Avenue for more choice of beaches and attractions, including **Sun Splash Beach, Frank Rendon Park** and **Lighthouse Point Park**, a 52acre/21ha stretch of nature trails, fishing, observation deck, swimming and picnicking (sunrise to sunset; $10/car). The tide here can retreat up to 500ft/150m and the beaches, open to the public year-round, tend to be quieter, though there can be some serious rip-tides (watch out for the beach signs). At the southern end is the **Ponce de Leon Inlet Lighthouse**, with 203 spiralling steps, a re-creation of 19th-century Florida maritime life from the top of America's second

Daytona Beach

tallest lighthouse, with a superb view (10am– 6pm, 9pm Jun–Aug; $6.95 adults, $1.95 under-12s; **ponceinlet.org**). It also has a lovely gift shop, while **Ponce Inlet Watersports** offers fishing, parasailing, kayaks, paddleboards and great dolphin eco-tours (**ponceinletwatersports.com**).

Marine Science Center: More family fun can be found round the corner from the lighthouse, showcasing mangrove, manatee and sea turtle exhibits, a seabird sanctuary and turtle rehab facility. It has a huge artificial reef aquarium, plus static and interactive educational displays. A boardwalk and nature trail extend through the Center, which also has a gift shop (10am–4pm Tues–Sat, noon–4pm Sun, closed Mon; $5 adults, $4 seniors, $2 under-13s; **marinesciencecenter.com**).

BRITTIP

Try a meal at the Hidden Treasure Rum Bar & Grill at Ponce Inlet for an eclectic Floridian experience.

Daytona Speedway: This is one of the biggest draws (p272), with three great tours of this amazing facility that has undergone a $400m transformation.

Three Brothers Boards: This family-run business of handcrafted stand-up paddleboards offers tours and rentals on the beautiful Halifax River, with its plentiful wildlife. They offer a fascinating 2hr Dolphin & Manatee Adventure through mangrove trails and bird sanctuaries (386 310 4927, **threebrothersboards.com**).

Hard Rock Hotel Daytona Beach

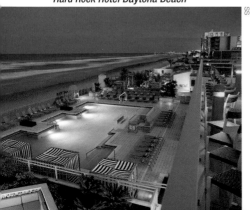

Where to stay: The **Wyndham Ocean Walk Resort** is a huge complex on the beach at Ocean Walk Village, with one, two and three-bed condos (all with kitchens and fab views). Family-friendly, with three outdoor pools, waterslide and lazy river, kids' water play area, two indoor pools, indoor mini-golf, kids' programmes, spa, lounge and food court, (386 323 4800, **wyndhamoceanwalk.com**). The nearby **Hilton Daytona Beach Oceanfront Resort** has spacious rooms, beachfront cabañas and suites, plus terrific dining (notably Hyde Park Prime Steakhouse), two pools and a fitness centre (386 254 8200, **daytonahilton.com**). **The Shores Resort & Spa** is a great boutique choice on a quieter stretch of the beaches, (386 767 7350, **shoresresort. com**), with extra-large rooms, Spa, gracious service and dining. For well-priced chain hotels on the seafront, try **Hyatt Place** (386 944 2010, **bit.ly/hyattdaytona**), **Residence Inn Oceanfront** (386 944 2000, **marriott. com**) or **Hampton Inn Beachfront** (386 944 2570, **hamptoninn3.hilton. com**). The new jewel in the crown is the fab **Hard Rock Hotel**, with extra-large rooms and rock-star vibe. Select the genre of music played in your room when you check in, or request an in-room guitar and amp to free your inner musician! The resort is right on the beach, with excellent onsite dining and memorabilia tours (386 947 7300; **hardrockhotels.com/daytona-beach**).

More info: Daytona Beach Area CVB (386 255 0415, **daytonabeach.com**).

New Smyrna Beach: Continue south on Highway 1 to this 13ml/20km stretch of pristine white sands with great surfing, shell collecting and boating. This is also a keen festival destination, notably for the **Beach Jazz Festival** in Sept (**https://nsbjazzfest.com/**). Other highlights include the shopping and dining of historic and pedestrian-friendly Canal Street, with a Saturday farmers' market (7am–12.30pm, **canalstreetnsb.com**), more shops and galleries along Flagler Avenue (**flaglerave.com**), the kid-friendly

Cook-it-yourself breakfast

Just north of DeLand in DeLeon Springs State Park is the unique Old Spanish Sugar Mill grill and griddle house, famous for hearty, cook-it-yourself breakfasts (9am–3.45pm; 8am at weekends), including pancakes, bacon, eggs, ham, sausage, home-made breads, French toast, sandwiches and salads. You'll struggle to pay more than $10/person and it's great fun, as well as a local institution. However, as it is inside the State Park, there is a $6/car entry fee (386 985 5644, **oldspanishsugarmill.com**). You can then try the park facilities, which include canoes, kayaks, hiking trails and boat tours (**floridastateparks.org**).

BRITTIP

With Florida's burgeoning craft brewery industry, you can find great beer across the state, including the excellent New Smyrna Beach Brewing Co. On Canal Street, it features seven regular beers – including their signature Shark Attack IPA – and various seasonal offerings (**newsmyrnabrewing.com**).

Marine Discovery Center (**marinediscoverycenter.org**) and two superb art centres, **Atlantic Center for the Arts** (**atlanticcenterforthearts. org**) and **The Hub on Canal** (**thehuboncanal.org**). For dining, don't miss **The Garlic**, with outdoor seating under huge oaks. **More info: https:// visitnsbfl.com/.**

Ormond Beach: Immediately to the north is another happening area with more smart resorts and beaches, notably at **Bicentennial Park** (with a nature walk, playground and fishing dock) and **Birthplace of Speed Park** (honouring the first beach automobile race in 1903). Don't miss **The Casements**, the restored former **John D Rockefeller House and Gardens**, with free tours twice a day Mon–Sat (**thecasements.net**). And, for a different shopping experience, **Dunn's Attic & Auction House** is an unusual venue (**dunnsattic.com,** closed Sun). Try a meal at the fun **Lulu's Oceanside Grill** with a great seafood menu, cocktails and weekend brunch, (**lulusoceansidegrill.com**). Or sample the chic **Rose Villa** (**rosevillarestaurant. com**), eclectic **Grind Gastropub & Kona Tiki Bar** (**grindgastropub.com**) and Speakeasy style of **31 Supper Club** (**31supperclub.com**). Another great locals' choice is the sprawling

RiverGrille overlooking the Tomoka River, which is fabulous at sunset with its outdoor decks and Cajun-inspired food (**rivergrillc.net/**).

The Space Coast

Further south on the Atlantic seaboard is the 'Space Coast', home to the iconic Kennedy Space Center (p213).

BRITTIP

For good info on all Kennedy Space Center rocket launches, especially good public viewing locations, see **spacecoastlaunches.com**

Cocoa Beach: Closest to Orlando, barely 50mins east (on the Beachline Expressway 528, then south on Highway A1A), this area has two excellent public beaches plus trademark shopping at Ron Jon's Surf Shop, a massive neon emporium of all things water related. As it's the Atlantic, the sea can be chilly Nov–Apr, but its resort style ensures good facilities (**cocoabeach.com**). If you haven't tried an airboat ride, you should definitely head for **Midway Airboats** on the nearby St John River (daily from 9am; 407 568 6790,

RiverGrille

airboatridesatmidway.com), and don't forget **Island Boat Lines** (p263).

Cocoa Village: This little town on the intracoastal waterway just inland from Cocoa Beach offers a fun array of shopping and dining, with some original boutiques, the historic Cocoa Village Playhouse and two of our favourite restaurants on the coast (**visitcocoavillage.com**). For casual dining, try **Murdock's Southern Bistro** (**murdocksbistro.com**) while **Café Margaux** offers fine dining continental style, with a creative twist (**margaux.com/**).

Titusville: Head here for attractions like the US Space Walk of Fame (a river walk with displays of memorabilia, plaques and public art depicting America's history in space), **Merritt Island National Wildlife Refuge** (a 6ml/9km driving tour adjacent to the Kennedy Space Center) and the fascinating and rather moving **American Police Hall of Fame & Museum**, with all you ever wanted to know about the history of crime and law enforcement, and a tribute to police officers who have died in the line of duty (**aphf.org**). **Dixie Crossroads** is a local institution for great Florida seafood (**dixiecrossroads.com**).

Aviation fans will enjoy the **Valiant Air Command Warbird Museum**, with dozens of vintage warplanes and fully guided tours through the exhibits and history of military aviation, as well as their dedicated restoration programme (**valiantaircommand.com**). Look out for the three-day **Warbird Air Show** each March, and **Tico Belle** C-47 that carried paratroops on D-Day.

Melbourne: Family-friendly **Brevard Zoo** is well worth a visit, with almost 500 animals in six themed areas, including the excellent Cheetah Complex in the Expedition Africa exhibit. Other highlights include La Selva (South America), Wild Florida, Paws On Play, where children can enjoy water play, Caribbean Trail and the Kangaroo-centric area of Lands of Change: Australia and Beyond (9.30am–5pm; $19.70 adults, $18.70 seniors, $14.70 2–12s; 321 254 9453, **brevardzoo.org**).

——————BRITTIP

For top value at Brevard Zoo, try an Explore! Package (admission, train ride, giraffe and lorikeet feeding at $24, $23 and $19) or Adventure! Package (kayaking in Expedition Africa, giraffe and lorikeet feeding at $30, $29 and $25).

Where to stay: Try lively, surf-themed **Four Points by Sheraton Cocoa Beach** (321 783 8717, **bit.ly/brit-4points** or **International Palms Resort** (321 783 2271, **internationalpalmscocoabeach.com**).

More info: 321 433 4470 or **visitspacecoast.com**.

The Beach at St Andrews State Park

Emerald Coast

For one of Florida's hidden gems (albeit not during the pre-Easter Spring Break holiday when it is Party Central!), head north-west to the 'Panhandle,' where this charming nature-based stretch of coastline offers fabulous sightseeing, nature tours and downhome local style, as well as the prime attraction – 100 miles of stunning beaches and emerald green waters. It's a long drive from Orlando but it is blissful from mid-Aug to late Oct. **Panama City Beach** is the heart of this coast, which is where you'll find the natural wonders of **St Andrews** and **Camp Helen State Parks,** and you can see it all via helicopter tours, sunset cruises, paddleboarding, kayaking, snorkelling and hiking. **Gulf World Marine Park** is a local institution and the sea hereabouts is often full of dolphins, turtles, rays, tarpon and even the occasional shark. Dining is full of one-off choices, notably the fun beachfront vibe of **Barefoot Hide-A-Way Grill (barefootrestaurants. com)**, the elegant chic of **Firefly (fireflypcb.com)**, and local seafood specialities of **Capt Anderson's (captanderson.com)**. **Turkey Creek Park** and **John C. Beasley Park** provide more natural wonders in the Destin/Fort Walton Beach area, while **Big Kahuna's** water park offers great family fun (**https:// bigkahunas.com/**). For dinner, don't miss **Brotula's Seafood House & Steamer** for a great location and the freshest local seafood (**brotulas.com**).

Where to stay: Try the modern condo-style **Tidewater Beach Resort**, with one, two and three-bed units (850 234 9645**, wyndhamvacationrentals.com**), the superbly equipped **Edgewater Beach & Golf Resort** (855 512 3843, **edgewaterbeachresort.com**), or, in Destin, **The Henderson** for a truly memorable stay (1855 741 2777, **hendersonbeachresort.com**). **More info:** look up, **visitpanamacitybeach.com** and **emeraldcoastfl.com**.

Tampa

Going west from Orlando brings you down I-4 to the bright city of Tampa, right on a major sea bay and with some excellent attractions of its own (including Busch Gardens, p200).

Dinosaur World: Right on I-4 as you head to Tampa (Exit 17) is this family-run attraction ideal for 3–8s. With several hundred life-sized dinosaurs in a lush, natural setting, plus walking trails, picnic area, playground and gift shop, it makes a good diversion for several hours. There are no rides, but there are life-size animatronic set-pieces – including a triceratops and pterodactyl – plus a Prehistoric Museum featuring authentic fossils, from dinosaur eggs to raptor claws and mammoth teeth. The shaded boardwalks feature more dino models with explanatory signs, plus a hands-on cave exploration show with a palaeontologist and the Triviasaurus Rex game show (with a chance to win prizes!). There is an extensive play area, and an expanded fossil dig with fossils you can take home (9am–5pm; $16.95 adult, $14.95 seniors, $11.95 3–12s, under-3 free; 813 717 9865; **dinosaurworld.com/florida**).

Florida Aquarium: In the heart of Tampa is this superb child-friendly draw with a series of galleries, from Wetlands and Journey to Madagascar, to Bays & Beaches and Dragons Down Under. The Splash Pad water-play area adds squirt fountains, dump buckets and sandbox play, plus Sandy's Snack Shack and Café Ray. There's a daily Penguin Meet & Greet, and swim adventures, including Dive With The Sharks, where scuba-certified 15s and older can join the daily dive into the lagoon ($160/ person, reservations required on 813 273 4015), a daily 20min non-scuba 'Swim with the fishes' reef swim ($85/ person), a daily Behind The Scenes tour and Penguins Backstage Pass (a 30min penguin interaction at $30/ person). There's also a twice-daily (weather permitting) Wild Dolphin Cruise on their 130-passenger catamaran, (9.30am–5pm daily, closed Thanksgiving, Christmas Day; parking $6; pricing varies by day: $25.95-33.70 adults, $23.453–0.45 seniors, $22.20–28.70 under-12s; there are also combo tickets with the Wild Dolphin Cruise, Behind The Scenes Tour and Close-Up Critters Tour; 813 273 4000, **flaquarium.org**; also on Tampa CityPass, p281).

> **BRITTIP**
> Book online for the Florida Aquarium and save up to $4 per person on general admission.

ZooTampa at Lowry Park: Rated one of the top zoos in America, this lush 60acre/24ha spread showcases manatees, koalas, elephants, tigers, penguins, giraffes and orang-utans among its more than 1,000 animals. Kids will also enjoy the water-play areas, educational shows and even rides, like Tasmanian Tiger coaster, Expedition Africa (a 15min safari ride) and Roaring Springs water ride (with a 30ft/10m splashdown!). There are extensive natural animal habitats and the chance (for a few extra dollars) to interact with some of them, including a koala photo and rhino feeding (9.30am–5pm; $33.95 adults, $24.95 3–11s; **zootampa.org**; also on Tampa CityPass, p281). Animal lovers should also make a note of **Big Cat Rescue**, a non-profit park. It runs 90min tours

Mum Ceduna and her new joey, Heathcliff, at Zoo Tampa

© Zoo Tampa

and all proceeds go into the care and rehab of their 100-plus animals. Other options include Feeder, Keeper and Private tours (3pm Mon, Tues, Wed and Fri, 10am and 3pm Sat and Sun, $39/person, over 10s only; under-10s tour noon Sat & Sun for $29; other tours $65–125; 813 920 4130, **bigcatrescue.org**).

Museum of Science and Industry: More family fun (especially for 4–12s) can be found at this entertaining science centre, with three floors of educational exhibits, activities and the Saunders Planetarium, with tours of the night sky several times daily. There are seven exhibit sections, from A Look Inside (a peek inside the human body) to Mission: Moonbase (NASA's vision for living on other planets). Other activities include Sky Trail Ropes Course (weather permitting) and a Virtual Reality simulator, while there are periodic travelling exhibits. (10am–5pm closed Thanksgiving and Christmas; $12.95 adults, $10.95 seniors, $7.95 3–12s; add a Planetarium show for $5; Ropes Course is $7 extra with admission; 813 987 6000, **mosi.org**; also on Tampa CityPass, p281).

Ybor City: Tampa's historic district can be found in the rejuvenated Cuban quarter of the city, where a fine mix of shops and restaurants provide a lively vibe by day and night. Dining choices include **Ybor Chophouse** (fine steaks and seafood), Asiatic Streetfood & Noodle Bar, and **Samurai Blue** (sushi and sake). A lively bar scene offers **Centro Cantina, Reservoir Bar**, the **Brass Tap** (craft beers and live music) and British-run **Tampa Bay Brewing Co,** with a varied menu, great beers, multiple TV screens and pool table (**tbbc.beer/home**). Find more fun at upscale arcade **Game Time**, the **AMC Classic Centro Ybor 10** cinema multiplex and **Improv Comedy Theatre**, busiest on Fri and Sat but bustling most nights (**centroybor.com**). For more exotic tastes, **Florida Cane Distillery** (**floridacane.com**) offers an eclectic mix of tastings to go with its own-brand vodka, gin, rum, whiskey and moonshine (Thurs–Sun), while

Cigar City Cider & Mead features fab home-brewed ciders and meads (Wed-Sun, **cigarcitycider.com**). Start at the **Visitor Center & Museum**, which shows a fascinating film on city history, and the well-presented **Ybor City Museum** on East 9th Avenue (9am–5pm Wed–Sun; $4/person, under-6s free; **ybormuseum.org**).

TECO Line Streetcar: Much of downtown Tampa is linked by replicas of authentic electric trams, which are now free to ride, every day of the week (7am–11pm Mon–Thurs, 7–2am Fri, 8.30–2am Sat, 8.30am–11pm Sun; **tecolinestreetcar.org**).

> ───── **BRITTIP** ⚔
> Don't miss Columbia Restaurant in Ybor City. Opened in 1905, it covers a whole city block that was slowly absorbed into this Spanish/Cuban bar-diner. Ask if they can give you a tour, with the story of the Gonzmart family (813 248 4961, **columbiarestaurant.com**).

Brewery Central: Tampa is a major centre for breweries and craft beer, with one of the biggest real ale profiles in the US. There are more than 30 breweries producing high-quality ales, lagers, ciders and more. Many offer tours and the chance to sample their wares, while the brew-pub phenomenon is going gangbusters. You can also try guided tours like **The Brew Bus** (**brewbususa.com**) and **Tampa Brew Tours**, travelling by stretch limo (**tampabrewtours.com**). For a good sample, try:

Cigar City Brewing: Celebrating Tampa's Cuban heritage, Cigar City features some wildly creative beers, like their Jai Alai IPA and Maduro Brown Ale, and with 4 tours a day (11am-11pm; tours $8/person Weds-Sun, noon, 1.30, 4 & 5.30pm; **cigarcitybrewing.com**). **Coppertail Brewing:** This features at least 8 beers, including a great IPA and Wheat Ale, with tours Thurs–Sun ($7.50/person, 5–8pm Thurs and Fri, 2–7pm Sat and Sun; **coppertailbrewing.com**). **Angry Chair Brewing:** Another hugely creative brewery with a great Tasting Room,

in the trendy Seminole Heights area that also boasts several other brew-pubs (Mon–Wed 4–10pm, Thurs 3–11pm, Fri and Sat noon–midnight, Sun noon–9pm, **angrychairbrewing.com**).

Where to stay: Arguably the most distinctive place in town is the **Epicurean Hotel**, a fabulously stylish boutique property with a blissful Spa and superb dining. It features designer rooms and suites, gourmet restaurant Elevage and gorgeous rooftop cocktail bar Edge (813 999 8700, **epicureanhotel.com**). Equally upmarket is **Le Meridien**, a sumptuous conversion of the old Federal Court building into an ultra-chic modern hotel (813 221 9555, **bit.ly/brit-lemeridien**). Another gem is the **Grand Hyatt**, tucked away in a quiet corner of Tampa Bay and offering a terrific array of activities and dining, including the fab Oystercatchers for fresh seafood (813 874 1234, **bit.ly/brit-grandhyatt**).

More info: Visitor Center on N. Franklin St, 10am–5.30pm Mon–Sat, noon–5pm Sun; 813 223 2752 or **visittampabay.com**.

> ───── **BRITTIP** ⚔
> The Tampa Bay CityPass card can provide BIG savings on five main attractions, including Busch Gardens, Clearwater Marine Aquarium, the Florida Aquarium and ZooTampa at Lowry Park. $109 adults and $99 3–9s. **citypass.com/tampa**.

Florida Aquarium has a programme for returning sea turtles to their natural habitat

© Florida Aquarium

St Pete/Clearwater

Continue west and you have the gorgeous Gulf Coast, a 2hr drive down I-4 and through Tampa on I-275 south to St Pete Beach (105ml/169km) or Clearwater Beach (110ml/177km), with a string of beautiful resorts in between, all featuring white-sand beaches, water sports and fewer crowds than you would think, plus the smart Beach Walk in Clearwater. The sea is a bit warmer and calmer on this side of Florida so is more suitable for small children. The 35ml/56km stretch from St Pete–Clearwater represents the heart of the Sunshine State beach experience and is one of the most popular two-centre options. It has a wonderful array of attractions and averages 361 days of sun a year.

BRITTIP

Do the 'stingray shuffle' in the sea from Apr–Oct. Move your feet through the sand without lifting them up to alert the odd stingray to your presence, then they will move away. Neosporin is a good antiseptic if you are stung.

St Petersburg: This city, just across the Howard Frankland Bridge from Tampa, is a wonderful mix of the old and the new, with an impressive Art District (10 museums, dozens of galleries and counting) and a real café society feel. Take time for the world-renowned **Dali Museum** (10am–5.30pm, 8pm Thurs; $24 adults, $22 seniors, $17 13–18s and students, $10 6–12s; **thedali.org**), and the **Chihuly Collection** across the street from **Morean Arts Center**, a superb showcase of the American glass artist, with guided tours each hour. There's also a separate glass studio and hot shop nearby (9am–5pm Mon–Sat, noon–5pm Sun; $19.95 adults, $17.95 seniors, $12.95 students and children over 5; 727 822 7872, **moreanartscenter.org**; also on Tampa CityPass, see left).

Other highlights include the elegant **Museum of Fine Arts**, with its two interior gardens (**fine-arts.org**), the **St Petersburg Museum of History** (**spmoh.com**), and fascinating **Great Explorations Children's Museum** (**greatex.org**). Pedestrian-friendly streets provide plenty of interest, while the fan-friendly **Tropicana Field** hosts the Tampa Bay Rays baseball team (Apr–Sept) for terrific local entertainment ($20–350; **mlb.com/rays**). Central Avenue South is the city's funky, happening district, with a great array of one-off shops, cafés and restaurants, like eclectic **The Lure** (**thelurestpete.com**), **Cycle Brewing** (**cyclebrewing.com**) and Portuguese **Iberian Rooster** (**iberianrooster.com**). **Magic Carpet Glide**, on Beach Drive in downtown, feature two-wheeled Segway tours for a superb view of the city's miles of waterfront parks, beaches and residences with a knowledgeable guide (ages 10 and over; 90min and 2hr tours daily at 10am, 1pm and 5.30pm, $55 and $65; call for reservations on 727 498 2322, **stpetesegwaytours.com**).

Weedon Island Preserve: Enjoy the rich cultural history of this 3,700acre/1,500ha seaside nature park in St Petersburg. Start at the Natural History Center (the main entrance is at the back) and learn about the prehistoric and Native American settlements here (plus periodic exhibitions), then go up to the open-air observation deck. There are several miles of boardwalks and trails around the tidal wetlands, which are home to ospreys, turtles, spoonbills, mangrove crabs, raccoons and gopher tortoises, with guided hikes Sats at 9am (call to register; Center open 9am–4pm Thurs–Sat, 11am–4pm Sun, free entry; Preserve open 7am–dusk; 727 453 6500, **weedonislandpreserve. org**). You could try a paddle round the shallow waters with **Sweetwater Kayaks**. This close encounter with nature (stingrays, jumping mullet and the odd manatee) is offered on an hourly or 4hr basis (9am–5pm daily; single kayaks $17, $34, $40 for 1, 2 4hrs, double kayaks $25, $50, $56, paddleboards $20, $40, $50; booking advised on 727 570 4844 or **sweetwaterkayaks.com**).

BRITTIP

Insect repellent is essential for any visit to Weedon Island Preserve as it is not sprayed for mosquitoes, and the little pests will feed on tourists!

Beaches: You are spoiled for choice, from the 1,100acre/445ha **Fort De Soto Park** in the south to stunning **Caladesi Island State Park** in the north (regularly voted in America's Top 10). There is plenty to do, too, with the likes of Treasure Island, Sand Key and St Pete Beach all receiving the Blue Wave Award for cleanliness and safety. **John's Pass Village** is an eclectic shopping district and marina full of shops and restaurants, plus the fun **Pirate Cruise** – a replica sailing ship offering a 2hr party cruise ($39 adults, $33 65 and over, $29 under-20s, $10 under-3s, inclusive of beer, wine and soft drinks; 11am, 2pm and sunset), and 90min **Dolphin Quest** tour at noon, 2, 4 and 6pm daily ($24.50 adults, $22.50 seniors, $19.50 under 20s; call for reservations on 727 423 7824, boattoursjohnspass.com). Parasailing, jet-skiing, fishing, boat rentals and tours are also popular (johnspass.com).

Dolphin Landings: A 'Don't miss' in St Pete Beach, with a pair of 51ft/15.5m yachts that sail on 2hr trips along the calm inland waterway (9.30am, noon and 2.15pm, Mon–Sat, noon and 2.15pm Sun; $40 adults, $30 children) for close-up dolphin-watch cruises and sunset sailings, plus a Sunset Sail, 4hr trip around beautiful Egmont Key and a 3½hr trip to Shell Key, with up to 2hrs on the beach ($45–50; 727 360 7411, dolphinlandings.com).

BRITTIP

Most public beaches will have toilets, changing facilities and picnic tables, but there is usually a parking fee.

Seaside Seabird Sanctuary: Further north at Indian Shores is America's largest wild bird hospital, caring for injured birds including birds of prey, pelicans, spoonbills and egrets, with feeding options and bird presentations periodically. Entry is free but they do ask for donations to visit this non-profit rehabilitation centre (8am–4pm, 727 391 6211, seabirdsanctuary.com).

Clearwater Beach: Continue north to acres of clean, white sands and the must-visit **Clearwater Marine Aquarium**, a wonderful non-profit organisation that rescues and rehabilitates injured dolphins, turtles, river otters and more (especially good for under-12s). There are 17 main exhibits, including Turtle Cove, Otter Oasis, Shark Pass and Shipwreck Alley but much of the focus is on the area's Hollywood 'star', Winter the tail-less dolphin in the Winter Zone.

BRITTIP

Don't leave without visiting the area's top attraction, a dolphin called Winter, the star of films *Dolphin Tale* and *Dolphin Tale 2* with Morgan Freeman. Rescued from a crab trap, her tail had to be amputated and she was not expected to survive. Happily, she not only lived but has learned to swim with a prosthetic tail!

There are dolphin presentations (into behaviour and care – not 'shows') three times a day and interactive animal encounters, plus a Dolphin & Animal Care Assistant programme, at $399/person. Take a behind-the-scenes tour or 2hr Sea Life Safari (great for kids) that goes out on the coastal waterway. There are another seven animal encounters, including dolphins, pelicans and sharks, two additional boat tours, and a Dolphin Care Experience at $249/person (10am–6 or 8pm daily, $24.95 adults, $22.95 seniors, $19.95 3-12s; behind-the-scenes tour $18/$16/$13; Sea Life Safari $27/$24/$18; save 25% by buying all three together; 727 441 1790, seewinter.com; also on Tampa CityPass, p281).

The Beach Walk: The heart of the area is a winding beachside promenade that links a ½ml/1km stretch of resorts, shops and restaurants (like the fun **Frenchy's** and **Crabby's Dockside**) to Pier 60 for the daily sunset celebration (with craft stalls and music). Also here is the marina where you can catch the 2hr **Captain Memo's Pirate Cruise** (10am and 2pm daily; $36 adults, $33 seniors, $31 teens, $28 under-13s, $11 under 3s) or **Sunset Champagne Cruise** (at 4.30 and 7pm, $39, $33, $31, $28, $11; online discounts at **captainmemo.com**) and the fab **Sea Screamer**, a huge power boat that goes out into the Gulf and often attracts dolphins jumping in its wake (noon, 2 and 4pm daily; $25 adults, $19 5–12; **seascreamer.com**).

Sugar Sand Festival: While Clearwater Beach is fun at all times of the year, it is at its best for April's 10-day Pier 60 Sugar Sand Festival with sand-sculpting competitions, concerts, films and other special events (**sugarsandfestival.com**).

Suncoast Beach Trolley: Avoid driving with this excellent bus service (5.20am–11.16pm Sun–Thurs, 12.40am Fri–Sat; 727 540 1900, **psta.net**) along the beaches and into St Petersburg for $2.25 a ride, $18 for a 3-day pass and $25 for a week. The **Jolly Trolley** runs north from Clearwater to the charming towns of Scottish-tinged **Dunedin**, with its Historical Museum, Dunedin Brewery (**dunedinbrewery. com/**), and 1920s period Fenway Hotel (**fenwayhotel.com), and Tarpon Springs**, which is hugely Greek influenced and offers great restaurants, Sponge Docks, Aquarium and Historic District, as well as the ornate Greek Orthodox Cathedral.

Restaurants: The area also boasts 2,000 restaurants, of which the Key

Bilmar Beach Resort

West bistro style of the five **Frenchy's Cafes** (Original Café, Rockaway Grill, South Beach and Saltwater Café all in Clearwater Beach, plus **Frenchy's Outpost** in Dunedin), the **Daiquiri Shak** (Madeira Beach), **Crabby's Dockside** (in Clearwater Beach), **RumFish Grill** at the RumFish Beach Resort (St Pete Beach) and the **Moon Under Water** (St Petersburg) are all worth visiting. The chic **Parkshore Grill** in downtown St Pete is ideal for a relaxing lunch or elegant dinner (727 896 9463, **parkshoregrill.com**), as is **400 Beach Seafood & Tap House**, which also features a fabulous Sunday brunch (727 896 2400, **400beachseafood.com**).

Where to stay: A range of **Superior Small Lodgings** combine beachfront locations with small-scale service. Weekly rates can be from $900 for a three-room apartment (1888 600 2468, **floridassl.com**). Upscale hotels include family-friendly **Tradewinds Island Resorts** on St Pete Beach, a 743-room complex with great facilities and dining in a blissful location (727 367 6461, **tradewindsresort.com**); the superb **Sandpearl Resort**, a four-star choice on Clearwater Beach, with a mix of stylish standard rooms and spacious suites. The pool, bar and grill are a beachfront sanctuary, and the modern Spa has a fab array of treatments. Caretta on the Gulf offers memorable dining with an inventive fusion cuisine (866 384 2995, **sandpearl.com**); and **Hyatt Regency Clearwater Beach Resort & Spa**, an all-suite hotel at the heart of Beach Walk with fantastic pool facilities and Gulf views, plus the eco-friendly Sandava Spa and excellent restaurant (727 373 1234, **bit.ly/hcclearwater**). More modest choices on the seafront in St Pete Beach are the chic motel style of **The Postcard Inn** (1800 237 8918, **postcardinn.com**) and funky **Bilmar Beach Resort**, with great self-catering rooms for a week or more (727 360 5531, **bilmarbeachresort. com**). By contrast, the **Vinoy Resort** (in St Petersburg) is the area's oldest formal hotel, a 1920s treasure that is well worth a look just for its

Spanish Revival style (727 894 1000, **bit.ly/brit-marriott**). Other hotels worth considering are the contemporary chic of **Opal Sands Resort** (727 450 0380, **opalsands.com**) and **Treasure Island Beach Resort** (855 660 6366, **treasureislandbeachresort.com**), plus the fun style of **Frenchy's Oasis Motel** (727 446 6835, **frenchysoasismotel.com**). **More info:** 727 464 7200, or **visitstpeteclearwater.com**.

BRITTIP
Don't miss the RumFish Grill (at the RumFish Beach Resort), with its great seafood and huge aquariums created by TV programme Tanked (**rumfishgrill. com**).

The south-west

Bradenton/Sarasota: Around 2hrs' drive from Orlando is this artsy area (take I-4 then I-75), which features the superb beachfronts of Anna Maria Island (charming and secluded beaches), Longboat Key and Venice ('the shark tooth capital of the world' and great for fossil hunters).

Sarasota is the spiritual home of the Ringling Circus, and there are many circus-influenced offerings here, including the unmissable **Ringling Estate and Museum of Art**, which includes the unique Circus Museum and Tibbals Learning Center (the world's largest scale model of a classic circus). The Museum of Art features a multi-million-dollar collection of Old Masters in a palatial setting while the former family home, the dazzling Ca d'Zan Mansion, grounds and gardens are also part of the entry fee (daily 10am–5pm, 8pm Thurs; closed Thanksgiving, Christmas, New Year's Day; $25 adults, $23 seniors, $5 6–17s and students; **ringling.org**). There is superb shopping at **St Armand's Circle** in Lido Key, and the **Mote Marine Laboratory** is also worthy of note. In Bradenton, don't miss the eclectic **Village of Arts** and family-friendly **South Florida Museum**, including the **Parker Manatee Aquarium** and **Bishop Planetarium**, where the 60,000-gallon pool is home

to rehabilitating manatees (10am–5pm Tues–Sat, noon–5pm Sun; $19 adults, $17 seniors, $14 4–11s; 941 746 4131, **southfloridamuseum.org**). Good food is always on the menu, including Spanish-Cuban **Columbia Restaurant** in St Armand's Circle (941 388 3987, **columbiarestaurant. com**), al fresco **Mattison's City Grille** in downtown Sarasota (941 330 0440, **mattisons.com**) and **Siesta Key Oyster Bar** in Siesta Key Village (941 346 5443, **skob.com**).

Where to stay: Anna Maria Island is full of small-scale B&Bs and cute beachfront inns, plus the stylish **Waterline Resort** with its huge, well-equipped suites (941 238 6262, **waterlineresort.com**) while Longboat Key boasts the superb new **Zota Beach Resort** (941 383 2451, **zotabeachresort.com**). The **Hyatt Regency Sarasota** is one of the top resorts (941 953 1234, **bit.ly/hrsarasola**), while the **Ritz-Carlton** is a Gulf Coast landmark (941 309 2000, **ritzcarlton. com/en/hotels/florida/sarasota**). For a great self-catering option, try the **Beach Club at Siesta Key** (941 552 9810, **beachclubatsiestakey.com**).

More info: Sarasota, call 941 706 1253 or **visitsarasota.com**; Bradenton and Anna Maria Island, 941 729 9177 or **bradentongulfislands.com**.

Charlotte Harbor: Go further south (170ml/272km from Orlando) and you have the lower-key destinations of Punta Gorda, Port Charlotte, Englewood and Boca Grande. Port Charlotte is the place to be for some of the best shelling in Florida, while kayakers should try the 'tunnel of love' mangrove tunnels and other nature adventures. Downtown Punta Gorda has free bike rentals and a lovely walk along the Peace River. If you are looking for 'small town America', this is it.

More info: 941 743 1900 or **pureflorida.com**.

Fort Myers/Sanibel: It's only a short drive to the mini tropical paradise of the Lee Island Coast, featuring history and nature-rich Fort Myers and funky Pine Island.

Among the many highlights are bustling family-orientated Fort Myers Beach; Sanibel Island, centred around its shell-strewn beaches; the bird-watching Mecca at the **Darling National Wildlife Refuge**; the shops and restaurants in Captiva Island; and Bonita Beach. Sanibel is home to the unique **Bailey-Matthews Shell Museum**, plus a quaint **Historical Museum & Village**, wildlife attractions, canoeing and nature tours.

Where to stay: There is a good mix of vacation homes and cottages in Fort Myers Beach and Sanibel, while the top hotels are **Lovers Key Resort** (1877 798 4879, **loverskey.com**) and **Sanibel Harbor Marriott Resort & Spa** (239 466 4000, **marriott.com**). Stay at **Hyatt Regency Coconut Point** and you can sample a full cross-section of the area, including sports, eco-tours, great dining, beautiful scenery and a secluded beach (239 444 1234, **hyatt. com/en-US/hotel/florida/hyatt-regency-coconut-point-resort-and-spa/naprn**). **More info:** 239 338 3500 or **fortmyers-sanibel.com**.

Paradise Coast: Continue south to the magnificent 'Paradise Coast' of Naples and Marco Island. Naples is a fresh, modern city with plenty of attractions, notably **The Baker Museum at Artis – Naples**, the **Conservancy of Southwest Florida's Nature Center** (**conservancy.org/nature-center**) and **Corkscrew Swamp Sanctuary**, plus ultra-chic shopping, as well as a top beach destination. Its art-tinged ambience is well-evidenced

Seminole Central

Head west out of Fort Lauderdale to Big Cypress and you find the rewarding Ah-Tah-Thi-Ki Museum, home to the Seminole tribe of Florida. See the Living Village and walk the 1ml/1.6km Boardwalk over the Cypress Swamp. Then try the Billie Swamp Safari, a 2,200-acre/1.6ha Cypress Reservation featuring close-ups of the wildlife (including snakes and gators) via its giant-wheeled buggy, airboat rides and swamp critter shows. And you can even stay overnight in its Chickee huts (863 983 6101, **floridaseminoletourism.com**).

in its two main areas of 5th Avenue South, with boutique shops, sidewalk cafés and art festivals, and Third Street South, with more distinctive stores, galleries and café society atmosphere (try the **Old Naples Pub** for fine food in a relaxed ambience with an outdoor patio and live music Thurs–Sat). On Fifth Avenue, each of **Ocean Prime** (superb steaks and seafood), Parisian style of **French Brasserie Rustique** and **Osteria Tulia**, with its rustic Italian vibe, offer great dining. The beaches are mere steps away; at the municipal beach, Naples Pier juts into placid Gulf waters, while Lowdermilk Beach is family-friendly, with volleyball and other facilities. Marco Island is the largest of the Ten Thousand Islands, consisting of Marco, known for its wide beach, fine resorts and sea-fishing charters; and Goodland, with its fish restaurants, and Everglades fishing charters.

Where to stay: Pick from high-quality resorts like **JW Marriott Marco Island** (239 394 2511, **jwmarco.com**), **Marco Beach Ocean Resort** (239 393 1400, **marcoresort.com**) and **Naples Grande Beach Resort** (239 227 2182, **naplesgrande.com**). We also like the small-scale Caribbean-tinged **Lemon Tree Inn** in Naples (239 262 1414, **lemontreeinn.com**) and the ultimate indulgence of **The Inn On Fifth**, right in the heart of ritzy Fifth Avenue (239 403 8777, **innonfifth.com**).

More info: 001 239 225 1013 or **paradisecoast.com**.

Corkscrew Swamp Sanctuary

Miami nice

If you see nothing else in Miami, do spend time in South Beach (or SoBe) and über-cool Ocean Drive, full of open-air cafés, art galleries and nightclubs. Tranquil during the day, non-stop at night, this is where the beautiful people hang out, or just cruise in their Ferraris.

BRITTIP

Naples/Marco Island is the perfect base from which to explore the Florida Everglades, though you can also reach them from Fort Lauderdale.

Treasure Coast

Returning to the Atlantic Coast, heading south on Highway 1 brings you to an often-overlooked Florida jewel, Vero Beach. Nicknamed the Treasure Coast (for its history of shipwrecks), it boasts the intriguing **McLarty Treasure Museum** and the **Pelican Island National Wildlife Refuge**. Vero Beach itself is located on the barrier island of North Hutchinson but spreads to the mainland, with art galleries, smart shops, restaurants, small resorts and beach parks, including a boardwalk atop the dunes.

Martin County is at the heart of the Treasure Coast and provides a fab microcosm of Florida, from great beaches and activities to fine dining and unique attractions. The Indian River Lagoon is a hugely bio-diverse ecosystem and offers many eco-tours, while the child-friendly **Florida Oceanographic Coastal Center** provides great insight into the marine wildlife. **Barley Barber Swamp** (barleybarber. org) is an ecological treasure (Oct-May), with tours into the freshwater wetlands around Lake Okeechobee from historic Indiantown. **Stuart** is another gem. Voted Happiest Seaside Town in 2016, it offers genuine small-town charm, with great dining and shopping, and represents a taste of the 'old Florida' before the tourist boom. For shipwreck history, the

House of Refuge Museum is a must-see.

Go south again and you reach the **Palm Beaches**, with the barrier island town of Palm Beach, one of Florida's most chic hangouts. A playground of the rich and famous, the fabulous **Flagler Museum** (formerly the rail tycoon's 1902-built Whitehall mansion) is a highlight, while the many restaurants are places to go celebrity-watching and **Worth Avenue** is one of America's most iconic shopping streets. Don't miss dining at Italian style **Bice** (561 835 1600 **bice-palmbeach.com**), the ultra-chic **Meat Market** (561 354 9800, **meatmarket.net/locations/palm-beach-steakhouse**), small-plate specialist **Buccan** (561 833 3450, **buccanpalmbeach.com**) and indulgent **HMF** at The Breakers, plus the celebrity bistro of **Ta-boo** (561 835 3500, **taboorestaurant.com**). This is also a great place to take a fishing charter or yacht hire, like **Palm Breeze Charters** (561 368 3566, **palmbreezecharters.com**). Also here is **Lion Country Safari**, with lions, elephants and giraffes (**lioncountrysafari.com**).

Where to stay: For true beach sophistication on secluded Hutchinson Island, head for the new **Hutchinson Shores Resort**, with wonderfully comfy rooms and a great restaurant, Drift Kitchen + Bar (772 334 1950, **hutchinsonshores. com**). Stuart offers an array of charming B&Bs, notably the **Inn Shepards Park** (772 781 4244, **innshepard.com**) and super-quaint **Old Colorado Inn** (772, 215 3437, **oldcoloradoinn.com**). The Palm Beaches boasts outstanding 5-star hotels in the blissful **Eau Palm Beach** (1888 306 4894; **eaupalmbeach.com**), Florida's iconic **The Breakers**, with breathtaking décor and design (844 568 0767, **thebreakers.com**) and **The Colony**, a distinguished 1960s haunt of the Duke and Duchess of Windsor (561 655 5430, **thecolonypalmbeach.com**).

More info: 1800 554 7256 or **thepalmbeaches.com**; 772 288 5451, **discovermartin.com**.

Miami and Fort Lauderdale

From Palm Beach, you reach increasingly built-up resort territory – Delray Beach, chic Boca Raton, Deerfield Beach, Pompano Beach and **Fort Lauderdale**, one of Florida's most upmarket destinations.

It also has a canal and waterway network that makes it the 'Venice of America', with water taxis being more plentiful than the wheeled variety.

Top things to see are the **Museum of Discovery & Science** (one of the state's finest), **Bonnet House Museum & Gardens**, **Old Fort Lauderdale Village & Museum** and **Las Olas Boulevard**, full of boutiques and restaurants. Shop at **Sawgrass Mills**, Florida's largest mall, which has more than 300 outlet-style stores from big-name designers, then sample the all-out fun of **Xtreme Action Park**, with go-karts, 10-pin bowling, roller-skating, escape room, rope course, 3-D video games and more (**xtremeactionpark.com**). Fort Lauderdale is also a perfect stay for a few days before or after a cruise, as both Port Everglades and Miami are only a short distance away, while you can also sample an array of sight-seeing cruises, including the Jungle Queen Riverboat (**junglequeen.com**).

Where to stay: Check out the **Superior Small Lodgings** or one of the high-class resorts like **Margaritaville Beach Resort**, with superb amenities, dining and rooms (954 874 4444, **margaritavillehollywoodbeachresort.com**), five-star **Ritz-Carlton** (954 465 2300, **ritzcarlton.com/en/hotels/florida/fort-lauderdale**) and action-packed **Marriott Harbor Beach Resort** (954 525 4000, **marriott.com**). For self-catering, the **Beachwalk Resort** has one, two and three-bed suites with full kitchens in an ideal location, plus a great pool deck and restaurant (954 266 0147, **beachwalkresortfl.com**). **More info:** 954 765 4466 or **sunny.org**.

Miami: Some 230 miles south of Orlando is Florida's biggest and trendiest city, with superb high-rise resorts, miles of open, accessible beaches, ultra-chic **South Beach** (with its Art Deco District), fantastic shopping, sports, restaurants and nightlife. The city is 5ml/8km from the beach area, which runs north for almost 15ml/24km along Collins Avenue, with most of the resorts and nightlife. High style is almost everywhere; a narrated boat tour (from Bayside Marketplace) shows off the mansions of the rich, while you should also tour Coral Gables and the older, neater Coconut Grove, with its **CocoWalk** shopping district and ornate **Vizcaya Museum**.

Other attractions include **Miami Seaquarium** on the island of Key Biscayne (**miamiseaquarium.com**), the amazing Venetian Pool at **Coral Gables** and the entertaining family attraction **Jungle Island**, a combination of zoo, animal shows and gardens with great up-close encounters (**jungleisland.com**). You are spoiled for choice for shopping, from fashion-conscious **Bal Harbor Shops**, to the massive **Aventura Mall** and funky **Lincoln Road** in South Beach. Or try the **Shops at Merrick Park** in Coral Gables, a Mediterranean-style outdoor mall with more designer style, including the iconic **Nordstrom** department store and superb dining, notably at fab Italian restaurant **Villagio** and gastropub **Yard House** (305 529 1215, **shopsatmerrickpark.com**).

Miami Food Tours: Try this fascinating insight into the Art Deco district's architecture and eclectic dining. Sample 'neighbourhood specialities' at five South Beach restaurants and cafés along this fun walking tour, while learning about the area's culture, history and unique building style (786 361 0991; **miamifoodtours.com**)

Dining: Consider the sumptuous Latin American cuisine of **Ola Miami** (305 695 9125; **olamiami.com**); fresh and authentic Northern Italian trattoria offerings at **Salumiera 104** (305 424 9588; **salumeria104.com**); and ultra-swanky **Casa Tua** 305 673 1010, **casatualifestyle.com/miami**).

Where to stay: There are boutique hotels and dazzling resorts aplenty, but two we like a lot are **The Beacon** in the heart of South Beach on Ocean Drive (305 674 8200; **beaconsouthbeach. com**) and the **Miami Beach Edition**, a chic conversion of the 1950s Seville Hotel (786 257 4500, **editionhotels.com/ miami-beach/**). **More info**: 305 539 3000 or **miamiandbeaches.com**.

Florida Keys

Leaving Miami behind on Highway 1 brings you to the unique Keys, a loose archipelago of 1,700 islands that arc down into the Caribbean. This is the laid-back 'Conch Republic', where shorts and flip-flops are official wear and the mix of influences merges into a 'Floribbean' culture. Scuba divers enjoy some of the world's best coral reefs, with renowned **John Pennekamp Coral Reef State Park** the highlight of miles of National Marine Sanctuary. Or try **Vandenberg Artificial Reef** off Key West, an old US Navy ship sunk in 2009 to create a man-made reef. The first city is **Key Largo**, followed by **Islamorada**, where you should see **Theater of the Sea**, with its dolphin and sea-lion programmes. Some of the best fishing charters are at Islamorada, Marathon and Big Pine Key.

Marathon is the starting point of the **Seven Mile Bridge**, the unofficial eighth wonder of the world, which connects the biggest gap between the islands, while **Big Pine Key** is home to **Bahia Honda State Park**, one of Florida's finest beaches. Finally, the 375ml/600km drive from Orlando brings you to America's southernmost city. **Key West** is possibly the most eclectic city in the US, a mix of the laid-back and outrageous, with street performers, sidewalk artists, cafés and bars, plus the former home of Ernest Hemingway. You should also see **Key West Aquarium** and **Key West Shipwreck Museum**, and the wonderful shops. You must be on the harbour front for the daily Sunset Celebration, when Key West's party spirit is in full force. The other great feature of Key West is its myriad ways to get around – you can try the **Conch Tour Train, Old Town Trolley Tours**, pedicabs and bicycles. Just don't expect your stay to be sedate!

Where to stay: Guest houses, inns and B&Bs are plentiful, like the ultra-chic **Marquesa Hotel** (305 292 1919, **marquesa.com**) in Key West's Old Town. Or go for the epic style of **Casa Marina**, a historic Waldorf Astoria hotel that has links to the grand Henry Flagler era (305 296 3535, **casamarinaresort.com**). For something special, try **Hawks Cay Resort** in secluded Duck Key (305 743 7000, **hawkscay.com**), luxurious **Isla Bella Beach Resort** in Marathon (844 885 4706, **islabellabeachresort. com**) or Key West's tropical island hideaway **Parrot Key** (888 211 0348, **parrotkeyhotel.com**). **More info**: 1800 352 5397 or **fla-keys.com**.

Cruise-and-stay

Taking a cruise is increasingly popular with an Orlando stay and there are well-priced 3, 4, 5 and 7-day sailings out of Port Canaveral, Tampa, Fort Lauderdale and Miami. From here, you can visit the Bahamas, much of the Caribbean, Mexico, Central and South America.

Select from **Disney Cruise Line** (from their own dedicated cruise terminal at Port Canaveral and Miami), with four fabulous ships and voyages from 3–7 days (0800 951 3532, **disneycruise.disney.go.com**); party-style **Carnival** (from Port Canaveral, Fort Lauderdale, Miami and Tampa), 3–7 days (0808 234 0680 in the UK, **carnival. co.uk**); **Royal Caribbean**, with some of the biggest ships (from all four ports) for 3–14 days (0344 493 4005, **royalcaribbean.co.uk**); **Norwegian Cruise Line** (from Port Canaveral, Miami and Tampa) from 3–7 days (0333 241 2319, **ncl.com/uk/en/**); **Holland America** 7-18 days (from Fort Lauderdale and Tampa; 1877 932 4259, **hollandamerica. com**); **Celebrity** 4-14 days (from Miami and Fort Lauderdale; 1888 751 7804, **celebritycruises.com**); **MSC Cruises** 3-22 days (from Miami; 0203 426 3010, **msccruises.co.uk**); and **Princess Cruises**, 7–14 days (from Fort Lauderdale; 1800 774 6237, **princess.com**).

Now we need to tell you about how to enjoy all the night-time entertainment …

10 Orlando by Night

or Burning the Candle at Both Ends

If Orlando and the parks are hot during the day, they positively sizzle at night, with yet more diverse and thrilling entertainment, most of it family friendly. Disney and Universal lead the way, but there is much to enjoy throughout the area.

The full range runs from purpose-built entertainment complexes and an amazing variety of dinner shows to a unique array of bars and nightclubs. The choice is widespread and almost always high quality. Downtown Orlando has some great offerings, as does International Drive, while Disney has two entertainment centres and Universal features its CityWalk district of live music, dining and fun.

Entertainment at Disney Springs
© Disney

BRITGUIDE 25

Church Street Station and Disney's Pleasure Island were the two big entertainment centres in 1995. Both have been overtaken by more dramatic developments ever since, along with six of nine dinner shows.

DISNEY SPRINGS

Disney's big shopping, dining and entertainment district has been transformed into a four-part adventure in recent years. The original Marketplace and West Side were joined in 2015 by The Landing (the old Pleasure Island area), with the Town Center added in 2016, featuring iconic restaurants, bars and live entertainment (see also Dining, p308; Shopping, p331).

BRITTIP

Photo ID is essential for all bars and clubs, even if you happen to be the 'wrong' side of 30. No ID equals no alcohol, and there are no exceptions. For Disney, a photocopy of your passport ID page is needed, along with your driving licence.

The Landing

Raglan Road: This pub features traditional live Irish music each night in its Grand Room 4.30pm–1.30am Mon– Fri, 12pm–1am Sat–Sun, plus Irish dancing 4.30–10pm daily. Enjoy its full bar, ample collection of genuine Irish whiskey, nine European beers, four beer flights, plus local brews, great bartenders and even better menu (p308) (407 938 0300, raglanroad.com).

The Boathouse: This bar-restaurant venue offers live music nightly, 8pm–midnight, but the real feature is the Amphicar rides. Each land-to-water car accommodates up to three guests and a Car Captain (provided driver), with 20min rides costing a whopping $125, but it's a unique opportunity. Tickets can be purchased at The Boathouse. For the best spectator value, watch the Amphicars on the lake from the comfort of the waterside Boathouse bar. Tours run 10am–10pm, weather permitting.

BRITTIP

If your tipple is vodka and lime, ask for vodka and a dash of lime cordial. For port and lemon, ask for port and Sprite. Otherwise you'll get a slice of citrus fruit with your alcohol.

The Edison: This massive 1920s-themed 'Industrial Gothic' destination offers a funky Catalogue of Parts (menu) featuring classic American food, craft cocktails, beer and wine. Live music Thurs–Sat. Period-style entertainment (9.30pm nightly) includes stilt walkers, jugglers and other variety acts. Eclectic? You bet! One of Disney's best night-time venues? No doubt about it! Ages 21 and up only after 10pm.

Jock Lindsey's Hangar Bar: Indiana Jones fans will love this wonderfully themed bar named for the pilot of the Indy films. There is a boat-themed patio and aeroplane memorabilia, plus reminders of the former Adventurer's Club at Pleasure Island, as well as a range of craft beers, cocktails and a small-plate dining menu.

Paddlefish: Housed in a replica paddleboat, this seafood-themed offering boasts a superb rooftop lounge and bar with a magnificent view, plus live music Fri–Sat, 9pm–midnight. Perfect for enjoying the sunset with an excellent craft beer or handcrafted cocktail (also see Dining p309).

Paradiso 37: This expansive, split-level bar-restaurant offers a fine array of food from Latin America plus a Tequila Bar featuring over 50 varieties. Live music adds to its picturesque waterfront location (p309).

STK Orlando: The latest outlet of this über-chic international steakhouse has a high-energy vibe that features an in-house DJ and a fabulous rooftop patio with great views over Disney Springs – ideal for cocktails and people-watching.

Enzo's Hideaway: Tucked away in a former underground tunnel for Cast Members, this speakeasy-style lounge is one of our favourites for small-plate, late-night bites and superb classic cocktails (lounge, 11.30am–midnight Sun–Thurs, Fri-Sat 11.30am–1am).

STK Orlando

© Disney

West Side

AMC® Dine-In Theaters Complex:
With 24 screens and 6,000 seats plus a
huge choice of snacks, drinks and
even its own bar, this superb cinema
multiplex shows first-run films in
state-of-the-art surroundings,
including the Enhanced Theatre
Experience (a bigger screen, with 3D
technology, 12-channel audio and
digital projection) and a Dine-In
option, with six of the auditoriums
converted to serve meals and drinks
while you watch. The menu includes
starters like wings and sushi rolls,
then salads, fish and chips, flatbreads,
burgers and milkshakes, plus wine,
beer and cocktails (tickets $11–18,
prices vary by show; food and drink
extra; call 407 827 1308 for show
times; under 18s must be
accompanied by an adult in Dine-In
theatres; **amctheatres.com**). Disabled
accessible; assisted listening devices
available at Guest Services.

BRITTIP

Some films have added features,
such as enhanced sound, larger
screen, or 3-D that will increase your ticket
price. However, you can save $2 on adult
tickets at the AMC® cineplex by visiting
before 3.55pm.

Cirque Du Soleil: The superb La
Nouba closed in 2017, but April 2020
will see the debut of a new Cirque

Cirque du Soleil at Disney Springs

© Disney

show in conjunction with Walt Disney
Animation Studios. It will feature a
variety of Disney characters in the
story of an animator's daughter, with
all the unique creativity, imagination
and breathtaking staging of Cirque
(1855 473 7783, **cirquedusoleil.com/at-
walt-disney-world**).

House of Blues: Free live music every
night at the Front Porch bar, with full
concerts at the separately accessed
music venue next to the restaurant.
The main venue offers a mix of big-
name headliners, up-and-coming
bands and local acts. Standing only.
Tickets required, no discounts for
children ($30–100 and up; 407 934
2583, **houseofblues.com**).

NBA Experience: OK, basketball fans,
here's a chance to dribble, shoot,
dunk and score in a specially-created
environment that puts guests in the
heart of a series of 13 NBA games
and events. Test your skills, take
part in trivia, enjoy 'Insider Access'
for an imaginary Draft Day and visit
the changing rooms of a typical
team. Arcade games, two mini-
cinemas with unique multi-media
presentations and a speciality shop
complete an absorbing picture, but it
might not mean much to non-fans of
the sport (ages 10 and up only, under
14s must be accompanied by an
adult; $34/person; **bit.ly/brit-nba**).

Splitsville: An imaginative venue in
which to 'dine, dance, drink – and
bowl'. But with a difference. Built in
best 1950s period style, this twin-level
entertainment palace offers 30 lanes
of bowling, multiple bars, billiard
tables and a full-service restaurant,
plus elegant indoor and outdoor
seating, including a 1st-floor patio for
a great view over Disney Springs. The
upper floor also has more of a grown-
up style in the evening, with DJs
adding a nightclub vibe. Walk-in rates
are $28/person Mon–Fri 10.30am–
4pm and $32 from 4pm; $32/person
all day Sat and Sun 10pm-close, with
Early Bird specials until noon. Book
a lane in advance by calling or online
(10.30–1am Mon– Fri; 10–2am Sat and
Sun; 407 938 7467, **splitsvillelanes.com**).

Town Center

While this is primarily a shopping area, with a few smart dining outlets like D-Luxe Burger, Wolfgang Puck's and Blaze Pizza, there are a couple of worthy candidates for evening fun.

Coca-Cola Store: Another iconic building, this is home to Coke products, gift items and memorabilia, and features a glamorous rooftop tasting bar.

Planet Hollywood Observatory: The new-look Planet Hollywood features a futuristic space observatory theme to go with its celebrity style. As well as the main restaurant, there's the Stargazers outdoor terrace and bar with live entertainment.

Marketplace

This area is again primarily about shopping and dining but there are still a couple of nice spots to stop for a drink, notably the **Lava Lounge** (beside the Rainforest Café and with a view over Crescent Lake), and **Dockside Margaritas**, an open-air terrace facing the water that also serves great cocktails.

Other entertainment: The evening sees a variety of live music performers throughout Disney Springs, from flamenco guitarists to classical quartets and more. Look for them in all four sections.

Disney Resorts

Disney's Boardwalk: Disney's other big entertainment offering is part of its impressive BoardWalk Resort, where the waterfront district contains several notable venues (not counting the excellent micro-brewery and restaurant of **Big River Grille and Brewing Works**, **ESPN Club** for sports fans and five-star **Flying Fish Café**). **Jellyrolls** is a variation on the duelling piano bar, with the pianists conjuring up a lively evening of audience participation (7pm–2am, music from 8pm; $15 cover charge; 21 and over only) while **Atlantic Dance Hall** features mainly modern dance music with house and guest DJs, plus occasional live music, a huge dance floor and a great bar service and ambience. Video DJs feature on Tues, Wed and Sat, with 'duelling DJs' on Thurs and Fri, and it's especially popular on Fri and Sat (9pm–2am; closed Sun and Mon; strictly 21 and over). The Boardwalk also features amusing live entertainers, like magicians and jugglers, while **ESPN Club** features regular celebrity (American) sports guests.

Coronado Springs Resort: A hidden gem here is the **Rix Sports Bar & Grill** with an elegant setting for a sports bar. It's stylish, lively and features hand-crafted cocktails and craft beers along with classic bar food, while multiple TVs show all the major sports (7am– midnight).

Abracadabar at Disney's Boardwalk

© Disney

Electrical Water Pageant: This is another nightly (and free!) alternative, a 'parade' that circles Bay Lake and the Seven Seas Lagoon. It lasts just 10mins, but it's almost a waterborne version of a typical Magic Kingdom parade, with thousands of twinkling lights on a cavalcade of pontoons, all set to music. The usual schedule is 9pm at the Polynesian Resort, 9.15 at Grand Floridian Resort & Spa (get a grandstand view in Narcoosee's restaurant), 9.35 at Wilderness Lodge, 9.45 on the shores of Fort Wilderness Resort and 10.05 at Contemporary Resort. It can also be seen outside the Magic Kingdom at 10.20pm during extended hours.

UNIVERSAL'S CITYWALK

As part of the big Universal Orlando development, this 30acre/12ha spread offers a bustling expanse of restaurants, snack bars, shops, open-air events and nightclubs. It offers a huge variety of cuisines, from fast food to fine dining, an unusual blend of speciality shops and an eclectic nightclub mix, from reggae and rock 'n' roll to salsa, jazz and high-energy disco, plus the superb **Blue Man Group** show and a karaoke theatre/bar. There's a $7 entry fee at the six clubs but you can buy a **CityWalk Party Pass** ($12) or **Party Pass with Movie** (one free film at the 20-screen Universal Cineplex; $15) for entry to all of them, while most multi-day tickets include a Party Pass. The area splits into the Main Plaza (shopping and dining), Lagoon Front (dining, live music and theatre) and the Promenade (dining and nightclubs). For dining, see p314.

The Groove at CityWalk

© Universal Orlando Resort

Blue Man Group: The most entertaining element here offers a unique brand of comedy, music and multi-media theatrics, adding something novel to the Universal line-up. In the hands (or mouths!) of the Blue Men, mundane items like pipes, paintballs, cereal, Gi-Pads, and even audience members become the instruments of wild creativity with sometimes stunning, occasionally slightly gross but always hilariously gratifying outcomes. There is a strong live music element and it can feel a bit like a rock concert. Their ability to drum up a tune on various bits and pieces is amazing. The wild finale, involving the whole theatre, is a real corker, and don't worry if you're seated in the 'poncho section'; the Blue Men will make sure you have adequate protection. An unforgettable evening of family entertainment, from $70/adults, $40/3–9s. Tickets are available at **universalorlando.com** or from the theatre box office (book online for a $10 discount).

Bob Marley – A Tribute to Freedom: A clever re-creation of Marley's Jamaica home is turned into a courtyard music venue and restaurant. The bands are excellent, the atmosphere authentic and the place comes alive at night (bar open until 2am, 21 and over only after 9pm; cover charge after 9pm).

> **BRITTIP**
> Park in Universal's multi-storey car park for all CityWalk venues – free after 6pm (except during special evening events).

The Groove: For club-minded visitors this is a high-tech dance venue designed like a Victorian theatre but with the latest in club music, lighting and special effects (9pm–2am; 21 and over only; attire casual chic, no hats, no sleeveless tops).

Hard Rock Live: A massive mock-Coliseum styled 2,500-seat theatre with high-tech staging and sound, big-name artists are on stage several times a week (Pat Benatar, Adam

Ant and the fab Classic Albums Live all appeared in 2019) in this slightly retro rock 'n' roll venue (407 351 5483, **hardrock.com**).

Jimmy Buffet's Margaritaville: Live music and three bars (10.30am–midnight Sun–Thurs, 10.30am–1am Fri–Sat). Band (and cover charge) starts at 10pm.

Red Coconut Club: Retro dance club with a trendy, tropical vibe. Live music, signature cocktails, tapas-style menu and eclectic South Seas décor make it a popular venue (8pm–2am daily; 21 and over only). DJ daily, live music Thurs–Sat.

Rising Star Karaoke: It's karaoke taken to the next level and it's hugely entertaining, with a live band, back-up singers, a large selection of songs and a host who makes every volunteer singer feel like a star. There is a full bar with speciality cocktails and appetisers (8pm– 2am nightly; 18 and over on Sun–Thurs; 21 + Fri–Sat). Tue–Sat live band, back-up singers and host; back-up singers and host only on Sun and Mon.

NBC Sports Grill & Brew: For a sports bar raised a level, this is perfect for live sporting events (or just a good meal or a drink at one of the two bars). The atmosphere is lively, its own brewery offers great beers and the many HD TV screens feature multiple views of the action. The food is well above usual sports bar cuisine, though, and even non-sports fans should feel comfortable with the more sophisticated style. We especially like the Crispy Pretzel Crusted Calamari, Cedar-Planked Salmon, Bang-Bang Chicken and succulent barbecue dishes (10.30am–midnight Sun–Thurs, 1am Fri–Sat).

Toothsome Chocolate Emporium & Savory Feast Kitchen: This temple to all things sweet is a work of art, with its steampunk décor and built-in gadgetry, as well as actors playing the roles of Penny Toothsome and robot companion Jaques. The entertainment value is high but the range of milkshakes, sundaes and desserts is dazzling. Look out for the Chocolate x 5 (with five different kinds of chocolate ladled into a milkshake), the Thrilla in Vanilla and the Chocolate Brownie Bark. The restaurant also serves excellent burgers, steak, pasta and seafood, but we're betting you're coming for the sweet stuff! There is also a gift shop (10.30am–midnight Sun–Thurs, 1am Fri–Sat).

Not breathless yet? Well, there's still the 20-screen **Universal Cineplex** with a capacity of 5,000 and Luxury Loungers and an XD auditorium for the latest in movie comfort. And, of course, there's the Hollywood Drive-In Golf (p268).

NBC Sports Grill and Brew

Orlando's 'Districts'

One of the biggest developments in Orlando in recent years has been the growth of hip, trendy 'Districts' that are great locals' hangouts as well as interesting places to explore. From SoDo, or 'South Downtown' to Ivanhoe Village and College Park to Curry Ford West, there are 10 distinct 'main street' neighbourhoods of shops, cafés, bars, breweries and nightlife, all of which have real tourist appeal if you're looking for an authentic local experience. They offer a more urban take on places like Winter Park and Winter Garden, and feature original dining, boutiques (notably antiques in Ivanhoe Village) and community events. You should definitely try the **Mills 50** district, with its strong Asian influences (like Vietnamese restaurant Little Saigon), and the **Milk District**, where the bars and coffee shops regularly win awards. Look up more at **orlandomainstreets.com**.

POINTE ORLANDO

This development on I-Drive, almost opposite the Convention Center, is a mix of shops, cinema, restaurants, live entertainment and the WonderWorks fun centre (with its magic-themed dinner show). The Pointe has day and night appeal.

BB King's Blues Club: Live jazz and blues make this a fine choice for a meal or drinks and a show in this imaginative venue, featuring a two-storey concert hall and a variety of bars. Live music nightly from 7pm with one of its two excellent house

BB King's Blues Club

bands, plus guests (407 370 4550, **bbkingclubs.com**).

Cuba Libre Restaurant and Rum Bar: Offers live Latin music on Fri and Sat nights, starting at 10pm (**cubalibrerestaurant.com**).

Main Event Entertainment: For active fun, this high-quality indoor complex – with state-of-the-art 10-pin bowling, ropes course, pool tables, mini-golf, karaoke, laser tag, rock climbing and video games – takes some beating. Especially clever is their multi-player virtual reality centre that pits guests in active, free-roaming challenges against zombies, robots and more. Another highlight is the extensive indoor/outdoor bar and dining room, with a great drinks menu and New American cuisine (11am–midnight Mon, 11pm Tues–Thurs and Sun, 1am Fri, 9am–1am Sat, **bit.ly/brit-mainevent**).

Orlando Improv Comedy Club and Fat Fish Blue: The Improv pulls in top name comedians from across the US, with shows ranging from mildly risqué to downright raucous. The theatre is intimate, making it easy for entertainers to interact with guests (often with hilarious results) and it is a terrific change of pace for a grown-up night out. Seating is first-come, first-seated, full food and drinks menu available, all shows 21 and over, with two performances on Fri and Sat (no shows Mon and Tues). Connected to the Improv is the bistro-style Fat Fish Blue, featuring American fare with a New Orleans accent. Full bar, a good range of speciality beers, and live music five nights a week. All ages welcome (407 480 5233, **theimprovorlando.com**).

Regal Cinema: State-of-the-art 21-screen movieplex (with IMAX screen) boasting stadium seating and the latest 4DX immersive technology (**bit.ly/brit-regal**).

Taverna Opa: A lively Greek option, with belly-dancing, other live entertainment and a great ouzo bar! (407 351 8660, **opaorlando.com**).

For more on Pointe Orlando, 407 248 2838 or **pointeorlando.com**. For the restaurant choices, see p322.

DOWNTOWN ORLANDO

Church Street is the epicentre of this nightlife hub, with a wide variety of dining choices, from the distinctive supper-club of **Kres Chophouse** and its elegant bar, the award-winning gastropub-style **Rusty Spoon** to the all-American burger bar frenzy of **Graffiti Junktion**. Add in high-energy bars **Latitudes**, **Cahoots** and **Chillers**, plus cabaret, theatre and live music, and this is Party Central at weekends. It's fairly lively Wed and Thurs, too. **Harry Buffalo** appeals to sports fans, while **Lion's Pride**, a soccer-themed pub, is a big fan favourite. Don't miss the eclectic **Mad Cow Theatre**, which presents major plays and theatrical events, including an annual Cabaret Festival (early May; 407 297 8788, **madcowtheatre. com**) and the atmospheric **Ceviche** lounge, offering live flamenco dance shows, outstanding cocktails with a Mediterranean twist and an extensive wine list to go with the restaurant's high-end cuisine (**ceviche. com**). **Hamburger Mary's** takes some beating, with its outrageous drag acts and live comedy (distinctly X-rated but lots of fun), to complement its great burgers, sandwiches, decadent desserts and cocktails. They feature Twisted Sisters Bingo on Tues, BOGO Thursday on Thurs, the Dining With The Divas Friday Show ('an interactive drag show'), Leigh Shannon's Cabaret on Sat and a Broadway Brunch on Sun (shows variously 6.30–7.30pm, 11am Brunch, booking highly advised; 321 319 0600, **hamburgermarys.com/orlando**). Nearby, **Wall Street Plaza**, between Orange Ave and N Court Ave, is equally lively Thurs–Sat as the locals bar-hop the eight bar venues, which include live music for special events (**wallstplaza.net**). More downtown entertainment can be had at **The Social**, an indie club staging eclectic bands most nights, plus a busy bar; the **Bosendorfer Lounge**, for great live jazz inside The Grand Bohemian Hotel; and **The Beacham**, a nightclub and concert venue next to The Social. The Speakeasy phenomenon can also be found here, with the 1920s 'hidden

bar' style well evidenced by **Hanson's Shoe Repair** (call in advance on 407 476 9446 and they will contact you with the nightly password!) and **The Treehouse** (407 205 2062, **thetreehouseorlando.com**).

DINNER SHOWS

Dinner shows are an Orlando phenomenon: live entertainment coupled with dinner and free soft drinks in a fantasy environment, where even the waiters and waitresses are in costume. They have strong family appeal and you are usually seated at large tables where you get to know other people, but at $32–69, they are not cheap (especially with taxes and tips). Be aware, too, of the attempts to extract more from you with photos, souvenirs and upgrades.

BRITTIP

American cinema popcorn is invariably SALTED. Sweet popcorn in the US is usually called Kettle Corn.

Pirate's Dinner Adventure

Disney shows

Visitors often overlook Walt Disney World's offerings unless they are staying at one of the hotel resorts, but they are worth considering.

Disney's Spirit of Aloha: For an excellent night of South Seas entertainment, go to Luau Cove at Disney's Polynesian Resort. It's a bit expensive at $78/adult (Category 1 main floor centre seating) and $46/under-10; or Cat 2 upper floor and sides $74 and $44; Cat 3 extreme sides or extreme upper level $66 and $39 – but good value as the 2hr show features some splendid entertainment, such as Hawaiian singers and dancers, and an amazing Samoan fire juggler. Tax and gratuity are included. The food is plentiful, with salad, barbecue ribs, roast chicken and vegetable medley, plus a pineapple coconut-guava cake (limited kid-friendly menu). Beer, wine and soft drinks are included, and shows are at 5.15 and 8.15pm Tues–Sat. Make reservations up to 180 days in advance, with full payment when booking.

Hoop-Dee-Doo Musical Revue: At Disney's Fort Wilderness Resort & Campground, this is a popular nightly dinner show that maintains the resort's Western theme, and has great food (all-you-can-eat ribs, fried chicken, salad, baked beans, corn bread and strawberry shortcake, plus unlimited beer, wine, sangria and soft drinks). Especially popular with children, it features the amusing song and dance of the Pioneer Hall Players in a merry American hoedown. We're slightly biased but we love this show as it's been running since 1974 and remains a Disney tradition, full of genuine wit and humour, plus a hugely energetic cast that keep things fresh every night. The Revue plays at 4, 6.15 and 8.30pm at the authentic Pioneer Hall, Category 1 seating (main floor centre) is $72/adult, $43/under-10; Cat 2 (back and balcony) $67 and $39; Cat 3 (side balconies) $64 and $38 (under-3s free; prices include tax and gratuity) and the show lasts almost two hours. Reservations are ALWAYS necessary and can be made up to 180 days in advance (full payment at booking).

BRITTIP

Most dinner shows can be quite chilly, especially those with animals, like Medieval Times, so bring a jacket or sweater to beat the air-conditioning.

Medieval Times

Spain in the 11th century is the entertaining setting for this two-hour extravaganza of medieval pageantry, falconry and robust horseback jousts. It's worth arriving early to appreciate the clever mock castle design as you are ushered into the pre-show hall before being taken into the arena. The show features jousting, sword-fighting and hand-to-hand combats, plus some superb horsemanship, with the basic idea of cheering on one of the Knights of the Realm in the six colour-coded sections. The weapons are all real and used with great skill, and there are some neat special effects. You need to be in full audience participation mode as you cheer on your knight in the traditional good-v-evil scenario, but kids (and many adults) get a huge kick out of it and they'll also love eating without cutlery (the soup bowls do have handles, though!). The elaborate staging is backed up by a succulent chicken dinner, with tomato soup, garlic bread, potatoes and corn, plus dessert (vegetarian meal available) and the serfs and wenches who serve you make it a fun experience. A basic Royalty Package upgrade for $12/person includes priority access, preferred seating, knight's cheering banner, and lanyard. The Queen's Royalty Package adds VIP first or second-row seating in the centre seating area, plus a framed group photo ($22); and the birthday Celebration Package includes a group photo per person, VIP seating, banner, lanyard, personalised announcement during the show and a slice of cake ($18 more). Doors open 90mins prior to show time (times vary seasonally; $64.95 adults, $36.95 3–12s; 407 396 2900, **medievaltimes.com**). The Castle is on Highway 192, 5ml/8km east of the junction with I-4 between Markers 14 and 15.

Pirate's Dinner Adventure

One of the most spectacular settings, this features a life-size pirate ship 'anchored' in a huge indoor lagoon – and a full pirate crew to fill it! It delivers good value with a pre-show, plentiful food and soft drinks. The hearty main meal features soup or salad, chicken or surf and turf with mash and seasonal vegetables, or vegetarian pasta, plus dessert. The story revolves around your invitation to the Governor's Ball, where you will meet a magical mermaid who possesses the legendary Serpent's Eye jewel. But evil Captain Sebastian the Black is plotting revenge, and it all devolves into chaos when he and his pirate crew stage a kidnapping that includes Princess Anita, the mermaid and YOU. That's the cue for duels, acrobatics, fights and trapeze acts, with plenty of audience participation. A Treasure Upgrade adds 2nd-row seating, guaranteed pirate interaction, unlimited soda and beer or two glasses of wine during the show, and gift shop discount ($25 adult, $20 child); a VIP Upgrade ($30 adult, $25 child) adds exclusive pre-show lounge, bar and restrooms, front-row seating, appetiser buffet, gift shop discount, guaranteed pirate interaction, unlimited beer and soft drinks or two glasses of wine during the show, plus guaranteed boarding of the ship for photos with the cast. It is located on Carrier Drive between I-Drive and Universal Boulevard, and runs at 5pm and 8pm Mon-Sat, 4.30pm and 7.30pm Sun, plus 2pm June 1-Sept 1. Appetisers are served for 45mins prior to seating ($63.95 adults, $37.95 3–12s, includes two rounds of beer during the show; see website for savings; 407 206 5102, **piratesdinneradventure.com**). Watch for themed Pirates Christmas and Halloween shows in December and October. There is a parking fee.

The Rock Show

Settle in for a live musical entertainment experience while you dine in this 300-seat venue on I-Drive. The 90-minute Las Vegas-style tribute concert experience starts at 6.30pm nightly (with pre-show at 7pm, show at 7.30pm) and features live music and an excellent dinner with a choice of chicken, braised short rib or veggie pasta, plus a full kids' menu. It continues with the signature concert on the main stage, including an aerialist, and concludes with a chance to meet the highly acclaimed performers and enjoy a drink at the eye-catching Orlando Forum's indoor/outdoor bar. It makes for a completely novel and interactive performance, and should suit fans of rock and pop legends like Elvis, Michael Jackson, Katy Perry and Justin Timberlake. There is a real high-energy, non-stop pace to the show, and the live band are a phenomenon in their own right. ($65 adults, $40 3–12s; 407 536 7943, **rockdinnershow.com**).

Sleuth's Mystery Dinner Shows

This is a live version of Cluedo acted out before your eyes in hilarious fashion while you enjoy a substantial meal with a main course choice of poussin, lasagne with or without meatballs (or, for $6 extra, prime rib) or a vegetarian meal, and unlimited beer, wine and soft drinks. You can choose between three theatres and 12 different plot situations (several of which have amusing British settings), including Squire's Inn, Roast 'Em & Toast 'Em and Lord Mansfield's Fox Hunt Banquet (mayhem at an English banquet), that add up to some elaborate murder mysteries. The action takes place all around you and members of the audience can take some cameo roles. The quick-witted cast keep things moving and keep you guessing during the theatrical part of the 2½-hour show, then during the main part of dinner you think up questions for interrogation (but the real murderer is allowed to lie!). Solve the crime and you win a prize, but that is pretty secondary to the overall enjoyment and this is a show we enjoy a lot, plus it's a terrific choice with teens ($65.95/adult, $29.95/3–11; times vary; 407 393 1985, **sleuths.com**).

Also check out their periodic Stand Up Comedy (see website for dates, times, and comedians). Sleuth's is in the plaza just past Ripley's Believe It Or Not on I-Drive, with three theatres, a smart pre-dinner bar area and gift shop.

WonderWorks: Outta Control Magic Comedy

This smaller-scale dinner show is at WonderWorks on I-Drive (at Pointe Orlando). A novel mixture of improvised comedy and magic, with all-you-can-eat pizza, salad, and dessert, plus beer, wine and Coke. Set in the intimate Shazam Theater, it features illusionist (and funny guy) Tony Brent serving up one-of-a-kind close-up sleight of hand with plenty of audience participation, especially if you sit close to the stage. Nightly at 6 or 8pm, it costs a good-value $32/ adult, $22/4–12 and seniors. A VIP Combo for the show and an All Access ticket to WonderWorks (open 9am until midnight, p236) is $60/$42 (407 351 8800, **wonderworksonline.com**).

Capone's Dinner & Show

Enter Miss Jewel's 1930s Prohibition-era Chicago speak-easy, where gangsters, dames and mobsters gather – and hapless Detective Marvel might make YOU part of his efforts to close the joint down. A mix of comedy and song and dance numbers tell the slapstick-style story, while a huge Italian-American buffet offers a pasta bar, 12-item hot bar, salad bar, carvery and side dishes so no-one goes home hungry! Unlimited Bud Light, a selection of wines and cocktails, plus soft drinks, juice, Kiddie Cocktails and Mama Capone's 'dessert surprise' round out the all-you-can-eat-and-drink menu ($70/ adult, $46/4–12, 3 and under free; 407 397 2378, **alcapones.com**).

BRITBONUS

Mention your Brit Guide and receive 50% off the General Admission for Capone's Dinner Show, plus $2 off per paid ticket. Not valid for New Year's Eve Gala.

LIVE MUSIC

Orlando's live music scene is lively and always changing but several venues can be relied on for quality entertainment. As already noted, the House of Blues and Hard Rock Live provide regular big-name concerts, while international acts appear at the state-of-the-art **Amway Center** in downtown (as well as the Orlando Magic, Orlando Predators and Orlando Solar Bears sports teams), including Ariana Grande, Pentatonix, Jennifer Lopez and Disturbed in 2019 (**amwaycenter.com**).

The **Dr Phillips Performing Arts Center** also features big-name concert performers as well as touring Broadway performances and the Orlando Ballet company (1844 513 2014, **drphillipscenter.org**).

SPORTS BARS

The sports bar is an American invention and if you'd like to sample the way the locals follow their sport (American football is usually the biggest at weekends Sept–Jan, but basketball is also popular along with baseball and ice-hockey) try these locations.

Buffalo Wild Wings: This popular national chain has nine Orlando locations (notably on I-Drive, 407 351 6200; Lake Buena Vista near Disney Springs, 407 827 0444; and ICON Park, 407 413 5115), where masses of chicken-based dishes (watch out for the Blazin' sauce – it's seriously hot!) are served up in a casual, lively atmosphere, highlighted by its Buzztime Trivia System at each table and multiple big-screen TVs (**buffalowildwings. com**). Be like the cool kids and call it 'B-Dubs.'

Disney: Boasts the excellent **ESPN Club** at Disney's BoardWalk Resort, a full-service restaurant with sports broadcast facilities, video games, more than 70 TV monitors, giant scoreboards and even a Little League menu for kids.

Miller's Ale House: Among the multitude of sports bars, one of our favourites has fine examples on Kirkman Road, opposite Universal Studios (407 248 0000) at Lake Buena Vista on Highway 535 near Disney Springs (407 239 1800), on I-Drive (407 370 6688), at ChampionsGate and the Kissimmee location on Highway 192 (407 238 4499). The Ale Houses feature more than 30 TVs (each!), classic American bar food, including their signature spicy 'chicken zingers' and an above-average range of beers (**millersalehouse.com**).

Other options: Look out for the revamped **Uno Chicago** chain (**unos.com**) or any **TGI Friday's**, **Graffiti Junktion** or **BJ's Brewhouse** outlet. Then there are **The Pub** and **Marlow's Tavern**, both at Pointe Orlando (p322). In the Dellagio complex on Sand Lake Road, **Miller's Field House** is the place to visit. **Universal CityWalk** boasts **NBC Sports Grill & Brew**, with more big-screen TV style and fab food in an elegant, comfortable atmosphere.

When you're close to Mall at Millennia, be sure to call in at family-friendly **Duffy's Sports Grill**, with a great array of sandwiches, burgers and steaks to go with their TVs (**duffysmvp.com**). Or, for possibly the most impressive TV screen, **Wreckers Sports Bar** at the Gaylord Palms resort takes some beating (as does its food). For something different, **Tomkos Tavern** has terrific appeal with its many sports simulators, as well as plenty of TVs and good food. Or try **Frankie Farrell's Irish Pub** at Lake Buena Vista Resort & Spa (next to the Factory Stores).

SOMETHING DIFFERENT

ICEBAR: Spend 45mins surrounded by 50 tons of carved ice while sipping a chilled vodka beverage, then warm up in the Nordic-inspired Fire Lounge, at this fun venue on I-Drive just north of WonderWorks. Coats and gloves are provided or you can upgrade to a glam mock fur coat for $10, and entry fee is $19.95 (drinks not included; save 25% by booking online). Open 5pm–12am Sun–Wed, 5pm–1am Thurs, 5pm–2am Fri–Sat, with the first ICEBAR entry time at 5.15pm; ages eight and up allowed 5pm–9pm only. No cover charge for Fire Lounge (which also features DJs), but no children. Happy Hour 7–9pm Sun–Thurs, and Expedition Package at $43.95 (online discount saves 27%), including one premium drink in ICEBAR and one in Fire Lounge (407 426 7555 or **icebarorlando.com**).

Howl at the Moon: If you're looking for a serious party, try Howl at the Moon on I-Drive, where the live music doesn't stop until the wee hours! An energetic piano-playing duo pound out a rockin' good time, highlighted by 'Showtime', when the whole bar joins in a choreographed dance-fest. Cocktails are available by the glass or the bucket(!), with drink specials nightly (21 and over only; 7pm–2am Sat–Thurs, 6pm–2am Fri; cover charge $5 Sun–Wed, $7 Thurs, $10 Fri and Sat; 407 354 5999, **howlatthemoon.com**).

Now you'll want to know a lot more about where, when and how to tackle that other holiday dilemma – where to eat. Read on…

ICEBAR Orlando

11 Dining Out

or Eat, Drink and Eat Again!

Orlando dazzles with its attractions, delights with its quality and bewilders with its quantity and variety. And that is also true when it comes to dining. There has never been more choice, in more ways and more alternatives than ever before. Hold on to your waistbands, we're going in....

Variety

The diversity of food on offer, from fast-food counters to five-star gourmet experiences, is now Orlando's speciality.

Chain restaurants are seemingly everywhere, and you need to know your Applebees from your Sweet Tomatoes. But, at the same time, there are a range of one-off restaurants of all kinds that maintain the local tradition for convenience, value and superiority.

As a rule, food is plentiful, relatively cheap, available 24 hours a day, and nearly always appetising and filling. You will find an increasing number of fine-dining possibilities, but the basic emphasis is on value, so unless we have marked somewhere as 'pricey', you'll find prices are fairly consistent. Portions are large, service is efficient and friendly, and it's hard to come by a bad meal. The one real exception is if you dine mainly at fast-food places and the likes of Dennys and Co, you won't find much fresh veg. But if you look up the vegetarian options, visit outlets like Sweet Tomatoes or ask for the vegetable option instead of fries or potatoes at other restaurants, you will find a balanced choice. Plus, salads are almost always on the menu.

BRITGUIDE 25

The big change in the dining scene since 1995 has been in the amazing growth of fine-dining restaurants. Where once was barely half a dozen, now there are 50 or more.

Exceptional deals

Most restaurants tend towards the informal (T-shirts and shorts are nearly always acceptable) and cater readily for families; you will always find a kids' menu, and many have activity packs. Many hotels and restaurants offer Kids-eat-free deals (from under-10 to under-14), provided parents are also dining. The age limits vary. The all-you-can-eat buffet is another common feature, where you can probably eat enough at breakfast to keep you going to dinner! Some places offer early-bird specials for dining before 5.30pm as 5.30–7.30pm is peak time for most restaurants. You may have a wait if you arrive between 6 and 8pm.

Don't be afraid to ask for the leftovers 'to go' and don't hesitate to say if something isn't right; the locals will readily complain (politely) if they are not happy, so restaurants are keen to ensure everything is to their diners' satisfaction. And, please, don't forget to tip; the basic wage for waiters and waitresses is low, so they rely heavily on tips as part of their income and are taxed on an assumed level of tips. Unless service really is shoddy (in which case mention it), the usual tip rate is 10% of your bill at buffet-style restaurants and 15–20% at full-service restaurants. Check if service is already added to your bill, though this isn't common. You will encounter a huge range of food types. Florida is renowned for its seafood, which comes much cheaper than in the Mediterranean: crab, lobster, shrimp (what we call king prawns), scallops and oysters, as well as several dozen varieties of fish, many unusual (like mahi mahi and grouper; take note, dolphin on a menu is dolphin fish, not the mammal!). Latin-style cuisines, notably Cuban and Mexican, are common, and the South American influences mean the delicious citrus-marinated seafood called ceviche is often featured. There is also plenty of Asian fare, from Chinese and Indian to Japanese, Thai and Vietnamese.

The big shopping malls all offer good-value food courts. 'Cracker' cooking is original Floridian fare, and the speciality is alligator, either stewed, barbecued, smoked, sautéed or braised. Fried gator tail 'nuggets' are a local favourite, as are catfish and frogs' legs. And do try key lime pie!

Vegetarian options

In a country where beef is king, vegetarians often find themselves hard done by. However, there are some bright spots. Most good-quality restaurants should provide a veggie option and are usually happy to provide something even if it's not on the menu. All Disney's full-service restaurants will be able to oblige, and most at Universal, too. There are also several vegetarian restaurants, including the Indian cuisine of **Woodlands** on S Orange Blossom Trail (407 854 3330, **woodlandsusa. com**; closed Mon); and **Ethos Vegan Kitchen** in Winter Park (407 228 3898, **ethosvegankitchen.com**); **Sanctum** in the trendy Mills 50 district east of downtown (407 757 0346, **thesanctumcafe.com**); and the bohemian **Market On South**, in Orlando's Milk District (407 613 5968, **marketonsouth.com**).

More mainstream is **Sweet Tomatoes,** with six outlets in the main tourist areas, notably on I-Drive by Kirkman Road; in the Crossroads Plaza at Lake Buena Vista; and just off West Highway 192 in Kissimmee on Rolling Oaks Blvd. It is a buffet restaurant, not totally vegetarian, but most of its fare – salads, soups, pastas, breads

Cold Stone Creamery

© Universal Orlando Resort

Belly up to the bar!

If you'd like just a snack or sample of a restaurant's fare, many places offer a bar or appetiser menu, including Bar Louie, Big Fin Seafood, Bonefish Grill, Capital Grille, Carrabba's, Eddie V's, Fishbones, Fleming's, Hillstone, House of Blues, Kres Chophouse, Luma on Park, Moonfish, Morton's, The Oceanaire, Old Hickory, Paddlefish, Rainforest Café, Ravenous Pig, Roy's, Seasons 52, Texas de Brazil, T-Rex Café and Urbain 40, plus Brio Tuscan Grille (weekdays only, in the bar), Landry's Seafood House (3–6pm Mon–Thurs, noon–4pm Sat, Sun), The Palm (5–7pm Sun–Fri) and the fab Nomads Lounge at Animal Kingdom.

and desserts – are either veggie or vegan, and all are clearly labelled.

BRITTIP

Sweet Tomatoes is a restaurant chain we recommend highly, and you can benefit from its enhanced dinner menu by arriving a little before 4pm but still paying only the lunch buffet price.

The all-you-can-eat lunch is $10.39, dinner (after 4pm) is $12.39, and both include the vast salad counter, freshly made soups, pizza, pasta, bread and pastries, plus fruit and frozen yoghurt. Drinks are $2.79 (refills free) and kids' meals are $4.39 3–6s and $6.39 7–12s. (11am–10pm daily; **souplantation.com**).

The **Panera Bread** chain also offers some decent veg options (and free wi-fi).

Drinking

Looking for a good beer or cocktail? Orlando definitely has you covered. You can run a tab in the majority of bars and pay when you leave. But be aware US licensing laws are stricter than ours and you MUST be 21 to drink alcohol in a bar or lounge. You'll often be asked for proof of age before you are served (or allowed into a club), so take your passport or

photo driving licence. No arguing: no photo ID, no beer!

Ice: Drinks usually come with a LOT of ice. If you want your whisky (or vodka, etc) without ice, ask for it 'straight up'. If you prefer soft drinks without the usual iceberg, ask for 'no ice' or 'light ice'.

Spirits: Called 'liquor' in the US, these come in a large selection, but beware of ordering just 'whisky' as you'll get bourbon. Specify if you want Scotch or Irish whiskey.

Cocktails: There is a massive choice of cocktails and most bars and restaurants have lengthy happy hours with good prices.

BRITTIP

Possibly the best Happy Hour deal is at swish Seasons 52, which offers a small-plate menu at $5/item 4–7pm Mon–Fri, plus select wines at $6/glass, beer $4 and cocktails $6–7.

Wines: Good-quality Californian wines are better value than European.

Soft drinks: If you stick to 'sodas' or coffee, most bars and restaurants give free refills.

Dollar Off Drinks Card: This programme does exactly what it says – provides a dollar off drinks (beer, wine, cocktails, sodas, tea and coffee) at more than 70 bars and restaurants around Orlando. It costs $15 for a card that can be used up to 30 days and is valid on all full-priced drinks (not happy hour or other specials), and can be used with *every* drinks order, so you could save $41 if you used it just four times a day for two weeks (potentially a lot more with greater use or a longer visit). Look up more at **dollaroffdrinks.com**.)

BRITBONUS

Order one **Dollar Off Drinks** card and get a second FREE with your *Brit Guide*. Just use the code BRITS in the 'Apply Coupon' box when ordering online.

Breweries

There's a huge craft beer scene in the US, with new breweries popping up all the time. Big-label beers (Budweiser, Coors and Miller Lite) leave a lot to be desired in taste terms, hence there's been big growth in national alternatives like Sam Adams, Leinenkugel's, Yuengling, Goose Island, Blue Moon and Kona. For the aficionado, Florida's brewery scene has mushroomed in recent years, and there is now the **Central Florida Ale Trail** to highlight the array of 24-plus on offer (**centralfloridaaletrail.com**). To get a representative taste – and don't be afraid to ask for a flight for a sampling selection – try any of the following.

Broken Cauldron: Just two blocks from Orlando City soccer stadium, this blend of two breweries (Broken Strings and Black Cauldron) is hugely popular with fans and offers a great variety in their taproom, with beers like Ruckus Red Amber Ale and Purple Mane that pay homage to the team (3–9pm Tues–Thurs, 1pm–midnight Fri, noon–11pm Sat; noon–7pm Sun, closed Mon; **brokencauldrontaproom.com**).

Bowigens Beer Company: This Casselberry brewery and taproom offers 10 drafts and more than 20 bottled beers, including staples like a Citrus Pale Ale, 7 Layer Stout and Peanut Butter Hefeweizen. (2–10pm Mon–Wed, 2–11pm Thurs, noon–midnight Sat, noon–8pm Sun; 407 960 7816, **bowigens.com**).

Crooked Can: In Winter Garden's Plant Street Market is this signature brewery, producing a wide range from a Belgian Golden Ale to Chocolate Stout and Cider. The taproom is open 11am–11pm Sun–Thurs and 11am–1am Fri and Sat, with food available from the neighbouring market stalls. Tours Sun noon–4pm ($5/person, includes a pint of your choice; 407 395 9520, **crookedcan.com**).

The Hourglass Brewery: Established in 2012 in the suburb of Longwood, this brewer has a reputation for unique beers – notably a barrel-aged selection – as well as flagship, year-round ales like the Belgian Saison and Frankie Rock hefeweizen (11am–11pm Mon–Thurs, 11am–1am Fri and Sat, noon–10pm Sun; 407 262 0056, **thehourglassbrewery.com**).

Ocean Sun: Another brewery and taproom with an imaginative range, including a great Porter, Kolsch and Westende, a fusion of Belgian Trippel ale and pale ale styles (3–10pm Mon–Thurs, noon–midnight Fri and Sat, noon–10pm Sun, 407 745 5551, **oceansunbrewing.com**).

Orlando Brewing Co: The oldest and biggest, and an organic brewer to boot, they feature a huge range of beers, from pale ales to stouts and porters, with more than 20 at any time. Just south of downtown (in an awkward location, but worth finding) they offer an excellent taproom (3–10pm Mon–Thurs, 1pm–midnight Fri and Sat, 1–9pm Sun) and free tours Mon–Sat at 6pm (407 872 1117, **orlandobrewing.com**).

Redlight Redlight: A Winter Park success story, with a regularly changing array of beers, lagers, cider and even barley wine (3.30–midnight Mon–Thurs, 3.30–2am Fri, 1pm–2am Sat, 1–11pm Sun, 407 893 9832, **redlightredlightbeerparlour.com**).

Ten10 Brewing: This lively brewer is in the heart of the Mills 50 district, hence popular with the locals for its tempting range, including a tasty Plum Fennel Farmhouse Ale and superbly sweet Sundae Best Brown. Their small-plate menu is good, too (11.30am–10pm Sun–Thurs, 11.30am–midnight Fri–Sat; 407 930 8993, **ten10brewingcompany.com**).

And don't forget Winter Park's Distilling Co and **Bear & Peacock Brewery** (p248) and **Cask & Larder** inside The Ravenous Pig (p329).

Crooked Can Brewing Company

Brew-pubs

These are also extremely popular and can be found in growing numbers, offering their own craft beers and surprisingly good food. The pick of the bunch include **Big River Grille & Brewing Works** at Disney's Boardwalk Resort; **NBC Sports Grill & Brew** at Universal's CityWalk; **BJ's Restaurant & Brewhouse** in five Central Florida locations (**bjsrestaurants.com**); **Seadog Brewing Company** in Lake Buena Vista; **The Yard House** at ICON Park; and the chic **Whisper Creek Farm: The Kitchen** at the JW Marriott hotel at the Grande Lakes Resort.

BRITTIP

If there are several of you drinking beer, ordering a pitcher will work out cheaper than buying it by the glass.

Magical dining

Orlando has become a foodie's paradise in recent years and, to celebrate, the period from Aug 23 to Sept 30 is officially **Magical Dining**, with a selection of more than 120 top restaurants offering a three-course prix fixe menu at $35/head, a great saving on regular prices. These have included A Land Remembered (Rosen Shingle Creek), Seasons 52, and the superb Urbain 40. Check out more at **bit.ly/brit-dining**.

Who's who

Despite the emerging foodie culture, most restaurants you encounter in the main tourist areas will still be the big chains, so here is a run-down of who they are (apart from the obvious fast-food places like McDonalds, KFC, Subway, Wendy's, etc).

Fast food: A few notable US additions to the burger scene, with a more distinctive touch, include BurgerFi, Five Guys Burgers & Fries, Fuddruckers, Steak 'n Shake and the fun drive-in option of Sonic.

Breakfast-style: Serving throughout the day but with a speciality for breakfast, and none of them serving alcohol: Bob Evans, Cracker Barrel, Dennys, Friendly's, IHOP, Panera Bread, Perkins, Village Inn, Waffle House and our recommendations of **First Watch** (**firstwatch.com**) and **Keke's Breakfast Café** (**kekes.com**).

BRITTIP

American bacon is always streaky crisp fried, and sausages are chipolata-like and slightly spicy. Very different from the British versions.

Buffet style: The all-you-can-eat options that tend to be cheap and cheerful: CiCi's Pizza, Golden Corral, Ponderosa, Shoney's and the excellent Sweet Tomatoes (**sweettomatoes.com**).

Bar-restaurant style: The full American dining experience, with typical bar food and drinks: Applebee's; Bahama Breeze (with a Caribbean twist); BJ's Brewhouse (wide-ranging menu and craft beers); Buffalo Wild Wings and Miller's Ale House (both in sports bar territory); Cheesecake Factory (a huge menu, and decadent desserts); Chilis and Chuys (with Tex-Mex flavours); Hooters (with their 'Hooter Girl' waitresses); Hurricane Grill & Wings (above average bar food and great wings); Manny's Chophouse (a local favourite); Red Robin (for some of the best burgers in town); Shake Shack (a lot more than just great milkshakes!); TGI Friday's (eclectic American style); Uno Pizzeria & Grill (with a more upmarket touch).

Steakhouse style: Where you'll get a really good steak, but also fish, chicken and salads: Capital Grille (the fancy touch); Charley's Steakhouse (also with a deluxe ambience); Logan's Roadhouse; Lone Star Steakhouse; Longhorn Steakhouse; Morton's Steakhouse (the sophisticated touch); Outback Steakhouse (Brit-popular and consistently good value); Ruth's Chris Steakhouse (another superb upmarket choice); Saltgrass Steak House (equally smart and classy);

Sonny's Real Pit Bar-B-Q (with the accent on barbecue everything); and Tony Roma's (especially good for ribs).

Italian flavours: With classic Italian menus: Brio Tuscan Grille (one of the best); Carrabba's; Macaroni Grill; Maggiano's Little Italy; Olive Garden.

Seafood specials: Where you can indulge in the full range of Floridian specialities like grouper and stone crabs: Bonefish Grill (with an upmarket touch); Boston Lobster Feast (pile 'em high!); Joe's Crab Shack (family-friendly style); Red Lobster.

Where to eat

That gives you the inside track on HOW to eat and drink like the locals. Now you need to know WHERE. There are 4,000-plus restaurants in the area, so the following selection covers the main ones, grouped by area.

As with most things Orlando, we start with Walt Disney World.

DISNEY DINING

Having said how Orlando is dominated by chain restaurants, you'll find little evidence of that in Walt Disney World, apart from one McDonalds near the All Star resorts; Earl of Sandwich, Starbucks, Planet Hollywood and House of Blues at Disney Springs; and niche upmarket names like Morimoto, Wolfgang Puck, Todd English and Shula's Steakhouse. Some of the most distinctive dining is from Disney's own creative team around the resorts, and we strongly recommend trying at least one of them.

Animal Kingdom Lodge: Jiko is one of Disney's finest dining choices, with a creative new world fusion cuisine boasting hints of Africa, India and the Mediterranean, as well as a superb South African wine list. **Sanaa** has similar African-Asian influence, but with more accent on Indian food and a couple of great curry dishes, all with a view over the animal savanna. For families, **Boma** is the ideal buffet choice, with a fabulous array of different dishes, both exotic and more familiar, and it's a great opportunity to sample more unusual offerings.

Contemporary Resort: The **California Grill** is the classic high-rise dining experience, with spectacular Pacific-coast flavours, including superb sushi and an amazing Sunday Brunch (with the price tag to match); **The Wave** offers another take on modern American cuisine in stylish

California Grill

© Disney

Our Disney Hotel Top 10

Ideal for a special occasion (p307–8):

1. Jiko
2. Bluezoo
3. Victoria & Albert's
4. California Grill
5. Shula's Steakhouse
6. Narcoossee's
7. Artist Point
8. Yachtsman Steakhouse
9. Sanaa
10. Flying Fish

surroundings, with a great cocktail bar, and not quite so expensive.

Disney's Boardwalk Inn: There is more wonderful seafood on offer at the **Flying Fish,** with eye-catching décor and superb cocktail lounge), where the culinary team serve up some of the best seafood in Orlando; **Trattoria al Forno** features classic Italian cuisine with regional specialities like Venetian mussels and Pettini di Mare, plus great desserts and an all-Italian wine list.

Grand Floridian: First-class seafood is on offer at gorgeous waterfront restaurant **Narcoossee's**, which is a great special-occasion choice, if a touch pricey; **Citricos** offers fine dining with a Mediterranean-infused twist; and **Victoria & Albert's** is Disney's crème-de-la-crème, a superb gourmet experience with white-glove service and New American cuisine.

Whispering Canyon Café

© Disney

Polynesian Village Resort: The full South Seas dining experience is on display at **'Ohana**, where food is served family-style, with large plates of food for the whole table, and as much as you can eat; **Kona Café** also offers a Polynesian and Asian-tinged menu but with a more sophisticated ambience.

Swan and Dolphin: The choice here is dazzling, from the elegant supper-club style of **Shula's Steakhouse** to the classic Italian of **Il Mulino**, an upmarket New York trattoria with lashings of style. Japanese cuisine and excellent sushi is on offer at **Kimonos**, with an interesting sushi menu, and there is also karaoke nightly. Todd English's **Bluezoo** is another sumptuous seafood choice, both for the décor and the cuisine, as well as another wonderful bar area and wine list.

Wilderness Lodge: A great fine-dining experience is on offer at **Artist Point,** where steaks and seafood are superbly cooked and presented in elegant surroundings with a Pacific North-West culinary touch; **Whispering Canyon Café** is a rowdy, family-style restaurant, where the food has an Old West style and is served family-style.

Yacht & Beach Club: Fine dining is on offer at the **Yachtsman Steakhouse**, where succulent steaks are the order of the day, as well as fine seafood and gracious service. It's not cheap but the quality is unarguable. **Cape May Café** is themed like a New England beachfront, with quality seafood to match, served buffet style.

That is Disney's signature resort dining, but there are other gems worth noting. Caribbean Beach Resort has **Sebastian's Bistro**, where American favourites are given a Caribbean twist and the quality is well above average. Coronado Springs has **Maya Grill,** a Latin-infused menu that elevates dining beyond the norm, and fabulous new rooftop option **Toledo–Tapas, Steak & Seafood**; and Port Orleans has the eye-catching **Boatwrights** serving tastes of Louisiana in its heavily themed interior, including jambalaya and catfish.

DISNEY SPRINGS

With all the new development here, the dining choice is now immense. Going through all four areas by turn, here's your choice. Just remember you're paying for the scenery and ambience as well as the food.

The Landing

The Boathouse: This is nautically themed, with the obvious focus on great seafood, but also excellent chicken, chops, salads, raw bar and some of the best steaks in Florida. A well-presented kids' menu is also available, and the presentation is stylish. There are three bars, outdoor dining, live music, gift shop, boat rides and a water view from each dining room, which makes for memorable dining, but with the price tag to match (11am–1.30am, 407 939 2628; **theboathouseorlando.com**).

BRITTIP

Maria & Enzo's offers an extensive prix-fixe brunch at $35 ($17, 9 and under), with starters, entrée and dessert. Add cocktails for an additional $5–7.

The Edison: This imposing 1930s-style nightclub/restaurant scores highly for its cabaret and live music, plus acrobats, jugglers and aerialists, but it also has an enticing range of artisanal snacks, small plates, flatbreads, sandwiches, charcuterie and desserts (don't miss the big-enough-for-two milkshakes!) to go with great handcrafted cocktails (407 560 9288, **theedisonfla.com**).

Maria & Enzo's Ristorante: This enormous split-level southern Italian offering serves up soups, salads, pasta, fish and meat in surroundings themed as a 1930s airport terminal, and with magnificent lakeside views. Again, desserts are a highlight (11.30am–10pm Mon–Thurs, 11.30am–pm Fri–Sat, 10.30am–10pm Sun; 407 560 8466, **patinagroup.com/maria-enzos**).

Chef Art Smith's Homecomin': Celebrity chef Art Smith brings true Florida cooking (and moonshine!) to this elaborate rustic setting, with an excellent bar and show kitchen. Smith specialises in old-time 'Cracker' fare, with a modern twist and fresh local ingredients. Try his cheese-laced drop biscuits, fried chicken, and shrimp and grits, plus the signature cakes and fresh fruit cobblers for dessert. The adjacent Shine Bar offers wonderful coolers, cocktails and punches (11am–11pm Mon–Thurs, midnight Fri, 9.30am–midnight Sat, 9.30am–11pm Sun; 407 560 0100, **homecominkitchen.com**).

Jock Lindsey's Hangar Bar: This Indiana Jones-themed lounge bar is packed with eye-catching novelties, as well as great cocktails, but it also serves up some excellent small-plate meals, like the Snakebite Sliders, Chen's BBQ Pork Skewers and Spicy Popcorn Chicken (noon–midnight Sun–Wed, 2am Thurs–Sat).

Morimoto Asia: We're big fans of the Pan-Asian style of Chef Masaharu Morimoto (of TV's *Iron Chef* fame), which puts the emphasis on Japanese cuisine, seafood and elaborate sushi offerings in a sleek two-storey setting. Exhibition kitchens, a contemporary cocktail lounge and patio dining add to the ambiance, while the menu features classics such as Orange Chicken and Dim Sum, plus plenty of contemporary twists. A 'Street Foods' patio window also serves small-scale tastes (11.30am–10pm Sun–Thurs, 1am Fri–Sun; 407 939 6686; **patinagroup.com/morimoto-asia**).

The Boathouse

© Disney

─────────**BRITTIP**

Make sure you taste Morimoto's Spare Ribs, deep-fried with a hoisin sweet chilli glaze – even if you only sample them from the Street Foods window. They are out-of-this-world and perfect for sharing, either as a half-rack starter or full-rack main course.

Paddlefish: The former Fulton's Crabhouse has been re-imagined to give it a smart new look to go with an excellent seafood menu, which includes Lobster guacamole and a shellfish-heavy Cioppino. It's not cheap but the rooftop lounge is worth visiting just for a drink (11.30am–11pm Sun–Thurs, midnight Fri–Sat; 407 934 2628, **paddlefishrestaurant.com**).

Paradiso 37: This 'Taste of the Americas' offers a wide variety of foods, much with a Latin-tinged flavour, and live music nightly. A tempting menu includes Argentinean skirt steak, Baha Fish Tacos, cocktails and tequila. The lively style, split-level restaurant, chic bar area (inside and out) and lakeside setting mark this out for a relaxing lunch or upbeat dinner (11am–2am daily, bar until 2am; 407 934 3700, **paradiso37.com**).

Terralina Crafted Italian: This replaced the old Portobello with even more authentic Italian flair under award-winning chef Tony Mantuano. It is built around a show-kitchen, with a broad range of Italian regional specialities, notably fried olives, house-made pastas, littleneck clams and artisanal wood-fired pizza, plus a kid's menu and a genuine, laid-back vibe (407 934 8888, **terralinacrafteditalian.com**).

Jock Lindsey's Hangar Bar

© Disney

Raglan Road: This Irish-themed pub, with lively music and a genuine Emerald Isle style, is where you really can enjoy the food as well as the craic. Much of the restaurant's interior was shipped over from Ireland (including four reclaimed 130-year-old bars), establishing an authentic backdrop to an original menu. Fresh, simple ingredients with an imaginative twist: shepherd's pie, drunk mussels, Mammy's chicken, Irish sausages, plus a range of original sandwiches at lunchtime and a healthy goat cheese terrine. Great weekend brunch and special dining events, and it's not too taxing on the wallet (11am–11pm, bar menu to 1am, 407 938 0300, **raglanroad.com**).

STK Orlando: This fabulous take on steakhouse chic brings a vibrant, edgy style to a traditional area, combining restaurant and lounge (with great cocktails). Instead of dark, brooding and formal, STK goes for playful and innovative (including a live DJ), with a creative touch to the décor and a decadent depth to their flavours. Rooftop dining – perfect for warm Floridian evenings – is another feature, along with trendy menu items that include grilled octopus, smoked spicy Maine Lobster, and Truffled Spring Pea Risotto, along with large, medium and small steaks, plus some sizzling signature cocktails (5pm–11pm Sun–Thurs, midnight Fri, Sat, brunch 11am–3pm Sat–Sun; late night happy hour until 2am, 407 917 7440, **bit.ly/brit-STK**).

Wine Bar George: This sparkling offering is the work of local master sommelier George Miliotes, who helped create Disney's California Grill and Seasons 52 restaurants. A rustic two-storey creation, it features delicious small-plate bites – like Grilled Octopus and Crispy Mac and Cheese – as well as huge 'sharing' dishes (don't miss the luscious Skirt Steak), plus a superb Wine Country Brunch at weekends. There is a dazzling array of 140 wines, by the ounce, glass or bottle, including some well-priced wineries sourced by George himself, plus signature cocktails, craft beers and ciders. And the Olive Oil Cake for dessert is to die for! (11am–midnight Sun–Wed, 2am Thurs–Sat, brunch 11am–3pm Sat–Sun, 407 490 1800, **winebargeorge.com**).

Other choices: To one side of Raglan Road is **Cookes of Dublin**, a chippie serving up real chips, beer-battered fish, gourmet battered sausages and 'Do bars' (deep-fried Snickers bars!). Chocolate lovers will want to make a bee-line for **The Ganachery** for some superb confectionery, including Disney character-themed chocolate lollipops! Fabulous Italian-style ice cream is on offer at **Vivoli Il Gelato** (direct from Florence) or head to **Joffrey's Coffee & Tea Co** for a really good cuppa. The quick-service **Pizza Ponte** next to Maria & Enzo's adds great pizza, Italian sandwiches and pastries, while the neighbouring **Enzo's Hideaway** combines a speakeasy vibe – and great beers, wines and cocktails – with Italian small-plate dining, from pasta dishes, meats and cheeses to fish dishes and even a full-scale sirloin steak.

━━━BRITTIP

For reservations at any Disney restaurant, call 407 939 3463 (407 WDW DINE), or book online at **disneyworld.co.uk**.

The Earl of Sandwich

© Disney

The Marketplace

While The Marketplace is largely a shopping area (p331), it also offers tempting dining.

Rainforest Café: With its safari-style 'adventures' under a spectacular volcano-topped exterior (that belches fire and smoke!), this is the place to entertain the family while they fill up on huge platefuls of chicken, pasta, steak, seafood and burgers, surrounded by audio-animatronic animals and periodic 'rainstorms', with an excellent kids menu. The Lava Lounge features small-plate appetisers from the main menu, great cocktails and other drink specials in a lakeside setting (11am–10.30pm Sun–Thurs, 11.30pm Fri and Sat; 407 827 8500, **rainforestcafe.com**).

T-Rex Café: Enter an audio-animatronic prehistoric world, with a vast series of themed areas like the Ice Cave and Jurassic Forest, which are home to all manner of roaring dinos, with meteor strikes and thunderstorms for good measure! The food is straightforward (albeit with wacky names like Chicken Fried Chicken and Boneyard Buffet) but portions are large and it is also somewhere you can pop into just for a drink (11am–11pm, midnight Fri and Sat, 407 828 8739. See more at **trexcafe.com**).

Other choices: Ghirardelli Ice Cream & Chocolate Shop is a great option for dessert or a milkshake. **The Earl of Sandwich** serves superb sandwiches and lighter meals, and **Wolfgang Puck Express** has quick-service Californian cuisine, while there are quick-bite counter service offerings at **The Daily Poutine** (Canadian-style French fries with different toppings), and **BB Wolf's Sausage Co** (tempting artisan sausages with a variety of toppings).

━━━BRITTIP

We think the best value at Disney Springs is the excellent Earl of Sandwich, where one of their hot sandwiches is often enough for two.

West Side

Back in the more hip night-time district of Disney Springs are another four options.

House of Blues®: Enjoy some rock'n' roll as you dine in 'backwoods Mississippi' style, plus a signature Gospel Brunch on Sun that offers fab food with a full gospel show (10.30am; $49/person). The main restaurant offers excellent Cajun and Creole specialities, notably seafood jambalaya and crawfish etouffee, with a weekend Bayou Brunch (10am–1pm; $33 adults, $15 3–9s) and live music (10.30am–11pm Sun–Thurs, 1am Fri–Sat; 407 934 2583, **houseofblues.com/orlando**).

Splitsville: OK, so it's a bowling alley, but the food and drink are good, so you might want to consider this as a dining option on its own. Fresh sushi is their speciality, but the menu also offers gourmet burgers, sandwiches, pizza, entrée salads and main-course dishes like a variety of bowls, fish 'n' chips, Ahi Tuna, grilled salmon, and Smothered Chicken. They feature sundaes for dessert and the cocktail menu is extremely tempting (10.30–midnight Mon–Fri, 10–midnight Sat–Sun; 407 938 7467, **splitsvillelanes.com**).

Jaleo: This authentic taste of Spain from influential Chef José Andrés features an extensive menu of tapas, cured meats, paella, cheese dishes, shellfish and favourites such as skirt steak and chorizo. Beer, wine and cocktails continue the Spanish influence and desserts are markedly Catalan, including a scrummy Olive Oil ice cream with grapefruit! (11.30am–1pm daily; 321 348 3211, **bit.ly/brit-jaleo**).

St Patrick's Day at Raglan Road

© Disney

City Works Eatery & Pour House: A new sports bar and brew pub, featuring three bars, large-screen TVs and a constantly rotating draft beer list, with an inviting open-air patio and menu.

Other choices: Grab a snack at **Wetzel's Pretzels**, pretzels, hot dogs and lemonade; **YeSake's** Asian bowls and wraps; try **Haagen-Dazs** ice-cream, or coffee at the inevitable **Starbucks**; or sample more fun offerings at the **Food Truck Park**, with a series of trucks offering fresh, local specialities like tacos and Mac & Cheese.

Town Center

This area of Disney Springs is focused firmly on shopping, but there are still several tempting food offerings, and the return of a stylish Californian.

Blaze Fast-Fire'd Pizza: For counter-service artisanal pizza, plus salads and desserts, this is another fresh choice, and at a lower price than many. Everything is flash-cooked in their 'blazing hot' ovens, so beware biting too soon! (10.30am–11pm Sun–Thurs, midnight Fri–Sat; 407 318 9128).

Chicken Guy!: Looking for fast-food chicken with a twist? Visit celebrity chef Guy Fieri's latest creation, with Chicken Tenders, signature Sandwiches and Salad Bowls all given a fresh burst of flavour, and enhanced by Guy's choice of 22 (!) sauces to go with them (407 560 8180, **https://chickenguy.com/**).

D-Luxe Burger: You'll need both hands for these huge gourmet burgers, each prepared to order from a relatively simple (but delicious) selection. Fries are separate and come with four dipping sauces, and there are magnificent milkshakes and soda floats for dessert (8.30am–11pm Sun–Thurs, 11.30am Fri–Sat; 407 934 3110).

BRITTIP

For a drink with a kick, try the alcoholic shakes at D-Luxe Burger, including a Godiva Chocolate and Strawberry, Smoked Bourbon and Vanilla Porter Gelato. A cocktail and dessert in one!

Frontera Cucina: Here's more celebrity chef style, with TV's Rick Bayless presenting his modern version of traditional Mexican cuisine in another imaginative setting. As well as tacos and his famous tortas (sandwiches), there are luscious chicken and shrimp dishes, plus a heavenly Carne Asada – red chilli-marinated Black Angus steak. For smaller tastes, there is a grab-and-go window (11am–11pm; 407 560 9197, **fronteracocina.com**).

Planet Hollywood Observatory: The largest and busiest of this worldwide chain underwent a major transformation in 2017 to a sleek, sophisticated observatory in keeping with the Disney Springs story. A new menu came with the new look, focused on familiar foods with an upscale twist, including long-time favourite World Famous Chicken Crunch, Florida Mahi Mahi, bbq ribs, and NY Strip Steak, along with salads, sandwiches and gigantic burgers designed by Guy Fieri. Save room for one of their outrageous desserts! Beer, wine and speciality cocktails are all available, and there are three bars, including outdoor Stargazers Bar, (11am–12am, bar until 1am; 407 827 7827).

Sprinkles: All the cupcakes (and cookies and ice-cream sundaes) you could imagine, in regular and mini sizes, served up with immense style in this modern bakery (but, again, with the price to match! 10am–midnight).

The Polite Pig: This delicious counter service addition, from the owners of Winter Park fave The Ravenous Pig, specialises in wood-fired fare straight from the smoker, such as pork ribs,

Our Disney Springs Top10

You'll definitely be in for a treat at this selection of fine-dining choices:

1. Wolfgang Puck's Bar & Grill
2. Morimoto Asia
3. Jaleo
4. Raglan Road
5. Chef Art Smith's Homecomin'
6. The Boathouse
7. STK Orlando
8. The Edison
9. The Polite Pig
10. Planet Hollywood Observatory

shoulder and brisket, plus hearty sandwiches (try the Fried Chicken or Southern Pig) and scrumptious sides. Healthy salads and decadent deserts round out your meal, with beer, wine and a bourbon bar. Kid-friendly meals available (11am–11pm Sun–Thurs, midnight Fri–Sat; 407 938 7444, **politepig.com**).

Wolfgang Puck Bar & Grill: Back in Disney Springs with a new 'farmhouse inspired' California concept, this tempting choice puts an emphasis on Puck's signature dishes highlighted by Mediterranean flavours. From homemade focaccia to artistic pizzas, burgers, salmon and minute steak, the menu is delightfully refined. Don't miss some delicious desserts, plus their Gelato Bar. Handcrafted cocktails, craft beer and wine round out some impressive offerings (11am–11pm daily; 407 815 2100, **bit.ly/brit-puck**).

Morimoto Asia

UNIVERSAL ORLANDO

Universal also has a terrific array of hotel dining, many of which are worth trying even if you're not staying there.

Aventura Hotel: This relative newcomer features superb rooftop dining 17 storeys high in **Bar 17 Bistro**, offering classic fare paired with custom-crafted cocktails, all with an amazing view – ideal at sunset.

Hard Rock Hotel: The Palm is a signature New York steak-and-lobster supper club restaurant, hence slightly more formal by Florida standards. The celebrity caricatures on the walls pay tribute to the original restaurant's roots in the Manhattan newspaper district, while the food features Nova Scotia lobster, prime cuts of meat and Italian specialities. **The Kitchen** epitomises more of the rock-star style with a livelier atmosphere and imaginative menu featuring flatbreads, burgers, pasta, excellent fish dishes and comfort foods with a modern twist, like bacon-wrapped meatloaf, and gourmet mac and cheese.

Portofino Bay Hotel: The jewel in the crown here is **Bice**, a superbly presented formal restaurant with genuine Italian flair and tastes. For a special night out it takes some beating, and their antipasto, organic pan-seared venison and Chilean

sea bass are divine. **Mama Della's Ristorante** is more Italian style, but with a more traditional touch in the fish and pasta dishes (still not cheap, though). **Trattoria del Porto** is more brasserie style, with sandwiches, salads and a great pasta selection.

Royal Pacific Resort: The **Islands Dining Room** is a good choice for dinner, with Wok specials and other Asian-influenced dishes, like Korean Bulgogi Ribeye.

Sapphire Falls Resort: Just one main restaurant at this hotel, but it's a highlight, with **Amatista Cookhouse** featuring a Caribbean-inspired menu, a show kitchen and views over the central lagoon, plus the lure of the adjacent **Strong Water Tavern** with its rum-based cocktails and excellent small-plate Caribbean cuisine.

> **BRITTIP**
>
> Toothsome Chocolate Emporium serves beer, wine, and creative hand-crafted cocktails in the surprisingly grown-up atmosphere of their upper-floor lounge. An excellent way to unwind after a day in the parks.

Universal CityWalk

Citywalk provides Universal's other great concentration of dining opportunities, with wonderful variety.

Antojitos Authentic Mexican Food: This cavernous party restaurant offers bags of Mexican style and atmosphere, from their own Mariachi band to fabulous cocktails. The menu is equally good, running the culinary gambit from street food (tacos, enchiladas, fajitas) to refined twists on traditional dishes such as Orange Salmon and Churrasco Steak, along with 203 authentic tequilas (4–11pm Sun–Thurs, 3pm–midnight Fri–Sat; 407 224 3663).

Bob Marley: Jamaican cuisine in a funky setting, featuring entrées such as curry, oxtail stew and Jamaican Jerk Chicken (4pm–2am daily; 21 and up after 9pm; 407 224 3663).

Hard Rock Hotel

© Universal Orlando Resort

Bubba Gump's Shrimp Co: This has the full *Forrest Gump* theme, and is heavy on seafood but also includes chicken, sandwiches, ribs, salads and more, with catchy names like Boat Trash With Maine Lobster (gluten-free menu available; 11am–midnight; 407 903 0044, **bubbagump.com**).

BRITTIP
Mention you are celebrating a birthday at Bubba Gump's and you'll find yourself the centre of attention!

The Cowfish: Fresh and innovative, this claims to be the world's first restaurant to feature great sushi AND burgers (hence their trademark 'Burgushi'), with a wide variety of both in an eclectic, lively setting. Spiked milkshakes, premium sakes, craft beers, wine and exotic martinis add to the temptations here, along with a great pure sushi bar (10.30am–midnight Sun–Thurs, 1am Fri–Sat; 407 224 3663, **thecowfish.com**).

BRITTIP
Looking for a pastry experience with a difference? Try the Voodoo Doughnut, with a dazzling array, including many vegan and gluten-free options. The Texas doughnut is big enough for 4!

Hard Rock Café: The largest one of this worldwide chain, with its rock 'n' roll memorabilia (including a pink 1959 Cadillac) and full concert venue, is hugely popular, so get in early for lunch or dinner, with their signature burgers, steaks, fajitas, ribs and sandwiches, or try breakfast until 11am (8.30am–midnight, Rock Bar until midnight; 407 351 7625, **hardrock.com/cafes/orlando**).

BRITTIP
After dining at the Hard Rock Café, ask for one of their VIBE Tours with a special 'rock guide'. You'll get an insight into their unique memorabilia, the history of the Café (which began in London), a look inside the John Lennon-themed VIP room and a tour of the music venue's back-stage areas. An amazing – and free – treat, available 1–9pm most days.

Our Universal Top 10

For a memorable meal, choose any of our Universal favourites:

1. Bice
2. The Toothsome Chocolate Emporium
3. Vivo Italian Kitchen
4. NBC Sports Grill & Brew
5. The Palm
6. Bigfire
7. Antojitos
8. The Cowfish
9. Amatista Cookhouse
10. The Kitchen

Hot Dog Hall of Fame: All kinds of hot-dogs, frankfurters and stuffed dumplings from around the US, with hundreds of condiment variations make this a fun offering (11am–11pm Sun–Thurs, 1am Fri–Sat, 407 224 3663).

Jimmy Buffet's Margaritaville: An island homage to Florida's laid-back musical hero, with 'Floribbean' cuisine (a mix of Key West and Caribbean), with the Volcano Bar, which 'erupts' margaritas periodically (10.30am–midnight Sun–Thurs, 1am Fri and Sat, live music until midnight; 407 224 2155, **margaritavilleorlando.com**)

NBC Sports Grill & Brew: Sophisticated and large scale, with more than 100 TV screens, an excellent menu and its own range

Pat O'Brien's

of beers. Two bars and most of the food comes from huge custom-made gas grills in the main show kitchen. The outdoor stadium-style screen sets the scene and there are a lot of smart touches inside, not least with the menu that includes Cedar-Planked Salmon, Bang-Bang Chicken and succulent pulled pork, as well as standards like burgers (10.30am–midnight Sun–Thurs, 1am Fri–Sat).

Pat O'Brien's: This is a reproduction of the famous New Orleans bar and restaurant with its Flaming Fountain courtyard, main bar and duelling piano bar. Excellent Cajun food and world-famous Hurricane cocktails. (4pm–2am; 5pm–2am for the piano bar, with a $7 cover charge after 9pm; 21 and over only; 407 224 2106, **bit.ly/brit-obrien**).

Red Oven Pizza Bakery: Authentic artisan pizza at this chic restaurant, with some imaginative flavours all baked in their signature 900º Red Oven (10.30am–midnight Sun–Thurs, 1.30am Fri–Sat).

Bigfire: New in 2019 was this open-fire cooking concept serving American 'campfire' favourites such as steak, bison burger and lake trout in a lakeside summer-house setting from a custom wood-fired grill. The smoky aromas are good enough on their own, but the 16oz Cowboy Ribeye is superb and the speciality S'mores, prepared tableside, are a must-try (10.30am–midnight Sun–Thurs, 1am Fri–Sat).

Toothsome Chocolate Emporium & Savory Feast Kitchen: This funky Steampunk-style venue is ice cream parlour, gift shop and spectacular restaurant in one. The vast menu features soups, salads, burgers, quiche, waffles and crêpes *before* you get to the entrees. Specialities include Beef Filet Mignon Oscar, Chicken Bourguignon and Brisket and Wild Mushroom Meatloaf. Start with their Warm Chocolate Almond Bread, but save room for dessert, massive milkshakes and killer cocktails (10.30am–midnight Sun–Thurs, 1am Fri-Sat; 407 224 3663).

Vivo Italian Kitchen: Fine Tuscan dining with fresh ingredients served from an open kitchen that offers a customisable menu for its pasta and other featured dishes. Everything is made from scratch and includes freshly pulled mozzarella, house-cured meats and slow-cooked ragu. Excellent wine and cocktail list (4–11pm Sun–Thurs, midnight Fri and Sat; 407 224 3663).

Other choices: Try **Menchie's** for fab frozen yoghurt, **Bread Box** for great sandwiches, **Cinnabon** for cinnamon rolls and other pastries, **Cold Stone Creamery** for indulgent ice-cream creations, **Voodoo Doughnut** for 'sinfully delicious' donuts, and the inevitable **Starbucks** coffee house. **The Top of the Walk** food court also features the **Burger King Whopper Bar, Panda Express, Moe's Southwest Grill** and **Fusion Bistro Sushi &**

Bigfire

Sake Bar. Look up more details at **bit.ly/brit-citywalk**.

> ───────────**BRITTIP** ◀┃▶
> Can't get in any of the CityWalk restaurants? Jump on a boat and you can usually dine without a wait at The Kitchen (Hard Rock), Trattoria del Porto or Mama Della's (Portofino Bay).

INTERNATIONAL DRIVE
Here's the best of the I-Drive dining. We divide it into I-Drive North, Sand Lake Road (the 'Restaurant Row' district west of the junction with I-Drive), I-Drive South, The Pointe and I-Drive 360.

I-Drive North
The section north of Sand Lake Road is largely fast-food and buffets, but with some exceptions.

> ───────────**BRITTIP** ◀┃▶
> A buffet breakfast at one of Golden Corral, Ponderosa or Shoney's should keep you going until tea-time and is a good way to start a theme-park day.

Fast food: Burger King, Dairy Queen, Del Taco, Dunkin' Donuts, Fuddruckers, KFC, McDonalds, Panda Express (Chinese), Pizza Hut, Pollo Tropical (Latin American), Popeye's (fried chicken), Starbucks (Orlando Premium Outlets), Sonic, Subway, Taco Bell, and Five Guys (Orlando Premium Outlets).

Breakfast style: Denny's, IHOP, Perkins, Ponderosa.

Buffet style: CiCi's Pizza, Sweet Tomatoes.

Bar-restaurant style: Applebee's, Buffalo Wild Wings, Chili's, TGI Friday's.

Steakhouse style: Black Angus.

Seafood specials: Fishbones, Red Lobster.

Individuals: Look for **Hash House A Go-Go**, for an inspired, fresh take on classic dishes like burgers, salads, meatloaf, chicken and waffles, and

huge portions (8am–10pm, 11pm Fri and Sat; **hashhouseagogo.com**); and the spectacular upmarket Brazilian steakhouse **Texas de Brazil**, which features a set-price all-you-can eat menu, with a huge salad bar and fresh-cut meats. Pricey but worth it (lunch noon–3.30pm, dinner 5–10pm Mon–Thurs, 5–10.30pm Fri, 4–10.30pm Sat, 4pm–9.30pm Sun; **texasdebrazil.com**).

Sand Lake Road
This is an area that has more notable one-off restaurants than almost anywhere in town.

Fast food: Chick-fil-A, Chipotle (more Mexican), Jimmy John's (sandwiches), McDonalds, Starbucks, Tijuana Flats (fresh Mexican style).

Breakfast style: First Watch, Panera Bread.

Steakhouse style: Ruth's Chris.

Seafood specials: Bonefish Grill, the beautifully upmarket **Ocean Prime** for a special dinner occasion, and the inventive **Moonfish**, with superb sushi, and more.

Amura: Some of Orlando's best sushi is in this eye-catching Japanese restaurant that also features Asian table barbecue, plus flavourful beef and chicken dishes and first-class seafood. 'Fresh, healthy and delicious,' they promise, and we agree (11.30am–3pm, 5–10.30pm Mon–Fri, 5–11pm Sat, noon–10pm Sun; 407 370 0007, **amura.com**).

Bar Louie: Another smart bar-restaurant chain with a wide-ranging menu (burgers and salads to flatbreads and fab chicken dishes), great wine and cocktails, live music on Thurs and a tempting happy hour 4–7pm Mon–Fri (11am–2am; 407 553 8502; **barlouie.com**).

Cedar's: Lebanese cuisine with some of the best chicken and lamb in town. A family-run Middle Eastern delight, it offers the full range of kebabs, falafel and hummus as well as specialities like fish tajen, grilled quail and baked kibbeh. A different alternative and an aromatic treat

Bartaco

(11.30am–10.30pm Mon–Thurs, 11.30–2am Fri, noon–2am Sat, noon–9.30pm Sun; 407 351 6000; **orlandocedars.com**).

Eddie V's: Supper-club style venue featuring succulent seafood with live jazz most evenings. A stylish option but with a more informal V Lounge that is first-come, first-served. The menu is a mouth-watering collection of fresh fish and shellfish, as well as fine steaks. Superb wine list and signature cocktails (4–11pm Sun–Thurs, midnight Fri and Sat; 407 355 3011, **eddiev.com**).

The Melting Pot: Every night is fondue night at this smart dining experience, which features seasoned vegetables, fresh-cut meats and artisan cheeses (5–10pm Mon–Thurs, 5–11pm Fri, noon–11pm Sat, noon–10pm Sun; 407 903 1100, **meltingpot.com/orlando-fl**).

Rocco's Tacos: Wildly eclectic but quality-conscious Mexican offering, great for a fun lunch or lively evening out. Start with their table-side guacamole, then consider one of the signature Molcajete dishes – a sizzling fajita choice served in a lava rock bowl with fresh flour tortillas. Their taco choice is equally tempting, as is the array of margaritas and speciality drinks from their Tequila Bar, where it is party night every night! (11.30–midnight Sun–Mon, 11.30am–2am Tues–Fri, 11am–2am Sat; 407 226 0550, **roccostacos.com**).

Roy's: Go upmarket Hawaii style where the Asia–Pacific fusion cuisine is as spectacular as the decor and service. Creator and celebrity chef Roy Yamaguchi offers Macadamia-Nut Crusted Mahi-Mahi, Blackened Island Ahi and Braised Short Ribs, as well as fabulous cocktails and an 'Aloha Hour' bar menu (3pm–7pm), with $7 appetisers, wines and cocktails (5pm–11pm Mon–Fri, 11am–11pm Sat, 11am–10pm Sun; 407 352 4844 **roysrestaurant.com**).

Saffron: Smart and stylish Indian choice, with fab-value lunch deals, weekend champagne brunch buffet and classic fine-dining dinner menu. All dishes can be prepared to individual levels of spiciness and the Chicken Xacutti and Jhinga Malabar (a shrimp dish in a coconut-based sauce) are worth coming in for alone (11.30am–2.30pm Mon–Fri, 5–10pm Sun–Thurs, 10.30 Fri–Sat; 407 674 8899 **saffronorlando.com**).

Seasons 52: A trendy national chain, with 10 outlets in Florida, we think this offers some of the best dining in the area, with a creative, seasonal, health-conscious menu. All appetisers, salads and soups range from 100–250 calories, and all mains are less than 475 calories. Seafood is the highlight but lamb, chicken, steaks and veggie options are equally tempting. The 'mini indulgence' desserts are ideal to finish a meal in style. The bar and outdoor terrace are equally stylish, ideal for a romantic occasion, and fab value for happy hour 3–7pm Mon–Fri (11.30am–10pm Sun–Thurs, 11pm Fri–Sat; 407 354 5212, **seasons52.com**).

The Whiskey: Great burgers, killer cocktails and almost 150 whiskies, ryes and bourbons are on offer at this chic bistro-pub, offering a friendly welcome, keen service, and excellent small-plate choices alongside their succulent burgers, chops, salmon and salads (11am–2am; 407 930 6517, **downatthewhiskey.com**).

Vine's Grille & Wine Bar: This upmarket restaurant and wine shop features live jazz to go with a tempting menu that runs from grilled octopus and oysters to excellent salads, fine steaks (including a 24oz Tomahawk bone-in rib steak) and fresh seafood. Another special occasion night out (4pm–11pm Mon–Thurs, midnight Fri–Sat, 10pm Sun; 407 351 1227, **vinesgrill.com**).

Sand Lake Road – Dr Phillips Plaza

Staying on Sand Lake Rd but moving into the Dr Phillips Plaza, there are:

Fast food: Chipotle, Pizza Hut, Starbucks, Subway, Toojay's Deli (excellent sandwich choice).

Breakfast style: Keke's.

Bar-restaurant style: World of Beer.

Steakhouse style: Morton's.

bartaco: A lively tapas-style restaurant in an urban-casual setting, their mini tacos, rice bowls, ceviche and fab chicken soup are all worth trying, while kids meals, desserts, beer, wine and signature cocktails are all reasonably priced. Be sure to start with the guacamole! (11am–11pm Sun–Wed, midnight Thurs–Sat; 407 801 8226; **bartaco.com**)

Bosphorous: Turkish flavours with a delicious range of authentic breads, hot and cold appetisers, salads, soups, pides (Turkish pizzas), kebabs and specialities like moussaka and baklava. Dine royally without breaking the bank. Try babaganoush (char-grilled aubergine with fresh herbs and spices), tabbuli, lamb kofte or chicken adana (11am–10pm Sun–Thurs, 11pm Fri and Sat; 407 352 6766, **bosphorousrestaurant.com**).

Christinis: an upmarket, formal Italian restaurant that has been around for 50 years and remains stylish and traditional, with a classic menu. Reservations usually required (6–11pm; 407 545 6867; **christinis.com**).

The H Cuisine: This new Turkish/Mediterranean offering specialises in charcoal oven dishes for a rich array of smoky delights, from meze dishes to steaks, plus a fab veggie stew (noon–3pm, 5–11pm Mon–Fri, 9am–3pm, 5pm–11pm Sat and Sun; 407 930 3020, **thehcuisine.com**).

Sand Lake Road – Dellagio complex

Moving on to the final part of Sand Lake Road is the **Dellagio** complex, with seven more worthy options.

Big Fin Seafood: One of Orlando's most imaginative seafood options, Big Fin is refined but relaxed, a big-scale experience that offers special-occasion atmosphere. The main dining room features a grand salon style but two smaller rooms are more intimate, while the Trophy Bar is ideal for a pre-dinner drink. The menu features sushi, sashimi, oysters and ceviche; classic salads and chowders; steak, chops and chicken; crab and lobster dishes; fresh fish and tempting pastas. Happy Hour is 5–7pm Mon–Sat, 5–9pm Sun, at the Bar with $7 drink specials and a reduced-price menu (5–10pm daily; 407 392 3904, **bigfinseafood.com**).

BRITBONUS

Show your copy of the *Brit Guide* on arrival at Big Fin Seafood Kitchen to receive 10% off all entrees. Not valid with any other offers/specials.

Dragonfly: Get ready for a Japanese taste sensation from the super-hot *Robata* grill that produces delicious fish, beef, chicken, shrimp and pork. Dragonfly also specialises in fresh sushi and sashimi, as well as its own cocktails and sake for an authentic dining experience (5–10pm Mon–Thurs, 11pm Fri–Sat, 11am–2pm and 5–10pm Sun; 407 370 3359, **dragonflyrestaurants.com**).

Fleming's: Award-winning steakhouse serving succulent cuts of the best meats, fish and chicken, notably a divine Wagyu New York Strip Steak. All can be enhanced with rubs, toppings and sauces for steak aficionados, but this is a premium experience, with all side dishes extra (407 352 5706; 5–10pm Sun–Thurs, 11pm Fri–Sat; **flemingssteakhouse.com**).

Miller's Field House: Great sports-bar territory, with more than 70 TVs showing all the action and an 'Owner's Box' for high rollers. The menu is sophisticated, with steaks and tacos as well as the usual burgers and wings, plus daily drink specials (3pm-2am Mon–Thurs, 11am–2am Fri–Sat; 407 248 3474, **fieldhouseorlando.com**).

The Pharmacy: Try the Speakeasy style here, behind fake elevator doors but ensuring you know the password (issued online) in advance! Great cocktails, a varied menu and lively atmosphere make for a fun night out (5–10pm Tues–Thurs, midnight Fri–Sat; 407 985 2972; **thepharmacyorlando.com**).

Slate: A smart upmarket restaurant at the far end of the Dellagio complex (just past Trader Joe's), featuring wood-grilled cuisine, with indoor and open-air dining. Imaginative menu offers pizza, pasta, salads, seafood and steaks with a lighter touch, plus a fab weekend brunch (11am-2pm and 5–10pm Mon–Thurs, 11am–2.30pm and 5–11pm Fri–Sat, 10.30am–2.30pm and 5pm-9pm Sun; 407 500 7528, **slateorlando.com**).

Urbain 40: Gorgeous 1940s style, from the décor to the music (but with a contemporary menu) is the key here, with a gracious, more formal style that includes live jazz most evenings. Billed as 'An American brasserie and lounge', its sumptuous main dining room is the place to be for a special night out, while the lounge is more casual. The food is exquisite, from salads and pastas to seafood and steaks, as are the cocktails and even a craft beer selection (4pm–11.30pm Sun–Wed, 4pm-midnight Thurs–Sat; 407 500 7528, **urbain40.com**).

Urbain 40

BRITTIP

For a taste of Urbain 40 without the full price, try their Happy Hour in the Lounge 4–7pm daily and soak up the wonderful ambience.

International Drive South

Heading back to I-Drive south of Sand Lake Road, you'll find a dazzling range of choice.

Fast food: Checkers, Domino's Pizza, Dunkin' Donuts, Firehouse Subs, McDonalds, Starbucks, Subway.

Breakfast style: Friendly's, Denny's, Panera Bread.

Buffet style: CiCi's Pizza, Golden Corral, Ponderosa.

Bar-restaurant style: BJ's Brewhouse, Bahama Breeze, Bar Louie, Brick House Tavern & Tap (good sports style), Buffalo Wild Wings, Chuys, Hooters, Hurricane Grill & Wings, Red Robin, Miller's Ale House, Senor Frogs, TGI Friday's, Twin Peaks, Uno Pizzeria & Grill.

Steakhouse style: Charley's, Longhorn, Saltgrass Steak House, Tony Roma's, Vito's Chophouse.

Italian flavours: Olive Garden.

Seafood specials: Boston Lobster Feast, Joe's Crab Shack, Red Lobster.

Café Tu Tu Tango: A wonderful tapas-style menu is boosted by live music and local artists at work in this Bohemian-style cafe. Vegetarians are well catered for, and you can try succulent pizzas, seafood, salads and soups, plus imaginative Mexican dishes and a thoughtful kids' menu (11am–midnight, Mon–Thurs, 1am Fri–Sat, 10am–11pm Sun; 407 248 2222, **cafetututango.com**).

Cooper's Hawk: Wine lovers are spoiled for choice here, with a massive range in their Tasting Room to complement an excellent wide-ranging menu that runs the gamut from burgers and flatbreads to seafood and prime steaks (11am–9.30pm Mon–Thurs, 10.30pm Fri–Sat, 11am–9pm Sun; 407 954 3400, **coopershawkwinery.com**).

Del Frisco's Double Eagle: I-Drive's new standard for fine steaks and stylish dining, with an amazing array of fresh-cut meats, plus seafood, chicken and great cocktails, but with the price to match. There are two gorgeous bars and a picturesque patio (5–10pm Mon–Thurs, 5–11pm Fri, 4–11pm Sat, 4–10pm Sun; 407 351 5074, **delfriscos.com**).

Everglades: Tucked away inside the Rosen Centre Hotel is this beautiful Florida speciality restaurant, specialising in great steaks and fine seafood. Don't miss the Broiled Florida Grouper and melt-in-the-mouth Filet Key Largo (5.30–10pm; 407 996 2385; **evergladesrestaurant.com**).

> **BRITTIP**
>
> For a great lunch or dinner alternative, visit Fogo de Chao and just sample their 30-item Market Table at $15 (lunch) or $30.95 (dinner). It is WAY more than just salad, with the likes of aged Parmesan, Italian salami and smoked salmon, and is wonderfully fresh and appetising.

Fogo De Chao: This Brazilian churrascaria is superbly authentic and flavourful, with an enchanting mix of elaborate serving style and succulent cuts of meat, all cooked on the traditional 'churrasco' skewer grill. It is a set-fee lunch or dinner, including a buffet-style Market Table ($36.95–54.95) for the full churrascaria experience, (noon–2.30pm and 5–10pm Mon–Thurs, noon–3pm, 5.30–10.30pm Fri, 11.30am–10.30am Sat, noon–9pm Sun; 407 370 0711, **fogodechao.com**).

Spencer's: The Hilton by the Convention Center is home to this beautiful restaurant that features magnificent steak, chops and seafood. Steaks are all pasture-raised without hormones or antibiotics, aged for 21 days and cooked in a custom-made grill (5.30–10pm Tues–Sat; 407 313 8625; **thehiltonorlando.com**).

ICON Park

This extensive entertainment complex is also a restaurant destination in its own right.

Fast food: Ben & Jerry's (ice cream), iCafe de Paris, Pretzelmaker.

Bar-restaurant style: Buffalo Wild Wings, Shake Shack.

Steakhouse style: Outback Steakhouse.

Italian flavours: Carrabba's.

iLounge Istanbul: Enjoy a glass of wine, a hookah and a snack (cheese platter, bruschetta, antipasta) at this trendy indoor/outdoor lounge (4pm-2am daily; 407 630 6001, **iloungeistanbul.com**).

> **BRITTIP**
>
> The legal age to purchase or smoke tobacco, or use tobacco-related devices in Florida is 18, and may soon rise to 21.

Sugar Factory: An 'American brasserie' catering to those of a sweet-toothed persuasion, it still serves crêpes, burgers, salads, flatbreads and sandwiches, but really dazzles with its ice-cream-based desserts, milkshakes and candy-inspired cocktails. Don't miss the coffee and

The Sugar Factory

milkshake window (11am–11pm Sun–Thurs, midnight Fri–Sat; 407 270 7082; **sugarfactory.com/orlando**).

Tapa Toro: Classic and contemporary Spanish specialities with a focus on tapas and paella, plus live music and tableside flamenco dancers in this elegant and multi-faceted restaurant (11am–11pm Sun–Thurs, midnight Fri–Sat; 407 490 1378; **tapatoro.restaurant**).

Tin Roof: Country music fans will love the live entertainment here, with a smattering of rock, soul, Americana and pop. The menu features Tex-Mex favourites, and specialities include Candy Pig Mac and Cheese, Voodoo Shrimp, and BBQ Pulled Pork. Full bar, funky style, and a somewhat raucous atmosphere after 10pm (11am–2am; 407 270 7926; **tinrooforlando.com**).

Yard House: With a huge selection of beers on tap and a wonderfully inventive menu, this isn't your typical bar. Its air of comfortable

refinement is also family-friendly, and the menu is several steps above the norm, featuring twists on bar favourites, plus other gourmet offerings. There is a good selection of healthy/vegetarian dishes, along with steaks, pizza, seafood, pasta and a kids menu (11–12.30am Sun–Thurs, 1.20am Fri–Sat; 407 351 8220; **yardhouse.com**).

Uncle Julio's: Get genuine made-from-scratch, Mesquite-grilled Mexican favourites with modern Tex-Mex twists at this lively bar/restaurant. Look out for their Swirl Margarita – layered with home-made sangria – among a great array of beers and cocktails, plus signature smoke-grilled fajitas, shrimp brochettes and salsas (11.30am–11.30pm Mon–Thurs, 1am Fri and Sat, 10am–12.30am Sun; **bit.ly/brit-julios**).

Ox Grill, **Mikado** and the southern flavours of **Ole Red** are slated to open in 2020.

Cuba Libre

Pointe Orlando

Head to this other I-Drive entertainment complex, and you'll find more great dining options.

Fast food: Ben & Jerry's.

Bar-restaurant style: Johnny Rockets (classic diner), Marlow's Tavern (above-average menu and live music).

Steakhouse style: Capital Grille.

Italian flavours: Maggiano's Little Italy.

BB King's Blues Club: Live jazz and blues (see p295) with a Southern comfort-food menu, such as Fried Shrimp Po Boy and Southern Fried Catfish, and a full bar (4pm–midnight Sun–Thurs, 1am Fri and Sat; 407 370 4550, **bbkings.com/orlando**).

Blue Martini: Upmarket bar with 42 signature martinis, plus beer, wine and cocktails. Light fare, flatbreads and signature dishes such as Lollipop Lambchops and Maine Lobster Salad. Live music nightly, plus a good happy hour 4–8pm each day (4pm–2am Mon–Fri, 3pm–2am Sat–Sun; 407 447 2583, **bluemartinilounge.com**).

Cuba Libre: This bar/restaurant adds a touch of 1940s Havana, featuring Latin-inspired cuisine with an exciting twist, from tasty tapas and ceviche to coconut crab fritters – and wicked cocktails! (5pm–10pm daily, bar and nightlife 11pm–2am Fri–Sat; 407 226 1600, **cubalibrerestaurant.com**).

Hopdoddy Burger Bar: A real twist on counter-service burger bars, with a classic menu given a modern re-styling for thick, juicy burgers, hand-cut fries, delicious milkshakes and a full bar (11am–10pm; 321 251 4500, **bit.ly/brit-hop**).

Itta Bena: A New Orleans-inspired piano bar, with contemporary Southern cuisine to go with the live music. Try their signature 16oz bone-in Ribeye Steak or the Blackened Gulf Red Snapper, or just chill out with a cocktail in the bar (5–10pm Sun–Thurs, 11pm Fri and Sat; 407 757 2910; **ittabenadining.com/orlando**).

Lafayette's: Get a great big helping of Cajun and Creole cuisine, along with cool Bluegrass, jazz, blues-rock and other live music in this rustic, Southern-inspired setting. The main restaurant is matched by a lively bar, with indoor and outdoor seating. Their Sunday Brunch is worth coming in for on its own (11am–midnight Sun–Thurs, 11am–2am Fri–Sat, 11am–3pm Sun brunch; 407 930 1655, **lafayettes.com/orlando**).

Lotus Asia House: New in 2019 was this upscale – and extensive – choice for memorable Chinese, Thai, Japanese and Vietnamese cuisines, boasting an indoor/outdoor sushi bar and superb sake-based cocktails (5-10.30pm Sun–Thurs, midnight Fri–Sat; 407 250 8888, **lotusasiahouse.com**).

The Oceanaire: Step back in time at this relaxed, stylish seafood room. The decor, reminiscent of a classic 1930s ocean liner, and mood music lead you into a fish and shellfish wonderland, complete with a superb oyster bar, as well as superb steaks and chicken. The raw bar alone is dazzling and the fish dishes are some of the best in town. Service is equally top-notch (5–10pm Sun–Thurs, 11pm Fri–Sat; 407 363 4801, **theoceanaire.com**).

The Pub: This huge pub-style offering features a wide variety of cosy seating nooks, a fantastic mix of UK and US beers (including the Orlando Brewing Co), a sharp menu and multiple TV screens for sports fans. The unique 'Pour Your Own Beer Walls' are a fun feature, as is Happy Hour Mon–Fri 3–7pm (11am–2am; 407 352 2305, **experiencethepub.com/orlando**).

Rodizio Grill: Replacing the former Copper Canyon Grill here in 2020 will be in this Brazilian steakhouse featuring gaucho servers and plenty of fresh-grilled meats served directly from skewers (**rodiziogrill.com**).

Taverna Opa: Lively Greek option, with an appetising menu, from hot and cold meze to moussaka, souvlaki, kebabs and signature lamb chops, but much more besides, like fine steaks, fresh seafood and a great ouzo bar. Watch for table dancing

Taverna Opa

and napkin throwing! (noon–11pm Sun–Thurs, 2am Fri–Sat; 407 351 8660, **opaorlando.com**).

> **BRITTIP**
> There is free valet parking at some Pointe Orlando restaurants if you're dining there, so ask about validation. Just pull in at the drop-off point next to Capital Grille (but don't forget to tip the valet when you pick up your car).

LAKE BUENA VISTA

At the junction of I-4 and Highway 535 (Apopka-Vineland Rd) is this busy area of hotels, shops and restaurants – lots of restaurants. It falls into two sections, east of I-4 and west of the motorway.

> **BRITTIP**
> Join the free Landry's Select Club and earn rewards points toward a $25 gift voucher each time you dine at a Landry's location, including Yak and Yeti restaurant in Disney's Animal Kingdom.

Lake Buena Vista West

Fast food: Burger King, Domino's Pizza, Dunkin' Donuts, Firehouse Subs, Flippers Pizzeria, Fuddruckers, McDonalds, Pizza Hut, Steak 'n Shake, Taco Bell.

Breakfast style: Denny's, IHOP, Perkins, Waffle House.

Buffet style: CiCi's Pizza, Shoney's, Sweet Tomatoes.

Bar-restaurant style: Buffalo Wild Wings, Chevys, Chili's, Giordano's

Frankie Farrell's

Join The (Curry) Club!

Viceroy Chipshop Curry Club is a new venture taking typical flavours into existing restaurants for a Curry Night several times a month. It costs $22/person and provides a set meal with a choice of entrée, with rice, naan, onion bhaji, samosa and vegetables. It is the brainchild of Paul and Jennie, a British couple who have run several successful dining ventures in Orlando. Book via **facebook.com/viceroycurry/** and order in advance. One of their regular locations is El Patron in Lake Buena Vista, and we are keen customers!

(pizza), Hooters, Manny's Chophouse, Miller's Ale House, Seadog Brew Pub, TGI Friday's, UNO Pizzeria & Grill.

Steakhouse style: Black Angus Steakhouse, Black Fire Brazilian Steakhouse, The Knife (South American churrascaria).

Italian flavours: Macaroni Grill, Olive Garden.

Seafood specials: Red Lobster.

El Patron: Reliable and great value-for-money Mexican choice, with good traditional dishes given a contemporary twist, like the pan-seared snapper and slow-braised pork, plus great artisan tacos (11am–10pm Mon–Fri, 11.30–10pm Sat–Sun; **elpatronorlando.com**).

Hemingway's: Worth finding inside the Hyatt Grand Cypress Resort is this gorgeous formal dining room that features superb seafood, steaks and more in a Key West ambience (6–10pm, 407 239 1234).

Sofrito Latin Café: Simon's favourite place for a quick lunch or dinner, serving traditional authentic South and Central American dishes. You order at the counter then wait at your table for the fresh-cooked meal, with tapas-style plates and main courses. No recommendations – just try anything! They also have local craft beers and wine, and a breakfast menu (7am–9pm Sun–Thurs, 10pm Fri–Sat; 407 778 4205, **sofritocafe.com**).

Lake Buena Vista East

Fast food: Chick-fil-A, Dunkin' Donuts, Starbucks, Subway, Wendy's.

Breakfast style: Panera Bread.

Buffet style: CiCi's Pizza, Golden Corral.

Bar-restaurant style: Applebee's, Bahama Breeze, BJ's Brewhouse, Hurricane Grill & Wings.

Steakhouse style: Longhorn Steakhouse, Outback Steakhouse (opposite Orlando Premium Outlets), Saltgrass Steak House.

Italian flavours: Carrabba's.

Frankie Farrell's: Inside the Lake Buena Vista Resort Village & Spa is this smart pub-style restaurant and bar with an imaginative menu, good range of beers and live entertainment (8.30am–11pm Mon–Fri, 8am–11pm Sat–Sun; 407 238 1003; **frankiefarrells.com**).

Landry's Seafood: This big-name company boasts an elegant touch, featuring fresh daily seafood platters and excellent salad bowls, with top-notch service and wine list. For a special occasion, the Stuffed Flounder and Seafood Feast for two is superb (3–10pm Mon–Thurs, 11pm Fri, 11.30am–11pm Sat, 10pm Sun; 407 827 6465, **landrysseafood.com**).

KISSIMMEE

Heading out into Highway 192, you are largely in fast-food territory, but there are some notable individuals. We divide it East and West of I-4.

Highway 192 East

Fast food: Arby's, Burger King, Checkers, Chick-Fil-A, Chipotle, Domino's Pizza, Dunkin' Donuts, Five Guys, Jimmy John's, KFC, McDonalds, Panda Express, Pizza Hut, Starbucks, Steak n Shake, Subway, Taco Bell, Wendy's.

Breakfast style: Cracker Barrel, Denny's, IHOP, Panera Bread, Perkins, Waffle House.

Buffet style: CiCi's Pizza, Golden Corral, Ponderosa.

Bar-restaurant style: Applebee's, Chili's, TGI Friday's, Uno Pizzeria & Grill.

Steakhouse style: Black Angus, Charley's Steakhouse, Longhorn Steakhouse, Logan's Roadhouse, Sonny's BBQ.

Italian flavours: Carrabba's, Macaroni Grill, Olive Garden.

Seafood specials: Joe's Crab Shack, Red Lobster.

Old Hickory Steakhouse: In the Gaylord Palms Resort is this five-star steakhouse set amid elaborate Everglades theming. Their steak needs no gimmicks as the house speciality of certified prime-aged beef is cooked to perfection. There are a few alternatives, such as fish, chicken and veggie, but all sides are extra and this is a pricey experience, albeit memorable (5.30–10pm; 407 586 1600).

Pacino's: A Highway 192 feature in Kissimmee for more than 25 years, this 'taste of Sicily' features a signature open-flame oven that delivers great pizza, seafood and steaks, as well as an authentic range of pasta dishes. Good wine cellar (4–11pm; 407 396 8022, **pacinos.com**).

Smokey Bones: With a rustic, log-cabin touch and succulent, deep-smoked BBQ, this eye-catching venue serves up fire-grilled steaks, salmon, chicken, burgers and salads. Try the BBQ platters and rib combos. Sports fans can also enjoy a huge array of TVs (11am–1am Mon–Sat, midnight Sun; 407 397 7102; **smokeybones.com**).

Pacino's

Highway 192 West

Fast food: Burger King, Burger Craft, Chick-Fil-A, Culver's (burgers), Domino's Pizza, Dunkin' Donuts, McDonalds, Panda Express, Pizza Hut, Pollo Tropical, Shula Burger, Starbucks, Subway, Taco Bell, Wendy's.

Breakfast style: Bob Evans, Cracker Barrel, Denny's, IHOP, Panera Bread, Perkins.

Buffet style: CiCi's Pizza, Golden Corral, Ponderosa, Sizzler, Sweet Tomatoes.

Bar-restaurant style: Applebee's, Bahama Breeze, Buffalo Wild Wings, Chuys, Giordano's, Flippers Pizza, Hooters, Miller's Ale House, On The Border (Mexican Grill and Cantina), Red Robin, TGI Friday's.

Steakhouse style: Black Angus, Logan's Roadhouse, Longhorn, Outback, Texas Roadhouse.

Italian: Carrabba's, Olive Garden.

Seafood specials: Bonefish Grill, Joe's Crab Shack, Red Lobster.

Manny's Chophouse: The Kissimmee version of this popular steak oriented chain with a 2-for-1 Happy Hour daily from 4–7pm. It is often packed by 6pm as locals and tourists alike flock here for the lively style and well-priced food (all steaks under $30, and many just $15–20), which also includes fab burgers, ribs, fajitas, seafood and chicken. They don't take reservations but do have Call-Ahead seating, which puts you on the waiting list in advance (4–10 pm Mon–Thurs, 10.30pm Fri–Sat, noon–10pm Sun; 407 396 8880; **mannyschophouse.com**).

Sunset Walk at Margaritaville: This self-contained area of shops, restaurants and entertainment next to the huge Margaritaville Resort now features 13 contrasting and lively places to eat, from the counter-service **Burger Fi**, **Coldstone Creamery** and **Bahama**

Buck's (shaved ice) to New York deli-style **Café D'Avignon, Capone's Coal-Fired Pizza**, Mexican vibe of **El Jefe Tequila Cocina & Cantina** and **Bento Asian Kitchen + Sushi**. Three others worthy of note are the "neighbourhood burger and beer joint" of **Ford's Garage**, the all-British style of **Yeoman's Cask & Lion** pub (when you need Shepherd's Pie and bangers and fish in an eclectic pop-art setting) and the sheer rockin' good fun of **Rock And Brews**, with an immense craft beer list accompanied by a comfort food menu featuring signature wings, salads, seafood and pasta. New in 2020 will be restaurant/nightclub **Estefan Kitchen**, a fresh take on Latin and Cuban flavours with the music – and dancing – to go with it (**sunsetwalk.com**).

Wildside Bar & Grill: Great barbecue here, with the first Kissimmee outlet of the Thornton Park-based restaurant. It serves up signature steaks and seafood, as well as burgers and sandwiches, but the real speciality is their delicious home-smoked pulled chicken and pork, smoked sausage, Angus brisket, smoked turkey, St Louis ribs and baby back ribs (4–11pm; 407 396 1166, **wildsiderestaurant.com**).

Mall at Millenia

In and around the upmarket Mall at Millenia you will find another tempting choice of restaurants.

Fast food: Burger 21, Jimmy John's, Krispy Kreme Doughnuts, McDonalds, Moe's Southwest Grill, Panda Express, Pollo Tropical, Subway, Wendy's, Zaxby's Chicken.

Breakfast style: Keke's.

Bar-restaurant style: BJ's Brewhouse, Cheesecake Factory, Johnny Rockets, TGI Friday's.

Steakhouse style: Capital Grille.

Italian flavours: Olive Garden.

The Cheesecake Factory

BRITTIP

The huge Cheesecake Factory at Mall of Millenia is a firm Brit favourite for its extensive (and surprisingly sophisticated) menu, huge portions – and amazing array of cheesecake choices. See more at **cheesecakefactory.com**.

Brio Tuscan Grille: Inside the Mall (and at Winter Park Village), this stylish Italian offering makes for a superb casual lunch or romantic dinner, with superb steaks, creative pastas and regional specialities like chicken limone and grilled pork chops, plus daily fish specials. The Tuscan country-style ambience and fresh kids' menu all add up to memorable dining. (11am–10pm Mon–Thurs, 11pm Fri and Sat, 10am–10pm Sun; 407 351 8909, **brioitalian.com**).

Duffy's Sports Grill: Sports bar and restaurant that features an extensive menu, great beers and cocktails, and a vast array of TVs for live sporting action (11am–11pm, midnight Fri-Sat; 407 930 2960; **duffysmvp.com**).

Earls Kitchen & Bar: Also in Mall at Millenia, this is an upscale choice for just a burger or one of their Black Angus beef steaks, plus fresh choices like sushi, rice and noodle bowls, ribs, chicken, fish, tacos and more (11.30am–11pm Mon–Thurs, 12.30am Fri, 11am–12.30pm Sat, 10am–11pm Sun; 407 345 8260, **bit.ly/brit-earls**).

PF Chang's China Bistro: Inside the Mall, this mixes classic Chinese fare with American bistro style that makes fans of virtually all who sample it. Try the Chang's Spicy Chicken, Oolong Chilean Sea Bass and fiery Beef à la Sichuan. There is also a good veggie selection (11am–11pm, midnight Fri–Sat, 10pm Sun; 407 345 2888, **pfchangs.com**).

EAT LIKE A LOCAL
A short drive to the more residential areas means you can sample off-the-beaten-track choices.

4 Rivers SmokeHouse: Annually rated the best barbecue in Central Florida, this Winter Park diner draws long queues at peak times, but it's worth the wait for their succulent pulled pork, brisket, ribs and chicken (11am–8pm Mon–Thurs, 9pm Fri–Sat; 1844 474 8377, **4rsmokehouse.com**).

Dixie Cream Café: When we want a 'home-cooked' breakfast or lunch, we head to this charming café/bakery/coffee shop in the heart of the ritzy suburb of Windermere and enjoy a

Orlando Top 10
Here's our 'Best Of' list for the Orlando area in general.

1. Urbain 40 (p320)
2. A Land Remembered (p329)
3. Capa (Four Seasons) (p328)
4. Hamilton's Kitchen (below)
5. The Ravenous Pig (p329)
6. Highball & Harvest (p329)
7. Cala Bella (p328)
8. The Boheme (p328)
9. Kres Chophouse (below)
10. Yellow Dog Eats (p328)

variety of Southern comfort food, burgers, sandwiches and salads (8am–2.30pm Tues–Sun; 407 217 5047, **dixiecreamcafe.com**).

Hamilton's Kitchen: For a stylish lunch or when we're feeling fancy, head to Winter Park for the chic, artsy feel of the Alfond Inn, where the signature restaurant is a treat and the food wonderfully fresh and inventive (7am–2pm and 6pm–9pm Sun–Wed, 10pm Thurs–Sat; 407 998 8089, **bit.ly/brit-alfond**).

BRITTIP
For something special, try Hamilton's Kitchen's Sunday Brunch (11am–2pm), then shop along Park Avenue to stroll it off.

Kres Chophouse: For an elegant night-on-the-town, this is a great choice in downtown Orlando, in the busy Church Street area. Ideal for pre-dinner cocktails, a late-night

Brio Tuscan Grille

nightcap or a full, elegant dinner, Kres features signature steaks, chops and seafood, plus a supper-club style that is genuinely classy (11.30am–midnight Mon–Fri, 5pm–midnight Sat, 5pm–11pm Sun; 407 447 7950, **kresrestaurant.com**).

The Glass Knife: Ready for dessert? This is the place to go in Winter Park, with a mouthwatering array of cakes, pastries, doughnuts and sandwiches, for breakfast, brunch or afternoon tea/coffee, as well as dinner, with some tempting soups, salads and flatbreads (8am–10pm Sun–Thurs, 11pm Fri–Sat; 407 500 2253, **theglassknife.com**).

The Taproom at Dubsdread: Yes, Dubsdread is a golf course (just west of downtown), but it boasts a great clubhouse restaurant with some of the best burgers in town. There are also great steaks, seafood and truly decadent desserts (11am–10pm Mon–Thurs, 11pm Fri–Sat, 9pm Sun; 407 650 0100, **taproomatdubsdread.com**).

Urban Flats: After a day in delightful Winter Garden), we often pop in to this great bar-restaurant for flatbreads and cocktails. Very much a locals' hangout, it is ideal for dinner before going to the Garden Theater (11am–10pm Sun–Thurs, 11pm Fri–Sat; 407 614 2765, **urbanflats-wintergarden.com**).

Yellow Dog Eats: Just past Windermere in rural Gotha is this eclectic deli-restaurant-country store with a hugely appealing mix of salads, sandwiches, tacos, nachos and veggie offerings, plus their succulent barbecue specialities. There is also a good beer and wine selection, plus Happy Hour 2–6pm and live music 6pm–10pm Thurs–Sat (11am–9pm Sun–Wed, 10pm Thurs–Sat; 407 296 0609, **yellowdogeats.com**).

Zen: For great Asian dining, the Omni Orlando Resort at ChampionsGate features this stylish restaurant, which also boasts a sake and sushi bar. An oasis of relaxed charm, highlights include the Szechwan-style Beef Tenderloin and Sautéed Shrimp in Black Pepper Sauce and Spinach. Or try the Zen Experience multi-course feast (6–10pm; 407 390 6664, **omnihotels.com**).

DELUXE DINING

This selection is when you really have something to celebrate.

Boca: This 'neighbourhood bar-kitchen-market' in Winter Park features fresh seasonal ingredients from local growers, with a cosy, European ambience that encourages visitors to slow down and join in the chat. Salads, flatbreads, sandwiches, seafood and daily specials are their stock in trade, but there is plenty of imagination (and organic produce) incorporated into dishes like smoked chimichurri chicken, bronzed sea scallops and their brie and apple flatbread (11am–11pm; 407 636 7022, **bocawinterpark.net**).

The Boheme: Elegantly tucked away inside the Grand Bohemian hotel in downtown Orlando is this original and artfully crafted restaurant that is ideal for a special couples' occasion. Boasting fabulous seafood, decadent steaks and exquisite cocktails, all with a New American cuisine twist, it also features a superb Sunday jazz brunch and is hugely popular with the locals (407 581 4700, **bit.ly/brit-boheme**).

Cala Bella: A proven winner at the stylish Rosen Shingle Creek Resort, this superb Italian-influenced restaurant is heavy on pasta and seafood, but also offers signature dishes like its sensational Cala Bella Lamb, Veal Marsala and Seafood Pescatore. Save room for dessert – the pastry chefs are among the best in America (5.30–10pm; 407 996 3663, **calabellarestaurant.com**).

Capa: The signature 17th floor rooftop restaurant at the Four Seasons hotel in Walt Disney World

The Bohème

is superb for style, elegance and the nightly views of the Magic Kingdom fireworks. Even better is its contemporary Spanish steakhouse cuisine, with dishes from delightful small plates, freshly shucked oysters and fine Florida seafood to succulent steaks from the wood-burning grill in the show kitchen (6–10pm; 407 313 7777 **bit.ly/brit-capa**).

Highball and Harvest: This exquisite choice in the Ritz-Carlton resort at Grande Lakes features Southern cuisine with an upmarket twist. Lightened-up favourites include Shrimp and Grits and Diver Scallops, plus an artisanal cheese plate and the signature Triple Dipped Fried Chicken. Belly up to the bar for a handcrafted cocktail (11am–11pm), drop by for lunch, and don't miss the Red Velvet Cake for dessert! (5.30am–10pm, 407 393 4422; **bit.ly/brit-ritz**).

Hillstone: This lakeside location in Winter Park provides a relaxed but upmarket choice for a casual lunch or full-scale dinner. Where the locals go for a 'power lunch,' it is also an evening oasis, with the chance to enjoy a drink on their pier or grab a patio table with a wonderful view of Lake Killarney. The menu varies from simple burgers and salads to epic fresh fish dishes, rotisserie chicken and succulent steaks. (11.30am–10pm Sun–Thurs, 10.30pm Fri–Sat; 407 740 4005, **www.hillstone.com**).

A Land Remembered: Inside the golf clubhouse of the Rosen Shingle Creek Resort (but open to non-residents), this is a superbly refined venue boasting exquisite service and an outstanding wine list. The lamb, chicken and short ribs are outstanding, but the all-natural prime black Angus beef is out of this world. Various cuts of steak and a surf and turf (with lobster) are among the most succulent meat dishes you will find and, while it is pricey, we believe it is worth every cent (5.30–10pm; 407 996 3663, **landrememberedrestaurant.com**).

Luma on Park: Also in Winter Park, this trendy gastropub can offer cuisine as simple as a well-cooked burger or pizza or a fabulous filet mignon. The mix of outdoor patio, lounge bar and great wine cellar makes it chic and lively. It also features a $35 three-course prix fixe Sun–Tues (4–10pm Mon–Thurs, 11pm Fri–Sat; 9pm Sun; 407 599 4111, **lumaonpark.com**).

BRITTIP

Check out our good friend, restaurant critic and foodie Scott Joseph for latest news, views and insights at scottjosephorlando.com. His 'Flog' (food blog) is essential, plus he offers coupons at local restaurants. Try his great Orlando Restaurant Guide or his free app from iTunes.

Ravenous Pig: Staying in Winter Park, local restaurateurs James and Julie Petrakis have crafted the British gastropub idea into a cosy hideaway that oozes style, whether you want great pub food or the full gourmet experience. Superb craft beer is supplied by their own Cask & Larder micro-brewery. Bookings are highly advisable though, as its popularity is widespread (11.30am–3pm lunch Wed–Sat, 5–10pm dinner Mon–Thurs, 5pm-11pm Fri–Sat, 5–9pm Sun, happy hour 3–5pm; 407 628 2333, **theravenouspig.com**).

OK, that's enough eating for now – on to another of our favourite topics – shopping…

Sunset on the pier at Hillstone

12 Shopping

or How to Send Your Credit Card into Meltdown

As well as being a theme park wonderland, this vast area of Florida is a shopper's paradise, with a dazzling array of specialist outlets, malls, flea markets and discount retailers. New centres spring up all the time, from smart malls to cheap gift shops – and you can't go a few paces in the tourist areas without a shop insisting it has the 'best bargains' of one sort or another.

With so much good shopping to be had for UK visitors, there's a danger of exceeding your baggage allowance for the flight home – or your duty-free allowance. American stores are genuinely fun just to browse, let alone splash out in and real bargains are to be had in jeans, trainers, sports equipment and cosmetics. Almost everywhere offers free, convenient parking, while shop assistants are polite and helpful.

Sales tax: Be aware of the hidden extra costs of shopping. Unlike our VAT, Florida sales tax is NOT part of the displayed purchase price, so you must add on 6% or 7% (it varies by county) for the final price. Also, some shops will ask for photo ID with credit card purchases, so have a photo driving licence or photo ID with you.

Allowances: Your limit in the catch-all duty category of 'gifts and souvenirs' is only £390 per person. If you exceed that, you need to keep your receipts and go through the 'goods to declare' channel (though paying the duty and VAT can still be cheaper than buying the same items at home). Some items, such as clothing and footwear for children, do not incur a VAT rate. However, restrictions apply to all reduced-rate VAT items, so be sure to check details with HM Revenue & Customs. Your ordinary duty-free allowances from America include 200 cigarettes and 1 litre of spirits or 2 litres of fortified wine or sparkling wine and 4 litres of still wine.

Disneystyle at Disney Springs

© Disney

BRITTIP

Don't buy electrical goods in the US – they won't work in the UK without a converter. Most games systems (notably X Box, Wii and PS4) are also NOT compatible with UK players. Hand-held games are fine.

Up, up and away!

In Disney Springs West Side, across the bridge from The Landing, is Aerophile, a wonderful tethered balloon ride that gently soars up to 400ft/122m high carrying up to 30 at a time in a 19ft/5.7m gondola on 6min rides. It provides a fab panorama of much of the huge extent of Walt Disney World and is a great photo opportunity by day or night (8.30am–midnight). It costs $20/adult and $15/3–9s. In certain weather conditions the number of passengers is limited, while it is grounded in high winds or heavy rain.

Customs duty: You pay duty (which varies depending on the item) on the total purchase price (i.e. inclusive of Florida sales tax) once you have exceeded £390, plus VAT at 20%. You CANNOT pool your allowances to cover one item that exceeds a single allowance. Hence, if you buy a single item that costs £700, you have to pay the duty on the full £700, and then VAT on top of that. However, if you have several items that add up to £390, and then another that exceeds that, you pay the duty and VAT only on the excess item (and customs officers usually give you the benefit of the lowest rate on what you pay for). Duty rates are updated regularly and vary from 2.5 to 14%. You pay 2.5% for goods worth up to £630, and then it depends on the type of goods above £630. For more info, contact the Customs and Excise National Advice Service on 0845 010 9000, **gov.uk/duty-free-goods**.

Alligator products constitute those of an endangered species (to UK authorities) so require an import licence. Consult the Global Wildlife Licensing and Registration Service for more info.

BRITGUIDE 25

Shopping has always been a big part of the Orlando experience, but it has also seen huge growth. Disney Springs, the two Orlando Premium Outlets centres, Lake Buena Vista Factory Stores, Mall at Millenia, The Loop and Winter Garden Village have all been built since 1995.

Disney Springs

This shopping and dining district splits into four sections: Marketplace, The Landing, Town Center and West Side. With imaginative architecture and one-off elements, it makes shopping a pleasure. There are 110 shops and 63 dining options, and a free water-taxi links each end as well as Disney's Old Key West, Port Orleans and Saratoga Springs Resorts.

Disney Springs can be found off exits 67 and 68 of I-4 and is well signposted (exit 68 can be congested at peak periods). Parking has been boosted by three new multi-storey car parks that feature clever technology to indicate every empty space on each floor (look for the green lights).

Marketplace: Don't miss the **World of Disney** store, the largest of its kind, with a mind-boggling array of Disney merchandise, from clothing and jewellery to toys and home goods. Equally impressive are **The LEGO Store** (an interactive playground and shop), the amazing **Art of Disney** and the **Marketplace Co-Op** (a number of small shops under one roof). **Once Upon a Toy** is a gigantic toy emporium complete with a host of classic games, many with a Disney theme, for kids to try. Here you will also find the **Bibbidi Bobbidi Boutique**, where young girls can have hair, make-up and nails done in true Princess style (and with the price to match!). The Knight Package ($20) gives boys a gel and confetti hairstyle, plus a sword and shield. Other worthwhile one-offs are the blissful **Basin** (for toiletries) and **Disney's Wonderful World of Memories** (for all scrapbook fans).

BRITTIP

Parents beware! The Bibbidi Bobbidi Boutique is hideously expensive. Packages range from $65–450! There is even a version for adults, Character Couture, at several Disney salons, from $80–120.

Princess Parade: Young girls in the princess mood may want to take part in the daily parade from the Bibbidi

Bobbidi Boutique at 1–2pm (weather permitting). It marches around the Marketplace, finishing at the Carousel, where all children get a free ride. Kids can dress up (or not) and there is NO fee.

Arribas Brothers is a big, attractive gift store, while those keen on pin-trading should check out **Pin Traders**. Then there's **Disney Design-A-Tee**, **Star Wars Trading Post**, **Tren-D**, a cutting edge Disney fashion store for women, **The Spice & Tea Exchange** (tea, food, housewares), **Pearl Factory** (clothes) and **Disney's Days of Christmas**.

Looking to outfit your home and kitchen in a Disney theme? **Mickey's Pantry** has you covered. Dancing fountains and squirt pools (where kids tend to get seriously wet) and the lakeside setting all add to the appeal. **Build-A-Dino** and **Dino Store** can be found inside T-Rex Café. There are several kiosk-style shops as well.

The Void: This virtual reality experience is ideal for Star Wars fans and shoot-'em-up gamers, as it's a cross between a 3-D video game and an immersive escape game. Teams of four suit up on a mission, choosing from **Star Wars: Secrets of the Empire**, where players aid the Rebellion and must navigate an

elaborate – and highly convincing – VR world on the planet Mustafar, with blasters and droids to help out, or **Ralph Breaks VR**, where gamers enter the world of Wreck It Ralph, and all mayhem breaks lose – including a food fight at Pancake Milkshake Diner! Each lasts around 30 minutes, with around 15 inside the game, and includes real-time effects and other props to enhance the reality. It all adds up to an experience gamers – and even non-gamers – will want to do again and again! (Sun–Thurs 10am-11pm, Fri–Sat 10am-11.30pm; Mon–Thurs $30/person, Fri–Sun, holidays and holiday weeks $33 www.thevoid.com/locations/orlando).

The Landing: Browse a variety of imaginative shops like **The Art of Shaving** (toiletries), **Chapel Hats** (funky/vintage hats), **Havaianas** (flip-flops), **Oakley** (apparel and accessories), **Sanuk** (shoes), **Erin McKenna's bakery NYC** (vegan/gluten-free baked goods), and **The Ganachery** (delicious chocolates). For dining, see chapter 11 (p308), while **Raglan Road** also has its own Irish-themed gift shop here.

West Side: This area offers the superb **AMC 24** cinema complex (p291), plus another 13 retail and dining outlets, notably **Disneystyle** and **Pelé Soccer**. **Pop Gallery** has collectable artwork while **Disney's Candy Cauldron** is a big hit with kids. Others include **Super Hero Headquarters** (apparel and collectables), **Star Wars Galactic Outpost, Curl by Sammy Duvall** (water sports), **Sunglass Icon** and **Fit2Run**. There are also gift shops for **House of Blues** and **Splitsville**, and this is where to find the **Food Truck Park**.

Town Center: The final part of Disney Springs is more like an upmarket mall, but there are still nice touches in the architecture and story of Disney Springs itself. The water features are extremely eye-catching and there are great back-stories at **Amorette's Patisserie** and **D-Luxe Burger** in particular (the former of which serves decadent cakes and pastries). Be sure to ask

D-Luxe Burger

© Disney

Zara at Disney Springs

the Cast Members about them. The stores are those you'll find in most good shopping centres (and at a premium price), but pick from the likes of **Everything But Water**, **Kipling**, **Lucky Brand**, **Tommy Bahama**, **Lilly Pulitzer**, **Kate Spade**, **Under Armour**, **Coach** and **Lacoste** for the latest fashions, apparel and sportswear. There are six jewellery shops, including **Vera Bradley**, **Alex and Ani** and **Pandora**, another five for footwear, including **UGG**, **Sperry** and **Trophy Room**, and four for cosmetics, notably **Sephora** and **L'Occitane**. For true one-offs, sample **Sprinkles** for wonderful cupcakes, ice cream and shakes; **Sugarboo** for arts and crafts; and the **Coca-Cola Store**, with its amazing array of products.

The shops of Disney Springs are open 10am–11pm or midnight. For more details, see **disneysprings.com**.

International Drive

This core tourist area is awash with shopping of all kinds, from the cheapest and tackiest plazas full of tourist gift shops, to four purpose-built centres. Some of the shops just north of the Sand Lake Road junction are best avoided, while the northern end of I-Drive has undergone a major redevelopment. This area is also renowned for discount outlet shopping – a local speciality – offering name brands at heavily reduced prices.

Universal CityWalk: Among the most original of the 12 shops are **Quiet Flight**, for radical surf and beachwear; the retro-American

decor of **Fossil** for leather goods, watches and sunglasses; **Fresh Produce** for swimwear, casual clothing and accessories; **Rock Shop** clothing; **P!Q** toys and household; the large **Island Clothing Store** for Tommy Bahama clothing and merchandise; and **Hart & Huntington Orlando Tattoo Shop** with an array of permanent tattoos, as well as clothing and accessories. Again, none of these are anything special but the huge **Universal Studios Store** offers a wide range of park souvenirs and merchandise.

Artegon Marketplace: This outlet has largely closed, but the big **Bass Pro Shops** and **Cinemark** multi-screen cinema remain for the time being.

Orlando International Premium Outlets: At the top of I-Drive, this attractive 175-shop 'lifestyle centre' has gone all out for the big, semi-open-air style that encourages people to wander the long promenades full of shop fronts and big-name brands.

Boasting a landscaped canal running through the centre, outdoor seating, cafés, a Market Place food court and a Guest Services centre, it provides a luxury touch. Major brands include **Kate Spade New York**, **Calvin Klein**, **Lacoste** and **Michael Kors**. Other familiar names include **Nike Factory Store**, **Tommy Hilfiger**, **Dooney & Bourke**, **Banana Republic**, **Bath & Body Works**, **Aeropostale** and **Brooks Brothers**, plus, inevitably, a Starbucks. With its attractive food court, including the popular Five Guys Burgers, Panera Bread and

Sugarboo at Disney Springs

Sbarro pizza, plus Italian restaurant Vinito, you have one of the area's brightest shopping centres that is also at the top of the I-Ride Trolley route daily; **bit.ly/brit-premium**).

Pointe Orlando: In the heart of I-Drive, this is a good choice for an evening out with some retail therapy. With 13 smart stores, you can indulge your passion for fashion at **Tommy Hilfiger** and **Hollister** or stock up on gifts and souvenirs at **1 For the Road**, **Charming Charlie**, **Design By U**, **Moon Dance**, **Redi to Pedi**, **Flow** and **Tharoo & Co** jewellery. For the lowdown on places to eat at Pointe Orlando (p321). Parking is in the multi-storey car park, but some stores and restaurants will redeem your parking ticket if you shop there (11am-9pm; later at the bars and restaurants; 407 248 2838, **pointeorlando.com**).

ICON Park: This entertainment and dining complex (p230) has a selection of shops, including the big chemist and general store **Walgreens**, **Tervis** (durable drinkware), **Caleoni Sunglasses**, **360 Gifts** (ICON Park souvenirs) and the **Flip Flop Shop**.

Old Town Kissimmee

A Kissimmee tradition

Old Town is home to some weekly events that appeal to both locals and tourists alike. **The Saturday Nite Cruise** at 8.30pm is a trademark drive-past of 300-plus vintage and collector cars (the biggest in America; viewing starts at 1pm). A **Friday Nite Muscle Car Cruise** features cars built between 1964 and today (viewing starts at 4pm, cruise starts at 8.30pm), and **Thursday Night Bike Night** with classic and modern motorcycles and trikes, (from 5pm–11pm). There is live music, fairground stalls and prizes, and it can get fairly raucous later on, with plenty of alcoholic libations (witness the Sun on the Beach bar!).

Kissimmee

Along the tourist territory of Highway 192, you will again find a complete mix of outlets, with a profusion of the cheap and cheerful, but also several highly enticing possibilities.

Old Town: This is Kissimmee's version of the purpose-built tourist shopping centre, an Old Florida style offering with an eclectic mix of shops, restaurants, bars and fairground attractions set out along brick-lined streets. The shops range from standard souvenirs and novel T-shirt outlets to sportswear, and collectibles (check out the **Old Town General Store** for a step back in time, or the **Old Town Portrait Gallery** for period-style photos). The individual style of **Out of This World Embroidery** offers a 'you name it, we'll stitch it' service, while, **Filthy Rich** jewellery, **Wild Billie's Gifts** and **Lucky Mouse** are all great for gifts. There are also 15 restaurants or snack bars. For lunch or dinner, try **Shoney's**, **Southern Breeze** or the fun style of **Froggers Bar & Grill**. **Flippers**

Pizzeria and **El Borrego** are also worth trying, while there are other snack outlets, with offerings from popcorn to candy and the wonderful **Sweet Dreams Ice Cream Café**. **Sun on the Beach** is a good nightclub in evenings (until 2am). Parking is free (10am–11pm daily; 407 396 4888; **myoldtownusa.com**).

Downtown Kissimmee: This offers the more local, authentic face of shopping in Florida, with the charming Main Street area featuring antique shops, one-off boutiques, cafés and restaurants. Much attention has been paid to the historic district in recent years, and it is now a relaxing place for a wander and a meal. **The Welcome Station** on Main Street (formerly an old-fashioned petrol station) is a great place to start, and even has local crafts, keepsakes, and books focusing on Floridian history (9am–5pm Mon–Fri). Then look into the likes of local landmarks **Lanier's**, **Makinson Hardware** (the oldest hardware store in Florida), and **Echoes of Yesterday** antiques. Try the casual sports-bar style of **Broadway Pizza**, or the smart **3 Sisters Speakeasy** wine bar and café, which has **Trivia Night Tuesdays**, an **Antique Car** Show on the first Fri every month and live music Wed–Sat (times vary; 407 201 3270, **3sistersspeakeasy.com**). For a truly charming local experience, be sure to check out **Diane's Tea Room** on Broadway, while there is usually free parking available on E. Deakin Avenue and Pleasant Street.

BRITTIP

For something different, don't miss **Abracadabra Ice Cream Factory**, just outside Kissimmee town centre (on North Main Street). Here, they mix fantastic creamy creations using a wonderful variety of ingredients – and flash freeze it all with liquid nitrogen for a true taste sensation! It's open 11am–10pm daily.

The Loop and The Loop West: Apart from Old Town and Downtown, the Kissimmee area is largely short of quality shopping, but head to the

Osceola Parkway (at the junction with John Young Parkway), running parallel to Highway 192, to find these extensive developments. They offer an enticing mix of shopping and dining, plus a 16-screen Regal Cinema in a pedestrian-friendly setting, with the shops grouped around two large car parks. Many of the shops may be unfamiliar but are worth visiting. Of note at The Loop are **Ross** (a huge discount warehouse of clothes, shoes, linens, cosmetics and more), **Kohl's** (a well-priced department store), **Bed, Bath & Beyond** (household), **Old Navy** (clothing), **Michaels** (arts and crafts), **Famous Footwear** (discounted shoes) and a hairdresser, nail salon and chemist (**CVS**). At The Loop West, look for the big department stores of **JC Penney** (clothing and housewares) and **Sketchers** (footwear), plus **Ulta** (cosmetics), **TJ Maxx** (clothing) and **DSW** (shoes), plus several other shops.

The extensive dining choice includes classic 1950s diner **Johnny Rockets**, **Ben & Jerry's** ice cream, the counter-service of **Pei Wei Asian Diner**, Mexican choice **Abuelo's**, **Noodles & Company** and the big-name chains of **Chick-Fil-A**, **Chili's**, **Panera Bread**, **Bonefish Grill** and the distinctive **BJ's Brewhouse** offering great burgers, sandwiches, salads and steaks, plus an impressive beer choice (407 932 5245, **bjsbrewhouse.com**). The shops are open 10am–9.30pm Mon–Sat, 11am–6pm Sun, later at the restaurants and cinemas (407 343 9223; **experiencetheloop.com**).

Abracadabra Ice Cream Factory

Lake Buena Vista

The Lake Buena Vista area offers two of the best discount outlet centres, with a great range and prices.

Orlando Vineland Premium Outlets: High on your 'must visit' list, this is a huge hit with UK visitors. With a fresh look and ambience, and a legion of big-name designers, it is the sister centre of the I-Drive version, with a number of similarities but also its own style and range of shops. It can be found on Vineland Avenue between I-Drive and I-4 (just south of SeaWorld; or exit 68 off I-4).

BRITTIP
Although it can be a battle to find a parking spot in the main open-air car park at Orlando Vineland Premium Outlets, the multi-storey car park now charges $10.

In all, it offers more than 150 stores of well-known brand names (like **Diesel, Armani Exchange**, **Perry Ellis**, **Banana Republic**, **Prada**, **Coach**, **Kate Spade** and **Calvin Klein**) in a semi-covered pedestrian plaza, with free open-air parking and the convenience of being at the south end of the I-Ride Trolley. Other signature shops are **Samsonite Company Store**, **Burberry**, **UGG Australia** (Ugg boots), **OshKosh B'Gosh** (baby/toddler clothes), **Famous Footwear** (a mini-warehouse of footwear fashion) and **Perfumania**. Watch out also for big Disney bargains at the **Disney Outlet**, which offers the previous season's items. The adjoining expansion of The Promenade adds 12 more stores, including a two-storey **Sak's Fifth Avenue Off 5th**, **Tommy Bahama** and **Forever 21**. The food court is quite tempting, too, with 15 outlets, from **Villa Fresh Italian Kitchen** and **Maki of Japan** to **Starbucks**, **Ben & Jerry's** and **Subway**. There is even a beer and wine kiosk.

The Lynx bus service stops here, while **Mears Transport** has taxi stands. Premium Outlets is open daily 10am–11pm (407 238 0703; **bit.ly/brit-premium**).

BRITTIP
Want to see a REAL shopping frenzy? Visit either Orlando Premium Outlets centre for Midnight Madness on the Fri after Thanksgiving when they open at midnight and stay open for 24 hours – and thousands pour in to shop!

Lake Buena Vista Factory Stores: Get ready for more big-name products at discount prices here, from **Fossil**, **Converse**, **Reebok**, **Tommy Hilfiger**, **OshKosh B'Gosh** superstore and (the better-priced) **Carter's For Kids**. It is another open-air plaza, with 44 stores spread over 6acres/2.5ha and with plentiful parking. It's slightly off the beaten track and therefore not quite as busy as some of the others.

Another option is **Theme Park Outlet** for Disney gifts and apparel. Some of the names may not be well known to us, but the likes of **Old Navy** (excellent-value casual clothing), **Crocs** (super-comfortable shoes), **Travelpro** (luggage and travel accessories) and **Rack Room Shoes** are worth discovering. **World of Coffee** is both an internet café and a great place to sip a latte and enjoy a cake or pastry, with its outdoor terrace and bird cages (plus British snacks and chocs!). There is also a decent food court with a pleasant outdoor deck and kids' playground. Worth noting at the neighbouring Lake Buena Vista Resort Village and Spa are the fab **Reflections Spa** for a bit of pampering after a day's shopping, and **Frankie Farrells Irish Pub** (p324).

The Factory Stores are on SR 535 (2ml/3km south off exit 68 on I-4) and are open 10am–9pm (7pm Sun, later in peak season). Their shuttle service picks up at 60 hotels and condos in a 10ml/16km radius (407 238 9301, **lbvfs.com**).

BRITTIP
Don't miss the Lake Buena Vista Factory Stores website for valuable weekly coupons and do 'friend' their Facebook page for even more special offers and discounts. Or just visit Travelpro store for a coupon booklet.

Malls

Head out slightly beyond the main tourist territory and you will discover the further choice and style of the area's many malls. They contain a huge range of shops and, if you take advantage of their periodic sales, you will be firmly back on the bargain trail. The top two locally are the Florida Mall and the Mall at Millenia, and both offer a contrasting experience.

Florida Mall: The largest in central Florida, this features more than 230 shops, with four large department stores and a huge food court, plus a children's play area, and the popular fresh offerings of **Nature's Table** and hearty **Buca di Beppo**. Located on the South Orange Blossom Trail, on the corner of Sand Lake Road, this spacious and smart mall is open 10am–9pm Mon–Fri, 10am-10pm Sat, noon–8pm Sun. Highlights are the department stores, led by the upmarket **Macy's**, plus **JC Penney**, **Sears** and **Dillard's**. Other shops worth looking out for are **Bath & Body Works**, **Gap**, **PacSun** (beachwear and more) and the **Build-a-Bear Workshop**, **Game Stop** and the fun **M&M's World** store. Also here is the massive **Crayola Experience** (interactive fun and design for kids; **crayolaexperience.com/orlando**). Guest services offers a discount booklet with a handy international size chart, while there is also free wi-fi throughout the mall, free wheelchair use, pushchair rental and foreign currency exchange. **JC Penney** even has a hair styling salon (407 851 7234; **simon.com/mall/the-florida-mall**). The Mall also benefits from the integral **Florida Hotel**, with **Cricket's Bar**.

BRITTIP

With 25 hands-on attractions – from melting, moulding, spinning, and painting to drawing, doodling, and digital design, plus an indoor play area – the marvellous **Crayola Experience** is a top choice when it's too hot or wet for the parks. There is even a Crayola Café for lunch or a snack. Admission is $25pp, under-3s free.

Mall at Millenia: If the Florida Mall is the biggest shopping venue, this is the smartest. Just off I-4 to the north of Universal Orlando, it is among the most dramatic centres in Florida, with famous New York department stores **Bloomingdale's, Neiman Marcus** and **Macy's** among top-name boutiques like **Louis Vuitton**. The entrance features a huge glass rotunda with a water garden theme and a concièrge desk (valet parking is available). As well as five restaurants, it also offers a high-quality food court featuring **Bistro Europa** (salads, soups, wraps), **Firehouse Subs**, **Sbarro**, the Mandarin-style of **Chinatown**, **Chipotle Mexican Grill** (salads, tacos and burritos) and **Haagan-Dazs** ice cream, plus **Gourmet Grill** (burgers, hot dogs, Philly cheesesteak).

BRITTIP

Visit the Mall at Millenia Concièrge, located inside the main entrance on level 1, and show this book to receive a complimentary savings book.

The grand architecture is also focused on five separate courts along a flattened, serpentine S-shape, topped by an arched glass roof. On two airy levels (three in Bloomingdale's and Macy's) and with eight Juliet balconies connecting the two sides, the mall

Florida Mall

© Disney

consists of a colossal amount of glass, plus a stunning Grand Court, featuring a dozen 20ft/6m columns capped by curved plasma video screens. And, while around 20% of the 150 stores are upmarket (**Cartier**, **Jimmy Choo**, **Burberry** and **Gucci**), there are regular-priced shops like **Urban Outfitters**, **Apple**, **MAC Cosmetics**, **Anthropologie**, **Abercrombie & Fitch**, **Hollister**, **Gap**, **Banana Republic** and **Victoria's Secret**. The five main restaurants are also first class: **The Cheesecake Factory**, **Earl's Kitchen + Bar**, **PF Chang's China Bistro**, the stylish **Brio Tuscan Grille**, and the swanky **Capital Grille**. On top of that there is the excellent fresh sandwich style of **Charlie's Philly Steaks**, the **California Pizza Kitchen** and a **Johnny Rockets** diner. This is also the only mall with a US post office inside (NB: Standard postcards to the UK cost $1.15). A currency exchange is available, as are international phone cards (10am–9pm Mon–Sat, 11am–7pm Sun; 407 363 3555; **mallatmillenia.com**).

Altemonte Mall

Other malls: The **Altamonte Mall** is on Altamonte Avenue in the suburb of Altamonte Springs (take exit 92 off I-4 and head east for ½ml/800m on Route 436, then turn left); **Seminole Towne Center**, just off I-4 to the north of Orlando on the outskirts of Sanford (exit 101C off I-4); and **Oviedo Mall**, to the east of Orlando (right off exit 41 of Central Florida Greeneway, 417). The Altamonte Mall is the best of the bunch and well off the beaten tourist track, featuring 94 speciality shops, three major department stores – **Macy's**, **Dillard's** and **JC Penney** – and 24 eateries, including the fun **Bahama Breeze**, **iSpice** Indian cuisine, and pub-style **Miller's Ale House** (p325). An 18-screen cinema and children's soft-play area round out the offerings. Open 10am–9pm Mon–Sat, noon–6pm Sun, the Customer Service Centre offers a VIP savings book to visitors (**altamontemall.com**). During the week you'll feel as if you have the place to yourself!

BRITTIP

Popular comic book and fantasy gaming store **Gods and Monsters** can be found in Orlando Crossings Plaza on upper International Drive (**godmonsters.com**).

Winter Garden Village: A final recommendation, 10ml/16km north of Walt Disney World on Highway 535 at the junction with toll road 429, which is primarily a locals' centre but still has visitor appeal. The expansive open-plan design, set around key stores like **Super Target**, **Best Buy**, **Ross**, **Marshall's**, **Home Goods** and **Beall's**, features a mix of the big names and smaller boutiques, with notable speciality stores like **World Market**, as well as an array of 21 cafes and restaurants. Look for the upmarket seafood choice of **Bonefish Grill**, the elegant **Longhorn Steakhouse**, family-style **Chili's**, **Cracker Barrel**, **UNO Chicago Grill** and **Village Inn**, or the counter-service options like **Five Guys Burgers**, **Panda Express**, **Coldstone Creamery** and **Chick-Fil-A**, and our favourite burger restaurant, **Red Robin** (**facebook.com/wintergardenvillage**).

Specialist shops

Wal-Mart: High on many people's lists, this warehouse-like store sells just about everything. There are 25 Wal-Marts in central Florida, 16 of which are 24hr Supercenters. The main tourist area stores are on Highway 27 (just north of 192); Highway 192 by Medieval Times (between markers 14 and 15); Osceola Parkway (at Buenaventura Lakes); John Young Parkway (at Sand Lake Road); on Kirkman Road (north of Universal Boulevard); by Highway 535 and Osceola Parkway; on Old Lake Wilson Road at the junction with Highway 192; and on Turkey Lake Road.

> **BRITTIP**
> Lucky's Market is the ideal place to assemble a meal or picnic from their prepared foods, including pizza, sandwiches, pre-cooked meats and veg or just cheese, biscuits and a bottle of wine.

Other supermarkets: There are plenty of other choices, including the ubiquitous **Publix**, and local chain **Winn-Dixie**, but the real Rolls-Royce of food stores, **Whole Foods Market**, has a branch on Turkey Lake Road, with its signature fresh produce emporium and salad bar, plus a magnificent hot-food counter to grab a meal (**wholefoodsmarket.com**). By the same token, **Fresh Market** (with five Central Florida locations) is a great choice for high-quality grocery shopping (**thefreshmarket.com**). Our new favourite grocer, **Lucky's Market**, has opened at 11601 Regency Village Drive, near Premium Outlets, and it carries the area's best fresh produce,

groceries, hot and cold prepared foods, a sushi and noodle bar, meat and fish counter, plus beer and wine you can drink while you shop! (407 778 3232, **luckysmarket.com**).

For clothes, DIY, home furnishings, electrical goods, household items, gifts, toys and groceries, visit **Target** (its superstores on Highway 192 just west of Highway 535, near Mall at Millenia and Winter Garden Village are fine examples). The big chemists ('drug stores') of **Walgreens** and **CVS** also carry a wide range of goods.

> **BRITTIP**
> Wal-Mart offers 1hr photo printing at great savings on UK prices, as do branches of Walgreens.

Individual outlets: Ross (10 in Orlando, see **rossstores.com**) carries a huge range of discounted brand-name clothes, shoes, linens, towels, etc (hours vary by store, roughly 9.30am–9.30pm), while **Marshalls** (five in Orlando, **marshallsonline.com**) and **TJ Maxx** (also five, **tjmaxx.com**) are similar. For American sports gear visit **Academy Sports** stores (**academy.com**), while golfers should visit **Edwin Watts Golf** (including the Turkey Lake Road clearance centre; **worldwidegolfshops. com**), or **Special Tee Golf & Tennis** shops. You can pick up some great deals on golf clubs in particular. By the same token, anglers can stock up on the latest gear at bargain prices at **Bass Pro Shops** (at the former Artegon Marketplace; **basspro.com**).

But now the shopping is done, it's time to think about going home…

Winter Garden Village

And so, dog-tired, lighter in the wallet but (hopefully) blissfully happy and with a wealth of lovely memories, it's time to deal with that bane of all holidays – the journey home.

Now you have come through the last two weeks relatively unscathed, here's how to avoid any last-minute pitfalls.

The car

Returning the hire car can take time if you used an off-airport car depot, so allow an extra half hour; the process is much slicker with firms that operate directly from the airports, as nearly all now do. Most airlines require you to arrive 3hrs before an international flight, so don't be tempted to leave your check-in until the last minute. The off-airport check-in facility for Virgin Holidays (at Disney Springs by the Cirque du Soleil® theatre) is a major bonus in making this process smoother.

Now you'll have time to kill, so here is a guide to the two main Orlando airports.

Dockside Margaritas at Disney Springs

© Disney

Orlando International

Timing: Orlando's biggest airport is 46ml/74km from Cocoa Beach and 54ml/87km from Daytona Beach on the east coast, 84ml/135km from Tampa and 110ml/177km from Clearwater and St Petersburg to the west, 25ml/40km from Walt Disney World and 10ml/16km from Universal Orlando, so always allow plenty of time for the return journey, check-in and security procedure. The Beachline Expressway (528) can get congested in late afternoon, for example, and the Central Florida Greeneway (417) is often better.

Should you have more than 3hrs to spare, it's worth taking the 15min taxi ride to the Florida Mall.

The car: A convenient 'quick turnaround' area for hire cars allows most of the big hire companies to have onsite locations, a huge boon especially when returning the car.

Facilities: One of America's biggest and rated top for passenger satisfaction, this modern airport handles 47 million passengers a year, which is more than Gatwick and San Francisco. It can get busy at peak times, but its 1,000acre/405ha complex usually handles crowds with ease, and this is one of the most comfortable airports you could find. It boasts great facilities and its wide, airy concourses make it feel more like an elegant hotel (one end is actually the airport-owned Hyatt Hotel). Be aware the airport is now engaged in a $3b expansion to increase capacity, mainly with a new South Terminal for 2021. This should have minimal effect on arrivals but could affect departures – another reason not to cut it fine with check-in.

The airport always aims to stay a step ahead, with environmentally friendly enhancements, smart restrooms and a wide selection of food and drink outlets. It boasts a major food court, multiple restaurant options, good shops and plenty of seating.

Facilities for the disabled: Ramps, restrooms, wide lifts and large open areas ensure easy wheelchair access, and there are features like TDD and amplified telephones, wheelchair-height drinking fountains, Braille lift controls and companion-care restrooms for any travellers with disabilities.

BRITTIP

You are advised to leave all luggage unlocked (no combination locks or padlocks) when you check in for your flight, as the TSA security staff open a LOT of bags during screening and have the right to access any case, locked or not. TSA approved locks are suggested, if you prefer to lock your cases.

Landside

As with all international airports, there is a division between LANDSIDE (for visitors) and AIRSIDE (where you must have a ticket). There are three levels to Orlando's Landside.

- Level 1 is for ground transportation, tour operator desks, parking, buses and car rental agencies, plus the Virgin Atlantic baggage claim.
- Level 2 is for main Baggage Claim and private vehicles meeting passengers.
- Level 3 is where you enter on your return journey, as it holds the check-in desks, shops and restaurants.

The main area of Level 3 is further divided into interconnected sections:

Landside A: This houses the check-in for Gates 1–29 and 100–129. Here you'll find Aer Lingus, Southwest, JetBlue, Norwegian and Virgin Atlantic (though Aer Lingus, Norwegian and Virgin Atlantic depart from Gates 70–99).

Landside B: Check-in here for Gates 30–99 and American Airlines, Air Canada, BA, Delta, Icelandair, Lufthansa, United and Spirit (Icelandair departs from Gates 1–29).

Shopping: Once you've checked in, you can explore the East and West Halls of the Level 3 concourse. These house a good mix of shops and restaurants, plus currency exchange, information desks and ATMs, while the Hyatt Hotel is in the East Hall. The East and West Halls are linked by the restaurants, shops and services of the North and South Walks. In total, there are 137 places to shop and eat, including the food court, and it's almost like being in a smart shopping mall.

Many shops feature outstanding design and even photo opportunities: see the **Disney**, **Universal**, **SeaWorld/Busch Gardens** and **Kennedy Space Center** stores (two of each!). Other notable shops are **Guess** apparel, **Brookstone**, **Ron Jon Surf Shop**, **Lids** (sports hats and clothes) and **Hudson News**.

Dining: Another pleasure here, the eight-counter food court features **Carvel** ice-cream, **Sbarro** pizza, **Qdoba Mexican Grill**, **McDonalds** and **Panda Express**, plus the slightly healthier option of **Chick-Fil-A**. **Macaroni Grill** is a tasty full-service Italian restaurant option, while **City Pub** adds a multi-screen TV set-up themed to Orlando's football team. Upstairs at the West Hall is **Chili's Too**.

The East Hall is quieter and more picturesque as it is dominated by the eight-storey Hyatt Hotel atrium. Up the escalator is the main entrance, and, to see out your visit in style, **McCoy's Bar & Grill** (up and turn right) is a smart bar-restaurant with a superb airport view and a menu

Airport map

that includes a **Sushi Bar** and fresh salads, sandwiches, flatbreads and small plates ideal for sharing or lighter appetites (11am–12:30am, Sushi Bar 4–11pm; 407 825 1234, **orlandoairport.regency.hyatt.com**).

To go really upmarket, take the lift to the 9th-floor **Hemisphere** restaurant (breakfast and dinner only). You'll have an even more impressive view, and its made-for-sharing small-plate menu is packed with a variety of taste sensations, from grilled octopus to spiced duck (breakfast 5.30am–11am Mon–Fri, noon Sat–Sun; dinner 5–10pm Mon–Sat).

BRITTIP

If the queues at security for Gates 70–99 look long, you can use the other side, for Gates 100–129, as you end up in the same place after screening. Just remember to get the tram to Gates 70–99.

Airside

Once it's time to move to your departure gate, be aware of the four satellite 'arms' that make up Airside. This is where you will probably need to queue as the security screening

takes time, and you should allow AT LEAST 30mins. The arms are divided into Gates 1–29 and 30–59 at the West end, and 70–99 (UK international departures) and 100–129 (all American domestic flights) at the East. All the departure gates are here, plus duty-free shops and more cafés.

The four satellites are each connected to the main building by an automated tram, so you need to be alert when it comes to finding your departure gate. There are no Tannoy announcements for flights, so check your departure gate and time when you check in. However, there are large monitors in the terminal with all departure info. The usual gates are:

- **1–29:** Icelandair and JetBlue.

- **30–59:** American, Spirit and United.

- **70–99:** Air Canada, Aer Lingus, Bahamasair, British Airways, Delta, Lufthansa, Norwegian, Thomas Cook and Virgin Atlantic.

- **100–129:** Southwest and Alaska Air.

Airside is clean and efficient. There's less choice than the main terminal but there are two duty-free shops (your purchases are delivered to the departure gate for you to collect as you board). Both stores include designer sunglasses, jewellery, handbags, fashion watches, perfumes and a selection of travel retail exclusives.

BRITTIP
Orlando International Airport offers free WiFi throughout its main concourse and satellite arms.

Gates 1–29: Here you'll find the first duty-free shop, **Hudson News** (newsagent), **ZaZa Cuban Café**, **On the Border Mexican Cantina**, and a mini food court with **Starbucks**, **Burger King**, **Cold Stone Creamery**, **Brioche Doree**, **Famous Famiglia**, **UrbanCrave** street food and **Le Grand Comptoir** bar.

Gates 30–59: These have **Qdoba Mexican Grill**, **Manchu Wok**, **Nature's Table**, **Wendy's**, **Freshens Treats**, **ZaZa**, full-service **Ruby Tuesday**, the fresh grab-and-go or bar style of **Camden Food Co**, **Hudson News** (books and gifts) and **Natalie's Candy**.

Gates 70–99: The main satellite for UK flights offers a good duty-free shop, currency exchange, **Stellar News & Gifts**, the speciality **See's Candy**, **CNN Kiosk** and **XpresSpa**. A food court contains **Nathan's Hot Dogs**, **Carvel**, **Starbucks** and fresh deli style of **MCO/MKT**, plus the full-service **Outback Steakhouse** and bar, tropical **Bahama Breeze Island Grille**, and a small **Cibo Express** grab-and-go and bar.

Gates 100–129: This revamped satellite offers a food court with **Asian Chao**, **Green Leaf's & Bananas** (salads, smoothies and frozen yoghurt), **Jersey Mike's Subs**, **Chipotle**, **McDonalds**, **Starbucks**, **Villa Italian Kitchen** and the grab-and-go **The Market by Villa**. Even better is a full restaurant from **Cask & Larder**, one of Orlando's best gastropubs, plus eight shops and the **Terminal Getaway Spa**.

More info: See **orlandoairports.net**, with live flight details.

Orlando Sanford

Returning to the gateway for some British charter flights should be relatively simple, providing you retrace your route on the Central Florida Greeneway (following signs for Orlando Sanford Airport, NOT Orlando International) and come off at exit 49. Turn first right at the lights, then first right again on to Lake Mary Boulevard and follow it to the airport. Alamo and Dollar's efficient car return makes it easy.

BRITTIP
The airport turn-off sign is right after the toll plaza before exit 49 and is easy to miss; once you go through that toll plaza, take the very next turn-off.

Orlando Sanford was created as a full international airport in 1996, as an initiative between the airport authorities and British tour operators. TUI and various US domestic airlines all use this simpler option, as well as Belgian and Dutch charter flights. You are further north, so your journey time is 35mins longer with an extra $4–5 in tolls compared with the journey to and from Orlando International, but providing you follow the simple directions, you should have no problem.

And, while this charter gateway is smaller than Orlando International, it boasts a spacious check-in area and works hard to make the departure as painless as the arrival, especially with its **Royal Palm Lounge** facility. TUI and any other charters check in at Terminal A, with the departure lounge upstairs. Terminal B is for domestic flights only.

There are no food or beverage outlets at the check-in level at Terminal A, but you can walk across to Terminal B where there is a **Café Ritazza** and a food court featuring **Sanford Grill**, **Port Paradise Cinnabon**, **Cheeseburger Cheeseburger** and **Starbucks**. Once checked in, you need to pass through security (allow at least 30mins) to reach the International Departure Lounge.

Your chance to give something back

After a wonderful trip, you might be interested in two charities that help children with serious illnesses to have an equally memorable holiday.

Give Kids the World Village is an amazing organisation in Kissimmee, working with wish-granting foundations worldwide to provide an unforgettable week's holiday for children with life-threatening illnesses and their families. It is set up as a resort and includes meals, accommodation, transport, themed venues, donated park tickets and other thoughtful touches in a magical setting. It's a charity we support ourselves and we hope you will, too. You can donate via its website, **gktw.org**.

Dreamflight takes seriously ill and disabled children from the UK on a 'Holiday of a Lifetime' to the theme parks of Orlando, bringing fun and joy into the lives of children whose illnesses and treatments have brought pain, distress and disruption to their lives. Each October Dreamflight takes 192 children aged 8–14 from all over the UK. For many, it will be their first time away and most will require medical treatment or supervision. One adult accompanies every two children, a high proportion from the medical professions. Helpers in Orlando accompany each child in the parks on a one-to-one basis.

Since 1987, thousands of children have enjoyed what in many cases is a life-changing experience. Priority is given to children who would not otherwise be able to have such an opportunity. They meet others with similar experiences, form many long-term friendships and return with increased confidence and self-esteem. For further information or to make a donation please see **dreamflight.org**.

Thanks in advance for any contributions to these worthwhile organisations.

Here you have the **Budweiser Tap Room**, which serves a good selection of international beers, plus quick-serve **Dunkin Donuts**, **American Grill** and **Jetway Cafe**.

There's an extensive duty-free store, **Hudson News**, **KidWorks** for educational games, books and toys, plus **Discover Sanford Orlando** gifts, a currency and info exchange and smoking deck.

Royal Palm Lounge: An oasis of quiet in a separate annexe, open to all passengers, relax here for your final few hours. There's a pleasant café bar for unlimited soft drinks

The Give Kids The World village

and snacks (with two glasses of beer or wine for over-21s), two lounges with widescreen TV; a quiet reading room; computer terminals; a youth entertainment centre with Sony PlayStations; toddlers' playroom; and a left-luggage area. Well worth the extra cost ($30/adult, $20/4–20s, under-4s free). Most tour operators offer it in advance at a discount, or you can book on arrival or through your resort reps. See the Royal Palm Lounge and more about the airport at **orlandosanfordairport.com or email royal.palm@tbiusinc.aero**.

From either airport, your return flight will be about 1hr shorter than the journey out, thanks to the Atlantic jetstreams. But you'll get home more jetlagged because the time difference is more noticeable. Avoid alcohol on the flight if you will be driving when you land. By far the best way to beat Florida jetlag is to enjoy the memories from this trip – then start planning your next Orlando holiday! Believe us, the lure of this wonderland is hard to resist – you WILL be back!

14 Your Holiday Planner

Example: 2 weeks with Disney's 7-Day Ultimate, Universal 3-Park Explorer & SeaWorld 3-Park Tickets

(Disney's Ultimate Tickets give 7, 14 or 21 days of unlimited admission at their 4 main theme parks, plus visits to Blizzard Beach, Typhoon Lagoon and ESPN World Of Sports™, valid for 7, 14 or 21 days from first use. Universal 3-Park Explorer Ticket is valid for all 3 parks – including the new Volcano Bay – and CityWalk for 14 days from first use. SeaWorld 3-Park ticket includes SeaWorld, Busch Gardens and Aquatica for 14 consecutive days).

Day	Our Example	Your Planner
1 (Mon)	Arrive 2.40pm local time, Orlando Sanford airport; transfer to resort – check out local shops and restaurants	
2 (Tues)	Start with a full day at SEAWORLD	
3 (Wed)	Start day at UNIVERSAL STUDIOS for Wizarding World of Harry Potter; then VOLCANO BAY	
4 (Thur)	Morning at MAGIC KINGDOM; take a break and return for Happily Ever After fireworks at 9pm	
5 (Fri)	Rest day – take in some shopping and have afternoon at SeaWorld's AQUATICA water park	
6 (Sat)	All the fun of DISNEY'S HOLLYWOOD STUDIOS; stay for evening shows	
7 (Sun)	Enjoy Universal's ISLANDS OF ADVENTURE park; evening at CityWalk or VOLCANO BAY	
8 (Mon)	Take a trip to WILD FLORIDA; evening at leisure (dinner show or I-Drive 360)	
9 (Tues)	A day at BUSCH GARDENS; consider evening at SEAWORLD if back in time	
10 (Wed)	A full day at Disney's EPCOT park, with the IllumiNations show at 9pm	
11 (Thur)	An early start for all the Pandora attractions at DISNEY'S ANIMAL KINGDOM; Rivers of Light at 9.15pm	
12 (Fri)	A Disney chillout day – spend time between TYPHOON LAGOON and Disney Springs	
13 (Sat)	The best of UNIVERSAL STUDIOS and ISLANDS OF ADVENTURE; or Kennedy Space Center	
14 (Sun)	Back to our favourite Disney parks – perhaps ANIMAL KINGDOM and MAGIC KINGDOM	
15 (Mon)	Gatorland/Back to airport; return flight at 5.30pm	

Busy Day Guide

NB: This is a *general* guide only as the parks do change their hours frequently and often without notice. However, this guide will still be accurate for the busiest times of the year.

Day	Busiest	Average	Lightest
Mon	Animal Kingdom, Universal Studios	Magic Kingdom, EPCOT, Islands of Adventure	Disney's Hollywood Studios, SeaWorld, Busch Gardens; Kennedy Space Center, water parks
Tues	Magic Kingdom, EPCOT	Disney's Hollywood Studios, Universal Studios, Kennedy Space Center	Animal Kingdom, Islands of Adventure, SeaWorld, Busch Gardens, water parks
Wed	Animal Kingdom	Magic Kingdom, Disney's Hollywood Studios, Islands of Adventure, SeaWorld	EPCOT, Universal Studios, Busch Gardens, Kennedy Space Center, water parks
Thurs	EPCOT	Disney's Hollywood Studios, Islands of Adventure, Kennedy Space Center, SeaWorld	Magic Kingdom, Animal Kingdom, Universal Studios, Busch Gardens, water parks
Fri	Magic Kingdom, Islands of Adventure	Disney's Hollywood Studios, Animal Kingdom, Universal Studios, Kennedy Space Center, Busch Gardens, water parks	EPCOT, SeaWorld
Sat	Animal Kingdom, Universal Studios, Islands of Adventure, SeaWorld, Busch Gardens, Kennedy Space Center, water parks	Magic Kingdom, EPCOT	Disney's Hollywood Studios
Sun	Disney's Hollywood Studios, EPCOT, Universal Studios, Islands of Adventure, SeaWorld, water parks	Magic Kingdom, Busch Gardens, Kennedy Space Center	Animal Kingdom

Only here for a week? Here's our suggestion for an action-packed 7 nights in Orlando:

Day 1: Arrive; visit EPCOT in evening for IllumiNations

Day 2: Up early for Magic Kingdom

Day 3: All day at Universal and Islands of Adventure

Day 4: EPCOT for the day; Disney's Hollywood Studios for evening

Day 5: Disney's Animal Kingdom for a full day

Day 6: SeaWorld with mid-day break at Aquatica

Day 7: Hollywood Studios for the day, Magic Kingdom evening

Day 8: Shopping and return flight

Index

ACKNOWLEDGEMENTS

Acknowledgements

The authors wish to acknowledge the help of the following in the production of this book: Visit Orlando, Experience Kissimmee, Walt Disney Attractions Inc., Universal Orlando, SeaWorld Parks & Entertainment, Visit Florida, St Petersburg/Clearwater Area Convention and Visitors Bureau, Seminole County Convention & Visitors Bureau, Visit Tampa Bay, Space Coast Office of Tourism, Discover Crystal River, Visit West Volusia, Amelia Island Tourist Development Council, Martin County Florida, Greater Orlando Aviation Authority, Orlando Sanford International Airport and Alamo Rent A Car. In person: Amy Rodenbrock, Cory O'Born (Visit Orlando), Jo Thomas (Experience Kissimmee), Hannah Mulvey and Gill Standeven (Visit Florida), Patrick Harrison, Kevin Wiatrowski (Visit Tampa Bay), Todd Heiden, Dave Coombs, Nikki Palmas Jennie Hess (Walt Disney), Rebecca Romzek (Busch Gardens), Georgia Turner (Visit West Volusia), Miles Saunders (Discover Crystal River), Nerissa Okiye (Martin County Florida), Kate Harris (Amelia Island), Laura Myers (Florida Keys), Kevin Gibson, Jon Hornbuckle, Ali Beemer (Universal), Rebecca Shireman, Kenna Pell (Kennedy Space Center), Brittany Williams (LEGOLAND Florida), Carolyn Fennell, Rod Johnson (Orlando Aviation Authority), Tori Sullivan (Gray Line Orlando), Brandon Bruce, Adam Goldman (SeaWorld Parks & Entertainment), Rose Vignetti-Garlick (Downtown Orlando), Sam Haught (Wild Florida), Kathy Hernandez (Gatorland), Shaira Graulau (Medieval Times), Dana Berry (Four Seasons Orlando), Laura Richeson (Richeson Communications), Scott Joseph (ScottJosephOrlando.com), Michael Caires (Orlando Sanford International Airport), Allan Oakley (Alexander Homes & Associates), Donna Ernbro (Sleuths), Mary Deatrick (Deatrick PR for Rosen Hotels), Chris Brumbaugh (Gaylord Palms Resort), plus all our ATD friends! Reader feedback via email: Rupert Myers, Paul Davis, Bernard Mayo, Tim Limbach, David Gordon, Caroline Porter. Nick & Fiona Chapman.

Check out *Attractions Magazine* (who we also write for) for more info and features on this great destination, www.attractionsmagazine.com, and don't forget to join us on the discussion forums at www.attraction-tickets-direct.co.uk. Got a red-hot Brit Tip to pass on? We want to hear from YOU to keep improving the guide each year. Drop us a line at: Brit's Guide (Orlando), W. Foulsham & Co. Ltd, The Old Barrel Store, Drayman's Lane, Marlow, Bucks SL7 2FF. Or e-mail britsguide@yahoo.com.

Bye...come back soon!

© Disney